T0214528

Lecture Notes in Computer Science 11138

Commenced Publication in 1973
Founding and Former Series Editors:
Gerhard Goos, Juris Hartmanis, and Jan van Leeuwen

More information about this series at http://www.springer.com/series/7408

Shuvendu K. Lahiri · Chao Wang (Eds.)

Automated Technology for Verification and Analysis

16th International Symposium, ATVA 2018
Los Angeles, CA, USA, October 7–10, 2018
Proceedings

 Springer

Editors
Shuvendu K. Lahiri
Microsoft Research
Redmond, WA
USA

Chao Wang
University of Southern California
Los Angeles, CA
USA

ISSN 0302-9743   ISSN 1611-3349 (electronic)
Lecture Notes in Computer Science
ISBN 978-3-030-01089-8   ISBN 978-3-030-01090-4 (eBook)
https://doi.org/10.1007/978-3-030-01090-4

Library of Congress Control Number: 2018955278

LNCS Sublibrary: SL2 – Programming and Software Engineering

This Springer imprint is published by the registered company Springer Nature Switzerland AG
The registered company address is: Gewerbestrasse 11, 6330 Cham, Switzerland

Preface

This volume contains the papers presented at the 16th International Symposium on Automated Technology for Verification and Analysis (ATVA 2018) held during October 7–10, 2018, in Los Angeles, California, USA.

ATVA is a series of symposia dedicated to the promotion of research on theoretical and practical aspects of automated analysis, verification, and synthesis by providing a forum for interaction between the regional and the international research communities and industry in the field. Previous events were held in Taipei (2003–2005), Beijing (2006), Tokyo (2007), Seoul (2008), Macao (2009), Singapore (2010), Taipei (2011), Thiruvananthapuram (2012), Hanoi (2013), Sydney (2014), Shanghai (2015), Chiba (2016), and Pune (2017).

ATVA 2018 received 82 high-quality paper submissions, each of which received three reviews on average. After careful review, the Program Committee accepted 27 regular papers and six tool papers. The evaluation and selection process involved thorough discussions among members of the Program Committee through the Easy-Chair conference management system, before reaching a consensus on the final decisions.

To complement the contributed papers, we included in the program three keynote talks and tutorials given by Nikolaj Bjørner (Microsoft Research, USA), Corina Păsăreanu (NASA Ames Research Center, USA), and Sanjit Seshia (University of California, Berkeley, USA), resulting in an exceptionally strong technical program.

We would like to acknowledge the contributions that made ATVA 2018 a successful event. First, we thank the authors of all submitted papers and we hope that they continute to submit their high-quality work to ATVA in future. Second, we thank the Program Committee members and external reviewers for their rigorous evaluation of the submitted papers. Third, we thank the keynote speakers for enriching the program by presenting their distinguished research. Finally, we thank Microsoft and Springer for sponsoring ATVA 2018.

We sincerely hope that the readers find the ATVA 2018 proceedings informative and rewarding.

October 2018

Shuvendu K. Lahiri
Chao Wang

Organization

Steering Committee

E. Allen Emerson	University of Texas, Austin, USA
Teruo Higashino	Osaka University, Japan
Oscar H. Ibarra	University of California, Santa Barbara, USA
Insup Lee	University of Pennsylvania, USA
Doron A. Peled	Bar Ilan University, Israel
Farn Wang	National Taiwan University, Taiwan
Hsu-Chun Yen	National Taiwan University, Taiwan

Program Committee

Aws Albarghouthi	University of Wisconsin-Madison, USA
Cyrille Valentin Artho	KTH Royal Institute of Technology, Sweden
Gogul Balakrishnan	Google, USA
Roderick Bloem	Graz University of Technology, Austria
Tevfik Bultan	University of California, Santa Barbara, USA
Pavol Cerny	University of Colorado at Boulder, USA
Sagar Chaki	Mentor Graphics, USA
Deepak D'Souza	Indian Institute of Science, Bangalore, India
Jyotirmoy Deshmukh	University of Southern California, USA
Constantin Enea	University Paris Diderot, France
Grigory Fedyukovich	Princeton University, USA
Masahiro Fujita	The University of Tokyo, Japan
Sicun Gao	University of California, San Diego, USA
Arie Gurfinkel	University of Waterloo, Canada
Fei He	Tsinghua University, China
Alan J. Hu	The University of British Columbia, Canada
Joxan Jaffar	National University of Singapore, Singapore
Akash Lal	Microsoft, India
Axel Legay	IRISA/Inria, Rennes, France
Yang Liu	Nanyang Technological University, Singapore
Zhiming Liu	Southwest University, China
K. Narayan Kumar	Chennai Mathematical Institute, India
Doron Peled	Bar Ilan University, Israel
Xiaokang Qiu	Purdue University, USA
Giles Reger	The University of Manchester, UK
Sandeep Shukla	Indian Institute of Technology Kanpur, India
Oleg Sokolsky	University of Pennsylvania, USA
Armando Solar-Lezama	MIT, USA
Neeraj Suri	TU Darmstadt, Germany

Aditya Thakur   University of California, Davis, USA
Willem Visser   Stellenbosch University, South Africa
Bow-Yaw Wang   Academia Sinica, Taiwan
Farn Wang   National Taiwan University, Taiwan
Georg Weissenbacher   Vienna University of Technology, Austria
Naijun Zhan   Chinese Academy of Sciences, China

Additional Reviewers

Akshay, S.   Lewchenko, Nicholas V.   Sangnier, Arnaud
Alt, Leonardo   Li, Yangjia   Sankaranarayanan, Sriram
Bastani, Osbert   Lin, Wang   Song, Fu
Bouajjani, Ahmed   Liu, Wanwei   Srivathsan, B.
Chen, Mingshuai   Luo, Chen   Suresh, S. P.
Chen, Wei   Maghareh, Rasool   Ting, Gan
Chen, Zhenbang   Matteplackel, Raj Mohan   Tizpaz Niari, Saeid
Ebrahim, Masoud   McClurg, Jedidiah   Trung, Ta Quang
Ge, Ning   Mordvinov, Dmitry   Wang, Chao
Habermehl, Peter   Pick, Lauren   Wang, Lingtai
Jansen, Nils   Poulsen, Danny   Xue, Bai
Karl, Anja   Poulsen, Dany   Yang, Zhibin
Katelaan, Jens   Praveen, M.   Yin, Liangze
Katis, Andreas   Qamar, Nafees   Zhang, Xin
Khalimov, Ayrat   Quilbeuf, Jean
Koenighofer, Bettina   Riener, Martin

$Z3^{Azure}$ and $Azure^{Z3}$
(Abstract)

Nikolaj Bjørner[1], Marijn Heule[2], Karthick Jayaraman[3],
and Rahul Kumar[1]

[1] Microsoft Research
{nbjorner,rahulku}@microsoft.com
[2] UT Austin
marijn@heule.nl
[3] Microsoft Azure
karjay@microsoft.com

Azure to the power of Z3: Cloud providers are increasingly embracing network verification for managing complex datacenter network infrastructure. Microsoft's Azure cloud infrastructure integrates the SecGuru tool, which leverages the Z3 SMT solver, for assuring that the network is configured to preserve desired intent. SecGuru statically validates correctness of access-control policies and routing tables of hundreds of thousands of network devices. For a structured network such as for Microsoft Azure data-centers, the intent for routing tables and access-control policies can be automatically derived from network architecture and metadata about address ranges hosted in the datacenter. We leverage this aspect to perform local checks on a per router basis. These local checks together assure reachability invariants for availability and performance. To make the service truly scalable, while using modest resources, SecGuru integrates a set of domain-specific optimizations that exploit properties of the configurations it needs to handle. Our experiences exemplify integration of general purpose verification technologies, in this case bit-vector solving, for a specific domain: the overal methodology available through SMT formalisms lowers the barrier of entry for capturing and checking contracts. They also alleviate initial needs for writing custom solvers. However, each domain reveals specific structure that produces new insights in the quest for scalable verification: for checking reachability properties in networks, methods for capturing symmetries in networks and header spaces can speed up verification by several orders of magnitude; for local checks on data-center routers we exploit common patterns in configurations to take the time it takes to check a contract from a few seconds to a few milliseconds.

Z3 to the power of Azure: Applications that rely on constraint solving may be in a fortunate situation where efficient solving technologies are adequately available. Several tools building on Z3 rely on this being the common case scenario. Then useful feedback can be produced within the attention span of a person performing program verification, and then the available compute time on a machine or a cluster is sufficient to complete thousands of small checks. As long as this fortunate situation holds, search techniques for SMT is a solved problem. Yet, in spite of rumors to the contrary, SAT and SMT is by no means a solved problem. When current algorithmic techniques, in particular modern SAT solving search methods based on conflict-driven clause learning, are insufficient to quickly find solutions, a next remedy is to harness computational resources at problems. In the context of SAT solving, the method of Cube & Conquer, has been used with significant success to solve hard combinatorial problems from mathematical conjectures. These are relatively small formulas, but require a substantial search space for analysis. Formulas from applications, such as scheduling and timetabling, are significantly larger and have wildly different structural properties. In spite of these differences, we found that the Cube & Conquer methodology can make a substantial difference as fixing even a limited number of variables can drastically reduce the overhead solving subformulas. We describe a distributed version of Z3 that scales with Azure's elastic cloud. It integrates recent advances in lookahead and distributed SAT solving for Z3's engines for SMT. A multi-threaded version of the Cube & Conquer solver is also available parallelizing SAT and SMT queries.

Contents

Temporal Logic Verification of Stochastic Systems Using Barrier
Certificates   177
    Pushpak Jagtap, Sadegh Soudjani, and Majid Zamani

Bisimilarity Distances for Approximate Differential Privacy   194
    Dmitry Chistikov, Andrzej S. Murawski, and David Purser

A Symbolic Algorithm for Lazy Synthesis of Eager Strategies   211
    Swen Jacobs and Mouhammad Sakr

Modular Verification of Concurrent Programs via Sequential
Model Checking   228
    Dan Rasin, Orna Grumberg, and Sharon Shoham

Quantifiers on Demand   248
    Arie Gurfinkel, Sharon Shoham, and Yakir Vizel

Signal Convolution Logic   267
    Simone Silvetti, Laura Nenzi, Ezio Bartocci, and Luca Bortolussi

Efficient Symbolic Representation of Convex Polyhedra
in High-Dimensional Spaces   284
    Bernard Boigelot and Isabelle Mainz

Accelerated Model Checking of Parametric Markov Chains   300
    Paul Gainer, Ernst Moritz Hahn, and Sven Schewe

Continuous-Time Markov Decisions Based on Partial Exploration   317
    Pranav Ashok, Yuliya Butkova, Holger Hermanns, and Jan Křetínský

A Fragment of Linear Temporal Logic for Universal Very Weak Automata . . .   335
    Keerthi Adabala and Rüdiger Ehlers

Quadratic Word Equations with Length Constraints, Counter Systems,
and Presburger Arithmetic with Divisibility   352
    Anthony W. Lin and Rupak Majumdar

Round-Bounded Control of Parameterized Systems   370
    Benedikt Bollig, Mathieu Lehaut, and Nathalie Sznajder

PSense: Automatic Sensitivity Analysis for Probabilistic Programs   387
    Zixin Huang, Zhenbang Wang, and Sasa Misailovic

Information Leakage in Arbiter Protocols   404
    Nestan Tsiskaridze, Lucas Bang, Joseph McMahan, Tevfik Bultan,
    and Timothy Sherwood

Invited Papers

DeepSafe: A Data-Driven Approach for Assessing Robustness of Neural Networks

Divya Gopinath[1], Guy Katz[3], Corina S. Păsăreanu[1,2(✉)], and Clark Barrett[3]

[1] Carnegie Mellon University, Silicon Valley, Mountain View, USA
`divgml@gmail.com`
[2] NASA Ames Research Center, Mountain View, USA
`corina.s.pasareanu@nasa.gov`
[3] Stanford University, Stanford, USA
`{guyk,barrett}@cs.stanford.edu`

Abstract. Deep neural networks have achieved impressive results in many complex applications, including classification tasks for image and speech recognition, pattern analysis or perception in self-driving vehicles. However, it has been observed that even highly trained networks are very vulnerable to *adversarial perturbations*. Adding minimal changes to inputs that are correctly classified can lead to wrong predictions, raising serious security and safety concerns. Existing techniques for checking *robustness* against such perturbations only consider searching locally around a few individual inputs, providing limited guarantees. We propose DeepSafe, a novel approach for automatically assessing the overall robustness of a neural network. DeepSafe applies clustering over known labeled data and leverages off-the-shelf constraint solvers to automatically identify and check *safe regions* in which the network is robust, i.e. *all* the inputs in the region are guaranteed to be classified correctly. We also introduce the concept of *targeted robustness*, which ensures that the neural network is guaranteed not to misclassify inputs within a region to a specific target (adversarial) label. We evaluate DeepSafe on a neural network implementation of a controller for the next-generation Airborne Collision Avoidance System for unmanned aircraft (ACAS Xu) and for the well known MNIST network. For these networks, DeepSafe identified many regions which were safe, and also found adversarial perturbations of interest.

1 Introduction

Machine learning techniques such as deep neural networks (NN) are increasingly used in a variety of applications, achieving impressive results in many domains, and matching the cognitive ability of humans in complex tasks. In this paper, we study a common use of NN as classifiers that take in complex, high dimensional input, pass it through multiple layers of transformations, and finally assign to it a specific output label or class. These networks can be used to perform pattern analysis, image classification, or speech and audio recognition, and are now being

© Springer Nature Switzerland AG 2018
S. K. Lahiri and C. Wang (Eds.): ATVA 2018, LNCS 11138, pp. 3–19, 2018.
https://doi.org/10.1007/978-3-030-01090-4_1

integrated into the perception modules of autonomous or semi-autonomous vehicles, at major car companies such as Tesla, BMW, Ford, etc. It is expected that this trend will continue and intensify, with neural networks being increasingly used in safety critical applications which require high assurance guarantees.

However, it has been observed that state-of-the-art networks are highly vulnerable to *adversarial perturbations*: given a correctly-classified input x, it is possible to find a new input x' that is very similar to x but is assigned a different label [17]. The vulnerability of neural networks to adversarial perturbations is thus a major safety and security concern, and it is essential to explore systematic methods for evaluating and improving the robustness of neural networks against such attacks.

To date, researchers have mostly focused on efficiently finding adversarial perturbations around select individual input points. The problem is typically cast as an optimization problem: for a given network F and an input x, find an x' such that F assigns different labels to x and x' (denoted $F(x') \neq F(x)$), while minimizing the distance $\|x - x'\|$, for different distance metrics. In other words, the goal is to find an input x' as close as possible to x such that x' and x are labeled differently. Finding the optimal solution for this problem is computationally difficult, and so various approximation approaches have been proposed [3,5,6,17]. There are also techniques that focus on generating *targeted attacks*: adversarial perturbations that result in the network assigning the perturbed input a specific target label [5,6,17].

The approaches for finding adversarial perturbations have successfully demonstrated the weakness of many state-of-the-art networks. However, using these techniques in assessing a network's robustness against adversarial perturbations is difficult, for two reasons. First, these approaches are heuristic-based, and provide no formal guarantees that they have not overlooked some adversarial perturbations; and second, these approaches only operate on individual input points, which may not be indicative of the network's robustness around other points. Approaches have also been proposed for training networks that are robust against adversarial perturbations, but these, too, provide no formal assurances [13].

Formal methods present a promising way for obtaining formal guarantees about the robustness of networks. Recent approaches tackle neural network verification [7,10] by casting it as an SMT solving problem. Reluplex [10] can check the *local robustness* at input point x, by checking if there is another point x' within a close distance δ to x ($\|x - x'\| < \delta$) for which the network assigns a different label. The initial value δ is picked arbitrarily and is tightened iteratively until the check holds. Similarly, DLV [7] searches locally around given inputs x within a small δ distance, but unlike Reluplex, it adopts discretization of the input space to reduce the search space.

These techniques are still limited to checking local robustness around a few individual points, giving no indication about the overall robustness of the network. In principle, one can apply the local check to a set of inputs that are drawn from some random distribution thought to represent the input space. However, this would require coming up with minimally acceptable distance δ values for all these checks, which can vary greatly between different input points. Furthermore, the check will likely fail (and produce invalid adversarial examples) for the input points that are close to the legitimate boundaries between different labels.

The concept of *global robustness* is defined in [10,11], which could be checked by Reluplex (we give the formal definition in Sect. 6). Whereas local robustness is measured for a specific input point, global robustness applies to all inputs simultaneously. The check requires encoding two side-by-side copies of the NN in question, operating on separate input variables, and checking that the outputs are similar. Global adversarial robustness is harder to prove than local robustness for two reasons: (1) encoding two copies of the network results in twice as many network nodes to analyze and (2) the problem is not restricted to a small domain, and therefore can not take advantage of Reluplex's heuristics, which work best when the check is restricted to small neighborhoods. Furthermore, it requires more manual tuning, as the user needs to provide minimally acceptable values for two parameters (δ and ϵ). As a result this global check could not be applied in practice to any realistic network [10].

Thus the problem of assessing the overall robustness of a network remains open.

DeepSafe. We propose DeepSafe, an automatic, data-driven approach for assessing the *overall robustness* of a neural network. The key idea is to effectively leverage the inputs with known correct labels to automatically identify *regions* in the input space which have a high chance of being labelled consistently or uniformly, thereby making global robustness checks achievable.

Specifically, DeepSafe applies a clustering algorithm over the labeled inputs to group them into *clusters*, which are sets of inputs that are close to each other (with respect to some given distance metric) and share the same label. The labeled inputs can be drawn from the training set or can be generated directly from executing the network on some random inputs; in the latter case the user needs to validate that the labels are correct. We use k-means clustering [9], which we modified to be guided by the labels of known inputs, but other clustering algorithms could be employed as well.

Each cluster defines a *region* which is a hypersphere in the input space, where the centroid is automatically computed by the clustering algorithm and the radius is defined as the average distance of any element in the cluster from the centroid. Our hypothesis it that the NN should assign the same label to *all* the inputs in the region, not just to the elements (inputs with known labels) that are used to form the cluster. The rationale is that even highly non-linear networks should display consistent behavior in the neighborhoods of *groups of similar inputs* known to share the same true label. We check this hypothesis by formulating it as a query for an off-the-shelf constraint solver. For our experiments we use the state-of-the-art tool Reluplex, but other solvers can be used. If the solver finds no solutions, it means that the region is *safe* (all inputs are labeled the same). If a solution is found, this indicates a potential adversarial input. We use the adversarial example as feedback to iteratively reduce the radius of the region, and repeat the check until the region is proved to be safe. If a time-out occurs during this process, we can not provide any guarantee for that region (although the likely answer is that it is safe). The result of the analysis is a set of well-defined input regions in which the NN is guaranteed to be robust and s set of examples of adversarial inputs that may be of interest to the developers of the NN, and can be used in retraining.

Thus, DeepSafe decomposes the global robustness requirements into a set of local robustness checks, one for each region, which can be solved efficiently with a tool like Reluplex. These checks do not require two network copies and are restricted to small input domains, as defined by the regions. The distance used for the local checks is not picked arbitrarily as in previous approaches, but instead it is the radius computed for each regions, backed up by the labeled data. Furthermore regions define natural decision boundaries in the input domain, thereby increasing the chances of producing valid proofs or of finding valid adversarial examples.

We introduce the concept *targeted robustness* in line with *targeted attacks* [5,6,17]. Targeted robustness ensures that there are no inputs in a region that are mapped by the NN to a specific incorrect label. Therefore, even if in that region the NN is not completely robust against adversarial perturbations, we can give guarantees that it is robust against specific targeted attacks. As a simple example, consider a NN used for perception in an autonomous car that classifies the images of a traffic light as red, green or yellow. Even if it is not the case that the NN never misclassifies a red light, we may be willing to settle for a guarantee that it never misclassifies a red light as a green light—leaving us with the more tolerable case in which a red light is misclassified as yellow.

We implemented a prototype of DeepSafe and evaluated it on a neural network implementation of a controller for the next-generation Airborne Collision Avoidance System for unmanned aircraft (ACAS Xu) and on the well known MNIST dataset. For these networks, our approach identified regions which were completely safe, regions which were safe with respect to some target labels, and also adversarial perturbations that were of interest to the network's developers.

2   Background

2.1   Neural Networks

Neural networks and deep belief networks have been used in a variety of applications, including pattern analysis, image classification, speech and audio recognition, and perception modules in self-driving cars. Typically, the objects in such domains are high dimensional and the number of classes that the objects need to be classified to is also high—and so the classification functions tend to be highly non-linear over the input space. Deep learning operates with the underlying rationale that groups of input parameters can be merged to derive higher-level abstract features, which enable the discovery of a more linear and continuous classification function. Neural networks are often used as *classifiers*, meaning they assign to each input an output label/class. Such a neural network

F can thus be regarded as a function that assigns to input x an output label y, denoted as $F(x) = y$.

Internally, a neural network is comprised of multiple layers of nodes, called neurons. Each node refines and extracts information from values computed by nodes in the previous layer. The structure of a typical 3 layer neural network would be as follows: the first layer is the *input* layer, which takes in the input variables (also called features) $x_1, x_2, \ldots, x_n$. The second layer is a *hidden* layer: each of its neurons computes a weighted sum of the input variables according to a unique weight vector and a bias value, and then applies a non-linear *activation function* to the result. The sigmoid function ($f(x) = 1/(1 + e^{-x})$) is a widely used activation function. Most recent networks use rectified linear units (ReLUs) activation functions. A rectified linear unit has output 0 if the input is less than 0, and raw output otherwise; $f(x) = max(x, 0)$. The last layer uses a softmax function to assign an the output class is the input. The softmax function squashes the outputs of each node of the previous layer to be between 0 and 1, equivalent to a categorical probability distribution. The number of nodes in this layer is equal to the number of output classes and their respective outputs gives the probability of the input being classified to that class.

2.2   Neural Network Verification

Traditional verification techniques often cannot directly be applied to neural networks, and this has sparked a line of work focused on transforming the problem into a format more amenable to existing tools, such as LP and SMT solvers [4,7,15,16]. DeepSafe, while is not restricted to, currently uses the recently-proposed Reluplex tool, which has been shown to perform better than other solvers, such as Z3, CVC4, Yices or MathSat [10]. Reluplex is a sound and complete simplex-based verification procedure, specifically tailored to achieve scalability on deep neural networks. It is designed to operate on networks with piecewise linear activation functions, such as ReLU. Intuitively, the algorithm operates by eagerly solving the linear constraints posed by the neural network's weighted sums, while attempting to satisfy the non-linear constraints posed by its activation functions in a lazy manner. This often allows Reluplex to safely disregard many of these non-linear constraints, which is where the bulk of the problem's complexity originates.

Reluplex has been used in evaluating techniques for finding and defending against adversarial perturbations [2], and it has also been successfully applied to a real-world family of deep neural networks, designed to operate as controllers in the next-generation Airborne Collision Avoidance System for unmanned aircraft (ACAS Xu) [10]. However, as discussed, Reluplex could only be used to check local robustness around a few individual points, giving limited guarantees about the *overall* robustness of these networks.

2.3 Clustering

Clustering is an approach used to divide a population of data-points into sets called clusters, such that the data-points in each cluster are more similar (with respect to some metric) to other points in the same cluster than to the rest of the data-points. Here we focus on a particularly popular clustering algorithm called *kMeans* [9] (although our approach could be implemented using different clustering algorithms as well). Given a set of n data-points $\{x_1, \ldots, x_n\}$ and k as the desired number of clusters, the algorithm partitions the points into k clusters, such that the variance (also referred to as "within cluster sum of squares") within each cluster is minimal. The metric used to calculate the distance between points is customizable, and is typically the Euclidean distance (L_2 norm) or the Manhattan distance (L_1 norm). For points $x_1 = \langle x_1^1, \ldots, x_n^1 \rangle$ and $x_2 = \langle x_1^2, \ldots, x_n^2 \rangle$ these are defined as:

$$\|x_1 - x_2\|_{L_1} = \sum_{i=1}^{n} |x_i^1 - x_i^2|, \qquad \|x_1 - x_2\|_{L_2} = \sqrt{\sum_{i=1}^{n} (x_i^1 - x_i^2)^2} \qquad (1)$$

The kMeans clustering algorithm is an iterative refinement algorithm, which starts with k random points considered as the means (the *centroids*) of k clusters. Each iteration is then comprised of two main steps:(i) assign each data-point to the cluster whose centroid is closest to it with respect to the chosen distance metric; and (ii) re-calculate the new means of the clusters, which will serve as the new centroids. The iterations continue until the assignment of data-points to clusters does not change. This indicates that the clusters satisfy the constraints that the variance within each cluster is minimal and that the data-points within each cluster are closer to the centroid of that cluster than to the centroid of any other cluster.

3 The DeepSafe Approach

The *DeepSafe* approach is illustrated in Fig. 1. DeepSafe has two main components: clustering and verification. The inputs with known labels are fed into a clustering module which implements a modified version of the kMeans algorithm (as described in Sect. 3.1). The module generates clusters of similar inputs (wrt some distance metric) known to have the same label. Every such cluster defines a *region* characterized by a centroid (*cen*), radius (*r*) and label (*l*), which corresponds to the label of the inputs used to form the cluster. Thus, a cluster is a subset of the inputs while a region is the geometrical hypersphere defined by the cluster; for the rest of the paper we sometimes use regions and clusters interchangeably, when the meaning is clear from the context.

For every region, the verification module is invoked (as described in Sect. 3.2). This module uses Reluplex to check if there exists any input within the region for which the neural network assigns a different label than l (the *score* in the figure will be explained below). This check is done separately for each label l' other than

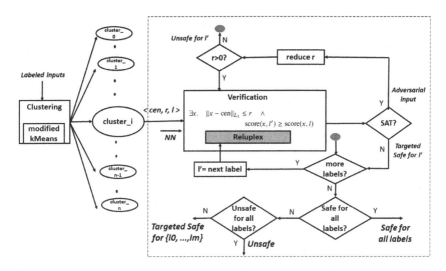

Fig. 1. The DeepSafe approach

l. If such an input is found (formula is SAT), then this is a potential adversarial example that is reported to the user. The radius is then reduced to exclude the adversarial input and the check is repeated. When no such adversarial example is found, the network is declared to be robust with respect to target l', and correspondingly the region is declared *targeted safe* for that label l'. If for a particular l', the solver keeps finding adversarial examples until r gets reduced to 0, the region is considered unsafe w.r.t. that label. If no adversarial examples are found for all the checks, the region is *completely safe*. If adversarial cases are found for all labels, it is *unsafe*.

3.1 Labeled-Guided Clustering

We employ a modified version of the kMeans clustering algorithm to perform clustering over the inputs with known correct labels. These inputs can be drawn from the training data or can be generated randomly and labeled according to the outputs given by a trained network. The kMeans approach is typically an unsupervised technique, meaning that the clustering is based purely on the similarity of the data-points themselves. Here, however, we use the labels to guide the clustering algorithm into generating clusters that have consistent labels (in addition to containing points that are similar to each other). The number of clusters, which is an input parameter of the kMeans algorithm, is often chosen arbitrarily but in our case the algorithm starts by setting the number of clusters, k, to be equal to the number of unique labels. Once the clusters are obtained, we check whether each cluster contains only inputs with the same label. kMeans is then applied again on each cluster that is found to contain multiple labels, with k set to the number of unique labels within that cluster. This effectively breaks the

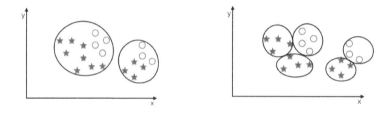

Fig. 2. Original clusters with k = 2 (left), Clusters with modified kMeans (right)

"problematic" cluster into multiple sub-clusters. The process is repeated until all the clusters contain inputs which share a single label.

To illustrate the clustering, let us consider a small example with training data labeled as either stars or circles. Each training data point is characterized by two dimensions/attributes (x,y). The original kMeans algorithm with $k = 2$, will partition the training inputs into 2 groups, purely based on proximity w.r.t. the 2 attributes (Fig. 2a). However, this simple approach would group stars and circles together. Our modified algorithm creates the same partitions in its first iteration, but because each cluster contains training inputs with multiple labels, it then proceeds to iteratively divide each cluster into sub-clusters. This finally creates 5 clusters as shown in (Fig. 2b): three with label star and two with label circle. This example is typical for domains such as image classification, where even a small change in some attribute value for certain inputs could change their label.

Distance Metrics. We note that the similarity of the inputs within a cluster is determined by the distance metric used for calculating the proximity of the inputs. Therefore, it is important to choose a distance metric that generates acceptable levels of similarity for the domain under consideration. We assume that inputs are representable as vectors of numeric attributes and hence can be considered as points in Euclidean space. The Euclidean distance (Eq. 1) is a commonly used metric for measuring the proximity of points in Euclidean space. However, recent studies indicate that the usefulness of Euclidean distance in determining the proximity between points diminishes as the dimensionality increases [1]. The Manhattan distance (Eq. 1) has been found to capture proximity more accurately in high dimensions. Therefore, in our experiments, we set the distance metric depending on the dimensionality of the input space (Sect. 4).

The clustering algorithm aims to produce neighborhoods of consistently-labeled inputs. The underlying assumption of our approach is that each such cluster will define a *safe region*, in which all inputs (and not just the inputs used to form the cluster) should be labeled consistently. We define the regions to have the centroid cen computed by kMeans and the radius to be the *average distance r* of any instance from the centroid. Note that we use the average instead of maximum distance. The reason is that kMeans typically generates clusters that are convex, compact and spherically shaped. However, the ideal boundaries of regions encompassing consistently labeled points need not conform to this.

Further, while inputs deep within a region are expected to be labeled consistently, the points that are close to the boundaries may have different labels. We therefore *shrink* the radius to increase the chances of obtaining a region that is indeed safe.

3.2   Region Verification

In this step, we check if the regions defined by the clusters formed in the previous step are *safe* for a given NN. The main hypothesis behind our approach is as follows:

Hypothesis 1. *For a given region R, with centroid cen and radius r, any input x within distance r from cen has the same true label l as that of the region:*

$$\|x - cen\| \leq r \quad \Rightarrow \quad label(x) = l$$

If this hypothesis holds, it follows that any point x' in the region which is assigned a different label $F(x') \neq l$ by the network constitutes an adversarial perturbation. To illustrate this on our example; a NN, may represent an input which is close to other stars in the input layer as a point further away from them in the inner layers. Therefore, it may incorrectly classify it as a circle.

We use Reluplex [10] to check the satisfiability of a formula representing the negation of Hypothesis 1 for every cluster for every label. The encoding is as follows://shown in Eq. 2:

$$\exists x. \quad \|x - cen\|_{L_1} \leq r \quad \wedge \quad score(x, l') \geq score(x, l) \tag{2}$$

Here, x represents an input point, and cen, r and l represent the centroid, radius and label of the region, respectively. l' represents a specific label, different from l. Reluplex models the network without the final softmax layer, and so the outputs of the model correspond to the outputs of the second last layer of the NN [REF]. This layer consists of as many nodes as the number of labels and the output value for each node corresponds to the level of *confidence* that the network assigns to that label for the given input. We use $score(x, y)$ to denote the level of confidence assigned to label y at point x.

The above formula holds for a given l' if and only if there exists a point x within distance at most r from cen, for which l' is assigned higher confidence than l. Consequently, if the property does *not* hold, then for every x within the cluster l, its score is higher than l'. This ensures *targeted robustness* of the network for label l': the network is guaranteed to never map any input within the region to the target label l'. The formula in Eq. 2 is checked for every possible $l' \in L - \{l\}$, where L denotes the set of all possible labels. If the query is unsatisfiable for all l', it ensures *complete robustness of the network for the region*; i.e., the network is guaranteed to map all the inputs in the region to the same label as the centroid. This can be expressed formally as follows:

$$\forall x. \|x - cen\|_{L_1} \leq r \quad \Rightarrow \quad \forall l \in L - \{l\}. \quad score(x, l) \geq score(x, l') \tag{3}$$

from which it follows that Hypothesis 1 holds, i.e. that:

$$\forall x. \ \|x - \text{cen}\|_{L_1} \leq r \quad \Rightarrow \quad label(x) = l \tag{4}$$

Note that as is the case with many SMT-based solvers, Reluplex typically solves satisfiable queries more quickly than unsatisfiable ones. Therefore, in order to optimize performance, we test the possible target labels l' in descending order based on the scores that they are assigned at the centroid, score(cen, l'). Intuitively, this is because labels with higher scores are more likely to yield a satisfiable query.

Encoding Distance Metrics in Reluplex. Reluplex takes as input a conjunction of linear equations and certain piecewise-linear constraints. Consequently, it is straightforward to model the neural network itself and the query in Eq. 2. Our ability to encode the distance constraint from the equation, $\|x - \text{cen}\| \leq r$, depends on the distance metric being used. While L_1 is piecewise linear and can be encoded, L_2 unfortunately cannot. When dealing with domains where L_2 distance is a better measure of proximity, we thus use the following approximation. We perform the clustering phase using the L_2 distance metric as described before and for each cluster obtain the radius r. When verifying the property in Eq. 2, however, we use the L_1 norm. Because $\|x - \text{cen}\|_{L_1} \leq \|x - \text{cen}\|_{L_2}$, it is guaranteed that any adversarial perturbation discovered would have also been discovered using the L_2 norm. If no such adversarial perturbation is discovered, however, we can only conclude that the portion of the corresponding region that was checked is safe. This limitation could be overcome by using a tool that directly supports L_2 (however no such tools currently exist), or by enhancing Reluplex to support it.

Safe Regions and Scalability. The main source of computational complexity in neural network verification is the presence of non-linear, non-convex activation functions. However, when restricted to a small domain of the input space, these functions may exhibit linear behavior—in which case they can be disregarded and replaced with a linear constraint, which greatly simplifies the problem. Consequently, performing verification within the small regions discovered by DeepSafe is beneficial, as many activation functions can often be disregarded.

The search space within a region is further reduced by restricting the range of values for each input attribute (input variable to the NN model). We calculate the minimum and maximum values for every attribute based on the instances with known labels encompassed within a cluster. Reluplex has built-in *bound tightening* [10] functionality. We leverage this by setting the lower and upper bounds for each of the input variables within the cluster based on the respective minimum and maximum values.

Our approach lends itself to more scalable verification also through parallelization. Because each region involves stand-alone verification queries, their verification can be performed in parallel. Also, because Eq. 2 can be checked independently for every l', these queries can be performed in parallel—expediting the process even further.

4   Case Studies

We implemented DeepSpace using MATLAB R2017a for the clustering algorithm and Reluplex v1.0 for verification. The runs were dispatched on a 8-Core 64GB server running Ubuntu 16.0.4. We evaluated DeepSpace on two case studies. The first network is part of a real-world controller for the next-generation Airborne Collision Avoidance System for unmanned aircraft (ACAS Xu), a highly safety-critical system. The second network is a digit classifier over the popular MNIST image dataset.

Table 1. Summary of the analysis for the ACAS Xu network for 210 clusters

Property	# clusters	Min radius	Time (hours)	# queries
Safe	125	0.084	4	11.8
Targeted safe	52	0.135	7.6	14.4
Time out	33	NA	12	NA

4.1   ACAS Xu

ACAS X is a family of collision avoidance systems for aircraft which is currently under development by the Federal Aviation Administration (FAA) [8]. ACAS Xu is the version for unmanned aircraft control. It is intended to be airborne and receive sensor information regarding the drone (the *ownship*) and any nearby intruder drones, and then issue horizontal turning advisories aimed at preventing collisions. The input sensor data includes: (i) ρ: distance from ownship to intruder; (ii) θ: angle of intruder relative to ownship heading direction; (iii) ψ: heading angle of intruder relative to ownship heading direction; (iv) v_{own}: speed of ownship; (v) v_{int}: speed of intruder; (vi) τ: time until loss of vertical separation; and (vii) a_{prev}: previous advisory. The five possible output actions are as follows: Clear-of-Conflict (COC), Weak Right, Weak Left, Strong Right, and Strong Left. Each advisory is assigned a score, with the lowest score corresponding to the best action. The FAA is currently exploring an implementation of ACAS Xu that uses an array of 45 deep neural networks. These networks were obtained by discretizing the two parameters, τ and a_{prev}, and so each network contains five input dimensions and treats τ and a_{prev} as constants. Each network has 6 hidden layers and a total of 300 hidden ReLU activation nodes.

We applied our approach to several of the ACAS XU networks. We describe here in detail the results for one network. Each input consists of 5 dimensions and is assigned one of 5 possible output labels, corresponding to the 5 possible turning advisories for the drone (0:COC, 1:Weak Right, 2:Weak Left, 3:Strong Right, and 4:Strong Left). We were supplied a set of cut-points, representing valid important values for each dimension, by the domain experts [8]. We generated 2662704 inputs (cartesian product of the values for all the dimensions). The network was

Table 2. Details of the analysis for some clusters for ACAS Xu

Cluster#	Safe for label	Radius	# queries	Time (min)	Slice (Y/N)
5282	1	0.04	1	5.45	N
label:0	2	0.04	1	3.91	N
	3	0.04	1	3.57	N
	4	0.04	1	4.01	N
1783	1	0.16	4	1.28	Y
label:0	2	0.17	1	279	N
	3	0.17	1	236	N
	4	0.17	1	223	N
2072	0	0.06	1	11.51	N
label:1	2	0.014	9	0.98	N
	3	0.011	7	0.71	N
	4	0.012	5	0.58	N
6138	1	0.089	9	103.2	N
label:0	2	0.11	4	2.86	N

executed on these inputs and the output advisories (labels) were verified. These were considered as the inputs with known labels for our experiments.

The labeled-guided clustering algorithm was applied on the inputs using the L_2 distance metric. Clustering yielded 6145 clusters with more than one input and 321 single-input clusters. The clustering took 7 h. For each cluster we computed a region, characterized by a centroid (computed by kMeans), radius (average distance of every cluster instance from the centroid), and the expected label (the label of all the cluster instances).

We first evaluated the network on all the centroids as they are considered representative of the entire cluster and should ideally have the expected label. The network assigned the expected label for the centroids of 5116 clusters (83% of total number of clusters). For the remaining 1029 clusters, we found that they contained few labeled instances spread out in large areas. Therefore, we considered these clusters were not precise and our analysis was inconclusive. For singleton clusters, we fall back to checking local robustness using previous techniques [10]. These stand-alone points serve to identify portions of the input space which require more training data, thus potentially more vulnerable to adversarial perturbations.

Amongst the remaining 5116 clusters, we picked randomly 210 clusters to illustrate our technique. These clusters contain 659315 labeled inputs (24% of the total inputs with known labels). For each region corresponding to the respective clusters, we applied DeepSafe to check equation 2 for every label. The distance metric used was L_1 since L_2 can not be handled by Reluplex (see Sect. 3 that explains why this is still safe). The results are presented in Tables 1 and 2. The *min radius* in Table 1, refers to the average minimum radius around the centroid of each region for which the safety guarantee applies (averaged over the total number of regions for that safety type). The # *queries* refers to the number of times the solver had to be invoked until an UNSAT was obtained, averaged over all the regions for that property.

DeepSafe was able to identify 125 regions which are completely *safe*, i.e. the network yields a label consistent with the neighboring labeled inputs within the region. 52 regions are *targeted safe*, the network is safe against misclassifying inputs to certain labels. For instance, the inputs within region 6138 (Table 2) with an expected label 0 (COC), were safe against misclassification only to labels 1 (weak right) and 2 (weak left). The solver timed out without returning any result for the remaining labels. The analysis timed out without returning a concrete result for any label for 33 clusters. A time out does not allow to provide a proof for the regions, although the likely answer is safe (generally, solvers take much longer when there is no solution).

The *min radius* in Table 1, refers to the average minimum radius around the centroid of each region for which the safety guarantee applies (averaged over the total number of regions for that safety type).

The # *queries* refers to the number of times the solver had to be invoked until an UNSAT was obtained, averaged over all the regions for that property.

4.2   MNIST Image Dataset

The MNIST database is a large collection of handwritten digits that is commonly used for training various image processing systems [12]. The dataset has 60,000 training input images, each characterized by 784 attributes and belonging to one of 10 labels. We used a network that comprised of 3 layers, each with 10 ReLU activation nodes. Clustering was applied using the L_1 distance metric. It yielded 6654 clusters with more than one input and 5681 single-input clusters. The clustering consumed 10 h. A separate process for verification of each cluster was spawned with a time-out of 12 h.

Table 3. Summary of the analysis for MNIST network for 80 clusters

Property	# clusters	Min radius	Time (hours)	# queries
Safe	7	2.46	11.27	2.85
Targeted safe	63	5.19	11.02	4.87
Time out	10	NA	12	NA

For the singleton clusters, as is the case with ACAS Xu, we performed local robustness checking as in previous approaches.

Table 3 shows the summary of the results for the runs for 80 clusters that we selected for evaluation. In past studies, the MNIST network has been shown to be extremely vulnerable to misclassification on adversarial perturbations even

with state-of-the art networks [3]. Therefore, as expected, it is easy to determine
SAT solutions and they were discovered very fast (within a minute). However,
it is very time consuming to prove safety; the verification time is much higher
than that of the ACAS Xu application as it is mainly impacted by the large
number of input variables (784 attributes). We would like to highlight that our
work is the first to successfully identify safety regions for MNIST even on a fairly
vulnerable network.

For 7 clusters, the solver returned UNSAT for all labels within 12 h. For 30
clusters, the solver returned UNSAT only for few labels but timed out before
returning any solution for the other labels. These have been included in the
targeted safe property in the table. Additionally, based on the nature of this
domain, we can consider it safe to assume that if for any label the solver does
not return a SAT solution within 10 h, then it is safe w.r.t. that label even
if it does not prove unsatisfiability within this time. This happened to be the
case for 33 clusters, where the solver could not find a solution for a specific
target label despite executing for more than 10 h. These have been included in
the *targeted safe* type as well. For 10 of the remaining clusters, the solver kept
finding adversarial examples despite iterative reductions of the radius and the
time-out occurred before the radius reduced to 0. These have been included as
time out in the table, since we cannot determine for sure if the region should be
marked unsafe for the specific labels.

5   Discussion

We compared DeepSafe with a method of randomly choosing inputs with known
labels and checking for local adversarial robustness using previous work [10].
This technique searches for inputs around the given fixed input, by varying each
input variable (dimension) in the range of $[fixedvalue - \epsilon, fixedvalue + \epsilon]$ (L_∞
distance metric). It checks if there exists any input in this range, for which the
network assigns a higher score to any other label than that of the fixed input.
The algorithm starts with a standard epsilon value of 0.1 and iteratively reduces
the value until UNSAT is obtained or the value reduces to 0.01. We chose 210
random points for ACAS Xu and 80 random points for MNIST respectively, in
line with the number of regions that we checked with DeepSafe.

We found that for MNIST, local robustness checking found no safe regions
around any of the 80 points, whereas DeepSafe found 7 safe regions and 63
targeted safe regions. For ACAS Xu, this technique yielded only 62 safe regions
which are completely safe compared to 125 safe regions that were found using
DeepSafe. This experiment shows that the choice of input points and the delta
around these points play an important role in effective adversarial robustness
checking. We also looked at the validity of the adversarial examples generated
by DeepSafe. If an adversarial example is invalid or spurious, it indicates that
the expected label is incorrect for that input and that the label generated by the
network is in fact correct. During our analysis for ACAS Xu we found adversarial
examples, which were validated by domain experts. The adversarial cases were

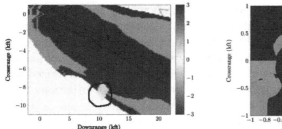
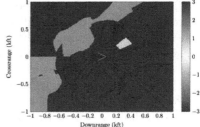

Fig. 3. Inputs highlighted in light blue are mis-classified as Strong Right instead of COC (left). Inputs highlighted in light blue are mis-classified as Strong Right instead of Strong Left(right).

Fig. 4. Images of 1 misclassified as 8, 4, and 3

found to be valid, albeit not of high criticality. The adversarial examples for MNIST were converted to images and manually verified to be valid (see Fig. 4).

There could be scenarios where both the region and the network agree on the labels for all inputs, and still this could not be the desired behavior. This would impact the *validity of the safety guarantees* provided by DeepCheck. We addressed this issue by validating the safety regions for ACAS Xu with the domain experts. The mismatch of labels for the centroid of a region does potentially indicate an imprecise oracle. However, we found that the number of such regions is not high (1029 out of 6145 clusters for ACAS Xu).

6   Related Work

The vulnerability of neural networks to adversarial perturbations was first discovered by Szegedy et al. in 2013 [17]. They model the problem of finding the adversarial example as a constrained minimization problem. Goodfellow et al. [6] introduced the Fast Gradient Sign Method for crafting adversarial perturbations using the derivative of the model's loss function with respect to the input feature vector. Jacobian-based Saliency Map Attack (JSMA) [14] proposed a method for targeted misclassification by exploiting the forward derivative of an NN to find an adversarial perturbation that will force the model to misclassify into a specific target class.

Carlini and Wagner [3] recently proposed an approach that could not be resisted by state-of-the-art networks such as those using defensive distillation.

Their optimization algorithm uses better loss functions and parameters (empirically determined) and uses three different distance metrics. Deep Learning Verification (DLV) [7] is an approach that defines a region of safety around a known input and applies SMT solving for checking robustness. They search for possibly-adversarial inputs by manipulating the given valid input in a discretized input space. They can only guarantee freedom of adversarial perturbations within the discrete points that are explored. Our clustering approach can potentially improve the technique by constraining the discrete search within regions.

Recent work [11] using Reluplex discusses in depth refined versions of global and local robustness, which take into account the *confidence* (C) that the network is placing on its predictions. For instance, the local robustness at input x_0 is defined as $\forall x. \|x - x_0\| < \delta \implies \forall l.\|C(F, x, l) - C(F, x_0, l)\| < \epsilon$. Similarly, the global robustness, informally introduced in [10], is defined as $\forall x, x'. \|x - x'\| < \delta \implies \forall l.\|C(F, x, l) - C(F, x, l)\| < \epsilon$. However, this check is expensive and also requires user input for acceptable values for both δ and ϵ. The motivation for taking into account the confidence is to better handle the inputs that lay on *boundaries* between labels, in the sense that there should be no spikes greater than ϵ in the levels of confidence that the network assigns to each labels for these points. However, the value of δ and *epsilon* need not be the same for all inputs and all labels respectively. For instance, points embedded deep inside consistently labeled regions, the δ should be large while for points on the boundaries between labels only a small δ could be tolerable. Nevertheless, we believe that DeepSafe can be used beneficially with the above approach, by automatically finding regions that can then be checked using the more refined local check.

7   Conclusion

This paper presents a data-guided technique for assessing the adversarial robustness of neural networks. The technique can find adversarial perturbations or prove they cannot occur within well-defined geometric regions in the input space that correspond to clusters of similar inputs known to share the same label. In doing so, the approach identifies and provides proofs for regions of safety in the input space within which the network is robust with respect to target labels. Experiments with the ACAS Xu and MNIST networks highlight the potential of the approach in providing formal guarantees about the robustness of neural networks in a scalable manner. Checking robustness for deep neural networks is an active area of research. As part of future work, we plan to integrate our approach with other solvers that will broaden the application of DeepSpace to other kinds of neural networks and also investigate testing, guided by the computed regions, as an alternative to verification for increased scalability.

Acknowledgements. This work was partially supported by grants from NASA, NSF, FAA and Intel.

References

1. Aggarwal, C.C., Hinneburg, A., Keim, D.A.: On the surprising behavior of distance metrics in high dimensional space. In: Van den Bussche, J., Vianu, V. (eds.) ICDT 2001. LNCS, vol. 1973, pp. 420–434. Springer, Heidelberg (2001). https://doi.org/10.1007/3-540-44503-X_27
2. Carlini, N., Katz, G., Barrett, C., Dill, D.: Ground-truth adversarial examples. Technical Report (2017). arXiv:1709.10207
3. Carlini, N., Wagner, D.: Towards evaluating the robustness of neural networks. In: Proceedings of 38th IEEE Symposium on Security and Privacy (2017)
4. Ehlers, R.: Formal verification of piece-wise linear feed-forward neural networks. In: D'Souza, D., Narayan Kumar, K. (eds.) ATVA 2017. LNCS, vol. 10482, pp. 269–286. Springer, Cham (2017). https://doi.org/10.1007/978-3-319-68167-2_19
5. Feinman, R., Curtin, R.R., Shintre, S, Gardner, A.B.: Detecting adversarial samples from artifacts. Technical Report (2017). arXiv:1703.00410
6. Goodfellow, I.J., Shlens, J., Szegedy, C.: Explaining and harnessing adversarial examples. Technical Report (2014). arXiv:1412.6572
7. Huang, X., Kwiatkowska, M., Wang, S., Wu, M.: Safety verification of deep neural networks. In: Majumdar, R., Kunčak, V. (eds.) CAV 2017. LNCS, vol. 10426, pp. 3–29. Springer, Cham (2017). https://doi.org/10.1007/978-3-319-63387-9_1
8. Julian, K., Lopez, J., Brush, J., Owen, M., Kochenderfer, M.: Policy compression for aircraft collision avoidance systems. In: Proceedings of 35th Digital Avionics System Conference (DASC), pp. 1–10 (2016)
9. Kanungo, T., Mount, D.M., Netanyahu, N.S., Piatko, C.D., Silverman, R., Angela, Y.Wu.: An efficient k-means clustering algorithm: analysis and implementation. IEEE Trans. Pattern Anal. Mach. Intell. **24**(7), 881–892 (2002)
10. Katz, G., Barrett, C., Dill, D.L., Julian, K., Kochenderfer, M.J.: Reluplex: an efficient SMT solver for verifying deep neural networks. In: Majumdar, R., Kunčak, V. (eds.) CAV 2017. LNCS, vol. 10426, pp. 97–117. Springer, Cham (2017). https://doi.org/10.1007/978-3-319-63387-9_5
11. Katz, G., Barrett, C., Dill, D., Julian, K., Kochenderfer, M.: Towards proving the adversarial robustness of deep neural networks. In: Proceedings of 1st Workshop on Formal Verification of Autonomous Vehicles (FVAV), pp. 19–26 (2017)
12. LeCun, Y., Cortes, C., Burges, C.J.C.: The MNIST database of handwritten digits. http://yann.lecun.com/exdb/mnist/
13. Papernot, N., McDaniel, P.D.: On the effectiveness of defensive distillation. Technical Report (2016). arXiv:1607.05113
14. Papernot, N., McDaniel, P.D., Jha, S., Fredrikson, M., Celik, Z.B., Swami, A.: The limitations of deep learning in adversarial settings. In: Proceedings of 1st IEEE European Symposium on Security and Privacy (EuroS&P), pp. 372–387 (2016)
15. Pulina, L., Tacchella, A.: An abstraction-refinement approach to verification of artificial neural networks. In: Touili, T., Cook, B., Jackson, P. (eds.) CAV 2010. LNCS, vol. 6174, pp. 243–257. Springer, Heidelberg (2010). https://doi.org/10.1007/978-3-642-14295-6_24
16. Pulina, L., Tacchella, A.: Challenging SMT solvers to verify neural networks. AI Commun. **25**(2), 117–135 (2012)
17. Szegedy, C., et al.: Intriguing properties of neural networks. Technical Report (2013). arXiv:1312.6199

Formal Specification for Deep Neural Networks

Sanjit A. Seshia$^{(\boxtimes)}$, Ankush Desai, Tommaso Dreossi, Daniel J. Fremont, Shromona Ghosh, Edward Kim, Sumukh Shivakumar, Marcell Vazquez-Chanlatte, and Xiangyu Yue

University of California, Berkeley, USA
sseshia@berkeley.edu

Abstract. The increasing use of deep neural networks in a variety of applications, including some safety-critical ones, has brought renewed interest in the topic of verification of neural networks. However, verification is most meaningful when performed with high-quality formal specifications. In this paper, we survey the landscape of formal specification for deep neural networks, and discuss the opportunities and challenges for formal methods for this domain.

1 Introduction

Deep neural networks (DNNs) are increasingly being deployed in domains where trustworthiness is a major concern, including automotive systems [41], health care [3], computer vision [35], and cyber security [13,53]. This increasing use of DNNs has brought with it a renewed interest in the topic of verification of neural networks, and more generally, in the topics of *verified artificial intelligence (AI)* and *AI safety* [4,47,52].

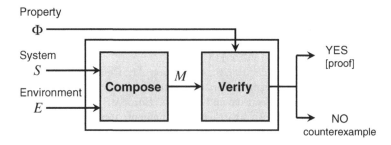

Fig. 1. Typical formal verification procedure: S is the system under verification, E is a model (or specification) of its environment, and Φ is the specification that system S must satisfy when composed with E.

Verification is most meaningful when performed with high-quality formal specifications, i.e., with a high-quality, mathematically rigorous specification of

S. K. Lahiri and C. Wang (Eds.): ATVA 2018, LNCS 11138, pp. 20–34, 2018.
https://doi.org/10.1007/978-3-030-01090-4_2

desired behavior that lends itself to algorithmic checking. As shown in Fig. 1, a typical formal verification procedure takes in not only a representation of the system under verification, but also the specification to be verified as well as a model (or specification) of the environment. Even as there is growing interest in the verification of DNNs (e.g., [20,32]), there is surprisingly little that has been written about formal specification for deep neural networks, in particular about properties that are particularly relevant for neural networks as opposed to other types of systems.

In this paper, we seek to address this gap by exploring the landscape of formal specification for deep neural networks (DNNs). We begin by exploring the use cases of neural networks in learning-based systems today, presenting a brief taxonomy of DNN-based systems under verification. We then consider the literature on the design, (adversarial) analysis, and verification of DNNs. These works have implicitly or explicitly specified a variety of properties. We present these properties, organizing them along two dimensions. First, we present a *semantic* classification of properties, based on their meaning and relevance for the verification of systems based on deep neural networks. Second, we present a *trace-theoretic* classification, where we take the standard view of properties defined using sets of traces, and discuss how the various properties fit into those categories.

Our overall goal is to lay an initial foundation for formalizing and reasoning about properties of DNNs, and for using these properties in a rigorous design and verification methodology. We conclude with a brief discussion of challenges and opportunities for applying formal methods to the design and analysis of DNNs.[1]

2   Deep Neural Networks: Background and Use Cases

We are assuming that the reader is familiar with the basics of deep neural networks (DNNs). For those not familiar with DNNs, we suggest one of the books on the topic (e.g., [25]). The goal of this section is to define basic notation and describe common patterns of DNN-based systems.

2.1   Notation

We will use fairly standard notation about machine learning in the supervised setting.

Consider a sample space Z of the form $X \times Y$, and an ordered training set $S = ((x_i, y_i))_{i=1}^{m}$, where $x_i \in X$ is the data and $y_i \in Y$ is the corresponding label. Let H be a hypothesis space (e.g., a particular neural network architecture parameterized by a weight vector w). If the network computes a function from X to Y, we will denote it by f_w; i.e., $f_w(x) = y$. There is a loss (or risk) function $\ell : H \times Z \mapsto \mathbb{R}$ so that given a hypothesis $w \in H$ and a sample $(x, y) \in Z$, we

---

[1] An early version of this paper appeared in [51].

obtain a loss $\ell(w, (x, y))$. We consider the case where we want to minimize the average loss over the training set S,

$$L_S(w) = \frac{1}{m} \sum_{i=1}^{m} \ell(w, (x_i, y_i)) + \lambda \mathcal{R}(w).$$

In the equation given above, $\lambda > 0$ and the term $\mathcal{R}(w)$ is called the *regularizer*; the latter seeks to enforce a notion of "simplicity" in w. Since S is fixed, we sometimes denote $\ell_i(w) = \ell(w, (x_i, y_i))$ as a function only of w. The training problem is to find a w that minimizes $L_s(w)$; i.e., we wish to solve the following optimization problem:

$$\min_{w \in H} L_S(w)$$

This optimization problem is also sometimes termed *empirical risk minimization*.

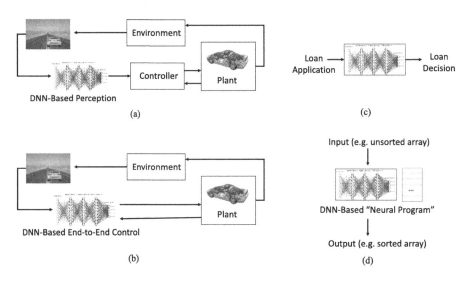

Fig. 2. Four use cases for DNNs in systems: (a) only for perception in a larger closed-loop system; (b) for end-to-end decision making, from perception to control, in a closed-loop system; (c) for open-loop decision making, and (d) for general-purpose programming.

2.2   DNN-Based Systems

DNNs have been used in a variety of systems. Figure 2 shows a selection of the types of DNN-based systems developed in research and development. Arguably their biggest impact to date has been in perceptual tasks, such as vision, natural language processing, speech recognition, etc. Thus, a major use case for DNNs is to perform perceptual tasks within the context of a larger closed-loop system, such as an autonomous vehicle, depicted in Fig. 2(a). An example of such a system is the automatic emergency braking system (AEBS) described by Dreossi et al. [15], where images taken by a camera mounted in front of an autonomous vehicle are fed to a DNN performing object detection and classification, whose output is sent to a controller that controls the steering angle and throttle of the autonomous vehicle. This vehicle then interacts with the rest of its environment (other vehicles, pedestrians, etc.) and the resulting interaction generates new sensor (image) data, closing the loop. In this case, the DNN is one component of a larger engineered system, which usually has its own specification that provides context for the design of the DNN.

The use of DNNs has also been demonstrated for so-called "end-to-end control", where neural networks go from sensor data to generating decisions and controlling actuation, as shown in Fig. 2(b). This example differs from Fig. 2(a) in that the DNN is used not just for perception, but also control. An example is an experimental self-driving system developed by a team at Nvidia [7].

Open-loop decision-making systems based on DNNs have also been proposed, such as a system that decides which loan applications to approve. This kind of system is depicted in Fig. 2(c). In this case, the DNN is the overall system under design and analysis.

Finally, the versatility of DNNs has also been demonstrated in general-purpose programming, such as learning programs for tasks such as sorting or string processing, shown in Fig. 2(d). This use case for DNNs has specifications similar to those arising in traditional program verification problems.

There are other use cases for DNNs not shown in Fig. 2, such as the use of stateful neural networks (e.g., recurrent neural networks) or the use of DNNs for reinforcement learning, where the DNN is used for sequential prediction and decision-making tasks.

Each of these use cases throws up different requirements. We will discuss the corresponding kinds of formal specifications in the following section.

3 Semantic Classification

We classify properties of deep neural networks based on the type of semantic behavior they capture. Each semantic category appears in a separate sub-section below; however, we note that these are not strict partitions, and there are some properties that fall into multiple categories.

3.1 System-Level Specification

Several systems use DNNs as one component in a larger system targeting a particular application. For example, consider the use of a DNN for object detection in an autonomous vehicle. In such settings, the end goal can typically be captured naturally in terms of a *system-level* specification—a property over the entire system that addresses the target application. As argued in recent papers (e.g. [18,52]), if the DNN is used for a perceptual task that mimics human perception, then it is very hard, if not impossible, to write a formal specification for that task. The overall system's specification, in contrast, can be described precisely, at least for engineered systems. Traditional specification formalisms, such as temporal logics, may be employed for the system-level specification.

An example of this approach is to specify the behavior of the automatic emergency braking system whose closed-loop diagram is shown in Fig. 2(a). The function of this system is to automatically actuate the brakes on the vehicle when it detects an environment object (obstacle) to be close. The objective is to maintain, at all times, a minimum safe distance between the autonomous vehicle (AV) and environment objects while the AV is in motion. We can write this specification in a standard specification language such as signal temporal logic (STL), as follows:

$$\mathbf{G} \ [\text{AV\_moving} \Rightarrow \text{dist}(\mathbf{x}_{AV}, \mathbf{x}_{env}) > \Delta]$$

However, to scale to large systems, compositional (modular) reasoning is necessary. This poses a challenge to perform compositional verification in the absence of traditional, assume-guarantee style compositional specifications [50]. In prior work [15,16,50], we have shown how to derive constraints on the input space of the DNN from a system-level specification. However, these constraints are a guidance on where to search for counterexamples rather than a specification for the DNN itself.

3.2   Input-Output Robustness

In recent years, a significant amount of work has addressed the robustness (or lack thereof) of neural networks to so-called "adversarial perturbations" of their inputs (for example, [5,9,27,38,42,43,54,58]). Techniques used to demonstrate a lack of robustness are often referred to as "adversarial analysis."

Optimization Formulation of Local Robustness: A common approach to adversarial analysis involves solving an optimization problem of the following form, given a fixed input x:

$$\min_{\delta} \mu(\delta)$$
$$\text{s.t. } \delta \in \Delta \qquad\qquad (1)$$
$$f_w(x + \delta) \in T(x)$$

Here μ is a cost function defined on the perturbations, typically a distance metric based on a norm ($L_1, L_2, or \ L_\infty$), Δ is a constrained domain set for δ, the constraint $f_w(x + \delta) \in T(x)$ ensures that the output of the NN to the perturbed input lies in the adversary's *target output set* $T(x)$ (which can be a function of x, e.g., $Y \setminus \{y\}$ where y is the correct label). Typically Δ is set to be the same as the domain of x, e.g., $\mathbb{R}^n$. This property is referred to as "local" robustness since it concerns robustness around a given input x.

For a recent survey (from a formal methods perspective) of techniques for analyzing robustness, see [18].

Decision Formulation of Local Robustness: The decision version of this optimization problem states that, given a bound β and input x, the adversarial analysis problem is to find a perturbation δ such that the following formula is satisfied:

$$\varphi(\delta) \doteq \mu(\delta) < \beta \wedge \delta \in \Delta \wedge f_w(x + \delta) \in T(x)$$

In other words, the robustness property is the negation of the above formula, $\neg\varphi(\delta)$:

$$[\mu(\delta) < \beta \wedge \delta \in \Delta] \Rightarrow [f_w(x + \delta) \notin T(x)]$$

Global Robustness: One can generalize the previous notion of robustness by universally quantifying over all inputs x, to get the following formula, for a fixed β:

$$\forall x. \; \forall \delta. \; \neg\varphi(\delta)$$

This is referred to as "global" robustness as we are not limited to analyzing robustness around a fixed point.

An alternative formulation of global robustness involves specifying that the DNN outputs a similar answer on all pairs of inputs (x_1, x_2) that are "close", as follows:

$$\forall x_1, x_2. \; [\mu(x_1 - x_2) < \beta \wedge (x_1 - x_2) \in \Delta] \Rightarrow [f_w(x_1) \approx f_w(x_2)]$$

where "$\approx$" is a suitably-defined notion of similarity between outputs of the DNN. *Loss-based Robustness:* Another formulation (e.g., [38]) involves finding a δ that maximizes the loss:

$$\mathbb{E}_{(xy)\sim D}[\max_{\delta \in \Delta} \ell(w, (x + \delta, y))] \tag{2}$$

where D is the distribution of the input space. In [38], the authors use the L_∞ norm to describe Δ as a bounded neighborhood around x.

This is a probabilistic formulation that involves knowledge of the distribution. In the absence of such knowledge, one may consider the worst case over the (x, y) space.

Additional Robustness Properties: Other authors have proposed alternative definitions of robustness in the literature. For instance, Bastani et al. [5] define notions of *adversarial frequency* (how often the DNN fails to be locally robust) and *adversarial severity* (the average robustness value exceeding a given threshold, averaged over inputs x chosen from some given input distribution). Cheng et al. [11] provide a definition of *maximum resilience* that is a global notion of robustness applying to multi-classification DNNs.

While these notions of robustness have been useful in demonstrating the limitations of DNNs for classification and other prediction tasks, as has been recently argued [18], they are not enough by themselves. We need to tie them to the overall application semantics. We discuss this point further in Sect. 3.

3.3 Input-Output Relations

Feedforward neural networks are programs that compute functions of their input. For such programs, one can write formal specifications in the standard manner: assuming a pre-condition on the inputs, $P(x)$, guarantee a post-condition $Q(x, y)$, i.e., $\forall x, y. \; P(x) \Rightarrow Q(x, y)$, where x and y are the inputs and outputs of the DNN respectively.

Researchers have identified special cases of pre/post-condition pairs for deep neural networks. For example, Dutta et al. [19] analyze properties of the form $P(x) \implies Q(y)$ where P and Q are restricted to certain kinds of geometric regions. Similarly, Dvijotham et al. [20] give examples of a similar class of restricted pre/post-condition pairs. These are typically partial specifications of sequential program correctness.

Deep neural networks are being used for other kinds of functional computations, such as neural Turing machines [30] and other neural programming architectures [8]. This case is depicted in Fig. 2(d). For these programs and formalisms, traditional classes of functional program specifications, those that provide complete specifications of program behavior, will also apply.

3.4 Semantic Invariance

For some applications, the input space X can be partitioned into equivalence classes $X_1, X_2, X_3, \ldots$, such that for each equivalence class $X_i \subseteq X$, and pair of inputs $x_{i1}, x_{i2} \in X_i$, we require that $f_w(x_{i1}) = f_w(x_{i2})$.

For instance, consider a DNN that must detect whether or not there is a car in an image. One may want to specify that the binary output of the network (car, ¬car) be invariant to translation or scaling of objects in the image. Examples of such properties are typically domain-specific. We refer to such properties as *semantic invariance*, an example of which is *geometric invariance* (see, for example, [14, 21, 26, 34, 37]).

3.5 Monotonicity

In certain applications, the input space X admits a natural partial order $\preceq$, and one expects the output of the classifier to be monotonic with respect to this ordering. A common example is a DNN used for approving loan applications: if Applicant A's income is strictly greater than Applicant B's, all else being equal, then one might expect that A's application would be granted if B's was.

One can formalize this property as follows:

$$\forall x_1, x_2 \in X . x_1 \preceq_X x_2 \implies f_w(x_1) \preceq_Y f_w(x_2)$$

where $\preceq_X$ indicates a preference order on X while $\preceq_Y$ denotes such an ordering on the output space Y.

For examples of papers discussing monotonicity properties, see [20, 59].

3.6 Fairness

Over the last decade, there is a growing literature on the need to ensure that machine learning (ML) systems produce outputs that are "fair" in some way. The notion of fairness typically has to do with certain attributes of the input vector x being sensitive, and that the decisions should not be influenced (perhaps in a statistical way) by those sensitive attributes. For DNNs, fairness is typically discussed in the context of decision-making systems similar to the one shown in Fig. 2(c).

This is still an evolving area, and there are many different formulations of fairness; see, e.g., [1,2,6,23,24,31,36]. One aspect shared by many is that they are probabilistic properties.

One class of fairness properties are *similarity-based fairness* properties, such as *individual fairness* (IF), which states that the neural network (ML model) maps similar inputs to similar outputs. This shares similarities with semantic invariance and robustness, except that the notion of similarity is different.

Another class of fairness properties are defined at the population level. An example is *demographic parity* which states that the probability of getting a particular output value is independent of the values of the sensitive attributes. In this respect, this property shares similarities with the notion of *non-interference* that has been researched in the formal methods and programming languages literature.

Yet another notion of fairness is counterfactual, relying on causal models (e.g. [36]). In this version of fairness, a decision output by a DNN is fair towards a particular input (individual) if that decision is the same in both the actual world and a counterfactual world where the input has a different value for one or more "protected" attributes (features).

3.7 Input/Distributional Assumptions

Many theoretical guarantees about machine learning algorithms are predicated on the assumption that the learned model is tested only on input drawn from the distribution it was trained on. Such distributional assumptions therefore form an important class of specifications. A specification language that captures such assumptions must inherently be probabilistic. We believe probabilistic programming languages (e.g., [10,28,29,39,45]), offer a natural and expressive way to specify distributions over the input space, and are thus a natural fit for such specifications. As an example, a recent probabilistic programming language for specifying input scenarios that can be used to generate input data for neural networks is described in [22].

3.8 Coverage Criteria

Formal specification can be useful even for testing or semi-formal verification of a system. This has been amply demonstrated in the design of digital circuits, where simulation-based verification of temporal logic assertions is standard. In this setting, formal specifications are often used to formalize *design coverage* objectives, e.g., to ensure that certain conditions are activated by a test suite.

We believe formal specifications could play a similar role for the analysis of DNNs. It is still unclear what sort of coverage properties are required. Some initial progress on coverage-driven testing of DNNs has been reported by Pei et al. [44].

3.9   Temporal Specifications

Stateful neural networks, such as recurrent neural networks (RNNs), essentially implement state machines. For such neural networks, the formalisms used to specify properties of state machines, and more broadly, of reactive systems, would apply. Temporal logics provide a suitable formalism to specify properties of such systems. An example of previous work in such a direction is that of Rodrigues et al. [46], while Taylor and Farrah [55] describe extracting rules from neural networks for verification, testing, and other purposes.

Another use of DNNs for stateful systems exhibiting temporally-varying behavior is in *deep reinforcement learning* (e.g., see [40]). In reinforcement learning (RL), an intelligent agent interacts with its environment through actions, observations and rewards [33]. Traditionally, specifications for RL have been given as quantitative objective (cost and reward) functions; however, there is also a large body of work on using temporal logics for specifying RL objectives (see, e.g., [48,57]).

3.10   Specifications on Learning Algorithms

Finally, one might want to specify properties on the learning algorithms themselves (and their implementations), rather than on specific learned models. Stochastic gradient descent (SGD) is a commonly used algorithm for training DNNs. As an example, we point out the recent work by Selsam et al. [49] on using interactive theorem proving to detect errors in systems that implement machine learning algorithms based on stochastic computation graphs.

3.11   Bridging System-Level Specifications with Component-Level Specifications

It has been recently observed [18] that although adversarial analysis of DNNs is useful, it is not sufficient. The relevance of adversarial attacks can be questioned when the impact on the overall system within which the DNN is used is unclear. Not all misclassifications are equally important. Thus, it is necessary to increase the use of application-level or system-level *semantics* in adversarial analysis and design of DNNs. There is a need to bridge system-level specifications with component-level specifications.

To this end, we believe it is important to devise a good notion of *semantic robustness* of DNNs to adversarial perturbations of the input. In order to do this, one needs to define the *semantic feature space* of the DNN—i.e., the feature space that captures application-level semantics and not just raw inputs (e.g., the pixel space for images). The raw input is obtained from the semantic feature vector through a process of "rendering", where we borrow the term from the rendering of images from high-level semantic configurations. As an example, consider the application of a DNN to perform object detection and classification in images captured for autonomous driving. In this case, the semantic feature space is one that captures high-level semantics of the scene around the vehicle – i.e., other agents that are present (cars, pedestrians, bicyclists, etc.) and their properties, parameters of the road and traffic scene, and other relevant characteristics. In this respect, this problem is similar to that of capturing input assumptions (see Sect. 3.7), although the emphasis here is more on the semantic features of the environment and less on the underlying distributions.

Let S represent the semantic feature space. Given $s \in S$, we obtain an input $x \in X$ by a process we will call *rendering* or *concretization*. (X is sometimes referred to as the "concrete feature space" to distinguish it from S.) Let R denote the rendering procedure; i.e., $R(s) = x$. Then, we introduce a notion of (global) *semantic robustness* as follows:

$$\forall s, s', x, x'. \, [s \approx_S s' \wedge R(s) = x \wedge R(s') = x'] \Rightarrow [f_w(x) \approx f_w(x')]$$

Similar to the notion of robustness described in Sect. 3.2, the above definition is based on a notion of similarity in the semantic feature space ($\approx_S$) and one on the output space of the DNN ($\approx$). Such a notion of similarity may well be based on a suitably-chosen norm and bound such as β or δ used in Sect. 3.2. However, we prefer the more abstract version given above given that much more work remains to be done in characterizing semantic feature spaces and their relation to the operation of the DNN. Further, the rendering procedure R may take in additional parameters (similar to those of the DNN w), which we hide here for simplicity.

Initial work on defining semantic feature spaces and bridging system-level specifications with component-level ones is just emerging. To our knowledge, the first work in this direction was [15,16], which uses a simple "modification" space to represent semantic transformations to images. Fremont et al. [22] present a more expressive language to capture semantic properties of a scene. However, these are very preliminary results, and much more remains to be done, as described in [18].

4   Trace-Theoretic Classification

We conclude with a brief categorization of the above types of properties with respect to their trace-theoretic nature.

Most properties in the formal methods literature tend to be *trace properties*; i.e., the property is equivalent to specifying a set of correct or desired behaviors of the system. For such properties, one can examine a single trace (input-output behavior) of the system and determine whether or not it violates the property.

However, certain properties are not trace properties, but are instead characterized as sets of trace sets (or a set of correct systems)—these are called *hyperproperties* [12]. Notable examples of such properties include determinism and security properties such as confidentiality and integrity. For such properties, one must examine an ensemble of two or more traces in order to determine whether the property has been violated. Hyperproperties cover all non-trace properties.

4.1   Trace Properties

Several system-level properties, such as those specified in linear temporal logic or metric temporal logics, are trace properties. Similarly input-output relations, temporal specifications for stateful NNs, and specifications on machine learning algorithms tend to be trace properties. Input-output robustness for a fixed input is a trace property. Certain coverage properties can be evaluated over single traces (e.g., whether specific neurons were activated on an input).

4.2   Hyperproperties

Some system-level properties, such as those specifying security policies, can be hyperproperties. Input-output robustness in the general case (for all inputs) is a hyperproperty; one must examine all pairs of inputs to determine if the system is robust. Similarly, semantic invariance and monotonicity involve reasoning over pairs of (related) traces. We note that all of the hyperproperties in this context are so-called two-safety properties, and so in theory are not much harder to verify or test than ordinary safety properties [56].

Fairness and average-case robustness are also hyperproperties, but of a probabilistic nature. Distributional assumptions on the input space are also properties of an ensemble of traces. Finally, some coverage properties are aggregate measures over sets of traces and thus are naturally hyperproperties.

5   Conclusion

In order to understand the design and verification problem for deep neural networks, it is essential to have a good understanding of the landscape of formal specification for DNNs. In this paper, we have presented a classification of the kinds of specifications that have been found useful for reasoning about neural networks and the systems that employ them. This serves as a starting point for creating a more systematic design methodology for DNNs.

Formal specifications can be used not only for verification and testing, but also for retraining, e.g., using counterexamples [17], or by using specification-guided cost functions or features (say by augmenting the regularizer $\mathcal{R}(w)$) in the training process. Specifications are also crucial to capture, in a rigorous manner, the assumptions made during the design process of DNNs, so that these can be taken into account during the design and operation of the overall system containing the DNN. We believe the field of formal methods for the design and analysis of deep neural networks, and of machine learning systems in general, will be a rich domain for research for the foreseeable future, and that formal specification will play a foundational role in this research.

Acknowledgments. The work of the authors on this paper was funded in part by the NSF VeHICaL project (#1545126), NSF projects #1646208 and #1739816, NSF Graduate Research Fellowships, DARPA under agreement number FA8750-16-C0043, the DARPA Assured Autonomy program, Berkeley Deep Drive, and by Toyota under the iCyPhy center. This paper was the outcome of discussions amongst the co-authors in early 2018. It has additionally benefited from conversations with Somesh Jha, Susmit Jha, Pushmeet Kohli, Aditya Nori, Jerry Zhu, and several participants in Dagstuhl Seminar 18121.

References

1. Albarghouthi, A., D'Antoni, L., Drews, S., Nori, A.: Fairness as a program property (2016), arXiv:1610.06067
2. Albarghouthi, A., D'Antoni, L., Drews, S., Nori, A.V.: Fairsquare: probabilistic verification of program fairness. In: Proceedings of the ACM on Programming Languages (2017)
3. Alipanahi, B., Delong, A., Weirauch, M.T., Frey, B.J.: Predicting the sequence specificities of DNA-and RNA-binding proteins by deep learning. Nat. Biotechnol. **33**, 831–838 (2015)
4. Amodei, D., Olah, C., Steinhardt, J., Christiano, P.F., Schulman, J., Mané, D.: Concrete problems in AI safety. ArXiV e-prints abs/1606.06565 (2016)
5. Bastani, O., Ioannou, Y., Lampropoulos, L., Vytiniotis, D., Nori, A., Criminisi, A.: Measuring neural net robustness with constraints. In: Lee, D.D., Sugiyama, M., Luxburg, U.V., Guyon, I., Garnett, R. (eds.) Advances in Neural Information Processing Systems (NIPS), vol. 29, pp. 2613–2621. MIT Press, Cambridge (2016)
6. Binns, R.: Fairness in machine learning: lessons from political philosophy (2017), arXiv:1712.03586
7. Bojarski, M., et al.: End to end learning for self-driving cars. arXiv preprint arXiv:1604.07316 (2016)
8. Cai, J., Shin, R., Song, D.: Making neural programming architectures generalize via recursion. arXiv preprint arXiv:1704.06611 (2017)
9. Carlini, N., Wagner, D.: Towards evaluating the robustness of neural networks. In: IEEE Symposium on Security and Privacy (SP) (2017)
10. Carpenter, B., et al.: Stan: a probabilistic programming language. J. Stat. Softw. **76**(1), 1–32 (2017)
11. Cheng, C.-H., Nührenberg, G., Ruess, H.: Maximum resilience of artificial neural networks. In: D'Souza, D., Narayan Kumar, K. (eds.) ATVA 2017. LNCS, vol. 10482, pp. 251–268. Springer, Cham (2017). https://doi.org/10.1007/978-3-319-68167-2_18
12. Clarkson, M.R., Schneider, F.B.: Hyperproperties. J. Comput. Secur. **18**(6), 1157–1210 (2010)
13. Dahl, G.E., Stokes, J.W., Deng, L., Yu, D.: Large-scale malware classification using random projections and neural networks. In: Proceedings of the IEEE International Conference on Acoustics, Speech and Signal Processing (ICASSP). pp. 3422–3426. IEEE (2013)

14. Dai, J., et al.: Deformable convolutional networks. In: IEEE International Conference on Computer Vision (2017)
15. Dreossi, T., Donzé, A., Seshia, S.A.: Compositional falsification of cyber-physical systems with machine learning components. In: NASA Formal Methods Symposium (2017)
16. Dreossi, T., Donzé, A., Seshia, S.A.: Compositional falsification of cyber-physical systems with machine learning components. In: Barrett, C., Davies, M., Kahsai, T. (eds.) NFM 2017. LNCS, vol. 10227, pp. 357–372. Springer, Cham (2017). https://doi.org/10.1007/978-3-319-57288-8_26
17. Dreossi, T., Ghosh, S., Yue, X., Keutzer, K., Sangiovanni-Vincentelli, A., Seshia, S.A.: Counterexample-guided data augmentation. In: 27th International Joint Conference on Artificial Intelligence (IJCAI) (2018)
18. Dreossi, T., Jha, S., Seshia, S.A.: Semantic adversarial deep learning. In: 30th International Conference on Computer Aided Verification (CAV) (2018)
19. Dutta, S., Jha, S., Sanakaranarayanan, S., Tiwari, A.: Output range analysis for deep neural networks (2017), arXiv:1709.09130
20. Dvijotham, K., Stanforth, R., Gowal, S., Mann, T., Kohli, P.: A dual approach to scalable verification of deep networks (2018), arXiv:1803.06567
21. Fawzi, A., Frossard, P.: Manitest: Are classifiers really invariant? (2017), arXiv:1507.06535
22. Fremont, D., Yue, X., Dreossi, T., Ghosh, S., Sangiovanni-Vincentelli, A.L., Seshia, S.A.: Scenic: Language-based scene generation. Technical report UCB/EECS-2018-8. EECS Department, University of California, Berkeley, April 2018. http://www2.eecs.berkeley.edu/Pubs/TechRpts/2018/EECS-2018-8.html
23. Friedler, S.A., Scheidegger, C., Venkatasubramanian, S.: On the (im) possibility of fairness (2016), arXiv:1609.07236
24. Friedler, S.A., Scheidegger, C., Venkatasubramanian, S., Choudhary, S., Hamilton, E.P., Roth, D.: A comparative study of fairness-enhancing interventions in machine learning (2018), arXiv:1802.04422
25. Goodfellow, I., Bengio, Y., Courville, A.: Deep Learning. MIT Press, Cambridge (2016). http://goodfeli.github.io/dlbook/
26. Goodfellow, I., Lee, H., Le, Q.V., Saxe, A., Ng, A.Y.: Measuring invariances in deep networks. In: Advances in Neural Information Processing Systems (2009)
27. Goodfellow, I.J., Shlens, J., Szegedy, C.: Explaining and harnessing adversarial examples (2014), arXiv:1412.6572
28. Goodman, N.D., Mansinghka, V.K., Roy, D., Bonawitz, K., Tenenbaum, J.B.: Church: a language for generative models. In: Proceedings of the Twenty-Fourth Conference on Uncertainty in Artificial Intelligence, pp. 220–229. UAI'08 (2008)
29. Gordon, A.D., Henzinger, T.A., Nori, A.V., Rajamani, S.K.: Probabilistic programming. In: FOSE 2014, pp. 167–181. ACM (2014)
30. Graves, A., Wayne, G., Danihelka, I.: Neural turing machines. arXiv preprint arXiv:1410.5401 (2014)
31. Hardt, M., Price, E., Srebro, N., et al.: Equality of opportunity in supervised learning. In: Advances in Neural Information Processing Systems (2016)
32. Huang, X., Kwiatkowska, M., Wang, S., Wu, M.: Safety verification of deep neural networks. In: Majumdar, R., Kunčak, V. (eds.) CAV 2017. LNCS, vol. 10426, pp. 3–29. Springer, Cham (2017). https://doi.org/10.1007/978-3-319-63387-9_1
33. Kaelbling, L.P., Littman, M.L., Moore, A.W.: Reinforcement learning: a survey. J. Artif. Intell. Res. **4**, 237–285 (1996)
34. Kanbak, C., Moosavi-Dezfooli, S.M., Frossard, P.: Geometric robustness of deep networks: analysis and improvement (2017), arXiv:1711.09115

35. Krizhevsky, A., Sutskever, I., Hinton, G.E.: Imagenet classification with deep convolutional neural networks. In: Advances in Neural Information Processing Systems, pp. 1097–1105 (2012)
36. Kusner, M.J., Loftus, J., Russell, C., Silva, R.: Counterfactual fairness. In: Advances in Neural Information Processing Systems (2017)
37. Lowe, D.G.: Object recognition from local scale-invariant features. In: IEEE International Conference on Computer Vision (1999)
38. Madry, A., Makelov, A., Schmidt, L., Tsipras, D., Vladu, A.: Towards deep learning models resistant to adversarial attacks (2017), arXiv:1706.06083
39. Milch, B., Marthi, B., Russell, S.: Blog: Relational modeling with unknown objects. In: ICML 2004 Workshop on Statistical Relational Learning and its Connections to Other Fields, pp. 67–73 (2004)
40. Mnih, V., et al.: Human-level control through deep reinforcement learning. Nature **518**(7540), 529 (2015)
41. NVIDIA: Nvidia tegra drive px: Self-driving car computer (2015), http://www.nvidia.com/object/drive-px.html
42. Papernot, N., McDaniel, P., Jha, S., Fredrikson, M., Celik, Z.B., Swami, A.: The limitations of deep learning in adversarial settings. In: Proceedings of the 1st IEEE European Symposium on Security and Privacy. arXiv preprint arXiv:1511.07528 (2016)
43. Papernot, N., McDaniel, P., Wu, X., Jha, S., Swami, A.: Distillation as a defense to adversarial perturbations against deep neural networks. arXiv preprint arXiv:1511.04508 (2015)
44. Pei, K., Cao, Y., Yang, J., Jana, S.: Deepxplore: automated whitebox testing of deep learning systems. In: Proceedings of the 26th Symposium on Operating Systems Principles, pp. 1–18. ACM (2017)
45. Pfeffer, A.: Figaro: an object-oriented probabilistic programming language. Technical report, Charles River Analytics (2009)
46. Rodrigues, P., Costa, J.F., Siegelmann, H.T.: Verifying properties of neural networks. In: Mira, J., Prieto, A. (eds.) IWANN 2001. LNCS, vol. 2084, pp. 158–165. Springer, Heidelberg (2001). https://doi.org/10.1007/3-540-45720-8_19
47. Russell, S., et al.: Letter to the editor: research priorities for robust and beneficial artificial intelligence: an open letter. AI Mag. **36**(4), 3–4 (2015)
48. Sadigh, D., Kim, E.S., Coogan, S., Sastry, S., Seshia, S.A.: A learning based approach to control synthesis of markov decision processes for linear temporal logic specifications. In: Proceedings of the 53rd IEEE Conference on Decision and Control (CDC), pp. 1091–1096, December 2014
49. Selsam, D., Liang, P., Dill, D.L.: Developing bug-free machine learning systems with formal mathematics. In: International Conference on Machine Learning, pp. 3047–3056 (2017)
50. Seshia, S.A.: Compositional verification without compositional specification for learning-based systems. Technical report UCB/EECS-2017-164. EECS Department, University of California, Berkeley, November 2017. http://www2.eecs.berkeley.edu/Pubs/TechRpts/2017/EECS-2017-164.html
51. Seshia, S.A., et al.: Formal specification for deep neural networks. Technical report UCB/EECS-2018-25. EECS Department, University of California, Berkeley, May 2018. http://www2.eecs.berkeley.edu/Pubs/TechRpts/2018/EECS-2018-25.html
52. Seshia, S.A., Sadigh, D., Sastry, S.S.: Towards Verified Artificial Intelligence. ArXiv e-prints, July 2016

53. Shin, E.C.R., Song, D., Moazzezi, R.: Recognizing functions in binaries with neural networks. In: 24th USENIX Security Symposium (USENIX Security 15), pp. 611–626 (2015)
54. Szegedy, C., et al.: Intriguing properties of neural networks (2013), arXiv:1312.6199
55. Taylor, B.J., Darrah, M.A.: Rule extraction as a formal method for the verification and validation of neural networks. In: IEEE International Joint Conference on Neural Networks (IJCNN), vol. 5, pp. 2915–2920. IEEE (2005)
56. Terauchi, T., Aiken, A.: Secure information flow as a safety problem. In: Hankin, C., Siveroni, I. (eds.) SAS 2005. LNCS, vol. 3672, pp. 352–367. Springer, Heidelberg (2005). https://doi.org/10.1007/11547662_24
57. Wen, M., Ehlers, R., Topcu, U.: Correct-by-synthesis reinforcement learning with temporal logic constraints. In: 2015 IEEE/RSJ International Conference on Intelligent Robots and Systems (IROS), pp. 4983–4990 (2015)
58. Weng, T.W., et al.: Evaluating the robustness of neural networks: an extreme value theory approach (2018), arXiv:1801.10578
59. You, S., Ding, D., Canini, K., Pfeifer, J., Gupta, M.: Deep lattice networks and partial monotonic functions. In: Advances in Neural Information Processing Systems (2017)

Regular Papers

Optimal Proofs for Linear Temporal Logic on Lasso Words

David Basin, Bhargav Nagaraja Bhatt[✉], and Dmitriy Traytel[✉]

Institute of Information Security, Department of Computer Science, ETH Zürich,
Zurich, Switzerland
`bhargav.bhatt.n@gmail.com, traytel@inf.ethz.ch`

Abstract. Counterexamples produced by model checkers can be hard
to grasp. Often it is not even evident why a trace violates a specification. We show how to provide easy-to-check evidence for the violation
of a linear temporal logic (LTL) formula on a lasso word, based on a
novel sound and complete proof system for LTL on lasso words. Valid
proof trees in our proof system follow the syntactic structure of the formula and provide insight on why each Boolean or temporal operator
is violated or satisfied. We introduce the notion of optimal proofs with
respect to a user-specified preference order and identify sufficient conditions for efficiently computing optimal proofs. We design and evaluate
an algorithm that performs this computation, demonstrating that it can
produce optimal proofs for complex formulas in under a second.

1 Introduction

Model checking is a successful formal verification technique. Designing an error-
free system using a model checker follows the cycle: (1) model the system and
formulate the specification it should adhere to, (2) run the model checker, (3)
if the tool finds an error, determine whether the error is in the model or the
specification, and (4) go back to Step 1 and change the model or the specification accordingly. Our focus in this paper is on Step 3, which can be extremely
challenging and time-consuming. To succeed there, the user must understand
the interaction between the model, the specification, and the counterexample.
Many prior approaches focus on explaining the interaction between the model
and the counterexample [3, 12–14], while neglecting the specification.

In many cases, the interaction between the specification and the counterexample is non-trivial to understand. Hence the question "Why does this counterexample violate this specification?" may be a hard one. Our work focuses
on this question in the context of model checking properties expressed in linear
temporal logic with past and future (LTL), where counterexamples are finite
words or infinite but ultimately periodic words (also called *lasso* words). In this
paper, we restrict our attention to lasso word counterexamples, although it is
possible to transfer most of our results to finite words.

© Springer Nature Switzerland AG 2018
S. K. Lahiri and C. Wang (Eds.): ATVA 2018, LNCS 11138, pp. 37–55, 2018.
https://doi.org/10.1007/978-3-030-01090-4_3

Given our restriction, we refine the question that we investigate to "Why does the counterexample uv^ω violate the LTL formula φ?" This question is independent of the specific model checking technique used to find the counterexample. Ignoring the "Why" in the question, we obtain the *LTL path-checking* problem [21], a core decision problem in for runtime verification. A decision procedure for this problem, namely a path-checking algorithm, computes a Boolean result which provides no insight into why the formula is violated. However, the algorithm itself knows why the formula is violated.

To expose the internal knowledge of an LTL path-checking algorithm, we must fix a suitable representation of this information. Our approach is to devise a *proof system* for LTL on lasso words, where proof search amounts to solving LTL path checking. Then, *proof trees* (or just *proofs*) in this setting capture the knowledge of the proof search algorithm and are the data structure that we output to explain violations. To be understandable, the proof system's rules must be as simple and as close to the standard semantics of LTL as possible. In particular, they should *not* be tainted with algorithmic details such as LTL's unrolling equations used in many path-checking algorithms.

Typically there are multiple (often infinitely many) different proof trees for a given formula and lasso word. Each proof tree represents a different way to explain the violation. Deciding which proof among the set of all valid proofs helps the user best understand the violation depends on the application scenario and the user. If the user's objective is to identify the most severe violation given an ordering of severity on atomic events, then he or she may be interested in proofs that focus on the particular events. For example, consider the formula $\Box(PipeSealed \wedge LightsOn)$, stating that the pipe is always sealed and the light is always turned on. When there are different violations, we might prefer learning about the more severe cases of pipe leakage than about the lights being switched off. In addition, it is useful to learn about the earliest point in time when the pipe started to leak. The proofs in our proof system can represent this information. Moreover, it might be preferable to give the user a concise proof. To flexibly handle different scenarios, we allow the user to specify a *preference order* on proofs. For preference orders that satisfy some monotonicity conditions, we devise a proof search algorithm that computes an optimal proof with respect to the order.

In summary, we make the following contributions. We describe a sound and complete proof system for LTL on lasso words, where proof search amounts to path-checking (Sect. 3). We define a notion of optimal proofs in our proof system with respect to a user-specified preference order. Since computing optimal proofs can be intractable for arbitrary orders, we identify sufficient conditions on the preference order for which an optimal proof can be efficiently computed (Sect. 4) and we use these conditions to devise an algorithm that computes an optimal proof (Sect. 5). Taken together, these contributions provide a new approach to explaining counterexamples generated by LTL model checkers. Finally, we evaluate and demonstrate the effectiveness of a prototype implementation of our algorithm on realistic examples (Sect. 6). We postpone the discussion of related work until after the presentation of our technical contributions (Sect. 7).

2 Linear Temporal Logic

We briefly recapitulate the syntax and semantics of *linear temporal logic (LTL)*. The set of LTL formulas over a set of atomic propositions P is defined inductively:

$$\varphi = p \mid \neg\varphi \mid \varphi \vee \varphi \mid \varphi \wedge \varphi \mid \varphi \, \mathcal{S} \, \varphi \mid \varphi \, \mathcal{U} \, \varphi,$$

where $p \in P$. Along with the standard Boolean operators, LTL includes the temporal operator $\mathcal{S}$ *(since)* and $\mathcal{U}$ *(until)*, which may be nested freely. For simplicity, we omit *next* and *previous*; however, all results in this paper can be easily extended to accommodate them. LTL formulas are evaluated on words over the alphabet $\Sigma = 2^P$. A word is an infinite sequence $\rho = \rho(0), \rho(1), \rho(2), \ldots$, where each $\rho(i) \in 2^P$. Whether an LTL formula is satisfied at time-point i for a fixed word ρ is defined inductively as follows.

$$
\begin{aligned}
&i \models p && \text{iff } p \in \rho(i) && i \models \neg\varphi && \text{iff } i \not\models \varphi \\
&i \models \varphi_1 \vee \varphi_2 && \text{iff } i \models \varphi_1 \text{ or } i \models \varphi_2 && i \models \varphi_1 \wedge \varphi_2 && \text{iff } i \models \varphi_1 \text{ and } i \models \varphi_2 \\
&i \models \varphi_1 \, \mathcal{S} \, \varphi_2 && \text{iff } j \models \varphi_2 \text{ for some } j \leq i \text{ and } k \models \varphi_1 \text{ for all } j < k \leq i \\
&i \models \varphi_1 \, \mathcal{U} \, \varphi_2 && \text{iff } j \models \varphi_2 \text{ for some } j \geq i \text{ and } k \models \varphi_1 \text{ for all } i \leq k < j
\end{aligned}
$$

Note that here, and in subsequent definitions, the dependence on ρ is left implicit.

A *lasso (word)* has the form $\rho = uv^\omega$, where u and v are finite words over the alphabet 2^P and $|v| \neq 0$. We refer to u as the *prefix* and v as the *loop* of the lasso word ρ.

Let $\mathsf{SF}(\varphi)$ denote the set of φ's strict subformulas (i.e., excluding φ) defined as usual. We pick some well-founded total order $\sqsubset$ over $\mathsf{SF}(\varphi)$ that respects the subformula ordering: if $\varphi_1 \in \mathsf{SF}(\varphi_2)$, then $\varphi_1 \sqsubset \varphi_2$. For a formula φ, the *past height* $h_p(\varphi)$ and the *future height* $h_f(\varphi)$ are defined as the number of nested past operators and future operators in φ, respectively. The *temporal height* $h(\varphi)$ is defined as $h_p(\varphi) + h_f(\varphi)$.

3 Proof System for LTL on Lasso Words

We introduce a proof system for LTL *path checking*. Proofs in this system witness the satisfaction or violation of an LTL formula with respect to a given lasso $\rho = uv^\omega$. Although we are primarily interested in violations, in the presence of negation it is convenient to reason about satisfaction as well. Our proof system therefore consists of two mutually dependent judgments: $\vdash^+$ (satisfaction) and $\vdash^-$ (violation), and is defined as the least relation satisfying the deduction rules shown in Fig. 1. The names of the satisfaction and violation judgment rules are suffixed by $^+$ and $^-$, respectively.

The satisfaction rules ap^+, $\neg^+$, $\vee_L^+$, $\vee_R^+$, $\wedge^+$, $\mathcal{U}^+$, and $\mathcal{S}^+$ directly follow the semantics of the corresponding LTL operators. For example, in the case of $\mathcal{S}^+$, the premise for $i \vdash^+ \varphi_1 \, \mathcal{S} \, \varphi_2$ includes a witness time-point j such that $j \vdash^+ \varphi_2$ and a finite sequence of satisfaction proofs of φ_1 for all $k \in (j, i]$. The violation rules for the non-temporal operators ap^-, $\neg^-$, $\vee^-$, $\wedge_L^-$, and $\wedge_R^-$ are dual. The

$$\frac{a \in \rho(i)}{i \vdash^+ a} \, ap^+ \qquad \frac{i \vdash^- \varphi}{i \vdash^+ \neg\varphi} \, \neg^+ \qquad\qquad \frac{a \notin \rho(i)}{i \vdash^- a} \, ap^- \qquad \frac{i \vdash^+ \varphi}{i \vdash^- \neg\varphi} \, \neg^-$$

$$\frac{i \vdash^+ \varphi_1}{i \vdash^+ \varphi_1 \vee \varphi_2} \, \vee_L^+ \qquad \frac{i \vdash^+ \varphi_2}{i \vdash^+ \varphi_1 \vee \varphi_2} \, \vee_R^+ \qquad\qquad \frac{i \vdash^- \varphi_1 \quad i \vdash^- \varphi_2}{i \vdash^- \varphi_1 \vee \varphi_2} \, \vee^-$$

$$\frac{i \vdash^+ \varphi_1 \quad i \vdash^+ \varphi_2}{i \vdash^+ \varphi_1 \wedge \varphi_2} \, \wedge^+ \qquad\qquad \frac{i \vdash^- \varphi_1}{i \vdash^- \varphi_1 \wedge \varphi_2} \, \wedge_L^- \qquad \frac{i \vdash^- \varphi_2}{i \vdash^- \varphi_1 \wedge \varphi_2} \, \wedge_R^-$$

$$\frac{j \le i \quad j \vdash^+ \varphi_2 \quad \forall k \in (j, i].\, k \vdash^+ \varphi_1}{i \vdash^+ \varphi_1 \, \mathcal{S} \, \varphi_2} \, \mathcal{S}^+ \qquad\qquad \frac{j \le i \quad j \vdash^- \varphi_1 \quad \forall k \in [j, i].\, k \vdash^- \varphi_2}{i \vdash^- \varphi_1 \, \mathcal{S} \, \varphi_2} \, \mathcal{S}^-$$

$$\frac{j \ge i \quad j \vdash^+ \varphi_2 \quad \forall k \in [i, j).\, k \vdash^+ \varphi_1}{i \vdash^+ \varphi_1 \, \mathcal{U} \, \varphi_2} \, \mathcal{U}^+ \qquad\qquad \frac{j \ge i \quad j \vdash^- \varphi_1 \quad \forall k \in [i, j].\, k \vdash^- \varphi_2}{i \vdash^- \varphi_1 \, \mathcal{U} \, \varphi_2} \, \mathcal{U}^-$$

$$\frac{\forall k \in [0, i].\, k \vdash^- \varphi_2}{i \vdash^- \varphi_1 \, \mathcal{S} \, \varphi_2} \, \mathcal{S}_\infty^- \qquad\qquad \frac{\forall k \in [i, max(i, |u| + h_p(\varphi_2) \times |v|) + |v|).\, k \vdash^- \varphi_2}{i \vdash^- \varphi_1 \, \mathcal{U} \, \varphi_2} \, \mathcal{U}_\infty^-$$

Fig. 1. Proof system for a fixed lasso word $\rho = uv^\omega$

violation rules for the temporal operators are more interesting. To arrive at $\mathcal{S}^-$ and $\mathcal{S}_\infty^-$, we negate and rewrite the semantics of $\mathcal{S}$:

$$i \nvDash \varphi_1 \, \mathcal{S} \, \varphi_2 \text{ iff } \forall j \le i.\, j \nvDash \varphi_2 \vee (\exists k \in (j, i].\, k \nvDash \varphi_1)$$
$$\text{iff } (\exists j \le i.\, j \nvDash \varphi_1 \wedge (\forall k \in [j, i].\, k \nvDash \varphi_2)) \vee (\forall k \le i.\, k \nvDash \varphi_2) \quad (\text{Eq. } \equiv_\mathcal{S})$$

The rules $\mathcal{S}^-$ and $\mathcal{S}_\infty^-$ correspond to the two disjuncts in the last right-hand side. Using this particular format for the rules (as opposed, for example, to the first right hand side, which requires deciding between two choices for all previous time-points) is a deliberate design decision. The violation proof $j \vdash^- \varphi_1$ in $\mathcal{S}^-$ allows us to disregard all the previous time-points at which φ_2 held, since these previous time-points cannot witness the satisfaction of $\varphi_1 \, \mathcal{S} \, \varphi_2$ exactly because of $j \vdash^- \varphi_1$. The second rule $\mathcal{S}_\infty^-$ covers the case when there is no such j with $j \vdash^- \varphi_1$. Then, to violate $\varphi_1 \, \mathcal{S} \, \varphi_2$ at i, the formula φ_2 must have previously always been violated.

For the future operator $\mathcal{U}$, we consider the dual semantic equation:

$$i \nvDash \varphi_1 \, \mathcal{U} \, \varphi_2 \text{ iff } (\exists j \ge i.\, j \nvDash \varphi_1 \wedge (\forall k \in [i, j].\, k \nvDash \varphi_2)) \vee (\forall k \ge i.\, k \nvDash \varphi_2) \quad (\text{Eq. } \equiv_\mathcal{U})$$

The rules $\mathcal{U}^-$ and $\mathcal{U}_\infty^-$ model the two disjuncts. Yet the assumption in $\mathcal{U}_\infty^-$ appears to be much weaker than what the right disjunct demands: instead of providing infinitely many violation proofs for φ_2 for every time-point $\ge i$, the rule requires only a finite number (that depends on the past height of φ_2, $|u|$ and $|v|$) of violation proofs for φ_2. This rule's soundness follows by taking the cyclic nature of the fixed lasso word into account. To see this, we recall a theorem from Markey and Schnoebelen [21] that states that the satisfiability of φ is periodic on lasso words after a certain threshold time-point.

Lemma 1. *Fix a lasso* $\rho = uv^\omega$. *For all* φ *and* $k > |u| + h_p(\varphi) \cdot |v|$, *we have* $k \vDash \varphi$ *iff* $k + |v| \vDash \varphi$.

Proof. By structural induction on φ with an arbitrary k.   □

Another induction extends this result to cover all time-points modulo $|v|$, starting from the threshold.

Corollary 1. *Fix a lasso $\rho = uv^\omega$. For all φ, $n \in \mathbb{N}$, and $k > |u| + h_p(\varphi) \cdot |v|$, we have $k \models \varphi$ iff $k + n \cdot |v| \models \varphi$.*

Proof. Induction over n with an arbitrary k using Lemma 1 in the induction step.   □

Corollary 1 yields that if $k \not\models \varphi$ for $k \in [thr, thr + |v|)$ (where $thr \geq |u| + h_p(\varphi) \times |v|$), then $\forall k \geq thr.\ k \not\models \varphi$. Intuitively, if we can prove often enough that a formula does not hold, then it will never hold. From this, the soundness of $\mathcal{U}_\infty^-$ follows easily. So does the soundness and completeness of the entire proof system.

Theorem 1. *Fix a lasso $\rho = uv^\omega$. For all φ and $i \in \mathbb{N}$, we have $i \vdash^+ \varphi$ iff $i \models \varphi$ and $i \vdash^- \varphi$ iff $i \not\models \varphi$.*

Proof. ($\Longrightarrow$, *Soundness*): Mutual induction over the structure of the derivations $\vdash^+$ and $\vdash^-$ using the Equations $\equiv_\mathcal{U}$ and $\equiv_\mathcal{S}$ for the temporal operators and Corollary 1.
($\Longleftarrow$, *Completeness*): Induction over the structure of φ for an arbitrary i.   □

We conclude this section with an example.

Example 1. Let $\rho = \{a, c\}(\{a, b\}\{c\})^\omega$ and $\varphi = a\,\mathcal{U}\,(b \wedge c)$. Here is a proof of $0 \not\models \varphi$:

$$\cfrac{\cfrac{\cfrac{b \notin \{a, c\}}{0 \vdash^- b}\ ap^-}{0 \vdash^- b \wedge c}\ \wedge_L^-\quad \cfrac{\cfrac{c \notin \{a, b\}}{1 \vdash^- c}\ ap^-}{1 \vdash^- b \wedge c}\ \wedge_R^-\quad \cfrac{\cfrac{b \notin \{c\}}{2 \vdash^- b}\ ap^-}{2 \vdash^- b \wedge c}\ \wedge_L^-}{0 \vdash^- a\,\mathcal{U}\,(b \wedge c)}\ \mathcal{U}_\infty^-$$

Such proofs explain why a formula is satisfied or violated on a lasso word. In this example, we immediately see that the $\mathcal{U}$ operator is violated because its second argument $b \wedge c$ is always violated. The proof provides witnesses for the violation of $b \wedge c$ at the first three time-points.

4   Proof Trees

To manipulate and compare proofs in the above system, we make them explicit. Namely, we define an inductive syntax for satisfying ($\mathfrak{sp}$) and violating ($\mathfrak{vp}$) proofs built using the rules in our proof system.

$$\mathfrak{sp} = ap^+(\mathbb{N}, \Sigma) \mid \neg^+(\mathfrak{vp}) \mid \wedge^+(\mathfrak{sp}, \mathfrak{sp}) \mid \vee_L^+(\mathfrak{sp}) \mid \vee_R^+(\mathfrak{sp}) \mid \mathcal{S}^+(\mathfrak{sp}, \overline{\mathfrak{sp}}) \mid \mathcal{U}^+(\mathfrak{sp}, \overline{\mathfrak{sp}})$$
$$\mathfrak{vp} = ap^-(\mathbb{N}, \Sigma) \mid \neg^-(\mathfrak{sp}) \mid \wedge_L^-(\mathfrak{vp}) \mid \wedge_R^-(\mathfrak{vp}) \mid \vee^-(\mathfrak{vp}, \mathfrak{vp}) \mid \mathcal{S}^-(\mathfrak{vp}, \overline{\mathfrak{vp}}) \mid \mathcal{U}^-(\mathfrak{vp}, \overline{\mathfrak{vp}})$$
$$\phantom{\mathfrak{vp} = } \mid \mathcal{S}_\infty^-(\overline{\mathfrak{vp}}) \mid \mathcal{U}_\infty^-(\overline{\mathfrak{vp}})$$

Here, $\overline{\mathfrak{sp}}$ and $\overline{\mathfrak{vp}}$ abbreviate finite sequences $[\mathfrak{sp}, \ldots, \mathfrak{sp}]$ and $[\mathfrak{vp}, \ldots, \mathfrak{vp}]$ of sub-proofs. The proof from Example 1 can be written as $P_1 = \mathcal{U}_\infty^-([\wedge_L^-(ap^-(0, b)),$ $\wedge_R^-(ap^-(1, c)), \wedge_L^-(ap^-(2, b))])$ using this syntax. In the following, we treat satisfaction and violation proofs uniformly, operating on the disjoint union $\mathfrak{p} = \mathfrak{sp} \uplus \mathfrak{vp}$. For a proof $p \in \mathfrak{p}$, we define $\mathbb{V}(p)$ to be $\top$ if $p \in \mathfrak{sp}$ and $\bot$ otherwise.

Observe that the time-points are only stored in the proofs of the atomic propositions. This is sufficient to associate each proof tree p with a time-point $i(p)$. For example, $i(\mathcal{S}^+(p, [q_1, \ldots, q_n]))$ is $i(q_n)$ if $n > 0$ and $i(p)$ otherwise. If the proof additionally passes a few syntactic checks with respect to a given formula φ (such as the constructors in the proof match the constructors in the formula) and a lasso word ρ (for atomic propositions), we call it valid for φ at $i(p)$ in ρ, written $p \vdash \varphi$ (again leaving the dependence on ρ implicit). We omit the straightforward formal definitions of $i(p)$ and $p \vdash \varphi$. It is easy to see that when $p \vdash \varphi$, we have that $\mathbb{V}(p)$ implies $i(p) \vdash^+ \varphi$ and $\neg \mathbb{V}(p)$ implies $i(p) \vdash^- \varphi$.

For a time-point i and a formula φ, multiple (in fact, potentially infinitely many) valid proofs may exist. For example, two additional valid proofs for the formula and the lasso word from Example 1 at time-point 0 are $P_2 = \mathcal{U}^-(ap^-(2, a), [\wedge_L^-(ap^-(0, b)), \wedge_R^-(ap^-(1, c)), \wedge_L^-(ap^-(2, b))])$ and $P_3 = \mathcal{U}^-(ap^-(4, a), [\wedge_L^-(ap^-(0, b)), \wedge_R^-(ap^-(1, c)), \wedge_L^-(ap^-(2, b)), \wedge_R^-(ap^-(3, c)),$ $\wedge_L^-(ap^-(4, b))])$. Let us compare the three proofs. The proof using $\mathcal{U}_\infty^-$ is smaller in size. In contrast, the proofs using $\mathcal{U}^-$ might be preferable as the $\mathcal{U}^-$ rule is very close to $\mathcal{U}$'s semantics and thus easy to understand (whereas understanding $\mathcal{U}_\infty^-$ requires understanding Lemma 1). Of the two $\mathcal{U}^-$ proofs, the shorter one is easier to digest. Still, different proofs might be preferable in different situations.

With no reasonable way to decide which proof to present to a user, we offer users a way to specify their preference using a *well-quasi-order* (*wqo*) $\preceq \subseteq \mathfrak{p} \times \mathfrak{p}$. A wqo is a well-founded preorder: a transitive and reflexive relation $\preceq$ for which the induced strict relation $\prec$ (defined as $p \prec q \iff p \preceq q \wedge q \not\preceq p$) is well-founded.

Example 2. Let $w :: \Sigma \to \mathbb{N}$ be a *weight function* on the set Σ of atomic predicates. We define, the weighted size $|-|_w :: \mathfrak{p} \to \mathbb{N}$ of a proof tree recursively as follows:

$$|ap^+(i, a)|_w = w(a) \qquad\qquad |ap^-(i, a)|_w = w(a)$$
$$|\neg^+(p)|_w = 1 + |p|_w \qquad\qquad |\neg^-(p)|_w = 1 + |p|_w$$
$$|\vee_L^+(p)|_w = 1 + |p|_w \qquad\qquad |\wedge_L^-(p)|_w = 1 + |p|_w$$
$$|\vee_R^+(p)|_w = 1 + |p|_w \qquad\qquad |\wedge_R^-(p)|_w = 1 + |p|_w$$
$$|\wedge^+(p_1, p_2)|_w = 1 + |p_1|_w + |p_2|_w \qquad\qquad |\vee^-(p_1, p_2)|_w = 1 + |p_1|_w + |p_2|_w$$
$$|\mathcal{S}^+(p, \overline{q})|_w = 1 + |p|_w + \sum_{i=1}^n |q_i|_w \qquad\qquad |\mathcal{S}^-(p, \overline{q})|_w = 1 + |p|_w + \sum_{i=1}^n |q_i|_w$$
$$|\mathcal{U}^+(p, \overline{q})|_w = 1 + |p|_w + \sum_{i=1}^n |q_i|_w \qquad\qquad |\mathcal{U}^-(p, \overline{q})|_w = 1 + |p|_w + \sum_{i=1}^n |q_i|_w$$
$$|\mathcal{S}_\infty^-(\overline{q})|_w = 1 + \sum_{i=1}^n |q_i|_w \qquad\qquad |\mathcal{U}_\infty^-(\overline{q})|_w = 1 + \sum_{i=1}^n |q_i|_w$$

Here, $\overline{q}$ abbreviates $[q_1, \ldots, q_n]$. The weighted size induces a total wqo on proofs by $p \preceq_{size}^w q \iff |p|_w \leq |q|_w$. If the weight function is the constant function $w(a) = 1$ for all $a \in \Sigma$, then $|p|_w$ is the number of constructors occurring in p, written $|p|$. We write $\preceq_{size}$ for the corresponding wqo. For the above proofs for the formula and lasso word from Example 1, we have $|P_1| = 7$, $|P_2| = 8$, and $|P_3| = 12$. Hence, $P_1 \preceq_{size} P_2 \preceq_{size} P_3$.

Our goal is to compute *optimal* proofs with respect to a user-supplied relation $\preceq$. We call p optimal for φ at $i(p)$ if for all valid proofs q for φ at $i(p)$, we have $q \not\prec p$. Note that at least one valid satisfaction or violation proof always exists by the completeness of our proof system and (non-unique) minimal elements of non-empty sets of proofs exist by the well-foundedness of $\prec$.

The existence of optimal proofs does not provide us with an algorithm to compute them. In general, it is impossible to compute the minimal elements of an infinite set of proofs with respect to a wqo $\preceq$. As a first step towards an algorithm, we restrict our attention to relations on which the proof constructors behave in a monotone fashion.

Definition 1. *A relation $\preceq$ is* constructor-monotone *if it satisfies:*

1. *If $i \leq j$ then $ap^+(i,a) \preceq ap^+(j,a)$ and $ap^-(i,a) \preceq ap^-(j,a)$ for any atom a.*
2. *If $p \preceq p'$ then $\neg^+(p) \preceq \neg^+(p')$, $\vee_R^+(p) \preceq \vee_R^+(p')$, $\vee_L^+(p) \preceq \vee_L^+(p')$, $\wedge_R^-(p) \preceq \wedge_R^-(p')$, and $\wedge_L^-(p) \preceq \wedge_L^-(p')$.*
3. *If $p_1 \preceq p_1'$ and $p_2 \preceq p_2'$ then $\wedge^+(p_1,p_2) \preceq \wedge^+(p_1',p_2')$ and $\vee^-(p_1,p_2) \preceq \vee^-(p_1',p_2')$.*
4. *If $m \leq n$, $p \preceq p'$, and $q_i \preceq q_i'$ for each $i \in \{1,\ldots,m\}$ then $\mathcal{S}^+(p,[q_1,\ldots,q_m]) \preceq \mathcal{S}^+(p',[q_1',\ldots,q_n'])$, $\mathcal{S}^-(p,[q_1,\ldots,q_m]) \preceq \mathcal{S}^-(p',[q_1',\ldots,q_n'])$, and $\mathcal{S}_\infty^-([q_1,\ldots,q_m]) \preceq \mathcal{S}_\infty^-([q_1',\ldots,q_n'])$.*
5. *If $m \leq n$, $p \preceq p'$, and $q_i \preceq q_i'$ for each $i \in \{m,\ldots,n\}$ then $\mathcal{U}^+(p,[q_m,\ldots,q_n]) \preceq \mathcal{U}^+(p',[q_1',\ldots,q_n'])$, $\mathcal{U}^-(p,[q_m,\ldots,q_n]) \preceq \mathcal{U}^-(p',[q_1',\ldots,q_n'])$, and $\mathcal{U}_\infty^-([q_m,\ldots,q_n]) \preceq \mathcal{U}_\infty^-([q_1',\ldots,q_n'])$.*

Lemma 1 only guarantees the equisatisfiability of a formula at time-points k and $k+|v|$, for k suitably large. Constructor-monotonicity can be used to significantly generalize this result to a proof comparison with respect to $\preceq$ at those time-points as follows.

Theorem 2. *Given a lasso $\rho = uv^\omega$, an LTL formula φ, and a constructor-monotone relation $\preceq$, if $k > |u| + h_p(\varphi) \cdot |v|$ then for all valid proofs q of φ with $i(q) = k + |v|$ there exists a valid proof p of φ with $i(p) = k$ and $p \preceq q$.*

Proof. Proof by induction on structure of φ with an arbitrary k.

– Case $\varphi = a$ directly follows from the constructor-monotonicity condition 1.
– Cases $\varphi = \neg\psi$, $\varphi = \varphi_1 \wedge \varphi_2$, and $\varphi = \varphi_1 \vee \varphi_2$ directly follow from the constructor-monotonicity conditions 2 and 3 and the induction hypotheses.
– Case $\varphi = \varphi_1 \, \mathcal{S} \, \varphi_2$. Let $thr(\varphi) = |u| + h_p(\varphi) \cdot |v|$. Suppose $k + |v| \models \varphi$. Let $P = \mathcal{S}^+(p,[q_{j+1},\ldots,q_{k+|v|}])$ be some valid proof of φ at $k + |v|$, i.e., there exists a $j \leq k + |v|$ such that p as a valid proof of φ_2 at j and the q_i are valid proofs for φ_1 at i for $i \in j+1,\ldots,k+|v|$. If $j \leq k$ then $P' = \mathcal{S}^+(p,[q_{j+1},\ldots,q_k])$ is a valid proof for φ at k. Moreover, $P' \preceq P$ by the constructor-monotonicity condition 4. (Here, we need the condition to apply

to finite sequences of different length.) Otherwise if $k < j$, then we have $j > k > thr(\varphi) >= thr(\varphi_2) + |v|$ and thus $j - |v| > thr(\varphi_2)$. Thus we can use the induction hypothesis on φ_2 (and p at $j - |v|$) and on φ_1 (and each of the q_i for $i \in \{j+1,\ldots,k+|v|\}$ at $i - |v|$) to obtain valid proofs p' of φ_2 at $j - |v|$ and q_i' for φ_1 at $i - |v|$ such that $p' \preceq p$ and $q_i' \preceq q_i$ for each $i \in \{j+1,\ldots,k+|v|\}$. Then $P' = \mathcal{S}^+(p', [q_{j+1}',\ldots,q_k'])$ is a valid proof of φ at k and moreover by the constructor-monotonicity condition 4 we have $P' \preceq P$.

Similarly for the case $k + |v| \not\models \varphi$, any proof P for φ at $k + |v|$ must either have the form $\mathcal{S}^-(p, [q_j,\ldots,q_{k+|v|}])$ or $\mathcal{S}_\infty^-([q_0,\ldots,q_{k+|v|}])$. In the former case, the reasoning to obtain a proof $P' \preceq P$ of φ at k is very similar to the case where $k + |v| \models \varphi$. In the latter case, it suffices to take $P' = \mathcal{S}_\infty^-([q_0,\ldots,q_k])$ to obtain $P' \preceq P$ by the constructor-monotonicity condition 4.

– Case $\varphi = \varphi_1 \mathcal{U} \varphi_2$ is similar to the $\varphi_1 \mathcal{S} \varphi_2$ case. For a valid proof P of φ at $k + |v|$, all immediate subproofs of P are proofs at future time-points, i.e., at least $k + |v|$. Thus the induction hypothesis is immediately applicable (unlike in the $\mathcal{S}$ case, where a case distinction was required). Thus, we obtain a valid proof P' of φ at k that has exactly the same structure as P, in particular regarding the lengths of the finite sequences of immediate subproofs in P and P'. Using the constructor-monotonicity condition 5, we can conclude $P' \preceq P$.

□

Theorem 2 allows us to stop the search for an optimal proof after a finite number of time-points. Thus, we could in principle compute a finite set of candidate proofs that is guaranteed to contain an optimal one and select a minimal element from this set. Such an algorithm would not be very efficient, as the set of candidate proofs might become extremely large. Instead, we give an algorithm that selects minimal elements eagerly and lifts optimal proofs of temporal connectives from time-points $i - 1$ (for $\mathcal{S}$) and $i + 1$ (for $\mathcal{U}$) to a proof at i. We first define the operator $+\!\!\!+$ that performs this lifting by combining subproofs of temporal formulas. We thereby abbreviate $[q_1,\ldots,q_n]$ by $\bar{q}$.

$$\mathcal{S}^+(p,\bar{q}) +\!\!\!+ r = \mathcal{S}^+(p, [q_1,\ldots,q_n,r]) \qquad \mathcal{U}^+(p,\bar{q}) +\!\!\!+ r = \mathcal{U}^+(p, [r,q_1,\ldots,q_n])$$
$$\mathcal{S}^-(p,\bar{q}) +\!\!\!+ r = \mathcal{S}^-(p, [q_1,\ldots,q_n,r]) \qquad \mathcal{U}^-(p,\bar{q}) +\!\!\!+ r = \mathcal{U}^-(p, [r,q_1,\ldots,q_n])$$
$$\mathcal{S}_\infty^-(\bar{q}) +\!\!\!+ r = \mathcal{S}_\infty^-([q_1,\ldots,q_n,r]) \qquad \mathcal{U}_\infty^-(\bar{q}) +\!\!\!+ r = \mathcal{U}_\infty^-([r,q_1,\ldots,q_n])$$

For a valid satisfaction proof p of $\varphi_1 \mathcal{S} \varphi_2$ at $i - 1$ (or $\varphi_1 \mathcal{U} \varphi_2$ at $i + 1$) and a valid satisfaction proof r of φ_1 at i, $p +\!\!\!+ r$ is a valid satisfaction proof of $\varphi_1 \mathcal{S} \varphi_2$ (or $\varphi_1 \mathcal{U} \varphi_2$) at i. Similarly, for a valid violation proof p of $\varphi_1 \mathcal{S} \varphi_2$ at $i - 1$ (or $\varphi_1 \mathcal{U} \varphi_2$ at $i+1$) and a valid violation proof r of φ_2 at i, $p +\!\!\!+ r$ is a valid violation proof of $\varphi_1 \mathcal{S} \varphi_2$ (or $\varphi_1 \mathcal{U} \varphi_2$) at i.

Constructor-monotonicity does not ensure that composing optimal proofs p and r will yield an optimal proof $p +\!\!\!+ r$. We therefore further extend our requirements on $\preceq$.

Definition 2. *A constructor-monotone $\preceq$ is* monotone *if it additionally satisfies:*

6. *If $p \preceq p'$ and $r \preceq r'$ then $p + \!\!\!+\, r \preceq p' + \!\!\!+\, r'$.*

We conclude this section by providing some (counter)examples of monotone wqos. The relation induced by the (weighted) size $\preceq_{size}$ (Example 2) is a monotone (total) wqo. Moreover, the relation $\preceq_{reach}$ defined as $p \preceq_{reach} q = reach(p) \le reach(q)$ where $reach(p)$ is the largest time-point occurring in the proof p is a monotone (total) wqo. The dual relation that maximizes the smallest occurring time-point is neither monotone nor well-founded. Given two monotone wqos $\preceq_1$ and $\preceq_2$, the Cartesian product $p \preceq_{\times} q \iff (p \preceq_1 q \wedge p \preceq_2 q)$ is a monotone wqo too. A more exotic example of a monotone wqo is the multiset extension of a total order on atomic propositions. Finally, the relation that compares the sets of occurring atomic propositions by inclusion is not monotone.

5   Computing Optimal Proofs

We now describe a *proof search* algorithm O that takes as input the prefix u and the loop v of a lasso word $\rho = uv^{\omega}$, an LTL formula φ, a time-point i, and a monotone wqo $\preceq$ and computes an optimal (with respect to $\preceq$) valid proof for the violation or satisfaction of φ at i. The algorithm determines whether the formula is satisfied or violated during proof search; it thereby solves the LTL path-checking problem along the way. Because our proof system is complete, O always returns a proof of either satisfaction or violation. This is in contrast to a previously proposed proof search algorithm for LTL [8] that computes (non-optimal) proofs in an incomplete proof system.

Our algorithm exploits the monotonicity of the $\preceq$ relation to both bound the number of proofs that must be considered and eagerly combine optimal proofs for subformulas to obtain an optimal proof for the entire formula. In other words, we compute proofs in a bottom-up manner (in terms of formula structure), such that proofs of φ are constructed using only the optimal proofs of φ's immediate subformulas. For a fixed monotone wqo $\preceq$ and $\rho = uv^{\omega}$, our algorithm consists of two mutually recursive functions $O(i, \varphi)$ and $C(i, \varphi)$, shown in Fig. 2. The *optimal proof* function $O(i, \varphi)$ merely selects an optimal proof from a small set of *candidate proofs* (computed by C) at time-point i. The function $C(i, \varphi)$ composes optimal proofs (computed by O) for φ's subformulas at the current time-point i and optimal proofs for φ at the previous $(i-1)$ and next $(i+1)$ time-points, exploiting the standard unrolling equations for $\mathcal{S}$ and $\mathcal{U}$.

The function $C(i, \varphi)$ is defined by pattern matching on the formula φ's structure. The cases for atomic propositions and Boolean connectives are simple; for conjunction and disjunction we use the auxiliary functions $doDisj$ and $doConj$ (Fig. 3) to compose optimal proofs of the subformulas. The precise outcome depends on whether the subformulas are satisfied or violated. For example, for $\varphi_1 \wedge \varphi_2$, we obtain a $\wedge^+$ proof only if both subformulas are satisfied, i.e., $\mathbb{V}(p_1)$ and $\mathbb{V}(p_2)$ are $\top$.

$\mathsf{C}(i, a) =$
   if $a \in \rho(i)$ then $\{ap^+(i,a)\}$ else $\{ap^-(i,a)\}$
$\mathsf{C}(i, \neg\varphi) =$
   let $p = \mathsf{O}(i, \varphi)$ in
   if $\mathbb{V}(p)$ then $\{\neg^-(p)\}$ else $\{\neg^+(p)\}$
$\mathsf{C}(i, \varphi_1 \vee \varphi_2) =$
   $doDisj(\mathsf{O}(i, \varphi_1), \mathsf{O}(i, \varphi_2))$
$\mathsf{C}(i, \varphi_1 \wedge \varphi_2) =$
   $doConj(\mathsf{O}(i, \varphi_1), \mathsf{O}(i, \varphi_2))$
$\mathsf{C}(i, \varphi_1 \, \mathcal{S} \, \varphi_2) =$
   if $i = 0$ then
      let $p_2 = \mathsf{O}(i, \varphi_2)$ in
      if $\mathbb{V}(p_2)$ then $\{\mathcal{S}^+(p_2, [])\}$ else $\{\mathcal{S}^-_\infty([p_2])\}$
   else
      $doSince(\mathsf{O}(i, \varphi_1), \mathsf{O}(i, \varphi_2), \mathsf{O}(i-1, \varphi_1 \, \mathcal{S} \, \varphi_2))$
$\mathsf{C}(i, \varphi_1 \, \mathcal{U} \, \varphi_2) =$
   $doUntil^\omega(i, \varphi_2) \cup doUntil^n(i, \varphi_1, \varphi_2)$

$\mathsf{O}(i, \varphi) = \min_\preceq(\mathsf{C}(i, \varphi))$

$doUntil^\omega(i, \varphi_2) =$
   if $i < |u| + h_p(\varphi_2) \cdot |v|$ then $\{\}$
   else
      let $ps_2 = [\mathsf{O}(i, \varphi_2), \ldots, \mathsf{O}(i+|v|-1, \varphi_2)]$ in
      if $\forall x \in ps_2. \neg\mathbb{V}(x)$ then $\{\mathcal{U}^-_\infty(ps_2)\}$ else $\{\}$

$doUntil^n(i, \varphi_1, \varphi_2) =$
   if $i < |u| + h_p(\varphi_1 \, \mathcal{U} \, \varphi_2) \cdot |v|$
   then
      $doUntil(\mathsf{O}(i, \varphi_1), \mathsf{O}(i, \varphi_2), \mathsf{O}(i+1, \varphi_1 \, \mathcal{U} \, \varphi_2))$
   else
      let $ps_1 = [\mathsf{O}(i, \varphi_1), \ldots, \mathsf{O}(i+|v|-1, \varphi_1)]$ in
      let $ps_2 = [\mathsf{O}(i, \varphi_2), \ldots, \mathsf{O}(i+|v|-1, \varphi_2)]$ in
      $\{\mathcal{U}^+(ps_2[j], [ps_1[0], \ldots, ps_1[j-1]]) \mid j < |v| \wedge$
        $\mathbb{V}(ps_2[j]) \wedge \forall k < j. \, \mathbb{V}(ps_1[k])\} \cup$
      $\{\mathcal{U}^-(ps_1[j], [ps_2[0], \ldots, ps_2[j]]) \mid j < |v| \wedge$
        $\neg\mathbb{V}(ps_1[j]) \wedge \forall k \leq j. \, \neg\mathbb{V}(ps_2[k])\}$

Fig. 2. Optimal proof algorithm: functions C, O, $doUntil^\omega$ and $doUntil^n$

Temporal operators are more challenging to deal with. Setting the special case of $i = 0$ aside, C computes for the formula $\varphi_1 \, \mathcal{S} \, \varphi_2$ optimal proofs of φ_1 and φ_2 at i and an optimal proof of φ at $i - 1$. These proofs are given to the auxiliary $doSince$ function (Fig. 4) that performs a case distinction on their truth values $\mathbb{V}(-)$ and accordingly constructs a set of proofs unrolling $\mathcal{S}$: $i \models \varphi_1 \, \mathcal{S} \, \varphi_2$ iff $i \models \varphi_2 \vee i \models \varphi_1 \wedge i-1 \models \varphi_1 \, \mathcal{S} \, \varphi_2$. Note that the set $\mathsf{C}(i, \varphi_1 \, \mathcal{S} \, \varphi_2)$ contains at least one and at most two elements. For example, if $i \models \varphi_2$, $i \models \varphi_2$, and $i - 1 \models \varphi_1 \, \mathcal{S} \, \varphi_2$ all hold (and we have computed the optimal proofs for them), then there are two candidate proofs for $\varphi_1 \, \mathcal{S} \, \varphi_2$ corresponding to the two disjuncts in the unrolling equation.

Performing a dual unrolling for $\mathcal{U}$ would immediately lead to non-termination. However, since ρ is a lasso word, we can bound the proof search using Theorem 2. The case $\mathsf{C}(i, \varphi_1 \, \mathcal{U} \, \varphi_2)$ splits the proof search in two parts: $doUntil^\omega$ which corresponds to applying the rule $\mathcal{U}^-_\infty$ and $doUntil^n$ which corresponds to either extending any $\mathcal{U}$ proof at time-point $i + 1$ or applying $\mathcal{U}^+$ or $\mathcal{U}^-$ with a fixed bound on the time-point j occurring in the assumptions of those rules. The function $doUntil^\omega$ checks whether the premises of $\mathcal{U}^-_\infty$ holds (i.e., $i > |u| + h_p(\varphi_2) \cdot |v|$ and $\forall k \in [i, i+|v|). \, k \not\models \varphi_2$) and either returns a single $\mathcal{U}^-_\infty$ proof or an empty set (if some premise is violated). The function $doUntil^n$ checks if the time-point i is larger than $|u| + h_p(\varphi_1 \, \mathcal{U} \, \varphi_2) \cdot |v|$, which is the threshold after which the measure of valid proofs of $\varphi_1 \, \mathcal{U} \, \varphi_2$ cannot decrease anymore by Theorem 2. For time-points before the threshold, the unrolling characterization of $\mathcal{U}$ is used to construct the proofs using $doUntil$ (similar to $doSince$). For time-points after the threshold, it is sufficient to only search for proofs that use as subproofs only those proofs of φ_1 and φ_2 at time-points less than $i+|v|$, which ensures termination of the entire algorithm. Because of the soundness and com-

$\mathbb{V}(p_1)$	$\mathbb{V}(p_2)$	$doDisj(p_1,p_2)$	$doConj(p_1,p_2)$
$\top$	$\top$	$\{\vee_L^+(p_1),\vee_R^+(p_2)\}$	$\{\wedge^+(p_1,p_2)\}$
$\top$	$\bot$	$\{\vee_L^+(p_1)\}$	$\{\wedge_R^-(p_2)\}$
$\bot$	$\top$	$\{\vee_R^+(p_2)\}$	$\{\wedge_L^-(p_1)\}$
$\bot$	$\bot$	$\{\vee^-(p_1,p_2)\}$	$\{\wedge_L^-(p_1),\wedge_R^-(p_2)\}$

Fig. 3. Functions $doDisj$ and $doConj$

$\mathbb{V}(p_1)$	$\mathbb{V}(p_2)$	$\mathbb{V}(p')$	$doSince(p_1,p_2,p')$	$doUntil(p_1,p_2,p')$
$\top$	$\top$	$\top$	$\{\mathcal{S}^+(p_2,[]),p'\mathbin{+\!\!+}p_1\}$	$\{\mathcal{U}^+(p_2,[]),p'\mathbin{+\!\!+}p_1\}$
$\top$	$\bot$	$\top$	$\{p'\mathbin{+\!\!+}p_1\}$	$\{p'\mathbin{+\!\!+}p_1\}$
$\bot$	$\bot$	$\top$	$\{\mathcal{S}^-(p_1,[p_2])\}$	$\{\mathcal{U}^-(p_1,[p_2])\}$
$\top$	$\bot$	$\bot$	$\{p'\mathbin{+\!\!+}p_2\}$	$\{p'\mathbin{+\!\!+}p_2\}$
$\bot$	$\bot$	$\bot$	$\{\mathcal{S}^-(p_1,[p_2]),p'\mathbin{+\!\!+}p_2\}$	$\{\mathcal{U}^-(p_1,[p_2]),p'\mathbin{+\!\!+}p_2\}$
	otherwise		$\{\mathcal{S}^+(p_2,[])\}$	$\{\mathcal{U}^+(p_2,[])\}$

Fig. 4. Functions $doSince$ and $doUntil$

pleteness of the proof system, exactly one of the sets is necessarily non-empty in the union returned in the else branch of $doUntil^n$.

We prove that our algorithm always terminates.

Lemma 2. $\mathsf{C}(i,\varphi)$ *(and thus also* $\mathsf{O}(i,\varphi)$*) terminates for any* i, φ, ρ, *and* $\preceq$.

Proof. We define the function $\mathsf{dist}(i,\varphi)$ as $|u| + h_\rho(\varphi) \cdot |v| - i$ if $\varphi = \varphi_1 \,\mathcal{U}\, \varphi_2$ and as i otherwise. Consider the well-founded relation $\ll$ defined as the lexicographic product of the subformula relation $\sqsubset$ and a dist-comparison, i.e., $(i,\varphi) \ll (j,\psi) \iff \varphi \sqsubset \psi \vee (\varphi = \psi \wedge \mathsf{dist}(i,\varphi) < \mathsf{dist}(j,\psi))$. The relation $\ll$ is decreasing along the call graph of C (after unfolding the definition of O). $\square$

We now prove our algorithm's correctness. We fix a lasso word $\rho = uv^\omega$ and a monotone wqo $\preceq$. We first establish properties of the auxiliary functions $doConj$, $doDisj$, and $doSince$. The case of $\mathcal{U}$ is a bit subtle as the proof search is split between the functions $doUntil^\omega$ and $doUntil$; hence we reason about them together in the following lemma.

Lemma 3. *For a time-point* i, *let* p_1 *and* p_2 *be optimal proofs of* φ_1 *at* i *and* φ_2 *at* i, *respectively.*

- *Let* $\varphi = \varphi_1 \,\mathcal{S}\, \varphi_2$ *and* p' *be an optimal proof of* φ *at* $i-1$. *If* $i \neq 0$, *then all proofs in* $doSince(p_1,p_2,p')$ *are valid proofs of* φ *at* i *and an optimal proof is contained among them.*
- *The same holds for* $doDisj(p_1,p_2)$ *for* $\varphi = \varphi_1 \vee \varphi_2$ *and* $doConj(p_1,p_2)$ *for* $\varphi = \varphi_1 \wedge \varphi_2$.
- *Let* $\varphi = \varphi_1 \,\mathcal{U}\, \varphi_2$ *and* p' *be an optimal proof of* φ *at* $i+1$. *Then all proofs in* $doUntil^\omega(i,\varphi_2) \cup doUntil(p_1,p_2,p')$ *are valid proofs of* φ *at* i *and an optimal proof is contained among them.*

Proof (sketch for $\mathcal{S}$). We make a case distinction on the truth values $\mathbb{V}(p_1)$, $\mathbb{V}(p_2)$, and $\mathbb{V}(p')$. Here, we only consider the case where $\mathbb{V}(p_1) = \mathbb{V}(p_2) = \mathbb{V}(p') = \top$. Then $doSince(p_1, p_2, p') = \{\mathcal{S}^+(p_2, []), p' \mathbin{+\!\!+} p_1\}$. Any valid proof of φ at i is either of the form $\mathcal{S}^+(q_2, [])$ or $q' \mathbin{+\!\!+} q_1$. Using the constructor-monotonicity condition 4, the monotonicity condition 6, and the optimality of p_1, p_2, p', we conclude that either $\mathcal{S}^+(p_2, [])$ or $p' \mathbin{+\!\!+} p_1$ is optimal. The other cases follow by similar arguments using the appropriate (constructor-)monotonicity conditions. □

We next prove the soundness and optimality of C, from which the same properties of O follow (also by induction hypotheses for the recursive calls to O in this proof itself).

Theorem 3. *Let $C = \mathsf{C}(i, \varphi)$ for a fixed lasso $\rho = uv^\omega$ and a monotone wqo $\preceq$. We have:*

Soundness *All proofs in C are valid proofs of φ at i.*
Optimality *An optimal proof of φ at i is contained in C.*

Proof. (sketch). Proof by well-founded induction on $\ll$, the relation used to establish the termination of C in the proof of Lemma 2. As before, we write $thr(\varphi)$ to abbreviate the threshold $|u| + h_p(\varphi) \cdot |v|$. We perform a case distinction on φ. The cases for atomic propositions, Boolean operators, and $\mathcal{S}$ are either simple or follow directly from Lemma 3. We focus on optimality in the $\varphi = \varphi_1 \mathcal{U} \varphi_2$ case.

Suppose $i < thr(\varphi)$. Then $\mathsf{C}(i, \varphi) = doUntil^\omega(i, \varphi_2) \cup doUntil(p_1, p_2, p'_\varphi)$ with $p_1 = \mathsf{O}(i, \varphi_1)$, $p_2 = \mathsf{O}(i, \varphi_2)$, and $p' = \mathsf{O}(i + 1, \varphi)$. (Note that $doUntil^\omega(i, \varphi_2) = \{\}$ for $i < thr(\varphi_2)$.) Using the induction hypothesis, we have the optimality of p_1, p_2, and p'. The case follows using Lemma 3.

Suppose $i \geq thr(\varphi)$. Then the set of candidate proofs computed by $doUntil^n$ consists of only valid $\mathcal{U}^+$ and $\mathcal{U}^-$ proofs of φ whose immediate subproofs are proofs at time-points up to $i + |v|$. As before, $doUntil^\omega(i, \varphi)$ accounts for a potential proof of φ obtained using the $\mathcal{U}^-_\infty$ rule at i. We know that the proofs in ps_1 and ps_2 are optimal by the induction hypothesis. Suppose there exists an optimal proof at i that goes beyond $i + |v|$. Assume it is a satisfaction proof P of the form $\mathcal{U}^+(p, [q_i, \ldots, q_k])$ for some $k > i + |v|$ (the case for violation proofs follows analogously). Then there exist $k_1 > 0$ and $k_2 < |v|$ such that $k = i + k_1 \cdot |v| + k_2$. By the constructor-monotonicity condition 5, for the proof $P' = \mathcal{U}^+(p, [q_{i + k_1 \cdot |v|}, \ldots, q_k])$ of φ at $i + k_1 \cdot |v|$ we have $P' \preceq P$. Using Theorem 2 k_1 times, we obtain another proof $P'' = \mathcal{U}^+(p', [q'_i, \ldots, q'_{k_2}])$ of φ at i with $P'' \preceq P'$. Because of the transitivity of $\preceq$ and the optimality of P, P'' is another optimal proof of φ at i. But P'' belongs to the set of proofs computed by $doUntil^n$. □

Corollary 2. *For a fixed lasso word ρ and a monotone wqo $\preceq$, the function $\mathsf{O}(i, \varphi)$ outputs an optimal (with respect to $\preceq$) valid proof p of φ at i.*

Finally, we discuss the time complexity of O.

Theorem 4. *For a fixed lasso $\rho = uv^\omega$ and a monotone wqo $\preceq$, an upper bound for the time complexity of $\mathsf{O}(0, \varphi)$ is $\mathcal{O}((|u| + h(\varphi) \cdot |v|) \cdot |\mathsf{SF}(\varphi)| \cdot f(\preceq) \cdot w(\preceq) \cdot |v|)$, where $f(\preceq)$ is the complexity of comparing proofs with respect to $\preceq$ and $w(\preceq)$ is the width of $\preceq$, i.e., the maximum size of an antichain in $\preceq$.*

Proof (sketch). To compute $\mathsf{O}(0, \varphi)$, the largest k at which $\mathsf{O}(k, \varphi)$ can be recursively called is $thr(\varphi) = |u| + h_p(\varphi) \cdot |v|$. Furthermore, to compute $\mathsf{O}(i, \psi)$ at $i \geq thr(\varphi)$ for some subformula ψ of φ, the largest time-point at which O is recursively called on immediate subformulas is $i + |v|$ if $\varphi = \varphi_1 \, \mathcal{U} \, \varphi_2$ and it is zero otherwise. Therefore, the largest time-point at which O is recursively called is $thr(\varphi) + h_f(\varphi) \cdot |v| = |u| + h(\varphi) \cdot |v|$. In the worst case, for each time-point i, O can be called for every subformula. Hence, the parametrized time complexity is $\mathcal{O}((|u| + h(\varphi) \cdot |v|) \cdot |\mathsf{SF}(\varphi)| \cdot f(\preceq) \cdot w(\preceq) \cdot M)$, where M is the largest cardinality of a set returned by C. Note that the $\mathcal{O}(f(\preceq) \cdot w(\preceq) \cdot M)$ is an upper bound on the complexity of computing a minimal element with respect to $\preceq$ in a set of size M [9]. If $\varphi = \varphi_1 \, \mathcal{U} \, \varphi_2$ and $i \geq thr(\varphi)$, then M is bounded by $|v|$ and otherwise it is at most 2. Hence, the calls $\mathsf{O}(i, \varphi)$ that trigger an expensive minimum computation are very rare compared to the overall number of calls. Also note that in case $\preceq$ is total, we have $w(\preceq) = 1$.

We ignored above that O may be called several times with the same arguments. Memoizing O provides a countermeasure against this potential inefficiency. $\square$

6   Implementation and Evaluation

We implemented the presented algorithm in a publicly available prototype [1]. The implementation is concise: altogether about 1500 lines of OCaml code. Our tool supports a much richer LTL syntax than the one shown in this paper: users can write formulas involving *true, false, (bi)implications* → and ↔, *next* ○, *previous* ●, *eventually* ◇, *always* □, *once* ◆, and *historically* ■. All of these operators are treated as first class citizens: optimal proofs are computed in an extended proof system containing inference rules for each of the new operators. In principle, we could have defined operators like ◇ in terms of $\mathcal{U}$. However, we want to provide proofs precisely for a formula the user wrote, rather than an equivalent version of it, as these will be easier for the user to understand.

We observed earlier that repeated calls to C (and O) with the same arguments may occur. We therefore memoize the function C to avoid expensive recomputations. The memoization is performed using a hash-table that stores the already computed results of C for its arguments. To hash formulas efficiently, we use hash-consing [10]. Hash-consing of proofs would also improve the space efficiency of our algorithm by sharing subproofs, but we have not implemented this optimization yet. In our experiments, space consumption was not a bottleneck.

Our tool parses the output of the NuSMV model checker [2]. In case of violations, this output contains the LTL formula and the lasso word counterexample—the inputs for our algorithm. The user can choose between a few predefined monotone wqos (or Cartesian products thereof) for optimization. The textual representation of the optimal proof computed is pretty printed separating the different levels in the proof by indentation.

We evaluate our algorithm on counterexamples generated by the NuSMV model checker on realistic models and specifications [18,25]. The LTL formulas we consider include freely nested past and future operators, with temporal heights ranging from 3 to 8. We used NuSMV release 2.1.2 to regenerate the counterexamples, as some of the models were not compatible with the latest release of NuSMV (2.6.1). We ran our experiments on an Intel Core i7 2.5 GHz processor with 16 GB RAM. Figure 5 shows the $|-|$ and *reach* of optimal proofs found by our tool with respect to three monotone wqos: $\preceq_{size}$ and $\preceq_{reach}$ induced by $|-|$ and *reach* (as described in Sect. 4) and their Cartesian product $\preceq_\times$ (defined as $p \preceq_\times q = p \preceq_{size} q \wedge p \preceq_{reach} q$). Columns $|u|$ and $|v|$ show the lengths of the prefix and the loop of the lasso word, whereas h_p and h_f show the past and future height of the specification. In all but one example, optimal proofs with respect to the partial order Cartesian product $\preceq_\times$ result in minimal $|-|$ and *reach* values.

The generated proofs helped explain the violations. Figure 6 (left) shows two proofs P (optimal with respect to $\preceq_{reach}$) and Q (optimal with respect to $\preceq_{size}$) output by our tool for the formula φ_0 on the counterexample lasso word uv^ω generated by NuSMV for the model *srg5* (a 5-bit counter). The textual representation includes the aforementioned additional constructors for $\rightarrow$, $\square$, and $\diamond$. For example, P demonstrates the satisfaction of the implication by providing evidence for the conclusion's satisfaction ($\rightarrow_R^+ (\ldots)$). In contrast, Q shows that the implication can also be vacuously satisfied by providing evidence for the assumption's violation ($\rightarrow_L^+ (\ldots)$). The implication's vacuous satisfaction is not desirable and indicates a problem with the specification (which is amended in φ_1). Yet the vacuity is far from obvious when just given the trace.

Figure 6 (right) shows the atomic propositions occurring in each of the proofs. In the visualization, which our tool can also output, each column corresponds to a single alphabet letter. A gray box in a row labeled by an atomic predicate denotes that the predicate is true (and white denotes that the predicate is false) at that letter. The marked boxes are solely *responsible* for φ_0's violation in P or Q respectively: flipping non-responsible atomic propositions in the trace will not affect P's or Q's validity. The visualization is helpful even though it discards most of the information present in the proof. Support for interactively selecting subformulas and visualizing the responsible atomic propositions in the corresponding subproofs would further improve the usability.

As another example, our tool computed an optimal proof of φ_2's violation with respect to $\preceq_{reach}$ for the lasso word counterexample generated from the model *dme4*. This proof uses the time-point (82) as the earliest possible witness of a violation of $\square$ in the counterexample of length 280. At that time-point, p is true in the lasso word and $\neg p \, \mathcal{S} \, (p \, \mathcal{S} \, q)$ is violated (witnessed by a recursive subproof, which does not look beyond the time-point 82). For the *1394-3-*

Model	Spec	$|u|$	$|v|$	h_p	h_f	$\preceq_{size}$ $|p|$	reach(p)	$\preceq_{reach}$ $|p|$	reach(p)	$\preceq_\times$ $|p|$	reach(p)
srg5	φ_0	15	2	4	4	7	16	8	6	7	16
srg5	φ_1	0	16	4	4	621	70	621	33	621	33
dme2	φ_2	0	111	2	1	11	242	14	20	11	20
dme3	φ_2	0	216	2	1	11	494	14	62	11	62
dme4	φ_2	0	280	2	1	11	642	14	82	11	82
abp	φ_3	18	20	2	2	7	59	7	3	7	3
1394-3-2	φ_4	15	2	1	2	7	18	7	18	7	18

$$\psi = ((\Diamond\Box(\neg p) \wedge \Box\Diamond q) \wedge \Box\Diamond x_0) \rightarrow \Diamond(x_0 \, \mathcal{S} \, (x_1 \, \mathcal{S} \, (x_2 \, \mathcal{S} \, (x_3 \, \mathcal{S} \, x_4))))$$
$$\varphi_0 = \neg\psi \qquad \varphi_1 = \neg(\psi \wedge ((\Diamond\Box(\neg p) \wedge \Box\Diamond q) \wedge \Box\Diamond x_0))$$
$$\varphi_2 = \Box(p \rightarrow \neg(\neg p \, \mathcal{S} \, (p \, \mathcal{S} \, q))) \qquad \varphi_3 = \Box(p \rightarrow \bullet\blacksquare\neg p) \qquad \varphi_4 = \neg\Diamond\Box(p \rightarrow \neg(\neg q \, \mathcal{S} \, r))$$

Fig. 5. Evaluation results and LTL properties

2 counterexample, the computed proofs made it evident that the implication $p \rightarrow \neg(\neg q \, \mathcal{S} \, r)$ was vacuously satisfied, resulting in φ_4's violation.

Our tool has good performance with memoization being a key optimization. Prior to its use, computation on some of the examples took several minutes. With memoization in place, optimal proofs were generated within one second for each of the examples.

7 Related work

Markey and Schnoebelen [21] provide a comprehensive overview of the *path-checking* problem for various fragments of LTL. They reduce LTL path checking on lasso words to LTL path checking on finite words. We build upon the core argument behind this result, reproduced in our Lemma 1. We further generalize their result to reasoning about optimal proofs in our Theorem 2. The best known upper bound for LTL path checking is provided by Kuhtz and Finkbeiner [15], showing that it can be efficiently parallelized.

Several proof systems [5,19] for LTL have been previously proposed to check a formula's *validity*. However, these proof systems are significantly different from ours, which checks the satisfaction (or violation) of a formula on a particular lasso word. An LTL proof system for checking satisfaction (or violation) closely related to ours was proposed by Cini and Francalanza [8]. They focus on *runtime verification* and provide an online proof search algorithm that processes letter-wise a word's finite prefix. Their proof system is sound but not complete: it cannot prove the violation of liveness properties (or the satisfaction of safety properties), which is natural in a runtime verification application. They are mainly concerned with solving the path-checking problem by proof search and do not focus on leveraging the found proofs as explanations.

Chechik and Gurfinkel [6] give a sound and complete proof system for CTL to explain violations of model-checkers and to debug specifications, in line with

$$P = \neg^- (\rightarrow^+_R (\Diamond^+$$
$$(\mathcal{S}^+(\mathcal{S}^+(\mathcal{S}^+(\mathcal{S}^+(ap^+(x_4, 6), []), []), []), [])))) $$
$$Q = \neg^- (\rightarrow^+_L (\wedge^-_R (\Box^- (\Diamond^-$$
$$([ap^-(x_0, 15), ap^-(x_0, 16)]))))) $$

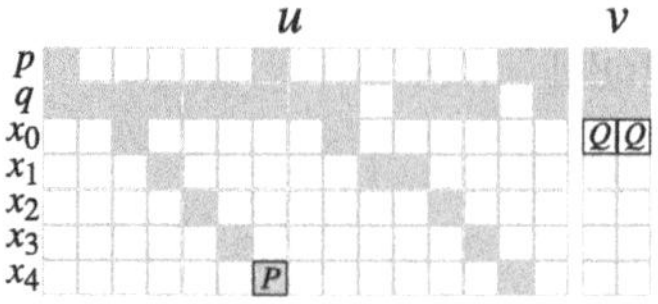

Fig. 6. Two example proofs

our goals. They also develop an interactive user interface for exploring different counterexamples for a model and the corresponding proofs. Their proof system is arguably more complex and thus harder to understand than ours: partly as it handles a branching-time logic and partly because they rely on the unrolling equations of the temporal operators and state summaries to finitely represent the infinite proof trees that arise when considering negations of temporal operators, instead of employing a simple meta-argument (Lemma 1) as we do. They do not consider past operators nor the optimality of the proof trees. Similar unrolling-based proof systems were developed for model-checking games [17]. Winning strategies in such games are certain notions of proof. In general, we argue that unrolling may be a good approach to solving the path-checking problem. However, it is not ideal for explaining a violation to a user who wrote the specification having LTL's standard semantics in mind rather than the recursive equations that underly the unrolling technique.

Sulzmann and Zechner's [26] proof system for LTL on finite words is also motivated by using proofs as explanations. However, they neither support past operators nor lasso words. Moreover, they only consider formulas in negation normal form, but neglect dual future operators, which significantly limits their language's expressiveness. Even if the dual operators were supported, imposing a normal form is problematic when a proof should serve as an explanation. Users typically do not think in term of normal forms but prefer to freely use the syntax of LTL; hence the explanation given should be as close as possible to the users' mindset. Sulzmann and Zechner compute optimal proofs with respect to a particular monotone order (lexicographic combination of the proof size and the relation that prefers $\vee^+_L$ over $\vee^+_R$), which is an instance in our generalized technique.

There has been significant work in the model checking community to address the problem of understanding counterexamples [3,12–14]. Most of these works focus on the interaction of the system model being verified and the counterexample. Our approach explores the interaction of the LTL property and the counterexample, without knowing the system model. An ideal explanation should combine all three components. We believe that our work is an important step towards achieving this goal.

The notion of *causality* [4,27] has been used to explain model checking counterexamples. Causality can be encoded as a relation in our framework, but it is not monotone. This is not surprising since the problem of computing the minimal causal set is NP hard and the existing solutions therefore settle for approximations. Our algorithm is more tractable, but can only optimize for simpler relations.

The size of the counterexample input to our algorithm affects the resulting proof tree's size: smaller counterexamples typically result in smaller proof trees. Our work can thereby directly benefit from past work on computing short counterexamples [11, 25]. Other lines of work aim at identifying the vacuous satisfaction of properties [16, 20] or justifying why the system satisfies a property when no counterexample is found [22–24]. We provide such a justification for a single trace, but not for an entire system model.

Finally, we refer to a survey on *provenance in databases* [7], which aims at identifying the root cause of violations, yet without taking the temporal dimension into account.

8   Conclusion

We have proposed a sound and complete proof system for LTL on lasso words. A proof tree in this system carries all the information necessary to witness and explain a formula's satisfaction or violation. We have devised and implemented an algorithm for computing a proof tree that is minimal with respect to a given monotone well-quasi-order $\preceq$. The parametrization by $\preceq$ allows the algorithm's users to optimize for different statistics (such as $|-|$ or *reach*) of the proof tree or even their combinations.

Our work lays the foundation for explaining the counterexamples generated by model checking tools. There are several natural continuations. In real world examples, even optimal proof trees can be too large to examine in practice. Devising user-friendly ways to explore them is therefore a practically relevant information visualization challenge. On the theoretical side, an open problem is to develop analogous techniques for other specification languages used by model checkers. Finally it would be interesting to adapt our proof search algorithm to work in an online fashion. This would enable its use to explain online, the verdicts produced by runtime verification algorithms.

Acknowledgment. We thank Srđan Kristić, Felix Klaedtke, and Joshua Schneider for discussions on using proof trees as explanations. Srđan Kristić, Karel Kubíček, and anonymous reviewers provided useful comments on early drafts of this paper. This work is supported by the Swiss National Science Foundation grant Big Data Monitoring (167162).

References

1. Explanator: Send in the Explanator–it explains satisfaction/violation of LTL formulas on lasso words (2018). https://bitbucket.org/traytel/explanator
2. NuSMV: a new symbolic model checker (2018). http://nusmv.fbk.eu/
3. Ball, T., Naik, M., Rajamani, S.K.: From symptom to cause: Localizing errors in counterexample traces. In: Aiken, A., Morrisett, G. (eds.) POPL 2003, pp. 97–105. ACM (2003)

4. Beer, I., Ben-David, S., Chockler, H., Orni, A., Trefler, R.J.: Explaining counterexamples using causality. Form. Methods Syst. Des. **40**(1), 20–40 (2012)
5. Brünnler, K., Lange, M.: Cut-free sequent systems for temporal logic. J. Log. Algebr. Program. **76**(2), 216–225 (2008)
6. Chechik, M., Gurfinkel, A.: A framework for counterexample generation and exploration. STTT **9**(5–6), 429–445 (2007)
7. Cheney, J., Chiticariu, L., Tan, W.C.: Provenance in databases: Why, how, and where. Found. Trends Databases **1**(4), 379–474 (2009)
8. Cini, C., Francalanza, A.: An LTL proof system for runtime verification. In: Baier, C., Tinelli, C. (eds.) TACAS 2015. LNCS, vol. 9035, pp. 581–595. Springer, Heidelberg (2015). https://doi.org/10.1007/978-3-662-46681-0_54
9. Daskalakis, C., Karp, R.M., Mossel, E., Riesenfeld, S., Verbin, E.: Sorting and selection in posets. SIAM J. Comput. **40**(3), 597–622 (2011)
10. Filliâtre, J., Conchon, S.: Type-safe modular hash-consing. In: ACM Workshop on ML, pp. 12–19. ACM (2006)
11. Gastin, P., Moro, P.: Minimal counterexample generation for SPIN. In: Bošnački, D., Edelkamp, S. (eds.) SPIN 2007. LNCS, vol. 4595, pp. 24–38. Springer, Heidelberg (2007). https://doi.org/10.1007/978-3-540-73370-6_4
12. Groce, A., Chaki, S., Kroening, D., Strichman, O.: Error explanation with distance metrics. STTT **8**(3), 229–247 (2006)
13. Groce, A., Kroening, D.: Making the most of BMC counterexamples. Electr. Notes Theor. Comput. Sci. **119**(2), 67–81 (2005)
14. Groce, A., Visser, W.: What went wrong: explaining counterexamples. In: Ball, T., Rajamani, S.K. (eds.) SPIN 2003. LNCS, vol. 2648, pp. 121–136. Springer, Heidelberg (2003). https://doi.org/10.1007/3-540-44829-2_8
15. Kuhtz, L., Finkbeiner, B.: LTL path checking is efficiently parallelizable. In: Albers, S., Marchetti-Spaccamela, A., Matias, Y., Nikoletseas, S., Thomas, W. (eds.) ICALP 2009. LNCS, vol. 5556, pp. 235–246. Springer, Heidelberg (2009). https://doi.org/10.1007/978-3-642-02930-1_20
16. Kupferman, O.: Sanity checks in formal verification. In: Baier, C., Hermanns, H. (eds.) CONCUR 2006. LNCS, vol. 4137, pp. 37–51. Springer, Heidelberg (2006). https://doi.org/10.1007/11817949_3
17. Lange, M., Stirling, C.: Model checking games for branching time logics. J. Log. Comput. **12**(4), 623–639 (2002)
18. Latvala, T., Biere, A., Heljanko, K., Junttila, T.: Simple is better: efficient bounded model checking for past LTL. In: Cousot, R. (ed.) VMCAI 2005. LNCS, vol. 3385, pp. 380–395. Springer, Heidelberg (2005). https://doi.org/10.1007/978-3-540-30579-8_25
19. Manna, Z., Pnueli, A.: The Temporal Logic of Reactive and Concurrent Systems - Specification. Springer, New York (1992)
20. Maretic, G.P., Dasthi, M.T., Basin, D.A.: Semantic vacuity. In: Grandi, F., Lange, M., Lomuscio, A. (eds.) TIME 2015, pp. 111–120. IEEE Computer Society (2015)
21. Markey, N., Schnoebelen, P.: Model checking a path. In: Amadio, R., Lugiez, D. (eds.) CONCUR 2003. LNCS, vol. 2761, pp. 251–265. Springer, Heidelberg (2003). https://doi.org/10.1007/978-3-540-45187-7_17
22. Namjoshi, K.S.: Certifying model checkers. In: Berry, G., Comon, H., Finkel, A. (eds.) CAV 2001. LNCS, vol. 2102, pp. 2–13. Springer, Heidelberg (2001). https://doi.org/10.1007/3-540-44585-4_2
23. Peled, D., Pnueli, A., Zuck, L.: From falsification to verification. In: Hariharan, R., Vinay, V., Mukund, M. (eds.) FSTTCS 2001. LNCS, vol. 2245, pp. 292–304. Springer, Heidelberg (2001). https://doi.org/10.1007/3-540-45294-X_25

24. Peled, D., Zuck, L.: From model checking to a temporal proof. In: Dwyer, M. (ed.) SPIN 2001. LNCS, vol. 2057, pp. 1–14. Springer, Heidelberg (2001). https://doi.org/10.1007/3-540-45139-0_1

25. Schuppan, V., Biere, A.: Shortest counterexamples for symbolic model checking of LTL with past. In: Halbwachs, N., Zuck, L.D. (eds.) TACAS 2005. LNCS, vol. 3440, pp. 493–509. Springer, Heidelberg (2005). https://doi.org/10.1007/978-3-540-31980-1_32

26. Sulzmann, M., Zechner, A.: Constructive finite trace analysis with linear temporal logic. In: Brucker, A.D., Julliand, J. (eds.) TAP 2012. LNCS, vol. 7305, pp. 132–148. Springer, Heidelberg (2012). https://doi.org/10.1007/978-3-642-30473-6_11

27. Wang, C., Yang, Z., Ivančić, F., Gupta, A.: Whodunit? causal analysis for counterexamples. In: Graf, S., Zhang, W. (eds.) ATVA 2006. LNCS, vol. 4218, pp. 82–95. Springer, Heidelberg (2006). https://doi.org/10.1007/11901914_9

What's to Come is Still Unsure*
Synthesizing Controllers Resilient to Delayed Interaction**

Mingshuai Chen[1]([✉])[iD], Martin Fränzle[2][iD], Yangjia Li[1,3][iD],
Peter N. Mosaad[2][iD], and Naijun Zhan[1][iD]

[1] State Key Lab. of Computer Science, Institute of Software,
CAS, University of Chinese Academy of Sciences, Beijing, China
chenms@ios.ac.cn, znj@ios.ac.cn
[2] Department of Computing Science, Carl von Ossietzky Universität Oldenburg,
Oldenburg, Germany
fraenzle@informatik.uni-oldenburg.de,
peter.nazier.mosaad@informatik.uni-oldenburg.de
[3] University of Tartu, Tartu, Estonia
yangjia@ios.ac.cn

Abstract. The possible interactions between a controller and its environment can naturally be modelled as the arena of a two-player game, and adding an appropriate winning condition permits to specify desirable behavior. The classical model here is the positional game, where both players can (fully or partially) observe the current position in the game graph, which in turn is indicative of their mutual current states. In practice, neither sensing or actuating the environment through physical devices nor data forwarding to and signal processing in the controller are instantaneous. The resultant delays force the controller to draw decisions before being aware of the recent history of a play. It is known that existence of a winning strategy for the controller in games with such delays is decidable over finite game graphs and with respect to ω-regular objectives. The underlying reduction, however, is impractical for non-trivial delays as it incurs a blow-up of the game graph which is exponential in the magnitude of the delay. For safety objectives, we propose a more practical incremental algorithm synthesizing a series of controllers handling increasing delays and reducing game-graph size in between. It is demonstrated using benchmark examples that even a simplistic explicit-state implementation of this algorithm outperforms state-of-the-art symbolic synthesis algorithms as soon as non-trivial delays have to be handled. We furthermore shed some light on the practically relevant case of non-order-preserving delays, as arising in actual networked control, thereby

---

*William Shakespeare, Twelfth Night/What You Will, Act 2, Scene 3.
**The first and fifth authors are funded partly by NSFC under grant No. 61625206 and 61732001, by "973 Program" under grant No. 2014CB340701, and by the CAS/SAFEA International Partnership Program for Creative Research Teams. The second and fourth authors are supported by DFG under grant No. DFG RTG 1765 SCARE. The third author is funded by NSFC under grant No. 61502467 and by the US AFOSR via AOARD grant No. FA2386-17-1-4022.

S. K. Lahiri and C. Wang (Eds.): ATVA 2018, LNCS 11138, pp. 56–74, 2018.
https://doi.org/10.1007/978-3-030-01090-4_4

considerably extending the scope of regular game theory under delay pioneered by Klein and Zimmermann.

Keywords: Safety games · Control under delay
Efficient algorithmic synthesis

1   Introduction

Algorithmic game theory is an established approach to the synthesis of correct-by-construction reactive controllers [13,16]. A finite game graph is used to formalize the possible actions of the players; it is complemented by a winning condition specifying desirable properties of infinite paths by means of an acceptance condition or a specification in temporal logic. Frequently, the game is played on a finite graph alternating moves by two players; the first player is the controller (sometimes called "ego" player) and the second player is its environment ("alter"), which may be uncooperative, erratic, or even malicious. Correct controllers thus have to be able to counteract any environmental actions, i.e., they need a sure winning strategy in the game. Controller synthesis can thus be understood as search for a winning strategy for ego. In this paper, we are interested in the synthesis problem when the interaction of a controller and its environment is described by a safety game [13], i.e., an infinite two-player game on finite graphs comprising "unsafe" states that the controller should avoid visiting.

These safety games have traditionally been investigated in a setting where the current position in the game is either fully known ("perfect information") or known up to certain observability constraints ("imperfect/incomplete information"). In this article, we address the problem of control under delays in perception and action. This can be understood as a form of imperfect information, as decisions by the controller have to be drawn based on delayed state observation—i.e., with the recent game history being opaque to the controller—and in advance—i.e., well before the actual situation where the action takes effect is fully determined. Such games have numerous practical applications, especially in networked control settings like cooperative driving, where observation of and influence on other cars' states are delayed by communication protocols severely restricting frequency of certain message types in order to keep overall channel usage sustainable under the pertinent severe bandwidth constraints.

It is intuitively obvious that such delay renders control harder: the controller has to decide in advance and based on dated information, which may no longer be fully indicative of the current situation. The existence of a winning strategy for the controller under such delays is decidable over finite game graphs and with respect to ω-regular objectives [10,11]. The underlying reduction to delay-free games, however, is impractical for non-trivial delays as it incurs a blow-up of the game graph which is strictly exponential in the magnitude of the delay, as also observed by Tripakis [20].

In this article, we follow Tripakis' quest for more efficient algorithms. For safety objectives, we propose a more practical incremental algorithm synthesizing a series of controllers handling increasing delays and reducing game-graph size in between. We demonstrate on benchmark examples that even a simplistic explicit-state implementation of this algorithm outperforms state-of-the-art symbolic synthesis algorithms as soon as non-trivial delays have to be handled. We furthermore shed some light on the practically relevant case of non-order-preserving delays, as arising in actual networked control, thereby considerably extending the scope of regular game theory under delay/lookahead pioneered by Klein and Zimmermann in [10,11,22] and explained below. Detailed proofs, extra examples and other materials are listed in the appendixes of [8].

Related work. In the literature on games, constraints on observation and interaction are reflected by corresponding restrictions on the information frames available to the players. The majority of the results about two-player games played on graphs adopt the hypothesis of *perfect information*, where fixed-point algorithms for the computation of winning strategies exist [5,6,16]. In this case, the controller is aware of the exact current (and past) state of its environment when selecting its next control action. Reif [17] has studied games of *incomplete information* and Kupferman and Vardi in [12] have extended the work of Pnueli and Rosner [15] about the synthesis of reactive modules to consider incomplete information . Similarly [21] and [16] study two-player games on graphs with ω-regular objectives subject to partial observability of the current (and past) game state. Recent state information is available, however; no restriction concerning the minimum age of observable state information is imposed. As the latter is an increasingly relevant problem in, e.g., networked control with its non-trivial end-to-end communication latencies, we here address the problem of two-player safety games subject to *delayed observation* and *delayed action* of the controlled process, obtaining a specific (and practically extremely relevant) case of imperfect information amenable to optimized synthesis algorithms.

The notion of control under delayed information exchange between the controller and the environment, where both the ego and the alter player suffer from having to operate under dated information about their mutual adversary's state, is complementary to the notion of delayed ω-regular games investigated by Zimmermann et al. [10,11]. In their setting, a delayed output player lags behind the input player in that the output player has to produce the i-th letter of the output string only when $i + \sum_{j=0}^{i} f(j)$ letters of the input string are available, with $\forall j : f(j) \geq 0$. Thus, delay essentially comes as an advantage, as the input player grants the output player a lookahead—the burden for the output player is "just" that she may have to memorize (a finite abstraction of) infinite lookahead if delay is unbounded in that $\sum_{j=0}^{i} f(j)$ diverges. In Zimmermann's terminology, our setting can be understood as asking for a strategy of the input player—whose strategic strength suffers from having to grant a lookahead—rather than for the output player and under the condition that delay is constant, i.e., $f(0) > 0$ and $\forall i > 0 : f(i) = 0$. We exploit a similar reduction to games of perfect information as the oblivious-delay construction of Zimmermann [22], which in the case of constant delay exploits a product construction on the game graph essentially representing a synchronous concurrent composition of the graph with a shift register implementing the delays. In contrast to Zimmermann et al., we do not grant introspection into the shift register, i.e., lookahead into an adversary's future actions. We do instead adopt the perspective of their input player, who has to submit her actions without knowledge of the recent history, as is frequently the case in practice. For this setting, the above reduction by means of a shift register also provides a consistent semantics of playing under delay.

It is worth noting that the notion of delay employed in this paper and by Klein and Zimmermann in [11] is different from that in timed games and their synthesis algorithms, like UPPAAL-TIGA [2], as well as from that used in the discrete-event system community, e.g. [1,14]. In timed games, delay refers to the possibility to deliberately delay the next control action, i.e., a single event. Up-to-date positional information, however, is always fully transparent to both players in timed games. In our setting, delay refers to a time lag imposed when obtaining positional information, modelling the end-to-end latency of information distribution in a communication network. Up-to-date positional information thus is opaque to the players as long as it resides in a queue modelling the network, where state information as well as control events of multiple different ages coexist and pipeline towards delivery. Such pipelining of control actions is lacking in the model of delay from [14], where only one controllable event can be latent at any time and just the time of its actual execution is determined by the environment. Meanwhile, the model of delay in [1] is different from ours as it leads to non-regular languages.

2 Safety Games under Delayed Information

Notation. Given a set A, we denote its powerset by 2^A, the set of finite sequences over A by A^*, and the set of infinite sequences over A by A^ω. The relative complement of a set B in A is denoted $A \setminus B = \{x \in A \mid x \notin B\}$. An empty sequence is denoted by ε.

2.1 Games with Perfect Information

The plays we consider are played on finite bipartite game graphs as known from ω-regular games, see e.g. [19]:

Definition 1 (Two-player game graph). *A finite game graph is of the form* $G = \langle S, s_0, S_0, S_1, \Sigma, \rightarrow \rangle$, *where S is a finite (non-empty) set of states, S_0, S_1 define a partition of S (S_i containing the states where it is the turn of player i to perform an action), $s_0 \in S_0$ is the initial state, Σ is a finite alphabet of actions for player 0 (while any action for player 1 is abstracted as $u \notin \Sigma$), and $\rightarrow \subseteq S \times (\Sigma \cup \{u\}) \times S$ is a set of labeled transitions satisfying the following four conditions:*

Bipartition: *if* $s \in S_i$ *and* $s \xrightarrow{\sigma} s'$ *for some* $\sigma \in \Sigma \cup \{u\}$ *then* $s' \in S_{1-i}$;

Absence of deadlock: *for each* $s \in S$ *there exist* $\sigma \in \Sigma \cup \{u\}$ *and* $s' \in S$ *s.t.*
$s \xrightarrow{\sigma} s'$;

Alphabet restriction on actions: *if* $s \xrightarrow{\sigma} s'$ *for some* $\sigma \in \Sigma \cup \{u\}$ *then* $\sigma \in \Sigma$
iff $s \in S_0$ *(and consequently,* $\sigma = u$ *iff* $s \in S_1$*)*;

Determinacy of Σ **moves:** *if* $s \in S_0$ *and* $s \xrightarrow{\sigma} s_1$ *and* $s \xrightarrow{\sigma} s_2$ *then* $s_1 = s_2$.

The state space is required to be deadlock-free and bipartite with respect to the transitions, which thus alternate between S_0 and S_1 states. Furthermore, the actions of player 0 are from Σ and deterministic, while all actions of player 1 are lumped together into a non-deterministic u action, since we are interested in synthesizing a winning strategy merely for player 0 who models the controller.

The game is played by a controller (player 0, ego) against an environment (player 1, alter) in turns. Starting from $s = s_0$ and in each second turn, the controller chooses an action $\sigma \in \Sigma$ that is enabled in the current state s. By $s \xrightarrow{\sigma} s'$, this leads the game to a unique successor state $s' \in S_1$. From s', it now is the environment's turn to select an action, which it does by selecting a successor state $s'' \in S_0$ with $s' \xrightarrow{u} s''$. As s'' again is a position controlled by player 0, the game alternates between moves of player 0 (the controller) and player 1 (the environment) forever, leading to the following definition.

Definition 2 (Infinite play). *A* play *on game graph* $G = \langle S, s_0, S_0, S_1, \Sigma, \rightarrow \rangle$ *is an infinite sequence* $\pi = \pi_0 \sigma_0 \pi_1 \ldots \sigma_{n-1} \pi_n \sigma_n \ldots$ *s.t.* $\pi_0 = s_0$, *and* $\forall i \in \mathbb{N}$:
$\pi_i \xrightarrow{\sigma_i} \pi_{i+1}$.

The game graph is accompanied by a *winning condition*. In a *safety game*, this is a set of *unsafe positions* $\mathcal{U} \subseteq S$ and the controller loses (and thus the environment wins) as soon as the play reaches an unsafe state $s_i \in \mathcal{U}$. Conversely, the controller wins (and the environment loses) iff the game goes on forever without ever visiting $\mathcal{U}$.

Definition 3 (Two-player safety game). *A* two-player safety game *is of the form* $G = \langle S, s_0, S_0, S_1, \Sigma, \mathcal{U}, \rightarrow \rangle$, *where* $G' = \langle S, s_0, S_0, S_1, \Sigma, \rightarrow \rangle$ *is a finite game graph and* $\mathcal{U} \subseteq S$ *is a set of* unsafe positions.
$\Pi(G)$ *denotes the set of plays over the underlying game graph* G'. *Play* $\pi_0 \sigma_0 \pi_1 \ldots \in \Pi(G)$ *is won by player 0 iff* $\forall i \in \mathbb{N} : \pi_i \notin \mathcal{U}$ *and won by player 1 otherwise.*

The objective of the controller in a safety game thus is to always select actions avoiding unsafe states, while the hostile or just erratic environment would try to drive the game to a visit of an unsafe state by picking adequate successor states on u actions.

For a given play $\pi \in \Pi(G)$, its *prefix* up to position π_n is denoted $\pi(n)$. This prefix thus is the finite sequence $\pi(n) = \pi_0 \sigma_0 \pi_1 \ldots \sigma_{n-1} \pi_n$, whose *length* is $|\pi(n)| = n + 1$ and whose *last* element is $\text{Tail}(\pi(n)) = \pi_n$. The set of prefixes of all plays in $\Pi(G)$ is denoted by $\text{Pref}(G)$, in which we denote those ending in a controller state by $\text{Pref}_c(G) = \{\rho \in \text{Pref}(G) \mid \text{Tail}(\rho) \in S_0\}$. Likewise,

$\text{Pref}_e(G) = \{\rho \in \text{Pref}(G) \mid \text{Tail}(\rho) \in S_1\}$ marks prefixes of plays ending in environmental positions.

For a game $G = \langle S, s_0, S_0, S_1, \Sigma, \mathcal{U}, \to \rangle$, a *strategy* for the controller is a mapping $\xi : \text{Pref}_c(G) \mapsto 2^\Sigma$ s.t. all $\sigma \in \xi(\rho)$ are enabled in $\text{Tail}(\rho)$ and $\xi(\rho) \neq \emptyset$ for any $\rho \in \text{Pref}_c(G)$. The *outcome* of the strategy ξ in G is defined as $O(G, \xi) = \{\pi = \pi_0 \sigma_0 \pi_1 \ldots \in \Pi(G) \mid \forall i \in \mathbb{N} : \sigma_{2i} \in \xi(\pi(2i))\}$ and denotes all plays possible when player 0 respects strategy ξ while player 1 plays arbitrarily.

Definition 4 (Winning strategy for the controller). *A strategy ξ for the controller in a safety game $G = \langle S, s_0, S_0, S_1, \Sigma, \mathcal{U}, \to \rangle$ is* winning for the controller *(or just* winning *for short) iff* $\forall \pi = \pi_0 \sigma_0 \pi_1 \ldots \in O(G, \xi). \forall k \in \mathbb{N} : \pi_k \notin \mathcal{U}$.

A winning strategy for the environment can be defined similarly as being a mapping $\tilde{\xi} : \text{Pref}_e(G) \mapsto 2^{S_0}$ with equivalent well-defined conditions as above. It is a classical result of game theory that such safety games under perfect observation are determined: one of the two players has a sure winning strategy enforcing a win irrespective of the opponent's choice of actions.

Theorem 1 (Determinacy [9]**).** *Safety games are determined, i.e., in each safety game $G = \langle S, s_0, S_0, S_1, \Sigma, \mathcal{U}, \to \rangle$ exactly one of the two players has a winning strategy.*

We call a (controller) strategy $\xi : \text{Pref}_c(G) \mapsto 2^\Sigma$ *positional* (or *memoryless*) if for any ρ and $\rho' \in \text{Pref}_c(G)$, $\text{Tail}(\rho) = \text{Tail}(\rho')$ implies $\xi(\rho) = \xi(\rho')$. Being positional implies that at any position in a play, the next decision of a controller which follows the strategy only depends on the current position in the game graph and not on the history of the play. As a consequence, such a positional strategy can also be described by a function $\xi' : S_0 \mapsto 2^\Sigma$ that maps every state of the controller in the game to a set of actions to be performed whenever the state is visited. The reduction to positional strategies is motivated by the fact that in delay-free safety games, whenever there exists a winning strategy for the controller, then there also exists a positional strategy for it.

Theorem 2 (Computing positional strategies [7,19]**).** *Given a two-player safety game G, the set of states from which player 0 (player 1, resp.) can enforce a win is computable, and memoryless strategies are sufficient for the winning party.*

The construction of a positional strategy builds on backward fixed-point iteration computing the set of states from which a visit in $\mathcal{U}$ can be enforced by player 1 [19].

2.2 Games under Delayed Control

As immediately obvious from the fact that memoryless strategies suffice in the above setting, being able to fully observe the *current* state and to react on it immediately is an essential feature of the above games. In practice, this is often impossible due to delays between sensing the environmental state, computing the control action, submitting it, and it taking effect. The strategy, if existent, thus cannot resort to the full state history, but only to a proper prefix thereof due to the remainder becoming visible too late.

If the delay is constant and equates to $\delta \in \mathbb{N}$ steps, then the controller would have to decide about the action to be taken after some finite play $\pi_0\sigma_0\pi_1\ldots\pi_{2n}$ already after just seeing its proper prefix $\pi_0\sigma_0\pi_1\ldots\pi_{2n-\delta}$. Furthermore, a constant strategy not dependent on any historic observations would have to be played by the controller initially for the first δ steps. That motivates the following definition:

Definition 5 (Playing under delay). *Given a delay $\delta \in \mathbb{N}$, a strategy for the controller under delay δ is a map $\xi : \mathrm{Pref}_x(G) \mapsto 2^\Sigma$, where $x = c$ if δ is even and $x = e$ else, together with a non-empty set $\alpha \subseteq \Sigma^{\lceil\frac{\delta}{2}\rceil}$ of initial action sequences. The outcome of playing strategy (α, ξ) in G under delay δ is $O(G, \alpha, \xi, \delta) =$*

$$
\left\{ \pi = \pi_0\sigma_0\pi_1\ldots \in \Pi(G) \;\middle|\;
\begin{array}{l}
\exists a = a_0 \ldots a_{\lceil\frac{\delta}{2}\rceil-1} \in \alpha. \forall i \in \mathbb{N}: \\
\left(\begin{array}{l} 2i < \delta \Rightarrow \sigma_{2i} = a_i \\ \wedge\; 2i \geq \delta \Rightarrow \sigma_{2i} \in \xi(\pi(2i - \delta)) \end{array} \right)
\end{array}
\right\}.
$$

We call the strategy (α, ξ) playable by the controller iff it always assigns permitted moves, i.e., iff for each prefix $\pi_0\sigma_0\pi_1\ldots\sigma_{2n-1}\pi_{2n-1}$ of a play in $O(G, \alpha, \xi, \delta)$, we have that the set of next actions

$$
\Sigma_n = \begin{cases} \{a_n \mid \langle\sigma_0, \sigma_2, \sigma_4, \ldots, \sigma_{2n-2}, a_n\rangle \text{ is a prefix of a word in } \alpha\} & \text{iff } 2n < \delta, \\ \xi(\pi(2n - \delta)) & \text{iff } 2n \geq \delta \end{cases}
$$

suggested by the strategy is non-empty and contains only actions enabled in π_{2n-1}. Strategy (α, ξ) is winning (for the controller) under delay δ iff it is playable and for each $\pi = \pi_0\sigma_0\pi_1\ldots \in O(G, \alpha, \xi, \delta)$, the condition $\forall k \in \mathbb{N}: \pi_k \notin \mathcal{U}$ holds, i.e., no unsafe state is ever visited when playing the strategy.

Playing under a delay of δ thus means that for a play $\pi = \pi_0\sigma_0\pi_1\ldots$, the choice of actions suggested by the winning strategy at state π_{2i} has to be predecided at state $\pi_{2i-\delta}$ for any $i \geq \lceil\frac{\delta}{2}\rceil$ and decided without recourse to positional information for the first $\delta - 1$ steps. Playing under delay 0 is identical to playing under complete information.

From Definition 5 it is obvious that existence of a (delay-free) winning strategy in the complete information game G is a necessary, yet not sufficient condition for existence of a strategy that is winning under a delay of $\delta > 0$. Likewise, existence of a strategy winning under some relatively small delay δ is a necessary, yet not sufficient condition for existence of a strategy that is winning under a delay of $\delta' > \delta$: the strategy for δ' can be played for δ by simply waiting $\delta' - \delta$ steps before implementing the control action.

Remark 1. The reader may wonder why Definition 5 assumes strictly sequential delay, i.e., in-order delivery of the delayed information, which cannot be guaranteed in many practical applications of networked control. The reason is that random out-of-order delivery with a maximum delay of δ has in-order delivery with an exact delay of δ as its worst-case instance: whenever a data item is delivered out-of-order then it is delivered before δ, implying earlier availability of more recent state information and thus enhanced controllability. In a qualitative setting, as addressed in this article, solving the control problem for out-of-order delivery with a maximum delay of δ is consequently—up to delaying data items arriving early—identical to solving the control problem under in-order delivery with an exact delay of δ, as the latter is the former's worst case.

Issues are, however, different in a stochastic setting, where out-of-order delivery with a maximum delay of δ induces a reduced expected message delay strictly smaller than δ, i.e., it even truly enhances controllability. Dealing with this basic quantitative case and furthermore exploiting constructive means of control on message delay, like setting a network's QoS parameters, for control will be subject of future research.

2.3   Insufficiency of Memoryless Strategies

Recall that in safety games with complete information, the existence of a winning strategy for the controller implies existence of a memoryless strategy for player 0. For games with delayed information, however, memoryless strategies are not powerful enough:

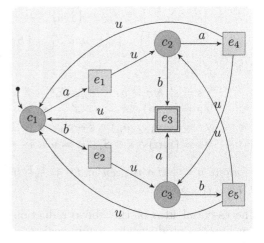

Example 1. Consider the safety game $G = \langle S, s_0, S_0, S_1, \Sigma, \mathcal{U}, \rightarrow \rangle$, shown in Fig. 1, where $S = S_0 \cup S_1$, $S_0 = \{c_1, c_2, c_3\}$, $S_1 = \{e_1, e_2, e_3, e_4, e_5\}$, $s_0 = c_1$, $\Sigma = \{a, b\}$, and $\mathcal{U} = \{e_3\}$. Player 0 can obviously win this safety game if no delay is involved.

Fig. 1. A safety game winnable with memoryless strategies for delay $\delta \leq 1$, yet not beyond.

Now consider a memoryless strategy $\xi' : S_0 \mapsto 2^{\Sigma}$ for the controller under delay 2. We obviously need $\xi'(c_2) = \{b\}$, indicating that the controller executes b two steps later at either c_1 or c_3, as a at c_3 would yield the unsafe state e_3. Analogously, we have $\xi'(c_3) = \{a\}$. It is a different matter when arriving at c_1, where the controller has to draw a pre-decision for both c_2 and c_3. If the controller picks a (or b) at c_1, then two steps later at c_3 (c_2, resp.) it executes the unsafe action a (b, resp.). For a win, extra memory keeping track of the historic sequence of actions is necessary such that the controller can determine whether it will visit c_2 or c_3 from c_1.

The above example shows that memoryless strategies are generally insufficient for winning a safety game under delays. A straightforward generalization of the situation shown in Fig. 1, namely deeply nesting triangles of the shape spanned by c_1, c_2, and c_3, demonstrates that the amount of memory needed will in worst case be exponential in the delay. Any reduction to safety games under complete information will have to introduce a corresponding blow-up of the game graph.

2.4 Reduction to Delay-Free Games

As playing a game under delay δ amounts to pre-deciding actions δ steps in advance, the problem of finding a winning strategy for the controller in $G = \langle S, s_0, S_0, S_1, \Sigma, \mathcal{U}, \rightarrow \rangle$ that wins under delay δ can be reduced to the problem of finding an undelayed winning strategy for the controller in a related safety game:

Lemma 1. *Let $G = \langle S, s_0, S_0, S_1, \Sigma, \mathcal{U}, \rightarrow \rangle$ be a safety game and $\delta \in \mathbb{N}$ a delay. Then the controller has strategy that wins G under a delay δ iff the controller has a winning strategy in the game $\widehat{G} = \langle S', s_0', S_0', S_1', \Sigma \cup \Sigma^{\lceil \frac{\delta}{2} \rceil}, \mathcal{U}', \rightarrow' \rangle$ given by*

1. $S' = \left(S \times \Sigma^{\lceil \frac{\delta}{2} \rceil} \right) \uplus \{ s_0' \} \uplus \left(\{ s_0' \} \times \Sigma^{\lceil \frac{\delta}{2} \rceil} \right)$, *where $\uplus$ denotes disjoint union,*
   $S_0' = \left(S_0 \times \Sigma^{\lceil \frac{\delta}{2} \rceil} \right) \cup \{ s_0' \}$, *and* $S_1' = \left(S_1 \times \Sigma^{\lceil \frac{\delta}{2} \rceil} \right) \cup \left(\{ s_0' \} \times \Sigma^{\lceil \frac{\delta}{2} \rceil} \right)$,

2. $s \xrightarrow{\sigma}' s'$ *iff*

$$ s = s_0' \wedge \sigma = a_1 \ldots a_n \in \Sigma^n \wedge s' = (s_0', a_1 \ldots a_n) $$
$$ \vee \, s = (s_0', \alpha) \wedge \sigma = u \wedge s' = (s_0, \alpha) $$
$$ \vee \, s = (\hat{s}, a_1 \ldots a_n) \wedge \hat{s} \in S_0 \wedge \sigma \in \Sigma \wedge \hat{s} \xrightarrow{a_1} \hat{s}' \wedge s' = (\hat{s}', a_2 \ldots a_n \sigma) $$
$$ \vee \, s = (\hat{s}, \alpha) \wedge \hat{s} \in S_1 \wedge \sigma = u \wedge \hat{s} \xrightarrow{u} \hat{s}' \wedge s' = (\hat{s}', \alpha), $$

where $n = \frac{\delta}{2}$ if δ is even and $n = \frac{\delta+1}{2}$ if δ is odd.
3. $\mathcal{U}' = \mathcal{U} \times \Sigma^{\lceil \frac{\delta}{2} \rceil}$.

The essential idea of the above reduction is to extend the game graph by a synchronous product with a shift register appropriately delaying the implementation of the control action decided by the controller. The blow-up in graph size incurred is by a factor $|\Sigma|^{\lceil \frac{\delta}{2} \rceil}$ and thus exponential in the delay. It is obvious that due to this, a winning strategy for the controller in the delayed game can, if existent, be synthesized with $|\Sigma|^{\lceil \frac{\delta}{2} \rceil}$ memory.

Note that the above reduction to delay-free safety games does not imply that games under delay are determined, as the claim in Lemma 1 is not symmetric for the environment. A simple guessing game, where player 1 guesses in each step either a 0 or a 1 and player 0 has to repeat the exact guess, losing as soon as she fails to properly repeat, reveals that player 0 has a sure winning strategy under delay 0, but none of the two players has one under any positive delay.[1] Determinacy is only obtained if one of the players is granted a lookahead

---

[1] While player 1 could enforce a win with probability 1 in a probabilistic setting by just playing a random sequence, she cannot enforce a win in the qualitative setting where player 0 may just be lucky to draw the right guesses throughout.

equivalent to the other's delay, as in Klein and Zimmermann's setting [11]. Such lookahead does not, however, correspond to any physical reality in distributed control, where both players are subject to the same end-to-end latency (i.e., delay) in their mutual feedback loop.

3   Synthesizing Controllers

As stated above, controller synthesis for games under delay can be obtained using a reduction to a delay-free safety game involving the introduction of a shift register. The exponential blow-up incurred by this reduction, however, seems impractical for any non-trivial delay. We therefore present a novel incremental synthesis algorithm, which starts from synthesizing a winning strategy for the underlying delay-free safety game and then incrementally hardens the strategy against larger and larger delays, thus avoiding explicit reductions. We further optimize the algorithm by pruning the otherwise exponentially sized game graph after each such hardening step: as controllability (i.e., the controller wins) under delay k is a necessary condition for controllability under delay $k' > k$, each state uncontrollable under delay k can be removed before proceeding to the next larger delay. The algorithm thus alternates between steps extending memory, as necessary for winning under delay, and steps compressing the game graph.

The key idea of the synthesis procedure (Algorithm 1) is to compute a series of finite-memory winning strategies $\hat{\xi}_k$ while increasing delays from $k = 0$ to the final delay of interest $k = \delta$. The algorithm takes as input a delayed safety game G_δ and returns either WINNING paired with a winning strategy $(\alpha, \hat{\xi}_\delta)$ for the controller if G_δ is controllable, or LOSING otherwise with an integer m indicating that the winning strategy vanishes when lifting delay to m. Line 2 invokes the classical fixed-point iteration (cf. Appx. C in [8]) to generate the *maximally permissive strategy* for the controller in G under no delay. The procedure **FPIteration** first conducts a backward fixed-point iteration computing the set L of states from which a visit to $\mathcal{U}$ can be enforced by the alter player 1 [19]. The maximally permissive strategy for the controller is then obtained by admitting in each state from $S_0 \setminus L$ exactly those actions leading to a succesor in $S_1 \setminus L$. Then the delays are lifted from $k = 0$ to δ by a while loop in line 3, and within each step of the loop the strategy $\hat{\xi}_{k+1}$ is computed based on $\hat{\xi}_k$ as follows:

1. If $k + 1$ is an odd delay, the controller needs to make pre-decisions at safe states of the environment, namely at each $s \in S_1 \setminus \mathcal{U}$. The controller needs to pre-decide at s a set of actions that are safe to perform at any successor $s' \in \texttt{Succ}(s)$, for which the winning actions have already been encoded in the strategy $\hat{\xi}_k(s', \cdot)$. This is achieved, in line 7, by taking an intersection of $\hat{\xi}_k(s', \rho)$ for all $s' \in \texttt{Succ}(s)$ with the same history sequence of actions ρ. The derived strategy can be spurious however, inasmuch as the intersection involves only immediate successors of s, yet without observing the entire strategy space. At line 9 we therefore remove all uncontrollable predecessors of freshly unwinnable states by a **Shrink** procedure depicted in Algorithm 2, which will be explained below.

Algorithm 1: Synthesizing winning finite-memory strategy

---

input : $G = \langle S, s_0, S_0, S_1, \Sigma, \mathcal{U}, \rightarrow \rangle$, a safety game played under delay δ.

/* initialization */

1 $k \leftarrow 0$; $\alpha \leftarrow \{\varepsilon\}$;

/* computing maximally permissive strategy under no delay */

2 $\hat{\xi}_0 \leftarrow$ **FPIteration**(G);

/* lifting delays from 0 to δ */

3 **while** $k < \delta$ **do**

    /* with an odd delay $k+1$ */

4   **if** $k \equiv 0 \pmod 2$ **then**

5   **for** $s \in S, \sigma_1 \ldots \sigma_{\frac{k}{2}} \in \alpha$ **do**

6   **if** $s \in S_1 \setminus \mathcal{U}$ **then**

7                $\hat{\xi}_{k+1}(s, \sigma_1 \ldots \sigma_{\frac{k}{2}}) \leftarrow \bigcap_{s': s \xrightarrow{u} s'} \hat{\xi}_k(s', \sigma_1 \ldots \sigma_{\frac{k}{2}})$;

                /* shrinking the possibly-spurious strategy */

8   **if** $\hat{\xi}_{k+1}(s, \sigma_1 \ldots \sigma_{\frac{k}{2}}) = \emptyset$ **and** $\bigwedge_{s': s \xrightarrow{u} s'} \hat{\xi}_k(s', \sigma_1 \ldots \sigma_{\frac{k}{2}}) \neq \emptyset$

                then

9   **Shrink**$(\hat{\xi}_{k+1}, \hat{\xi}_k, G, (s, \sigma_1 \ldots \sigma_{\frac{k}{2}}))$;

10   **else**

11                $\hat{\xi}_{k+1}(s, \sigma_1 \ldots \sigma_{\frac{k}{2}}) \leftarrow \emptyset$;

12        $\alpha \leftarrow \{\sigma_0 \sigma_1 \cdots \sigma_{\frac{k}{2}} \mid s_0 \xrightarrow{\sigma_0} s', \sigma_1 \cdots \sigma_{\frac{k}{2}} \in \alpha, \hat{\xi}_{k+1}(s', \sigma_1 \cdots \sigma_{\frac{k}{2}}) \neq \emptyset\}$;

13   **if** $\alpha = \emptyset$ **then**

14   **return** (LOSING, $k+1$);

    /* with an even delay $k+1$ */

15   **else**

16   **for** $s \in S, \sigma_1 \ldots \sigma_{\frac{k-1}{2}} \in \alpha$ **do**

17   **if** $s \in S_0 \setminus \mathcal{U}$ **then**

18   **for** $\sigma_0, s' : s \xrightarrow{\sigma_0} s'$ **do**

19                      $\hat{\xi}_{k+1}(s, \sigma_0 \sigma_1 \ldots \sigma_{\frac{k-1}{2}}) \leftarrow \hat{\xi}_k(s', \sigma_1 \ldots \sigma_{\frac{k-1}{2}})$;

20   **else**

21                $\hat{\xi}_{k+1}(s, \sigma_0 \sigma_1 \ldots \sigma_{\frac{k-1}{2}}) \leftarrow \emptyset$;

22    $k \leftarrow k+1$;

23 **return** (WINNING, $(\alpha, \hat{\xi}_k)$);

---

2. In case of an even delay $k+1$, the controller needs to make pre-decisions at safe states of its own, i.e. at each $s \in S_0 \setminus \mathcal{U}$. In contrast to an intersection in the odd case, the controller can inherit the winning strategy $\hat{\xi}_k(s', \rho)$ directly from each successor s' of s. However, we have to prepend, if $s \xrightarrow{\sigma_0} s'$, the action σ_0 to the history sequence ρ to record the choice in the shift register (line 19).

The synthesis algorithm may abort at line 14 if the controller does not have available actions to pick anymore at the initial state s_0, declaring LOSING at $k+1$ where the winning strategy vanishes. Otherwise, the algorithm continues and eventually produces a winning strategy $\hat{\xi}_\delta$ for the controller in G.

Only when a fresh unwinnable state s for the controller is detected (line 8), the **Shrink** function (Algorithm 2) will be launched to carry out two tasks in a recursive manner: (1) it traverses the graph backward and removes from the current strategy all the actions that may lead the play to this unwinnable state, and consequently (2) it gives a state-space pruning that removes all states no longer controllable under the given delay before proceeding to the next larger delay. The latter accelerates synthesis, while the former is a key ingredient to the correctness of Algorithm 1, as can be seen from the proof of Theorem 3: it avoids "blind alleys" where locally controllable actions run towards subsequently deadlocked states.

Algorithm 2: Shrink: Shrinking the possibly-spurious strategy

input : $\hat{\xi}_{2n+1}$, the strategy under an odd delay $2n+1$;
$\hat{\xi}_{2n}$, the strategy under an even delay $2n$;
$G = \langle S, s_0, S_0, S_1, \Sigma, \mathcal{U}, \rightarrow \rangle$, a safety game played under delay δ;
$(s, \sigma_1 \ldots \sigma_n)$, a fresh unwinnable state with the sequence of actions.

1 **for** $s' : s' \xrightarrow{\sigma} s$ **do**
2   **if** $\sigma_n \in \hat{\xi}_{2n}(s', \sigma\sigma_1 \ldots \sigma_{n-1})$ **then**
3         $\hat{\xi}_{2n}(s', \sigma\sigma_1 \ldots \sigma_{n-1}) \leftarrow \hat{\xi}_{2n}(s', \sigma\sigma_1 \ldots \sigma_{n-1}) \setminus \{\sigma_n\}$;
       /* $\tilde{s} < s$ indicates the existence of $\hat{\xi}_{2n+1}(\tilde{s}, \cdot)$, i.e., we visit merely states that have already been attached with (possibly deadlocking) actions by Algorithm 1 */
4   **for** $\tilde{s} : \tilde{s} \xrightarrow{u} s'$ and $\tilde{s} \notin \mathcal{U}$ and $\tilde{s} < s$ **do**
5   **if** $\sigma_n \in \hat{\xi}_{2n+1}(\tilde{s}, \sigma\sigma_1 \ldots \sigma_{n-1})$ **then**
6               $\hat{\xi}_{2n+1}(\tilde{s}, \sigma\sigma_1 \ldots \sigma_{n-1}) \leftarrow \hat{\xi}_{2n+1}(\tilde{s}, \sigma\sigma_1 \ldots \sigma_{n-1}) \setminus \{\sigma_n\}$;
7   **if** $\hat{\xi}_{2n+1}(\tilde{s}, \sigma\sigma_1 \ldots \sigma_{n-1}) = \emptyset$ **then**
8   **Shrink**$(\hat{\xi}_{2n+1}, \hat{\xi}_{2n}, G, (\tilde{s}, \sigma\sigma_1 \ldots \sigma_{n-1}))$;

The worst-case complexity of Algorithm 1 follows straightforwardly as $O(\delta \cdot |S_0| \cdot |S_1| \cdot |\Sigma|^{\lfloor \frac{\delta}{2} \rfloor})$, as is the case for the reduction to a delay-free safety games. In practice, the advantage however is that we avoid explicit construction of the graph of the corresponding delay-free game, which yields an exponential blow-up, and interleave the expansion by yet another shift-register stage with state-set shrinking removing uncontrollable states.

Theorem 3 (Correctness and Completeness). *Algorithm 1 always terminates. If its output is* (WINNING, $(\alpha, \hat{\xi})$) *then* $(\alpha, \hat{\xi})$ *is a winning strategy of* G_δ; *otherwise, with output* (LOSING, $k+1$) *of the algorithm,* G_δ *has no winning strategy.*

Proof. Elaborated in Appx. A of [8].

Example 2. Consider the safety game G under delayed information in Fig. 1. The series of finite-memory winning strategies produced by Algorithm 1 is:

$$\hat{\xi}_0(c_1, \varepsilon) = \{a, b\}, \qquad \hat{\xi}_0(c_2, \varepsilon) = \{a\}, \qquad \hat{\xi}_0(c_3, \varepsilon) = \{b\}.$$

$$\hat{\xi}_1(e_1, \varepsilon) = \{a\}, \quad \hat{\xi}_1(e_2, \varepsilon) = \{b\}, \quad \hat{\xi}_1(e_3, \varepsilon) = \emptyset, \quad \hat{\xi}_1(e_4, \varepsilon) = \{b\}, \quad \hat{\xi}_1(e_5, \varepsilon) = \{a\}.$$

$$\hat{\xi}_2(c_1, a) = \{a\}, \qquad \hat{\xi}_2(c_2, a) = \{b\}, \qquad \hat{\xi}_2(c_3, a) = \emptyset,$$

$$\hat{\xi}_2(c_1, b) = \{b\}, \qquad \hat{\xi}_2(c_2, b) = \emptyset, \qquad \hat{\xi}_2(c_3, b) = \{a\}.$$

Winning strategies for the controller vanish when the delay reaches 3.

4   Case Study and Experimental Evaluation

Avoiding collisions is a central issue in transportation systems as well as in many other applications. The task of a collision avoidance (CA) system is to track objects of potential collision risk and determine any action to avoid or mitigate a collision. One of the challenges in designing a CA system is determining the correct action in presence of the end-to-end latency of the overall control system.

In the context of avoiding collisions, we present an escape game as an artificial scenario to illustrate our approach. The game is a two-player game between a robot (i.e., the controller) and a kid (i.e., the dynamical part of its environment), which are moving in a closed room with some fixed obstacles as shown in Fig. 2. In this scenario, the robot has to make decisions (*actions*) under δ-*delayed information*.

Definition 6 (Two-player escape game in a $p \times q$ room under delay). *A two-player escape game under delay δ is of the form $\widehat{G} = \langle S, s_0, S_0, S_1, \mathcal{O}, \Sigma, \mathcal{U}, \rightarrow \rangle$, where*

- $S = X \times Y \times X \times Y \times \mathbb{B}$ *is a non-empty set of states providing* $x \in X = \{0, \ldots, p-1\}$ *and* $y \in Y = \{0, \ldots, q-1\}$ *coordinates for the robot as well as for the kid, together with a flag denoting whose move is next. Concretely, a state* (x_0, y_0, x_1, y_1, b) *encodes that the robot currently is at position* (x_0, y_0), *while the kid is at* (x_1, y_1), *and that the next move is the robot's iff b holds. Here* $p, q \in \mathbb{N}_{\geq 1}$ *denote the width and length of the room.*
- $\mathcal{O} \subseteq X \times Y$ *is a finite set of positions occupied by fixed obstacles.*
- Σ *is a finite alphabet of actions for player 0 (i.e., the robot), which consists of kinematically constrained moves explained below.*
- $\mathcal{U} \subseteq S$ *is the finite set of undesirable states, which are characterized by featuring collisions with the obstacles or the kid.*
- $\rightarrow \subseteq S \times (\Sigma \cup \{u\}) \times S$ *is a set of labelled transitions, and*
- δ *is the delay in information retrieval s.t. the robot has to react on δ old information.*

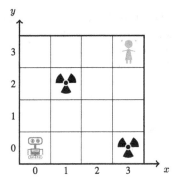

Fig. 2. The robot escape game

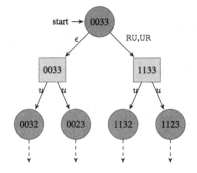

Fig. 3. A snippet of the game graph

In our scenario, we first consider a room of extent 4×4, as shown in Fig. 2. The fixed obstacles are located at $o_1 = (1,2)$ and $o_2 = (3,0)$ and the initial state s_0 where the robot and the kid are located in the room is $s_0 = (0,0,3,3,\text{true}) \in S_0$. The kid can move in the room and her possible moves (i.e., the *uncontrollable actions*) are unilaterally denoted u for unpredictable, yet amount to moves either one step to the right R, left L, up U, or down D. The robot has a finite set of moves (i.e., *controllable actions*), which are kinematically constrained as being a combination of two moves, e.g., up then right UR, denoted as $\Sigma = \{\text{RU}, \text{UR}, \text{LU}, \text{UL}, \text{RD}, \text{DR}, \text{LD}, \text{DL}, \epsilon\}$, and ϵ means doing nothing. We assume that the two players respect the geometry of the room and consequently never take any action leaving the inside area of the room or running through an obstacle, which can be achieved by specifying two groups of constraints $\mathcal{C}$ and $\mathcal{E}$ (exemplified in Appx. D of [8]) respectively for the robot and the kid, defining their legal actions. Representing a state (x_0, y_0, x_1, y_1, b) as $x_0 y_0 x_1 y_1$ inside a blue circular node if b (robot's turn) and inside a red square node if $\neg b$ (kid's turn), the game graph spanned by the legal actions looks as shown in Fig. 3.

The safety objective for the robot is to move inside the working room while avoiding to ever be collocated with the kid or the fixed obstacles. We consequently define the set of unsafe states as $\mathcal{U} = \{(x_0, y_0, x_1, y_1, b) \mid (x_0, y_0) \in \mathcal{O} \vee (x_0, y_0) = (x_1, y_1)\}$.

There obviously exists a winning strategy for the robot in a delay-free setting, namely to cycle around the obstacle at o_1 to avoid being caught by the kid. To investigate the controllability resilient to delays, we first construct the graph structure from the symbolic description by a C++ program. It consists of 224 states, 16 unsafe states, and 738 legal transitions satisfying the respective conditions $\mathcal{C}$ and $\mathcal{E}$. The obtained game graph is then used as input to a prototypical implementation in Mathematica[2] of Algorithm 1, which declares WINNING paired with a finite-memory winning strategy (i.e., a safe controller) $\hat{\xi}_\delta$ under delays

---

[2] Both the prototype implementation and the evaluation examples used in this section can be found at http://lcs.ios.ac.cn/~chenms/tools/DGame.tar.bz2. We opted for an implementation in Mathematica due to its built-in primitives for visualization.

$0 \leq \delta \leq 2$ (see Appx. E in [8]), while LOSING when the delay is 3. The latter indicates that the problem is uncontrollable under any delay $\delta' \geq 3$.

To further investigate the scalability and efficiency of our method, we have evaluated the implementation on two additional examples (Appx. B in [8]) as well as evasion games instantiated to rooms of different sizes (marked with prefix Escp.). A slightly adapted scenario (denoted by prefix Stub.) was also investigated, where the kid plays in a rather stubborn way, namely she always moves either one step to the left or down, yet never goes right nor up, which yields potentially larger affordable delays for the robot. In particular, a comparison of the performance of our incremental algorithm was done with respect to two points of reference: to the same Mathematica-based algorithm using $\delta = 0$ (the underlying explicit-state delay-free safety synthesis) employed after reducing the games to delay-free ones by shift registers (cf. Lemma 1), and to the state-of-the-art synthesizer SafetySynth[3] for solving safety games applied to an appropriate symbolic form of that shift-register reduction. All experiments were pursued on a 2.5 GHz Intel Core-i7 processor with 8GB RAM running 64-bit Ubuntu 17.04.

From the upper part of Table 1, it can be seen that our incremental algorithm significantly outperforms the use of the shift-register reduction . On all cases involving delay, Algorithm 1 is faster than the same underlying explicit-state implementation of safety synthesis employed to the reduction of Lemma 1. The benefits from not resorting to an explicit reduction, instead taking advantage of incrementally generated strategies and on-the-fly pruning of already-uncontrollable branches, are thus obvious. In contrast, the reduction-based approach suffers inevitably from the state-explosion problem: for e.g. Escp.4×5 under $\delta = 3$, the reduction yields a game graph comprising 29242 states and 107568 transitions.

Within the lower part of Table 1, the performance of the current explicit-state implementation of Algorithm 1 is compared with that of SafetySynth, the winner in the sequential safety synthesis track of the 3rd and 4th Reactive Synthesis Competition[4] (SYNTCOMP 2016 and 2017). In order to be able to examine the efficiency of our incremental algorithm under larger delays, we used a slight modification of the escape game forbidding the kid to take moves to the right or up, thus increasing the controllability for the robot. Note that Algorithm 1 completes synthesis faster in these "stubborn" scenarios due to the reduced action set. SafetySynth implements a symbolic backward fixed-point algorithm for solving delay-free safety games using the CUDD package. Its input is an extension of the AIGER[5] format known from hardware model-checking and synthesis. We therefore provided symbolic models of the escape games in Verilog[6] and compiled them to AIGER format using Yosys[7]. Verilog supports compact symbolic modelling of the coordinates other than an explicit representation of the game

---

[3] Available at https://www.react.uni-saarland.de/tools/safetysynth/.
[4] http://www.syntcomp.org/.
[5] http://fmv.jku.at/aiger/.
[6] http://www.verilog.com/.
[7] http://www.clifford.at/yosys/.

Table 1. Benchmark results in relation to reduction-based approaches (time in seconds)

Benchmark				Reduction + Explicit-State Synthesis						Algorithm 1						
name	$|S|$	$|\rightarrow|$	$|\mathcal{U}|$	δ_{max}	$\delta=0$	$\delta=1$	$\delta=2$	$\delta=3$	$\delta=4$	δ_{max}	$\delta=0$	$\delta=1$	$\delta=2$	$\delta=3$	$\delta=4$	%
Exmp.3 [8]	14	20	4	≥ 22	0.00	0.00	0.01	0.02	0.02	≥ 30	0.00	0.00	0.00	0.01	0.01	81.97
Exmp.4 [8]	14	22	4	$= 2$	0.00	0.01	0.01	0.02	–	$= 2$	0.00	0.00	0.00	0.01	–	99.02
Escp.4×4	224	738	16	$= 2$	0.08	11.66	11.73	1059.23	–	$= 2$	0.08	0.13	0.22	0.25	–	99.02
Escp.4×5	360	1326	20	$= 2$	0.18	34.09	33.80	3084.58	–	$= 2$	0.18	0.27	0.46	0.63	–	98.98
Escp.5×5	598	2301	26	≥ 2	0.46	96.24	97.10	?	?	$= 2$	0.46	0.68	1.16	1.71	–	99.00
Escp.5×6	840	3516	30	≥ 2	1.01	217.63	216.83	?	?	$= 2$	1.00	1.42	2.40	4.30	–	98.97
Escp.6×6	1224	5424	36	≥ 2	2.13	516.92	511.41	?	?	$= 2$	2.06	2.90	5.12	10.30	–	98.99
Escp.7×7	2350	11097	50	≥ 2	7.81	2167.86	2183.01	?	?	$= 2$	7.71	10.67	19.04	52.47	–	99.01
Escp.7×8	3024	14820	56	≥ 0	13.07	?	?	?	?	$= 2$	13.44	18.25	32.69	108.60	–	

Benchmark		Reduction + Yosys + SafetySynth[4] (symbolic)							Algorithm 1 (simple explicit-state implementation)							
name	δ_{max}	$\delta=0$	$\delta=1$	$\delta=2$	$\delta=3$	$\delta=4$	$\delta=5$	$\delta=6$	$\delta=0$	$\delta=1$	$\delta=2$	$\delta=3$	$\delta=4$	$\delta=5$	$\delta=6$	%
Stub.4×4	$= 2$	1.07	1.24	1.24	1.80	–	–	–	0.04	0.07	0.12	0.18	–	–	–	98.98
Stub.4×5	$= 2$	1.16	1.49	1.49	2.83	–	–	–	0.08	0.14	0.25	0.44	–	–	–	98.97
Stub.5×5	$= 2$	1.19	2.61	2.50	13.67	–	–	–	0.21	0.37	0.63	1.17	–	–	–	98.97
Stub.5 ×6	$= 2$	1.18	2.60	2.59	23.30	–	–	–	0.42	0.69	1.20	2.49	–	–	–	98.96
Stub.6×6	$= 4$	1.17	2.76	2.74	19.96	19.69	655.24	–	0.93	1.47	2.60	5.79	7.54	7.60	–	99.89
Stub.7×7	$= 4$	1.23	2.50	2.48	24.57	23.01	2224.62	–	3.60	5.52	10.08	22.75	31.18	32.98	–	99.88

δ_{max}: the maximum delay under which G'_δ is controllable.
$\delta_{max} = \delta'$: G_δ is verified controllable under delays $0 \leq \delta \leq \delta'$ while uncontrollable under any delay $\delta > \delta'$.
$\delta_{max} \geq \delta'$: G_δ is verified controllable under delays $0 \leq \delta \leq \delta'$ within 1 h CPU time bound, yet unknown under $\delta > \delta'$ due to the limitation of computing capability.
–: already for smaller δ the controller has no winning strategy.
?: algorithm fails to answer the control/synthesis problem within 1 h of CPU time.
%: percentage of savings in state space compared to the reduction-based methods, as obtained on $\delta_{max} + 1$.

graph as in Fig. 3, and further admits direct use of shift registers for memorizing actions of the robot under delays. Therefore, as visible in Table 1, SafetySynth outperforms our explicit-state safety synthesis for some large room sizes under small delays. For larger delays it is, however, evident that our incremental algorithm always wins, despite its use of non-symbolic encodings.

Remark 2 It would be desirable to pursue a comparison on standard benchmarks like the synthesis track of SYNTCOMP. As these are conveyed in AIGER format only and not designed for modifiability, like the introduction of shift registers , this unfortunately is not yet possible. Likewise, other state-of-the-art synthesizers from the SYNTCOMP community, like AbsSynthe [4], could not be used for comparison as they do not support the state initializations appearing in the AIGER translations of the escape game.

5   Conclusions

Designing controllers that work safely and reliably when exposed to delays is a crucial challenge in many application domains, like transportation systems or industrial robots. In this paper, we have used a straightforward, yet exponential reduction to show that the existence of a finite-memory winning strategy for the controller in games with delays is decidable with respect to safety objectives. As such a reduction being exponential in the magnitude of the delay would rapidly become unwieldy, we proposed an algorithm that incrementally synthesizes a series of controllers withstanding increasingly larger delays, thereby interleaving the unavoidable introduction of memory with state-space pruning removing all states no longer controllable under the given delay before proceeding to the next larger delay. To the best of our knowledge, we also provided the first implementation of such a state-space pruning within an algorithm for solving games with delays, and we demonstrated the beneficial effects of this incremental approach on a number of benchmarks.

The benchmarks used were robot escape games indicative of collision avoidance scenarios in, e.g., traffic maneuvers. Control under delay here involves selecting appropriate safe actions or movements without yet knowing the most recent positions of the other traffic participants. Experimental results on such escape games demonstrate that our incremental algorithm outperforms reduction-based safety synthesis, irrespective of whether this safety synthesis employs naïve explicit-state or state-of-the-art symbolic synthesis methods, as available in Saarbrücken's SafetySynth tool.

An extension to hybrid control, dealing with infinite-state game graphs described by hybrid safety games, is currently under development and will be exposed in future work. We are also moving forward to a more efficient implementation of Algorithm 1 based on symbolic encodings, like BDDs [18] or SAT [3]. A further subject of future investigation is stochastic models of out-of-order delivery of messages. As these result in a high likelihood of state information being available before the maximum transportation delay, such models can quantitatively guarantee better controllability than the worst-case scenario of always delivering messages with maximum delay addressed in this paper. We will therefore attack synthesis towards quantitative safety targets in such stochastic settings and may also exploit constructive means of manipulating probability distributions of message delays, like QoS control, within the synthesis.

Acknowledgements. The authors would like to thank Bernd Finkbeiner and Ralf Wimmer for insightful discussions on the AIGER format for synthesis and Leander Tentrup for extending his tool SafetySynth by state initialization, thus facilitating a comparison.

References

1. Balemi, S.: Communication delays in connections of input/output discrete event processes. CDC **1992**, 3374–3379 (1992)
2. Behrmann, G., Cougnard, A., David, A., Fleury, E., Larsen, K.G., Lime, D.: UPPAAL-Tiga: time for playing games!. In: Damm, W., Hermanns, H. (eds.) CAV 2007. LNCS, vol. 4590, pp. 121–125. Springer, Heidelberg (2007). https://doi.org/10.1007/978-3-540-73368-3_14
3. Bloem, R., Könighofer, R., Seidl, M.: SAT-based synthesis methods for safety specs. In: McMillan, K.L., Rival, X. (eds.) VMCAI 2014. LNCS, vol. 8318, pp. 1–20. Springer, Heidelberg (2014). https://doi.org/10.1007/978-3-642-54013-4_1
4. Brenguier, R., Pérez, G.A., Raskin, J., Sankur, O.: AbsSynthe: abstract synthesis from succinct safety specifications. In: SYNT 2014, volume 157 of EPTCS, pp. 100–116 (2014)
5. Brenguier, R., Pérez, G.A., Raskin, J., Sankur, O.: Compositional algorithms for succinct safety games. SYNT **2015**, 98–111 (2015)
6. Büchi, J., Landweber, L.: Solving sequential conditions by finite-state strategies. Trans. Am. Math. Soc. **138**, 295–311 (1969)
7. Büchi, J.R., Landweber, L.H.: Solving sequential conditions by finite-state strategies. Trans. Am. Math. Soc. **138**(1), 295–311 (1969)
8. Chen, M., Fränzle, M., Li, Y., Mosaad, P.N., Zhan, N.: What's to come is still unsure: synthesizing controllers resilient to delayed interaction (full version). [Online]. http://lcs.ios.ac.cn/~chenms/papers/ATVA2018_FULL.pdf
9. Gale, D., Stewart, F.M.: Infinite games with perfect information. In: Kuhn, H.W., Tucker, A.W. (eds.) Contributions to the Theory of Games II, Annals of Mathematics Studies 28, pp. 245–266. Princeton University Press, 1953
10. Klein, F., Zimmermann, M.: How much lookahead is needed to win infinite games? In: Halldórsson, M.M., Iwama, K., Kobayashi, N., Speckmann, B. (eds.) ICALP 2015. LNCS, vol. 9135, pp. 452–463. Springer, Heidelberg (2015). https://doi.org/10.1007/978-3-662-47666-6_36
11. Klein, F., Zimmermann, M.: What are strategies in delay games? Borel determinacy for games with lookahead. In: CSL 2015, volume 41 of Leibniz International Proceedings in Informatics, pp. 519–533 (2015)
12. Kupferman, O., Vardi, M.Y.: Synthesis with incomplete information. In: Advances in Temporal Logic, pp. 109–127. Springer, Berlin (2000)
13. McNaughton, R.: Infinite games played on finite graphs. Ann. Pure Appl. Logic **65**(2), 149–184 (1993)
14. Park, S., Cho, K.: Delay-robust supervisory control of discrete-event systems with bounded communication delays. IEEE Trans. Autom. Control **51**(5), 911–915 (2006)

15. Pnueli, A., Rosner, R.: On the synthesis of an asynchronous reactive module. In: Ausiello, G., Dezani-Ciancaglini, M., Della Rocca, S.R. (eds.) ICALP 1989. LNCS, vol. 372, pp. 652–671. Springer, Heidelberg (1989). https://doi.org/10.1007/BFb0035790

16. J. Raskin, K. Chatterjee, L. Doyen, and T. A. Henzinger. Algorithms for omega-regular games with imperfect information. Logical Methods Comput. Sci. **3**(3) (2007)

17. Reif, J.H.: The complexity of two-player games of incomplete information. J. Comput. Syst. Sci. **29**(2), 274–301 (1984)

18. Somenzi, F.: Binary decision diagrams. In: Calculational System Design, Volume 173 of NATO Science Series F: Computer and Systems Sciences, pp. 303–366. IOS Press (1999)

19. Thomas, W.: On the synthesis of strategies in infinite games. In: Mayr, E.W., Puech, C. (eds.) STACS 1995. LNCS, vol. 900, pp. 1–13. Springer, Heidelberg (1995). https://doi.org/10.1007/3-540-59042-0_57

20. Tripakis, S.: Decentralized control of discrete-event systems with bounded or unbounded delay communication. IEEE Trans. Autom. Control **49**(9), 1489–1501 (2004)

21. De Wulf, M., Doyen, L., Raskin, J.-F.: A lattice theory for solving games of imperfect information. In: Hespanha, J.P., Tiwari, A. (eds.) HSCC 2006. LNCS, vol. 3927, pp. 153–168. Springer, Heidelberg (2006). https://doi.org/10.1007/11730637_14

22. Zimmermann, M.: Finite-state strategies in delay games. In: GandALF 2017, Volume 256 of EPTCS, pp. 151–165 (2017)

A Formally Verified Motion Planner
for Autonomous Vehicles

Albert Rizaldi[1](✉), Fabian Immler[2], Bastian Schürmann[1],
and Matthias Althoff[1]

[1] Institut für Informatik, Technische Universität München, Munich, Germany
{rizaldi,bastian.schuermann,althoff}@in.tum.de
[2] Computer Science Department, Carnegie Mellon University, Pittsburgh, USA
immler@cmu.edu

Abstract. Autonomous vehicles are safety-critical cyber-physical systems. To ensure their correctness, we use a proof assistant to prove safety properties deductively. This paper presents a formally verified motion planner based on manoeuvre automata in Isabelle/HOL. Two general properties which we ensure are numerical soundness (the absence of floating-point errors) and logical correctness (satisfying a plan specified in linear temporal logic). From these two properties, we obtain a motion planner whose correctness only depends on the validity of the models of the ego vehicle and its environment.

Keywords: Motion primitives · Manoeuvre automata · Motion planning · Theorem proving · Linear temporal logic · Reachability analysis · Autonomous vehicles

1 Introduction

Autonomous vehicles' planning and control are hard. Not only are they required to consider complex vehicle dynamics, but they must also deal with possibly unknown and dynamically changing environments. To tackle these complexities, most symbolic motion planners abstract continuous systems by discrete representations in either an *environment-driven* [6,12] or a *controller-driven* manner [14,16]. The former partitions the environment into cells, such as triangles or squares, while the latter partitions the controller into several primitives, such

A. Rizaldi and B. Schürmann—This work is partially supported by the DFG Graduiertenkolleg 1840 (PUMA) and the European Comission project UnCoVer-CPS under grant number 643921.

F. Immler—Supported by DFG Koselleck grant NI 491/16-1. Moreover, this material is based upon work supported by the Air Force Office of Scientific Research under grant number FA9550-18-1-0120. Any opinions, finding, and conclusion or recommendations expressed in this material are those of the author(s) and do not necessarily reflect the views of the United States Air Force.

© Springer Nature Switzerland AG 2018
S. K. Lahiri and C. Wang (Eds.): ATVA 2018, LNCS 11138, pp. 75–90, 2018.
https://doi.org/10.1007/978-3-030-01090-4_5

as `turn-left` or `turn-right`. Which discretisation is preferred for autonomous vehicles?

Environment-driven discretisation is preferred when *(1)* we have static, a priori known, and geometrically complex environments; or *(2)* one has to handle expressive specifications, such as those expressed in Linear Temporal Logic (LTL). However, environment-driven discretisation usually works only for systems with simple dynamics [5]. On the contrary, controller-driven discretisation is preferred when we have dynamic, possibly unknown, and geometrically simple environments. Controllers designed with this discretisation can handle complex dynamics and navigate the environment by chaining a series of well-tested motion primitives [14]. However, specification languages for this discretisation in the literature, such as in [10], are very close to the implementation level; often, we want to specify *what* to achieve rather than *how* to achieve it.

Most vehicle models for autonomous vehicles are complex, making controller-driven discretisation a natural choice. In this work, we shall use manoeuvre automata-based motion planners [35], where each motion primitive is encoded as a state in our manoeuvre automaton. However, autonomous vehicles operate in dynamic and possibly unknown environments, where they could benefit from specification languages such as LTL—usually associated with environment-driven discretisation. This work aims to combine the advantages of both discretisation strategies by interpreting LTL over manoeuvre automata. To the best of our knowledge, this paper is the first work to tackle this challenge.

To prove correctness of our motion planner, we use the generic theorem prover Isabelle [28], as opposed to the specialised theorem prover KeYmaera X [15], which is tailored for proving the correctness of hybrid systems. This choice is motivated by eliminating numerical errors in computations with real numbers, which is largely ignored in motion planning [30]. Isabelle's libraries of approximation and affine arithmetic allow us to eliminate these errors [19,20]. Our contributions are as follows[1]:

- We provide a formally verified construction of manoeuvre automata (Sect. 3). More precisely, we interface Isabelle with MATLAB for solving optimisation problems and use the formalised algorithm for continuous reachability analysis [22]; both optimisation and reachability analysis are needed for constructing manoeuvre automata formally.
- We show how to eliminate numerical errors for functions involving real numbers (Sect. 4). To this end, we provide a verified translation between the representation of floating-points used by Isabelle and that of IEEE-754 used by MATLAB. Additionally, we extend the work in [22] to handle the trigonometric functions sine and cosine required in this work.
- We show how to plan autonomous vehicles' motions with temporal logic and manoeuvre automata (Sect. 5). More precisely, we interpret LTL over manoeuvre automata and formally perform satisfiability checking—as opposed to model checking—in order to find a sequence of manoeuvres which is guaranteed to satisfy a plan formalised in LTL.

---

[1] The formalisation is in https://gitlab.lrz.de/ga96tej/manoeuvre-automata.

2   Preliminaries

Notations used in this paper closely resemble Isabelle/HOL's syntax. Function application is always written in an uncurried form: instead of writing $f\ x\ y$ as in the λ-calculus, we always write $f(x, y)$. We write $t :: \tau$ to indicate that term t has type τ. Types used in this paper could either be a base type such as $\mathbb{R}$ for real numbers, or constructed via type constructors such as α *list* and α *set* for list of type α and set of type α, respectively. Another type constructor is the function type; a function from type α to β is written as (has the type of) $\alpha \Rightarrow \beta$. We use '$\Longrightarrow$' and '$\longrightarrow$' to denote deduction (inference) and implication, respectively. The set of all objects of type α is $UNIV :: \alpha$. Isabelle[2] also supports the **case** construct as in functional programming:

$$\textbf{case } t \textbf{ of } pat_1 \Rightarrow t_1 \mid \ \ldots \ \mid pat_n \Rightarrow t_n.$$

One of the most frequently used data structures in this work are *affine forms*. An affine form A is defined by a sequence $(A_i)_{i \in \mathbb{N}}$ with only finitely many nonzero elements. We write A_i to refer to the i-th element of the affine form A. An affine form is interpreted for a valuation $\varepsilon : \mathbb{N} \to [-1, 1]$ as:

$$[\![A]\!]_\varepsilon := A_0 + \sum_i \varepsilon_i \cdot A_i.$$

We could also think of ε as a vector taken from an interval vector $[-\mathbf{1}, \mathbf{1}]$, where $\mathbf{1}$ is a vector of ones. One calls the terms ε_i noise symbols, A_0 the centre, and the remaining A_i generators. The idea is that noise symbols are shared between affine forms and that they are treated symbolically: the sum of two affine forms is given by the pointwise sum of their generators, and multiplication with a constant factor is also done componentwise:

$$[\![(A + B)]\!]_\varepsilon := (A_0 + B_0) + \sum_i \varepsilon_i \cdot (A_i + B_i).$$

$$[\![(k \cdot A)]\!]_\varepsilon := k \cdot A_0 + \sum_i \varepsilon_i \cdot (k \cdot A_i).$$

For $A_0, A_i :: \mathbb{R}^n$, the affine form A is a data structure to represent a specific type of set $\mathcal{Z} :: \mathbb{R}^n$ *set* (see the notation of type constructor for sets) called *zonotope*— a special class of polytopes. By defining a function *range* which represents all possible valuations of an affine form, the relationship between an affine form A and a zonotope $\mathcal{Z}$ is formalised as $range(A) = \mathcal{Z}$. Figure 1 provides the graphical illustration of the set of all points belonging to a zonotope.

If we represent an affine form concretely by a pair of its centre c and a list of its generators gs, then the *Minkowski sum* of two affine forms $A = (c, gs)$ and $A' = (c', gs')$ is defined as:

$$msum\,(A, A') = (c + c',\ msum\text{-}gens\,(A, A'))\ ,$$
$$msum\text{-}gens\,(A, A') = gs\ @\ gs',$$

---

[2] From now on, 'Isabelle' refers to 'Isabelle/HOL' for simplicity.

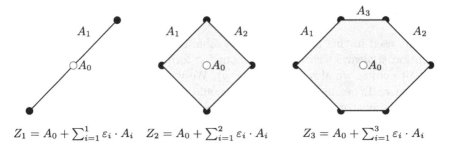

Fig. 1. Three zonotopes with $A_0 = (0,0)$, $A_1 = (1,1)$, $A_2 = (1,-1)$, and $A_3 = (1,0)$. Black circles represent the extreme points of each zonotope.

where function @ denotes list concatenation. Figure 1 provides graphical illustrations of the Minkowski sum: $Z_2 = msum(Z_1, Z_2')$, $Z_3 = msum(Z_2, Z_3')$ where $Z_2' = \mathbf{0} + A_2$ and $Z_3' = \mathbf{0} + A_3$.

3   Constructing Manoeuvre Automata

A manoeuvre automaton (MA) [14] is an automaton whose states represent manoeuvres (motion primitives) which an autonomous system could execute. For helicopters, these could be standard manoeuvres such as `hover` and `land`, or more aggressive movements such as `hammerhead` and `loop`. For autonomous vehicles, these could be basic manoeuvres such as `turn-left` and `turn-right`, or more ambitious manoeuvres such as `hard-left` and `hard-right`. A transition between two states in an MA means that the system can execute those two manoeuvres successively.

Definition 1. *We define a manoeuvre automaton as a tuple* $MA = (M, jump, ode)$ *where*

– M *is a predefined type for manoeuvre labels;*
– $jump :: (M \times M)\,set$ *is the transition relation between manoeuvre labels; and*
– $ode\,(m) :: \mathbb{R} \times \mathbb{R}^n \Rightarrow \mathbb{R}^n$ *is the corresponding ordinary differential equation (ODE) for manoeuvre* m.

If we assume that the $ode\,(m)$ has the general form of

$$\dot{x} = f(x, u_m), \tag{1}$$

then the $ode\,(m)$ represents a fixed system model f—such as a point-mass or as a kinematic single-track model for autonomous vehicles [3]—with a fixed input trajectory u_m for manoeuvre m. For an initial state x_{init} and a final state x_{final}, a controller must choose a trajectory $u_m \in \mathcal{U}_m$ which steers x_{init} to x_{final}. We refrain from discussing the design of such controllers, as this work focusses more on the verification aspect; interested readers can consult the work in [35].

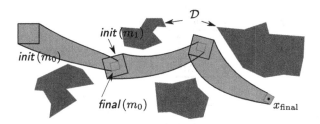

Fig. 2. Ensuring the safety of a path from an MA.

For safety verification purposes, it is paramount to compute the *reachable set* of a manoeuvre m—denoted by *reach*(m). This set represents the set of all states x which could be reached by the system f in (1) from an initial set denoted by *init*(m) with trajectory u_m. A manoeuvre m is safe with respect to a given unsafe set $\mathcal{D}$ if and only if *reach*(m) does not intersect with the unsafe set: *reach*$(m) \cap \mathcal{D} = \emptyset$ (see Fig. 2). A formally verified computation of reachable sets of continuous systems with the theorem prover Isabelle has been previously researched by one of the authors in [22] and we shall use it here.

How can we incorporate the reachable set of each manoeuvre to ensure the safety of a path? A safe path from an MA is a series of manoeuvres $m = m_0, m_1, \ldots, m_n$ which: *(a)* respects the transition relation *jump* in Definition 1, i.e., $(m_i, m_{i+1}) \in$ *jump* for $0 \leq i < n$; *(b)* ensures that the reachable set of each manoeuvre does not intersect with an unsafe set; and *(c)* for every chain (m_i, m_{i+1}) in the series, the final set of m_i—denoted by *final*(m_i)—must be contained by the initial set of m_{i+1}, i.e., *final*$(m_i) \subseteq$ *init*(m_{i+1}) (see [35]). Figure 2 illustrates these requirements of ensuring the safety of a path from an MA.

The first technical challenge for formally constructing manoeuvre automata, as proposed in this work, is how to interface the controller design in [35] implemented in MATLAB and the reachability analysis in [22] formalised in Isabelle. Figure 3 illustrates how we interface Isabelle and MATLAB by using the C programming language as a *lingua franca*. Functions programmed in MATLAB are callable from C by using the MATLAB API. Isabelle, on the other hand, can call functions in Standard ML (SML) directly but not those in C. Fortunately, there is a Foreign Function Interface (FFI) between SML and C which enables us to call functions in C and, hence, MATLAB indirectly. Therefore, we need to provide the corresponding wrapper for each MATLAB function required by Isabelle at the SML and C levels.

The second technical challenge is to bridge the different types of floating-point representation between Isabelle and MATLAB. Isabelle uses arbitrary precision floating-point numbers ($m \cdot 2^e$ for potentially unbounded $m, e \in \mathbb{Z}$) and MATLAB uses IEEE-754 floating point-numbers (with fixed precision). How to obtain a formally correct conversion between arbitrary precision floating-point numbers (as used in Isabelle/HOL) and IEEE floating-point numbers (as used in MATLAB) is discussed in the next section.

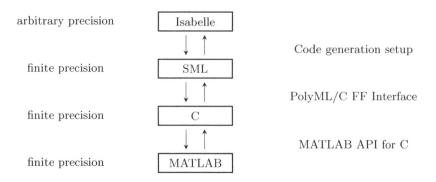

Fig. 3. Block diagram for interfacing Isabelle and MATLAB.

4 Affine Arithmetic and Floating-Point Numbers

This section considers rounding errors when using finite precision floating-point numbers to ensure soundness of our proofs. To achieve this, we use rigorous numerics, which encloses real numbers by sets. This means, for example, the function $\times :: real \Rightarrow real \Rightarrow real$ is "lifted" to a new function $\otimes :: real\,set \Rightarrow real\,set \Rightarrow real\,set$ with the correctness theorem $\forall x, y. \quad x \in X \wedge y \in Y \longrightarrow x \times y \in X \otimes Y$. The first problem entailed by this decision is how to choose the proper data structure to represent the abstract type $real\,set$. Following the decision made in our previous work [20], we use affine arithmetic [13] for this purpose. There are other approaches such as intervals [27] and Taylor models [7] whose discussion is out of the scope of this paper. The second problem is how to approximate functions operating on reals with functions operating on sets correctly. Previous work in [20] has covered affine approximation of arithmetic functions such as addition, multiplication, subtraction, and division, but not trigonometric functions. For this particular work, we need affine approximations of trigonometric functions such as sine and cosine occuring in model f in (1) (the specific model can be found in (5), Sect. 5).

4.1 Affine Approximation of Trigonometric Functions

To simplify formal proofs, modularity and abstraction are important. As a basis for all operations that follow, we use a generic linear operation that involves round-off operations and also adds a noise symbol for further uncertainties (this is also discussed by Stolfi and de Figueredo [13]). The idea is to define a generic linear operation $\textit{affine-unop}(\alpha, \beta, \delta, X)$ that encloses the linear function $x \mapsto \alpha \cdot x + \beta$ with an uncertainty of δ for every valuation $\varepsilon \in \mathbb{N} \to [-1, 1]$:

$$|\alpha \cdot [\![X]\!]_\varepsilon + \beta - [\![\textit{affine-unop}(\alpha, \beta, \delta, X)]\!]_\varepsilon| \le \delta.$$

The motivation behind $\textit{affine-unop}(\alpha, \beta, \delta, X)$ is that $\alpha \cdot x + \beta$ approximates some (possibly nonlinear) function f up to an error δ, i.e.,

$$|f(x) - (\alpha \cdot x + \beta)| \le \delta \ , \tag{2}$$

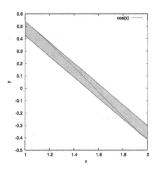

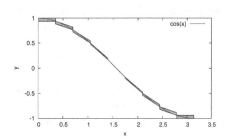

Fig. 4. Min-range approximation of $\cos [1, 2]$.

Fig. 5. Min-range approximations (nine subdivisions) of $\cos [0, \pi]$

up to a certain interval $x \in [l, u]$. There are various degrees of freedom for linearising a non-linear function f such that (2) holds. In this work, we use the *min-range approximation* [13,34] for the sake of ease of implementation and verification; other techniques such as interval approximation [13,34] and first-order Tchebychev approximation [13,34] exist.

The idea behind the min-range approximation is to maximize the slope of the enclosure while fixing the range of the approximation. Consider Fig. 4, which illustrates a min-range approximation of cosine on the interval $[1, 2]$; it does not exceed the interval $[\cos(2), \cos(1)]$. Any smaller slope would be just as safe, but the slope could not be chosen to be larger. The following theorem guides us to find suitable values of α, β, and δ.

Proposition 1 (Min-range approximation).

$$\forall x \in [l, u].\ |f(x) - (\alpha \cdot x + \beta)| \leq \delta$$

if the following conditions are satisfied:

1. $\forall y \in [l, u].\ \alpha \leq f'(y)$;
2. $\delta \geq \frac{f(u) - f(l) - \alpha \cdot (u - l)}{2} + |(f(l) + f(u) - \alpha \cdot (l + u))/2 - \beta|.$

Parameter α needs to be a lower bound on the derivative while parameters β and δ need to be chosen such that they account for the error of the linear function centred between $f(u)$ and $f(l)$ as well as for the error that β makes with respect to the centre (the second summand on the right of the inequality bounding δ). This is a slight generalisation of what is demanded in the literature [13,34], where one assumes a convex function f. This ensures that the derivative f' attains its maximum at one of the endpoints of the interval. Something that is not mentioned in the statement of the lemma should be noted: the approximation using α, β is close to the optimal approximation only if the function f is increasing on $[l, u]$ (otherwise the theorem still holds, but δ is unnecessarily large). However, a similar approximation lemma can be easily obtained for the case when f is decreasing.

Trigonometric Functions. The trigonometric functions sine and cosine pose the problem that they are not monotonic. This can be alleviated in two steps (similar to the treatment of periodic functions in [2]). The first step, range reduction, exploits periodicity to reduce the argument to the range $[0, 2\pi]$. Range reduction (shifting the argument x by $-2\pi \cdot \lfloor \frac{x}{2\pi} \rfloor$) is computed using interval arithmetic. The second step is a case distinction if the argument is contained in the decreasing part $[0, \pi]$ or the monotone part $[\pi, 2\pi]$ (for cosine). It is possible that this distinction cannot be decided (if e.g., the argument interval straddles π), but then the only valid min-range approximation is the interval approximation (with 1 as upper bound). A series of such computed min-range approximations is shown in Fig. 5.

4.2 From Isabelle's to IEEE-754's Floating-Point Representation

Affine arithmetic in Isabelle is implemented with arbitrary-precision floating-point numbers, hereafter denoted by $float_\infty$. Software floating point numbers (the formalisation in Isabelle originates from Obua's work [29]) are the subset of real numbers that can be represented by two arbitrary-precision integers: mantissa (or significand) m and exponent e. Mantissa and exponent together represent the real number $m \cdot 2^e$:

$$float_\infty := \{ m \cdot 2^e \mid m, e \in \mathbb{Z} \}.$$

Arbitrary-precision floating-point numbers are convenient for formal reasoning because arithmetic operations can be carried out without round-off errors. For efficiency, however, we do use explicit round-off operations overapproximately to reduce the size of the mantissa. The explicit separation of operation and rounding helps keeping the formalisation modular.

The representation used by MATLAB is IEEE-754 floating-point numbers. A specification of floating-point numbers (with a fixed precision of 52 bits for the mantissa and 11 bits for the exponent of double-precision floating point numbers) according to the IEEE-754 standard was formalized in Isabelle by Yu [37].[3] We denote IEEE-754 floating-point numbers with $float_{ieee}$. They are represented by triples $(s, e, f) \in \mathbb{N} \times \mathbb{N} \times \mathbb{N}$ to represent sign s, exponent e, and fraction f. There are special representations for special values like infinity or NaN (Not-a-Number); everything else represents *finite* numbers. A predicate *is-finite* encodes whether a triple represents a finite number. Finite IEEE floating point numbers can be normal ($e \neq 0$) or denormal ($e = 0$) and are interpreted as a real number differently using *to-real*:

$$to\text{-}real(s, e, f) = \begin{cases} (-1)^s \cdot 2^{-1022} \cdot (f \cdot 2^{-52}) & \text{if } e = 0, \\ (-1)^s \cdot 2^{e-1023} \cdot (1 + f \cdot 2^{-52}) & \text{if } e \neq 0. \end{cases}$$

---

[3] Yu's formalisation was inspired by Harrison's [18] extensive formalisation in HOL Light. More work on floating-point numbers in theorem provers has been done in the comprehensive formalisation of floating-point numbers by Boldo and Melquiond [9] in Coq as well as early efforts in ACL2 [26].

We provide functions *of-ieee* and *to-ieee* which convert between a subset of arbitrary-precision floating-point numbers and IEEE floating-point numbers. The bijection is guarded by *is-valid* (to ensure that the arbitrary precision floating-point number is actually of suitable finite precision) and *is-finite* (to exclude special values).

$$\textit{is-finite}(s, e, f) \implies \textit{of-ieee}(s, e, f) = \textit{to-real}(s, e, f),$$

$$\textit{is-valid}(m \cdot 2^e) \implies \textit{to-real}(\textit{to-ieee}(m, e)) = m \cdot 2^e.$$

We implemented this (based on work by Fabian Hellauer, which we gratefully acknowledge here) using the IEEE-754 formalisation in the archive of formal proofs [37]. Note that since Isabelle's floating-point representation can have arbitrary precision, we have to ensure that the floating-point numbers used in Isabelle's theories are guaranteed to have at most 53-bit precision (i.e., *is-valid* holds) to be able to pass them down to SML, C, and MATLAB.

5   Motion Planning with Manoeuvre Automata

5.1   Interpreting LTL over Manoeuvre Automata

Definition 2 (Linear Temporal Logic for MA). *If AP is the type for all atomic propositions, then we can create a new compound data type*

$$\textbf{datatype } atom \ = \ AP^+ \mid AP^-,$$

where we label an atomic proposition with either a positive or negative sign. The syntax of LTL for manoeuvre automata is defined by the following grammar:

$$\phi ::= \textit{true} \mid \pi \mid \phi_1 \wedge \phi_2 \mid \neg\phi \mid \mathsf{X}\phi \mid \phi_1 \, \mathsf{U} \, \phi_2, \tag{3}$$

where $\pi :: atom$. Constant false, logical operators disjunction and implication, and temporal operators F and G are defined as usual [11].

Atomic propositions in path planning with LTL are used to represent objects of interest. For example, atomic propositions in our work could be defined as follows:

$$\textbf{datatype } AP \ = \ \textit{left-boundary} \mid \textit{right-boundary} \mid \textit{obstacle} \mid \textit{goal}$$

Definition 3 (Semantics of LTL for MA over finite-length traces). *Suppose that the state space for the model $ode(m)$ in Definition 1 is of type $\mathbb{R}^n$, and there is an interpretation function $\llbracket \_ \rrbracket :: AP \Rightarrow \mathbb{R}^n$ set. Additionally, for a finite sequence of sets $\sigma = \mathcal{A}_0, \mathcal{A}_1, \ldots, \mathcal{A}_n$, we denote the j-th suffix of σ by $\sigma[j..] := \mathcal{A}_j, \ldots, \mathcal{A}_n$ for $0 \leq j \leq n$. We can define a semantics of LTL* *for MA over a finite sequence of sets* $\sigma = \mathcal{A}_0, \mathcal{A}_1, \ldots, \mathcal{A}_n$, *where* $\mathcal{A}_i :: \mathbb{R}^n$ *set for* $0 \leq i \leq n$, *as follows:*

$$\sigma \models true$$
$$\sigma \models \pi^+ \qquad \Longleftrightarrow \qquad \mathcal{A}_0 \subseteq [\![\pi]\!]$$
$$\sigma \models \pi^- \qquad \Longleftrightarrow \qquad \mathcal{A}_0 \cap [\![\pi]\!] = \emptyset$$
$$\sigma \models \neg\phi \qquad \Longleftrightarrow \qquad \sigma \not\models \phi$$
$$\sigma \models \phi_1 \wedge \phi_2 \qquad \Longleftrightarrow \qquad \sigma \models \phi_1 \text{ and } \sigma \models \phi_2$$
$$\sigma \models X\phi \qquad \Longleftrightarrow \qquad \text{if } \sigma[1..] \text{ is defined then } \sigma[1..] \models \phi$$
$$\sigma \models \phi_1 \cup \phi_2 \qquad \Longleftrightarrow \qquad \exists j.\ \sigma[j..] \models \phi_2 \ \wedge \ \forall i.0 \leq i < j \longrightarrow \sigma[i..] \models \phi_1.$$

Comparison with standard LTL. The differences with standard LTL's syntax and semantics primarily lie in the additional sign for each atomic proposition and their denotations. To illustrate these differences more concretely, consider the formalisation of reach-avoid plans in standard LTL. Fainekos et al. [11] formalised these plans with $\neg obstacle \cup goal$; this is fine if we interpret LTL over a single trajectory. For an interpretation over a set of trajectories, we can lift the denotation for atomic propositions used by Fainekos et al. [11] into $\sigma \models \pi :: AP \iff \mathcal{A}_0 \subseteq [\![\pi]\!]$ (see [33]). This denotation implies $\sigma \models \neg obstacle$ if and only if $\mathcal{A}_0 \not\subseteq [\![obstacle]\!]$ and, if we assume further that $\mathcal{A}_0 \cap [\![obstacle]\!] \neq \emptyset$, then there could be a trajectory which visits the obstacle before it reaches the goal. This means the safety of σ cannot be guaranteed anymore.

The syntax and semantics in Definitions 2 and 3 provide a solution to this problem. Each atomic proposition can be labelled either with a positive or negative sign, and the root cause of the unsafety in the previous argument is due to the additional assumption $\mathcal{A}_0 \cap [\![obstacle]\!] \neq \emptyset$. The semantics solves this problem by enforcing that all negatively labelled atomic propositions have the denotation that all trajectories in $\mathcal{A}_0$ cannot be located at $[\![\pi]\!]$, i.e., $\mathcal{A}_0 \cap [\![\pi]\!] = \emptyset$. Positively labelled atomic propositions, meanwhile, have the obvious denotation that all trajectories in the initial set $\mathcal{A}_0$ must also be located inside $[\![\pi]\!]$, i.e., $\mathcal{A}_0 \subseteq [\![\pi]\!]$. In case $\mathcal{A}_0 \not\subseteq [\![\pi]\!]$ and $\mathcal{A}_0 \cap [\![\pi]\!] \neq \emptyset$, there might be a trajectory which always stays in $[\![\pi]\!]$ or lies outside of $[\![\pi]\!]$ completely, but this should not justify $\sigma \models \pi^+$ or $\sigma \models \pi^-$ because we choose soundness over completeness.

Checking zonotope inclusion and intersection freedom. The semantics in Definition 3 does not stipulate any concrete type of sets. To demonstrate our approach, we use zonotopes in this work to check $\sigma \models \pi^+$ (using an inclusion check) and $\sigma \models \pi^-$ (checking for intersection freedom) in $\mathbb{R}^2$ since higher dimensions are not required in this work. We define the function *zono-contain2D* $(prec, Z, Z')$ to check whether zonotope *range* (Z) is a subset of zonotope *range* (Z'). This is performed[4] by first enumerating all extreme points of zonotope *range* (Z)—via the function *extreme-pts* (Z)—initially (see Fig. 1) and then checking whether each of these extreme points belongs to the zonotope *range* (Z_2) as partially done in [21].

---

[4] For high-dimensional zonotopes, please consult the technique described in CORA [1].

Theorem 1 *By defining* zono-contain2D$(prec, Z, Z')$ *as:*

$$zono\text{-}contain2D(prec, Z, Z') := \textbf{case } extreme\text{-}pts(Z) \textbf{ of}$$
$$[] \Rightarrow Z_0 \in_{zono} Z'$$
$$| ps \Rightarrow \forall p.\ p \in set(ps) \longrightarrow p \in_{zono} Z',$$

we have the correctness condition:

$$zono\text{-}contain2D(prec, Z, Z') \implies range(Z) \subseteq range(Z'),$$

for any precision prec *and any two zonotopes* Z, Z' *of type* $\mathbb{R}^2$.

We also define the function *collision-freedom2D*$(prec, Z, Z')$ to check whether zonotope *range*(Z) does *not* intersect with *range*(Z') based on [17] which we proved formally in Isabelle too.

Theorem 2 *Suppose that affine forms* Z *and* Z' *have the centres of* Z_0 *and* Z_0', *respectively, and* $Z_0' - Z_1'$ *denotes the vector difference of* Z_0' *and* Z_1', *then*

$$\underbrace{Z_0' - Z_1' \notin range(msum\text{-}gens(Z, Z'))}_{:=\ collision\text{-}freedom2D\,(prec, Z, Z')} \implies range(Z) \cap range(Z') = \emptyset.$$

Note that the two theorems above take the precision $prec :: \mathbb{N}$ into account to ensure numerical soundness.

5.2   Satisfiability Checking of LTL over Manoeuvre Automata

The problem of finding a path in MA which satisfies a plan formalised in LTL can now be stated formally as satisfiability checking.

Definition 4 (Satisfiability checking). *An LTL formula* ϕ *is satisfiable with respect to a manoeuvre automaton* $MA = (M, jump, ode)$ *if there is a path* $\tau = m_0, m_1, \ldots m_{n-1}$ *such that* $m_i :: M$ *for all* $0 \le i < n$ *and*

$$reach(m_0), reach(m_1), \ldots, reach(m_{n-1}) \models \phi.$$

Satisfiability checking is a search problem and since *(1)* time efficiency is paramount, and *(2)* a path satisfying a plan usually has a finite duration, we use a depth-limited search strategy for satisfiability checking. Since each manoeuvre lasts for 1 s and a sensible duration for a plan is supposed to be less than 10 s, the maximum depth is set to be 10. Note that the search strategy can be improved further by using an informed search strategy. However, since our main focus is correctness, we choose a simpler yet sufficient depth-limited search strategy for satisfiability checking.

As an example, we construct an intentionally simple, formally verified manoeuvre automaton with three motion primitives which last for 1 s each:

$$\textbf{datatype } M = go\text{-}straight \mid turn\text{-}left \mid turn\text{-}right, \tag{4}$$

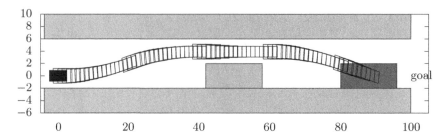

Fig. 6. Example of reach-avoid scenario. The vehicle is represented as the solid black rectangle. Red-coloured rectangles are the objects the vehicle has to avoid. The blue-coloured rectangle is the area which the vehicle has to reach eventually (Color figure online).

where any two manoeuvres can be composed, i.e., *jump* := *UNIV*:: $M \times M$. Note that the duration for each motion primitive need not to be the same; some primitives could last for, e.g., 0.1 s and others could last for 5 s. We use the following kinematic model of autonomous vehicles:

$$\dot{v} = a; \quad \dot{\Psi} = b; \quad \dot{x} = v \cdot \cos(\Psi); \quad \dot{y} = v \cdot \sin(\Psi). \qquad (5)$$

State variables v and Ψ are speed and orientation, respectively, while x and y are the positions in Cartesian coordinates. Inputs to the system are a and b, which denote acceleration and normalised steering angle, respectively. The initial set *init* (m) is set to be the same for all manoeuvres:

$$[19.8, 20.2]\,\mathrm{m\,s^{-1}} \times [-0.02, 0.02]\,\mathrm{rad} \times [-0.2, 0.2]\,\mathrm{m} \times [-0.2, 0.2]\,\mathrm{m}.$$

Meanwhile, the final states are $(20, 0, 20, 0)$ for *go-straight*, $(20.2, 0.2, 19.87, 0.2)$ for *turn-left*, and $(20.2, -0.2, 19.87, -0.2)$ for *turn-right*. We use the controller design in [35] to obtain a set of trajectories for each manoeuvre and use the verified implementation in [22] to compute the reachable sets for each time.

According to the third requirement to ensure the safety of a path from an MA in Sect. 3, we must ensure the enclosure property *final* $(m_1) \subseteq$ *init* (m_2) holds for any two manoeuvres $(m_1, m_2) \in$ *jump*. However, the concrete numbers above show that *final* (*go-straight*) $\not\subseteq$ *init* (*go-straight*). This does not mean we cannot compose two *go-straight* primitives. To achieve this, the initial set can be shifted in position and orientation—due to position and orientation invariance in (5).

We consider the reach-avoid scenario for autonomous vehicles (Fig. 6) for motion planning. The road is divided into two four-meter-wide lanes and bounded by left and right boundaries. There is also a $16\,\mathrm{m} \times 4\,\mathrm{m}$-rectangle located at $(50, 0)$ which serves as an obstacle in our scenario. The autonomous vehicle has the length and width of 5 m and 1.75 m, respectively. It is located initially at $(0, 0)$ and must reach the goal represented by a $16\,\mathrm{m} \times 4\,\mathrm{m}$ rectangle which is located at $(80, 0)$.

The reach-avoid plan is formalised with the following LTL formula:

$$\phi := (\textit{left-boundary}^- \wedge \textit{right-boundary}^- \wedge \textit{obstacle}^-) \, \mathsf{U} \, \textit{goal}^+.$$

After performing satisfiability checking, the search returned the following plan as shown in Fig. 6:

$$\tau := \text{ turn-left , turn-right , go-straight , turn-right , go-straight.}$$

Regarding the search strategy for satisfiability checking, there are two properties we proved: termination and soundness. The former is proved with the aid of the function package in Isabelle [23] by specifying a measure function which decreases after each recursive call. Meanwhile, the latter is ensured due to the following two facts: *(1)* we use the formalised LTL monitoring function from our previous work [32] to check whether current nodes satisfy the LTL formula, and *(2)* we interpret each atomic proposition over-approximatively either due to inherent uncertainty or numerical round-offs.

Two remarks worth mentioning here. Firstly, note that the main scientific dimension considered in this work is the correctness of a motion planner achieved with the aid of a theorem prover. Hence, we prioritise correctness over other dimensions such as coverage, efficiency, and scalability. The example provided in this section should be perceived as an evidence that the formalisation in Isabelle is implementable (code generation); this section by no means is an evaluation of the coverage of our framework which we plan to do in future with other scenarios in [3]. Secondly, readers might question the fidelity of the model in (5). However, Schürmann et al. [36] have provided a framework such that a relatively simple model like ours with added uncertainties from a higher fidelity model or a real vehicle could adequately ensure the safety of a plan in a real vehicle.

6   Related Work and Conclusions

Fainekos et al. [12] and Plaku et al. [30] use satisfiability checking (or falsification) of temporal logic for finding a path which satisfies a plan formalised in (a fragment of) LTL. Fainekos et al. [12] expanded and contracted objects which must be avoided and reached, respectively, in order to have a robust interpretation of LTL. Plaku et al. [30] ignore the issue of numerical soundness when checking whether a path satisfies an LTL formula. Our approach, meanwhile, uses sets (zonotopes) as the main data structure which means we can handle robustness and numerical soundness simultaneously.

Interpreting LTL formulae over a set of trajectories has also been studied by Roehm et al. [33]. The difference between our semantics is in the way we treat the negation operator. In their work, the negation operator is allowed for formulae without any temporal operators only. Our approach, however, does not have this restriction—hence ours is more expressive—but it comes with an additional requirement of labelling each atomic proposition with a positive or negative sign.

Mitsch et al. [25] use the theorem prover KeYmaera X [15] to prove safety properties of autonomous vehicles. The main difference to our work is the approach to formal reasoning. Theirs is *proof-theoretic*: *(a)* they specify the physical model of autonomous vehicles with hybrid programs and the property with differential dynamic logic [31]; then *(b)* they use the proof system's inference rules to deduce that the hybrid program indeed satisfies the specified property. As pointed out by Anand and Knepper [4], KeYmaera X does not consider the possibility of round-off errors in floating-point numbers. This issue has been addressed by Bohrer et al. [8] where they introduce a framework called VeriPhy.

Our approach is *model-theoretic*: *(1)* we model autonomous vehicles with manoeuvre automata in which each state (manoeuvre) is assigned with reachable sets of the physical behaviour; *(2)* we specify the property in a modified LTL which takes the reachable sets into account; and *(3)* we enumerate all possible paths in the manoeuvre automaton and find a path which satisfies the property according to the predefined semantics of the modified LTL. The role of the Isabelle theorem prover in our work is to prove that each step is implemented correctly. Compared to VeriPhy, we use affine arithmetic and VeriPhy uses interval arithmetic—a special case of affine arithmetic. However, our approach needs to trust the code generation setup provided by Isabelle, whereas VeriPhy uses a sound compilation technique to generate code in CakeML [24].

Anand and Knepper [4] use the Coq theorem prover to implement a framework to specify the physical model and controller of robots for the Robot Operating System (ROS). Compared to our formalisation, theirs is closer to the implementation level; ours assumes that the optimal controller can be implemented correctly in the hardware. However, their implementation assumes that the high-level plan is given, whereas we derive a high-level plan and a low-level controller. Both works guarantee numerical soundness, but with a different technique; theirs uses constructive reals, whereas we use floating-point numbers.

Belta et al. [5] have outlined that the challenge for symbolic motion planning and control is to tie the *top-down approaches*, which use temporal logic on rather abstract models, and *bottom-up approaches*, whose aim is to construct manoeuvre automata effectively for formal analysis. We solve this challenge by adapting the syntax and semantics of LTL for manoeuvre automata. The main finding for this work is that *reachability analysis* is the key ingredient to solve this problem. It allows us to compute the reachable sets of each motion primitive and subsequently to define the satisfaction relation of motion primitives with formulae in LTL. We also address the challenge of formal verification of cyber-physical systems, where numerical soundness is largely ignored. By using a generic theorem prover such as Isabelle, we can guarantee both mathematical correctness and numerical soundness.

References

1. Althoff, M.: An introduction to CORA 2015. In: Proceedings of the Workshop on Applied Verification for Continuous and Hybrid Systems (2015)
2. Althoff, M., Grebenyuk, D.: Implementation of interval arithmetic in CORA 2016. In: Proceedings of the 3rd International Workshop on Applied Verification for Continuous and Hybrid Systems, pp. 91–105 (2016)

3. Althoff, M., Koschi, M., Manzinger, S.: CommonRoad: composable benchmarks for motion planning on roads. In: Proceedings of the IEEE Intelligent Vehicles Symposium, pp. 719–726 (2017)
4. Anand, A., Knepper, R.A.: ROSCoq: robots powered by constructive reals. In: Proceedings of the 6th International Conference on Interactive Theorem Proving, pp. 34–50 (2015)
5. Belta, C., Bicchi, A., Egerstedt, M., Frazzoli, E., Klavins, E., Pappas, G.J.: Symbolic planning and control of robot motion [grand challenges of robotics]. IEEE Robot. Autom. Mag. **14**(1), 61–70 (2007)
6. Belta, C., Isler, V., Pappas, G.J.: Discrete abstractions for robot motion planning and control in polygonal environments. IEEE Trans. Robot. **21**(5), 864–874 (2005)
7. Berz, M., Makino, K.: Verified integration of ODEs and flows using differential algebraic methods on high-order Taylor models. Reliab. Comput. **4**(4), 361–369 (1998)
8. Bohrer, B., Tan, Y.K., Mitsch, S., Myreen, M., Platzer, A.: Veriphy: Verified controller executables from verified cyber-physical system models. In: Proceedings of the ACM SIGPLAN Conference on Programming Language Design and Implementation (2018). https://doi.org/10.1145/3192366.3192406
9. Boldo, S., Melquiond, G.: Flocq: a unified library for proving floating-point algorithms in Coq. In: Proceedings of the IEEE Computer Arithmetic Symposium, pp. 243–252 (2011)
10. Egerstedt, M.B., Brockett, R.W.: Feedback can reduce the specification complexity of motor programs. IEEE Trans. Autom. Control **48**(2), 213–223 (2003)
11. Fainekos, G.E., Kress-Gazit, H., Pappas, G.J.: Temporal logic motion planning for mobile robots. In: Proceedings of the IEEE International Conference on Robotics and Automation, pp. 2020–2025 (2005)
12. Fainekos, G.E., Girard, A., Kress-Gazit, H., Pappas, G.J.: Temporal logic motion planning for dynamic robots. Automatica **45**(2), 343–352 (2009)
13. de Figueiredo, L., Stolfi, J.: Affine arithmetic: concepts and applications. Numer. Algorithms **37**(1–4), 147–158 (2004)
14. Frazzoli, E., Dahleh, M.A., Feron, E.: Maneuver-based motion planning for nonlinear systems with symmetries. IEEE Trans. Robot. **21**(6), 1077–1091 (2005)
15. Fulton, N., Mitsch, S., Quesel, J.-D., Völp, M., Platzer, A.: KeYmaera X: an axiomatic tactical theorem prover for hybrid systems. In: Felty, A.P., Middeldorp, A. (eds.) CADE 2015. LNCS (LNAI), vol. 9195, pp. 527–538. Springer, Cham (2015). https://doi.org/10.1007/978-3-319-21401-6_36
16. Gavrilets, V., Mettler, B., Feron, E.: Human-inspired control logic for automated maneuvering of miniature helicopter. J. Guidance Control Dyn. **27**(5), 752–759 (2004)
17. Guibas, L.J., Nguyen, A., Zhang, L.: Zonotopes as bounding volumes. In: Proceedings of the Fourteenth Annual ACM-SIAM Symposium on Discrete Algorithms, pp. 803–812 (2003)
18. Harrison, J.: Floating-point verification using theorem proving. In: Proceedings of the 6th International Conference on Formal Methods for the Design of Computer, Communication, and Software Systems, pp. 211–242 (2006)
19. Hölzl, J.: Proving inequalities over reals with computation in Isabelle/HOL. In: Proceedings of the ACM International Workshop on Programming Languages for Mechanized Mathematics Systems, pp. 38–45 (2009)
20. Immler, F.: Formally verified computation of enclosures of solutions of ordinary differential equations. In: Proceedings of the 6th International Symposium of NASA Formal Methods, pp. 113–127 (2014)

21. Immler, F.: A verified algorithm for geometric zonotope/hyperplane intersection. In: Proceedings of International Conference on Certified Programs and Proofs, pp. 129–136 (2015)
22. Immler, F.: Verified reachability analysis of continuous systems. In: Proceedings of the 21st International Conference on Tools and Algorithms for the Construction and Analysis of Systems, pp. 37–51 (2015)
23. Krauss, A.: Automating recursive definitions and termination proofs in higher-order logic, Ph.D. thesis, Technical University Munich (2009)
24. Kumar, R., Myreen, M.O., Norrish, M., Owens, S.: CakeML: a verified implementation of ML. In: Proceedings of the ACM SIGPLAN-SIGACT Symposium on Principles of Programming Languages, pp. 179–191 (2014)
25. Mitsch, S., Ghorbal, K., Vogelbacher, D., Platzer, A.: Formal verification of obstacle avoidance and navigation of ground robots. Int. J. Robot. Res. **36**(12), 1312–1340 (2017)
26. Moore, J.S., Lynch, T., Kaufmann, M.: A mechanically checked proof of the correctness of the kernel of the AMD5K86 floating-point division algorithm. IEEE Trans. Comput. **47**(9), 913–926 (1996)
27. Moore, R.E.: Methods and Applications of Interval Analysis. SIAM, Philadelphia (1979)
28. Nipkow, T., Wenzel, M., Paulson, L.C. (eds.): Isabelle/HOL. LNCS, vol. 2283. Springer, Heidelberg (2002). https://doi.org/10.1007/3-540-45949-9
29. Obua, S.: Flyspeck II: The Basic Linear Programs, Ph.D. thesis, Technische Universität München, München (2008)
30. Plaku, E., Kavraki, L.E., Vardi, M.Y.: Falsification of LTL safety properties in hybrid systems. Int. J. Softw. Tools Technol. Transf. **15**(4), 305–320 (2013)
31. Platzer, A.: Differential dynamic logic for hybrid systems. J. Automa. Reason. **41**(2), 143–189 (2008)
32. Rizaldi, A., Keinholz, J., Huber, M., Feldle, J., Immler, F., Althoff, M., Hilgendorf, E., Nipkow, T.: Formalising traffic rules for autonomous vehicles involving multiple lanes in Isabelle/HOL. In: Proceedings of the 13th International Conference on integrated Formal Methods, pp. 50–66 (2017)
33. Roehm, H., Oehlerking, J., Heinz, T., Althoff, M.: STL model checking of continuous and hybrid systems. In: Proceedings of 14th International Symposium on Automated Technology for Verification and Analysis, pp. 412–427 (2016)
34. Rump, S.M., Kashiwagi, M.: Implementation and improvements of affine arithmetic. Nonlinear Theory Appl. IEICE **6**(3), 341–359 (2015)
35. Schürmann, B., Althoff, M.: Convex interpolation control with formal guarantees for disturbed and constrained nonlinear systems. In: Proceedings of the Hybrid Systems: Computation and Control, pp. 121–130 (2017)
36. Schürmann, B., Heß, D., Eilbrecht, J., Stursberg, O., Köster, F., Althoff, M.: Ensuring drivability of planned motions using formal methods. In: Proceedings of the Intelligent Transportation Systems Conference, pp. 1661–1668 (2017)
37. Yu, L.: A formal model of IEEE floating point arithmetic. Arch. Form. Proofs (2018). http://isa-afp.org/entries/IEEE_Floating_Point.html. ISSN: 2150-914x

Robustness Testing of Intermediate Verifiers

YuTing Chen[(✉)] and Carlo A. Furia

Chalmers University of Technology, Gothenburg, Sweden
yutingc@chalmers.se
bugcounting.net

Abstract. Program verifiers are not exempt from the bugs that affect nearly every piece of software. In addition, they often exhibit *brittle* behavior: their performance changes considerably with details of how the input program is expressed—details that should be irrelevant, such as the order of independent declarations. Such a lack of robustness frustrates users who have to spend considerable time figuring out a tool's idiosyncrasies before they can use it effectively. This paper introduces a technique to detect lack of robustness of program verifiers; the technique is lightweight and fully automated, as it is based on *testing* methods (such as mutation testing and metamorphic testing). The key idea is to generate many simple variants of a program that initially passes verification. All variants are, by construction, equivalent to the original program; thus, any variant that fails verification indicates lack of robustness in the verifier. We implemented our technique in a tool called μgie, which operates on programs written in the popular Boogie language for verification—used as intermediate representation in numerous program verifiers. Experiments targeting 135 Boogie programs indicate that brittle behavior occurs fairly frequently (16 programs) and is not hard to trigger. Based on these results, the paper discusses the main sources of brittle behavior and suggests means of improving robustness.

1 Introduction

Automated program verifiers have become complex pieces of software; inevitably, they contain bugs that make them misbehave in certain conditions. *Verification tools need verification too.*

In order to apply verification techniques to program verifiers, we have to settle on the kind of (correctness) properties to be verified. If we simply want to look for basic *programming errors*—such as memory allocation errors, or parsing failures—the usual verification[1] techniques designed for generic software—from random testing to static analysis—will work as well on program verifiers. Alternatively, we may treat a program verifier as a *translator* that encodes the semantics of a program and specification language into purely logic constraints—which

---

[1] In this paper, the term "verification" also designates *validation* techniques such as testing.

© Springer Nature Switzerland AG 2018
S. K. Lahiri and C. Wang (Eds.): ATVA 2018, LNCS 11138, pp. 91–108, 2018.
https://doi.org/10.1007/978-3-030-01090-4_6

can be fed to a generic theorem prover. In this case, we may pursue a correct-by-construction approach that checks that the translation preserves the intended semantics—as it has been done in few milestone research achievements [20].

There is a third kind of analysis, however, which is peculiar to automated program verifiers that aim at being sound. Such tools input a program complete with specification and other auxiliary annotations, and output either "✔ SUCCESS" or "✘ FAILURE". Success means that the verifier proved that the input program is correct; but failure may mean that the program is incorrect or, more commonly, that the verifier needs more information to verify the program—such as more detailed annotations. This asymmetry between "verified" and "don't know" is a form of incompleteness, which is inevitable for sound verifiers that target expressive, undecidable program logics. Indeed, using such tools often requires users to become acquainted with the tools' idiosyncrasies, developing an intuition for what kind of information, and in what form, is required for verification to succeed. To put it in another way, program verifiers may exhibit *brittle, or unstable, behavior*: tiny changes of the input program that ought to be inconsequential have a major impact on the effectiveness achieved by the program verifier. For instance, Sect. 2 details the example of a small program that passes or fails verification just according to the relative order of two unrelated declarations. Brittle behavior of this kind compromises the usability of verification tools.

In this work, we target this kind of *robustness (stability) analysis* of program verifiers. We call an automated verifier *robust* if its behavior is not significantly affected by small changes in the input that should be immaterial. A verifier that is not robust is *brittle* (unstable): it depends on idiosyncratic features of the input. Using brittle verifiers can be extremely frustrating: the feedback we get as we try to develop a verified program incrementally is inconsistent, and we end up running in circles—trying to fix nonexistent errors or adding unnecessary annotations. Besides being a novel research direction for the verification of verifiers, identifying brittle behavior has the potential of helping develop more robust tools that are ultimately more usable.

More precisely, we apply *lightweight verification techniques* based on *testing*. Testing is a widely used technique that cannot establish correctness but is quite effective at findings bugs. The goal of our work is to automatically generate tests that reveal brittleness. Using the approach described in detail in Sect. 3, we start from a *seed*: a program that is correct and can be verified by an automated verifier. We *mutate* the seed by applying random sequences of predefined mutation operators. Each mutation operator captures a simple variation of the way a program is written that *does not change its semantics*; for example, it changes the order of independent declarations. Thus, every mutant is a *metamorphic transformation* [4] of the seed—and equivalent to it. If the verifier *fails* to verify a mutant we found a bug that exposes brittle behavior: seed and mutant differ only by small syntactic details that should be immaterial, but such tiny details impact the verifier's effectiveness in checking a correct program.

While our approach to *robustness testing* is applicable in principle to any automated program verifier, the mutation operators depend to some extent on the semantics of the verifier's input language, as they have to be semantic preserving. To demonstrate robustness testing in practice, we focus on the Boogie language [17]. Boogie is a so-called *intermediate verification language*, combining an expressive program logic and a simple procedural programming language, which is commonly used as an intermediate layer in many verification tools. Boogie's popularity[2] makes our technique (and our implementation) immediately useful to a variety of researchers and practitioners.

As we describe in Sect. 3, we implemented robustness testing for Boogie in a tool called μgie. In experiments described in Sect. 4, we ran μgie on 135 seed Boogie programs, generating and verifying over 87000 mutants. The mutants triggered brittle behavior in 16 of the seed programs; large, feature-rich programs turned out to be particularly brittle, to the point where several different mutations were capable of making Boogie misbehave. As we reflect in Sect. 6, our technique for robustness testing can be a useful complement to traditional testing techniques, and it can help buttress the construction of more robust, and thus ultimately more effective and usable, program verifiers.

Tool availability. The tool μgie, as well as all the artifacts related to its experimental evaluation, are publicly available [23]. A few additional details about the experiments are available in a longer version of this paper [6].

2   Motivating Example

Let's see a concrete example of how verifiers can behave brittlely. Figure 1 shows a simple Boogie program consisting of five declarations, each listed on a separate numbered line.

```
1 function h(int) returns (int);
2 axiom (∀ x, y: int • x > y ⟹ h(x) > y);
3 const a: [int] int;
4 axiom (∀ i: int • 0 ≤ i ⟹ a[i] < a [i + 1]);
5 procedure p(i: int) returns (o: int)
       requires i ≥ 0; ensures o > a[i]; { o := h(a[i + 1]); }
```

Fig. 1. A correct Boogie program that exposes the brittleness of verifiers: changing the order of declarations may make the program fail verification.

The program introduces an integer function h (ln. 1), whose semantics is partially axiomatized (ln. 2); a constant integer map a (ln. 3), whose elements at nonnegative indexes are sorted (ln. 4); and a procedure p (ln. 5, spanning two physical lines in the figure)—complete with signature, specification, and implementation—which returns the result of applying h to an element of a. Never mind about the specific nature of the program; we can see that procedure p is correct with respect to its specification: a[i + 1] > a[i] from the axiom

---

[2] http://boogie-docs.readthedocs.io/en/latest/#front-ends-that-emit-boogie-ivl.

about a and p's precondition, and thus $h(a[i+1]) > a[i] = o$ from the axiom about h. Indeed, Boogie successfully checks that p is correct.

There is nothing special about the order of declarations in Fig. 1—after all, "the order of the declarations in a [Boogie] program is immaterial" [17, Sec. 1]. A different programmer may, for example, put a's declarations before h's. In this case, surprisingly, Boogie fails verification warning the user that p's postcondition may not hold.

A few more experiments show that there's a fair chance of running into this kind of brittle behavior. Out of the $5! = 120$ possible permutations of the 5 declarations in Fig. 1—each an equivalent version of the program—Boogie verifies exactly half, and fails verification of the other half. We could not find any simple pattern in the order of declarations (such as "line x before line y") that predicts whether a permutation corresponds to a program Boogie can verify.

To better understand whether other tools' SMT encodings may be less brittle than Boogie's, we used b2w [1] to translate all 120 permutations of Fig. 1 to WhyML—the input language of the Why3 intermediate verifier [9]. Why3 successfully verified all of them—using Z3 as SMT solver, like Boogie does—which suggests that some features of Boogie's encoding (as opposed to Z3's capabilities) are responsible for the brittle behavior on the example.

Such kinds of brittleness—a program switching from verified to unverified based on changes that should be inconsequential—can greatly frustrate users, and in particular novices who are learning the ropes and may get stuck looking for an error in a program that is actually correct—and could be proved so if definitions were arranged in a slightly different way. Since brittleness hinders scalability to projects of realistic size, it can also be a significant problem for advanced users; for example, the developers behind the Ironclad Apps [14] and IronFleet [13] projects reported[3] that "solvers' instability was a major issue" in their verification efforts.

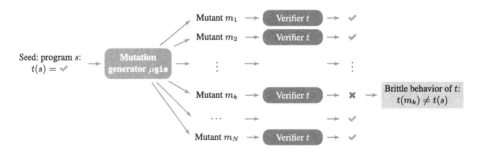

Fig. 2. How robustness testing of Boogie programs works. We start with a correct program s that some Boogie tool t can successfully verify; mutation generator μgie mutates s in several different ways, generating many different *mutants* m_k equivalent to s; each mutant undergoes verification with tool t; a mutant m_k that *fails verification* with t exposes *brittle behavior* of t on the two equivalent correct programs $s \equiv m_k$

---

[3] By an anonymous reviewer of FM 2018.

3   How Robustness Testing Works

Robustness testing is a technique that "perturbs" a correct and verified program by introducing small changes, and observes whether the changes affect the program's verifiability. The changes should be inconsequential, because they are designed not to alter the program's behavior or specification; if they do change the verifier's outcome, we found lack of robustness. While robustness testing is applicable to any automated program verifier, we focus the presentation on the popular Boogie intermediate verification language. Henceforth, a "program" is a program (complete with specification and other annotations) written in the Boogie language. Figure 2 illustrates how robustness testing works at a high level; the rest of the section provides details.

In general terms, testing requires to build a valid *input*, feed it to the system under test, and compare the system's output with the *expected* output—given by a testing *oracle*. Testing the behavior of a verifier according to this paradigm brings challenges that go beyond those involved in generating tests for general programs. First, a verifier's input is a whole *program*, complete with specification and other annotations (such as lemmas and auxiliary functions) for verification. Second, robustness testing aims at exposing subtle inconsistencies in a verifier's output, and not basic programming errors—such as memory access errors, parsing errors, or input/output errors—that every piece of software might be subject to. Therefore, we need to devise suitable strategies for *input generation* and *oracle generation*.

3.1   Mutation Operators

Input generation. In order to expose brittleness of verifiers, we need to build complex input programs of significant size, complete with rich specifications and all the annotations that are necessary to perform automated verification. While we may use grammar-based generation techniques [28] to automatically build syntactically correct Boogie programs, the generated programs would either have trivial specifications or not be semantically correct—that is, they would not pass verification. Instead, robustness testing starts from a collection of *verified programs*—the *seeds*—and automatically generates simple, semantically equivalent variants of those programs.[4] This way, we can seed robustness testing with a variety of sophisticated verification benchmarks, and assess robustness on realistic programs of considerable complexity.

Mutation operators. Given a seed s, robustness testing generates many variants $M(s)$ of s by "perturbing" s. Building on the basic concepts and terminology of mutation testing [16],[5] we call *mutant* each variant m of a seed s obtained by applying a random sequence of *mutation operators*.

---

[4] [6] describes some experiments with seeds that *fail* verification. Unsurprisingly, random mutations are unlikely to turn an unverified program into a verified one—therefore, the main paper focuses on using verified programs as seeds.

[5] See Sect. 5 for a discussion of how robustness testing differs from traditional mutation testing.

A mutation operator captures a simple syntactic transformation of a Boogie program; crucially, mutation operators should *not change a program's semantics* but only introduce equivalent or redundant information. Under this fundamental condition, every mutant m of a seed s is equivalent to s in the sense that s and m should both pass (or both fail) verification. This is an instance of *metamorphic testing*, where we transform between equivalent inputs so that the seed serves as an oracle to check the expected verifier output on all of the seed's mutants.

Table 1. Mutation operators of Boogie code in categories structural, local, and generative. Operators do not change the semantics of the code they are applied to (except possibly G_2, which is used separately)

STRUCTURAL	LOCAL	GENERATIVE
S_1 Swap any two declarations	L_1 Swap any two local variable declarations	G_1 Add **true** as pre-/postcondition, intermediate assertion, or loop invariant clause
S_2 Split a procedure definition into declaration and implementation	L_2 Split a declaration of multiple variables into multiple declarations	G_2 Remove a trigger annotation
S_3 Move any declaration into a separate file (and call Boogie on both files)	L_3 Join any two preconditions into a conjunctive one	
	L_4 Join any two postconditions into a conjunctive one	
	L_5 Swap any two pre-/postcondition, intermediate assertion, or loop invariant clauses	
	L_6 Complement an **if** condition and switch its **then** and **else** branches	

Based on our experience using Boogie and working around its brittle behavior, we designed the mutation operators in Table 1, which exercise different language features:

Structural mutation operators change the overall structure of top-level declarations—by changing their relative order (S_1), separating declarations and implementations (S_2), and splitting into multiple files (S_3).

Local mutation operators work at the level of procedure bodies—by changing the relative order of or splitting on multiple lines local variable declarations (L_1 and L_2), merging two pre- or postcondition clauses x and y into a conjunctive clause x $\wedge$ y (L_3 and L_4), changing the relative order of assertions of the same program element (L_5), and permuting the **then** and **else** branches of a conditional (L_6).

Generative mutation operators alter redundant information—by adding trivial assertions (G_1), and removing quantifier instantiation suggestions ("triggers" in G_2).

We stress that our mutation operators do not alter the semantics of a Boogie program according to the language's specification [17]: in Boogie, the order of declarations is immaterial (S_1, L_1, L_2); a procedure's implementation may be

```
input  : seed program s
input  : weight w(o) for each mutation operator o
input  : number of mutants N_M
output: set of mutants M of s

M ← {s}                                    // initialize pool of mutants to seed
attempts ← 0                               // number of main loop iterations
while |M| < N_M do                         // repeat until N_M mutants are generated
    if attempts > MAX_ATTEMPTS then
    │   break
    end
    p ← any program in M
    o ← any mutation operator                    // draw with probability w(o)
    m ← o(p)                                 // apply mutation operator o to p
    M ← M ∪ {m}                                      // add m to pool M
    attempts ← attempts + 1
end
return M
```
Algorithm 1: Mutant generation algorithm

with its declaration or be separate from it (S_2); multiple input files are processed as if they were one (S_3); multiple specification elements are implicitly conjoined, and their relative order does not matter (L_3, L_4, L_5); a conditional's branches are mutually exclusive (L_6); and true assertions are irrelevant since Boogie only checks partial correctness (G_1).

Triggers. G_2 is the only mutation operator that may alter the semantics of a Boogie program in practice: while triggers are suggestions on how to instantiate quantifiers, they are crucial to guide SMT solvers and increase stability in practice [5,19]. Therefore, **we do not consider G_2 semantics-preserving**; our experiments only apply G_2 in a separate experimental run to give an idea of its impact in isolation.

More mutation operators are possible, but the selection in Table 1 should strike a good balance between effectiveness in setting off brittle behavior and feasibility of studying the effect of each individual operator in isolation.

3.2 Mutation Generation

Given a seed s, the generation of mutants repeatedly draws random mutation operators and applies them to s, or to a previously generated mutant of s, until the desired number N_M of mutants is reached.

Algorithm 1 shows the algorithm to generate mutants. The algorithm maintains a pool M of mutants, which initially only includes the seed s. Each iteration of the main generation loop proceeds as follows: 1. pick a random program p in the pool M; 2. select a random mutation operator o; 3. apply o to p, giving mutant m; 4. add m to pool M (if it is not already there).

Users can bias the random selection of mutation operators by assigning a weight $w(o)$ to each mutation operator o in Table 1: the algorithm draws an operator with probability proportional to its weight, and operators with zero weight are never drawn.

Besides the mutation operator selection, there are two other passages of the algorithm where random selection is involved: a program p is drawn uniformly at random from M; and applying an operator o selects uniformly at random program locations where o can be applied. For example, if o is S_1 (swap two top-level declarations), applying o to p involves randomly selecting two top level declarations in p to be swapped.

Any mutation operator can generate only finitely many mutants; since the generation is random, it is possible that a newly generated mutant is identical to one that is already in the pool. In practice, this is not a problem as long as the seed s is not too small or the enabled operators too restrictive (for example, S_2 can only generate 2^D mutants, where D is the number of procedure definitions in s). The generation loop has an alternative stopping conditions that gives up after MAX_ATTEMPTS iterations that have failed to generate enough distinct mutants.

Robustness testing. After generating a set $M(s)$ of mutants of a seed s, robustness testing runs the Boogie tool on each mutant in $M(s)$. If Boogie can verify s but fails to verify any mutant $m \in M(s)$, we have found an instance of *brittle behavior*: s and m are equivalent by construction, but the different form in which m is expressed trips up Boogie and makes verification fail on an otherwise correct program.

3.3   Implementation

We implemented robustness testing as a commandline tool μgie (pronounced "moogie"). μgie implements in Haskell the mutation generation Algorithm 1, and extends parts of Boogaloo's front-end [25] for parsing and typechecking Boogie programs.

4   Experimental Evaluation

Robustness testing was initially motivated by our anecdotal experience using intermediate verifiers. To rigorously assess to what extent they are indeed brittle, and whether robustness testing can expose their brittleness, we conducted an experimental evaluation using μgie. This section describes design and results of these experiments.

4.1   Experimental Design

A run of μgie inputs a *seed* program s and outputs a number of metamorphic mutants of s, which are then verified with some tool t (see Fig. 2).

Seed selection. We prepared a curated collection of seeds by selecting Boogie programs from several different sources, with the goal of having a diverse representation of how Boogie may be used in practice. Each example belongs

Table 2. Boogie programs ("seeds") and Boogie tool versions used in the experiments.

			LOC			
GROUP	# SEEDS	MIN	MEDIAN	MEAN	MAX	TOTAL
A	10	17	34	44	152	439
D	26	2 000	4 076	4 465	8 533	116 101
E	10	13	18	23	49	230
P	30	986	1 665	1 911	5 737	57 330
S	51	6	126	1 047	7 286	67 006
T	8	11	41	1 662	7 378	18 283
all	135	6	642	1 718	8 533	259 389

(a) Selection of Boogie programs used as seeds: for each GROUP, the number of programs in that group (# SEEDS), and their MINimum, MEDIAN, MEAN, MAXimum, and TOTAL size in non-blank non-comment lines of code. Row *all* summarizes measures over all groups.

TOOL	COMMIT	DATE	Z3
BOOGIE 4.1.1	b2d448	2012-09-18	4.1.1
BOOGIE 4.3.2	97fde1	2015-03-10	4.3.2
BOOGIE 4.4.1	75b5be	2015-11-19	4.4.1
BOOGIE 4.5.0	63b360	2017-07-06	4.5.0

(b) Selection of Boogie versions used in the experiments. For every version of the Boogie TOOL, the corresponding COMMIT hash in Boogie's Git repository, the DATE of the commit, and the matching Z3 version.

to one of six groups according to its origin and characteristics; Table 2a displays basic statistics about them. Group **A** contains basic **A**lgorithms (search in an array, binary search trees, etc.) implemented directly in Boogie in our previous work [10]; these are relatively simple, but non-trivial, verification benchmarks. Group **T** is a different selection of mainly algorithmic problems (bubble sort, Dutch flag, etc.) included in Boogie's distribution **T**ests. Group **E** consists of small **E**xamples from our previous work [5] that target the impact of different trigger annotations in Boogie. Group **S** collects large Boogie programs that we generated automatically from fixed, repetitive structures (for example, nested conditionals); in previous work [5] we used these programs to evaluate **S**calability. Groups **D** and **P** contain Boogie programs automatically generated by the **D**afny [18] and Auto**P**roof [11] verifiers (which use Boogie as intermediate representation). The Dafny and Eiffel programs they translate come from the tools' galleries of verification benchmarks [2,8]. As we see from the substantial size of the Boogie programs they generate, Dafny and AutoProof introduce a significant overhead as they include axiomatic definitions of heap memory and complex types. In all, we collected 135 seeds of size ranging from just 6 to over 8500 lines of Boogie code for a total of nearly 260000 lines of programs and specifications.

Tool selection. In principle, μgie can be used to test the robustness of any verifier that can input Boogie programs: besides Boogie, tools such as Boogaloo [25], Symbooglix [21], and blt [5]. However, different tools target different kinds of analyses, and thus typically require different kinds of seeds to be tested properly and meaningfully compared. To our knowledge, no tools other than Boogie itself support the full Boogie language, or are as mature and as effective as Boogie for sound verification (as opposed to other analyses, such as the symbolic execution performed by Boogaloo and Symbooglix) on the kinds of examples we selected. We intend to perform a different evaluation of these tools using μgie in the future, but for consistency and clarity we focus on the Boogie tool in this paper.

In order to understand whether Boogie's robustness has changed over its development history, our experiments include different versions of Boogie. The Boogie repository is not very consistent in assigning new version numbers, nor does it tag specific commits to this effect. As a proxy for that, we searched through the logs of Boogie's repository for commit messages that indicate updates to accommodate new features of the Z3 SMT solver—Boogie's standard and main backend. For each of four major versions of Z3 (4.1.1, 4.3.2, 4.4.1, and 4.5.0), we identified the most recent commit that refers explicitly to that version (see Table 2b); for example, commit `63b360` says "Calibrated test output to Z3 version 4.5.0". Then, we call "Boogie v" the version of Boogie at the commit mentioning Z3 version v, running Z3 version v as backend.

To better assess whether brittle behavior is attributable to Boogie's encoding or to Z3's behavior, we included two other tools in our experiments: CVC4 refers to the SMT solver CVC4 v. 1.5 inputting Boogie's SMT2 encoding of verification condition (the same input that is normally fed to Z3); Why3 refers to the intermediate verifier Why3 v. 0.86.3 using Z3 4.3.2 as backend, and inputting WhyML translations of Boogie programs automatically generated by `b2w` [1].

Table 3. Definitions and descriptions of the experimental measures reported in Table 4.

	DEFINITION	DESCRIPTION
S		set of all seeds
$M_O(s)$		set of all mutants of seed s (generated with mutation operators O)
$S_t^{\checkmark}$	$\{s \in S \mid t(s)\}$	seeds that pass verification with tool t
$M_O(s)_t^{\times}$	$\{m \in M_O(s) \mid \neg t(m)\}$	mutants of seed s that fail verification with tool t
$S_t^{\checkmark \rightsquigarrow \times}$	$\{s \in S_t^{\checkmark} \mid \lvert M_O(s)_t^{\times}\rvert > 0\}$	passing seeds with at least one mutant failing with tool t
$M_O(s)_t^{\infty}$	$\{m \in M_O(s) \mid t(m)\ \text{times out}\}$	failing mutants of seed s that time out with tool t
# PASS	$\lvert S_t^{\checkmark}\rvert$	number of seeds that pass verification with tool t
# ∃FAIL	$\lvert S_t^{\checkmark \rightsquigarrow \times}\rvert$	number of verified seeds with at least one failing mutant with tool t
% ∃FAIL	$100 \cdot \lvert S_t^{\checkmark \rightsquigarrow \times}\rvert/\lvert S_t^{\checkmark}\rvert$	percentage of verified seeds with at least one failing mutant with tool t
% FAIL	$100 \cdot mean_{s \in S_t^{\checkmark}}\lvert M_O(s)_t^{\times}\rvert/\lvert M_O(s)\rvert$	average percentage of failing mutants per verified seed with tool t
% TIMEOUT	$100 \cdot mean_{s \in S_t^{\checkmark}}\lvert M_O(s)_t^{\infty}\rvert/\lvert M_O(s)\rvert$	average percentage of timed out mutants per verified seed with tool t
% ∃FAIL	$100 \cdot mean_{s \in S_t^{\checkmark \rightsquigarrow \times}}\lvert M_O(s)_t^{\times}\rvert/\lvert M_O(s)\rvert$	average percentage of failing mutants per verified seed with some failing mutants

Experimental setup. Each experiment has two phases: first, *generate mutants* for every seed; then, *run Boogie* on the mutants and check which mutants still verify.

For every seed $s \in S$ (where S includes all 135 programs summarized in Table 2a), we generate different *batches* $M_O(s)$ of mutants of s by enabling specific mutation operators O in μgie. Precisely, we generate 12 different batches for every seed:

$M_*(s)$ consists of 100 different mutants of s, generated by picking uniformly at random among all mutation operators in Table 1 **except G_2** (that is, each mutation operator gets the same positive weight, and G_2 gets weight zero);

$M_J(s)$, for J one of the 11 operators in Table 1, consists of 50 different mutants of s generated by only applying mutation operator J (that is, J gets a positive weight, and all other operators get weight zero).

Batch M_* demonstrates the effectiveness of robustness testing with general settings; then, the smaller batches M_J focus on the individual effectiveness of one mutation operator at a time. Operator G_2 is only used in isolation (and not at all in M_*) since it may change the semantics of programs indirectly by guiding quantifier instantiation.

Let t be a tool (a Boogie version in Table 2b, or another verifier). For every seed $s \in S$, we run t on s and on all mutants $M_O(s)$ in each batch. For a run of t on program p (seed or mutant), we write $t(p)$ if t verifies p successfully; and $\neg t(p)$ if t fails to verify p (because it times out, or returns with failure). Based on this basic data, we measure robustness by counting the number of verified seeds whose mutants fail verification: see the measures defined in Table 3 and the results described in detail in Sect. 4.2.

Running times. The experiments ran on a Ubuntu 16.04 LTS GNU/Linux box with Intel 8-core i7-4790 CPU at 3.6 GHz and 16 GB of RAM. Generating the mutants took about 15 min for the batch M_* and 10 min for each batch M_J. Each verification run was given a timeout of 20 s, after which it was forcefully terminated by the scheduler of GNU `parallel` [27].

4.2   Experimental Results

Overall results: batch M_*. Our experiments, whose detailed results are in Table 4, show that robustness testing is *effective* in exposing *brittle behavior*, which is *recurrent* in Boogie: for 12% of the seeds that pass verification,[6] there is at least one mutant in batch M_* that fails verification.

Not all seeds are equally prone to brittleness: while on average only 3% of one seed's mutants fail verification, it is considerably easier to trip up seeds that are *susceptible* to brittle behavior (that is such that at least one mutant fails verification): 27% of mutants per such seeds fail verification.

When the verifier times out on a mutant, it may be because: (i) the timeout is itself unstable and due to random noise in the runtime environment; (ii) the mutant takes longer to verify than the seed, but may still be verified given longer time; (iii) verification time diverges.

We ruled out (i) by repeating experiments 10 times, and reporting a timeout only if all 10 repetitions time out. Thus, we can generally consider the timeouts in Table 4 indicative of a genuine degrading of performance in verification—which affected 3% of one seed's mutants on average.

Boogie versions. There is little difference between Boogie versions, with the exception of Boogie 4.1.1. This older version does not support some language features used extensively in many larger examples that also tend to be more brittle (groups D and P). As a result, the percentage of verified seeds with mutants

---

[6] For clarity, we initially focus on Boogie 4.5.0, and later discuss differences with other versions.

Table 4. Experimental results of robustness testing with μgie. For each GROUP of seeds, for each TOOL: number of seeds passing verification (# PASS), number and percentage of passing seeds for which at least one mutant fails verification (#∃FAIL and % ∃FAIL), average percentage of mutants per passing seed that fail verification (% FAIL), average percentage of mutants per passing seed that time out (% TIMEOUT), average percentage of mutants that fail verification per passing seed with at least one failing mutant (% ∃FAIL). The middle section of the table records experiments with batch M_*; each of the 11 rightmost columns records experiments with batch M_J, for J one of the mutation operators in Table 1.

				BATCH M_*				# ∃FAIL OF M_J										
GROUP	TOOL	# PASS	# ∃FAIL	% ∃FAIL	% FAIL	% TIMEOUT	% ∃FAIL	S_1	S_2	S_3	L_1	L_2	L_3	L_4	L_5	L_6	G_1	G_2
A	4.1.1	10	2	20%	9%	5%	45%	1	0	1	0	0	0	1	1	0	0	0
	4.3.2	10	1	10%	4%	0%	42%	0	0	0	0	0	0	1	1	0	0	0
	4.4.1	10	1	10%	4%	0%	42%	0	0	0	0	0	0	1	1	0	0	0
	4.5.0	10	1	10%	4%	0%	42%	0	0	0	0	0	0	1	1	0	0	0
	CVC4	6	0	0%	0%	0%	–	0	0	0	0	0	0	0	0	0	0	0
	WHY3	7	0	0%	0%	0%	–											
D	4.1.1	0	0	–	–	–	–	0	0	0	0	0	0	0	0	0	0	0
	4.3.2	24	7	29%	7%	4%	23%	6	0	5	0	0	5	4	4	0	3	17
	4.4.1	24	7	29%	7%	5%	23%	6	0	5	0	0	5	4	4	0	3	17
	4.5.0	24	6	25%	8%	6%	33%	5	0	5	0	0	8	4	4	0	1	17
	CVC4	0	0	–	–	–	–	0	0	0	0	0	0	0	0	0	0	0
	WHY3	0	0	–	–	–	–											
E	4.1.1	5	0	0%	0%	0%	–	0	0	0	0	0	0	0	0	0	0	3
	4.3.2	7	0	0%	0%	0%	–	0	0	0	0	0	0	0	0	0	0	3
	4.4.1	7	0	0%	0%	0%	–	0	0	0	0	0	0	0	0	0	0	3
	4.5.0	7	0	0%	0%	0%	–	0	0	0	0	0	0	0	0	0	0	3
	CVC4	4	0	0%	0%	0%	–	0	0	0	0	0	0	0	0	0	0	3
	WHY3	7	0	0%	0%	0%	–											
P	4.1.1	0	0	–	–	–	–	0	0	0	0	0	0	0	0	0	0	0
	4.3.2	14	6	43%	1%	0%	2%	4	0	7	0	0	1	1	0	0	0	10
	4.4.1	13	5	38%	1%	0%	2%	3	0	6	0	0	0	0	0	0	0	9
	4.5.0	13	5	38%	1%	0%	2%	4	0	6	0	0	0	0	0	0	0	9
	CVC4	0	0	–	–	–	–	0	0	0	0	0	0	0	0	0	0	0
	WHY3	0	0	–	–	–	–											
S	4.1.1	51	0	0%	0%	0%	–	0	0	0	0	0	0	0	0	0	0	0
	4.3.2	51	0	0%	0%	0%	–	0	0	0	0	0	0	0	0	0	0	0
	4.4.1	51	0	0%	0%	0%	–	0	0	0	0	0	0	0	0	0	0	0
	4.5.0	51	0	0%	0%	0%	–	0	0	0	0	0	0	0	0	0	0	0
	CVC4	51	0	0%	0%	0%	–	0	0	0	0	0	0	0	0	0	0	0
	WHY3	40	2	5%	1%	1%	25%											
T	4.1.1	8	1	12%	5%	5%	39%	1	0	1	0	0	1	1	1	0	1	1
	4.3.2	8	1	12%	8%	8%	62%	1	0	1	0	0	1	1	1	0	1	1
	4.4.1	8	1	12%	8%	8%	60%	1	0	1	0	0	1	1	1	0	1	1
	4.5.0	8	1	12%	12%	12%	96%	1	0	1	0	0	1	1	1	0	1	1
	CVC4	4	0	0%	0%	0%	–	0	0	0	0	0	0	0	0	0	0	1
	WHY3	3	0	0%	0%	0%	–											
all	4.1.1	74	3	4%	2%	1%	43%	2	0	2	0	0	1	2	2	0	1	4
	4.3.2	114	15	13%	2%	2%	18%	11	0	13	0	0	7	7	6	0	4	31
	4.4.1	113	14	12%	2%	2%	20%	10	0	12	0	0	6	6	6	0	4	30
	4.5.0	113	13	12%	3%	2%	27%	10	0	12	0	0	9	6	6	0	2	30
	CVC4	65	0	0%	0%	0%	–	0	0	0	0	0	0	0	0	0	0	4
	WHY3	57	2	4%	1%	1%	25%											

that fail verification is spuriously lower (4%) but only because the experiments with Boogie 4.1.1 dodged the harder problems and performed similarly to the other Boogie versions on the simpler ones.

Intermediate verifier vs. backend. Is the brittleness we observed in our experiments imputable to Boogie or really to Z3? To shed light on this question, we tried to verify every seed and mutant using CVC4 instead of Z3 with Boogie's encoding; and using Why3 on a translation [1] of Boogie's input. Since the seeds are programs optimized for Boogie verification, CVC4 and Why3 can correctly process only about half of the seeds that Boogie can. This gives us too little evidence to answer the question conclusively: while both CVC4 and Why3 behaved robustly, they could verify none of the brittle seeds (that is, verified seeds with at least one failing mutant), and thus behaved as robustly as Boogie on the programs that both tools can process.[7] In cases such as the simple example of Sect. 2 (where Why3 was indeed more robust than Boogie), it is really the interplay of Boogie and Z3 that determines brittle behavior. While SMT solvers have their own quirks, Boogie is meant to provide a stable intermediate layer; in all, it seems fair to say that Boogie is at least partly responsible for the brittleness.

Program groups. Robustness varies greatly across groups, according to features and complexity of the seeds that are mutated. Groups D and P are the most brittle: about $1/3$ of passing seeds in D, and about $2/5$ of passing seeds in P, have at least one mutant that fails verification. Seeds in D and P are large and complex programs generated by Dafny and AutoProof; they include extensive definitions with plenty of generic types, complex axioms, and instantiations. The brittleness of these programs reflects the hardness of verifying strong specifications and feature-rich programming languages: the Boogie encoding must be optimized in every aspect if it has to be automatically verifiable; even a modicum of clutter—introduced by μgie—may jeopardize successful verification.

By the same token, groups A, E, and T's programs are more robust because they have a smaller impact surface in terms of features and size. Group S's programs are uniformly robust because they have simple, repetitive structure and weak specifications despite their significant size; Boogie scales effortlessly on such examples.

Mutation operators and batches M_J. Figure 3 and the rightmost columns of Table 4 explore the relative effectiveness of each mutation operator. S_2, L_1, L_2, and L_6 could not generate any failing mutant—suggesting that Boogie's encoding of procedure declarations, of local variables, and of conditionals is fairly robust. In contrast, all other operators could generate at least one failing mutant; Fig. 3 indicates that L_3 and S_3 generated failing mutants for respectively 2 seeds and 1 seed that were robust in batch M_* (using all mutation operators with the same frequency)—indicating that mutation operators are complementary to a certain extent in the kind of brittleness they can expose.

---

[7] Additionally, Why3 times out on 51 mutants of 2 seeds in group S; this seems to reflect an ineffective translation performed by b2w [1] rather than brittleness of Why3.

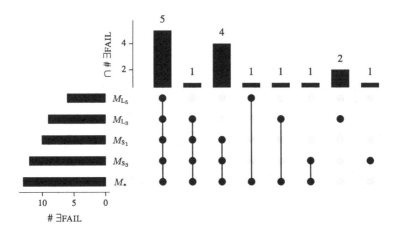

Fig. 3. For each of 16 verified seeds with at least one failing mutant with Boogie 4.5.0, which batches all exclusively include a failing mutant of those seeds. G_2 is excluded and analyzed separately; S_2, L_1, L_2, L_6 could not generate any failing mutant; L_4 generated failing mutants for a strict subset of those in M_*; G_1 generated failing mutants for a strict subset of those in M_{L_5}

Failures. Overall, 13 brittle seeds are revealed by 350 failing mutants in M_* with Boogie 4.5.0. Failures are of three kinds: *(a)* timeouts (6 seeds, 252 mutants); *(b)* type errors (5 seeds, 10 mutants); *(c)* explicit verification failures (2 seeds, 88 mutants). *Timeouts* mainly occur in group D (5 seeds), where size and complexity of the code are such that any mutation that slows down verification may hit the timeout limit; verification of some mutants seems to be non-terminating, whereas others are just slowed down by some tens of seconds. *Type errors* all occur in group P and only when mutation S_3 splits the seed in a way that procedure `update_heap` (part of AutoProof's heap axiomatization) ends up being declared after its first usage; in this case, Boogie cannot correctly instantiate the procedure's generic type, which triggers a type error even before Z3 is involved. *Verification failures* occur in seeds of group A and D. In particular, a binary search tree implementation in group A fails verification when the relative order of two postconditions is swapped by L_5; while Why3 cannot prove the whole example, it can prove the brittle procedure alone regardless of the postcondition order. In all, it is clear that Boogie's encoding is quite sensitive to the order of declarations and assertions even when it should not matter.

Triggers. Remember that mutation operator G_2 is the only one that modifies triggers, and was only applied in isolation in a separate set of experiments. As we expected from previous work [19], altering triggers is likely to make verification fail (30 seeds and 276 mutants overall; 20 seeds are only brittle if triggers are modified); most of these failures (26 seeds and 250 mutants) are timeouts, since removing triggers is likely to at least slow down verification—if not make it diverge. Operator G_2 is very effective at exposing brittleness mainly with the complex examples in groups D and P, which include numerous axioms and extensive quantification patterns. Group E's programs are a bit special because they are brittle—they are designed to be so—but are only affected by mutation operators that remove the trigger annotations on which they strongly depend; in contrast, they are robust against all other mutation operators.

5   Related Work

Robustness. This paper's robustness testing aims at detecting so-called *butterfly effects* [19]—macroscopic changes in a verifier's output in response to minor modifications of its input. Program provers often incur volatile behavior because they use automated theorem provers—such as SMT solvers—which in turn rely on heuristics to handle efficiently, in many practical cases, complex proofs in undecidable logics.

Random testing. Our approach uses *testing* to expose brittle behavior of verifiers. By automatically generating test inputs, *random testing* has proved to be extremely effective at detecting subtle errors in programs completely automatically. Random testing can generate instances of complex data types by recursively building them according to their inductive structure—as it has been done for functional [7] and object-oriented [24] programming languages. Random testing has also been successfully applied to security testing—where it is normally called "fuzzing" [12]—as well as to compiler testing [28]—where well-formed programs are randomly generated according to the input language's grammar.

Mutation testing. This paper's robustness testing is a form of random testing, in that it applies random mutation operators to transform a program into an equivalent one. The terminology and the idea of applying mutation operators to transform between variants of a program come from *mutation testing* [16]. However, the goals of traditional mutation testing and of this paper's robustness testing are specular. Mutation testing is normally used to assess the robustness of a test suite—by applying error-inducing mutations to correct programs, and ascertaining whether the tests fail on the mutated programs. In contrast, we use mutation testing to assess the *robustness of a verifier*—by applying semantic-preserving mutations to correct (verified) programs, and ascertaining whether the mutated programs still verify. Therefore, the mutation operators of standard mutation testing introduce bugs in a way that is representative of common programming mistakes; the mutation operators of robustness testing (see Table 1) do not alter correctness but merely represent alternative syntax expressing the same behavior in a way that is representative of different styles of programming.

Metamorphic testing. In testing, generating inputs is only half of the work; one also has to compare the system's output with the *expected output* to determine whether a test is passing or failing. The definition of correct expected output is given by an *oracle* [3]. The more complex the properties we are testing for, the more complex the oracle: a crash oracle (did the program crash?) is sufficient to test for simple errors such as out-of-bound memory access; finding more complex errors requires some form of *specification* [15] of expected behavior
.

Even when directly building an oracle is as complex as writing a correct program, there are still indirect ways of extrapolating whether an output is correct.

In *differential testing* [22], there are variants of the program under test; under the assumption that not all variants have the same bugs, one can feed the same input to every variant, and stipulate that the output returned by the majority is the expected one—and any outlier is likely buggy. In *metamorphic testing* [26], an input is transformed into an equivalent one according to *metamorphic relations*; equivalent inputs that determine different outputs are indicative of error. Our robustness testing applies mutation operators that determine identity metamorphic relations between Boogie programs, since they only change syntactic details and not the semantics of programs.

6 Discussion and Future Work

Our experiments with μgie confirm the intuition—bred by frequently using it in our work—that Boogie is prone to brittle behavior. How can we shield users from this brittle behavior, thus improving the usability of verification technology?

Program verifiers that use Boogie as an intermediate representation achieve this goal to some extent: the researchers who built the verifiers have developed an intuitive understanding of Boogie's idiosyncrasies, and have encoded this informal knowledge into their tools. End users do not have to worry about Boogie's brittleness but can count on the tools to provide an encoding of their input programs that has a good chance of being effective.

In contrast, developers of program verifiers still have to know how to interact with Boogie and be aware of its peculiarities.

Robustness testing may play a role not only in exposing brittle behavior—the focus of this paper—but in precisely tracking down the sources of brittleness, thus helping to debug them. To this end, we plan to address *minimization* and *equivalency detection* of mutants in future work. The idea is that the number of failing mutants that we get by running μgie are not directly effective as debugging aids, because it takes a good deal of manual analysis to pinpoint the precise sources of failure in large programs with several mutations. Instead, we will apply techniques such as delta debugging [29] to reduce the size of a failing mutant as much as possible while still triggering failing behavior in Boogie. Failing mutants of minimal size will be easier to inspect by hand, and thus will point to concrete aspects of the Boogie translation that could be made more robust.

To further investigate to what extent it is Z3 that is brittle, and to what extent it is Boogie's encoding of verification condition—an aspect only partially addressed by this paper's experiments—we will apply robustness testing directly to SMT problems, also to understand how Boogie's encoding can be made more robust.

Robustness testing could become a useful help to developers of program and intermediate verifiers, to help them track down sources of brittleness during development, ultimately making verification technology easier to use and more broadly applicable.

References

1. Ameri, M., Furia, C.A.: Why just Boogie? In: Ábrahám, E., Huisman, M. (eds.) IFM 2016. LNCS, vol. 9681, pp. 79–95. Springer, Cham (2016). https://doi.org/10.1007/978-3-319-33693-0_6
2. AutoProof verified code repository. http://tiny.cc/autoproof-repo
3. Barr, E.T., Harman, M., McMinn, P., Shahbaz, M., Yoo, S.: The oracle problem in software testing: a survey. IEEE Trans. Softw. Eng. **41**(5), 507–525 (2015)
4. Chen, T.Y., Cheung, S.C., Yiu, S.M.: Metamorphic testing: a new approach for generating next test cases. Technical Report HKUST-CS98-01, Department of Computer Science, Hong Kong University of Science and Technology (1998)
5. Chen, Y.T., Furia, C.A.: Triggerless happy. In: Polikarpova, N., Schneider, S. (eds.) IFM 2017. LNCS, vol. 10510, pp. 295–311. Springer, Cham (2017). https://doi.org/10.1007/978-3-319-66845-1_19
6. Chen, Y.T., Furia, C.A.: Robustness testing of intermediate verifiers. http://arxiv.org/abs/1805.03296 (2018)
7. Claessen, K., Hughes, J.: Quickcheck: a lightweight tool for random testing of Haskell programs. In: ICFP, pp. 268–279. ACM (2000)
8. Dafny examples and tests. https://github.com/Microsoft/dafny/tree/master/Test
9. Filliâtre, J.-C., Paskevich, A.: Why3—where programs meet provers. In: Felleisen, M., Gardner, P. (eds.) ESOP 2013. LNCS, vol. 7792, pp. 125–128. Springer, Heidelberg (2013). https://doi.org/10.1007/978-3-642-37036-6_8
10. Furia, C.A., Meyer, B., Velder, S.: Loop invariants: analysis, classification, and examples. ACM Comput. Surv. 46(3) (2014)
11. Furia, C.A., Nordio, M., Polikarpova, N., Tschannen, J.: AutoProof: auto-active functional verification of object-oriented programs. STTT **19**(6), 697–716 (2016)
12. Godefroid, P., Levin, M.Y., Molnar, D.A.: SAGE: whitebox fuzzing for security testing. Commun. ACM **55**(3), 40–44 (2012)
13. Hawblitzel, C., Howell, J., Kapritsos, M., Lorch, J.R., Parno, B., Roberts, M.L., Setty, S.T.V., Zill, B.: IronFleet: proving practical distributed systems correct. In: SOSP, pp. 1–17. ACM (2015)
14. Hawblitzel, C., Howell, J., Lorch, J.R., Narayan, A., Parno, B., Zhang, D., Zill, B.: Ironclad Apps: end-to-end security via automated full-system verification. In: USENIX OSDI, pp. 165–181. USENIX Association (2014)
15. Hierons, R.M., et al.: Using formal specifications to support testing. ACM Comput. Surv. **41**(2), 9:1–9:76 (2009)
16. Jia, Y., Harman, M.: An analysis and survey of the development of mutation testing. IEEE Trans. Softw. Eng. **37**(5), 649–678 (2011)
17. Leino, K.R.M.: This is Boogie 2 (2008). http://goo.gl/QsH6g
18. Leino, K., Rustan, M.: Dafny: an automatic program verifier for functional correctness. In: Clarke, E.M., Voronkov, A. (eds.) LPAR 2010. LNCS (LNAI), vol. 6355, pp. 348–370. Springer, Heidelberg (2010). https://doi.org/10.1007/978-3-642-17511-4_20
19. Leino, K.R.M., Pit-Claudel, C.: Trigger selection strategies to stabilize program verifiers. In: CAV, pp. 361–381. Springer, Berlin (2016)
20. Leroy, X.: Formal verification of a realistic compiler. Commun. ACM **52**(7), 107–115 (2009)
21. Liew, D., Cadar, C., Donaldson, A.F.: Symbooglix: A symbolic execution engine for boogie programs. In: ICST, pp. 45–56. IEEE Computer Society (2016)

22. McKeeman, W.M.: Differential testing for software. Digit. Tech. J. **10**(1), 100–107 (1998)
23. μgie repository. https://emptylambda.github.io/mu-gie/
24. Pacheco, C., Lahiri, S.K., Ernst, M.D., Ball, T.: Feedback-directed random test generation. In: ICSE, pp. 75–84. IEEE Computer Society (2007)
25. Polikarpova, N., Furia, C.A., West, S.: To run what no one has run before: executing an intermediate verification language. In: Legay, A., Bensalem, S. (eds.) RV 2013. LNCS, vol. 8174, pp. 251–268. Springer, Heidelberg (2013). https://doi.org/10.1007/978-3-642-40787-1_15
26. Segura, S., Fraser, G., Sanchez, A.B., Ruiz-Cortés, A.: A survey on metamorphic testing. IEEE Trans. Softw. Eng. **42**(9), 805–824 (2016)
27. Tange, O.: GNU parallel—the command-line power tool. Login: USENIX Mag. **36**, 42–47 (2011)
28. Yang, X., Chen, Y., Eide, E., Regehr, J.: Finding and understanding bugs in C compilers. ACM SIGPLAN Not. ACM **46**, 283–294 (2011)
29. Zeller, A., Hildebrandt, R.: Simplifying and isolating failure-inducing input. IEEE Trans. Softw. Eng. **28**(2), 183–200 (2002)

Simulation Algorithms for Symbolic Automata

Lukáš Holík[1], Ondřej Lengál[1(✉)], Juraj Síč[1,2], Margus Veanes[3],
and Tomáš Vojnar[1]

[1] FIT, Brno University of Technology, IT4Innovations Centre of Excellence, Brno,
Czech Republic
lengal@fit.vutbr.cz

[2] Faculty of Informatics, Masaryk University, Brno, Czech Republic

[3] Microsoft Research, Redmond, USA

Abstract. We investigate means of efficient computation of the simulation relation over symbolic finite automata (SFAs), i.e., finite automata with transitions labeled by predicates over alphabet symbols. In one approach, we build on the algorithm by Ilie, Navaro, and Yu proposed originally for classical finite automata, modifying it using the so-called mintermisation of the transition predicates. This solution, however, generates all Boolean combinations of the predicates, which easily causes an exponential blowup in the number of transitions. Therefore, we propose two more advanced solutions. The first one still applies mintermisation but in a local way, mitigating the size of the exponential blowup. The other one focuses on a novel symbolic way of dealing with transitions, for which we need to sacrifice the counting technique of the original algorithm (counting is used to decrease the dependency of the running time on the number of transitions from quadratic to linear). We perform a thorough experimental evaluation of all the algorithms, together with several further alternatives, showing that all of them have their merits in practice, but with the clear indication that in most of the cases, efficient treatment of symbolic transitions is more beneficial than counting.

1 Introduction

We investigate algorithms for computing simulation relations on states of symbolic finite automata. *Symbolic finite automata* (SFAs) [1,2] extend the classical (nondeterministic) finite automata (NFAs) by allowing one to annotate a transition with a predicate over a possibly infinite alphabet. Such *symbolic* transitions then represent a set of all (possibly infinitely many) concrete transitions over all the individual symbols that satisfy the predicate. SFAs offer a practical solution for automata-based techniques whenever the alphabet is prohibitively large to be processed with a standard NFA, for instance, when processing Unicode-encoded text (e.g., within various security-related analyses) or in automata-based decision procedures for logics such as MSO or WS1S [3,4]. Applications of SFAs

© Springer Nature Switzerland AG 2018
S. K. Lahiri and C. Wang (Eds.): ATVA 2018, LNCS 11138, pp. 109–125, 2018.
https://doi.org/10.1007/978-3-030-01090-4_7

over arithmetic alphabets and formulas arise also when dealing with symbolic transducers in the context of various sanitizer and encoder analyses [4].

A *simulation relation* on an automaton underapproximates the inclusion of languages of individual states [20]. This makes it useful for reducing non-deterministic automata and in testing inclusion and equivalence of their languages [5,6,20]. Using simulation for these purposes is often the best compromise between two other alternatives: (i) the cheap but strict bisimulation and (ii) the liberal but expensive language inclusion.

The obvious solution to the problem of computing simulation over an SFA is to use the technique of *mintermisation*: the input SFA is transformed into a form in which predicates on transitions partition the alphabet. Predicates on transitions can then be treated as ordinary alphabet symbols and most of the existing algorithms for NFAs can be used out of the box, including a number of algorithms for computing simulations. We, in particular, consider mintermisation mainly together with the algorithm by Ilie, Navaro, and Yu from [7] (called INY in the following), and, in the experiments, also with the algorithm by Ranzato and Tapparo (called also RT) [19]. A fundamental problem is that mintermisation can increase the number of transitions exponentially due to generating all Boolean combinations of the original transition predicates. Moreover, this problem is not only theoretical, but causes a significant blowup in practice too, as witnessed in the experiments presented in this paper.

We therefore design algorithms that do not need mintermisation. We take as our starting point the algorithm INY, which has the best available time complexity $\mathcal{O}(nm)$ in terms of the number of states n and transitions m of the input NFA. We propose two generalisations of this algorithm. The first one (called LOCALMIN) reflects closely the ideas that INY uses to achieve the low complexity. Instead of applying INY on a globally mintermised SFA, it, however, requires only a *locally mintermised form*: for every state, the predicates on its outgoing transitions partition the alphabet. Local mintermisation is thus exponential only to the maximal out-degree of a state.

Our second algorithm (called NOCOUNT) is fundamentally different from LOCALMIN because it trades off the upfront mintermisation cost against working with predicates in the algorithm, and therefore has a different worst case computational complexity wrt the number of transitions. We show experimentally that this trade-off pays off. To facilitate this trade-off, we had to drop a counting technique that INY uses to improve its time complexity from $\mathcal{O}(n^2m)$ to $\mathcal{O}(nm)$ and that replaces repeated tests for existence of transitions with certain properties by maintaining their number in a dedicated counter and testing it for zero. Dropping the counter-based approach (which depends on at least local mintermisation) in turn allowed an additional optimisation based on aggregating a batch of certain expensive operations (satisfiability checking) on symbolic transitions into one. Overall, this improves the efficiency and ultimately reduces a worst-case 2^m cost, which is typically *independent* of the Boolean algebra, to the cost of inlining the Boolean algebra operations, which may be polynomial or even (sub)linear in m.

In our experiments, although each of the considered algorithms wins in some cases, our new algorithms performed overall significantly better than INY with global mintermisation. NoCount performed the best overall, which suggests that avoiding mintermisation and aggregating satisfiability tests over transition labels is practically more advantageous than using the counting technique of INY. We have also compared our algorithms with a variant [8] of the RT algorithm, one of the fastest algorithms for computing simulation, run on the globally mintermised automata (we denote the combination as GlobRT). The main improvement of RT over INY is its use of partition-relation pairs, which allows one to aggregate operations with blocks of the so-far simulation indistinguishable states. Despite this powerful optimisation and the fine-tuned implementation of RT in the Vata library [9], NoCount has a better performance than GlobRT on automata with high diversity of transition predicates (where mintermisation significantly increases the number of transitions).

Related work. Simulation algorithms for NFAs might be divided between *simple* and *partition-based.* Among the simple algorithms, the algorithm by Henzinger, Henzinger, and Köpke [10] (called HHK) is the first algorithm that achieved the time complexity $\mathcal{O}(nm)$ on Kripke structures. The later algorithm INY [7] is a small modification of HHK and works on finite automata in a time at worst $\mathcal{O}(nm)$. The automata are supposed to be complete (every state has an outgoing transition for every alphabet symbol). INY can be adapted for non-complete automata by adding an initialisation step which costs $\mathcal{O}(\ell n^2)$ time where ℓ is the size of the alphabet, resulting in $\mathcal{O}(nm + \ell n^2)$ overall complexity (cf. Sect. 3.1).

The first partition-based algorithm was RT, proposed in [19]. The main innovation of RT is that the overapproximation of the simulation relation is represented by a so-called *partition-relation pair*. In a partition-relation pair, each class of the partition of the set of states represents states that are simulation-equivalent in the current approximation of the simulation, and the relation on the partition denotes the simulation-bigger/smaller classes. Working with states grouped into blocks is faster than working with individual states, and in the case of the most recent partition-based algorithms for Kripke structures [11], it allows to derive the time complexity $\mathcal{O}(n'm)$ where n' is the number of classes of the simulation equivalence (the partition-based algorithms are also significantly faster in practice, although their complexity in terms of m and n is still $\mathcal{O}(nm)$). See e.g. [11] for a more complete overview of algorithms for computing simulation over NFAs and Kripke structures.

Our choice of INY over HHK among the simple algorithms is justified by a smaller dependence of the data structures of INY on the alphabet size. The main reason for basing our algorithms on one of the simple algorithms is their relative simplicity. Partition-based algorithms are intricate as well as the proofs of their small asymptotic complexity. Moreover, they compute predecessors of dynamically refined blocks of states via individual alphabet symbols, which seems to be a problematic step to efficiently generalise for symbolic SFA transitions. Having said that, it remains true that the technique of representing preorders through partition-relation pairs is from the high-level perspective orthogonal to the techniques we have developed to generalise INY. Combining both types of optimisations would be a logical continuation of this work. It is, however, questionable if generalising already very complex partition-based algorithms, such as [11, 19], is the best way to approach computing simulations over SFAs. Most of the intricacy of the partition-based algorithms aims at combining the counting technique with the partition-relation pairs. Our experimental results suggest, however, that rather than using the counting technique, it is more important to optimise the treatment of symbolic transitions and to avoid mintermisation.

Our work complements other works on generalising classical automata algorithms to SFAs, mainly the deterministic minimisation [12] and computing of bisimulation [13].

2   Preliminaries

Throughout the paper, we use the following notation: If $R \subseteq A_1 \times \cdots \times A_n$ is an n-ary relation for $n \geq 2$, then $R(x_1, \ldots, x_{n-1}) \stackrel{\text{def}}{=} \{y \in A_n \mid R(x_1, \ldots, x_{n-1}, y)\}$ for any $x_1 \in A_1, \ldots, x_{n-1} \in A_{n-1}$. Let $R^{\complement} \stackrel{\text{def}}{=} (A_1 \times \ldots \times A_n) \setminus R$.

Effective Boolean algebra. An *effective Boolean algebra* is defined as a tuple $\mathcal{A} = (\mathfrak{D}, \mathbb{P}, \llbracket \cdot \rrbracket, \vee, \wedge, \neg)$ where $\mathbb{P}$ is a set of *predicates* closed under predicate transformers $\vee, \wedge : \mathbb{P} \times \mathbb{P} \to \mathbb{P}$ and $\neg : \mathbb{P} \to \mathbb{P}$. A first order interpretation (denotation) $\llbracket \cdot \rrbracket : \mathbb{P} \to 2^{\mathfrak{D}}$ assigns to every predicate of $\mathbb{P}$ a subset of the *domain* $\mathfrak{D}$ such that, for all $\varphi, \psi \in \mathbb{P}$, it holds that $\llbracket \varphi \vee \psi \rrbracket = \llbracket \varphi \rrbracket \cup \llbracket \psi \rrbracket$, $\llbracket \varphi \wedge \psi \rrbracket = \llbracket \varphi \rrbracket \cap \llbracket \psi \rrbracket$, and $\llbracket \neg \varphi \rrbracket = \mathfrak{D} \setminus \llbracket \varphi \rrbracket$. For $\varphi \in \mathbb{P}$, we write $IsSat(\varphi)$ when $\llbracket \varphi \rrbracket \neq \emptyset$ and say that φ is *satisfiable*. The predicate $IsSat$ and the predicate transformers $\wedge, \vee$, and $\neg$ must be effective (computable). We assume that $\mathbb{P}$ contains predicates $\top$ and $\bot$ with $\llbracket \top \rrbracket = \mathfrak{D}$ and $\llbracket \bot \rrbracket = \emptyset$. Let Φ be a subset of $\mathbb{P}$. If the denotations of any two distinct predicates in Φ are disjoint, then Φ is called a *partition* (of the set $\bigcup_{\varphi \in \Phi} \llbracket \varphi \rrbracket$). The set $Minterms(\Phi)$ of *minterms* of a finite set Φ of predicates is defined as the set of all satisfiable predicates of $\{\bigwedge_{\varphi \in \Phi'} \varphi \wedge \bigwedge_{\varphi \in \Phi \setminus \Phi'} \neg \varphi \mid \Phi' \subseteq \Phi\}$. Notice that every predicate of Φ is equivalent to a disjunction of minterms in $Minterms(\Phi)$.

Below, we assume that it is possible to measure the size of the predicates of the effective Boolean algebra $\mathcal{A}$ that we work with. We denote by $\mathcal{C}_{sat}(x, y)$ the worst-case complexity of constructing a predicate obtained by applying x operations of $\mathcal{A}$ on predicates of the size at most y and checking its satisfiability.

Symbolic finite automata. We define a *symbolic finite automaton* (SFA) as a tuple $M = (Q, \mathcal{A}, \Delta, I, F)$ where Q is a finite set of *states*, $\mathcal{A} = (\mathfrak{D}, \mathbb{P}, \llbracket \cdot \rrbracket, \vee, \wedge, \neg)$ is an effective Boolean algebra, $\Delta \subseteq Q \times \mathbb{P} \times Q$ is a finite *transition relation*, $I \subseteq Q$ is a set of *initial states*, and $F \subseteq Q$ is a set of *final states*. An element (q, ψ, p) of Δ is called a *(symbolic) transition* and denoted by $q\text{-}\{\psi\}\text{↦}p$. We write $\llbracket q\text{-}\{\psi\}\text{↦}p \rrbracket$ to denote the set $\{q\text{-}\{a\}\text{↦}p \mid a \in \llbracket \psi \rrbracket\}$ of *concrete transitions* represented by $q\text{-}\{\psi\}\text{↦}p$, and we let $\llbracket \Delta \rrbracket \stackrel{\text{def}}{=} \bigcup_{q\text{-}\{\psi\}\text{↦}p \in \Delta} \llbracket q\text{-}\{\psi\}\text{↦}p \rrbracket$. For $q \in Q$ and $a \in \mathfrak{D}$ let $\Delta(q, a) \stackrel{\text{def}}{=} \{p \in Q \mid q\text{-}\{a\}\text{↦}p\}$.

In the following, it is assumed that predicates of all transitions of an SFA are satisfiable unless stated otherwise. A sequence $\rho = q_0 a_1 q_1 a_2 \cdots a_n q_n$ with $q_{i-1} \text{-} \{a_i\} \mapsto q_i \in [\![\Delta]\!]$ for every $1 \leq i \leq n$ is a *run* of M over the word $a_1 \cdots a_n$. The run ρ is *accepting* if $q_0 \in I$ and $q_n \in F$, and a word is *accepted* by M if it has an accepting run. The *language* $\mathcal{L}(M)$ of M is the set of all words accepted by M.

An SFA M is *complete* iff, for all $q \in Q$ and $a \in \mathfrak{D}$, there is $p \in Q$ with $p \text{-} \{a\} \mapsto q \in [\![\Delta]\!]$. An SFA can be completed in a straightforward way: from every state q, we add a transition from q labelled with $\neg \bigvee \{\varphi \mid \exists p \in Q : q \text{-} \{\varphi\} \mapsto p \in \Delta\}$ to a new non-accepting sink state, if the disjunction is satisfiable.

An SFA M is *globally mintermised* if the set $\mathbb{P}_\Delta \stackrel{\text{def}}{=} \{\varphi \in \mathbb{P} \mid \exists p, q : p \text{-} \{\varphi\} \mapsto q \in \Delta\}$ of the predicates appearing on its transitions is a partition. Every SFA can be made globally mintermised by replacing each $p \text{-} \{\varphi\} \mapsto q \in \Delta$ by the set of transitions $\{p \text{-} \{\omega\} \mapsto q \mid \omega \in Minterms(\mathbb{P}_\Delta) \wedge IsSat(\omega \wedge \varphi)\}$ (see e.g. [12] for an efficient algorithm), where $IsSat(\omega \wedge \varphi)$ is an implementation of the test $[\![\omega]\!] \subseteq [\![\varphi]\!]$, because if ω is a minterm of $\mathbb{P}_\Delta$ and $\varphi \in \mathbb{P}_\Delta$ then $[\![\omega]\!] \cap [\![\varphi]\!] \neq \emptyset$ implies that $[\![\omega]\!] \subseteq [\![\varphi]\!]$. Since for a set of predicates Φ, the size of $Minterms(\Phi)$ is at worst $2^{|\Phi|}$, global mintermisation is exponential in the number of transitions.

A classical *(nondeterministic) finite automaton* (NFA) $N = (Q, \Sigma, \Delta, I, F)$ over a finite alphabet Σ can be seen as a special case of an SFA where Δ contains solely transitions of the form $q \text{-} \{a\} \mapsto r$ s.t. $a \in \Sigma$ and $[\![a]\!] = \{a\}$ for all $a \in \Sigma$. Below, we will sometimes interpret an SFA $M = (Q, \mathcal{A}, \Delta, I, F)$ as its *syntactic NFA* $N = (Q, \mathbb{P}_\Delta, \Delta, I, F)$ in which the predicates are treated as syntactic objects.

Simulation. Let $M = (Q, \mathcal{A}, \Delta, I, F)$ be an SFA. A relation S on Q is a *simulation* on M if whenever $(p, r) \in S$, then the following two conditions hold: (C1) if $p \in F$, then $r \in F$, and (C2) for all $a \in \mathfrak{D}$ and $p' \in Q$ such that $p \text{-} \{a\} \mapsto p' \in [\![\Delta]\!]$, there is $r' \in Q$ such that $r \text{-} \{a\} \mapsto r' \in [\![\Delta]\!]$ and $(p', r') \in S$. There exists a unique maximal simulation on M, which is reflexive and transitive. We call it the *simulation (preorder)* on M and denote it by $\preceq_M$ (or $\preceq$ when M is clear from the context). Computing $\preceq$ on a given SFA is the subject of this paper. A simulation that is symmetric is called a *bisimulation*, and *the bisimulation equivalence* is the (unique) largest bisimulation, which is always an equivalence relation.

3   Computing Simulation over SFAs

In this section, we present our new algorithms for computing the simulation pre-order over SFAs. We start by recalling an algorithm for computing the simulation preorder on an NFA of Ilie, Navarro, and Yu from [7] (called INY), which serves as the basis for our work. Then, we introduce three modifications of INY for SFAs: (i) GLOBINY, (ii) LOCALMIN, and (iii) NOCOUNT. GLOBINY is merely an application of the mintermisation technique: first globally mintermise the SFA and then use INY to compute the NFA simulation preorder over the result. The main contribution of our paper lies in the other two algorithms, which are subtler modifications of INY that avoid global mintermisation by reasoning about the semantics of transition predicates of SFAs.

Before turning to the different algorithms, we start by explaining how $\preceq_M$ can be computed by an abstract fixpoint procedure and provide the intuition behind how such a procedure can be lifted to the symbolic setting.

Abstract procedure for computing $\preceq_M$. We start by presenting an *abstract fixpoint procedure* for computing the simulation $\preceq_M$ on an SFA $M = (Q, \mathcal{A}, \Delta, I, F)$. We formulate it using the notion of *minimal nonsimulation* $\npreceq_M$ (which is a dual concept to the maximal simulation $\preceq_M$ introduced before), defined as the least subset $\npreceq \subseteq Q \times Q$ s.t. for all $s, t \in Q$, it holds that

$$s \npreceq t \Leftrightarrow (s \in F \wedge t \notin F) \vee$$
$$\underbrace{\exists i \in Q.\, \exists a \in \mathfrak{D}.(s \xrightarrow{\{a\}} i \wedge \forall j \in Q.(t \xrightarrow{\{a\}} j \Rightarrow i \npreceq j))}_{(1^*)}. \tag{1}$$

Informally, s cannot be simulated by t iff (line 1) s is accepting and t is not, or (line 2) s can continue over some symbol a into i, while t cannot simulate this move by any of its successors j. It is easy to see that $\preceq_M = \npreceq_M^{\complement}$. The algorithms for computing simulation over NFAs are efficient implementations of such a fixpoint procedure using *counter-based* implementations for evaluating (1^*). Namely, for every symbol a and a pair of states t and i, it keeps count of those states j that could possibly contradict the universally quantified property. The count dropping to zero means that the property holds universally.

Symbolic abstract procedure for computing $\preceq_M$. When the domain $\mathfrak{D}$ is very large or infinite, then evaluating (1^*) directly is infeasible. If $Minterms(\mathbb{P}_\Delta)$ is exponentially larger than the set $\mathbb{P}_\Delta$, then evaluating (1^*) with a ranging over $Minterms(\mathbb{P}_\Delta)$ may also be infeasible. Instead, we want to utilize the operations of the algebra $\mathcal{A}$ without explicit reference to elements in $\mathfrak{D}$ and without constructing $Minterms(\mathbb{P}_\Delta)$. The key insight is that condition (1^*) is equivalent to

$$IsSat(\varphi_{si} \wedge \neg \Gamma(t, \npreceq^{\complement}(i))) \tag{2}$$

where, for $t, s, i \in Q$ and $J \subseteq Q$, we define $\varphi_{si} \stackrel{\text{def}}{=} \bigvee_{(s,\psi,i) \in \Delta} \psi$ and $\Gamma(t, J) \stackrel{\text{def}}{=} \bigvee_{j \in J} \varphi_{tj}$, i.e., $\Gamma(t, \npreceq^{\complement}(i))$ is a disjunction of predicates on all transitions leaving t and entering a state that simulates i. Using (2) to compute (1^*) in the abstract procedure thus eliminates the explicit quantification over $\mathfrak{D}$ and avoids computation of $Minterms(\mathbb{P}_\Delta)$. The equivalence between (1^*) and (2) holds because, for all $a \in \mathfrak{D}$ and $R \subseteq Q \times Q$, we have

$$a \in \llbracket \neg\Gamma(t, R^{\complement}(i)) \rrbracket \Leftrightarrow \neg\exists j(t \xrightarrow{\{a\}} j \wedge (i,j) \in R^{\complement}) \Leftrightarrow \forall j(t \xrightarrow{\{a\}} j \Rightarrow (i,j) \in R).$$

The fixpoint computation based on (2) is used in our algorithm NOCOUNT, which does not require mintermisation. Its disadvantage is that it is not compatible with the counting technique. Our algorithm LOCALMIN is then a compromise between mintermisation and NOCOUNT that retains the counting technique for the price of using a cheaper, local variant of mintermisation.

Algorithm 1: INY

Input: An NFA $N = (Q, \Sigma, \Delta, I, F)$
Output: The simulation preorder $\preceq_N$

1 **for** $p, q \in Q, a \in \Sigma$ **do** $N_a(q, p) := |\Delta(q, a)|$
2 $Sim := Q \times Q$;
3 $NotSim := F \times (Q \setminus F) \cup \{(q, r) \mid \exists a \in \Sigma : \Delta(q, a) \neq \emptyset \wedge \Delta(r, a) = \emptyset\}$;
4 **while** $NotSim \neq \emptyset$ **do**
5   remove some (i, j) from $NotSim$ and Sim;
6   **for** $t \dashv\{a\}\!\!\mapsto\!\! j \in \Delta$ **do**
7          $N_a(t, i) := N_a(t, i) - 1$;
8   **if** $N_a(t, i) = 0$ **then**   // $t^a_i = \emptyset$
9   **for** $s \dashv\{a\}\!\!\mapsto\!\! i \in \Delta$ s.t. $(s, t) \in Sim$ **do**
10                  $NotSim := NotSim \cup \{(s, t)\}$;
11 **return** Sim;

3.1 Computing Simulation over NFAs (INY)

In Algorithm 1, we give a slightly modified version of the algorithm INY from [7] for computing the simulation preorder over an NFA $N = (Q, \Sigma, \Delta, I, F)$.

The algorithm refines an overapproximation Sim of the simulation preorder until it satisfies the definition of a simulation. The set $NotSim$ is used to store pairs of states (i, j) that were found to contradict the definition of the simulation preorder. $NotSim$ is initialised to contain (a) pairs that contradict condition C1 and (b) pairs that cannot satisfy condition C2 regardless of the rest of the relation, as they relate states with incompatible outgoing symbols. All pairs (i, j) in $NotSim$ are subsequently processed by removing (i, j) from Sim and propagating the change of Sim according to condition C2: for all transitions $t \dashv\{a\}\!\!\mapsto\!\! j \in \Delta$, it is checked whether j was the last a-successor of t that could be simulation-greater than i (hence there are no more such transitions after removing (i, j) from Sim). If this is the case, then t cannot simulate any a-predecessor s of i, and so all such pairs $(s, t) \in Sim$ are added to $NotSim$. In order to have the previous test efficient (a crucial step for the time complexity of the algorithm), the algorithm uses a three-dimensional array of counters $N_a(t, i)$, whose invariant at line 5 is $N_a(t, i) = |t^a_i|$ where t^a_i is the set $\Delta(t, a) \cap Sim(i)$ of successors of t over a that simulate i in the current simulation approximation Sim. In order to test $t^a_i = \emptyset$—i.e. the second conjunct of (1*)—, it is enough to test if $N_a(t, i) = 0$.

The lemma below shows the time complexity of INY in terms of $n = |Q|$, $m = |\Delta|$, and $\ell = |\Sigma|$. The original paper [7] proves the complexity $O(nm)$ for complete automata, in which case $m \geq \ell n$, so the factor ℓn^2 is subsumed by nm. Since completion of NFAs can be expensive, the initialization step on line 3 of our algorithm is modified (similarly as in [14]) to start with considering states with different sets of symbols appearing on their outgoing transitions as simulation-different; the cost of this step is subsumed by the factor ℓn^2 (see [21] for the proof of our formulation of the algorithm).

Lemma 1. INY computes $\preceq_N$ in time $\mathcal{O}(nm + \ell n^2)$.

Algorithm 2: GLOBINY

Input: An SFA $M = (Q, \mathcal{A}, \Delta, I, F)$
Output: The simulation preorder $\preceq_M$
1 $\Delta_G :=$ globally mintermised Δ;
2 **return** INY$((Q, \mathbb{P}_{\Delta_G}, \Delta_G, I, F))$;

3.2 Global Mintermisation-based Algorithm for SFAs (GlobINY)

The algorithm GLOBINY (Algorithm 2) is the initial solution for the problem of computing the simulation preorder over SFAs. It first globally mintermises the input automaton $M = (Q, \mathcal{A}, \Delta, I, F)$, then interprets the result as an NFA over the alphabet of the minterms, and runs INY on the NFA. The following lemma (together with Lemma 1) implies the correctness of this approach.

Lemma 2. *Let $N = (Q, \mathbb{P}_\Delta, \Delta, I, F)$ be the syntactic NFA of a globally minter-mised SFA $M = (Q, \mathcal{A}, \Delta, I, F)$. Then $\preceq_M = \preceq_N$.*

The lemma below shows the time complexity of GLOBINY in terms of $n = |Q|$, $m = |\Delta|$, and the size k of the largest predicate used in Δ.

Lemma 3. GLOBINY *computes $\preceq_M$ in time $\mathcal{O}(nm2^m + \mathcal{C}_{sat}(m,k)2^m)$.*

Intuitively, the complexity follows from the fact each transition of Δ can be replaced by at most 2^m transitions in Δ_G since there can be at most 2^m minterms in $Minterms(\mathbb{P}_\Delta)$. Nevertheless, 2^m minterms will always be generated (some of them unsatisfiable, though), each of them generated from m predicates of size at most k. More details are available in [21].

3.3 Local Mintermisation-based Algorithm for SFAs (LocalMin)

Our next algorithm, called LOCALMIN (Algorithm 3), represents an attempt of running INY on the original SFA without the global mintermisation used above. The main challenge in LOCALMIN is how to symbolically represent the counters $N_a(q, r)$—representing them explicitly would contradict the idea of symbolic automata and would be impossible if the domain $\mathfrak{D}$ were infinite. We will there-fore use counters $N_\psi(q, r)$ indexed with labels ψ of outgoing transitions of q to represent all counters $N_a(q, r)$, with $a \in [\![\psi]\!]$. A difficulty here is that if the automaton is not globally mintermised, then for some $q\text{-}\{\varphi\}\text{-}p$ and $a, b \in [\![\varphi]\!]$, the sizes of $q\overset{a}{\curvearrowright}r$ and $q\overset{b}{\curvearrowright}r$ may differ and hence cannot be represented by a single counter. [1] For example, if the only outgoing transition of q other than $q\text{-}\{\varphi\}\text{-}p$ is $q\text{-}\{\psi\}\text{-}r$ with $(p, r) \in Sim$, $[\![\varphi]\!] = \{a, b\}$, and $[\![\psi]\!] = \{b\}$, then $|q\overset{a}{\curvearrowright}r| = 1$ while $|q\overset{b}{\curvearrowright}r| = 2$. To avoid this problem, we introduce the so-called local mintermised form, in which only labels on outgoing transitions of every state must form a partition.

---

[1] When describing an algorithm that works over an SFA, we use the notation $q\overset{a}{\curvearrowright}r$ to represent the set $[\![\Delta]\!](q, a) \cap Sim(r)$, i.e., it refers to the *concrete* transitions of $[\![\Delta]\!]$.

Algorithm 3: LOCALMIN

    Input: A complete SFA $M = (Q, \mathcal{A}, \Delta, I, F)$
    Output: The simulation preorder $\preceq_M$

1 $\Delta_L :=$ locally mintermised form of Δ;
2 **for** $p, q \in Q, q\text{-}\{\psi\}\text{-}t \in \Delta_L$ **do**
3 | $N_\psi(q, p) := |\Delta_L(q, \psi)|$;
4 $Sim := Q \times Q; \ NotSim := F \times (Q \setminus F)$
5 **while** $NotSim \neq \emptyset$ **do**
6 | remove some (i, j) from $NotSim$ and Sim;
7 | **for** $t\text{-}\{\psi_{tj}\}\text{-}j \in \Delta_L$ **do**
8 | | $N_{\psi_{tj}}(t, i) := N_{\psi_{tj}}(t, i) - 1$;
9 | | **if** $N_{\psi_{tj}}(t, i) = 0$ **then**   // $t^{\psi_{tj}}i = \emptyset$
10 | | | **for** $s\text{-}\{\varphi_{si}\}\text{-}i \in \Delta$ s.t. $(s, t) \in Sim$ **do**
11 | | | | **if** $IsSat(\psi_{tj} \wedge \varphi_{si})$ **then**
12 | | | | | $NotSim := NotSim \cup \{(s, t)\}$;
13 **return** Sim;

Formally, we say that an SFA $M = (Q, \mathcal{A}, \Delta, I, F)$ is *locally mintermised* if for every state $p \in Q$, the set $\mathbb{P}_{\Delta,p} \stackrel{\text{def}}{=} \{\varphi \in \mathbb{P} \mid \exists q : p\text{-}\{\varphi\}\text{-}q \in \Delta\}$ of the predicates used on the transitions starting from p is a partition. A locally mintermised form is obtained by replacing every transition $p\text{-}\{\varphi\}\text{-}q$ by the set of transitions $\{p\text{-}\{\omega\}\text{-}q \mid \omega \in Minterms(\mathbb{P}_{\Delta,p}) \wedge IsSat(\omega \wedge \varphi)\}$. Local mintermisation can hence be considerably cheaper than global mintermisation as it is only exponential to the maximum out-degree of a state (instead of the number of transitions of the whole SFA). The key property of a locally mintermised SFA M_L is the following: for any transition $q\text{-}\{\varphi\}\text{-}p$ of M_L and a state $r \in Q$, and for any value of Sim, it holds that $|q^a r|$ is the same for all $a \in [\![\varphi]\!]$. This means that the set of counters $\{N_a(q, r) \mid a \in [\![\varphi]\!]\}$ for all symbols in the semantics of φ can be represented by a single counter $N_\varphi(q, r)$.

The use of only locally mintermised transitions also necessitates a modification of the **for** loop on line 6 of INY. In particular, the test on line 9 of INY, which determines the states s that cannot simulate t over the symbol a, only checks syntactic equivalence of the symbols. This could lead to incorrect results because (syntactically) different local minterms of different source states t and s can still have overlapping semantics. It can, in particular, happen that if a counter $N_{\psi_{tj}}(t, i)$, for some predicate ψ_{tj}, reaches zero on line 9 of LOCALMIN, there is a transition from state s to i over a predicate φ_{si} different from ψ_{tj} but with some symbol $a \in [\![\varphi_{si}]\!] \cap [\![\psi_{tj}]\!]$. Because of a, the state t cannot simulate s, but this would not happen if the two predicates were only compared syntactically. LOCALMIN solves this issue on lines 10 and 11, where it iterates over all transitions entering i and leaving a state s simulated by t (wrt Sim), and tests whether the predicate φ_{si} on the transition semantically intersects with ψ_{tj}.

LOCALMIN is correct only if the input SFA is complete. As mentioned in Sect. 2, this is, however, not an issue, since completion of an SFA is, unlike for

NFAs, straightforward, and its cost is negligible compared with the complexity of LOCALMIN presented below.

The lemma below shows the time complexity of LOCALMIN in terms of $n = |Q|$, $m = |\Delta|$, the size k of the largest predicate used in Δ, the *out-degree* m_q for each $q \in Q$ (i.e. the number of transitions leaving q), and the overall *maximum out-degree* $W = \max\{m_q \mid q \in Q\}$.

Lemma 4. LOCALMIN *derives* $\preceq_M$ *in time*

$$\mathcal{O}\Big(n \sum_{q \in Q} m_q 2^{m_q} + m\mathcal{C}_{sat}(W, k) \sum_{q \in Q} 2^{m_q}\Big).$$

As shown in more detail in [21], the result can be proved in a similar way as in the case of INY and GLOBINY, taking into account that each transition is, again, replaced by its mintermised versions. This time, however, the mintermised versions are computed independently and locally for each state (and the complexities are summed). Consequently, the factor 2^m gets replaced by 2^{m_q} for the different states $q \in Q$ (together with the replacement of $\mathcal{C}_{sat}(m, k)$ by $\mathcal{C}_{sat}(W, k)$), which can significantly decrease the complexity. On the other hand, as mintermisation is done separately for each state (which can sometimes lead to re-doing some work done only once in GLOBINY) and as one needs the satisfiability test on line 11 of LOCALMIN instead of the purely syntactic test on line 9 of INY, on which GLOBINY is based, GLOBINY can sometimes win in practice. This fact shows up even in our experiments presented in Sect. 4.

3.4   Counter-Free Algorithm for SFAs (NoCount)

Before we state our last algorithm, named NOCOUNT (Algorithm 4), let us recall that given an SFA $M = (Q, \mathcal{A}, \Delta, I, F)$, a set $S \subseteq Q$, and a state $q \in Q$, we use $\Gamma(q, S)$ to denote the disjunction of all predicates that reach S from q. We will also write $q \to S$ to denote that there is a transition from q to some state in S.

In NOCOUNT, we sacrifice the counting technique in order to avoid the local mintermisation (which is still a relatively expensive operation). The obvious price for dropping the counters and local mintermisation is that the emptiness of $t\overline{\gamma}i$ for symbols $a \in \psi_{ti}$ can no more be tested in a constant time by asking whether $N_{\psi_{ti}}(t, i) = 0$ as on line 9 of LOCALMIN. It does not even hold any more that $t\overline{\gamma}i$ is uniformly empty or non-empty for all $a \in \psi_{ti}$. To resolve the issue, we replace the test from line 9 of LOCALMIN by computing the formula $\psi = \Gamma(t, Sim(i))$ on line 7 of NOCOUNT, which is then used in the test on line 9. Intuitively, ψ represents all b's such that $t\overline{\gamma}i$ is *not* empty. By taking the negation of ψ, the test on line 9 of NOCOUNT then explicitly asks whether there is some $a \in [\![\varphi_{si}]\!]$ for which s can go to i and t cannot simulate this move.

Further, notice that NOCOUNT uses the set Rm for the following optimisation. Namely, if the use of Rm were replaced by an analogy of line 6 from LOCALMIN, it could choose a sequence of several $j \in Q$ such that $(i, j) \in NotSim$, and then the same ψ would be constructed for each j and tested against

---

Algorithm 4: NoCount

Input: A complete SFA $M = (Q, \mathcal{A}, \Delta, I, F)$
Output: The simulation preorder $\preceq_M$

1   $Sim := Q \times Q; NotSim := F \times (Q \setminus F)$;
2   **while** $\exists i \in Q : NotSim(i) \neq \emptyset$ **do**
3      $Rm := \{t \mid t \rightarrow NotSim(i)\}$;
4      $Sim(i) := Sim(i) \setminus NotSim(i)$;
5      $NotSim(i) := \emptyset$;
6   **for** $t \in Rm$ **do**
7         $\psi := \Gamma(t, Sim(i))$;
8   **for** $s \xrightarrow{\{\varphi_{si}\}} i \in \Delta$ s.t. $(s, t) \in Sim$ **do**
9   **if** $IsSat(\neg\psi \wedge \varphi_{si})$ **then**
10             $NotSim := NotSim \cup \{(s, t)\}$;
11   **return** Sim;

---

the same φ_{si}. In contrast, due to its use of Rm, NoCount will process all $j \in NotSim(i)$ in a single iteration of the main **while** loop, in which ψ is computed and tested against φ_{si} only once.

Lemma 5 shows the complexity of NoCount in the terms used in Lemma 4.

Lemma 5. NoCount computes $\preceq_M$ in time $\mathcal{O}\left(n \sum_{q \in Q} m_q^2 + m^2 \mathcal{C}_{sat}(W, k)\right)$.

Observe that $\sum_{q \in Q} m_q = m$ and $W \leq n$, so the above complexity is bounded by $\mathcal{O}\left(m^2 \mathcal{C}_{sat}(n, k)\right)$. Out-degrees are, however, typically small constants.

The proof of the lemma can be found in [21]. Compared with the time complexity of LocalMin, we can see that, by sacrificing the use of the counters, the complexity becomes quadratic in the number of transitions (since the decrement of the counter on line 8 followed by the test of the counter being zero on line 9 in LocalMin is replaced by the computation of Γ on line 7 combined with the test on line 9 in NoCount). On the other hand, since we completely avoid mintermisation, the 2^{m_q} factors are lowered to at most m (m_q in the left-hand side term).

The overall worst-case complexity of NoCount is thus clearly better than those of GlobINY and LocalMin. Moreover, as shown in Sect. 4, NoCount is also winning in most of our experiments. Another advantage of avoiding mintermisation is that it often requires a lot of memory. Consequently, GlobINY and LocalMin can run out of memory before even finishing the mintermisation, which is also witnessed in our experiments. If m_q is small for all $q \in Q$ and the predicates do not intersect much, the number of generated minterms can, however, be rather small compared with the number of transitions, and LocalMin can in some cases win, as witnessed in our experiments too.

4   Experimental Evaluation

We now present an experimental evaluation of the algorithms from Sect. 3 implemented in the Symbolic Automata Toolkit [2]. All experiments were run on

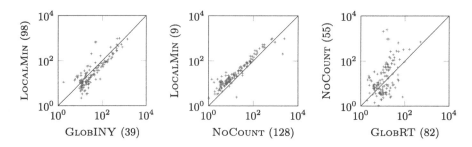

Fig. 1. Comparison of runtimes of algorithms on SFAs from REGEX. Times are in milliseconds (logarithmic scale).

an Intel Core i5-3230M CPU@2.6 GHz with 8 GiB of RAM. We used the following two benchmarks:

REGEX. We evaluated the algorithms on SFAs created from 1,921 regular expressions over the UTF-16 alphabet using the $\mathbf{BDD}_{16}$ algebra, which is the algebra of *binary decision diagrams* over 16 Boolean variables representing particular bits of the UTF-16 encoding. These regular expressions were taken from the website [15], which contains a library of regular expressions created for different purposes, such as matching email addresses, URIs, dates, times, street addresses, phone numbers, etc. The SFAs created from these regular expressions were used before when evaluating algorithms minimising (deterministic) SFAs [12] and when evaluating bisimulation algorithms for SFAs [13]. The largest automaton has 3,190 states and 10,702 transitions; the average transition density of the SFAs is 2.5 transitions per state. Since the UTF-16 alphabet is quite large, a symbolic representation is needed for efficient manipulation of these automata. WS1S. For this benchmark, we used 131 SFAs generated when deciding formulae of the *weak-monadic second order logic of one successor* (WS1S) [16]. We used two batches of SFAs: 93 deterministic ones from the tool MONA [17] and 38 nondeterministic from DWINA [18]. These automata have at most 2,508 states and 34,374 transitions with the average transition density of 6 transitions per state. These SFAs use the algebra $\mathbf{BDD}_k$ where k is the number of variables in the corresponding formula.

4.1   Comparison of Various Algorithms for Computing Simulation

We first evaluate the effect of our modifications of INY presented in Sect. 3. The results presented below clearly show the superiority of our new algorithms over GLOBINY, with NOCOUNT being the overall winner. In addition, we also compare the performance of our new algorithms to a version of the RT algorithm from [19], which is one of the best simulation algorithms. In particular, we use its adaptation for NFAs, which we run after global mintermisation (similarly as INY in GLOBINY). We denote the whole combination GLOBRT. RT is much faster than INY due to its use of the so-called partition-relation pairs to represent the intermediate preorder. Its $C++$ implementation in the VATA library [9] is also much more optimised than the $C\#$ implementation of our algorithms.

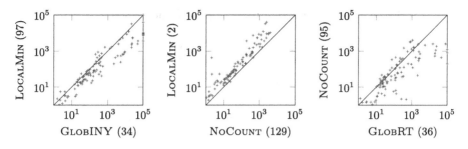

Fig. 2. Comparison of runtimes of algorithms on SFAs from WS1S. Times are in miliseconds (logarithmic scale).

Despite that, the comparison on automata with many global minterms is clearly favourable to our new algorithms.

To proceed to concrete data, Figs. 1 and 2 show scatter plots with the most interesting comparisons of the runtimes of the considered algorithms on our benchmarks (we give in parentheses the number of times the corresponding algorithm *won* over the other one). The timeout was set to 100 s. Fig. 1 shows the comparison of the algorithms on SFAs from the REGEX benchmark. In this experiment, we removed the SFAs where all algorithms finished within 10 ms (to mitigate the effect of imprecise measurement and noise caused by the C# runtime), which gave us 138 SFAs. Moreover, we also removed one extremely challenging SFA, which dominated the whole benchmark (we report on that SFA, denoted as M_c, later), which left us with the final number of 137 SFAs. On the other hand, Fig. 2 shows the comparison for WS1S. We observe the following phenomena: (i) LOCALMIN is in the majority of cases faster than GLOBINY, (ii) NOCOUNT clearly dominates LOCALMIN, and (iii) the comparison of NOCOUNT and GLOBRT has no clear winner: on the REGEX benchmark, GLOBRT is more often faster, but on the WS1S benchmark, NOCOUNT wins (in many cases, quite significantly).

Further, we also give aggregated results of the experiment in Table 1. In the table, we accumulated the runtimes of the algorithms over the whole benchmark (column "time") and the number of times each algorithm was the best among all algorithms (column "wins"). The column "fails" shows how many times the respective algorithm failed (by being out of time or memory). In the parentheses, we give the number of times the failure occurred already in the mintermisation. When a benchmark fails, we assign it the time 100 s (the timeout) for the computation of "time". The times of the challenging SFA M_c from REGEX were: 21 s for GLOBINY, 16 s for LOCALMIN, 25 s for NOCOUNT, and 148 s for GLOBRT. Obviously, including those times would bias the whole evaluation.

Observe that in this comparison, the performance of the algorithms on the two benchmarks differs—although GLOBRT wins on the REGEX benchmark and the other three algorithms have a comparable overall time (but NOCOUNT still wins in the majority of SFAs among the three), on the more complex benchmark (WS1S), NOCOUNT is the clear winner. The distinct results on the two

Table 1. Aggregated results of the performance experiment.

Algorithm	REGEX		WS1S		
	Time	Wins	Time	Wins	Fails
GLOBINY	12.3 s	2	1,258 s	1	9 (2)
LOCALMIN	11.9 s	0	316 s	0	1 (1)
NOCOUNT	12.4 s	54	44 s	94	0 (0)
GLOBRT	2.8 s	81	594 s	36	3 (2)

benchmark sets can be explained by a different diversity of predicates used on the transitions of SFA. In the REGEX benchmark, the globally mintermised automaton has on average 4.5 times more transitions (with the ratio ranging from 1 to 13), while in the WS1S benchmark, the mintermised automaton has on average 23.5 times more transitions (with the ratio ranging from 1 to 716). This clearly shows that our algorithms are effective in avoiding the potential blow-up of mintermisation. As expected, they are slower than RT on examples where the mintermisation is cheap since they do not use the partition-relation data structure.

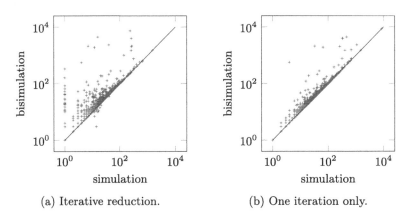

(a) Iterative reduction.   (b) One iteration only.

Fig. 3. Simulation vs. bisimulation-based reduction: the number of transitions of the reduced automaton.

4.2   Comparison of Simulation and Bisimulation

In the second experiment, we evaluate the benefit of computing simulation over computing bisimulation (we use the implementation of bisimulation computation from [13]). In particular, we focus on an application of (bi-)simulation for (language-preserving) reduction of SFAs from the whole REGEX benchmark.

For every SFA M from the benchmark, we compute its simulation preorder $\preceq_M$, take its biggest symmetric fragment (which constitutes an equivalence), and for each of its classes, merge all states of the class into a single state.

We also eliminate simulation subsumed transitions (the so-called *little brothers*) using the technique introduced in [20]. In particular, for a state q s.t. there exist transitions $q\text{-}\{a\}\!\!\mapsto\!p$ and $q\text{-}\{a\}\!\!\mapsto\!p'$ with $p \preceq p'$, we remove the transition $q\text{-}\{a\}\!\!\mapsto\!p$ (and also the states that have become unreachable). After that, we reverse the automaton and repeat the whole procedure. These steps continue until the number of states no longer decreases. Similar steps apply to bisimulation (with the exception of taking the symmetric fragment and removing transitions as a bisimulation is already an equivalence).

The results comparing the number of transitions of the output SFAs are given in Fig. 3a, showing that the simulation-based reduction is usually much more significant.[2] Figure 3b shows the reduction after the first iteration (it corresponds to the "ordinary" simulation and bisimulation-based reduction).

The comparison of the numbers of states gives a very similar picture as the comparison of the numbers of transitions (cf. [21]) but simulation wins by a slightly larger margin when comparing the numbers of transitions. This is probably due to the use of the removal of simulation-subsumed transitions, which does not have a meaningful counterpart when working with bisimulations.

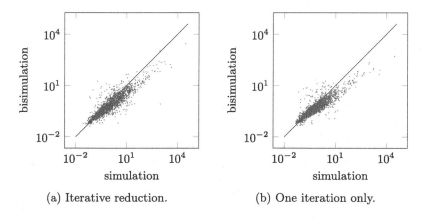

(a) Iterative reduction.   (b) One iteration only.

Fig. 4. Simulation vs. bisimulation-based reduction: runtime in miliseconds.

As for the runtimes, they differ significantly on the different case studies with some of the cases won by the simulation-based reduction process, some by the bisimulation-based reduction, as can be seen in Fig. 4. Figure 4a shows comparison of runtimes for the whole iterative process, Fig. 4b shows the comparison for the first iteration only—essentially the time taken by computing the simulation preorder or the bisimulation equivalence. One may see that bisimulation is notably cheaper, especially when the automata are growing larger and

---

[2] There are still some cases when bisimulation achieved a larger reduction than simulation, which may seem unintuitive since the largest bisimulation is always contained in the simulation preorder. This may happen, e.g., when a simulation-based reduction disables an (even greater) reduction on the subsequent reversed SFA.

both algorithms are taking more time (note the logarithmic scale). Computing simulation was, however, faster in surprisingly many cases.

5 Conclusion and Future Work

We have introduced two new algorithms for computing simulation over symbolic automata that do not depend on global mintermisation: one that needs a local and cheaper variant of mintermisation, and one that does not need mintermisation at all. They perform well especially on automata where mintermisation significantly increases the number of transitions. In the future, we would like to come up with a partition-based algorithm that could run on an SFA without the need of mintermisation. Such algorithm might, but does not necessarily need to, be based on an NFA partition-based algorithm such as RT. Further, we wish to explore the idea of encoding NFAs over finite alphabets compactly as SFAs over a fast Boolean algebra (such as bit-vector encoding of sets) and compare the performance of our algorithms with known NFA simulation algorithms.

Acknowledgements. This paper was supported by the Czech Science Foundation projects 16-17538S and 16-24707Y, the IT4IXS: IT4Innovations Excellence in Science project (LQ1602), and the FIT BUT internal project FIT-S-17-4014.

References

1. Watson, B.W.: Implementing and Using Finite Automata Toolkits. Cambridge University Press, New York (1999)
2. Veanes, M., Bjørner, N.: Symbolic automata: the toolkit. In: Flanagan, C., König, B. (eds.) TACAS 2012. LNCS, vol. 7214, pp. 472–477. Springer, Heidelberg (2012). https://doi.org/10.1007/978-3-642-28756-5_33
3. Veanes, M.: Applications of symbolic finite automata. In: Konstantinidis, S. (ed.) CIAA 2013. LNCS, vol. 7982, pp. 16–23. Springer, Heidelberg (2013). https://doi.org/10.1007/978-3-642-39274-0_3
4. D'Antoni, L., Veanes, M.: The power of symbolic automata and transducers. In: Majumdar, R., Kunčak, V. (eds.) CAV 2017. LNCS, vol. 10426, pp. 47–67. Springer, Cham (2017). https://doi.org/10.1007/978-3-319-63387-9_3
5. Abdulla, P.A., Chen, Y.-F., Holík, L., Mayr, R., Vojnar, T.: When simulation meets antichains. In: Esparza, J., Majumdar, R. (eds.) TACAS 2010. LNCS, vol. 6015, pp. 158–174. Springer, Heidelberg (2010). https://doi.org/10.1007/978-3-642-12002-2_14
6. Bonchi, F., Pous, D.: Checking NFA equivalence with bisimulations up to congruence. In: Proceeding of POPL'13, ACM (2013)
7. Ilie, L., Navarro, G., Yu, S.: On NFA reductions. In: Karhumäki, J., Maurer, H., Păun, G., Rozenberg, G. (eds.) Theory Is Forever. LNCS, vol. 3113, pp. 112–124. Springer, Heidelberg (2004). https://doi.org/10.1007/978-3-540-27812-2_11
8. Holík, L., Šimáček, J.: Optimizing an LTS-simulation algorithm. In: Masaryk, U. (ed.) Proceedings of MEMICS'09 (2009)
9. Lengál, O., Šimáček, J., Vojnar, T.: VATA: a library for efficient manipulation of non-deterministic tree automata. In: Flanagan, C., König, B. (eds.) TACAS 2012. LNCS, vol. 7214, pp. 79–94. Springer, Heidelberg (2012). https://doi.org/10.1007/978-3-642-28756-5_7

10. Henzinger, M.R., Henzinger, T.A., Kopke, P.W.: Computing simulations on finite and infinite graphs. In: Proceedings of FOCS'95, IEEE (1995)
11. Cécé, G.: Foundation for a series of efficient simulation algorithms. In: Proceedings of LICS'17, IEEE (2017)
12. D'Antoni, L., Veanes, M.: Minimization of symbolic automata. In: Proceedings of POPL'14, ACM (2014)
13. D'Antoni, L., Veanes, M.: Forward bisimulations for nondeterministic symbolic finite automata. In: Legay, A., Margaria, T. (eds.) TACAS 2017. LNCS, vol. 10205, pp. 518–534. Springer, Heidelberg (2017). https://doi.org/10.1007/978-3-662-54577-5_30
14. Eberl, M.: Efficient and verified computation of simulation relations on NFAs. Bachelor's thesis, TU Munich, 2012
15. Regular expression library. http://regexlib.com/
16. Comon, H., et al.: Tree automata techniques and applications (2007)
17. Elgaard, J., Klarlund, N., Møller, A.: MONA 1.x: new techniques for WS1S and WS2S. In: Hu, A.J., Vardi, M.Y. (eds.) CAV 1998. LNCS, vol. 1427, pp. 516–520. Springer, Heidelberg (1998). https://doi.org/10.1007/BFb0028773
18. Fiedor, T., Holík, L., Lengál, O., Vojnar, T.: Nested antichains for WS1S. In: Baier, C., Tinelli, C. (eds.) TACAS 2015. LNCS, vol. 9035, pp. 658–674. Springer, Heidelberg (2015). https://doi.org/10.1007/978-3-662-46681-0_59
19. Ranzato, F.: A more efficient simulation algorithm on Kripke structures. In: Chatterjee, K., Sgall, J. (eds.) MFCS 2013. LNCS, vol. 8087, pp. 753–764. Springer, Heidelberg (2013). https://doi.org/10.1007/978-3-642-40313-2_66
20. Bustan, D., Grumberg, O.: Simulation-based minimization. ACM Trans. Comput. Log. 4(2), 181–206 (2003)
21. Holík, L., Lengál, O., Síč, J., Veanes, M., Vojnar, T.: Simulation algorithms for symbolic automata (Technical Report). CoRR, arXiv:abs/1807.08487 (2018)

Quantitative Projection Coverage for Testing ML-enabled Autonomous Systems

Chih-Hong Cheng[1]([envelope]), Chung-Hao Huang[1]([envelope]), and Hirotoshi Yasuoka[2]

[1] fortiss - Landesforschungsinstitut des Freistaats Bayern, Munich, Germany
{cheng,huang}@fortiss.org
[2] DENSO CORPORATION, Tokyo, Japan
hirotoshi_yasuoka@denso.co.jp

Abstract. Systematically testing models learned from neural networks remains a crucial unsolved barrier to successfully justify safety for autonomous vehicles engineered using data-driven approach. We propose quantitative k-projection coverage as a metric to mediate combinatorial explosion while guiding the data sampling process. By assuming that domain experts propose largely independent environment conditions and by associating elements in each condition with weights, the product of these conditions forms scenarios, and one may interpret weights associated with each equivalence class as relative importance. Achieving full k-projection coverage requires that the data set, when being projected to the hyperplane formed by arbitrarily selected k-conditions, covers each class with number of data points no less than the associated weight. For the general case where scenario composition is *constrained* by rules, precisely computing k-projection coverage remains in NP. In terms of finding minimum test cases to achieve full coverage, we present theoretical complexity for important sub-cases and an encoding to 0-1 integer programming. We have implemented a research prototype that generates test cases for a visual object detection unit in automated driving, demonstrating the technological feasibility of our proposed coverage criterion.

1 Introduction

There is a recent hype of applying neural networks in automated driving, ranging from perception [3,9] to the creation of driving strategies [14,21] to even end-to-end driving setup [1]. Despite many public stories that seemly hint the technical feasibility of using neural networks, one fundamental challenge is to establish rigorous safety claims by considering all classes of relevant scenarios whose presence is subject to technical or societal constraints.

The key motivation of this work is that, apart from recent formal verification efforts [5,7,8,10] where scalability and lack of specification are obvious concerns, the most plausible approach, from a certification perspective, remains to be testing. As domain experts or authorities in autonomous driving may suggest n (incomplete) weighted criteria for describing the operating conditions such as weather, landscape, or partially occluding pedestrians, with these criteria one

S. K. Lahiri and C. Wang (Eds.): ATVA 2018, LNCS 11138, pp. 126–142, 2018.
https://doi.org/10.1007/978-3-030-01090-4_8

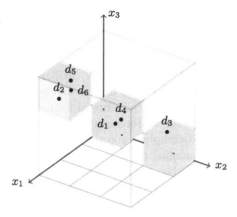

Fig. 1. A total of 6 data points and their corresponding equivalence classes (highlighted as bounding boxes).

can systematically partition the domain and weight each partitioned class based on its relative importance. This step fits very well to the consideration as in automotive safety standard ISO 26262, where for deriving test cases, it is highly recommended to *perform analysis of equivalence classes* (Chap 6, Table 11, item 1b). Unfortunately, there is an *exponential* number of classes being partitioned, making the naïve coverage metric of having at least one data point in each class unfeasible. In addition, such a basic metric is *qualitative* in that it does not address the relative importance among different scenarios.

Towards above issues, in this paper we study the problem of *quantitative k-projection coverage*, i.e., for arbitrary k criteria being selected ($k \ll n$ being a small *constant* value), the data set, when being projected onto the k-hyperplane, needs to have (in each region) data points no less than the associated weight. When k is a constant, the size of required data points to achieve full quantitative k-projection coverage remains polynomially bounded. Even more importantly, for the case where the composition of scenarios is *constrained* by rules, we present an NP algorithm to compute exact k-projection coverage. This is in contrast to the case without projection, where computing exact coverage is ♯P-hard.

Apart from calculating coverage, another crucial problem is to generate, based on the goal of increasing coverage, fewer scenarios if possible, as generating images or videos matching the scenario in autonomous driving is largely semi-automatic and requires huge human efforts. While we demonstrate that for *unconstrained* quantitative 1-projection, finding a minimum set of test scenarios to achieve full coverage remains in polynomial time, we prove that for 3-projection, the problem is NP-complete. To this end, we develop an efficient encoding to 0-1 integer programming which allows incrementally creating scenarios to maximally increase coverage.

To validate our approach, we have implemented a prototype to define and ensure coverage of a vision-based front-car detector. The prototype has integrated state-of-the-art traffic simulators and image synthesis frameworks [15, 25], in order to synthesize close-to-reality images specific to automatically proposed scenarios.

(**Related Work**) The use of AI technologies, in particular the use of neural networks, has created fundamental challenges in safety certification. Since 2017 there has been a tremendous research advance in formally verifying properties of neural networks, with focuses on neurons using piecewise linear activation function (ReLU). For sound-and-complete approaches, Reluplex and Planet developed specialized rules for managing the 0-1 activation in the proof system [7, 10]. Our previous work [4, 5] focused on the reduction to mixed integer liner programming (MILP) and applied techniques to compute tighter bounds such that in MILP, the relaxation bound is closer to the real bound. Exact approaches suffer from combinatorial explosion and currently the verification speed is not satisfactory. For imprecise yet sound approaches, recent work has been emphasizing linear relaxation of ReLU units by approximating them using outer convex polytopes [11, 20, 26], making the verification problem feasible for linear programming solvers. These approaches are even applied in the synthesis (training) process, such that one can derive provable guarantees [11, 20]. Almost all verification work (apart from [4, 7, 10]) targets robustness properties, which is similar to adversarial testing (e.g., FGSM & iterative attacks [24], deepfool [16], Carlini-Wagner attacks [2]) as in the machine learning community. All these approaches can be complemented with our approach by having our approach covering important scenarios, while adversarial training or formal verification measuring robustness within each scenario.

For classical structural coverage testing criteria such as MC/DC, they fail to deliver assurance promises, as satisfying full coverage either turns trivial (tanh) or intractable (ReLU). The recent work by Sun, Huang, and Kroening [22] borrows the concept of MC/DC and considers a structural coverage criterion, where one needs to find tests to ensure that for every neuron, its activation is supported by independent activation of neurons in its immediate previous layer. Such an approach can further be supported by concolic testing, as being recently demonstrated by same team [23]. Our work and theirs should be viewed as complementary, as we focus on the data space for training and testing neural networks, while they focus on the internal structure of a neural network. However, as in the original MC/DC concept, each condition in a conditional statement (apart from detecting errors in programming such as array out-of-bound which is not the core problem of neural networks) is designed to describe scenarios which should be viewed as natural consequences of input space partitioning (our work). Working on coverage criteria related to the internal structure of neural networks, provided that one cannot enforce the meaning of an individual neuron but can only empirically analyze it via reverse engineering (as in standard approaches like saliency maps [19]), is less likely provide direct benefits. Lastly, one major benefit of these structural testing approaches, based on the author claims, is to find adversarial examples via perturbation, but the benefit may be reduced due to new training methods with provable perturbation bounds [11, 20].

Lastly, our proposed metric tightly connects to the classic work of combinatorial testing and covering arrays [6,12,13,17,18]. However, as their application starts within hardware testing (i.e., each input variable being true or false), the quantitative aspects are not really needed and it does not need to consider constrained input cases, which is contrary to our practical motivation in the context of autonomous driving. For unconstrained cases, there are some results of NP-completeness in the field of combinatorial testing, which is largely based on the proof in [18]. It is not applicable to our case, as the proof is based on having freedom to define the set of groups to be listed in the projection. In fact, as listed in a survey paper [12], the authors commented that it remains open whether "the problem of generating a minimum test set for pairwise testing ($k = 2$) is NP-complete" and "existing proof in [13] for the NP-completeness of pairwise testing is wrong" (due to the same reason where pairwise testing cannot have freedom to define the set of groups). Our new NP-completeness result in this paper can be viewed as a relaxed case by considering $k = 3$ with sampling being quantitative than qualitative.

2   Discrete Categorization and Coverage

Let $\mathcal{DS} \subset \mathbb{R}^m$ be the *data space*, $\mathcal{D} \subset \mathcal{DS}$ be a finite set called *data set*, and $d \in \mathcal{DS}$ is called a *data point*. A *categorization* $\mathcal{C} = \langle C_1, \ldots, C_n \rangle$ is a list of functions that transform any data point d to a *discrete categorization point* $\mathcal{C}(d) = (C_1(d), \ldots, C_n(d))$, where for all $i \in \{1, \ldots, n\}$, C_i has co-domain $\{0, 1, \ldots, \alpha\}$. Two data points d_1 and d_2 are *equivalent by categorization*, denoted by $d_1 \equiv_{\mathcal{C}} d_2$, if $\mathcal{C}(d_1) = \mathcal{C}(d_2)$. The *weight* of a categorization $\mathcal{W} = \langle W_1, \ldots, W_n \rangle$ further assigns value $j \in \{0, 1, \ldots, \alpha\}$ in the co-domain of C_i with an integer value $W_i(j) \in \{0, \ldots, \beta\}$.

Next, we define constraints over categorization, allowing domain experts to express knowledge by specifying relations among categorizations. Importantly, for all data points in the data space, whenever they are transformed using $\mathcal{C}$, the transformed discrete categorization points satisfy the constraints.

Definition 1. (Categorization constraint) *A categorization constraint $\mathcal{CS} = \{CS_1, \ldots, CS_p\}$ is a set of constraints with each being a CNF formula having literals of the form $C_i(d)$ op α_i, where op $\in \{=, \neq\}$ and $\alpha_i \in \{0, \ldots, \alpha\}$.*

Let $\odot_{i \in \{1, \ldots, n\}} W_i(c_i)$ abbreviate $W_1(c_1) \odot \ldots \odot W_n(c_n)$, where $\odot \in \{+, \times, \max\}$ can be either scalar addition, multiplication, or max operators. In this paper, unless specially mentioned we always treat $\odot$ as scalar multiplication. Let $\mathcal{C}(\mathcal{D})$ be the multi-set $\{\mathcal{C}(d) \mid d \in \mathcal{D}\}$, and $\leq_{\odot}^{\mathcal{W}}$ be set removal operation on $\mathcal{C}(\mathcal{D})$ such that every categorization point $(c_1, \ldots, c_n) \in \mathcal{C}(\mathcal{D})$ has at most cardinality equal to $\odot_{i \in \{1, \ldots, n\}} W_i(c_i)$. We define *categorization coverage* by requiring that for each discrete categorization point $(c_1, \ldots, c_n)$, in order to achieve full coverage, have at least $\odot_{i \in \{1, \ldots, n\}} W_i(c_i)$ data points.

Definition 2. (Categorization coverage) *Given a data set $\mathcal{D}$, a categorization $\mathcal{C}$ and its associated weights $\mathcal{W}$, define the categorization coverage $cov_\mathcal{C}(\mathcal{D})$ for data set $\mathcal{D}$ over $\mathcal{C}$ and $\mathcal{W}$ to be $\frac{|\leq_\odot^\mathcal{W}(\mathcal{C}(\mathcal{D}))|}{\sum_{(c_1,\ldots,c_n)\in sat(\mathcal{CS})} \odot_{i\in\{1,\ldots,n\}} W_i(c_i)}$, where $sat(\mathcal{CS})$ is the set of discrete categorization points satisfying constraints $\mathcal{CS}$.*

(**Example 1**) In Fig. 1, let the data space $\mathcal{DS}$ be $[0,3) \times [0,3) \times [0,3)$ and the data set be $\mathcal{D} = \{d_1, \ldots, d_6\}$. By setting $\mathcal{C} = \langle C_1, C_2, C_3 \rangle$ where $C_i = \lfloor x_i \rfloor$ for $i \in \{1,2,3\}$, then for data points d_2, d_5 and d_6, applying C_1, C_2 and C_3 creates $\mathcal{C}(d_2) = \mathcal{C}(d_5) = \mathcal{C}(d_6) = (2,0,2)$, i.e., $d_2 \equiv_\mathcal{C} d_5 \equiv_\mathcal{C} d_6$. Similarly, $d_1 \equiv_\mathcal{C} d_4$.

- If $\mathcal{CS}$ is an empty set and $\forall i \in \{1,2,3\}, j \in \{0,1,2\} : W_i(j) = 1$, then $|sat(\mathcal{CS})| = 3^3 = 27$, $\leq_\odot^\mathcal{W}(\mathcal{C}(\mathcal{D}))$ removes $\mathcal{C}(d_2), \mathcal{C}(d_4), \mathcal{C}(d_5)$ by keeping one element in each equivalence class, and $cov_\mathcal{C}(\mathcal{D})$ equals $\frac{3}{27} = \frac{1}{9}$.
- If $\mathcal{CS} = \{(C_1(d) \neq 0 \vee C_2(d) = 2)\}$ and $\forall i \in \{1,2,3\}, j \in \{0,1,2\} : W_i(j) = 1$, then $|sat(\mathcal{CS})| = 21$ rather than 27 in the unconstrained case, and $cov_\mathcal{C}(\mathcal{D})$ equals $\frac{3}{21} = \frac{1}{7}$. Notice that all data points, once when being transformed into discrete categorization points, satisfy the categorization constraint.
- Assume that $\mathcal{CS}$ is an empty set, and $\forall i \in \{1,2,3\}, j \in \{0,1,2\}$, $W_i(j)$ always returns 1 apart from $W_1(2)$ and $W_3(2)$ returning 3. Lastly, let $\odot$ be scalar multiplication. Then for discrete categorization points having the form of $(2,-,2)$, a total of $W_1(2) \times W_3(2) = 9$ data points are needed. One follows the definition and computes $cov_\mathcal{C}(\mathcal{D})$ to be $\frac{3+1+1}{9\times3+3\times12+1\times12} = \frac{1}{13}$.

Achieving 100% categorization coverage is essentially hard, due to the need of exponentially many data points.

Proposition 1. *Provided that $\mathcal{CS} = \emptyset$ and $\forall i \in \{1,\ldots,n\}, j \in \{0,\ldots,\alpha\} : W_i(j) = 1$, to achieve full coverage where $cov_\mathcal{C}(\mathcal{D}) = 1$, $|\mathcal{D}|$ is exponential to the number of categorizations.*

Proof. Based on the given condition, $|sat(\mathcal{CS})| = (\alpha + 1)^n$, and for each $(c_i, \ldots, c_n) \in sat(\mathcal{CS})$, $\odot_{i\in\{1,\ldots,n\}} W_i(c_i) = 1$. Therefore, $cov_\mathcal{C}(\mathcal{D}) = \frac{|\leq_\odot^\mathcal{W}(\mathcal{C}(\mathcal{D}))|}{(\alpha+1)^n}$. As $|\leq_\odot^\mathcal{W}(\mathcal{C}(\mathcal{D}))| \leq |\mathcal{C}(\mathcal{D})|$, to achieve full coverage $|\mathcal{C}(\mathcal{D})|$ (and correspondingly $|\mathcal{D}|$) needs to be exponential to the number of categorizations. □

Proposition 2. *Computing exact $cov_\mathcal{C}(\mathcal{D})$ is $\sharp P$-hard.*

Proof. Computing the exact number of the denominator in Definition 2, under the condition of $\alpha = 1$, equals to the problem of model counting for a SAT formula, which is known to be $\sharp P$-complete. □

3   Quantitative Projection Coverage

The intuition behind quantitative projection-based coverage is that, although it is unfeasible to cover all discrete categorization points, one may degrade the confidence by asking if the data set has covered every pair or triple of possible categorization with sufficient amount of data.

Definition 3. *(k-projection) Let set $\Delta = \{\Delta_1, \ldots, \Delta_k\} \subseteq \{1, \ldots, n\}$ where elements in Δ do not overlap. Given $d \in \mathcal{D}$, define the projection of a discrete categorization point $\mathcal{C}(d)$ over Δ to be $\mathsf{Proj}_\Delta(\mathcal{C}(d)) = (C_{\Delta_1}(d), C_{\Delta_2}(d), \ldots, C_{\Delta_k}(d))$.*

Given a multi-set S of discrete categorization points, we use $\mathsf{Proj}_\Delta(S)$ to denote the resulting multi-set by applying the projection function on each element in S, and analogously define $\leq^{\mathcal{W}}_{\odot_\Delta}$ ($\mathsf{Proj}_\Delta(S)$) to be a function which removes elements in $\mathsf{Proj}_\Delta(S)$ such that every element $(c_{\Delta_1}, \ldots, c_{\Delta_k})$ has cardinality at most $W_{\Delta_1}(c_{\Delta_1}) \odot \ldots \odot W_{\Delta_k}(c_{\Delta_k})$. Finally, we define k-projection coverage based on applying projection operation on the data set $\mathcal{D}$, for all possible subsets of $\mathcal{C}$ of size k.

Definition 4. *(k-projection coverage) Given a data set $\mathcal{D}$ and categorization $\mathcal{C}$, define the k-projection categorization coverage $cov^k_{\mathcal{C}}(\mathcal{D})$ for data set $\mathcal{D}$ over $\mathcal{C}$ and $\mathcal{W}$ to be*

$$\frac{\sum_{\{\Delta\,:\,|\Delta|=k\}} |\leq^{\mathcal{W}}_{\odot_\Delta} (\mathsf{Proj}_\Delta(\mathcal{C}(\mathcal{D})))|}{\sum_{\{\Delta\,:\,|\Delta|=k\}} \sum_{(c_{\Delta_1},\ldots,c_{\Delta_k}) \in \text{to-set}(\mathsf{Proj}_\Delta(sat(\mathcal{CS})))} W_{\Delta_1}(c_{\Delta_1}) \odot \ldots \odot W_{\Delta_k}(c_{\Delta_k})}$$

where function to-set() translates a multi-set to a set without element repetition.

(Example) Consider again Fig. 1 with $\odot$ being scalar multiplication, $\mathcal{CS} = \emptyset$ and $\forall i \in \{1, 2, 3\}, j \in \{0, 1, 2\} : W_i(j) = 2$.

- For $k = 1$, one computes $cov^1_{\mathcal{C}}(\mathcal{D}) = \frac{5+5+5}{\binom{3}{1}3^1 2^1} = \frac{15}{18}$. In the denominator, Δ has $\binom{3}{1}$ choices, namely $\Delta = \{1\}$, $\Delta = \{2\}$, or $\Delta = \{3\}$. Here we do detailed analysis over $\Delta = \{1\}$, i.e., we consider the projection to C_1.
  - Since $\mathcal{CS} = \emptyset$, $sat(\mathcal{CS})$ allows all possible 3^3 assignments.
  - $\mathsf{Proj}_\Delta(sat(\mathcal{CS}))$ creates a set with elements 0, 1, 2 with each being repeated 9 times, and to-set($\mathsf{Proj}_\Delta(sat(\mathcal{CS}))$) removes multiplicity and creates $\{0, 1, 2\}$. The sum equals $W_1(0) + W_1(1) + W_1(2) = 6$.
  The "5" in the numerator comes from the contribution of $(2, 0, 2)$ with 2 (albeit it has 3 data points), $(1, 1, 1)$ with 2, and $(0, 2, 0)$ with 1.
- For $k = 2$, one computes $cov^2_{\mathcal{C}}(\mathcal{D}) = \frac{6+6+6}{\binom{3}{2}3^2 2^2} = \frac{1}{6}$. The denominator captures three hyper planes ($x_1 x_2$, $x_1 x_3$, $x_2 x_3$) with each having 3^2 grids and with each grid allowing 2^2 data points.

Notice that Definitions 2 and 4 are the same when one takes k with value n.

Proposition 3. $cov^n_{\mathcal{C}}(\mathcal{D}) = cov_{\mathcal{C}}(\mathcal{D})$.

Proof. When $k = n$, the projection operator does not change $sat(\mathcal{CS})$. Subsequently, to-set operator is not effective as $\mathsf{Proj}_\Delta(sat(\mathcal{CS})) = sat(\mathcal{CS})$ is already a set, not a multi-set. Finally, we also have $W_{\Delta_1}(c_{\Delta_1}) \odot \ldots \odot W_{\Delta_k}(c_{\Delta_k}) = \odot_{i \in \{1,\ldots,n\}} W_i(c_i)$. Thus the denominator part of Definitions 2 and 4 are computing the same value. The argument also holds for the numerator part. Thus the definition of $cov^n_{\mathcal{C}}(\mathcal{D})$ can be rewritten as $cov_{\mathcal{C}}(\mathcal{D})$. □

The important difference between categorization coverage and k-projection coverage (where k is a constant) includes the number of data points needed to achieve full coverage (exponential vs. polynomial), as well as the required time to compute exact coverage ($\sharp$P vs. NP).

Proposition 4. *If k is a constant, then to satisfy full k-projection coverage, one can find a data set $\mathcal{D}$ whose size is bounded by a number which is polynomial to n, α and β.*

Proof. In Definition 4, the denominator is bounded by $\binom{n}{k}(\alpha + 1)^k \beta^k$.

- The total number of possible Δ with size k equals $\binom{n}{k}$, which is a polynomial of n with highest degree being k.
- For each Δ, $(c_{\Delta_1}, \ldots, c_{\Delta_k}) \in \mathsf{to\text{-}set}(\mathsf{Proj}_\Delta(\mathsf{sat}(\mathcal{CS})))$ has at most $(\alpha + 1)^k$ possible assignments - this happens when $\mathcal{CS} = \emptyset$.
- For each assignment of $(c_{\Delta_1}, \ldots, c_{\Delta_k})$, $W_{\Delta_1}(c_{\Delta_1}) \odot \ldots \odot W_{\Delta_k}(c_{\Delta_k})$ can at most has largest value β^k.

As one can use one data point for each element in the denominator, $\mathcal{D}$ which achieves full coverage is polynomially bounded. □

(Example 2) Consider a setup of defining traffic scenarios where one has $\alpha = 3$ and $n = 20$. When $\mathcal{CS} = \emptyset$ and $\forall i \in \{1, \ldots, n\}, j \in \{0, \ldots, \alpha\} : W_i(j) = 1$, the denominator of categorization coverage as defined in Definition 2 equals 3486784401, while the denominator of 2-projection coverage equals 1710 and the denominator of 3-projection coverage equals 10260.

Proposition 5. *If k is a constant, then computing k-projection coverage can be done in NP. If $\mathcal{CS} = \emptyset$, then computing k-projection coverage can be done in P.*

Proof. – For the general case where $\mathcal{CS} \neq \emptyset$, to compute k-projection coverage, the crucial problem is to know the precise value of the denominator. In the denominator, the part "$(c_{\Delta_1}, \ldots, c_{\Delta_k}) \in \mathsf{to\text{-}set}(\mathsf{Proj}_\Delta(\mathsf{sat}(\mathcal{CS})))$" is actually only checking if for grid $(c_{\Delta_1}, \ldots, c_{\Delta_k})$ in the projected k-hyperplane, whether it is possible to be occupied due to the constraint of $\mathcal{CS}$. If one knows that it can be occupied, simply add to the denominator by $W_{\Delta_1}(c_{\Delta_1}) \odot \ldots \odot W_{\Delta_k}(c_{\Delta_k})$. This "occupation checking" step can be achieved by examining the satisfiability of $\mathcal{CS}$ with C_{Δ_i} being replaced by the concrete assignment $(c_{\Delta_1}, \ldots, c_{\Delta_k})$ of the grid. As there are polynomially many grids (there are $\binom{n}{k}$ hyperplanes, with each having at most $(\alpha + 1)^k$ grids), and for each grid, checking is done in NP (due to SAT problem being NP), the overall process is in NP.

- For the special case where $\mathcal{CS} = \emptyset$, the "occupation checking" step mentioned previously is not required. As there are polynomially many grids (there are $\binom{n}{k}$ hyperplanes, with each having at most $(\alpha + 1)^k$ grids), the overall process is in P. □

4   Fulfilling k-Projection Coverage

As a given data set may not fulfill full k-projection coverage, one needs to generate additional data points to increase coverage. By assuming that there exists a *data generator function* $\mathcal{G}$ which can, from any discrete categorization point $c \in \{0, \ldots, \alpha\}^n$, creates a new data point $\mathcal{G}(c)$ in $\mathcal{DS}$ such that $\mathcal{C}(\mathcal{G}(c)) = c$ and $\mathcal{G}(c) \notin \mathcal{D}$ (e.g., for image generation, $\mathcal{G}$ can be realized using techniques such as conditional-GAN [15] to synthesize an image following the specified criterion, or using manually synthesized videos), generating data points to increase coverage amounts to the problem of finding additional discrete categorization points.

Definition 5. (Efficiently increasing k-projection coverage) *Given a data set $\mathcal{D}$, categorization $\mathcal{C}$ and generator $\mathcal{G}$, the problem of increasing k-projection coverage refers to the problem of finding a minimum sized set $\Theta \subseteq \{0, \ldots, \alpha\}^n$, such that* $cov_{\mathcal{C}}^k(\mathcal{D} \cup \{\mathcal{G}(c) : c \in \Theta\}) = 1$.

(Book-keeping k-projection for a given data set) For $\Delta = \{\Delta_1, \ldots, \Delta_k\}$, we use $\boxed{C_{\Delta_1} \ldots C_{\Delta_k}}$ to represent the data structure for book-keeping the covered items, and use subscript "$_{\{\gamma\}}$" to indicate that certain categorization has been covered γ times by the existing data set.

(Example 3) Consider the following three discrete categorization points $\{(0, 0, 1, 1), (1, 0, 0, 0), (1, 0, 0, 1)\}$ under $\alpha = 1$. Results of applying 1-projection and 2-projection are book-kept in Eqs. 1 and 2 respectively.

$$\boxed{C_1} = \{0_{\{1\}}, 1_{\{2\}}\}, \boxed{C_2} = \{0_{\{3\}}, 1_{\{0\}}\}, \boxed{C_3} = \{0_{\{2\}}, 1_{\{1\}}\}, \boxed{C_4} = \{0_{\{1\}}, 1_{\{2\}}\} \tag{1}$$

$$\boxed{C_1 C_2} = \{00_{\{1\}}, 01_{\{0\}}, 10_{\{2\}}, 11_{\{0\}}\} \quad \boxed{C_1 C_3} = \{00_{\{0\}}, 01_{\{1\}}, 10_{\{2\}}, 11_{\{0\}}\}$$

$$\boxed{C_1 C_4} = \{00_{\{0\}}, 01_{\{1\}}, 10_{\{1\}}, 11_{\{1\}}\} \quad \boxed{C_2 C_3} = \{00_{\{2\}}, 01_{\{1\}}, 10_{\{0\}}, 11_{\{0\}}\}$$

$$\boxed{C_2 C_4} = \{00_{\{1\}}, 01_{\{2\}}, 10_{\{0\}}, 11_{\{0\}}\} \quad \boxed{C_3 C_4} = \{00_{\{1\}}, 01_{\{1\}}, 10_{\{0\}}, 11_{\{1\}}\} \tag{2}$$

(Full k-projection coverage under $\mathcal{CS} = \emptyset$) To achieve k-projection coverage under $\mathcal{CS} = \emptyset$, in the worst case, one can always generate $\binom{n}{k}(\alpha + 1)^k \beta^k$ discrete categorization points for $|\Theta|$ in polynomial time. Precisely, to complete coverage on a particular projection Δ, simply enumerate all possible assignments (a total of $(\alpha + 1)^k$ assignments, as k is a constant, the process is done in polynomial time) for all $(C_{\Delta_1}, \ldots, C_{\Delta_k})$, and extend them by associating C_i, where $i \in \{1, \ldots, n\} \setminus \Delta$, with arbitrary value within $\{0, \ldots, \alpha\}$, and do it for β^k times. For example, to increase 2-projection coverage in Eq. 2, provided that $W_i(j) = 1$, one first completes $\boxed{C_1 C_2}$ by adding $\{01\text{- -}, 11\text{- -}\}$ where "-" can be either 0 or 1. One further improves $\boxed{C_1 C_3}$ using $\{0\text{-}0\text{-}, 1\text{-}1\text{-}\}$, and subsequently all others.

As using $|\Theta|$ to be $\binom{n}{k}(\alpha + 1)^k \beta^k$ can still create problems when data points are manually generated from discrete categorization points, in the following, we demonstrate important sub-cases with substantially improved bounds over $|\Theta|$.

Data: $\boxed{C_{\Delta_1}}, \ldots, \boxed{C_{\Delta_n}}$ of a given data set, and weight function $\mathcal{W}$
Result: The minimum set Θ of additional discrete categorization points to
          guarantee full 1-projection

```
1  while true do
2  |    let c := (*, ..., *);
3  |    for i = 1, ..., n do
4  |    |    for j = 0, ..., α do
5  |    |    |    if |C_Δi|[j] < W_i(j) then
6  |    |    |    |    replace the i-th element of c by value j;
7  |    |    |    |    |C_Δi|[j] := |C_Δi|[j] + 1;
8  |    |    |    |    break /* inner-loop */;
9  |    |    |    end
10 |    |    end
11 |    end
12 |    if c == (*, ..., *) then return Θ else replace every * in c by value 0,
   |    Θ := Θ ∪ {c}
13 end
```

Algorithm 1: Algorithm for achieving 1-projection.

Proposition 6. (1-projection coverage). *Finding an additional set of discrete categorization points Θ to achieve 1-projection coverage, with minimum size and under the condition of $\mathcal{CS} = \emptyset$, can be solved in time $\mathcal{O}(\alpha^2 \beta n^2)$, with $|\Theta|$ being bounded by $(\alpha + 1)\beta$.*

Proof. We present an algorithm (Algorithm 1) that allows generating minimum discrete categorization points for full 1-projection coverage. Recall for 1-projection, our starting point is $\boxed{C_{\Delta_1}}, \ldots, \boxed{C_{\Delta_n}}$ with each $\boxed{C_{\Delta_i}}$ recording the number of appearances for element $j \in \{0, \ldots, \alpha\}$. We use $\boxed{C_{\Delta_i}}_{[j]}$ to denote the number of appearances for element j in $\boxed{C_{\Delta_i}}$.

In Algorithm 1, for every projection i, the inner loop picks a value j whose appearance in $\boxed{C_{\Delta_i}}$ is lower than $W_i(j)$ (line 5-9). If no value is picked for some projection i, then the algorithm just replaces $*$ by 0, before adding it to the set Θ used to increase coverage (line 13). If after the iteration, c remains to be $(*, \ldots, *)$, then we have achieved full 1-projection coverage and the program exits (line 12). The algorithm guarantees to return a set fulling full 1-projection with minimum size, due to the observation that each categorization is independent, so the algorithm stops so long as the categorization which misses most elements is completed. In the worst case, if projection i started without any data, after $(\alpha + 1)\beta$ iterations, it should have reached a state where it no longer requires additional discrete characterization points. Thus, $|\Theta|$ is guaranteed to be bounded by $(\alpha + 1)\beta$.

Consider the example in Eq. 1. When $W_i(j) = 1$, the above algorithm reports that only one additional discrete categorization point $(0, 1, 0, 0)$ is needed to satisfy full 1-projection.   □

On the other hand, efficiently increasing 3-projection coverage, even under the condition of $\mathcal{CS} = \emptyset$, is hard.

Proposition 7. *(Hardness of maximally increasing 3-projection coverage, when $\mathcal{CS} = \emptyset$) Checking whether there exists one discrete categorization point to increase 3-projection coverage from existing value χ to value χ', under the condition where $\odot$ is scalar multiplication, is NP-hard.*

Proof. (Sketch) The hardness result is via a reduction from 3-SAT satisfiability, where we assume that each clause has exactly three variables. This problem is known to be NP-complete. We consider the case where $\alpha = 2$ and $\beta = 1$, i.e., each categorization function creates values in $\{0, 1, 2\}$. Given a 3-SAT formula ϕ_{3SAT} with δ clauses, with each literal within the set of variables being $\{C_1, C_2, \ldots, C_n\}$, we perform the following construction.

- Set the weight of categorization such that $W_i(0) = W_i(1) = 1$ and $W_i(2) = 0$.
- For each clause such as $(C_x \vee \neg C_y \vee C_z)$, we create a discrete categorization point by setting $C_x = 0$, $C_y = 1$, $C_z = 0$ (i.e., the corresponding assignment makes the clause false) and by setting remaining C_i to be 2. Therefore, the process creates a total of δ discrete categorization points and can be done in polynomial time.
- Subsequently, prepare the data structure and record the result of 3-projection for the above created discrete categorization points. As there are at most $\binom{n}{3}$ boxes of form $\boxed{C_x C_y C_z}$, with each box having $|\{0, 1, 2\}|^3 = 27$ items, the construction can be conducted in polynomial time.
- One can subsequently compute the 3-projection coverage. Notice that due to the construction of $W_i(2) = 0$, all projected elements that contain value 2 should not be counted. The computed denominator should be $\binom{n}{3}(2)^3$ rather than $\binom{n}{3}(3)^3$ also due to $W_i(2) = 0$.

Then the ϕ_{3SAT} problem has a satisfying instance *iff* there exists a discrete categorization point which increases the 3-projection coverage from $\frac{a}{\binom{n}{3}(2)^3}$ to value $\frac{a + \binom{n}{3}}{\binom{n}{3}(2)^3}$.

- ($\Rightarrow$) If ϕ_{3SAT} has a satisfying instance, create a discrete categorization point where $C_i = 0$ ($C_i = 1$) if the satisfying assignment of ϕ_{3SAT}, C_i equals false (true). The created discrete categorization point, when being projected, will
  - not occupy the already occupied space (recall that overlapping with existing items in each box implies that the corresponding clause can not be satisfied), and
  - not occupy a grid having $C_i = 2$ (as the assignment only makes C_i to be 0 or 1), making the point being added truly help in increasing the numerator of the computed coverage.

Overall, each projection will increase value by 1, and therefore, the 3-projection coverage increases from $\frac{a}{\binom{n}{3}(2)^3}$ to value $\frac{a+\binom{n}{3}}{\binom{n}{3}(2)^3}$.

- ($\Leftarrow$) Conversely, if there exists one discrete categorization point to increase coverage by $\binom{n}{3}$, due to the fact that we only have one point and there are $\binom{n}{3}$ projections, it needs to increase in *each* box representing 3-projection, without being overlapped with existing items in that box and without having value 2 being used. One can subsequently use the value of the discrete categorization point to create a satisfying assignment. □

In the following, we present an algorithm which encodes the problem of finding a discrete categorization point with maximum coverage increase to a 0-1 integer programming problem. Stated in Algorithm 2, line 1 prepares variables and constraints to be placed in the 0-1 programming framework. For each categorization C_i, for each possible value we create an 0-1 variable $\mathsf{var}_{[C_i=j]}$ (line 3-5), such that $\mathsf{var}_{[C_i=j]} = 1$ iff the newly introduced discrete categorization point has C_i using value j. As the algorithm proceeds by only generating one discrete categorization point, only one of them can be true, which is reflected in the constraint $\sum_{j=0}^{\alpha} \mathsf{var}_{[C_i=j]} = 1$ in line 6.

Then starting from line 8, the algorithm checks if a particular projected value still allows improvement $\boxed{C_{\Delta_1} \dots C_{\Delta_k}}_{[v_{\Delta_1} \dots v_{\Delta_k}]} < W_{\Delta_1}(v_{\Delta_1}) \odot \dots \odot W_{\Delta_k}(v_{\Delta_k})$.

If so, then create a variable $\mathsf{occ}_{[C_{\Delta_1}=v_{\Delta_1},\dots,C_{\Delta_k}=v_{\Delta_k}]}$ (line 10) such that it is set to 1 iff the newly introduced discrete categorization point will occupy this grid when being projected. As our goal is to maximally increase k-projection coverage, $\mathsf{occ}_{[C_{\Delta_1}=v_{\Delta_1},\dots,C_{\Delta_k}=v_{\Delta_k}]}$ is introduced in the objective function (line 11 and 16) where the sum of all variables is the objective to be maximized. Note that $\mathsf{occ}_{[C_{\Delta_1}=v_{\Delta_1},\dots,C_{\Delta_k}=v_{\Delta_k}]}$ is set to 1 iff the newly introduced discrete categorization point guarantees that $C_{\Delta_1} = v_{\Delta_1} \wedge \dots \wedge C_{\Delta_k} = v_{\Delta_k}$. For this purpose, line 12 applies a standard encoding tactic in 0-1 integer programming to encode such a condition - If $\mathsf{var}_{[C_{\Delta_1}=v_{\Delta_1}]} = \dots = \mathsf{var}_{[C_{\Delta_k}=v_{\Delta_k}]} = 1$, then $\mathsf{var}_{[C_{\Delta_1}=v_{\Delta_1}]} + \dots + \mathsf{var}_{[C_{\Delta_k}=v_{\Delta_k}]} = k$. Thus $\mathsf{occ}_{[C_{\Delta_1}=v_{\Delta_1},\dots,C_{\Delta_k}=v_{\Delta_k}]}$ will be set to 1 to enforce satisfaction of the right-hand inequality of the constraint. Contrarily, if any of $\mathsf{var}_{[C_{\Delta_j}=v_{\Delta_j}]}$, where $j \in \{1,\dots,k\}$ has value 0, then $\mathsf{occ}_{[C_{\Delta_1}=v_{\Delta_1},\dots,C_{\Delta_k}=v_{\Delta_k}]}$ needs to set to 0, in order to enforce the left-hand inequality of the constraint. Consider the example in Eq. 2, where one has $\boxed{C_1 C_2} = \{00_{\{1\}}, 01_{\{0\}}, 10_{\{2\}}, 11_{\{0\}}\}$. For improving $01_{\{0\}}$, line 12 generates the following constraint $0 \leq \mathsf{var}_{[C_1=0]} + \mathsf{var}_{[C_2=1]} - 2\,\mathsf{occ}_{[C_1=0,C_2=1]} \leq 1$.

Line 14 will be triggered when no improvement can be made by every check of line 9, meaning that the system has already achieved full k-projection coverage. Lastly, apply 0-1 integer programming where one translates variable $\mathsf{var}_{[C_i=v_i]}$ having value 1 by assigning C_i to v_i in the newly generated discrete categorization point (line 17, 18).

Here we omit technical details, but Algorithm 2 can easily be extended to constrained cases by adding $\mathcal{CS}$ to the list of constraints.

Data: The set $\{\boxed{C_{\Delta_1}\dots C_{\Delta_k}}\}$ of the current k-projection records, and weight function $\mathcal{W}$

Result: One discrete categorization point $(c_1,\dots,c_n)$ which maximally increase coverage, or null if current records have achieved full coverage.

1 let $\mathsf{var}_{0/1} := \emptyset$, $\mathsf{constraints}_{0/1} := \emptyset$, $\mathsf{objvar}_{0/1} := \emptyset$,;

2 **forall the** $C_i,\ i \in \{1,\dots,n\}$ **do**

3   **forall the** $j \in \{0,\dots,\alpha\}$ **do**

4 | $\mathsf{var}_{0/1} := \mathsf{var}_{0/1} \cup \{\mathsf{var}_{[C_i=j]}\}$;

5   **end**

6     $\mathsf{constraints}_{0/1} := \mathsf{constraints}_{0/1} \cup \{\sum_{j=0}^{\alpha} \mathsf{var}_{[C_i=j]} = 1\}$;

7 **end**

8 **forall the** $\boxed{C_{\Delta_1}\dots C_{\Delta_k}}$ **do**

9   **if** $\boxed{C_{\Delta_1}\dots C_{\Delta_k}}_{[v_{\Delta_1}\dots v_{\Delta_k}]} < W_{\Delta_1}(v_{\Delta_1}) \odot \dots \odot W_{\Delta_k}(v_{\Delta_k})$ **then**

10        $\mathsf{var}_{0/1} := \mathsf{var}_{0/1} \cup \{\mathsf{occ}_{[C_{\Delta_1}=v_{\Delta_1},\dots,C_{\Delta_k}=v_{\Delta_k}]}\}$;

11        $\mathsf{objvar}_{0/1} := \mathsf{objvar}_{0/1} \cup \{\mathsf{occ}_{[C_{\Delta_1}=v_{\Delta_1},\dots,C_{\Delta_k}=v_{\Delta_k}]}\}$;

12        $\mathsf{constraints}_{0/1} := \mathsf{constraints}_{0/1} \cup \{0 \le$ $\mathsf{var}_{[C_{\Delta_1}=v_{\Delta_1}]} + \dots + \mathsf{var}_{[C_{\Delta_k}=v_{\Delta_k}]} - k\,\mathsf{occ}_{[C_{\Delta_1}=v_{\Delta_1},\dots,C_{\Delta_k}=v_{\Delta_k}]} \le k-1\}$;

13   **end**

14   **if** $\mathsf{objvar} = \emptyset$ **then return** null **else**

15   let $\mathsf{obj} := \sum_{\mathsf{var} \in \mathsf{objvar}} \mathsf{var}$;

16   let $\mathsf{assignment} :=$ 0/1-programming$_{\{\mathsf{var}_{0/1}\}}$(**maximize** obj **subject-to** $\mathsf{constraint}_{0/1}$);

17   **return** $(v_1,\dots,v_n)$ where in $\mathsf{assignment}\ \mathsf{var}_{[C_i=v_i]}$ is assigned to 1;

18   **end**

19 **end**

Algorithm 2: Finding a discrete categorization point which maximally increases k-projection coverage, via an encoding to 0-1 integer programming.

5 Implementation and Evaluation

We have implemented above mentioned techniques as a workbench to support training vision-based perception units for autonomous driving. The internal workflow of our developed tool is summarized in Fig. 2. It takes existing labelled/categorized data set and the user-specified k value as input, computes k-projection coverage, and finds a new discrete categorization point which can increase the coverage most significantly. For the underlying 0-1 programming solving, we use IBM CPLEX Optimization Studio[1].

To convert the generated discrete categorization points to real images, we have further implemented a C++ plugin over the Carla simulator[2], an open-source simulator for autonomous driving based on Unreal Engine 4[3]. The

---

[1] IBM CPLEX Optimization Studio: https://www.ibm.com/analytics/data-science/prescriptive-analytics/cplex-optimizer.

[2] Carla Simulator: http://carla.org/.

[3] Unreal Engine 4: https://www.unrealengine.com/.

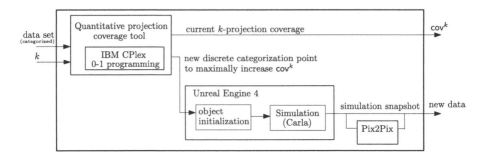

Fig. 2. Workflow in the developed prototype for quantitative projection coverage and generation of new synthetic data.

Fig. 3. Existing data points (E_1 to E_5), and the automatically generated data points (G_1 to G_6) to achieve full coverage.

plugin reads the scenario from the discrete categorization point and configures the ground truth, the weather, and the camera angle accordingly. Then the plugin starts the simulation and takes a snapshot using the camera mounted on the simulated vehicle. The camera can either return synthetic images (e.g., images in Fig. 3) or images with segmentation information, where for the latter one, one can further generate close-to-real image via applying conditional GAN framework Pix2Pix from NVIDIA[4]. Due to space limits, here we detail a small example by choosing the following operating conditions of autonomous vehicles as our categories.

- Weather = {Sunny, Cloudy, Rainy}
- Lane orientation = {Straight, Curvy}

[4] https://github.com/NVIDIA/pix2pixHD.

- Total number of lanes (one side) = $\{1, 2\}$
- Current driving lane = $\{1, 2\}$
- Forward vehicle existing = $\{\mathsf{true}, \mathsf{false}\}$
- Oncoming vehicle existing = $\{\mathsf{true}, \mathsf{false}\}$

Table 1. 2-projection coverage tables of the final data set

	1 Lane	2 Lanes
Sunny	G_2	G_1
Cloudy	G_4	G_3
Rainy	E_3	E_4

(a) Weather & #Lanes

	1st Lane	2nd Lane
Sunny	G_2	G_1
Cloudy	G_4	G_3
Rainy	E_5	G_5

(b) Weather & Current Lane

	Straight	Curvy
Sunny	G_1	G_6
Cloudy	G_4	G_3
Rainy	G_5	E_5

(c) Weather & Lane Curve

	No FC	FC
Sunny	G_1	G_2
Cloudy	G_4	G_3
Rainy	G_5	E_4

(d) Weather & Forward Car

	No OC	OC
Sunny	G_1	G_2
Cloudy	G_4	G_3
Rainy	G_5	E_4

(e) Weather & Oncoming Car

	1st Lane	2nd Lane
1 Lane	E_3	X
2 Lanes	E_2	G_1

(f) #Lanes & Current Lane

	Straight	Curvy
1 Lane	G_2	E_3
2 Lanes	E_1	E_2

(g) #Lanes & Lane Curve

	No FC	FC
1 Lane	E_3	G_2
2 Lanes	G_1	G_3

(h) #Lanes & Forward Car

	No OC	OC
1 Lane	G_4	E_3
2 Lanes	E_1	E_4

(i) #Lanes & Oncoming Car

	Straight	Curvy
1st Lane	E_1	E_2
2nd Lane	G_1	G_3

(j) Current Lane & Lane Curve

	No FC	FC
1st Lane	E_3	E_1
2nd Lane	G_1	G_3

(k) Current Lane & Forward Car

	No OC	OC
1st Lane	E_1	E_3
2nd Lane	G_1	G_3

(l) Current Lane & Oncoming Car

	No FC	FC
Straight	G_1	E_1
Curvy	E_3	E_2

(m) Lane Curve & Forward Car

	No OC	OC
Straight	E_1	G_2
Curvy	E_4	E_2

(n) Lane Curve & Oncoming Car

	No OC	OC
No FC	G_1	E_3
FC	E_2	E_4

(o) Forward Car & Oncoming Car

We used our test case generator to generate new data points to achieve full 2-projection coverage (with $W_i(j) = 1$) starting with a small set of randomly captured data points (Fig. 3, images E_1 to E_5). Images G_1 to G_6 are synthesized in sequence until full 2-projection coverage is achieved. The coverage condition of each 2-projection plane is shown in Table 1. Note that there exists one entry in the sub-table (f) which is not coverable (labelled as "X"), as there is a constraint stating that *if there exists only 1 lane, it is impossible for the vehicle to drive on*

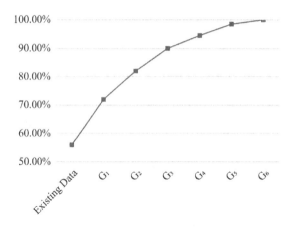

Fig. 4. Change of 2-projection coverage due to newly generated data.

the 2nd *lane.* Figure 4 demonstrates the growth of 2-projection coverage when gradually introducing images G_1 to G_6.

6 Concluding Remarks

In this paper, we presented quantitative k-projection coverage as a method to systematically evaluate the quality of data for systems engineered using machine learning approaches. Our prototype implementation is used to compute coverage and synthesize additional images for engineering a vision-based perception unit for automated driving. The proposed metric can further be served as basis to refine other classical metrics such as MTBF or availability which is based on statistical measurement.

Currently, our metric is to take more data points for important (higher weight) scenar ios. For larger k values, achieving full projection coverage may not be feasible, so one extension is to adapt the objective function of Algorithm 2 such that the generation process favors discrete categorization points with higher weights when being projected. Another direction is to improve the encoding of Algorithm 2 such that the algorithm can return multiple discrete categorization points instead of one. Yet another direction is to further associate temporal behaviors to categorization and the associated categorization constraints, when the data space represents a sequence of images.

References

1. Bojarski, M., et al.: End to end learning for self-driving cars. CoRR, abs/1604.07316 (2016)
2. Carlini, N., Wagner, D.: Towards evaluating the robustness of neural networks. In: 2017 IEEE Symposium on Security and Privacy (SP), pp. 39–57. IEEE (2017)

3. Chen, C., Seff, A., Kornhauser, A., Xiao, J.: Deepdriving: learning affordance for direct perception in autonomous driving. In: Proceedings of the IEEE International Conference on Computer Vision, pp. 2722–2730 (2015)
4. Cheng, C.-H., et al.: Neural networks for safety-critical applications challenges, experiments and perspectives. In: Design, Automation & Test in Europe Conference & Exhibition (DATE), 2018, pp. 1005–1006. IEEE (2018)
5. Cheng, C.-H., Nührenberg, G., Ruess, H.: Maximum resilience of artificial neural networks. In: International Symposium on Automated Technology for Verification and Analysis, pp. 251–268. Springer, Berlin (2017)
6. Colbourn, C.J.: Combinatorial aspects of covering arrays. Le Mat. **59**(1, 2), 125–172 (2004)
7. Ehlers, R.: Formal verification of piece-wise linear feed-forward neural networks. In: D'Souza, D., Narayan Kumar, K. (eds.) ATVA 2017. LNCS, vol. 10482, pp. 269–286. Springer, Cham (2017). https://doi.org/10.1007/978-3-319-68167-2_19
8. Huang, X., Kwiatkowska, M., Wang, S., Wu, M.: Safety verification of deep neural networks. In: Majumdar, R., Kunčak, V. (eds.) CAV 2017. LNCS, vol. 10426, pp. 3–29. Springer, Cham (2017). https://doi.org/10.1007/978-3-319-63387-9_1
9. Huval, B., et al.: An empirical evaluation of deep learning on highway driving. arXiv preprint arXiv:1504.01716 (2015)
10. Katz, G., Barrett, C., Dill, D.L., Julian, K., Kochenderfer, M.J.: Reluplex: an efficient SMT solver for verifying deep neural networks. In: Majumdar, R., Kunčak, V. (eds.) CAV 2017. LNCS, vol. 10426, pp. 97–117. Springer, Cham (2017). https://doi.org/10.1007/978-3-319-63387-9_5
11. Kolter, J.Z., Wong, E.: Provable defenses against adversarial examples via the convex outer adversarial polytope. arXiv preprint arXiv:1711.00851 (2017)
12. Lawrence, J., Kacker, R.N., Lei, Y., Kuhn, D.R., Forbes, M.: A survey of binary covering arrays. Electron. J. Comb. **18**(1), 84 (2011)
13. Lei, Y., Tai, K.-C.: In-parameter-order: a test generation strategy for pairwise testing. In: Proceedings of the Third IEEE International High-Assurance Systems Engineering Symposium, 1998, pp. 254–261. IEEE (1998)
14. Lenz, D., Diehl, F., Troung Le, M., Knoll, A.: Deep neural networks for Markovian interactive scene prediction in highway scenarios. In: IEEE Intelligent Vehicles Symposium (IV) 2017. IEEE (2017)
15. Mirza, M., Osindero, S.: Conditional generative adversarial nets. arXiv preprint arXiv:1411.1784 (2014)
16. Moosavi Dezfooli, S.M., Fawzi, A., Frossard, P.: Deepfool: a simple and accurate method to fool deep neural networks. In: Proceedings of 2016 IEEE Conference on Computer Vision and Pattern Recognition (CVPR) (2016)
17. Nie, C., Leung, H.: A survey of combinatorial testing. ACM Comput. Surv. (CSUR) **43**(2), 11 (2011)
18. Seroussi, G., Bshouty, N.H.: Vector sets for exhaustive testing of logic circuits. IEEE Trans. Inf. Theory **34**(3), 513–522 (1988)
19. Simonyan, K., Vedaldi, A., Zisserman, A.: Deep inside convolutional networks: visualising image classification models and saliency maps. arXiv preprint arXiv:1312.6034 (2013)
20. Sinha, A., Namkoong, H., Duchi, J.: Certifiable distributional robustness with principled adversarial training. arXiv preprint arXiv:1710.10571 (2017)
21. Sun, L., Peng, C., Zhan, W., Tomizuka, M.: A fast integrated planning and control framework for autonomous driving via imitation learning. arXiv preprint arXiv:1707.02515 (2017)

22. Sun, Y., Huang, X., Kroening, D.: Testing deep neural networks. arXiv preprint arXiv:1803.04792 (2018)
23. Sun, Y., Wu, M., Ruan, W., Huang, X., Kwiatkowska, M., Kroening, D.: Concolic testing for deep neural networks. arXiv preprint arXiv:1805.00089 (2018)
24. Szegedy, C., et al.: Intriguing properties of neural networks. arXiv preprint arXiv:1312.6199 (2013)
25. Wang, T.-C., Liu, M.-Y., Zhu, J.-Y., Tao, A., Kautz, J., Catanzaro, B.: High-resolution image synthesis and semantic manipulation with conditional gans. arXiv preprint arXiv:1711.11585 (2017)
26. Weng, T.-W., et al.: Towards fast computation of certified robustness for ReLU networks. arXiv preprint arXiv:1804.09699 (2018)

Recursive Online Enumeration of All Minimal Unsatisfiable Subsets

Jaroslav Bendík$^{(\boxtimes)}$, Ivana Černá, and Nikola Beneš

Faculty of Informatics, Masaryk University, Brno, Czech Republic
{xbendik,cerna,xbenes3}@fi.muni.cz

Abstract. In various areas of computer science, we deal with a set of constraints to be satisfied. If the constraints cannot be satisfied simultaneously, it is desirable to identify the core problems among them. Such cores are called minimal unsatisfiable subsets (MUSes). The more MUSes are identified, the more information about the conflicts among the constraints is obtained. However, a full enumeration of all MUSes is in general intractable due to the large number (even exponential) of possible conflicts. Moreover, to identify MUSes, algorithms have to test sets of constraints for their simultaneous satisfiability. The type of the test depends on the application domains. The complexity of the tests can be extremely high especially for domains like temporal logics, model checking, or SMT. In this paper, we propose a recursive algorithm that identifies MUSes in an *online* manner (i.e., one by one) and can be terminated at any time. The key feature of our algorithm is that it minimises the number of satisfiability tests and thus speeds up the computation. The algorithm is applicable to an arbitrary constraint domain. We benchmark our algorithm against the state-of-the-art algorithm Marco on the Boolean and SMT constraint domains and demonstrate that our algorithm really requires less satisfiability tests and consequently finds more MUSes in the given time limits.

1 Introduction

In many different applications we are given a set of constraints (requirements) with the goal to decide whether the set of constraints is satisfiable, i.e., whether all the constraints can hold simultaneously. In case the given set is shown to be unsatisfiable, we might be interested in an analysis of the unsatisfiability. Identification of minimal unsatisfiable subsets (MUSes) is a kind of such analysis. A minimal unsatisfiable subset is a set of constraints that are not simultaneously satisfiable, yet the elimination of any of them makes the set satisfiable. We illustrate the problem on two different applications.

In the *requirements analysis*, the constraints represent requirements on a system that is being developed. Checking for satisfiability (also called *consistency*) means checking whether all the requirements can be implemented at

N. Beneš—The author has been supported by the Czech Science Foundation grant No. GA18-00178S.

© Springer Nature Switzerland AG 2018
S. K. Lahiri and C. Wang (Eds.): ATVA 2018, LNCS 11138, pp. 143–159, 2018.
https://doi.org/10.1007/978-3-030-01090-4_9

once. If the set of requirements is unsatisfiable, the extraction of MUSes helps to identify and fix the conflicts among the requirements [5, 10].

In some model checking techniques, such as the *counterexample-guided abstraction refinement* (CEGAR) [16], we are dealing with the following question: is the counterexample that was found in an abstract model feasible also in the concrete model? To answer this question, a formula $cex \land conc$ encoding both the counterexample cex and the concrete model $conc$ is built and tested for satisfiability. If the formula is unsatisfiable, then the counterexample is *spurious* and the negation of the formula $cex \land conc$ is used to refine the abstract model. Since both cex and $conc$ are often formed as a conjunction of smaller subformulas, the whole formula can be seen as a set of conjuncts (constraints). Andraus et al. [1, 16] found out that instead of using the negation of $cex \land conc$ for the refinement, it is better to identify the MUSes of $cex \land conc$ and use the negations of the MUSes to refine the abstract model.

Yet another applications of MUSes arise for example during formal equivalence checking [17], proof based abstraction refinement [30], Boolean function bi-decomposition [13], circuit error diagnosis [25], type debugging in Haskell [37], or proof explanation in symbolic model checking [12, 23].

The individual applications differ in the constraint domain. Perhaps the most widely used are Boolean and SMT constraints; these types of constraints arise for example in the CEGAR workflow. In the requirements analysis, the most common constraints are those expressed in a temporal logic such as *Linear Temporal Logic* [34] or *Computational Tree Logic* [15]. The list of constraint domains in which MUS enumeration finds an application is quite long and new applications still arise. Therefore, we focus on MUS enumeration algorithms applicable in arbitrary constraint domains.

Main contribution. All algorithms solving the MUS enumeration problem have to get over two barriers. First, the number of all MUSes can be exponential w.r.t. the number of constraints. Therefore, the complete enumeration of all MUSes can be intractable. To overcome this limitation we present an algorithm for *online* MUS enumeration, i.e., an algorithm that enumerates MUSes one by one and can be terminated at any time.

Second, algorithms for MUS enumeration need to test whether a given set of constraints is satisfiable. This is typically a very hard task and it is thus desirable to minimise the overall number of satisfiability queries. To reduce the number of performed satisfiability queries, the majority of the state-of-the-art algorithms (for their detailed description see Sect. 4) try to exploit specific properties of particular constraint domains. Most of the algorithms were evaluated only in the SAT domain (the domain of Boolean constraints). The SAT domain enjoys properties that can be used to significantly reduce the number of satisfiability queries and the state-of-the-art algorithms are thus very efficient in this domain. However, this might not be the case in domains for which no such domain specific properties exist. Here, we present a novel algorithm that exploits both the domain specific as well as domains agnostics properties of the MUS enumeration

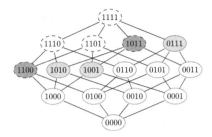

Fig. 1. Illustration of the power set of the set C of constraints from the Example 1. We encode individual subsets of C as bitvectors, e.g. the subset $\{c_1, c_3, c_4\}$ is written as 1011. The subsets with dashed border are the unsatisfiable subsets and the others are satisfiable subsets. The MUSes and MSSes are filled with a background colour.

problem. First, the algorithm employs, as a black-box subroutine, a domain specific single MUS extraction algorithm which allows it to exploit specific properties of particular domains. Second, it recursively searches for MUSes in smaller and smaller subsets of the given set of constraints which allows it to directly reduce the number of performed satisfiability queries.

2   Preliminaries and Problem Statement

We are given a finite set of constraints C with the property that each subset of C is either *satisfiable* or *unsatisfiable*. The notion of satisfiability may vary in different constraint domains. The only assumption is that if a set X, $X \subseteq C$, is unsatisfiable, then all supersets of X are unsatisfiable as well. The sets of interest are defined as follows.

Definition 1 (MUS, MSS, MCS). *Let C be a finite set of constraints and let $N \subseteq C$. N is a* minimal unsatisfiable subset *(MUS) of C if N is unsatisfiable and $\forall c \in N : N \setminus \{c\}$ is satisfiable. N is a* maximal satisfiable subset *(MSS) of C if N is satisfiable and $\forall c \in C \setminus N : N \cup \{c\}$ is unsatisfiable. N is a* minimal correction set *(MCS) of C if $C \setminus N$ is a MSS of C.*

   The maximality concept used in the definition of a MSS is the set maximality and not the maximum cardinality as in the MaxSAT problem. Thus a constraint set C can have multiple MSSes with different cardinalities.

Example 1. Assume that we are given a set $C = \{c_1, c_2, c_3, c_4\}$ of four Boolean satisfiability constraints $c_1 = a$, $c_2 = \neg a$, $c_3 = b$, and $c_4 = \neg a \vee \neg b$. Clearly, the whole set is unsatisfiable as the first two constraints are negations of each other. There are two MUSes of C, namely $\{c_1, c_2\}$, $\{c_1, c_3, c_4\}$. There are three MSSes of C, namely $\{c_1, c_4\}$, $\{c_1, c_3\}$, and $\{c_2, c_3, c_4\}$. Finally, there are three MCSes of C, namely $\{c_2, c_3\}$, $\{c_2, c_4\}$, and $\{c_1\}$. This example is illustrated in Fig. 1.

Another concept used in our work are the so-called *critical constraints* that are defined as follows:

Definition 2 (critical constraint). *Let C be a finite set of constraints and let $N \subseteq C$ be an unsatisfiable subset. A constraint $c \in N$ is a* critical constraint *for N if $N \setminus \{c\}$ is satisfiable.*

Note that N is a MUS of C if and only if each $c \in N$ is critical for N. Furthermore, if c is a critical constraint for C then c has to be contained in every unsatisfiable subset of C. Also, note that if S is a MSS of C and $\overline{S} = C \setminus S$ its complement (i.e. a MCS of C), then each $c \in \overline{S}$ is critical for $S \cup \{c\}$.

Example 2. We illustrate the concept of critical constraints on two sets, N and C, where C is the same set as in Example 1, and $N = C \setminus \{c_2\}$. The constraint c_1 is the only critical constraint for C whereas N has three critical constraints: c_1, c_3, and c_4.

Problem Formulation. Given a set of constraints C, enumerate all minimal unsatisfiable subsets of C in an online manner while minimising the number of constraints satisfiability queries. Moreover, we require an approach that is applicable to an arbitrary constraint domain.

3   Algorithm

We start with some observations about the MUS enumeration problem and describe the main concepts used in our algorithm.

The algorithm is given an unsatisfiable set of constraints C. To find all MUSes, the algorithm iteratively determines satisfiability of subsets of C. Initially, only the satisfiability of C is determined and at the end, satisfiability of all subsets of C is determined. The algorithm maintains a set *Unexplored* containing all subsets of C whose satisfiability is not determined yet. Recall that if a set of constraints is satisfiable then all its subsets are satisfiable as well. Therefore, if the algorithm determines some $N \subseteq C$ to be satisfiable, then not only N but also all of its subsets, denoted by $sub(N)$, become explored (i.e. are removed from the set *Unexplored*). Dually, if N is unsatisfiable then all of its supersets, denoted by $sup(N)$, are unsatisfiable and become explored.

Since there are exponentially many subsets of C, it is intractable to represent the set *Unexplored* explicitly. Instead, we use a symbolic representation that is common in contemporary MUS enumeration algorithms [11,23,28]. We encode $C = \{c_1, c_2, \ldots, c_n\}$ by using a set of Boolean variables $X = \{x_1, x_2, \ldots, x_n\}$. Each valuation of X then corresponds to a subset of C. This allows us to represent the set of unexplored subsets *Unexplored* using a Boolean formula $f_{Unexplored}$ such that each model of $f_{Unexplored}$ corresponds to an element of *Unexplored*. The formula is maintained as follows:

- Initially $f_{Unexplored} = True$ since all of $\mathcal{P}(C)$ are unexplored.
- To remove a satisfiable set $N \subseteq C$ and all its subsets from the set *Unexplored* we add to $f_{Unexplored}$ the clause $\bigvee_{i:c_i \notin N} x_i$.
- Symmetrically, to remove an unsatisfiable set $N \subseteq C$ and all its supersets from the set *Unexplored* we add to $f_{Unexplored}$ the clause $\bigvee_{i:c_i \in N} \neg x_i$.

To get an element of *Unexplored*, we ask a SAT solver for a model of $f_{Unexplored}$.

Example 3. Let us illustrate the symbolic representation on $C = \{c_1, c_2, c_3\}$. If all subsets of C are unexplored then $f_{Unexplored} = True$. If $\{c_1, c_3\}$ is determined to be unsatisfiable and $\{c_1, c_2\}$ to be satisfiable, then $f_{Unexplored}$ is updated to $True \land (\neg x_1 \lor \neg x_3) \land (x_3)$.

One of the approaches (see e.g. [11,27,35]) how to find a MUS of C is to find an unexplored unsatisfiable subset, called a *seed*, and then use any algorithm that finds a MUS of the seed (this algorithm is often denoted as a *shrink* procedure). In our algorithm we use a black-box subroutine for shrinking. This allows us to always employ the best available, domain specific, single MUS extraction algorithm.

The key question is how to find an unexplored unsatisfiable subset (a seed). Due to the monotonicity of the satisfiability of individual subsets (w.r.t. subset inclusion), satisfiable subsets are typically smaller and, dually, unsatisfiable subsets are more concentrated among the larger subsets. Therefore, we search for seeds among *maximal unexplored subsets*. A set S_{max} is a maximal unexplored subset of C iff $S_{max} \subseteq C$, $S_{max} \in$ *Unexplored*, and each of the proper supersets of S_{max} is explored. The maximal unexplored subsets correspond to the *maximal models* of $f_{Unexplored}$. Thus, in order to get a maximal unexplored subset S_{max}, we ask a SAT solver for such a model. If S_{max} is unsatisfiable, we use it as a seed for the shrinking procedure and compute a MUS of C.

The idea of searching for seeds among the maximal unexplored subsets is already used in some contemporary MUS enumeration algorithms [11,23,28,35]. However, none of the algorithms specify which maximal unexplored subset should be used for finding a seed. They just ask a SAT solver for an arbitrary maximal model of $f_{Unexplored}$ (maximal unexplored subset). We found that the choice of maximal unexplored subset to be used is very important. The complexity of the shrinking procedure, in general, depends on the cardinality (the number of constraints) of the seed. Thus, an ideal option would be to search for a seed among the maximal unexplored subsets with the minimum cardinality, i.e. to find a *minimum maximal model* of $f_{Unexplored}$. However, finding such a model is very expensive, especially compared to finding an arbitrary maximal model of $f_{Unexplored}$. In order to find an arbitrary maximal model, we can just instruct the SAT solver to use *True* as a default polarity of variables during solving (this can be done e.g. in the miniSAT [21] solver). On the other hand, finding a minimum maximal model of $f_{Unexplored}$ is a hard optimisation problem.

We propose a way of finding seeds that are relatively small, yet cheap to be found. To find the first seed we are repeatedly asking the SAT solver for an arbitrary maximal unexplored subset of C until we obtain some unsatisfiable

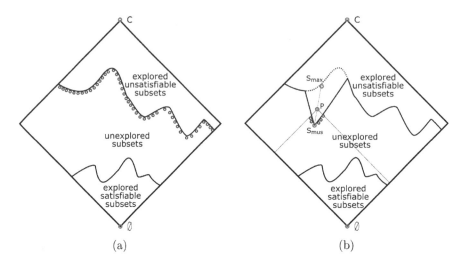

Fig. 2. Illustration of our seed selection approach. Figure 2a illustrates the division of subsets of C into explored satisfiable, explored unsatisfiable, and unexplored subsets. The blue circle nodes represent the maximal unexplored subsets of C. Figure 2b shows a previously used seed S_{max}, a MUS S_{mus} that was found based on the seed, a set P such that $S_{mus} \subseteq P \subseteq S_{max}$, and maximal unexplored subsets of P (blue circle nodes).

maximal unexplored subset S_{max}. Then, we use S_{max} as the first seed and shrink it to the first MUS S_{mus}. In order to find the next seed, we use a more sophisticated approach. Instead of searching for a seed among the maximal unexplored subsets of C, we restrict the search space so that the next seed is smaller than the previous one. In particular, we choose a set P such that $S_{mus} \subseteq P \subseteq S_{max}$ and search for the new seed among the maximal unexplored subsets of P. Note that the maximal unexplored subsets of P do not have to be maximal unexplored subsets of C. Furthermore, P is necessarily unsatisfiable and all seeds found within it are necessarily smaller than the previous seed S_{max} since $P \subseteq S_{max}$. By choosing the next seed among the maximal unexplored subsets of P, we de facto solve the problem in a recursive manner. Instead of finding a new MUS of C, we find a MUS of P, which is necessarily also a MUS of C. Each next seed is found based on the previous one, i.e. we keep to recursively reducing the search space as far as we can. Once we end up in a subset P of C such that the whole $\mathcal{P}(P)$ is explored, we backtrack from the recursion. The approach is illustrated in Fig. 2.

In our algorithm we also use critical constraints. For mining critical constraints we use the maximal unexplored subsets that are satisfiable. Every satisfiable maximal unexplored subset S_{max} of C is a maximal satisfiable subset (MSS) of C as every superset of S_{max} is explored. If it were satisfiable then due to monotonicity S_{max} should also be explored (which it is not). Thus, for every $c \in C \setminus S_{max}$ it holds that $S_{max} \cup \{c\}$ is unsatisfiable and c is a critical constraint for $S_{max} \cup \{c\}$.

The critical constraints are used in two different situations. The first situation arises when we are searching for a seed and the selected maximal unexplored subset S_{max} of C is satisfiable. In such a case we can try to pick another maximal unexplored subset of C and check it for satisfiability. However, for reasons mentioned above, we try to search for small seeds. Therefore we recursively search for a maximal unexplored subset of $S_{max} \cup \{c\}$, where c is a critical constraint for $S_{max} \cup \{c\}$. The set $S_{max} \cup \{c\}$ is definitely unsatisfiable and its cardinality is not greater than the cardinality of C.

Many modern shrinking algorithms [2,8,32] use critical constraints to speed up their computation. Every MUS of C has to contain all the critical constraints for C and this helps the shrinking procedure to narrow the search space. The critical constraints for C have to be delivered to the shrinking algorithm together with the seed. Our algorithm can compute and accumulate critical constraints effectively while recursively traversing the space. If X and Y are two sets of constraints such that $X \supseteq Y$, then every critical constraint for X is also a critical constraint for Y. The algorithm thus can utilise the known critical constraints even in its recursive part.

3.1   Description of the Algorithm

The pseudocode of our algorithm is shown in Algorithm 1. The computation of the algorithm starts with an initialisation phase followed by a call of the procedure FindMUSes, which is the core procedure of our algorithm.

The procedure FindMUSes has two input parameters: S and *criticals*. S is an unsatisfiable set of constraints and the procedure outputs MUSes of S. The set *criticals* contains (currently known) critical constraints for S and is used for the shrinking procedure. In each iteration, the procedure FindMUSes picks a maximal unexplored subset S_{max} of S and tests it for satisfiability. If S_{max} is satisfiable, then it is guaranteed to be a MSS of S. Thus, the complement $S_{mcs} = S \setminus S_{max}$ of S_{max} is an MCS of S and it can be used to obtain critical constraints. If $|S_{mcs}| = 1$, then the single constraint that forms S_{mcs} is guaranteed to be a critical constraint for S and it is thus added into *criticals*. Otherwise, the procedure recursively calls itself on $(S_{max} \cup \{c\}, \textit{criticals} \cup \{c\})$ for each $c \in S_{mcs}$ since each such c is guaranteed to be a critical constraint for $S_{max} \cup \{c\}$.

In the other case, when S_{max} is unsatisfiable, then S_{max} is shrunk to a MUS S_{mus} (note that the set *criticals* of critical constraints is provided to the shrinking procedure). The newly computed S_{mus} is used to reduce the dimension of the space in which another MUSes are searched for. Namely, the procedure picks some P, $S_{mus} \subset P \subset S_{max}$, and recursively calls itself on P. After the recursive call terminates, the procedure continues with the next iteration.

The main idea behind the recursion is to search for MUSes of sets smaller than S and thus lower the complexity of performed operations. Naturally, there is a trade-off between the complexity of operations and the expected number of MUSes occurring in the chosen subspace and thus it might be very tricky to find an optimal P. In our algorithm we choose P so that $|P| = 0.9 \cdot |S_{max}|$, where $|P|$ and $|S_{max}|$ are cardinalities of the two sets, respectively. We form P

Algorithm 1: ReMUS

---

1 **Function** Init(C):
    input : an unsatisfiable set of constraints C
2   $Unexplored \leftarrow \mathcal{P}(C)$
3   FindMUSes$(C, \emptyset)$

1 **Function** FindMUSes$(S, criticals)$:
2   **while** $Unexplored \cap \mathcal{P}(S) \neq \emptyset$ **do**
3       $S_{max} \leftarrow$ a maximal unexplored subset of S
4   **if** S_{max} *is satisfiable* **then**
5           $Unexplored \leftarrow Unexplored \setminus Sub(S_{max})$
6           $S_{mcs} \leftarrow S \setminus S_{max}$
7   **if** $|S_{mcs}| = 1$ **then**
8               $criticals \leftarrow criticals \cup S_{mcs}$
9   **else**
10   **for each** $c \in S_{mcs}$ **do**
11   FindMUSes$(S_{max} \cup \{c\}, criticals \cup \{c\})$
12   **else**
13          $S_{mus} \leftarrow$Shrink$(S_{max}, criticals)$
14   **output** S_{mus}
15          $Unexplored \leftarrow Unexplored \setminus (Sup(S_{mus}) \cup Sub(S_{mus}))$
16   **if** $|S_{mus}| < 0.9 \cdot |S_{max}|$ **then**
17              $P \leftarrow$ subset such that $S_{mus} \subset P \subset S_{max}, |P| = 0.9 \cdot |S_{max}|$
18   FindMUSes $(P, criticals)$

---

by adding a corresponding number of constraints from S_{max} to S_{mus}. Note that it might happen that $|S_{mus}| \geq 0.9 \cdot |S_{max}|$; in such a case the algorithm skips the recursion call and continues with the next iteration.

The set $Unexplored$ is updated appropriately during the whole computation. Note that the set $Unexplored$ is shared among the individual recursive calls; in particular if the algorithm determines some subset S to be unsatisfiable then all of its supersets (w.r.t. the original search space) are deduced to be unsatisfiable. On the other hand, the maximal unexplored subsets (and their complements) are local and are defined with respect to the current search space.

Correctness. The algorithm outputs only the results of *shrinking* which is assumed to be a correct MUS extraction procedure. Each MUS is produced only once since only unexplored subsets are shrunk and each MUS is removed from the set $Unexplored$ immediately after producing. Only subsets whose status is known are removed from the set $Unexplored$ thus no MUS is excluded from the computation. The algorithm terminates and all MUSes are found since the size of $Unexplored$ is reduced after every iteration.

4   Related Work

The list of existing approaches to the MUS enumeration problem is short, especially compared to the amount of work dealing with a single MUS extraction [6–9,31,33]. Moreover, existing algorithms for the MUS enumeration are tailored mainly to Boolean constraints [2,3,22,24] and cannot be applied to other constraints. The approaches that focus on MUS enumeration in general constraint systems can be divided into two categories: approaches that compute MUSes directly and those that rely on the *hitting set duality*.

Direct MUS enumeration. The early algorithms were based on explicit enumeration of every subset of the unsatisfiable constraint system. As far as we know, the MUS enumeration was pioneered by Hou [26] in the field of diagnosis. Hou's algorithm checks every subset for satisfiability starting with the whole set of constraints and exploring its power set in a tree-like structure. Also, some pruning rules that allow skipping irrelevant branches are presented. This approach was revisited and further improved by Han and Lee [25] and by de la Banda et al. [18]. Another approach using step-by-step powerset exploration was recently proposed by Bauch et al. [5]. The authors of this work focus on constraints expressed using LTL formulas; however, their algorithm can be used for any type of constraints. Explicit exploration of the power set is the bottleneck of all of the above mentioned algorithms as the size of the power set is exponential to the number of constraints in the system.

Liffiton et al. [27] and Silva et al. [35] developed independently two nearly identical algorithms: MARCO [27] and eMUS [35]. Both algorithms were later merged and presented [28] under the name of MARCO. Among the existing MUS enumeration algorithms, MARCO is perhaps the one most similar to ReMUS. It uses symbolic representation of the power set and is able to produce MUSes incrementally during its computation in a relatively steady rate. In order to find individual MUSes, it iteratively picks maximal unexplored subsets of the original set of constraints and checks them for satisfiability. The unsatisfiable subsets are shrunk, using a black-box procedure, into MUSes. Contrary to ReMUS, MARCO does not tend to reduce the size of the sets to be shrunk and thus to directly reduce the number of performed satisfiability checks. Instead, it assumes that the black-box shrinking procedure would do the trick. MARCO is very efficient in constraint domains for which efficient shrink procedures exist. However, in the other domains, it is less efficient. This is mainly due to the fact that it shrinks the maximal unexplored subsets of the original set of constraints, i.e. it shrinks relatively large sets.

In our previous work [11], we have presented the algorithm TOME that also produces MUSes in an online manner. It iteratively uses binary search to find the so-called local MUSes/MSSes. Each local MUS/MSS is optionally, based on its size (cardinality), shrunk/grown to a global MUS/MSS. TOME tries to predict the complexity of performing the shrinking/growing procedure and only those shrinks/grows that seem to be easy to perform are actually performed. TOME is very efficient in constraint domains for which no efficient shrinking and growing procedure exist. On the other hand, in domains like Boolean constraints, the effort needed to find local MUSes and MSSes outweighs the effort needed to perform the shrinks and grows.

Hitting set duality based approaches. There is a well known relationship between MUSes and MCSes based on the concept of *hitting sets*. Given a collection Ω of sets, a hitting set H for Ω is a set such that $\forall S \in \Omega : H \cap S \neq \emptyset$. A hitting set is called *minimal* if none of its proper subsets is a hitting set. If C is a set of constraints and $N \subseteq C$, then the *minimal hitting set duality* [36] claims that N is a MUS of C iff N is a minimal hitting set of the set of all the MCSes of C.

The hitting set duality is used for example in CAMUS [29] and DAA [4]. CAMUS works in two phases. It first computes all MCSes of a given constraint set and then finds all MUSes by computing all minimal hitting sets of these MCSes. A significant shortcoming of CAMUS is that the first phase can be intractable as the number of MCSes can be exponential in the number of constraints and all MCSes must be found before the first MUS can be produced.

The algorithm DAA [4] is able to produce some MUSes before the enumeration of MCSes is completed. DAA starts each iteration with computing a minimal hitting set H of currently known MCSes and tests H for satisfiability. If H is unsatisfiable, it is guaranteed to be a MUS. In the other case, H is *grown* into a MSS whose complement is a MCS, i.e. the set of known MCSes is enlarged. As in the case of MARCO, DAA can use any existing algorithm for a single MSS/MCS extraction to perform the grow.

MARCO, CAMUS and DAA were experimentally compared in the Boolean constraints domain [28] and CAMUS has shown to be the fastest in enumerating all MUSes in the tractable cases. However, in the intractable cases, MARCO was able to produce at least some MUSes, while CAMUS often got stuck in the phase of MCSes enumeration. DAA was much slower than CAMUS in the case of complete MUSes enumeration and also slower than MARCO in the case of partial MUS enumeration. The main drawbacks of DAA are the complexity of computing minimal hitting sets and no guarantee on the rate of MUS production.

Bacchus and Katsirelos proposed a MUS enumeration algorithm called MCS-MUS-BT [3] which is also based on recursion and uses MCSes to extract critical constraints. However, the algorithm is tailored for the SAT domain and, thus, cannot be applied in an arbitrary constraint domain. Moreover, the computation of MCSes is an integral part of MCS-MUS-BT, and the MCSes are computed in a different way taking up to linearly many satisfiability checks to compute each MCS. MCS-MUS-BT does not use black-box shrinking procedures and the recursion is not driven by previously found MUSes.

5   Implementation

We implemented ReMUS into a publicly available tool[1]. The tool currently supports three different constraint domains: SAT (Boolean constraints), SMT, and LTL. It employs several external tools. In particular, it uses the SAT solver miniSAT [21] for maintaining $f_{Unexplored}$, and miniSAT is also used as a satisfiability solver in the SAT domain. The tools Z3 [19] and SPOT [20] are used as satisfiability solvers in the SMT and LTL domains, respectively. Moreover, our tool uses the single MUS extractor MUSer2 [8] as a black-box shrink subroutine in the SAT domain. In the other domains, we use our custom implementation of the shrinking procedures.

6   Experimental Evaluation

Here, we report results of our experimental evaluation. Besides evaluating ReMUS, we also provide a comparison with the latest tool implementation[2] of the state-of-the-art MUS enumeration algorithm MARCO [28]. The comparison is done in the SAT and SMT domains since these are the domains supported by the MARCO tool. Note that MARCO uses the same external procedures as ReMUS, i.e. a satisfiability solver, a shrinking procedure, and a SAT solver for maintaining unexplored subsets. All these external procedures are implemented in the MARCO tool in the same way as in the ReMUS tool, i.e. using miniSAT [21], Z3 [19], and MUSer2 [8].

There are three main criteria for the comparison: (1) the number of output MUSes within a given time limit, (2) the number of satisfiability checks required to output individual MUSes, and (3) the time required to output individual MUSes.

6.1   Benchmarks and Experimental Setup

The experiments in the SAT domain were conducted on a collection of 292 Boolean CNF benchmarks that were taken from the MUS track of the SAT 2011 competition[3]. The benchmarks range in their size from 70 to 16 million constraints and use from 26 to 4.4 million variables. This collection of benchmarks has been already used in several papers that focus on the problem of MUS enumeration, see e.g. [11,27–29]. In the SMT domain, we used a set of 433 benchmarks that were used in the work by Griggio et al. [14]. The benchmarks were selected from the library SMT-LIB[4], and include instances from the QF_UF, QF_IDL, QF_RDL, QF_LIA and QF_LRA divisions. The size of the benchmarks ranges from 5 to 145422 constraints.

---

[1] https://www.fi.muni.cz/~xbendik/remus/.

[2] https://sun.iwu.edu/~mliffito/marco/.

[3] http://www.cril.univ-artois.fr/SAT11/.

[4] http://www.smt-lib.org/.

The experiments were run on an Intel(R) Xeon (R) CPU E5-2630 v2, 2.60GHz, 125 GB memory machine running Arch Linux 4.9.40-l-lts. All experiments were run using a time limit of 3600 s. Complete results are available at https://www.fi.muni.cz/~xbendik/remus/.

7   Experimental Results

7.1   Number of Output MUSes

In this section, we examine the performance of evaluated algorithms in terms of number of produced MUSes within the given time limit of 3600 s. Due to the potentially exponentially many MUSes in each instance, the complete MUS enumeration is generally intractable. Moreover, even producing a single MUS can be intractable for larger instances as it naturally includes solving the satisfiability problem, which is hard to solve in the SAT and SMT domains. Within the given time limit, both algorithms found more than two MUSes in only 216 SAT and 238 SMT instances. Furthermore, both algorithms finished the computation in only 24 SAT and 245 SMT instances.

Figure 3 provides scatter plots that compare both evaluated algorithms on individual benchmarks in the SAT and SMT domains. Each point in the plot represents the result achieved by the two compared algorithms on one particular instance; one algorithm determines the position on the vertical axis and the other one the position on the horizontal axis. MARCO found strictly more MUSes than ReMUS in 76 SAT and 15 SMT instances. On the other hand, ReMUS found strictly more MUSes than MARCO in 162 SAT and 118 SMT instances. Note

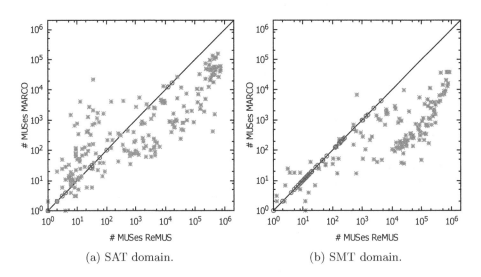

(a) SAT domain.   (b) SMT domain.

Fig. 3. Scatter plots comparing the number of produced MUSes. Blue points represent the benchmarks where both algorithms finished the computation.

that in the SMT domain, ReMUS was often better than MARCO by two orders of magnitude.

7.2   Performed Checks per MUS

In this section, we focus on the main optimisation criterion of our algorithm: the number of checks required to output individual MUSes. This number differs for different benchmarks since individual benchmarks vary in many aspects such as the size of the benchmarks and the size of the MUSes contained in the benchmarks. Therefore, we focus on average values. Plots in Fig. 4 show the average number of performed satisfiability checks required to output the first 750 MUSes. A point with coordinates (x, y) states that the algorithm needed to perform y satisfiability checks on average in order to output the first x MUSes. We used only a subset of the benchmarks to compute the average values since only for some benchmarks both algorithms found at least 750 MUSes. In particular, 70 and 51 benchmarks were used to compute the average values in the SAT and SMT domains, respectively.

ReMUS is clearly superior to MARCO in the number of satisfiability checks required to output individual MUSes. This happens both due to the fact that ReMUS gradually, in a recursive way, reduces the dimension of the search space (and thus shrink smaller seeds), as well as due the fact that ReMUS mines and accumulates critical constraints to speed up the shrinking procedures.

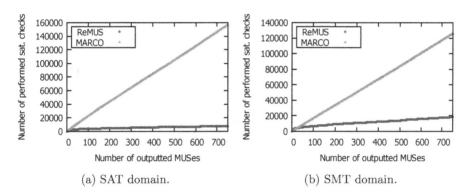

(a) SAT domain.   (b) SMT domain.

Fig. 4. Plots showing the average number of performed satisfiability checks required to output individual MUSes.

7.3   Elapsed Time per MUS

The fact that ReMUS requires less satisfiability checks than MARCO to output individual MUSes does not necessarily mean that it is also faster than MARCO in producing individual MUSes. The time spent by ReMUS to maintain the recursive calls while trying to save some satisfiability checks might not be worth it if the checks are easy to perform. We need to answer a domain specific question: is the price of performing satisfiability checks high enough?

To answer this question for the SAT and SMT domains, we took the 70 SAT and 51 SMT benchmarks in which both algorithms produced at least 750 MUSes and computed the average amount of time required to output individual MUSes. The results are shown in Fig. 5. A point with coordinates (x, y) states that in order to output the first x MUSes the algorithm required y seconds on average. In the SMT domain, ReMUS is significantly faster from the very beginning of the computation. In the SAT domain, MARCO is faster during the first three minutes, yet afterwards ReMUS becomes much faster.

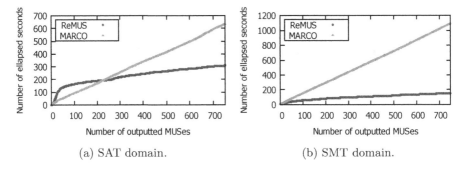

(a) SAT domain.   (b) SMT domain.

Fig. 5. Plots showing the average amount of time required to output individual MUSes.

7.4   Evaluation

Experimental results demonstrate that ReMUS outperformed MARCO on almost all the SMT instances and on a majority of the SAT instances. However, on some SAT instances, ReMUS was quite struggling, especially at the beginning of the computation. Here, we point out three characteristics of benchmarks/domains that affect the performance of ReMUS.

First, ReMUS tends to minimise the number of performed satisfiability checks. Therefore, the higher the complexity of the satisfiability checks, the more is the tendency to minimise the number of performed checks worth it. Second, the motivation behind finding small seeds for shrinking procedure is based on the fact that, in general, the larger the seed is, the more satisfiability checks are required. However, some constraint domains might enjoy domain specific properties that allow to shrink the seed very efficiently, regardless of the size of the seed. In particular, the CNF form of Boolean (SAT) formulas allows to significantly reduce the number of performed satisfiability checks [6,8,33]. Finally, the reduction of the search space is driven by the previously found MUSes. In order to perform deep recursion calls, the input instance has to contain many MUSes. Moreover, there have to be some similar MUSes, i.e. there has to be a subset that is relatively small and yet contains several MUSes.

In the SMT domain, the shrinking procedures are currently not so advanced as in the SAT domain, and the complexity of the satisfiability checks in the SMT domain is often larger than in the SAT domain. Thus, even a small reduction of the size of the seeds leads to a notable improvement in the overall efficiency. On the other hand, in the SAT domain, either a significant reduction of the size of the seeds (i.e. deep recursion calls) or a large number of cumulated critical constraints is required to speed up the shrinking.

8   Conclusion

We have presented the algorithm ReMUS for online enumeration of MUSes that is applicable to an arbitrary constraint domain. We observed that the time required to output individual MUSes generally correlates with the number of satisfiability checks performed to output the MUSes. The novelty of our algorithm lies in exploiting both the domain specific as well as domain agnostic properties of the MUS enumeration problem to reduce the number of performed satisfiability checks, and thus also reduce the time required to output individual MUSes. The main idea of the algorithm is to recursively search for MUSes in smaller and smaller subsets of a given set of constraints. Moreover, the algorithm cumulates critical constraints and uses them to speed up single MUS extraction subroutines. We have experimentally compared ReMUS with the state-of-the-art MUS enumeration algorithm MARCO in the SAT and SMT domains. The results show that the tendency to minimise the number of performed satisfiability checks leads to a significant improvement over the state-of-the-art.

References

1. Zaher, S.A., Mark, HL., Karem A.S.: Cegar-based formal hardware verification: a case study. Ann Arbor (2007)
2. Bacchus, F., Katsirelos, G.: Using minimal correction sets to more efficiently compute minimal unsatisfiable sets. In: Kroening, Daniel, Păsăreanu, Corina S. (eds.) CAV (2). LNCS, vol. 9207, pp. 70–86. Springer, Cham (2015). https://doi.org/10.1007/978-3-319-21668-3_5
3. Bacchus, F., Katsirelos, G.: Finding a collection of MUSes incrementally. In: CPAIOR (2016)
4. Bailey, J., Stuckey, P.J.: Discovery of minimal unsatisfiable subsets of constraints using hitting set dualization. In: Hermenegildo, M.V., Cabeza, D. (eds.) PADL 2005. LNCS, vol. 3350, pp. 174–186. Springer, Heidelberg (2005). https://doi.org/10.1007/978-3-540-30557-6_14
5. Barnat, J., Bauch, P., Beneš, N., Brim, L., Beran, J., Kratochvíla, T.: Analysing sanity of requirements for avionics systems. Formal Aspects of Computing (2016)
6. Belov, A., Heule, M., Marques-Silva, J.: MUS extraction using clausal proofs. In: SAT (2014)
7. Belov, A., Marques-Silva, J.: Accelerating MUS extraction with recursive model rotation. In: FMCAD (2011)
8. Belov, A., Marques-Silva, J.: MUSer2: An efficient MUS extractor. J. Satisf. Boolean Model. Comput. (2012)

9. Belov, A., Marques Silva, J.P.: Minimally unsatisfiable boolean circuits. In: SAT (2011)
10. Bendík, J.: Consistency checking in requirements analysis. In: ISSTA (2017)
11. Bendík, J., Benes, N., Cerná, I., Barnat, J: Tunable online MUS/MSS enumeration. In: FSTTCS (2016)
12. Bendík, J., Ghassabani, E., Whalen, M., Černá, I.: Online enumeration of all minimal inductive validity cores. In: Johnsen, E.B., Schaefer, I. (eds.) SEFM 2018. LNCS, vol. 10886, pp. 189–204. Springer, Cham (2018). https://doi.org/10.1007/978-3-319-92970-5_12
13. Chen, H., Marques-Silva, J.: Improvements to satisfiability-based boolean function bi-decomposition. In: VLSI-SoC (2011)
14. Cimatti, A., Griggio, A., Sebastiani, R.: Computing small unsatisfiable cores in satisfiability modulo theories. J. Artif. Intell. Res. (2011)
15. Clarke, E.M., Emerson, E.A.: Design and synthesis of synchronization skeletons using branching-time temporal logic. In: Logic of Programs (1981)
16. Clarke, E.M., Grumberg, Jha, S., Lu, Y., Veith, H,.: Counterexample-guided abstraction refinement. In: CAV (2000)
17. Cohen, O., Gordon, M., Lifshits, M., Nadel, A., Ryvchin, V.: Designers work less with quality formal equivalence checking. In: Design and Verification Conference (DVCon) (2010)
18. de la Banda, M.G., Stuckey, P.J., Wazny, J.: Finding all minimal unsatisfiable subsets. In: Proceedings of the 5th ACM SIGPLAN International Conference on Principles and Practice of Declaritive Programming (2003)
19. de Moura, L.M., Bjørner, N..: Z3: an efficient SMT solver. In: TACAS (2008)
20. Duret-Lutz, A., Lewkowicz, A., Fauchille, A., Michaud, T., Renault, E., Xu, L.: Spot 2.0 – a framework for LTL and ω-automata manipulation. In: ATVA (2016)
21. Eén, N., Sörensson, A.: An extensible sat-solver. In: SAT (2003)
22. Gasca, R.M., Del Valle, C., Gómez López, M.T., Ceballos, R.: NMUS: structural analysis for improving the derivation of all muses in over constrained numeric csps. In: CAEPIA (2007)
23. Ghassabani, E., Whalen, M.W., Gacek, A.: Efficient generation of all minimal inductive validity cores. In: FMCAD (2017)
24. Gleeson, J., Ryan, J.: Identifying minimally infeasible subsystems of inequalities. INFORMS J. Comput. (1990)
25. Han, B., Lee, S.-J.: Deriving minimal conflict sets by cs-trees with mark set in diagnosis from first principles. IEEE Trans. Syst. Man Cybern. Part B (1999)
26. Hou, A.: A theory of measurement in diagnosis from first principles. Artif. Intell. (1994)
27. Liffiton, M.H., Malik, A.: Enumerating infeasibility: finding multiple muses quickly. In: Gomes, C., Sellmann, M. (eds.) CPAIOR 2013. LNCS, vol. 7874, pp. 160–175. Springer, Heidelberg (2013). https://doi.org/10.1007/978-3-642-38171-3_11
28. Liffiton, M.H., Previti, A., Malik, A., Marques-Silva, J.: Fast, flexible MUS enumeration. Constraints (2015)
29. Liffiton, M.H., Sakallah, K.A.: Algorithms for computing minimal unsatisfiable subsets of constraints. J. Autom. Reason. (2008)
30. McMillan, K.L., Amla, N.: Automatic abstraction without counterexamples. In: TACAS (2003)
31. Nadel, A.: Boosting minimal unsatisfiable core extraction. In: FMCAD (2010)
32. Nadel, A., Ryvchin, V., Strichman, O.: Efficient MUS extraction with resolution. In: FMCAD (2013)

33. Nadel, A., Ryvchin, V., Strichman, O.: Accelerated deletion-based extraction of minimal unsatisfiable cores. In: JSAT (2014)
34. Pnueli, A.: The temporal logic of programs. In: FOCS (1977)
35. Previti, A., Marques-Silva, J.: Partial MUS enumeration. In: Proceedings of the Twenty-Seventh AAAI Conference on Artificial Intelligence, Bellevue, 14–18 July 2013
36. Reiter, R.: A theory of diagnosis from first principles. Artif. Intell. (1987)
37. Stuckey, P.J., Sulzmann, M., Wazny, J.: Interactive type debugging in haskell. In: Haskell (2003)

Synthesis in pMDPs: A Tale of 1001 Parameters

Murat Cubuktepe[1], Nils Jansen[2], Sebastian Junges[3(✉)], Joost-Pieter Katoen[3], and Ufuk Topcu[1]

[1] The University of Texas at Austin, Austin, TX, USA
[2] Radboud University, Nijmegen, The Netherlands
[3] RWTH Aachen University, Aachen, Germany
`sebastian.junges@rwth-aachen.de`

Abstract. This paper considers parametric Markov decision processes (pMDPs) whose transitions are equipped with affine functions over a finite set of parameters. The synthesis problem is to find a parameter valuation such that the instantiated pMDP satisfies a (temporal logic) specification under all strategies. We show that this problem can be formulated as a quadratically-constrained quadratic program (QCQP) and is non-convex in general. To deal with the NP-hardness of such problems, we exploit a convex-concave procedure (CCP) to iteratively obtain local optima. An appropriate interplay between CCP solvers and probabilistic model checkers creates a procedure—realized in the tool PROPheSY— that solves the synthesis problem for models with thousands of parameters.

1 Introduction

The parameter synthesis problem. Probabilistic model checking concerns the automatic verification of models such as Markov decision processes (MDPs). Unremitting improvements in algorithms and efficient tool implementations [15, 23,27] have opened up a wide variety of applications, most notably in dependability, security, and performance analysis as well as systems biology. However, at early development stages, certain system quantities such as fault or reaction rates are often not fully known. This lack of information gives rise to parametric models where transitions are functions over real-valued parameters [13,22,28], forming symbolic descriptions of (uncountable) families of concrete MDPs. The *parameter synthesis problem* is: Given a finite-state parametric MDP, find a parameter instantiation such that the induced concrete model satisfies a given specification. An inherent problem is *model repair*, where probabilities are changed ("repaired") with respect to parameters such that a model satisfies

---

Supported by the grants ONR N000141613165, NASA NNX17AD04G and AFRL FA8650-15-C-2546

Supported by the CDZ project CAP (GZ 1023), and the DFG RTG 2236 "UnRAVeL".

S. K. Lahiri and C. Wang (Eds.): ATVA 2018, LNCS 11138, pp. 160–176, 2018.
https://doi.org/10.1007/978-3-030-01090-4_10

a specification [5]. Concrete applications include adaptive software systems [9], sensitivity analysis [34], and optimizing randomized distributed algorithms [1].

State-of-the-art. First approaches to parameter synthesis compute a rational function over the parameters to symbolically express reachability probabilities [13,19,22]. Equivalently,[18,24] employ Gaussian elimination for matrices over the field of rational functions. Solving the (potentially very large, high-degree) functions is naturally a SAT-modulo theories (SMT) problem over nonlinear arithmetic, or a nonlinear program (NLP) [5,12]. However, solving such SMT problems is *exponential in the degree of functions and the number of variables* [24], and solving NLPs is *NP-hard in general* [29]. Specific approaches to model repair rely on NLP [5] or particle-swarm optimization (PSO) [10].

Finally, parameter synthesis is equivalent to computing finite-memory strategies for partially observable MDPs (POMDPs) [26]. Such strategies may be obtained, for instance, by employing sequential quadratic programming (SQP) [3]. Exploiting this approach is not practical, though, because SQP for our setting already requires a (feasible) solution satisfying the given specification. Overall, efficient implementations in tools like PARAM [22], PRISM [27], and PROPhESY [14] can handle thousands of states but only a *handful of parameters*.

Our approach. We overcome the restriction to few parameters by employing convex optimization [7]. This direction is not new; [12] describes a convexification of the NLP into a geometric program [6], which can still only handle up to about ten parameters. We take a different approach. First, we transform the NLP formulation [5,12] into a *quadratically-constrained quadratic program* (QCQP). As such an optimization problem is nonconvex in general, we cannot resort to polynomial-time algorithms for convex QCQPs [2]. Instead, to solve our NP-hard problem, we massage the QCQP formulation into a *difference-of-convex* (DC) problem. The convex-concave procedure (CCP) [30] yields local optima of a DC problem by a convexification towards a convex quadratic program, which is amenable for state-of-the-art solvers such as Gurobi [20].

Yet, blackbox CCP solvers [32,33] suffer from severe numerical issues and can only solve very small problems. We integrate the procedure with a probabilistic model checker, creating a method that—realized in the open-source tool PROPhESY [14]—yields (a) an improvement of multiple orders of magnitude compared to just using CCP as a black box and (b) ensures the correctness of the solution. In particular, we use probabilistic model checking to:

- rule out feasible solutions that may be spurious due to numerical errors,
- check if intermediate solutions are already feasible for earlier termination,
- compute concrete probabilities from intermediate parameter instantiations to avoid potential numerical instabilities.

An extensive empirical evaluation on a large range of benchmarks shows that our approach can solve the parameter synthesis problem for models with large state spaces and up to thousands of parameters, and is superior to all existing parameter synthesis tools [14,21,27], geometric programming [12], and an efficient re-implementation of PSO [10] that we create to deliver a better comparison. Contrary to the geometric programming approach in [12], we compute solutions that hold for all possible (adversarial) schedulers for parametric MDPs. Traditionally, model checking delivers results for such adversarial schedulers [4], which are for instance useful when the nondeterminism is not controllable and induced by the environment, which is the case in the example below.

An illustrative example. Consider the Carrier Sense Multiple Access/Collision Detection (CSMA/CD) protocol in Ethernet networks, which was subject to probabilistic model checking [17]. When two stations simultaneously attempt sending a packet (giving rise to a collision), a so-called randomized exponential back-off mechanism is used to avoid the collision. Until the k-th attempt, a delay out of 2^k possibilities is randomly drawn from a uniform distribution. An interesting question is if a uniform distribution is optimal, where optimality refers to the minimal expected time until all packets have been sent. A bias for small delays seems beneficial, but raises the collision probability. Using our novel techniques, within a minute we synthesize a different distribution, which induces less expected time compared to the uniform distribution. The used model has about 10^5 states and 26 parameters. We are not aware of any other parameter-synthesis approach being able to generate such a result within reasonable time.

2   Preliminaries

A *probability distribution* over a finite or countably infinite set X is a function $\mu\colon X \to [0, 1] \subseteq \mathbb{R}$ with $\sum_{x \in X} \mu(x) = 1$. The set of all distributions on X is denoted by $Distr(X)$. Let $V = \{x_1, \ldots, x_n\}$ be a finite set of *variables* over the real numbers $\mathbb{R}$. The set of multivariate polynomials over V is $\mathbb{Q}[V]$. An *instantiation* for V is a function $u\colon V \to \mathbb{R}$.

A function $f\colon \mathbb{R}^n \to \mathbb{R}$ is *affine* if $f(\boldsymbol{x}) = a^T \boldsymbol{x} + b$ with $a \in \mathbb{R}^n$ and $b \in \mathbb{R}$, and $f\colon \mathbb{R}^n \to \mathbb{R}$ is *quadratic* if $f(\boldsymbol{x}) = \boldsymbol{x}^T P \boldsymbol{x} + a^T \boldsymbol{x} + b$ with a, b as before and $P \in \mathbb{R}^{n \times n}$. A symmetric matrix $P \in \mathbb{R}^{n \times n}$ is *positive semidefinite* (PSD) if $\boldsymbol{x}^T P \boldsymbol{x} \geq 0 \ \forall \boldsymbol{x} \in \mathbb{R}^n$, or equivalently, if all eigenvalues of P are nonnegative.

Definition 1 ((Affine) pMDP) A *parametric Markov decision process (pMDP)* is a tuple $\mathcal{M} = (S, s_I, Act, V, \mathcal{P})$ with a finite set S of *states*, an *initial state* $s_I \in S$, a finite set Act of *actions*, a finite set V of real-valued variables *(parameters)* and a *transition function* $\mathcal{P}\colon S \times Act \times S \to \mathbb{Q}[V]$. A pMDP is *affine* if $\mathcal{P}(s, \alpha, s')$ is affine for every $s, s' \in S$ and $\alpha \in Act$.

For $s \in S$, $A(s) = \{\alpha \in Act \mid \exists s' \in S. \mathcal{P}(s, \alpha, s') \neq 0\}$ is the set of *enabled* actions at s. Without loss of generality, we require $A(s) \neq \emptyset$ for $s \in S$. If $|A(s)| = 1$ for all $s \in S$, $\mathcal{M}$ is a *parametric discrete-time Markov chain (pMC)*. We denote the transition function for pMCs by $\mathcal{P}(s, s')$. MDPs can be equipped with a state–action *cost function* $c\colon S \times Act \to \mathbb{R}_{\geq 0}$.

A pMDP $\mathcal{M}$ is a *Markov decision process (MDP)* if the transition function yields *well-defined* probability distributions, i.e., $\mathcal{P}\colon S \times Act \times S \to [0, 1]$ and $\sum_{s' \in S} \mathcal{P}(s, \alpha, s') = 1$ for all $s \in S$ and $\alpha \in A(s)$. Applying an *instantiation*

$u\colon V \to \mathbb{R}$ to a pMDP $\mathcal{M}$ yields $\mathcal{M}[u]$ by replacing each $f \in \mathbb{Q}[V]$ in $\mathcal{M}$ by $f[u]$. An instantiation u is *well-defined* for $\mathcal{M}$ if the resulting model $\mathcal{M}[u]$ is an MDP.

To define measures on MDPs, nondeterministic choices are resolved by a so-called *strategy* $\sigma\colon S \to Act$ with $\sigma(s) \in A(s)$. The set of all strategies over $\mathcal{M}$ is $Str^{\mathcal{M}}$. For the measures in this paper, memoryless deterministic strategies suffice [4]. Applying a strategy to an MDP yields an *induced Markov chain* where all nondeterminism is resolved.

For an MC $\mathcal{D}$, the *reachability specification* $\varphi_r = \mathbb{P}_{\leq\lambda}(\Diamond T)$ asserts that a set $T \subseteq S$ of *target states* is reached with probability at most $\lambda \in [0,1]$. If φ_r holds for $\mathcal{D}$, we write $\mathcal{D} \models \varphi_r$. Accordingly, for an *expected cost specification* $\varphi_c = \mathbb{E}_{\leq\kappa}(\Diamond G)$ it holds that $\mathcal{D} \models \varphi_c$ if and only if the expected cost of reaching a set $G \subseteq S$ is bounded by $\kappa \in \mathbb{R}$. We use standard measures and definitions as in [4, Ch. 10]. An MDP $\mathcal{M}$ satisfies a specification φ, written $\mathcal{M} \models \varphi$, if and only if *for all* strategies $\sigma \in Str^{\mathcal{M}}$ it holds that $\mathcal{M}^\sigma \models \varphi$.

3   Formal Problem Statement

Problem 1 (pMDP synthesis problem) Given a pMDP $\mathcal{M} = (S, s_I, Act, V, \mathcal{P})$, and a reachability specification $\varphi_r = \mathbb{P}_{\leq\lambda}(\Diamond T)$, compute a well-defined instantiation $u\colon V \to \mathbb{R}$ for $\mathcal{M}$ such that $\mathcal{M}[u] \models \varphi_r$.

Intuitively, we seek for an instantiation of parameters u that satisfies φ_r for all possible strategies for the instantiated MDP. We show necessary adaptions for an expected cost specification $\varphi_c = \mathbb{E}_{\leq\kappa}(\Diamond T)$ later.

For a given instantiation u, Problem 1 boils down to verifying if $\mathcal{M}[u] \models \varphi_r$. The standard formulation uses a linear program (LP) to minimize the probability p_{s_I} of reaching the target set T from the initial state s_I, while ensuring that this probability is realizable under any strategy [4, Ch. 10]. The straightforward extension of this approach to pMDPs in order to *compute* a suitable instantiation u yields the following nonlinear program (NLP):

$$\text{minimize} \quad p_{s_I} \tag{1}$$

$$\text{subject to}$$

$$\forall s \in T. \quad p_s = 1 \tag{2}$$

$$\forall s, s' \in S. \forall \alpha \in Act. \quad \mathcal{P}(s, \alpha, s') \geq 0 \tag{3}$$

$$\forall s \in S. \forall \alpha \in Act. \quad \sum_{s' \in S} \mathcal{P}(s, \alpha, s') = 1 \tag{4}$$

$$\lambda \geq p_{s_I} \tag{5}$$

$$\forall s \in S \setminus T. \forall \alpha \in Act. \quad p_s \geq \sum_{s' \in S} \mathcal{P}(s, \alpha, s') \cdot p_{s'}. \tag{6}$$

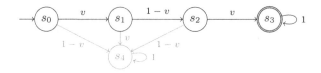

Fig. 1. A pMC with parameter v

For $s \in S$, the *probability variable* $p_s \in [0,1]$ represents an upper bound of the probability of reaching target set $T \subseteq S$, and the *parameters* in set V enter the NLP as part of the functions from $\mathbb{Q}[V]$ in the transition function $\mathcal{P}$.

Proposition 1. *The NLP in* (1)–(6) *computes the* minimal probability *of reaching T under a* maximizing *strategy.*

The probability to reach a state in T from T is one (2). The constraints (3) and (4) ensure *well-defined* transition probabilities. Constraint (5) is optional but necessary later, and ensures that the probability of reaching T is below the threshold λ. For each non-target state $s \in S$ and any action $\alpha \in Act$, the probability induced by the *maximizing scheduler* is a lower bound to the probability variables p_s (6). To assign probability variables the minimal values with respect to the parameters from V, p_{s_I} is minimized in the objective (1).

Remark 1 (Graph-preserving instantiations) In the LP formulation for MDPs, states with probability 0 to reach T are determined via a preprocessing on the underlying graph, and their probability variables are set to zero, to avoid an underdetermined equation system. For the same reason, we preserve the underlying graph of the pMDP, as in [14,22]. We thus exclude valuations u with $f[u] = 0$ for $f \in \mathcal{P}(s, \alpha, s')$ for all $s, s' \in S$ and $\alpha \in Act$. We replace (3) by

$$\forall s, s' \in S. \forall \alpha \in Act. \quad \mathcal{P}(s, \alpha, s') \geq \varepsilon_{\text{graph}}. \tag{7}$$

where $\varepsilon_{\text{graph}} > 0$ is a small constant.

Example 1 Consider the pMC in Fig. 1 with parameter set $V = \{v\}$, initial state s_0, and target set $T = \{s_3\}$. Let λ be an arbitrary constant. The NLP in (8)–(13) minimizes the probability of reaching s_3 from the initial state:

$$\text{minimize} \quad p_{s_0} \tag{8}$$
$$\text{subject to}$$
$$p_{s_3} = 1 \tag{9}$$
$$\lambda \geq p_{s_0} \geq v \cdot p_{s_1} \tag{10}$$
$$p_{s_1} \geq (1 - v) \cdot p_{s_2} \tag{11}$$
$$p_{s_2} \geq v \cdot p_{s_3} \tag{12}$$
$$1 - \varepsilon_{\text{graph}} \geq v \geq \varepsilon_{\text{graph}}. \tag{13}$$

Expected cost specifications. The NLP in (1)–(7) considers reachability probabilities. If we have instead an expected cost specification $\varphi_c = \mathbb{E}_{\leq \kappa}(\lozenge G)$, we replace (2), (5), and (6) in the NLP by the following constraints:

$$\forall s \in G. \quad p_s = 0, \tag{14}$$

$$\forall s \in S \setminus G. \forall \alpha \in A(s). \quad p_s \geq c(s, \alpha) + \sum_{s' \in S} \mathcal{P}(s, \alpha, s') \cdot p_{s'} \tag{15}$$

$$\kappa \geq p_{s_I}. \tag{16}$$

We have $p_s \in \mathbb{R}$, as these variables represent the expected cost to reach G. At G, the expected cost is set to zero (14), and the actual expected cost for other states is a lower bound to p_s (15). Finally, p_{s_I} is bounded by the threshold κ.

4   QCQP Reformulation of the pMDP Synthesis Problem

For the remainder of this paper, we restrict pMDPs to be affine, see Def. 1. For an affine pMDP $\mathcal{M}$, the functions in the resulting NLP (1)–(7) for pMDP synthesis from the previous section are affine in V. However, the functions in (6) are *quadratic*, as a result of multiplying affine functions occurring in $\mathcal{P}$ with the probability variables $p_{s'}$. We rewrite the NLP as a standard form of a *quadratically-constrained quadratic program* (QCQP) [7]. Afterwards, we examine this QCQP in detail and show that it is nonconvex.

In general, a QCQP is an optimization problem with a quadratic objective function and m quadratic constraints, written as

$$\text{minimize} \quad \boldsymbol{x}^T P_0 \boldsymbol{x} + q_0^T \boldsymbol{x} + r_0 \tag{17}$$
$$\text{subject to}$$
$$\forall i \in \{1, \dots, m\} \quad \boldsymbol{x}^T P_i \boldsymbol{x} + q_i^T \boldsymbol{x} + r_i \leq 0, \tag{18}$$

where $\boldsymbol{x}$ is a vector of *variables*, and the coefficients are $P_i \in \mathbb{R}^{n \times n}$, $q_i \in \mathbb{R}^n$, $r_i \in \mathbb{R}$ for $0 \leq i \leq m$. We assume $P_0, \dots, P_m$ are symmetric without loss of generality. Constraints of the form $\boldsymbol{x}^T P_i \boldsymbol{x} + q_i^T \boldsymbol{x} + r_i = 0$ are encoded by

$$\boldsymbol{x}^T P_i \boldsymbol{x} + q_i^T \boldsymbol{x} + r_i \leq 0 \text{ and } -\boldsymbol{x}^T P_i \boldsymbol{x} - q_i^T \boldsymbol{x} - r_i \leq 0.$$

Properties of QCQPs. We discuss properties of all matrices P_i for $0 \leq i \leq m$. If all $P_i = 0$, the function $q_i^T \boldsymbol{x} + r_i$ is *affine*, and the QCQP is in fact an LP. If every P_i is PSD, the function $\boldsymbol{x}^T P_i \boldsymbol{x} + q_i^T \boldsymbol{x} + r_i$ is *convex*, and the QCQP is a *convex optimization problem*, that can be solved in polynomial time [2]. If any P_i is not PSD, the resulting QCQP is nonconvex. The problem of finding a feasible solution in a nonconvex QCQP is NP-hard [8].

To ease the presentation, we transform the quadratic constraints in the NLP in (1)–(7) to the standard QCQP form in (17)–(18):

$$\text{minimize} \quad p_{s_I} \tag{19}$$

$$\text{subject to}$$

$$\forall s \in T. \quad p_s = 1 \tag{20}$$

$$\forall s, s' \in S. \forall \alpha \in A(s). \quad \mathcal{P}(s, \alpha, s') \geq \varepsilon_{\text{graph}} \tag{21}$$

$$\forall s \in S. \forall \alpha \in A(s). \quad \sum_{s' \in S} \mathcal{P}(s, \alpha, s') = 1 \tag{22}$$

$$\lambda \geq p_{s_I} \tag{23}$$

$$\forall s \in S \setminus T. \forall \alpha \in A(s). \quad p_s \geq \boldsymbol{x}^T P_{s,\alpha} \boldsymbol{x} + q_{s,\alpha}^T \boldsymbol{x}, \tag{24}$$

where $\boldsymbol{x}$ is a vector consisting of the probability variables p_s for all $s \in S$ and the pMDP parameters from V, i.e., $\boldsymbol{x}$ has $|S| + |V|$ rows. Furthermore, $P_{s,\alpha} \in \mathbb{R}^{(|S|+|V|) \times (|S|+|V|)}$ is a symmetric matrix, and $q_{s,\alpha} \in \mathbb{R}^{(|S|+|V|)}$.

Construction of the QCQP. We use the matrix $P_{s,\alpha}$ to capture the *quadratic* part and the vector $q_{s,\alpha}$ to capture the *affine* part in (24). More precisely, consider an affine function $\mathcal{P}(s, \alpha, s') = a \cdot v + b$ with $a, b \in \mathbb{R}$. The function occurs in the constraint (6) as part of the function $(a \cdot v + b) \cdot p_{s'}$. The quadratic part thus occurs as $a \cdot v \cdot p_{s'}$ and the affine part as $b \cdot p_{s'}$.

We first consider the product $\boldsymbol{x}^T P_{s,\alpha} \boldsymbol{x}$, which denotes the sum over all products of entries in $\boldsymbol{x}$. Thus, in $P_{s,\alpha}$, each row or column corresponds either to a probability variable p_s for a state $s \in S$ or to a parameter $v \in V$. In fact, the cells indexed $(v, p_{s'})$ and $(p_{s'}, v)$ correspond to the product of these variables. These two entries are summed in $\boldsymbol{x}^T P_{s,\alpha} \boldsymbol{x}$. In $P_{s,\alpha}$, the sum is reflected by two entries $a/2$ in the cells $(v, p_{s'})$ and $(p_{s'}, v)$. Then $P_{s,\alpha}$ is a symmetric matrix, as required. Similarly, we construct $q_{s,\alpha}$; the entry corresponding to $p_{s'}$ is set to b.

We do not modify the affine functions in (20)–(23) for the QCQP form.

Example 2 Recall Example 1. We reformulate the NLP in (8)–(13) as a QCQP in the form of (19)–(24) using the same variables.

$$\text{minimize} \quad p_{s_0}$$

$$\text{subject to}$$

$$p_{s_3} = 1$$

$$\lambda \geq p_{s_0} \geq \begin{bmatrix} v \\ p_{s_1} \end{bmatrix}^T P_{s_0} \begin{bmatrix} v \\ p_{s_1} \end{bmatrix} = \begin{bmatrix} v \\ p_{s_1} \end{bmatrix}^T \begin{bmatrix} 0 & 0.5 \\ 0.5 & 0 \end{bmatrix} \begin{bmatrix} v \\ p_{s_1} \end{bmatrix}$$

$$p_{s_1} \geq \begin{bmatrix} v \\ p_{s_2} \end{bmatrix}^T P_{s_1} \begin{bmatrix} v \\ p_{s_2} \end{bmatrix} = \begin{bmatrix} v \\ p_{s_2} \end{bmatrix}^T \begin{bmatrix} 0 & -0.5 \\ -0.5 & 0 \end{bmatrix} \begin{bmatrix} v \\ p_{s_2} \end{bmatrix} + p_{s_2}$$

$$p_{s_2} \geq \begin{bmatrix} v \\ p_{s_3} \end{bmatrix}^T P_{s_2} \begin{bmatrix} v \\ p_{s_3} \end{bmatrix} = \begin{bmatrix} v \\ p_{s_3} \end{bmatrix}^T \begin{bmatrix} 0 & 0.5 \\ 0.5 & 0 \end{bmatrix} \begin{bmatrix} v \\ p_{s_3} \end{bmatrix}$$

$$1 - \varepsilon_{\text{graph}} \geq v \geq \varepsilon_{\text{graph}}.$$

Theorem 1 *The QCQP in (19)–(23) is nonconvex in general.*

Proof The matrices $P_{s_0}, P_{s_1}, P_{s_2}$ in Example 2 have an eigenvalue of -0.5 and are not PSD. Thus, the constraints and the resulting QCQP are nonconvex. □

5   Efficient pMDP Synthesis via Convexification

The QCQP in (19)–(23) is nonconvex and hard to solve in general. We provide a solution by employing a heuristic called the *convex-concave procedure* (CCP) [30], which relies on the ability to efficiently solve convex optimization problems.

The CCP computes a *local optimum* of a non-convex *difference-of-convex* (DC) problem. A DC problem has the form

$$\text{minimize} \quad f_0(\boldsymbol{x}) - g_0(\boldsymbol{x}) \tag{25}$$
$$\text{subject to}$$
$$\forall i = 1, \ldots, m. \quad f_i(\boldsymbol{x}) - g_i(\boldsymbol{x}) \leq 0, \tag{26}$$

where for $i = 0, 1, \ldots, m$, $f_i(\boldsymbol{x}) \colon \mathbb{R}^n \to \mathbb{R}$ and $g_i(\boldsymbol{x}) \colon \mathbb{R}^n \to \mathbb{R}$ are convex. The functions $-g_i(\boldsymbol{x})$ are *concave*. Every quadratic function can be rewritten as a DC function. Consider the indefinite quadratic function $\boldsymbol{x}^T P_{s,\alpha} \boldsymbol{x} + q_{s,\alpha}^T \boldsymbol{x}$ from (24). We decompose the matrix $P_{s,\alpha}$ into the difference of two matrices

$$P_{s,\alpha} = P_{s,\alpha}^+ - P_{s,\alpha}^- \text{ with } P_{s,\alpha}^+ = P_{s,\alpha} + tI \text{ and } P_{s,\alpha}^- = tI,$$

where I is the identity matrix, and $t \in \mathbb{R}_+$ is sufficiently large to render $P_{s,\alpha}^+$ PSD, e.g., larger than the largest eigenvalue of $P_{s,\alpha}$. Then, we rewrite $\boldsymbol{x}^T P_{s,\alpha} \boldsymbol{x} + q_{s,\alpha}^T \boldsymbol{x}$ as $\left(\boldsymbol{x}^T P_{s,\alpha}^+ \boldsymbol{x} + q_{s,\alpha}^T \boldsymbol{x} \right) - \boldsymbol{x}^T P_{s,\alpha}^- \boldsymbol{x}$, which is in the form of (26).

Example 3 Recall the pMC in Fig. 1 and the QCQP from Example 2. All matrices P_s of the QCQP are not PSD. We construct a DC problem with $t = 1$ for all P_s:

$$\text{minimize} \quad p_{s_0}$$
$$\text{subject to}$$
$$p_{s_3} = 1$$
$$\lambda \geq p_{s_0} \geq \begin{bmatrix} v \\ p_{s_1} \end{bmatrix}^T \begin{bmatrix} 1 & 0.5 \\ 0.5 & 1 \end{bmatrix} \begin{bmatrix} v \\ p_{s_1} \end{bmatrix} - \begin{bmatrix} v \\ p_{s_1} \end{bmatrix}^T \begin{bmatrix} 1 & 0 \\ 0 & 1 \end{bmatrix} \begin{bmatrix} v \\ p_{s_1} \end{bmatrix}$$
$$p_{s_1} \geq \begin{bmatrix} v \\ p_{s_2} \end{bmatrix}^T \begin{bmatrix} 1 & -0.5 \\ -0.5 & 1 \end{bmatrix} \begin{bmatrix} v \\ p_{s_2} \end{bmatrix} - \begin{bmatrix} v \\ p_{s_2} \end{bmatrix}^T \begin{bmatrix} 1 & 0 \\ 0 & 1 \end{bmatrix} \begin{bmatrix} v \\ p_{s_2} \end{bmatrix} + p_{s_2}$$
$$p_{s_2} \geq \begin{bmatrix} v \\ p_{s_3} \end{bmatrix}^T \begin{bmatrix} 1 & 0.5 \\ 0.5 & 1 \end{bmatrix} \begin{bmatrix} v \\ p_{s_3} \end{bmatrix} - \begin{bmatrix} v \\ p_{s_3} \end{bmatrix}^T \begin{bmatrix} 1 & 0 \\ 0 & 1 \end{bmatrix} \begin{bmatrix} v \\ p_{s_3} \end{bmatrix}$$
$$1 - \varepsilon_{\text{graph}} \geq v \geq \varepsilon_{\text{graph}}.$$

We have $\boldsymbol{x} = (p_{s_1}, p_{s_2}, p_{s_3}, v)$ and an initial assignment $\hat{\boldsymbol{x}} = (\hat{p}_{s_1}, \hat{p}_{s_2}, \hat{p}_{s_3}, \hat{v})$.

CCP approach. For the resulting DC problem, we consider the iterative *penalty CCP method* [30]. The procedure is initialized with any initial assignment $\hat{x}$ of the variables $\boldsymbol{x}$. In the *convexification* stage, we compute affine approximations in form of a linearization of $g_i(\boldsymbol{x})$ around $\hat{x}$:

$$\bar{g}_i(\boldsymbol{x}) = g_i(\hat{x}) + \nabla g_i(\hat{x})^T (\boldsymbol{x} - \hat{x}),$$

where ∇g_i is the gradient of the functions $g_i(\boldsymbol{x})$ at $\hat{x}$. Then, we replace the DC function $f_i(\boldsymbol{x}) - g_i(\boldsymbol{x})$ by $f_i(\boldsymbol{x}) - \bar{g}_i(\boldsymbol{x})$, which is a *convex over-approximation* of the original function. A feasible assignment for the resulting over-approximated and *convex* DC problem is also feasible for the original DC problem.

To find such a feasible assignment, a *penalty variable* $k_{s,\alpha}$ for all $s \in S \setminus T$ and $\alpha \in Act$ is added to all convexified constraints. Solving the resulting problem then seeks to minimize the violation of the original DC constraints by minimizing the sum of the penalty variables. The resulting convex problem is written as

$$\text{minimize} \quad p_{s_I} + \tau \sum_{\forall s \in S \setminus T} \sum_{\forall \alpha \in Act} k_{s,\alpha} \tag{27}$$

subject to

$$\forall s \in T. \quad p_s = 1 \tag{28}$$

$$\forall s, s' \in S. \forall \alpha \in A(s). \quad \mathcal{P}(s, \alpha, s') \geq \varepsilon_{\text{graph}} \tag{29}$$

$$\forall s \in S. \forall \alpha \in A(s). \quad \sum_{s' \in S} \mathcal{P}(s, \alpha, s') = 1 \tag{30}$$

$$\lambda \geq p_{s_I} \tag{31}$$

$$\forall s \in S \setminus T. \forall \alpha \in A(s) \quad k_{s,\alpha} + p_s \geq \boldsymbol{x}^T P_{s,\alpha}^+ \boldsymbol{x} + q_{s,\alpha}^T \boldsymbol{x} - \hat{x}^T P_{s,\alpha}^- (2\boldsymbol{x} - \hat{x}) \tag{32}$$

$$\forall s \in S \setminus T. \forall \alpha \in A(s) \quad k_{s,\alpha} \geq 0, \tag{33}$$

where $\tau > 0$ is a fixed *penalty parameter*, and the gradient of $\boldsymbol{x}^T P_{s,\alpha}^- \boldsymbol{x}$ is $2 \cdot P_{s,\alpha}^- \hat{x}$. This convexified DC problem is in fact a convex QCQP. The changed objective now makes the constraint (31) important.

Example 4 Recall the pMC in Fig. 1 and the DC problem from Example 3. We introduce the penalty variables k_{s_i} and assume a fixed τ. We linearize around $\hat{x}$. The resulting convex problem is:

$$\text{minimize} \quad p_{s_0} + \tau \sum_{i=0}^{2} k_{s_i}$$

subject to

$$p_{s_3} = 1$$

$$\lambda \geq p_{s_0}$$

$$k_{s_0} + p_{s_0} \geq \begin{bmatrix} v \\ p_{s_1} \end{bmatrix}^T \begin{bmatrix} 1 & 0.5 \\ 0.5 & 1 \end{bmatrix} \begin{bmatrix} v \\ p_{s_1} \end{bmatrix} - \begin{bmatrix} \hat{v} \\ \hat{p}_{s_1} \end{bmatrix}^T \begin{bmatrix} 1 & 0 \\ 0 & 1 \end{bmatrix} \begin{bmatrix} 2 \cdot v - \hat{v} \\ 2 \cdot p_{s_1} - \hat{p}_{s_1} \end{bmatrix}$$

$$k_{s_1} + p_{s_1} \geq \begin{bmatrix} v \\ p_{s_1} \end{bmatrix}^T \begin{bmatrix} 1 & -0.5 \\ -0.5 & 1 \end{bmatrix} \begin{bmatrix} v \\ p_{s_2} \end{bmatrix} - \begin{bmatrix} \hat{v} \\ \hat{p}_{s_2} \end{bmatrix}^T \begin{bmatrix} 1 & 0 \\ 0 & 1 \end{bmatrix} \begin{bmatrix} 2 \cdot v - \hat{v} \\ 2 \cdot p_{s_2} - \hat{p}_{s_2} \end{bmatrix} + p_{s_2}$$

$$k_{s_2} + p_{s_2} \geq \begin{bmatrix} v \\ p_{s_3} \end{bmatrix}^T \begin{bmatrix} 1 & 0.5 \\ 0.5 & 1 \end{bmatrix} \begin{bmatrix} v \\ p_{s_3} \end{bmatrix} - \begin{bmatrix} \hat{v} \\ \hat{p}_{s_3} \end{bmatrix}^T \begin{bmatrix} 1 & 0 \\ 0 & 1 \end{bmatrix} \begin{bmatrix} 2 \cdot v - \hat{v} \\ 2 \cdot p_{s_3} - \hat{p}_{s_3} \end{bmatrix}$$

$$1 - \varepsilon_{\mathrm{graph}} \geq v \geq \varepsilon_{\mathrm{graph}}$$

$$k_{s_0} \geq 0, k_{s_1} \geq 0, k_{s_2} \geq 0.$$

If all penalty variables are assigned to zero, we can terminate the algorithm immediately, for the proof cf. [11]

Theorem 2 *A satisfying assignment of the convex DC problem in (27)–(33)*

$$\text{with} \qquad \tau \sum_{\forall s \in S \setminus T} \sum_{\forall \alpha \in Act} k_{s,\alpha} = 0$$

is a feasible solution to Problem 1.

If any of the penalty variables are assigned to a positive value, we update the penalty parameter τ by $\mu + \tau$ for a $\mu > 0$, until an upper limit for τ_{max} is reached to avoid numerical problems. Then, we compute a linearization of the g_i functions around the current (not feasible) solution and solve the resulting problem. This procedure is repeated until we find a feasible solution. If the procedure converges to an infeasible solution, it may be restarted with an adapted initial $\hat{x}$.

Efficiency Improvements in the Convex-Concave Procedure

Better convexification. We can use the previous transformation to perform CCP, but it involves expensive matrix operations, including computing the numerous eigenvalues. Observe that the matrices $P_{s,\alpha}$ and vectors $q_{s,\alpha}$ are sparse. Then, the eigenvalue method introduces more occurrences of the variables in every constraint, and thereby increases the approximation error during convexification. We use an alternative convexification: Consider the bilinear function $h = 2c \cdot yz$, where y and z are variables, and $c \in \mathbb{R}_+$. We rewrite h equivalently to $h + c(y^2 + z^2) - c(y^2 + z^2)$. Then, we rewrite $h + c(y^2 + z^2)$ as $c(y + z)^2$. We obtain $h = c(y + z)^2 - c(y^2 + z^2)$. The function $c(y + z)^2$ is a quadratic convex function, and we convexify the function $-c(y^2 + z^2)$ as $-c(\hat{y}^2 + \hat{z}^2) + 2c(\hat{y}^2 + \hat{z}^2 - y\hat{y} - z\hat{z})$, where $\hat{y}$ and $\hat{z}$ are the assignments as before. We convexify the bilinear function $h = 2c \cdot yz$ with $c \in \mathbb{R}_-$ analogously. Consequently, we reduce the occurrences of variables for sparse matrices compared to the eigenvalue method.

Integrating model checking with CCP. In each iteration of the CCP, we obtain values $\hat{v}$ which give rise to a parameter instantiation. Model checking at these instantiations is a good heuristic to allow for *early termination*. We check whether the values $\hat{v}$ already induce a feasible solution to the original NLP, even though the penalty variables have not converged to zero.

Additionally, instead of instantiating the initial probability values $\hat{p}_s$ in iteration $i+1$, we may use the model checking result of the MDP instantiated at $\hat{v}$ from iteration i. Model checking ensures that the probability variables are consistent with the parameter variables, i.e., that the constraints describing the transition relation in the original NLP are all met. Using the model checking results overcomes problems with local optima. Small violations in (32), i.e., small $k_{s,\alpha}$ values can lead to big differences in the actual probability valuations. Then, the CCP may be trapped in poor local optima, where the sum of constraint violations is small, but the violation for the probability threshold is too large.

Algorithmic improvements. We list three key improvements that we make as opposed to a naive implementation of the approaches. (1) We efficiently precompute the states $s \in S$ that reach target states with probability 0 or 1. Then, we simplify the NLP in (1)–(6) accordingly. (2) Often, all instantiations with admissible parameter values yield well-defined MDPs. We verify this property via an easy preprocessing. Then, we omit the constraints for the well-definedness. (3) Parts of the encoding are untouched over multiple CCP iterations. Instead of rebuilding the encoding, we only update constraints which contain iteration-dependent values. The update is based on a preprocessed representation of the model. The improvement is two-fold: We spend less time constructing the encoding, and the solver reuses previous results, making solving up to three times faster.

6   Experiments

6.1   Implementation

We implement the CCP with the discussed efficiency improvements from Sect. 5 in the parameter synthesis framework PROPhESY [14]. We use the probabilistic model checker Storm [15] to extract an explicit representation of an pMDP. We keep the pMDP in memory, and update the parameter instantiations using an efficient data structure to enable efficient repetitive model checking. To solve convex QCQPs, we use Gurobi 7.5 [20], configured for numerical stability.

Tuning constants. Optimally, we would initialize the CCP procedure, i.e., $\hat{v}$ (for the parameters) and $\hat{p}_s$ (for the probability variables), with a feasible point, but that would require to already solve Problem 1. Instead, we instantiate $\hat{v}$ as the center of the parameter space, and thereby minimize the worst-case distance to a feasible solution. For $\hat{p}_s$, we use the threshold λ from the specification $\mathbb{P}_{\leq\lambda}(\Diamond T)$ to initialize the probability variables, and analogously for expected cost. We initialize the penalty parameter $\tau = 0.05$ for reachability, and $\tau = 5$ for expected cost, a conservative number in the same order of magnitude as the values $\hat{p}_s$. As expected cost evaluations have wider ranges than probability evaluations, a larger τ is sensible. We pick $\mu = \max_{s \in S \setminus T} \hat{p}_s$. We update τ by adding μ after each iteration. Empirically, increasing τ with bigger steps is beneficial for the run time, but induces more numerical instability. In contrast, in the literature, the update parameter μ is frequently used as a constant, i.e., it is not updated between the iterations. In, e.g, [30], τ is multiplied by μ after each iteration.

6.2   Evaluation

Set-up. We evaluate on a HP BL685C G7 with 48 2 GHz cores, a 32 GB memory limit, and 1800 seconds time limit; the implementation only using a single thread. The task is to find feasible parameter valuation for pMCs and pMDPs with non-trivial upper/lower thresholds on probabilities/costs in the specifications, as in Problem 1. We ask for a well-defined valuation of the parameters, with $\varepsilon_{graph} = 10^{-5}$. We run all the approaches with the exact same configuration of Storm. For pMCs, we enable weak bisimulation, which is beneficial for all presented examples. We do not use bisimulation for pMDPs.

We compare runtimes with a particle-swarm optimization (PSO) and two SMT-based approaches. PSO is a heuristic sampling approach which searches the parameter space, inspired by [10]. For each valuation, PSO performs model checking *without* rebuilding the model, rather it adapts the matrix from previous valuations. As PSO is a randomized procedure, we run it with random seeds 0–19. The PSO implementation requires the well-defined parameter regions to constitute a hyper-rectangle, as proper sampling from polygons is a non-trivial task. The first SMT approach directly solves the NLP (2)–(7) using the SMT solver Z3 [25]. The second SMT approach preprocesses the NLP using state elimination [13] as implemented in, e.g., PARAM, PRISM and Storm.

We additionally compare against a prototype of the geometric programming (GP) approach [12] based on CvxPy [16] and the solver SCS [31], and the QCQP package [32], which implements several heuristics, including a naive CCP approach, for nonconvex QCQPs. Due to numerical instabilities, we could not automatically apply these two approaches to a wide range of benchmarks.

Benchmarks. We include the standard pMC benchmarks from the PARAM website, which contain two parameters.We furthermore have a rich selection of strategy synthesis problems obtained from partially observable MDPs (POMDPs), cf. [26]: GridX are gridworld problems with trap states (A), finite horizons (B), or movement costs (C). Maze is a navigation problem. Network and Repudiation originate from distributed protocols. We obtain the pMDP benchmarks either from the PARAM website, or as parametric variants to existing PRISM case studies, and describe randomized distributed protocols.

Results. Table 1 contains an overview of the results. The first two columns refer to the benchmark instance, the next column to the specification evaluated. We give the states (States), transitions (Trans.) and parameters (Par.) *in the bisimulation quotient*, which is then used for further evaluation. We then give the *minimum* (tmin), the *maximum* (tmax) and *average* (**tavg**) runtime (in seconds) for PSO with different seeds, the best runtime obtained using SMT (**t**), and the runtime for CCP (**t**). For CCP, we additionally give the fraction (in percent) of time spent in Gurobi (solv), and the number of CCP iterations (iter). Table 2 additionally contains the number of actions (Act) for pMDPs. The boldfaced measures **tavg**, and **t** for both SMT and CCP are the important measures to compare. Boldface values are the ones with the best performance for a specific benchmark.

Table 1. pMC benchmark results

prob			Info			PSO			SMT	CCP		
Set	Inst	Spec	States	Trans.	Par.	tmin	tmax	**tavg**	t	t	solv	iter
Brp	16,2	$\mathbb{P}_{\leq 0.1}$	98	194	2	0	0	**0**	40	0	30%	3
Brp	512,5	$\mathbb{P}_{\leq 0.1}$	6146	12290	2	24	36	**28**	TO	33	24%	3
Crowds	10,5	$\mathbb{P}_{\leq 0.1}$	42	82	2	4	5	5	8	**4**	2%	4
Nand	5,10	$\mathbb{P}_{\leq 0.05}$	10492	20982	2	21	51	28	TO	**22**	21%	2
Zeroconf	10000	$\mathbb{E}_{\leq 10010}$	10003	20004	2	2	4	**3**	TO	57	81%	3
GridA	4	$\mathbb{P}_{\geq 0.84}$	1026	2098	72	11	11	**11**	TO	22	81%	11
GridB	8,5	$\mathbb{P}_{\geq 0.84}$	8653	17369	700	409	440	427	TO	**213**	84%	8
GridB	10,6	$\mathbb{P}_{\geq 0.84}$	16941	33958	1290	533	567	553	TO	**426**	84%	7
GridC	6	$\mathbb{E}_{\leq 4.8}$	1665	305	168	261	274	267	TO	**169**	90%	23
Maze	5	$\mathbb{E}_{\leq 14}$	1303	2658	590	213	230	219	TO	**67**	89%	8
Maze	5	$\mathbb{E}_{\leq 6}$	1303	2658	590	–	–	TO	TO	**422**	85%	97
Maze	7	$\mathbb{E}_{\leq 6}$	2580	5233	1176	–	–	TO	TO	**740**	90%	60
Netw	5,2	$\mathbb{E}_{\leq 11.5}$	21746	63158	2420	312	523	359	TO	**207**	39%	3
Netw	5,2	$\mathbb{E}_{\leq 10.5}$	21746	63158	2420	–	–	TO	TO	**210**	38%	4
Netw	4,3	$\mathbb{E}_{\leq 11.5}$	38055	97335	4545	–	–	TO	TO	MO	-	-
Repud	8,5	$\mathbb{P}_{\geq 0.1}$	1487	3002	360	16	22	18	TO	**4**	36%	2
Repud	8,5	$\mathbb{P}_{\leq 0.05}$	1487	3002	360	273	324	293	TO	**14**	72%	4
Repud	16,2	$\mathbb{P}_{\leq 0.01}$	790	1606	96	–	–	TO	TO	**15**	78%	9
Repud	16,2	$\mathbb{P}_{\geq 0.062}$	790	1606	96	–	–	TO	TO	TO	-	-

Table 2. pMDP benchmark results

prob			Info				PSO			SMT	CCP		
Set	Inst	Spec	States	Act	Trans.	Par.	tmin	tmax	**tavg**	t	t	solv	iter
BRP	4,128	$\mathbb{P}_{\leq 0.1}$	17131	17396	23094	2	45	47	46	TO	**39**	33%	4
Coin	32	$\mathbb{E}_{\leq 500}$	4112	6160	7692	2	117	119	**118**	TO	TO	-	-
CoinX	32	$\mathbb{E}_{\leq 210}$	16448	24640	30768	2	1196	1222	1208	TO	**32**	78%	3
Zeroconf	1	$\mathbb{P}_{\geq 0.99}$	31402	55678	70643	3	18	19	**19**	TO	79	82%	2
CSMA	2,4	$\mathbb{E}_{\leq 69.3}$	7958	7988	10594	26	n.s.	n.s.	n.s.	TO	**79**	86%	10
Virus	-	$\mathbb{E}_{\leq 10}$	809	3371	6741	18	113	113	113	TO	**13**	76%	4
Wlan	0	$\mathbb{E}_{\leq 580}$	2954	3972	5202	15	n.s.	n.s.	n.s.	TO	**7**	72%	2

There is a constant overhead for model building, which is in particular large if the bisimulation quotient computation is expensive, see the small fraction of time spent solving CCPs for Crowds. For the more challenging models, this overhead is negligible. Roughly 80–90% of the time is spent within Gurobi in these models, the remainder is used to feed the CCPs into Gurobi. A specification threshold closer to the (global) optimum typically induces a higher number of iterations (see Maze or Netw with different threshold). For the pMDP Coin, optimal parameter values are on the boundary of the parameter space and quickly reached by

PSO. The small parameter values together with the rather large expected costs are numerically challenging for CCP. For CoinX, the parameter values are in the interior of the parameter space and harder to hit via sampling. For CCP, the difference between small and large coefficients is smaller than in Coin, which yields better convergence behavior. The benchmarks CSMA and WLAN are currently not supported by PSO due to the non-rectangular well-defined parameter space.

CCP does not solve all instances: In Netw (4,3), CCP exceeds the memory limit. In Repud, finding values close the global optimum requires too much time. While the thresholds used here are close to the global optima, actually finding the global optimum itself is always challenging.

Effect of integrating model checking for CCP. The benchmark-set Maze profits most: Discarding the model checking results in our CCP implementation always yields time-outs, even for the rather simple Maze, with threshold 14, which is solved with usage of model checking results within 30 seconds. Here, using model checking results thus yields a speed-up by a factor of at least 60. More typical examples are Netw, where discarding the model checking results yields a factor 5 performance penalty. The Repud examples do not significantly profit from using intermediate model checking results.

Evaluation of the QCQP package, GP and SMT. We evaluate the GP on pMCs with two parameters: For the smaller BRP instance, the procedure takes 90 seconds, for Crowds 14 seconds. Other instances yield timeouts. We also evaluate the QCQP package on some pMCs. For the smaller BRP instance, the package finds a feasible solution after 113 seconds. For the Crowds instance, it takes 13 seconds. For a Repud instance with 44 states, and 26 parameters, the package takes 54 seconds and returns a solution that violates the specification. CCP with integrated model checking takes less than a second.

The results in Tables 1 and 2 make obvious that *SMT is not competitive*, irrespectively whether the NLP is preprocessed via state elimination. Moreover, state elimination (for pMCs) within the given time limit *is only possible for those (considered) models with 2 parameters*, using either PRISM, PARAM, or Storm.

6.3   Discussion

A tuned variant of CCP improves the state-of-the-art. Just applying out-of-the-box heuristics for QCQPs—like realized in the QCQP package or using our CCP implementation without integrated model checking—does not yield a scalable method. To solve the nonconvex QCQP, we require a CCP with a clever encoding, cf. Sect. 5, and several algorithmic improvements. State space reductions shrink the encoding, and model checking after each CCP iteration to terminate earlier typically saves 20% of iterations. Especially when convergence is slow, model checking saves significantly more iterations. Moreover, feeding model checking results into the CCP improves runtime by up to an additional order of magnitude, at negligible costs. These combined improvements to the CCP method outnumbers any solver-based approach by orders of magnitude, and is often superior to sampling based approaches, especially in the presence of many parameters. Benchmarks with many parameters pose two challenges for sampling based approaches: Sampling is necessarily sparse due to the high dimension, and optimal parameter valuations for one parameter often depend significantly on other parameter values.

CCP performance can be boosted with particular benchmarks in mind. For most benchmarks, choosing larger values for τ and μ improves the performance. Furthermore, for particular benchmarks, we can find a better initial value for $\hat{p}_s$ and $\hat{v}$. These adaptions, however, are not suitable for a general framework. Values used here reflect a more balanced performance over several types of benchmarks. On the downside, the dependency on the constants means that minor changes in the encoding may have significant, but hard to predict, effect. For SMT-solvers, additional and superfluous constraints often help steering the solver, but in the context of CCP, it diminishes the performance.

Some benchmarks constitute numerically challenging problems. For specification thresholds close to global optima and for some expected cost specifications in general, feasible parameter values may be very small. Such extremal parameter values induce CCPs with large differences between the smallest and largest coefficient in the encoding, which are numerically challenging. The pMDP benchmarks are more susceptible to such numerical issues.

7   Conclusion and Future Work

We presented a new approach to parameter synthesis for pMDPs. To solve the underlying nonconvex optimization problem efficiently, we devised a method to efficiently employ a heuristic procedure with integrated model checking. The experiments showed that our method significantly improves the state-of-the-art.

In the future, we will investigate how to automatically handle nonaffine transition functions. To further improve the performance, we will implement a hybrid approach between PSO and the CCP-based method.

References

1. Aflaki, S., Volk, M., Bonakdarpour, B., Katoen, J.P., Storjohann, A.: Automated fine tuning of probabilistic self-stabilizing algorithms. In: SRDS, pp. 94–103. IEEE CS (2017)
2. Alizadeh, F., Goldfarb, D.: Second-order cone programming. Math. Program. **95**(1), 3–51 (2003)
3. Amato, C., Bernstein, D.S., Zilberstein, S.: Solving POMDPs using quadratically constrained linear programs. In: AAMAS, pp. 341–343. ACM (2006)
4. Baier, C., Katoen, J.P.: Principles of Model Checking. MIT Press, Cambridge (2008)
5. Bartocci, E., Grosu, R., Katsaros, P., Ramakrishnan, C.R., Smolka, S.A.: Model repair for probabilistic systems. In: Abdulla, P.A., Leino, K.R.M. (eds.) TACAS 2011. LNCS, vol. 6605, pp. 326–340. Springer, Heidelberg (2011). https://doi.org/10.1007/978-3-642-19835-9_30

6. Boyd, S., Kim, S.J., Vandenberghe, L., Hassibi, A.: A tutorial on geometric programming. Optim. Eng. 8(1) (2007)
7. Boyd, S., Vandenberghe, L.: Convex Optimization. Cambridge University Press, New York (2004)
8. Burer, S., Saxena, A.: The MILP road to MIQCP. Mixed Integer Nonlinear Programming, pp. 373–405 (2012)
9. Calinescu, R., Ghezzi, C., Kwiatkowska, M., Mirandola, R.: Self-adaptive software needs quantitative verification at runtime. Commun. ACM **55**(9), 69–77 (2012)
10. Chen, T., Hahn, E.M., Han, T., Kwiatkowska, M., Qu, H., Zhang, L.: Model repair for Markov decision processes. In: TASE, pp. 85–92. IEEE CS (2013)
11. Cubuktepe, M., Jansen, N., Junges, S., Katoen, J.P., Topcu, U.: Synthesis in pMDPs: a tale of 1001 parameters. CoRR abs/1803.02884 (2018)
12. Cubuktepe, M., et al.: Sequential convex programming for the efficient verification of parametric MDPs. In: Legay, A., Margaria, T. (eds.) TACAS 2017. LNCS, vol. 10206, pp. 133–150. Springer, Heidelberg (2017). https://doi.org/10.1007/978-3-662-54580-5_8
13. Daws, C.: Symbolic and parametric model checking of discrete-time Markov chains. In: Liu, Z., Araki, K. (eds.) ICTAC 2004. LNCS, vol. 3407, pp. 280–294. Springer, Heidelberg (2005). https://doi.org/10.1007/978-3-540-31862-0_21
14. Dehnert, C., et al.: PROPhESY: a probabilistic parameter synthesis tool. In: Kroening, D., Păsăreanu, C.S. (eds.) CAV 2015. LNCS, vol. 9206, pp. 214–231. Springer, Cham (2015). https://doi.org/10.1007/978-3-319-21690-4_13
15. Dehnert, C., Junges, S., Katoen, J.-P., Volk, M.: A storm is coming: a modern probabilistic model checker. In: Majumdar, R., Kunčak, V. (eds.) CAV 2017. LNCS, vol. 10427, pp. 592–600. Springer, Cham (2017). https://doi.org/10.1007/978-3-319-63390-9_31
16. Diamond, S., Boyd, S.: CVXPY: a python-embedded modeling language for convex optimization. J. Mach. Learn. Res. **17**(83), 1–5 (2016)
17. Duflot, M., et al.: Probabilistic model checking of the CSMA/CD protocol using PRISM and APMC. Electr. Notes TCS **128**(6), 195–214 (2005)
18. Filieri, A., Tamburrelli, G., Ghezzi, C.: Supporting self-adaptation via quantitative verification and sensitivity analysis at run time. IEEE Trans. Softw. Eng. **42**(1), 75–99 (2016)
19. Gainer, P., Hahn, E.M., Schewe, S.: Incremental verification of parametric and reconfigurable Markov chains. CoRR abs/1804.01872 (2018)
20. Gurobi Optimization Inc.: Gurobi optimizer reference manual. http://www.gurobi.com (2013)
21. Hahn, E.M., Hermanns, H., Wachter, B., Zhang, L.: PARAM: a model checker for parametric markov models. In: Touili, T., Cook, B., Jackson, P. (eds.) CAV 2010. LNCS, vol. 6174, pp. 660–664. Springer, Heidelberg (2010). https://doi.org/10.1007/978-3-642-14295-6_56
22. Hahn, E.M., Hermanns, H., Zhang, L.: Probabilistic reachability for parametric Markov models. STTT **13**(1), 3–19 (2010)
23. Hahn, E.M., Li, Y., Schewe, S., Turrini, A., Zhang, L.: iscasMc: a web-based probabilistic model checker. In: Jones, C., Pihlajasaari, P., Sun, J. (eds.) FM 2014. LNCS, vol. 8442, pp. 312–317. Springer, Cham (2014). https://doi.org/10.1007/978-3-319-06410-9_22
24. Hutschenreiter, L., Baier, C., Klein, J.: Parametric Markov chains: PCTL complexity and fraction-free Gaussian elimination. GandALF. EPTCS **256**, 16–30 (2017)

25. Jovanović, D., de Moura, L.: Solving non-linear arithmetic. In: Gramlich, B., Miller, D., Sattler, U. (eds.) IJCAR 2012. LNCS (LNAI), vol. 7364, pp. 339–354. Springer, Heidelberg (2012). https://doi.org/10.1007/978-3-642-31365-3_27
26. Junges, S., et al.: Finite-state controllers of POMDPs using parameter synthesis. In: UAI. AUAI Press, Canada (2018), to appear
27. Kwiatkowska, M., Norman, G., Parker, D.: PRISM 4.0: verification of probabilistic real-time systems. In: Gopalakrishnan, G., Qadeer, S. (eds.) CAV 2011. LNCS, vol. 6806, pp. 585–591. Springer, Heidelberg (2011). https://doi.org/10.1007/978-3-642-22110-1_47
28. Lanotte, R., Maggiolo-Schettini, A., Troina, A.: Parametric probabilistic transition systems for system design and analysis. Form. Asp. Comput. **19**(1), 93–109 (2007)
29. Linderoth, J.: A simplicial branch-and-bound algorithm for solving quadratically constrained quadratic programs. Math. Program. **103**(2), 251–282 (2005)
30. Lipp, T., Boyd, S.: Variations and extension of the convex-concave procedure. Optim. Eng. **17**(2), 263–287 (2016)
31. O'Donoghue, B., Chu, E., Parikh, N., Boyd, S.: Conic optimization via operator splitting and homogeneous self-dual embedding. J. Optim. Theory Appl. **169**(3), 1042–1068 (2016)
32. Park, J., Boyd, S.: General heuristics for nonconvex quadratically constrained quadratic programming. arXiv preprint arXiv:1703.07870 (2017)
33. Shen, X., Diamond, S., Gu, Y., Boyd, S.: Disciplined convex-concave programming. In: CDC, pp. 1009–1014. IEEE (2016)
34. Su, G., Rosenblum, D.S., Tamburrelli, G.: Reliability of run-time quality-of-service evaluation using parametric model checking. In: ICSE, pp. 073–84. ACM (2016)

Temporal Logic Verification of Stochastic Systems Using Barrier Certificates

Pushpak Jagtap[1], Sadegh Soudjani[2(✉)], and Majid Zamani[1]

[1] Technical University of Munich, Munich, Germany
{pushpak.jagtap,zamani}@tum.de
[2] Newcastle University, Newcastle upon Tyne, United Kingdom
Sadegh.Soudjani@ncl.ac.uk

Abstract. This paper presents a methodology for temporal logic verification of discrete-time stochastic systems. Our goal is to find a lower bound on the probability that a complex temporal property is satisfied by finite traces of the system. Desired temporal properties of the system are expressed using a fragment of linear temporal logic, called *safe LTL over finite traces*. We propose to use barrier certificates for computations of such lower bounds, which is computationally much more efficient than the existing discretization-based approaches. The new approach is discretization-free and does not suffer from the curse of dimensionality caused by discretizing state sets. The proposed approach relies on decomposing the negation of the specification into a union of sequential reachabilities and then using barrier certificates to compute upper bounds for these reachability probabilities. We demonstrate the effectiveness of the proposed approach on case studies with linear and polynomial dynamics.

1 Introduction

Verification of dynamical systems against complex specifications has gained significant attention in last few years [3,29]. The verification task is challenging for continuous-space dynamical systems under uncertainties and is hard to be performed exactly. There have been several results in the literature utilizing approximate finite models (a.k.a. abstractions) for verification of stochastic dynamical systems. Examples include results on verification of discrete-time stochastic hybrid systems against probabilistic invariance [23,25] and linear temporal logic specifications [1,30] using Markov chain abstractions. Verification of discrete-time stochastic switched systems against probabilistic computational tree logic formulae is discussed in [14] using interval Markov chains as abstract models. However, these abstraction techniques are based on state set discretization and face the issue of discrete state explosion. This scalability issue is only partly mitigated in [15,24] based on compositional abstraction of stochastic systems.

This work was supported in part by the German Research Foundation (DFG) through the grant ZA 873/1-1 and the TUM International Graduate School of Science and Engineering (IGSSE).

S. K. Lahiri and C. Wang (Eds.): ATVA 2018, LNCS 11138, pp. 177–193, 2018.
https://doi.org/10.1007/978-3-030-01090-4_11

On the other hand, a discretization-free approach, based on *barrier certificates*, has been used for verifying stochastic systems against simple temporal properties such as safety and reachability. Employing barrier certificates for safety verification of stochastic systems is initially proposed in [19]. Similar results are reported in [32] for switched diffusion processes and piecewise-deterministic Markov processes. The results in [9] propose a probabilistic barrier certificate to compute bounds on the probability that a stochastic hybrid system reaches unsafe region. However, in order to provide infinite time horizon guarantees, all of these results require an assumption that the barrier certificates exhibit *supermartingale* property which in turns presuppose stochastic stability and vanishing noise at the equilibrium point of the system.

In this work, we consider the problem of verifying discrete-time stochastic systems against complex specifications over finite time horizons *without* requiring any assumption on the stability of the system. This is achieved by relaxing supermartingale condition to *c-martingale* as also utilized in [27]. Correspondingly, instead of infinite-horizon specifications, we consider finite-horizon temporal specifications, which are more practical in the real life applications including motion planning problems [2,16,22]. In spirit, this work extends the idea of combining automata representation of the specification and barrier certificates, which is proposed in [33] for non-stochastic dynamics, to verify stochastic systems against specifications expressed as a fragment of LTL formulae, namely, safe LTL on finite traces. The authors in [6] also leverage the use of barrier certificates to provide deductive rules for synthesizing controllers for deterministic systems against alternating temporal logic whereas in this work we are dealing with the verification of stochastic systems against safe LTL specifications on finite traces.

To the best of our knowledge, this paper is the first one to use barrier certificates for algorithmic verification of stochastic systems against a wide class of temporal properties. Our main contribution is to provide a systematic approach for computing lower bounds on the probability that the discrete-time stochastic system satisfies given safe LTL specification over a finite time horizon. This is achieved by first decomposing specification into a sequence of simpler verification tasks based on the structure of the automaton associated with the negation of the specification. Next, we use barrier certificates for computing probability bounds for simpler verification tasks which are further combined to get a (potentially conservative) lower bound on the probability of satisfying the original specification. The effectiveness of the proposed approach is demonstrated using several case studies with linear and polynomial dynamics.

2   Preliminaries

2.1   Notations

We denote the set of nonnegative integers by $\mathbb{N}_0 := \{0, 1, 2, \ldots\}$ and the set of positive integers by $\mathbb{N} := \{1, 2, 3, \ldots\}$. The symbols $\mathbb{R}$, $\mathbb{R}^+$, and $\mathbb{R}_0^+$ denote the set of real, positive, and nonnegative real numbers, respectively. We use $\mathbb{R}^{n \times m}$

to denote the space of real matrices with n rows and m columns.

We consider a probability space $(\Omega, \mathcal{F}_\Omega, \mathbb{P}_\Omega)$ where Ω is the sample space, $\mathcal{F}_\Omega$ is a sigma-algebra on Ω comprising the subset of Ω as events, and $\mathbb{P}_\Omega$ is a probability measure that assigns probabilities to events. We assume that random variables introduced in this article are measurable functions of the form $X : (\Omega, \mathcal{F}_\Omega) \rightarrow (S_X, \mathcal{F}_X)$ as $Prob\{A\} = \mathbb{P}_\Omega\{X^{-1}(A)\}$ for any $A \in \mathcal{F}_X$. We often directly discuss the probability measure on $(S_X, \mathcal{F}_X)$ without explicitly mentioning the underlying probability space and the function X itself.

2.2   Discrete-Time Stochastic Systems

In this work, we consider discrete-time stochastic systems given by a tuple $S = (X, V_w, w, f)$, where X and V_w are Borel spaces representing state and uncertainty spaces of the system. We denote by $(X, \mathcal{B}(X))$ the measurable space with $\mathcal{B}(X)$ being the Borel sigma-algebra on the state space. Notation w denotes a sequence of independent and identically distributed (i.i.d.) random variables on the set V_w as $w := \{w(k) : \Omega \rightarrow V_w, \ k \in \mathbb{N}_0\}$. The map $f : X \times V_w \rightarrow X$ is a measurable function characterizing the state evolution of the system. For a given initial state $x(0) \in X$, the state evolution can be written as

$$x(k + 1) = f(x(k), w(k)), \quad k \in \mathbb{N}_0. \tag{1}$$

We denote the *solution process* generated over N time steps by $\mathbf{x}_N = x(0)$, $x(1), \ldots, x(N - 1)$. The sequence w together with the measurable function f induce a unique probability measure on the sequences $\mathbf{x}_N$.

We are interested in computing a lower bound on the probability that system $S = (X, V_w, w, f)$ satisfies a specification expressed as a temporal logic property. We provide syntax and semantics of the class of specifications dealt with in this paper in the next subsection.

2.3   Linear Temporal Logic Over Finite Traces

In this subsection, we introduce linear temporal logic over finite traces, referred to as LTL$_F$ [4]. LTL$_F$ uses the same syntax of LTL over infinite traces given in [3]. The LTL$_F$ formulas over a set Π of atomic propositions are obtained as follows:

$$\varphi ::= \ \text{true} \mid p \mid \neg\varphi \mid \varphi_1 \wedge \varphi_2 \mid \varphi_1 \vee \varphi_2 \mid \bigcirc\varphi \mid \Diamond\varphi \mid \Box\varphi \mid \varphi_1 \mathcal{U} \varphi_2,$$

where $p \in \Pi$, $\bigcirc$ is the next operator, $\Diamond$ is eventually, $\Box$ is always, and $\mathcal{U}$ is until. The semantics of LTL$_F$ is given in terms of *finite traces*, i.e., finite words σ, denoting a finite non-empty sequence of consecutive steps over Π. We use $|\sigma|$ to represent the length of σ and σ_i as a propositional interpretation at ith position in the trace, where $0 \leq i < |\sigma|$. Given a finite trace σ and an LTL$_F$ formula φ, we inductively define when an LTL$_F$ formula φ is true at the ith step $(0 \leq i < |\sigma|)$, denoted by $\sigma, i \models \varphi$, as follows:

- $\sigma, i \models \text{true}$;
- $\sigma, i \models p$, for $p \in \Pi$ iff $p \in \sigma_i$;
- $\sigma, i \models \neg\varphi$ iff $\sigma, i \not\models \varphi$;
- $\sigma, i \models \varphi_1 \wedge \varphi_2$ iff $\sigma, i \models \varphi_1$ and $\sigma, i \models \varphi_2$;
- $\sigma, i \models \varphi_1 \vee \varphi_2$ iff $\sigma, i \models \varphi_1$ or $\sigma, i \models \varphi_2$;
- $\sigma, i \models \bigcirc\varphi$ iff $i < |\sigma| - 1$ and $\sigma, i + 1 \models \varphi$;
- $\sigma, i \models \Diamond\varphi$ iff for some j such that $i \leq j < |\sigma|$, we have $\sigma, j \models \varphi$;
- $\sigma, i \models \Box\varphi$ iff for all j such that $i \leq j < |\sigma|$, we have $\sigma, j \models \varphi$;
- $\sigma, i \models \varphi_1 \mathcal{U} \varphi_2$ iff for some j such that $i \leq j < |\sigma|$, we have $\sigma, j \models \varphi_2$, and for all k s.t. $i \leq k < j$, we have $\sigma, k \models \varphi_1$.

The formula φ is true on σ, denoted by $\sigma \models \varphi$, if and only if $\sigma, 0 \models \varphi$. We denote the language of such finite traces associated with LTL$_F$ formula φ by $\mathcal{L}(\varphi)$. Notice that in this case we also have the usual boolean equivalences such as $\varphi_1 \vee \varphi_2 \equiv \neg(\neg\varphi_1 \wedge \neg\varphi_2)$, $\varphi_1 \implies \varphi_2 \equiv \neg\varphi_1 \vee \varphi_2$, $\Diamond\varphi \equiv \text{true}\,\mathcal{U}\varphi$, and $\Box\varphi \equiv \neg\Diamond\neg\varphi$.

In this paper, we consider only safety properties [12]. Hence, we use a subset of LTL$_F$ called safe LTL$_F$ as introduced in [22] and defined as follows.

Definition 1. *An LTL$_F$ formula is called a safe LTL$_F$ formula if it can be represented in positive normal form, i.e., negations only occur adjacent to atomic propositions, using the temporal operators next ($\bigcirc$) and always ($\Box$).*

Next, we define deterministic finite automata which later serve as equivalent representations of LTL$_F$ formulae.

Definition 2. *A deterministic finite automaton (DFA) is a tuple $\mathcal{A} = (Q, Q_0, \Sigma, \delta, F)$, where Q is a finite set of states, $Q_0 \subseteq Q$ is a set of initial states, Σ is a finite set (a.k.a. alphabet), $\delta : Q \times \Sigma \to Q$ is a transition function, and $F \subseteq Q$ is a set of accepting states.*

We use notation $q \xrightarrow{\sigma} q'$ to denote transition relation $(q, \sigma, q') \in \delta$. A finite word $\sigma = (\sigma_0, \sigma_1, \ldots, \sigma_{n-1}) \in \Sigma^n$ is accepted by a DFA $\mathcal{A}$ if there exists a finite state run $q = (q_0, q_1, \ldots, q_n) \in Q^{n+1}$ such that $q_0 \in Q_0$, $q_i \xrightarrow{\sigma_i} q_{i+1}$ for all $0 \leq i < n$ and $q_n \in F$. The accepted language of $\mathcal{A}$, denoted by $\mathcal{L}(\mathcal{A})$, is the set of all words accepted by $\mathcal{A}$.

According to [5], every LTL$_F$ formula φ can be translated to a DFA $\mathcal{A}_\varphi$ that accepts the same language as φ, i.e., $\mathcal{L}(\varphi) = \mathcal{L}(\mathcal{A}_\varphi)$. Such $\mathcal{A}_\varphi$ can be constructed explicitly or symbolically using existing tools, such as SPOT [7] and MONA [8].

Remark 1. For a given LTL$_F$ formula φ over atomic propositions Π, the associated DFA $\mathcal{A}_\varphi$ is usually constructed over the alphabet $\Sigma = 2^\Pi$. Solution process of a system S is also connected to the set of words by a labeling function L from the state space to the alphabet Σ. Without loss of generality, we work with the set of atomic propositions directly as the alphabet rather than its power set.

Property satisfaction by the solution process. For a given discrete-time stochastic system $S = (X, V_w, w, f)$ with dynamics (1), finite-time solution processes $\mathbf{x}_N$ are connected to LTL$_F$ formulae with the help of a measurable labeling function $L : X \to \Pi$, where Π is the set of atomic propositions.

Definition 3. *For a stochastic system $S = (X, V_w, w, f)$ and labeling function $L : X \rightarrow \Pi$, a finite sequence $\sigma_{\boldsymbol{x}_N} = (\sigma_0, \sigma_1, \dots, \sigma_{N-1}) \in \Pi^N$ is a finite trace of the solution process $\boldsymbol{x}_N = x(0), x(1), \dots, x(N-1)$ of S if we have $\sigma_k = L(x(k))$ for all $k \in \{0, 1, \dots, N-1\}$.*

Next, we define the probability that the discrete-time stochastic system S satisfies safe LTL$_F$ formula φ over traces of length $|\sigma| = N$.

Definition 4. *Let $Trace_N(S)$ be the set of all finite traces of solution processes of S with length $|\sigma_{\boldsymbol{x}_N}| = N$ and φ be a safe LTL$_F$ formula over Π. Then $\mathbb{P}\{Trace_N(S) \models \varphi\}$ is the probability that φ is satisfied by discrete-time stochastic system S over a finite time horizon $[0, N) \subset \mathbb{N}_0$.*

Remark 2. The set of atomic propositions $\Pi = \{p_0, p_1, \dots, p_M\}$ and the labeling function $L : X \rightarrow \Pi$ provide a measurable partition of the state space $X = \cup_{i=1}^{M} X_i$ as $X_i := L^{-1}(p_i)$. Without loss of generality, we assumed that $X_i \neq \emptyset$ for any i.

2.4   Problem Formulation

Problem 1. Given a system $S = (X, V_w, w, f)$ with dynamics (1), a safe LTL$_F$ specification φ of length N over a set $\Pi = \{p_0, p_1, \dots, p_M\}$ of atomic propositions, and a labeling function $L : X \rightarrow \Pi$, compute a lower bound on the probability that the traces of solution process of S of length N satisfies φ, i.e., a quantity ϑ such that $\mathbb{P}\{Trace_N(S) \models \varphi\} \geq \vartheta$.

Note that $\vartheta = 0$ is a trivial lower bound, but we are looking at computation of lower bounds that are as tight as possible. For finding a solution to Problem 1, we first compute an upper bound on the probability $\mathbb{P}\{Trace_N(S) \models \neg\varphi\}$. This is done by constructing a DFA $\mathcal{A}_{\neg\varphi} = (Q, Q_0, \Pi, \delta, F)$ that accepts all finite words over Π that satisfies $\neg\varphi$.

Example 1. Consider a two-dimensional stochastic system $S = (X, V_w, w, f)$ with $X = V_w = \mathbb{R}^2$ and dynamics

$$x_1(k + 1) = x_1(k) - 0.01x_2^2(k) + 0.1w_1(k),$$
$$x_2(k + 1) = x_2(k) - 0.01x_1(k)x_2(k) + 0.1w_2(k), \tag{2}$$

where $w_1(\cdot)$, $w_2(\cdot)$ are independent standard normal random variables. Let the regions of interest be given as

$$X_0 = \{(x_1, x_2) \in X \mid x_1 \geq -10, \ -10 \leq x_2 \leq 0, \ \text{and} \ x_1 + x_2 \leq 0\},$$
$$X_1 = \{(x_1, x_2) \in X \mid 0 \leq x_1 \leq 10, \ x_2 \leq 10, \ \text{and} \ x_1 + x_2 \geq 0\},$$
$$X_2 = \{(x_1, x_2) \in X \mid -10 \leq x_1 \leq 0 \ \text{and} \ 0 \leq x_2 \leq 10\}, \ \text{and}$$
$$X_3 = X \setminus (X_0 \cup X_1 \cup X_2).$$

The sets X_0, X_1, X_2, and X_3 are shown in Figure 1(a). The set of atomic propositions is given by $\Pi = \{p_0, p_1, p_2, p_3\}$, with labeling function $L(x) = p_i$ for any $x \in X_i$, $i \in \{0, 1, 2, 3\}$. We are interested in computing a lower bound on the probability that $Trace_N(S)$ of length N satisfies the following specification:

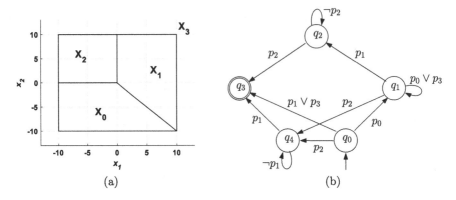

Fig. 1. (a) State space and regions of interest for Example 1, (b) DFA $\mathcal{A}_{\neg\varphi}$ that accepts all traces satisfying $\neg\varphi$ where φ is given in (3).

- Solution process should start in either X_0 or X_2. If it starts in X_0, it will always stay away from X_1 or always stay away from X_2 within time horizon $[0, N) \subset \mathbb{N}_0$. If it starts in X_2, it will always stay away from X_1 within time horizon $[0, N) \subset \mathbb{N}_0$.

This property can be expressed by the safe LTL$_F$ formula

$$\varphi = (p_0 \wedge (\Box\neg p_1 \vee \Box\neg p_2)) \vee (p_2 \wedge \Box\neg p_1). \tag{3}$$

The DFA corresponding to the negation of the safe LTL$_F$ formula φ in (3) is shown in Figure 1(b).   □

Next, we provide a systematic approach to solve Problem 1 by combining automata and barrier certificates introduced in the next section. We introduce the notion of barrier certificate similar to the one used in [19] and show how to use it for solving Problem 1 in Sects. 4-5.

3 Barrier Certificate

We recall that a function $B : X \to \mathbb{R}$ is a *supermartingale* for system $S = (X, V_w, w, f)$ if

$$\mathbb{E}[B(x(k+1)) \mid x(k)] \leq B(x(k)), \quad \forall x(k) \in X, \, k \in \mathbb{N}_0,$$

where the expectation is with respect to $w(k)$. This inequality requires that the expected value of $B(x(\cdot))$ does not increase as a function of time. To provide results for finite time horizon, we instead use a relaxation of supermartingale condition called *c-martingale*.

Definition 5. *Function* $B : X \to \mathbb{R}$ *is a c-martingale for system* $S = (X, V_w, w, f)$ *if it satisfies*

$$\mathbb{E}[B(x(k+1)) \mid x(k)] \leq B(x(k)) + c, \quad \forall x(k) \in X, \, k \in \mathbb{N}_0,$$

with $c \geq 0$ *being a non-negative constant.*

We provide the following lemma and use it in the sequel. This lemma is a direct consequence of [13, Theorem 1] and is also utilized in [27, Theorem II.1].

Lemma 1. *Let $B : X \to \mathbb{R}_0^+$ be a non-negative c-martingale for system S. Then for any constant $\lambda > 0$ and any initial condition $x_0 \in X$,*

$$\mathbb{P}\{ \sup_{0 \leq k \leq T_d} B(x(k)) \geq \lambda \mid x(0) = x_0 \} \leq \frac{B(x_0) + cT_d}{\lambda}. \tag{4}$$

Next theorem provides inequalities on a barrier certificate that gives an upper bound on reachability probabilities. This theorem is inspired by the result of [19, Theorem 15] that uses supermartingales for reachability analysis of continuous-time systems.

Theorem 1. *Consider a discrete-time stochastic system $S = (X, V_w, w, f)$ and sets $X_0, X_1 \subseteq X$. Suppose there exist a non-negative function $B : X \to \mathbb{R}_0^+$ and constants $c \geq 0$ and $\gamma \in [0, 1]$ such that*

$$B(x) \leq \gamma \qquad\qquad \forall x \in X_0, \tag{5}$$
$$B(x) \geq 1 \qquad\qquad \forall x \in X_1, \tag{6}$$
$$B(x) \text{ is c-martingale} \qquad\qquad \forall x \in X. \tag{7}$$

Then the probability that the solution process x_{T_d} of S starts from initial state $x(0) \in X_0$ and reaches X_1 within time horizon $[0, T_d] \subset \mathbb{N}_0$ is upper bounded by $\gamma + cT_d$.

Proof. Since $B(x(k))$ is non-negative and c-martingale, we conclude that (4) in Lemma 1 holds. Now using (5) and the fact that $X_1 \subseteq \{x \in X \mid B(x) \geq 1\}$, we have $\mathbb{P}\{x(k) \in X_1 \text{ for some } 0 \leq k \leq T_d \mid x(0) = x_0\} \leq \mathbb{P}\{\sup_{0 \leq k \leq T_d} B(x(k)) \geq 1 \mid x(0) = x_0\} \leq B(x_0) + cT_d \leq \gamma + cT_d$. This concludes the proof. □

Theorem 1 enables us to formulate an optimization problem by minimizing the value of γ and c in order to find an upper bound for finite-horizon reachability that is as tight as possible.

In the next section, we discuss how to translate LTL_F verification problem into the computation of a collection of barrier certificates each satisfying inequalities of the form (5)-(7). Then we show in Sect. 5 how to use Theorem 1 to provide a lower bound on the probability of satisfying LTL_F specifications over a finite time horizon.

4   Decomposition into Sequential Reachability

Consider a DFA $\mathcal{A}_{\neg\varphi} = (Q, Q_0, \Pi, \delta, F)$ that accepts all finite words of length $n \in [0, N] \subset \mathbb{N}_0$ over Π that satisfy $\neg\varphi$. Self-loops in the DFA play a central role in our decomposition. Let $Q_s \subseteq Q$ be a set of states of $\mathcal{A}_{\neg\varphi}$ having self-loops, i.e., $Q_s := \{q \in Q \mid \exists p \in \Pi, q \xrightarrow{p} q\}$.

Algorithm 1 Computation of sets $\mathcal{P}(\mathbf{q})$, $\mathbf{q} \in \mathcal{R}_{\leq N+1}$

Require: $\mathcal{G}, Q_s, N$
 1: Compute set $\mathcal{R}_{\leq N+1}$ by depth first search on $\mathcal{G}$
 2: **for all** $\mathbf{q} \in \mathcal{R}_{\leq N+1}$ and $|\mathbf{q}| \geq 3$ **do**
 3:     **for** $i = 0$ to $|\mathbf{q}| - 3$ **do**
 4:         $\mathcal{P}_1(\mathbf{q}) \leftarrow \{(q_i, q_{i+1}, q_{i+2})\}$
 5:         **if** $q_{i+1} \in Q_s$ **then**
 6:             $\mathcal{P}(\mathbf{q}) \leftarrow \{(q_i, q_{i+1}, q_{i+2}, N + 2 - |\mathbf{q}|)\}$
 7:         **else**
 8:             $\mathcal{P}(\mathbf{q}) \leftarrow \{(q_i, q_{i+1}, q_{i+2}, 1)\}$
     return $\mathcal{P}(\mathbf{q})$

Accepting state run of $\mathcal{A}_{\neg\varphi}$. Sequence $\mathbf{q} = (q_0, q_1, \ldots, q_n) \in Q^{n+1}$ is called an accepting state run if $q_0 \in Q_0$, $q_n \in F$, and there exist a finite word $\sigma = (\sigma_0, \sigma_1, \ldots, \sigma_{n-1}) \in \Pi^n$ such that $q_i \xrightarrow{\sigma_i} q_{i+1}$ for all $i \in \{0, 1, \ldots, n - 1\}$. We denote the set of such finite words by $\sigma(\mathbf{q}) \subseteq \Pi^n$ and the set of accepting runs by $\mathcal{R}$. We also indicate the length of $\mathbf{q} \in Q^{n+1}$ by $|\mathbf{q}|$, which is $n + 1$.

Let $\mathcal{R}_{\leq N+1}$ be the set of all finite accepting state runs of lengths less than or equal to $N + 1$ excluding self-loops,

$$\mathcal{R}_{\leq N+1} := \{\mathbf{q} = (q_0, q_1, \ldots, q_n) \in \mathcal{R} \mid n \leq N, \ q_i \neq q_{i+1}, \ \forall i < n, \ q_n \in F\}. \quad (8)$$

Computation of $\mathcal{R}_{\leq N+1}$ can be done efficiently using algorithms in graph theory by viewing $\mathcal{A}_{\neg\varphi}$ as a directed graph. Consider $\mathcal{G} = (\mathcal{V}, \mathcal{E})$ as a directed graph with vertices $\mathcal{V} = Q$ and edges $\mathcal{E} \subseteq \mathcal{V} \times \mathcal{V}$ such that $(q, q') \in \mathcal{E}$ if and only if $q' \neq q$ and there exist $p \in \Pi$ such that $q \xrightarrow{p} q'$. From the construction of the graph, it is obvious that the finite path in the graph of length $n + 1$ starting from vertices $q_0 \in Q_0$ and ending at $q_F \in F$ is an accepting state run $\mathbf{q}$ of $\mathcal{A}_{\neg\varphi}$ without any self-loop thus belongs to $\mathcal{R}_{\leq N+1}$. Then one can easily compute $\mathcal{R}_{\leq N+1}$ using variants of depth first search algorithm [21].

Decomposition into sequential reachability is performed as follows. For any $\mathbf{q} = (q_0, q_1, \ldots, q_n) \in \mathcal{R}_{\leq N+1}$, we define $\mathcal{P}(\mathbf{q})$ as a set of all state runs of length 3 augmented with a horizon,

$$\mathcal{P}(\mathbf{q}) := \{(q_i, q_{i+1}, q_{i+2}, T(\mathbf{q}, q_{i+1})) \mid 0 \leq i \leq n - 2\}, \quad (9)$$

where the horizon is defined as $T(\mathbf{q}, q_{i+1}) = N + 2 - |\mathbf{q}|$ for $q_{i+1} \in Q_s$ and 1 otherwise.

Remark 3. Note that $\mathcal{P}(\mathbf{q}) = \emptyset$ for $|\mathbf{q}| = 2$. In fact, any accepting state run of length 2 specifies a subset of the state space such that the system satisfies $\neg\varphi$ whenever it starts from that subset. This gives trivial zero probability for satisfying the specification, thus neglected in the sequel.

The computation of sets $\mathcal{P}(\mathbf{q})$, $\mathbf{q} \in \mathcal{R}_{\leq N+1}$, is illustrated in Algorithm 1 and demonstrated below for our demo example.

Example 2. (continuation of Example 1) For safe LTL$_F$ formula φ given in (3), Figure 1(b) shows a DFA $\mathcal{A}_{\neg\varphi}$ that accepts all words that satisfy $\neg\varphi$. From Figure 1(b), we get $Q_0 = \{q_0\}$ and $F = \{q_3\}$. We consider traces of maximum length $N = 5$. The set of accepting state runs of lengths at most $N + 1$ without self-loops is

$$\mathcal{R}_{\leq 6} = \{(q_0, q_4, q_3), (q_0, q_1, q_2, q_3), (q_0, q_1, q_4, q_3), (q_0, q_3)\}.$$

The set of states with self-loops is $Q_s = \{q_1, q_2, q_4\}$. Then the sets $\mathcal{P}(\mathbf{q})$ for $\mathbf{q} \in \mathcal{R}_{\leq 6}$ are as follows:

$$\mathcal{P}(q_0, q_3) = \emptyset, \quad \mathcal{P}(q_0, q_4, q_3) = \{(q_0, q_4, q_3, 4)\},$$
$$\mathcal{P}(q_0, q_1, q_2, q_3) = \{(q_0, q_1, q_2, 3), (q_1, q_2, q_3, 3)\},$$
$$\mathcal{P}(q_0, q_1, q_4, q_3) = \{(q_0, q_1, q_4, 3), (q_1, q_4, q_3, 3)\}.$$

For every $\mathbf{q} \in \mathcal{R}_{\leq 6}$, the corresponding finite words $\sigma(\mathbf{q})$ are listed as follows:

$$\sigma(q_0, q_3) = \{p_1 \vee p_3\}, \quad \sigma(q_0, q_4, q_3) = \{(p_2, p_1)\},$$
$$\sigma(q_0, q_1, q_2, q_3) = \{(p_0, p_1, p_2)\}, \quad \sigma(q_0, q_1, q_4, q_3) = \{(p_0, p_2, p_1)\}.$$

$\square$

5 Computation of Probabilities Using Barrier Certificates

Having the set of state runs of length 3 augmented with horizon, in this section, we provide a systematic approach to compute a lower bound on the probability that the solution process of S satisfies φ. Given DFA $\mathcal{A}_{\neg\varphi}$, our approach relies on performing a reachability computation over each element of $\mathcal{P}(\mathbf{q})$, $\mathbf{q} \in \mathcal{R}_{\leq N+1}$, where reachability probability is upper bounded using barrier certificates.

Next theorem provides an upper bound on the probability that the solution process of the system satisfies the specification $\neg\varphi$.

Theorem 2. *For a given safe LTL$_F$ specification φ, let $\mathcal{A}_{\neg\varphi}$ be a DFA corresponding to its negation, $\mathcal{R}_{\leq N+1}$ be the set of accepting state runs of length at most $N + 1$ as defined in* (8)*, and $\mathcal{P}$ be the set of runs of length 3 augmented with horizon as defined in* (9)*. Then the probability that the system satisfies $\neg\varphi$ within time horizon $[0, N] \subseteq \mathbb{N}_0$ is upper bounded by*

$$\mathbb{P}\{Trace_N(S) \models \neg\varphi\} \leq \sum_{q \in \mathcal{R}_{\leq N+1}} \prod \{(\gamma_\nu + c_\nu T) \mid \nu = (q, q', q'', T) \in \mathcal{P}(\mathbf{q})\}, \quad (10)$$

where $\gamma_\nu + c_\nu T$ is the upper bound on the probability of the trajectories of S starting from $X_0 := L^{-1}(\sigma(q, q'))$ and reaching $X_1 := L^{-1}(\sigma(q', q''))$ within time horizon $[0, T] \subseteq \mathbb{N}_0$ computed via Theorem 1.

Proof. Consider an accepting run $\mathbf{q} \in \mathcal{R}_{\leq N+1}$ and set $\mathcal{P}(\mathbf{q})$ as defined in (9). For an element $\nu = (q, q', q'', T) \in \mathcal{P}(\mathbf{q})$, the upper bound on the probability of trajectories of S stating from $L^{-1}(\sigma(q, q'))$ and reaching $L^{-1}(\sigma(q', q''))$ within time horizon T is given by $\gamma_\nu + c_\nu T$. This follows from Theorem 1. Now the upper bound on the probability of the trace of the solution process reaching accepting state following trace corresponding to $\mathbf{q}$ is given by the product of the probability bounds corresponding to all elements $\nu = (q, q', q'', T) \in \mathcal{P}(\mathbf{q})$ and is given by

$$\mathbb{P}\{\sigma_{\mathbf{x}_N}(\mathbf{q}) \models \neg\varphi\} \leq \prod \{(\gamma_\nu + c_\nu T) \mid \nu = (q, q', q'', T) \in \mathcal{P}(\mathbf{q})\}. \qquad (11)$$

Note that, the way we computed time horizon T, we always get the upper bound for the probabilities for all possible combinations of self-loops for accepting state runs of length less than or equal to $N + 1$. The upper bound on the probability that the solution processes of system S violate φ can be computed by summing the probability bounds for all possible accepting runs as computed in (11) and is given by

$$\mathbb{P}\{Trace_N(S) \models \neg\varphi\} \leq \sum_{\mathbf{q} \in \mathcal{R}_{\leq N+1}} \prod \{(\gamma_\nu + c_\nu T) \mid \nu = (q, q', q'', T) \in \mathcal{P}(\mathbf{q})\}.$$

□

Theorem 2 enables us to decompose the computation into a collection of sequential reachability, compute bounds on the reachability probabilities using Theorem 1, and then combine the bounds in a sum-product expression.

Remark 4. In case we are unable to find barrier certificates for some of the elements $\nu \in \mathcal{P}(\mathbf{q})$ in (10), we replace the related term $(\gamma_\nu + c_\nu T)$ by the pessimistic bound 1. In order to get a non-trivial bound in (10), at least one barrier certificate must be found for each $\mathbf{q} \in \mathcal{R}_{\leq N+1}$.

Corollary 1. *Given the result of Theorem 2, the probability that the trajectories of S of length N satisfies safe LTL$_F$ specification φ is lower-bounded by*

$$\mathbb{P}\{Trace_N(S) \models \varphi\} \geq 1 - \mathbb{P}\{Trace_N(S) \models \neg\varphi\}.$$

5.1   Computation of Barrier Certificate

Proving existence of a barrier certificate, finding one, or showing that a given function is in fact a barrier certificate are in general hard problems. But if we restrict the class of systems and labeling functions, we can provide computationally efficient techniques for searching barrier certificates of specific forms. One technique is to use sum-of-squares (SOS) optimization [17], which relies on the fact that a polynomial is non-negative if it can be written as sum of squares of different polynomials. Therefore, we raise the following assumption.

Assumption 1. System S has state set $X \subseteq \mathbb{R}^n$ and its vector field $f : X \times V_w \to X$ is a polynomial function of state x for any $w \in V_w$. Partition sets $X_i = L^{-1}(p_i)$, $i \in \{0, 1, 2, \ldots, M\}$, are bounded semi-algebraic sets, *i.e.*, they can be represented by polynomial equalities and inequalities.

Under Assumption 1, we can formulate (5)-(7) as an SOS optimization problem to search for a polynomial-type barrier certificate $B(\cdot)$ and the tightest upper bound $(\gamma + cT_d)$. The following lemma provides a set of sufficient conditions for the existence of such a barrier certificate required in Theorem 1, which can be solved as an SOS optimization.

Lemma 2. *Suppose Assumption 1 holds and sets X_0, X_1, X can be defined by vectors of polynomial inequalities $X_0 = \{x \in \mathbb{R}^n \mid g_0(x) \geq 0\}$, $X_1 = \{x \in \mathbb{R}^n \mid g_1(x) \geq 0\}$, and $X = \{x \in \mathbb{R}^n \mid g(x) \geq 0\}$, where the inequalities are defined element-wise. Suppose there exists a sum-of-squares polynomial $B(x)$, constants $\gamma \in [0, 1]$ and $c \geq 0$, and vectors of sum-of-squares polynomials $\lambda_0(x)$, $\lambda_1(x)$, and $\lambda(x)$ of appropriate size such that following expressions are sum-of-squares polynomials*

$$-B(x) - \lambda_0^T(x)g_0(x) + \gamma \tag{12}$$

$$B(x) - \lambda_1^T(x)g_1(x) - 1 \tag{13}$$

$$-\mathbb{E}[B(f(x, w))|x] + B(x) - \lambda^T(x)g(x) + c. \tag{14}$$

Then $B(x)$ satisfies conditions (5)-(7).

Proof. The proof is similar to that of Lemma 7 in [33] and is omitted due to lack of space. □

Remark 5. Assumption 1 is essential for applying the results of Lemma 2 to *any* LTL$_F$ specification. For a given specification, we can relax this assumption and allow some of the partition sets X_i to be unbounded. For this, we require that the labels corresponding to unbounded partition sets should only appear either on self-loops or on accepting runs of length less than 3. For instance, Example 1 has an unbounded partition set X_3 and its corresponding label p_3 satisfies this requirements (see Figure 1), thus the results are still applicable for verifying the specification.

5.2   Computational Complexity

Based on Lemma 2, a polynomial barrier certificate $B(\cdot)$ satisfying (5)-(7) and minimizing constants γ and c can be automatically computed using SOSTOOLS [20] in conjunction with a semidefinite programming solver such as SeDuMi [28]. We refer the interested reader to [27] and [19] for more discussions. Note that the value of the upper bound of violating the property depends highly on the selection of degree of polynomials in Lemma 2.

From the construction of directed graph $\mathcal{G} = (\mathcal{V}, \mathcal{E})$, explained in Sect. 4, the number of triplets and hence the number of barrier certificates needed to be computed are bounded by $|\mathcal{V}|^3 = |Q|^3$, where $|\mathcal{V}|$ is the number of vertices in $\mathcal{G}$.

Further, it is known [3] that $|Q|$ is at most $|\neg\varphi|2^{|\neg\varphi|}$, where $|\neg\varphi|$ is the length of formula $\neg\varphi$ in terms of number of operations, but in practice, it is much smaller than this bound [11].

Computational complexity of finding polynomials $B, \lambda_0, \lambda_1, \lambda$ in Lemma 2 depends on both the degree of polynomials appearing in (12)-(14) and the number of variables. It is shown that for fixed degrees the required computations grow polynomially with respect to the dimension [33]. Hence we expect that this technique is more scalable in comparison with the discretization-based approaches especially for large-scale systems.

6   Case Studies

In this section, we demonstrate the effectiveness of the proposed results on several case studies. We first showcase the results on the running example, which has nonlinear dynamics with additive noise. We then apply the technique to a ten-dimensional linear system with additive noise to show its scalability. The third case study is a three-dimensional nonlinear system with multiplicative noise.

6.1   Running Example

To compute an upper bound on reachability probabilities corresponding to each element of $\mathcal{P}(\mathbf{q})$ in Theorem 2, we use Lemma 2 to formulate it as a SOS optimization problem to minimize values of γ and c using bisection method. The optimization problem is solved using SOSTOOLS and SeDuMi, to obtain upper bounds in Theorem 2. The computed upper bounds on probabilities corresponding to the elements of $\mathcal{P}(\cdot)$, $(q_0, q_4, q_3, 4)$, $(q_0, q_1, q_2, 3)$, $(q_1, q_2, q_3, 3)$, $(q_0, q_1, q_4, 3)$, and $(q_1, q_4, q_3, 3)$ are respectively 0.00586, 0.00232, 0.00449, 0.00391, and 0.00488. Using Theorem 2, we get

$$\mathbb{P}\{Trace_N(S) \models \neg\varphi\} \le 0.00586 + 0.00232 \times 0.00449 + 0.00391 \times 0.00488 = 0.00589.$$

Thus, a lower bound on the probability that trajectories of S satisfy safe LTL_F property (3) over time horizon $N = 5$ is given by 0.99411. The optimization finds polynomials of degree 5 for B, λ, λ_0, and λ_1. Hence 4 barrier certificates are computed each with 245 optimization coefficients, which takes 29 minutes in total.

6.2   Thermal Model of a Ten-Room Building

Consider temperature evolution in a ten-room building shown schematically in Figure 2(a). We use this model to demonstrate the effectiveness of the results on large-dimensional state spaces. This model is adapted from [10] by discretizing it with sampling time $\tau_s = 5$ minutes and without including heaters.

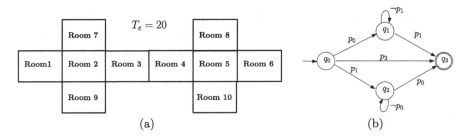

Fig. 2. (a) A schematic of a ten-room building, (b) DFA $\mathcal{A}_{\neg\varphi}$ that accepts all traces satisfying $\neg\varphi$ where φ is given in (15).

The dynamics of S are given as follows:

$$x_1(k+1) = (1 - \tau_s(\alpha + \alpha_{e1}))x_1(k) + \tau_s\alpha x_2(k) + \tau_s\alpha_{e1}T_e + 0.5w_1(k),$$
$$x_2(k+1) = (1 - \tau_s(4\alpha + \alpha_{e2}))x_2(k) + \tau_s\alpha(x_1(k) + x_3(k) + x_7(k) + x_9(k))$$
$$+ \tau_s\alpha_{e2}T_e + 0.5w_2(k),$$
$$x_3(k+1) = (1 - \tau_s(2\alpha + \alpha_{e1}))x_3(k) + \tau_s\alpha(x_2(k) + x_4(k)) + \tau_s\alpha_{e1}T_e + 0.5w_3(k),$$
$$x_4(k+1) = (1 - \tau_s(2\alpha + \alpha_{e1}))x_4(k) + \tau_s\alpha(x_3(k) + x_5(k)) + \tau_s\alpha_{e1}T_e + 0.5w_4(k),$$
$$x_5(k+1) = (1 - \tau_s(4\alpha + \alpha_{e2}))x_5(k) + \tau_s\alpha(x_4(k) + x_6(k) + x_8(k) + x_{10}(k))$$
$$+ \tau_s\alpha_{e2}T_e + 0.5w_5(k),$$
$$x_6(k+1) = (1 - \tau_s(\alpha + \alpha_{e1}))x_6(k) + \tau_s\alpha x_5(k) + \tau_s\alpha_{e1}T_e + 0.5w_6(k),$$
$$x_7(k+1) = (1 - \tau_s(\alpha + \alpha_{e1}))x_7(k) + \tau_s\alpha x_2(k) + \tau_s\alpha_{e1}T_e + 0.5w_7(k),$$
$$x_8(k+1) = (1 - \tau_s(\alpha + \alpha_{e1}))x_8(k) + \tau_s\alpha x_5(k) + \tau_s\alpha_{e1}T_e + 0.5w_8(k),$$
$$x_9(k+1) = (1 - \tau_s(\alpha + \alpha_{e1}))x_9(k) + \tau_s\alpha x_2(k) + \tau_s\alpha_{e1}T_e + 0.5w_9(k),$$
$$x_{10}(k+1) = (1 - \tau_s(\alpha + \alpha_{e1}))x_{10}(k) + \tau_s\alpha x_5(k) + \tau_s\alpha_{e1}T_e + 0.5w_{10}(k),$$

where x_i, $i \in \{1, 2, \ldots, 10\}$, denotes the temperature in each room, $T_e = 20°C$ is the ambient temperature, and $\alpha = 5 \times 10^{-2}$, $\alpha_{e1} = 5 \times 10^{-3}$, and $\alpha_{e2} = 8 \times 10^{-3}$ are heat exchange coefficients.

Noise terms $w_i(k)$, $i \in \{1, 2, \ldots, 10\}$, are independent standard normal random variables. The state space of the system is $X = \mathbb{R}^{10}$. We consider regions of interest $X_0 = [18, 19.75]^{10}$, $X_1 = [20.25, 22]^{10}$, $X_2 = X \setminus (X_0 \cup X_1)$. The set of atomic propositions is given by $\Pi = \{p_0, p_1, p_2\}$ with labeling function $L(x_i) = p_i$ for all $x_i \in X_i$, $i \in \{0, 1, 2\}$. The objective is to compute a lower bound on the probability that the solution process of length $N = 10$ satisfies the safe LTL$_F$ formula

$$\varphi = (p_0 \wedge \Box\neg p_1) \vee (p_1 \wedge \Box\neg p_0). \qquad (15)$$

The DFA $\mathcal{A}_{\neg\varphi}$ corresponding to $\neg\varphi$ is shown in Figure 2(b). We use Algorithm 1 to get $\mathcal{R}_{\leq 11} = \{(q_0, q_3), (q_0, q_1, q_3), (q_0, q_2, q_3)\}$, $\mathcal{P}(q_0, q_1, q_3) = \{q_0, q_1, q_3, 9\}$, and $\mathcal{P}(q_0, q_2, q_3) = \{q_0, q_2, q_3, 9\}$. As described in Sect. 5, we compute two barrier certificates and SOS polynomials satisfying inequalities of Lemma 2. The lower bound $\mathbb{P}\{Trace_N(S) \models \varphi\} \geq 0.9820$ is obtained using SOSTOOLS and SeDuMi for initial states starting from $X_0 \cup X_1$. The optimization procedure finds B, λ, λ_0, and λ_1 as quadratic polynomials. Hence, two barrier certificates are computed each with 255 optimization coefficients, which takes 18 minutes in total.

6.3 Lorenz Model of a Thermal Convection Loop

Our third case study is the Lorenz model of a thermal convection loop as used in [18] with multiplicative noise. The nonlinear dynamics of S is given as

$$
\begin{aligned}
x_1(k+1) &= (1-aT)x_1(k) + aTx_2(k) + 0.025x_1(k)w_1(k), \\
x_2(k+1) &= (1-T)x_2(k) - Tx_2(k)x_3(k) + 0.025x_2(k)w_2(k), \\
x_3(k+1) &= (1+bT)x_3(k) + Tx_1(k)x_2(k) + 0.025x_3(k)w_3(k), \quad (16)
\end{aligned}
$$

where $a = 10$, $b = 8/3$, and $T = 0.01$. Noise terms $w_1(k)$, $w_2(k)$, and $w_3(k)$ are independent standard normal random variables. We refer the interested readers to [31] for a detailed treatment of the model. The state space of the system is $X = \mathbb{R}^3$. We define regions of interest as $X_0 = [-10,10]^2 \times [2,10]$, $X_1 = [-10,10]^2 \times [-2,2]$, $X_2 = [-10,10]^2 \times [-10,-2]$, and $X_3 = X \setminus (X_0 \cup X_1 \cup X_2)$.

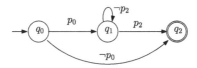

Fig. 3. DFA $\mathcal{A}_{\neg\varphi}$ that accepts all traces satisfying $\neg\varphi$ where $\varphi = p_0 \wedge \Box \neg p_2$.

The set of atomic propositions is given by $\Pi = \{p_0, p_1, p_2, p_3\}$ with labeling function $L(x_i) = p_i$ for all $x_i \in X_i$, $i \in \{0, 1, 2, 3\}$. We consider safe LTL$_F$ property $\varphi = p_0 \wedge \Box \neg p_2$ and time horizon $N = 10$. The DFA $\mathcal{A}_{\neg\varphi}$ corresponding to the negation of φ is shown in Figure 3. One can readily see that $\mathcal{R}_{\leq 11} = \{(q_0, q_1, q_2)\}$ with $\mathcal{P}(q_0, q_1, q_2) = (q_0, q_1, q_2, 9)$. Thus, we need to compute only one barrier certificate. We use inequalities of Lemma 2 and find a barrier certificate that gives a lower bound $\mathbb{P}\{Trace_N(S) \models \varphi\} \geq 0.9859$. The optimization procedure finds B, λ, λ_0, and λ_1 as polynomials of degree 4. Hence only one barrier certificate is computed with 53 optimization coefficients, which takes 3 minutes.

Remark that current implementations of discretization-based approaches (e.g., [26]) are not directly applicable to the models in Subsect. 6.1 and (16) due to the multiplicative noise in the latter and unbounded state space of the former. Application of these techniques to the model in Subsect. 6.2 will also be computationally much more expensive than our approach due to the existing exponential complexity as a function of state space dimension which is the case in discretization-based approaches.

7   Conclusions

In this paper, we proposed a discretization-free approach for formal verification of discrete-time stochastic systems. The approach computes lower bounds on the probability of satisfying a specification encoded as safe LTL over finite traces. It is based on computation of barrier certificates and uses sum-of-squares optimization to find such bounds. From the implementation perspective, we plan to generalize our code and make it publicly available so that it can be applied to systems and specifications defined by users.

References

1. Abate, A., Katoen, J.P., Mereacre, A.: Quantitative automata model checking of autonomous stochastic hybrid systems. In: Proceedings of the 14th International Conference on Hybrid systems: Computation and Control, pp. 83–92. ACM (2011)
2. Ayala, A.I.M., Andersson, S.B., Belta, C.: Probabilistic control from time-bounded temporal logic specifications in dynamic environments. In: 2012 IEEE International Conference on Robotics and Automation, pp. 4705–4710 (2012)
3. Baier, C., Katoen, J.P., Larsen, K.G.: Principles of Model Checking. MIT press, Cambridge (2008)
4. De Giacomo, G., Vardi, M.Y.: Linear temporal logic and linear dynamic logic on finite traces. In: International Joint Conference on Artificial Intelligence, vol. 13, pp. 854–860 (2013)
5. De Giacomo, G., Vardi, M.Y.: Synthesis for LTL and LDL on finite traces. In: International Joint Conference on Artificial Intelligence, vol. 15, pp. 1558–1564 (2015)
6. Dimitrova, R., Majumdar, R.: Deductive control synthesis for alternating-time logics. In: 2014 International Conference on Embedded Software (EMSOFT), pp. 1–10 (2014)
7. Duret-Lutz, A., Lewkowicz, A., Fauchille, A., Michaud, T., Renault, É., Xu, L.: Spot 2.0 — a framework for LTL and ω-automata manipulation. In: Artho, C., Legay, A., Peled, D. (eds.) ATVA 2016. LNCS, vol. 9938, pp. 122–129. Springer, Cham (2016). https://doi.org/10.1007/978-3-319-46520-3_8
8. Henriksen, J.G., Jensen, J., Jørgensen, M., Klarlund, N., Paige, R., Rauhe, T., Sandholm, A.: Mona: monadic second-order logic in practice. In: Brinksma, E., Cleaveland, W.R., Larsen, K.G., Margaria, T., Steffen, B. (eds.) TACAS 1995. LNCS, vol. 1019, pp. 89–110. Springer, Heidelberg (1995). https://doi.org/10.1007/3-540-60630-0_5
9. Huang, C., Chen, X., Lin, W., Yang, Z., Li, X.: Probabilistic safety verification of stochastic hybrid systems using barrier certificates. ACM Trans. Embed. Comput. Syst. **16**(5s), 186 (2017)
10. Jagtap, P., Zamani, M.: QUEST: a tool for state-space quantization-free synthesis of symbolic controllers. In: Bertrand, N., Bortolussi, L. (eds.) QEST 2017. LNCS, vol. 10503, pp. 309–313. Springer, Cham (2017). https://doi.org/10.1007/978-3-319-66335-7_21
11. Klein, J., Baier, C.: Experiments with deterministic ω-automata for formulas of linear temporal logic. Theor. Comput. Sci. **363**(2), 182–195 (2006)
12. Kupferman, O., Vardi, M.: Model checking of safety properties. In: International Conference on Computer Aided Verification, pp. 172–183. Springer, Berlin (1999)

13. Kushner, H.J.: On the stability of stochastic dynamical systems. Proc. Natl. Acad. Sci. **53**(1), 8–12 (1965)
14. Lahijanian, M., Andersson, S.B., Belta, C.: Formal verification and synthesis for discrete-time stochastic systems. IEEE Trans. Autom. Control **60**(8), 2031–2045 (2015)
15. Lavaei, A., Soudjani, S., Zamani, M.: From dissipativity theory to compositional construction of finite Markov decision processes. In: Hybrid Systems: Computation and Control (HSCC), pp. 21–30. ACM, New York (2018)
16. Maity, D., Baras, J.S.: Motion planning in dynamic environments with bounded time temporal logic specifications. In: 2015 23rd Mediterranean Conference on Control and Automation, pp. 940–946 (2015)
17. Parrilo, P.A.: Semidefinite programming relaxations for semialgebraic problems. Math. Program. **96**(2), 293–320 (2003)
18. Postoyan, R., Nesic, D.: Time-triggered control of nonlinear discrete-time systems. In: 2016 IEEE 55th Conference on Decision and Control, pp. 6814–6819 (2016)
19. Prajna, S., Jadbabaie, A., Pappas, G.J.: A framework for worst-case and stochastic safety verification using barrier certificates. IEEE Trans. Autom. Control **52**(8), 1415–1428 (2007)
20. Prajna, S., Papachristodoulou, A., Parrilo, P.A.: Introducing SOSTOOLS: a general purpose sum of squares programming solver. In: Proceedings of the 41st IEEE Conference on Decision and Control, vol. 1, pp. 741–746 (2002). http://www.cds.caltech.edu/sostools/
21. Russell, S.J., Norvig, P.: Artificial Intelligence: A Modern Approach, 2nd edn. Pearson Education, London (2003)
22. Saha, I., Ramaithitima, R., Kumar, V., Pappas, G.J., Seshia, S.A.: Automated composition of motion primitives for multi-robot systems from safe LTL specifications. In: 2014 IEEE/RSJ International Conference on Intelligent Robots and Systems, pp. 1525–1532 (2014)
23. Esmaeil Zadeh Soudjani, S., Abate, A.: Precise approximations of the probability distribution of a Markov process in time: an application to probabilistic invariance. In: Ábrahám, E., Havelund, K. (eds.) TACAS 2014. LNCS, vol. 8413, pp. 547–561. Springer, Heidelberg (2014). https://doi.org/10.1007/978-3-642-54862-8_45
24. Soudjani, S., Abate, A., Majumdar, R.: Dynamic Bayesian networks as formal abstractions of structured stochastic processes. In: 26th International Conference on Concurrency Theory, pp. 1–14. Dagstuhl Publishing, Madrid (2015)
25. Soudjani, S., Abate, A.: Adaptive and sequential gridding procedures for the abstraction and verification of stochastic processes. SIAM J. Appl. Dyn. Syst. **12**(2), 921–956 (2013)
26. Soudjani, S., Gevaerts, C., Abate, A.: FAUST^2: formal abstractions of uncountable-state stochastic processes. In: Baier, C., Tinelli, C. (eds.) Tools and Algorithms for the Construction and Analysis of Systems, pp. 272–286. Springer, Berlin (2015)
27. Steinhardt, J., Tedrake, R.: Finite-time regional verification of stochastic non-linear systems. Int. J. Robot. Res. **31**(7), 901–923 (2012)
28. Sturm, J.F.: Using SeDuMi 1.02, a MATLAB toolbox for optimization over symmetric cones. Optim. Methods Softw. **11**(1–4), 625–653 (1999). http://sedumi.ie.lehigh.edu/
29. Tabuada, P.: Verification and Control of Hybrid Systems: A Symbolic Approach. Springer Science & Business Media, Berlin (2009)

30. Tkachev, I., Abate, A.: Formula-free finite abstractions for linear temporal verification of stochastic hybrid systems. In: Proceedings of the 16th International Conference on Hybrid Systems: Computation and Control, pp. 283–292. ACM (2013)

31. Vincent, T.L., Yu, J.: Control of a chaotic system. Dyn. Control **1**(1), 35–52 (1991)

32. Wisniewski, R., Bujorianu, M.L.: Stochastic safety analysis of stochastic hybrid systems. In: 2017 IEEE 56th Annual Conference on Decision and Control, pp. 2390–2395 (2017)

33. Wongpiromsarn, T., Topcu, U., Lamperski, A.: Automata theory meets barrier certificates: temporal logic verification of nonlinear systems. IEEE Trans. Autom. Control **61**(11), 3344–3355 (2016)

Bisimilarity Distances for Approximate Differential Privacy

Dmitry Chistikov[1], Andrzej S. Murawski[2], and David Purser[1(✉)]

[1] Centre for Discrete Mathematics and its Applications (DIMAP)
and Department of Computer Science, University of Warwick, Coventry, UK
{D.J.Purser,d.chistikov}@warwick.ac.uk
[2] Department of Computer Science, University of Oxford, Oxford, UK

Abstract. Differential privacy is a widely studied notion of privacy for various models of computation. Technically, it is based on measuring differences between probability distributions. We study ϵ, δ-differential privacy in the setting of labelled Markov chains. While the exact differences relevant to ϵ, δ-differential privacy are not computable in this framework, we propose a computable bisimilarity distance that yields a sound technique for measuring δ, the parameter that quantifies deviation from pure differential privacy. We show this bisimilarity distance is always rational, the associated threshold problem is in **NP**, and the distance can be computed exactly with polynomially many calls to an **NP** oracle.

Keywords: Bisimilarity distances · Kantorovich metric
Differential privacy · Labelled Markov chains · Bisimulation
Analysis of probabilistic systems

1 Introduction

Bisimilarity distances were introduced by [16,17], as a metric analogue of classic probabilistic bisimulation [23], to overcome the problem that bisimilarity is too sensitive to minor changes in probabilities. Such robustness is highly desirable, because probabilistic automata arising in practice may often be based on approximate probability values, extracted or learnt from real world data.

In this paper, we study the computation of bisimilarity distances related to differential privacy. Differential privacy [18] is a security property that ensures that a small perturbation of the input leads to only a small perturbation in the output, so that observing the output makes it difficult to determine whether a particular piece of information was present in the input. A variant, ϵ-differential privacy, considers the ratio difference (rather than the absolute difference) between probabilities.

We will be concerned with the more general concept of ϵ, δ-differential privacy, also referred to as *approximate differential privacy*. The δ parameter allows one to assess to what degree ϵ-differential privacy ("pure differential privacy") was

© Springer Nature Switzerland AG 2018
S. K. Lahiri and C. Wang (Eds.): ATVA 2018, LNCS 11138, pp. 194–210, 2018.
https://doi.org/10.1007/978-3-030-01090-4_12

achieved. We will design a version of bisimilarity distance which will constitute a sound upper bound on δ, thus providing a reliable measure of security.

From a verification perspective, a natural question is how to analyse systems with respect to ϵ, δ-differential privacy. We carry out our investigations in the setting where the systems are *labelled Markov chains (LMC)*, abstractions of autonomous systems with probabilistic behaviour and under partial observability. States of an LMC $\mathcal{M}$ can be thought of as generating probability distributions on sets of traces, and these sets are taken to correspond to observable events. Let $\mathcal{M}$ be a system, and suppose s and s' are two states (configurations) of $\mathcal{M}$. Then we will say that s and s' satisfy ϵ, δ-differential privacy if the distributions on traces from these states are sufficiently close. We consider the following problem: given an LMC $\mathcal{M}$, states s and s', and a value of ϵ, determine δ such that s and s' satisfy ϵ, δ-differential privacy. Unfortunately, the smallest of such δ is not computable [22], which motivates our search for upper bounds.

In the spirit of generalised bisimilarity pseudometrics [12], our distance, denoted bd_α, is based on the Kantorovich-style lifting of distance between states to distance between distributions. However, because the underpinning distances in our case turn out not to be metrics, the setting does not quite fit into the standard picture, which presents a technical challenge. We discuss how the proposed distance may be computed, using techniques from linear programming, linear real arithmetic, and computational logic. Our first result is that the distance always takes on rational values of polynomial size with respect to the size of the LMC and the bit size of the probability values associated with transitions (Theorem 1).

This is then used to show that the associated threshold problem ("is bd_α upper-bounded by a given threshold value for two given states?") is in **NP** (Theorem 2). Note that the distance can be approximated to arbitrary precision by solving polynomially many instances of the threshold problem. Finally, we show that the distance can be computed exactly in polynomial time, given an **NP** oracle (Theorem 3). This places it in (the search version of) **NP**, leaving the possibility of polynomial-time computation open.

Related Work. Chatzikokolakis et al. [12] have advocated the development of Kantorovich pseudometrics, instantiated with any metric distance function (rather than absolute value) in the context of differential privacy. They did not discuss the complexity of calculating such pseudometrics, but asked whether it was possible to extend their techniques to ϵ, δ-differential privacy. Our paper shows the extent to which this can be achieved; the technical obstacle that we face is that our distances are not metrics. To the best of our knowledge, no complexity results on differential privacy for Markov chains have previously appeared in the literature, and we are the first to address this gap.

The computation of the standard bisimilarity distances has been the topic of a long running line of research [7], starting with approximation [8]. The distance was eventually determined to be computable in polynomial time using the ellipsoid method to solve an implicit linear program of exponential size [14]. This technique turns out slow in practice and further techniques have been developed which are faster but do not have such strong complexity guarantees [2,26]. Because of the two-sided nature of our distances, the main system of constraints that we introduce in our work involves a maximum of two quantities. This nonlinearity at the core of the problem prevents us from relying on the ellipsoid method and explains the gap between our **NP** upper bound and the polynomial-time algorithms of [14].

Tschantz et al. [28] first studied differential privacy using a notion similar to bisimulation, which was extended to a more general class of bisimulation relations by Xu et al. [31]. Both consider only ϵ-differential privacy, i.e. ratio differences, but do not examine how these could be computed.

An alternative line of research by Barthe et al. [5] concerns formal mechanised proofs of differential privacy. Recently, that direction has been related to coupling proofs [4] – this still requires substantial effort to choose the coupling, although recent techniques have improved this [1]. We complement this line of research by taking an algorithmic verification-centred approach.

The remainder of the paper is arranged as follows. Section 2 introduces the basic setting of labelled Markov chains. In Sect. 3, we discuss ϵ, δ-differential privacy and in Sect. 4 we define our distance. Section 5 develops technical results on our extended case of Kantorovich lifting. These are subsequently used in Sect. 6 to underpin techniques for computing the relevant distances.

2   Labelled Markov Chains

Given a finite set S, let $Dist(S)$ be the set of probability distributions on S.

Definition 1. *A labelled Markov chain (LMC) $\mathcal{M}$ is a tuple $\langle S, \Sigma, \mu, \ell \rangle$, where S is a finite set of states, Σ is a finite alphabet, $\mu : S \rightarrow Dist(S)$ is the transition function and $\ell : S \rightarrow \Sigma$ is the labelling function.*

Like in [2,7,14,26], our definition features labelled states. Variations, such as transition labels, can be easily accommodated within the setting. We also assume that all transition probabilities are rational, represented as a pair of binary integers. The bit sizes of these integers form part of the bit size of the representation $|\mathcal{M}|$. We will often write μ_s for $\mu(s)$.

In what follows, we study probabilities associated with infinite sequences of labels generated by LMC's. We specify the relevant probability spaces next using standard measure theory [3,6]. Let us start with the definition of cylinder sets.

Definition 2. *A subset $C \subseteq \Sigma^\omega$ is a* cylinder set *if there exists $u \in \Sigma^*$ such that C consists of all infinite sequences from Σ^ω whose prefix is u. We then write C_u to refer to C.*

Cylinder sets play a prominent role in measure theory in that their finite unions can be used as a generating family (an algebra) for the set $\mathcal{F}$ of measurable subsets of Σ^ω (the cylindric σ-algebra). What will be important for us is that any measure ν on $\mathcal{F}$ is uniquely determined by its values on cylinder sets. Next we show how to assign a measure ν_s on $\mathcal{F}$ to an arbitrary state of an LMC. We start with several auxiliary definitions.

Definition 3. *Given* $\mathcal{M} = \langle S, \Sigma, \mu, \ell \rangle$, *let* $\mu^+ : S^+ \to [0,1]$ *and* $\ell^+ : S^+ \to \Sigma^+$ *be the natural extensions of* μ *and* ℓ *to* S^+, *i.e.* $\mu^+(s_0 \cdots s_k) = \prod_{i=0}^{k-1} \mu(s_i)(s_{i+1})$ *and* $\ell^+(s_0 \cdots s_k) = \ell(s_0) \cdots \ell(s_k)$, *where* $k \geq 0$ *and* $s_i \in S$ $(0 \leq i \leq k)$. *Note that, for any* $s \in S$, *we have* $\mu^+(s) = 1$. *Given* $s \in S$, *let* $Paths_s(\mathcal{M})$ *be the subset of* S^+ *consisting of all sequences that start with* s.

Definition 4. *Let* $\mathcal{M} = \langle S, \Sigma, \mu, \ell \rangle$ *and* $s \in S$. *We define* $\nu_s : \mathcal{F} \to [0,1]$ *to be the unique measure on* $\mathcal{F}$ *such that for any cylinder* C_u *we have*

$$\nu_s(C_u) = \sum \{ \mu^+(p) \mid p \in Paths_s(\mathcal{M}), \ell^+(p) = u \}.$$

Our aim will be to compare states of labelled Markov chains from the point of view of differential privacy. Note that two states s, s' can be viewed as indistinguishable if $\nu_s = \nu_{s'}$. If they are not indistinguishable then the difference between them can be quantified using the *total variation distance*, defined by $tv(\nu, \nu') = \sup_{E \in \mathcal{F}} |\nu(E) - \nu'(E)|$. Given $\mathcal{M} = \langle S, \Sigma, \mu, \ell \rangle$ and $s, s' \in S$, we shall write $tv(s, s')$ to refer to $tv(\nu_s, \nu_{s'})$.

Remark 1. $tv(s, s')$ turns out surprisingly difficult to compute: it is undecidable whether the distance is strictly greater than a given threshold, and the non-strict variant of the problem ("greater or equal") is not known to be decidable [22].

To measure probabilities relevant to differential privacy, we will need to study a more general variant tv_α of the above distance, which we introduce next.

3 Differential Privacy

Differential privacy is a mathematical guarantee of privacy due to Dwork et al. [18]. It is a property similar to non-interference: the aim is to ensure that inputs which are related in some sense lead to very similar outputs. The notion requires that for two related states there only ever be a small change in output probabilities, and therefore discerning the two is difficult, which maintains the privacy of the states. Below we cast the definition in the setting of labelled Markov chains.

Definition 5. *Let* $\mathcal{M} = \langle S, \Sigma, \mu, \ell \rangle$ *be a labelled Markov chain and let* $R \subseteq S \times S$ *be a symmetric relation. Given* $\epsilon \geq 0$ *and* $\delta \in [0,1]$, *we say that* $\mathcal{M}$ *is* ϵ, δ-*differentially private (wrt* R*) if, for any* $s, s' \in S$ *such that* $(s, s') \in R$, *we have*

$$\nu_s(E) \leq e^\epsilon \cdot \nu_{s'}(E) + \delta$$

for any measurable set $E \in \mathcal{F}$.

Remark 2. Note that each state $s \in S$ can be viewed as defining a random variable X_s with outcomes from Σ^ω such that $P(X_s \in E) = \nu_s(E)$. Then the above can be rewritten as $P(X_s \in E) \leq e^\epsilon P(X_{s'} \in E) + \delta$, which matches the definition from [18], where one would consider $X_s, X_{s'}$ neighbouring in some natural sense.

The above formulation is often called *approximate differential privacy*. For $\delta = 0$, one talks about (pure) ϵ-*differential privacy*. Note that then the above definition boils down to measuring the ratio between the probabilities of possible outcomes. δ is thus an indicator of the extent to which ϵ-differential privacy holds for the given states. Intuitively, one could interpret ϵ, δ-differential privacy as "ϵ-differential privacy with probability at least $1 - \delta$" [29]. Our work is geared towards obtaining sound upper bounds on the value of δ for a given ϵ.

Remark 3. What it means for two states to be related (as specified by R) is to a large extent domain-specific. In general, R makes it possible to spell out which states should not appear too different and, consequently, should enjoy a quantitative amount of privacy. In the typical database scenario, one would relate database states that differ by just one person. In our case, we refer to states of a machine, for which we would like it to be indiscernible as to which was the start state (we assume the states are hidden and the traces are observable).

To rephrase the inequality underpinning differential privacy in a more succinct form, it will be convenient to work with the *skewed distance* Δ_α, first introduced by Barthe et al. [5] in the context of Hoare logics and ϵ, δ-differential privacy.

Definition 6 (Skewed Distance). *For $\alpha \geq 1$, let $\Delta_\alpha : \mathbb{R}_{\geq 0} \times \mathbb{R}_{\geq 0} \to \mathbb{R}_{\geq 0}$ be defined by $\Delta_\alpha(x, y) = \max\{x - \alpha y, y - \alpha x, 0\}$.*

Remark 4 It is easy to see that Δ_α is anti-monotone with respect to α. In particular, because $\alpha \geq 1$, we have $\Delta_\alpha(x, y) \leq \Delta_1(x, y) = |x - y|$. Observe that $\Delta_2(9, 3) = 9 - 2 \times 3 = 3$, $\Delta_2(9, 6) = 0$ and $\Delta_2(6, 3) = 0$. Note that $\Delta_2(x, y) = 0$ need not imply $x = y$, i.e. Δ_2 is not a metric. Note also that the triangle inequality may fail: $\Delta_2(9, 3) > \Delta_2(9, 6) + \Delta_2(6, 3)$, i.e. Δ_2 is not a pseudometric[1]. This will complicate our technical development, because we will not be able to use the framework of [12] directly.

The significance of the skewed distance will be seen shortly in Fact 1. We first introduce the skewed analogue of the total variation distance called tv_α, for which tv is a special case ($\alpha = 1$).

Definition 7. *Let $\alpha \geq 1$. Given two measures ν, ν' on $(\Sigma^\omega, \mathcal{F})$, let*

$$tv_\alpha(\nu, \nu') = \sup_{E \in \mathcal{F}} \Delta_\alpha(\nu(E), \nu'(E)).$$

Following the convention for tv, $tv_\alpha(s, s')$ will stand for $tv_\alpha(\nu_s, \nu_{s'})$. Fact 1 is an immediate corollary of Definitions 5, 6, and 7.

Fact 1. *$\mathcal{M}$ is ϵ, δ-differentially private wrt R if and only if, for all $s, s' \in S$ such that $(s, s') \in R$, we have $tv_\alpha(s, s') \leq \delta$, where $\alpha = e^\epsilon$.*

---

[1] A pseudometric must satisfy $m(x, x) = 0$, $m(x, y) = m(y, x)$ and $m(x, z) \leq m(x, y) + m(y, z)$. For metrics, one additionally requires that $m(x, y) = 0$ should imply $x = y$.

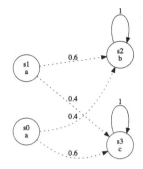

Fig. 1. States 1 and 2 are not bisimilar, but $tv_{1.5}(s_0, s_1) = 0$.

Some values of tv_α are readily known. For instance, the distance between any bisimilar states turns out to be zero.

Definition 8. *A probabilistic bisimulation on an LMC* $\mathcal{M} = \langle S, \Sigma, \mu, \ell \rangle$ *is an equivalence relation* $R \subseteq S \times S$ *such that if* $(s, s') \in R$ *then* $\ell(s) = \ell(s')$ *and for all* $X \in S/R$, $\sum_{u \in X} \mu(s)(u) = \sum_{u \in X} \mu(s')(u)$, *i.e. related states have the same label and probability of transitioning into any given equivalence class.*

It is known that probabilistic bisimulations are closed under union and hence there exists a largest one, written $\sim$ and called *probabilistic bisimilarity*. Two states are called *bisimilar*, written $s \sim s'$, if $(s, s') \in \sim$. Equivalently, this means that the pair (s, s') belongs to a probabilistic bisimulation. It follows from [14, Proposition 9, Lemma 10], that for bisimilar s, s', we have $tv_1(s, s') = 0$. As $tv_\alpha(s, s') \leq tv_1(s, s')$ we obtain the following.

Lemma 1. *If* $s \sim s'$ *then* $tv_\alpha(s, s') = 0$.

In contrast to [12], the converse will not hold.

Example 1. In the LMC shown in Fig. 1, states s_0 and s_1 are *not* bisimilar. To see this, observe first that s_2 must be the only state in its equivalence class with respect to $\sim$, because other states have different labels. Now note that the probabilities of reaching s_2 from s_0 and s_1 respectively are different (0.4 vs 0.6).

However, for $\alpha = 1.5$, we have $tv_\alpha(s_0, s_1) = 0$, because $\Delta_\alpha(0.6, 0.4) = \max(0.6 - 1.5 \cdot 0.4, 0.4 - 1.5 \cdot 0.6, 0) = 0$.

In an "acyclic" system, tv_α can be calculated by exhaustive search: the natural algorithm is doubly exponential, as one needs to consider all possible events over all possible traces. However, in general, tv_α is not computable (Remark 1). Thus, in the remainder of the paper, we shall introduce and study another distance bd_α. It will turn out possible to compute it and it will provide a sound method for bounding δ for $\ln(\alpha), \delta$-differential privacy. Our main result will be Theorem 3: the new distance can be calculated in polynomial time, assuming an **NP** oracle. Pragmatically, this means that this new distance can be computed efficiently, assuming access to an appropriate satisfiability or theory solver.

4   Skewed Bisimilarity Distance

Our distance will be defined in the spirit of bisimilarity distances [12,14,16, 17] through a fixed point definition based on a variation of the Kantorovich lifting. To motivate its shape, let us discuss how one would go about calculating tv_α recursively. If $\ell(s) \neq \ell(s')$ then $\nu_s(C_{\ell(s)}) = 1$, $\nu_{s'}(C_{\ell(s)}) = 0$, therefore $tv_\alpha(s, s') = 1$. So, let us assume $\ell(s) = \ell(s')$. Given $E \subseteq \Sigma^\omega$ and $a \in \Sigma$, let $E_a = \{w \in \Sigma^\omega \,|\, aw \in E\}$. Then we have:

$$tv_\alpha(\nu_s, \nu_{s'}) = \sup_{E \in \mathcal{F}} \Delta_\alpha(\nu_s(E), \nu_{s'}(E))$$

$$= \sup_{E_{\ell(s)} \in \mathcal{F}} \Delta_\alpha \Big(\sum_{u \in S} \mu_s(u)\, \nu_u(E_{\ell(s)}), \sum_{u \in S} \mu_{s'}(u)\, \nu_u(E_{\ell(s)}) \Big).$$

If we define $f : S \to [0,1]$ by $f(u) = \nu_u(E_{\ell(s)})$, this can be rewritten as

$$\sup_{E_{\ell(s)} \in \mathcal{F}} \Delta_\alpha \Big(\sum_{u \in S} \mu_s(u)\, f(u), \sum_{u \in S} \mu_{s'}(u)\, f(u) \Big).$$

We have little knowledge of f, otherwise we could compute tv_α, but from the definition of tv_α, we do know that $\Delta_\alpha(f(v), f(v')) \le tv_\alpha(v, v')$ for any $v, v' \in S$. Consequently, the following inequality holds.

$$tv_\alpha(s, s') \le \sup_{\substack{f : S \to [0,1] \\ \forall v,v' \in S\, \Delta_\alpha(f(v), f(v')) \le tv_\alpha(v, v')}} \Delta_\alpha \Big(\sum_{u \in S} \mu_s(u) f(u), \sum_{u \in S} \mu_{s'}(u) f(u) \Big)$$

The expression on the right is an instance of the Kantorovich lifting [15,21], which uses ("lifts") the distance tv_α between states s, s' to define a distance between the distributions $\mu_s, \mu_{s'}$ associated with the states. We recall the definition of the Kantorovich distance between distributions in the discrete case, noting that then, for $\mu \in Dist(S)$, we have $\int f d\mu = \sum_{u \in S} f(u)\, \mu(u)$.

Definition 9 (Kantorovich). *Given $\mu, \mu' \in Dist(S)$ and a pseudometric $m : S \times S \to [0,1]$, the Kantorovich distance between μ and μ' is defined to be*

$$K(m)(\mu, \mu') = \sup_{\substack{f : S \to [0,1] \\ \forall v,v' \in S\, |f(v) - f(v')| \le m(v,v')}} \Big| \int f d\mu - \int f d\mu' \Big|.$$

Remark 5. The Kantorovich distance is also known under other names (e.g. Hutchinson, Wasserstein distance), having been rediscovered several times in history [15]. Chatzikokolakis et al. [12] studied the Kantorovich distance and related bisimulation distances when the absolute value distance above is replaced with another metric. For our purposes, instead of $|...|$, we need to consider Δ_α, even though Δ_α is not a metric and m may not be a pseudometric.

Definition 10 (Skewed Kantorovich). *Given $\mu, \mu' \in Dist(S)$ and a symmetric distance $d : S \times S \to [0,1]$, the* skewed Kantorovich distance *between μ and μ' is defined to be*

$$K_\alpha(d)(\mu, \mu') = \sup_{\substack{f : S \to [0,1] \\ \forall v, v' \in S \; \Delta_\alpha(f(v), f(v')) \leq d(v, v')}} \Delta_\alpha \Big(\int f d\mu, \int f d\mu' \Big)$$

Note that setting $\alpha = 1$ gives the standard Kantorovich distance (Definition 9). Below we define a function operator, which will be used to define our distance.

Definition 11. *Let $\Gamma_\alpha : [0,1]^{S \times S} \to [0,1]^{S \times S}$ be defined as follows.*

$$\Gamma_\alpha(d)(s, s') = \begin{cases} K_\alpha(d)(\mu_s, \mu_{s'}) & \ell(s) = \ell(t) \\ 1 & \ell(s) \neq \ell(t) \end{cases}$$

Note that $[0,1]^{S \times S}$ equipped with the pointwise order, written $\sqsubseteq$, is a complete lattice and that Γ_α is monotone with respect that order (larger d permit more functions, thus larger supremum). Consequently, Γ_α has a least fixed point [27]. We take our distance to be exactly that point.

Definition 12 (Skewed Bisimilarity Distance). *Let $bd_\alpha : S \times S \to [0,1]$ be the least fixed point of Γ_α.*

Remark 6. Recall that the least fixed point is equal to the least pre-fixed point $(\min\{d \mid \Gamma_\alpha(d) \sqsubseteq d\})$.

Recall our initial remarks about the Kantorovich distance $K_\alpha(tv_\alpha)(\mu_s, \mu_{s'})$ over-approximating $tv_\alpha(s, s')$. They can be summarised by $tv_\alpha \sqsubseteq K_\alpha(tv_\alpha)$, i.e. tv_α is a post-fixed point of K_α. Since we want to bound tv_α as closely as possible, we can show that the least fixed point bd_α also bounds tv_α from above.

Lemma 2. $tv_\alpha \sqsubseteq bd_\alpha$.

Remark 7. The lemma is an analogue of Theorem 2 [12]. Its proof in [30] relied on the fact that the counterpart of Δ_α was a metric, which is not true in our case (unless $\alpha = 1$).

Just like Δ_α is anti-monotone with respect to α, so is bd_α. This means that $bd_\alpha \sqsubseteq bd_1$. The definition of bd_1 coincides with the definition of the classic bisimilarity pseudometric d_1 (see e.g. [14]), which satisfies $d_1(s, s') = 0$ if and only if s and s' are bisimilar. Consequently, we obtain the following corollary.

Corollary 1. *For any $\alpha \geq 1$, if $s \sim s'$ then $bd_\alpha(s, s') = 0$.*

As in the case of tv_α, we do not have the converse in our setting. Example 1 shows that $s_0 \not\sim s_1$ but we observe that $bd_{1.5}(s_0, s_1) = 0$. Observe:

$$bd_{1.5}(s_0, s_1) \leq$$
$$\max_f \Big(\sum_{s \in S} f(s)(\mu_{s_0}(s) - 1.5 \cdot \mu_{s_1}(s)), \sum_{s \in S} f(s)(\mu_{s_1}(s) - 1.5 \cdot \mu_{s_0}(s)) \Big)$$
$$= \max_f(f(s_2)(0.6 - 1.5 \cdot 0.4) + f(s_3)(0.4 - 1.5 \cdot 0.6),$$
$$f(s_2)(0.4 - 1.5 \cdot 0.6) + f(s_3)(0.6 - 1.5 \cdot 0.4)).$$

```
 1    diningCrypto(payingCryptographer):
 2       firstFlip  =  flip(p, 1−p)
 3       previousFlip  =  firstFlip
 4       for  cryptographer = 0 → n−1:
 5          if  cryptographer == n−1:
 6             thisFlip  =  firstFlip
 7          else :
 8             thisFlip  =  flip(p, 1−p)
 9          if  (cryptographer == payingCryptographer):
10             announce(previousFlip == thisFlip)
11          else :
12             announce(previousFlip != thisFlip)
13          previousFlip  =  thisFlip
```

Fig. 2. Simulation of Dining Cryptographers Protocol.

Notice the coefficients of $f(s)$ are all non-positive. Consequently, regardless of the restrictions on f, the maximising allocation will be $f(s) = 0$ and, thus, $bd_{1.5}(s_0, s_1) = 0$.

Example: Dining Cryptographers

In the dining cryptographer model [13], a ring of diners want to determine whether one of the diners paid or an outside body. If a diner paid, we do not want to reveal which of them it was. The protocol proceeds with each adjacent pair privately flipping a coin, each diner then reports the XOR of the two coin flips they observe, however if the diner paid he would report the negation of this. We can determine if one of them paid by taking the XOR of the announcements. With perfectly fair coins, the protocol guarantees privacy of the paying diner, but it is still differentially private if the coins are biased. If an outside body paid, there is no privacy to maintain so we only simulate the scenarios in which one of the diners did pay. The scenario where Cryptographer 0 paid must have similar output distribution to Cryptographer 1 paying, so that it can be determined that one of them did pay, but not which. The internal configuration of the machine is always assumed to be hidden, but the announcements are made public whilst maintaining the privacy of the participating Cryptographer (and the internal states).

The LMC in Fig. 3 shows the 2-person dining cryptographers protocol (Fig. 2) starting from Cryptographers 0 and 1 using weighted coins with $p = \frac{49}{100}$. The states of the machine encode the 5 variables that need to be tracked. To achieve ϵ, δ-differential privacy with $\alpha = e^\epsilon = 1.0002$ the minimal (true) value of δ is 0.00030004. Our methods generate a correct upper bound $bd_\alpha(s_0, s_1) = 0.0004$, showing $\ln(1.0002), 0.0004$-differential privacy. The protocol could be played with n players, requiring $O(n^2)$ states, for all possible assignments of paying cryptographer and current cryptographer. In a two-person scenario, the diners would know which of them had paid but an external observer of the output would only learn that one of them paid, not which.

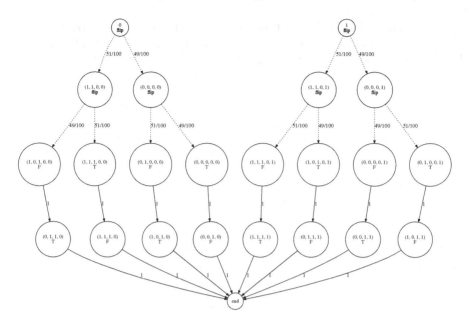

Fig. 3. Markov Chain for 2 dining cryptographers: state 0 (resp. 1) denotes Cryptographer 0 (resp. 1) paid. The first line of a node is the state name, the second line is the label of the state.

5   Skewed Kantorovich Distances

Here we discuss how to calculate our variant of the Kantorovich distance. This will inform the next section, in which we look into computing bd_α.

Recall the definition of $K_\alpha(d)(\mu, \mu')$ from Definition 10. In the general case of $\Delta_\alpha(a, b)$, both $a - \alpha b$ and $b - \alpha a$ could be negative, so the maximum with 0 is taken. However, within the Kantorovich function, the constant function $f(i) = 0$ is a valid assignment, which achieves 0 in either case ($0 - \alpha \times 0 = 0$). Consequently, we can simplify the definition of Δ_α to omit the 0 case inside K_α.

If $\alpha = 1$ then Δ_α is the absolute value function and it is known that the distance corresponds to a single instance of a linear programming problem [9]. However, this is no longer true in our case due to the shape of $\Delta_\alpha(x, y) = \max(x - \alpha y, y - \alpha x)$. Still, one can present the calculation as taking the maximum of a pair of linear programs. We shall refer to this formulation as the "primal form" of $K_\alpha(d)$. We give the first program below, the other is its symmetric variant with μ, μ' reversed. Below we write f_i for $f(i)$ and let i, j range over S, and assume that d is symmetric.

$$\max_{f \in [0,1]^S} \left(\sum_i f_i \mu(i) - \alpha \sum_i f_i \mu'(i) \right) \qquad \text{subject to} \qquad \forall i, j \quad f_i - \alpha f_j \leq d_{i,j}$$

The standard Kantorovich distance ($\alpha = 1$) is often presented in the following dual form when m is a pseudometric, based on the minimum coupling between the two distributions μ and μ', weighted by the distance function.

$$K(m)(\mu, \mu') = \min_{w \in [0,1]^{S \times S}} \sum_{i,j} w_{i,j} m_{i,j} \quad \text{subject to} \quad \begin{array}{l} \forall i \quad \sum_j w_{i,j} = \mu(i) \\ \forall j \quad \sum_i w_{i,j} = \mu'(j) \end{array}$$

Remark 8. The dual form can be viewed as an optimal transportation problem in which an arbitrarily divisible cargo must be transferred from one set of locations (represented by a copy S^L of S) to another (represented by a different copy S^R of S). Each state $s^R \in S^R$ must receive $\mu(s)$, while each state $s^L \in S^L$ must send $\mu'(s)$. If $w_{i,j}$ is taken to represent the amount that gets sent from j^L to i^R then the above conditions restrict w in accordance with the sending and receiving budgets. If $d_{i,j}$ represents the cost of sending from j^L to i^R then the objective function $\sum_{i,j} w_{i,j} \cdot d_{i,j}$ corresponds to the overall cost of transport. Consequently, the problem is referred to as a mass transportation problem [21].

To achieve a similar "dual form" in our case, we take the dual form of each of our linear programs. Then we can calculate the distance by taking the maximum of the two minima. The shape of the dual is given below on the right.

Lemma 3.

$$\max_{f \in [0,1]^S} \left(\sum_i f_i \mu(i) - \alpha \sum_i f_i \mu'(i) \right) = \min_{w \in [0,1]^{S \times S}, \tau, \gamma \in [0,1]^S} \sum_{i,j} w_{i,j} \cdot d_{i,j}$$

$$\begin{array}{cc} \textit{subject to} & \textit{subject to} \\ \forall i,j \ f_i - \alpha f_j \le d_{i,j} & \forall i : \sum_j w_{i,j} + \tau_i - \gamma_i = \mu(i) \\ & \forall j : \sum_i w_{i,j} + \frac{\tau_j - \gamma_j}{\alpha} \le \mu'(j) \end{array}$$

The dual form presented above is a simplified (but equivalent) form of the immediate dual obtained via the standard LP recipe. Note that the polytope we are optimising over is independent of d, which appears only in the objective function. The dual of the other linear program is obtained by swapping μ, μ'.

Remark 9. In the skewed case, we optimise over the following polytope

$$\Omega_{\mu,\mu'} = \left\{ w \in [0,1]^{S \times S} \ \middle| \ \exists \gamma, \tau \in [0,1]^S \ \begin{array}{l} \forall i : \sum_j w_{i,j} + \tau_i - \gamma_i = \mu(i) \\ \forall j : \sum_i w_{i,j} + \frac{\tau_j - \gamma_j}{\alpha} \le \mu'(j) \end{array} \right\}$$

One can also view it as a kind of transportation problem. As before, cargo can be transferred through the standard routes with w at a cost d, but there are additional, cost-free routes between corresponding pairs s^L and s^R (represented by τ_s) and back (represented by γ_s). These extra routes are quite peculiar. En route from s^L to s^R the cargo 'grows': when $\frac{\tau_s}{\alpha}$ is sent from s^L, a larger amount of τ_s is received at s^R. Overall, the total amount of cargo sent may be less than that received, so the sending constraints are now inequalities. From s^R to s^L the cargo 'shrinks': when γ_s is sent from s^R, only $\frac{\gamma_s}{\alpha}$ is received by s^L.

It is immediate that τ routes can be useful. The γ routes may be useful for optimisation under two conditions. Firstly the shrinkage of the cargo must be made up elsewhere, i.e., through 'growing' τ routes. Additionally the cost $\alpha \times d(s_1^L, s^R) + d(s^L, s_2^R)$ is lower than $d(s_1^L, s_2^R)$, which may well be the case due to the lack of triangle inequality. Note that it is not possible to satisfy the receiving constraints if, in total, more is sent through γ routes than received through τ routes, so $\sum_s(\tau_s - \gamma_s) \geq 0$. Therefore, the vector ω (the coupling) may be smaller than its equivalent in the standard Kantorovich case.

We arrive at the following formulation, which we call the "dual form":

$$K_\alpha(d)(\mu, \mu') = \max \left\{ \min_{\omega \in \Omega_{\mu,\mu'}} \sum_{i,j} \omega_{i,j} \cdot d_{i,j}, \; \min_{\omega \in \Omega_{\mu',\mu}} \sum_{i,j} \omega_{i,j} \cdot d_{i,j} \right\}.$$

Note that $K_\alpha(d)(\mu, \mu')$ can be computed in polynomial time as a pair of linear programs in either primal or dual form, and taking the maximum (in either case). In our calculations related to bd_α, the distributions μ, μ' will always be taken to be $\mu_s, \mu_{s'}$ respectively, for some $s, s' \in S$. The ability to switch between primal and dual form will play a useful role in our complexity-theoretic arguments.

6   Computing bd_α

We start off by observing that all distances $bd_\alpha(s, s')$ are rational and can be expressed in polynomial size with respect to $\mathcal{M}$. To that end, we exploit a result by Sontag [25], which states that, without affecting satisfiability, quantification in the first-order fragment of linear real arithmetic (LRA) can be restricted to rationals of polynomial size with respect to formula length (as long as all coefficients present in the formula are rational). Consequently, if we can express "there exists a least fixed point d of Γ_α" in this fragment (with a polynomial increase in size), we can draw the intended conclusion.

We give the relevant formula in Fig. 4. The formula asserts the existence of a distance d, which is a pre-fixed point of Γ_α ($\forall f. \phi(d, f)$) such that any other pre-fixed point d' of Γ_α is greater. Note that $\forall f. \phi(f, d)$ exploits the fact that $\max_f A(f) \leq d(s, s')$ is equivalent to $\forall f(A(f) \leq d(s, s'))$. Sontag's result then implies the following.

Theorem 1. *Values of bd_α are rational. There exists a polynomial p such that for any LMC $\mathcal{M}$ and $s, s' \in S$, the size of bd_α (in binary) can be bounded from above by a polynomial in $|\mathcal{M}|$.*

Remark 10. Sontag [25] uses the fact mentioned above to relate the alternation hierarchy within LRA to the polynomial hierarchy **PH**: formulae of the form $\exists x_1 \forall x_2 \ldots Q x_k F(x_1 \ldots x_k)$ (with quantifier-free F) correspond to Σ_k^P (and formulae starting with $\forall$ to Π_k^P). Recall that $\Sigma_1^P = \mathbf{NP}$.

$$\exists d \in [0,1]^{S \times S} \ (\forall f \in [0,1]^S \phi(d,f) \wedge \forall d' \in [0,1]^{S \times S}(\forall f \in [0,1]^S \ \phi(d',f) \implies \bigwedge_i d_i \le d'_i))$$

$$\phi(d,f) = \bigwedge_{s,s'} \begin{cases} d_{s,s'} = 1 & \ell(s) \ne \ell(s') \\ (\bigwedge_{i,j} f_i - \alpha f_j \le d_{i,j} \wedge f_j - \alpha f_i \le d_{i,j}) & \ell(s) = \ell(s') \\ \quad \implies (\sum_i f_i \mu_s(i) - \alpha \sum_i f_i \mu_{s'}(i) \le d_{s,s'} \\ \quad \wedge \sum_i f_i \mu_{s'}(i) - \alpha \sum_i f_i \mu_s(i) \le d_{s,s'}) \end{cases}$$

Fig. 4. Logical formulation of least pre-fixed point.

Next we focus on the following decision problem for bd_α.

BD-THRESHOLD: given $s, s' \in S$ and $\theta \in \mathbb{Q}$, is it the case that $bd_\alpha(s,s') \le \theta$?

Recall that the analogous problem for tv_α is undecidable (Remark 1). In our case, the problem turns out to be decidable and the argument does not depend on whether $<$ or $\le$ is used. To establish decidability we can observe that $bd_\alpha(s,s') \le \theta$ can be expressed in LRA simply by adding $d(s,s') \le \theta$ to the formula from Fig. 4. By Sontag's results, this not only yields decidability but also membership in Σ_2^P. Recall that $\mathbf{NP} \subseteq \Sigma_2^P \subseteq \mathbf{PH} \subseteq \mathbf{PSPACE}$.

We can simplify the formula, though, using $bd_\alpha = \min \{d \mid \Gamma_\alpha(d) \sqsubseteq d\}$. Then $bd_\alpha(s,s') \le \theta$ can be specified as the existence of a pre-fixed point d such that $d(s,s') \le \theta$. This can be done as follows, using $\phi(d,f)$ from Fig. 4.

$$\exists d \in [0,1]^{S \times S} \ (\ \forall f \in [0,1]^S \phi(d,f) \ \wedge \ d(s,s') \le \theta \ )$$

Note that the universal quantification over f remains, i.e. we can still only conclude that the problem is in Σ_2^P. To overcome this, we shall use the dual form instead (Lemma 3). This will enable us to eliminate the universal quantification and replace it with existential quantifiers using the fact that $\min_\omega A(\omega) \le B$ is equivalent to $\exists \omega(A(\omega) \le B)$. The resultant formula is shown in Fig. 5.

Note the formula is not linear due to $\omega_{i,j} \cdot d_{i,j}$. However, because we know (Theorem 1) that bd_α corresponds to an assignment of poly-sized rationals, we can consider the formula with d fixed at bd_α. Then it does become an LRA formula (of polynomially bounded length with respect to $|\mathcal{M}|$) and we can again conclude that the assignments of ω, γ, τ must also involve rationals whose size is polynomially bounded. Consequently, the formula implies membership of our problem in $\Sigma_1^P = \mathbf{NP}$: it suffices to guess the satisfying assignment, guaranteed to be rational and of polynomial size.

Theorem 2. BD-THRESHOLD *is in* $\mathbf{NP}$.

The decidability of BD-THRESHOLD makes it possible to approximate $bd_\alpha(s,s')$ to arbitrary (rational) precision ϵ by binary search. This will involve $O(|\epsilon|)$ calls to the oracle for BD-THRESHOLD (where $|\epsilon|$ is the number of bits required to represent ϵ in binary).

What's more, assuming the oracle, one can actually find the exact value of $bd_\alpha(s,s')$ in polynomial time (wrt $\mathcal{M}$). This exploits the fact that the value

$$\text{BD-THRESHOLD}(s, s', \theta) = \exists (d_{i,j})_{i,j \in S} \bigwedge_{i,j \in S} (0 \le d_{i.j} \le 1) \wedge \textit{prefixed}(d) \wedge d_{s,s'} \le \theta$$

$$\textit{prefixed}(d) = \bigwedge_{q,q' \in S} \begin{cases} d_{q,q'} = 1 & \ell(q) \ne \ell(q') \\ \textit{prefixed}_1(d, d_{q,q'}, q, q') & \ell(q) = \ell(q') \\ \quad \wedge \, \textit{prefixed}_1(d, d_{q,q'}, q', q) & \end{cases}$$

$$\textit{prefixed}_1(d, x, q, q') = \exists (\omega_{i,j})_{i,j \in S} \ \exists (\gamma_i)_{i \in S} \ \exists (\tau_i)_{i \in S} \ \sum_{i,j \in S} \omega_{i,j} \cdot d_{i,j} \le x$$

$$\wedge \bigwedge_{i,j \in S} (0 \le \omega_{i,j} \le 1) \wedge \bigwedge_{i \in S} (0 \le \gamma_i \le 1 \wedge 0 \le \tau_i \le 1)$$

$$\wedge \bigwedge_{i \in S} (\sum_{j \in S} \omega_{i,j} - \gamma_i + \tau_i = \mu_q(i)) \wedge \bigwedge_{j \in S} (\sum_{i \in S} \omega_{i,j} + \frac{\tau_j - \gamma_j}{\alpha} \le \mu_{q'}(j))$$

Fig. 5. NP Formula for BD-THRESHOLD.

of bd_α is rational and its size is polynomially bounded, so one can find it by approximation to a carefully chosen level of precision and then finding the relevant rational with the continued fraction algorithm [19,20].

Theorem 3. *bd_α can be calculated in polynomial time with an **NP** oracle.*

As a consequence, the problem of computing bd_α reduces to propositional satisfiability, i.e., can be encoded in SAT. This justifies, for instance, the following approach: treat every variable as a ratio of two integers from an exponential range, and give the system of resulting constraints to an Integer Arithmetic or SAT solver. While this might look like resorting to a general-purpose "hammer", Theorem 3 is necessary for this method to work: it is not, in fact, possible to solve general polynomial constraint systems relying just on SAT.[2]

We expect, however, this direct approach to be inferior to the following observation. Theorem 1 reveals that the variables in our constraint system need not assume irrational values or have large bit representations. Thus, one can give the system to a more powerful theory solver, or an optimisation tool, but to expect that the existence of simple and small models (solutions) will help the SMT heuristics (resp. optimization engines) to find them quickly.

7 Conclusion and Further Work

We have demonstrated that bisimilarity distances can be used to determine differential privacy parameters, despite their non-metric properties. We have established that the complexity of finding these values is polynomial, relative to

---

[2] More precisely, the existence of such a procedure would be a breakthrough in the computational complexity theory, showing that **NP** $= \exists \mathbb{R}$. This would imply that a multitude of problems in computational geometry could be solved using SAT solvers [11,24]. Unlike for bd_α, variable assignments in these problems may need to be irrational, even if all numbers in the input data are integer or rational.

an **NP** oracle. Yet, it may still be possible to obtain a polynomial algorithm—although much like in the case of the classical bisimilarity distances and linear programming, it may not necessarily outperform theoretically slower procedures.

We conjecture that bd_α, which we defined as the least fixed point of the operator Γ_α, may in fact be characterized as the unique fixed point of a similar operator. By the results of Etessami and Yannakakis [19], it would then follow that bd_α can be computed in **PPAD**, a smaller complexity class, improving upon our **NP** upper bound and matching the complexity of a closely related setting (see below). The reason is the continuity of Γ_α, which follows from the properties of the polytope over which f ranges (in the definition of $K_\alpha(d)$). Whether bd_α can in fact be computed in polynomial time or is **PPAD**-hard seems to be a challenging open question.

Our existing work is limited to labelled Markov chains, or fully probabilistic automata. However, the standard bisimulation distances can also be defined on deterministic systems, where their computational complexity is **PPAD** [10]. In our scenario, the privacy can only be analysed between two start states, but it is also reasonable to allow an input in the form of a trace or sequence of actions; the output would also be a trace. Here the choice of labels (at a specific state) would correspond to decisions taken by the user, and the availability of only one label would mean that this is the output. This setting would support a broader range of scenarios that could be modelled and verified as differentially private.

Acknowledgment. David Purser gratefully acknowledges funding by the UK Engineering and Physical Sciences Research Council (EP/L016400/1), the EPSRC Centre for Doctoral Training in Urban Science. Andrzej Murawski is supported by a Royal Society Leverhulme Trust Senior Research Fellowship and the International Exchanges Scheme (IE161701).

References

1. Albarghouthi, A., Hsu, J.: Synthesizing coupling proofs of differential privacy. Proc. ACM Program. Lang. **2**, 58:1–58:30 (2018)
2. Bacci, G., Bacci, G., Larsen, K.G., Mardare, R.: On-the-fly exact computation of bisimilarity distances. In: Piterman, N., Smolka, S.A. (eds.) TACAS 2013. LNCS, vol. 7795, pp. 1–15. Springer, Heidelberg (2013). https://doi.org/10.1007/978-3-642-36742-7_1
3. Baier, C., Katoen, J.P.: Principles of Model Checking. MIT Press, Cambridge (2008)
4. Barthe, G., Espitau, T., Grégoire, B., Hsu, J., Stefanesco, L., Strub, P.-Y.: Relational reasoning via probabilistic coupling. In: Davis, M., Fehnker, A., McIver, A., Voronkov, A. (eds.) LPAR 2015. LNCS, vol. 9450, pp. 387–401. Springer, Heidelberg (2015). https://doi.org/10.1007/978-3-662-48899-7_27
5. Barthe, G., Köpf, B., Olmedo, F., Zanella Béguelin, S.: Probabilistic relational reasoning for differential privacy. In: POPL, pp. 97–110. ACM (2012)
6. Billingsley, P.: Probability and Measure, 2nd edn. Wiley, New York (1986)
7. van Breugel, F.: Probabilistic bisimilarity distances. ACM SIGLOG News **4**(4), 33–51 (2017)

8. van Breugel, F., Sharma, B., Worrell, J.: Approximating a behavioural pseudometric without discount for probabilistic systems. In: Seidl, H. (ed.) FoSSaCS 2007. LNCS, vol. 4423, pp. 123–137. Springer, Heidelberg (2007). https://doi.org/10.1007/978-3-540-71389-0_10

9. van Breugel, F., Worrell, J.: An algorithm for quantitative verification of probabilistic transition systems. In: Larsen, K.G., Nielsen, M. (eds.) CONCUR 2001. LNCS, vol. 2154, pp. 336–350. Springer, Heidelberg (2001). https://doi.org/10.1007/3-540-44685-0_23

10. van Breugel, F., Worrell, J.: The complexity of computing a bisimilarity pseudometric on probabilistic automata. In: van Breugel, F., Kashefi, E., Palamidessi, C., Rutten, J. (eds.) Horizons of the Mind. A Tribute to Prakash Panangaden. LNCS, vol. 8464, pp. 191–213. Springer, Cham (2014). https://doi.org/10.1007/978-3-319-06880-0_10

11. Cardinal, J.: Computational geometry column 62. SIGACT News **46**(4), 69–78 (2015)

12. Chatzikokolakis, K., Gebler, D., Palamidessi, C., Xu, L.: Generalized bisimulation metrics. In: Baldan, P., Gorla, D. (eds.) CONCUR 2014. LNCS, vol. 8704, pp. 32–46. Springer, Heidelberg (2014). https://doi.org/10.1007/978-3-662-44584-6_4

13. Chaum, D.: The dining cryptographers problem: Unconditional sender and recipient untraceability. J. Cryptol. **1**(1), 65–75 (1988)

14. Chen, D., van Breugel, F., Worrell, J.: On the complexity of computing probabilistic bisimilarity. In: Birkedal, L. (ed.) FoSSaCS 2012. LNCS, vol. 7213, pp. 437–451. Springer, Heidelberg (2012). https://doi.org/10.1007/978-3-642-28729-9_29

15. Deng, Y., Du, W.: The Kantorovich metric in computer science: a brief survey. Electron Notes Theor. Comput. Sci. **253**(3), 73–82 (2009)

16. Desharnais, J., Gupta, V., Jagadeesan, R., Panangaden, P.: Metrics for labelled Markov processes. Theor. Comput. Sci. **318**(3), 323–354 (2004)

17. Desharnais, J., Jagadeesan, R., Gupta, V., Panangaden, P.: The metric analogue of weak bisimulation for probabilistic processes. In: LICS, pp. 413–422. IEEE (2002)

18. Dwork, C., McSherry, F., Nissim, K., Smith, A.: Calibrating noise to sensitivity in private data analysis. In: Halevi, S., Rabin, T. (eds.) TCC 2006. LNCS, vol. 3876, pp. 265–284. Springer, Heidelberg (2006). https://doi.org/10.1007/11681878_14

19. Etessami, K., Yannakakis, M.: On the complexity of Nash equilibria and other fixed points. SIAM J. Comput. **39**(6), 2531–2597 (2010)

20. Grötschel, M., Lovász, L., Schrijver, A.: Geometric Algorithms and Combinatorial Optimization, Algorithms and Combinatorics, vol. 2. Springer, Berlin (1988)

21. Kantorovich, L.V.: On the translocation of masses. Doklady Akademii Nauk SSSR **37**(7–8), 227–229 (1942)

22. Kiefer, S.: On computing the total variation distance of hidden Markov models. In: ICALP, pp. 130:1–130:13 (2018)

23. Larsen, K.G., Skou, A.: Bisimulation through probabilistic testing. Inf. Comput. **94**(1), 1–28 (1991)

24. Schaefer, M., Stefankovic, D.: Fixed points, Nash equilibria, and the existential theory of the reals. Theory Comput. Syst. **60**(2), 172–193 (2017)

25. Sontag, E.D.: Real addition and the polynomial hierarchy. IPL **20**(3), 115–120 (1985)

26. Tang, Q., van Breugel, F.: Computing probabilistic bisimilarity distances via policy iteration. In: CONCUR, pp. 22:1–22:15. Leibniz-Zentrum (2016)

27. Tarski, A.: A lattice-theoretical fixpoint theorem and its applications. Pac. J. Math. **5**(2), 285–309 (1955)

28. Tschantz, M.C., Kaynar, D., Datta, A.: Formal verification of differential privacy for interactive systems. ENTCS **276**, 61–79 (2011)
29. Vadhan, S.P.: The complexity of differential privacy. In: Tutorials on the Foundations of Cryptography, pp. 347–450. Springer, Berlin (2017)
30. Xu, L.: Formal verification of differential privacy in concurrent systems. Ph.D. thesis, Ecole Polytechnique (Palaiseau, France) (2015)
31. Xu, L., Chatzikokolakis, K., Lin, H.: Metrics for differential privacy in concurrent systems. In: Ábrahám, E., Palamidessi, C. (eds.) FORTE 2014. LNCS, vol. 8461, pp. 199–215. Springer, Heidelberg (2014). https://doi.org/10.1007/978-3-662-43613-4_13

A Symbolic Algorithm for Lazy Synthesis of Eager Strategies

Swen Jacobs and Mouhammad Sakr$^{(\boxtimes)}$

CISPA and Saarland University, Saarbrucken, Germany
{jacobs,sakr}@react.uni-saarland.de

Abstract. We present an algorithm for solving two-player safety games that combines a mixed forward/backward search strategy with a symbolic representation of the state space. By combining forward and backward exploration, our algorithm can synthesize strategies that are eager in the sense that they try to prevent progress towards the error states as soon as possible, whereas standard backwards algorithms often produce permissive solutions that only react when absolutely necessary. We provide experimental results for two new sets of benchmarks, as well as the benchmark set of the Reactive Synthesis Competition (SYNT-COMP) 2017. The results show that our algorithm in many cases produces more eager strategies than a standard backwards algorithm, and solves a number of benchmarks that are intractable for existing tools. Finally, we observe a connection between our algorithm and a recently proposed algorithm for the synthesis of controllers that are robust against disturbances, pointing to possible future applications.

1 Introduction

Automatic synthesis of digital circuits from logical specifications is one of the most ambitious and challenging problems in circuit design. The problem was first identified by Church [1]: given a requirement ϕ on the input-output behavior of a Boolean circuit, compute a circuit C that satisfies ϕ. Since then, several approaches have been proposed to solve the problem [2,3], which is usually viewed as a game between two players: the system player tries to satisfy the specification and the environment player tries to violate it. If the system player has a winning strategy for the game, then this strategy represents a circuit that is guaranteed to satisfy the specification. Recently, there has been much interest in approaches that leverage efficient data structures and automated reasoning methods to solve the synthesis problem in practice [4–9].

In this paper, we restrict our attention to safety specifications. In this setting, most of the successful implementations *symbolically* manipulate sets of states via their characteristic functions, represented as Binary Decision Diagrams (BDDs) [10]. The "standard" algorithm works backwards from the unsafe states and computes the set of all states from which the environment can force the system into these states. The negation of this set is the (maximal) winning

© Springer Nature Switzerland AG 2018
S. K. Lahiri and C. Wang (Eds.): ATVA 2018, LNCS 11138, pp. 211–227, 2018.
https://doi.org/10.1007/978-3-030-01090-4_13

region of the system, i.e., the set of all states from which the system can win the game. Depending on the specification, this algorithm may be suboptimal for two reasons: first, it may spend a lot of time on the exploration of states that are unreachable or could easily be avoided by the system player, and second, it may compute winning regions that include such states, possibly making the resulting strategy of controller more permissive and complicated than necessary. Additionally, for many applications it is preferable to generate strategies that avoid progress towards the error whenever possible, e.g., if the system should be tolerant to hardware faults or perturbations in the environment [11].

To keep the reachable state space small, some kind of forward search from the initial states is necessary. However, for forward search no efficient symbolic algorithm is known.

Contributions. In this work, we introduce a lazy synthesis algorithm that combines a forward search for candidate solutions with backward model checking of these candidates. All operations are such that they can be efficiently implemented with a fully symbolic representation of the state space and the space of candidate solutions. The combined forward/backward strategy allows us to find much smaller winning regions than the standard backward algorithm, and therefore produces less permissive solutions than the standard approach and solves certain classes of problems more efficiently.

We evaluate a prototype implementation of our algorithm on two sets of benchmarks, including the benchmark set of the Reactive Synthesis Competition (SYNTCOMP) 2017 [12]. We show that on many benchmarks our algorithm produces winning regions that are remarkably smaller: on the benchmark set from SYNTCOMP 2017, the biggest measured difference is by a factor of 10^{68}. Moreover, it solves a number of instances that have not been solved by any participant in SYNTCOMP 2017.

Finally, we observe a relation between our algorithm and the approach of Dallal et al. [11] for systems with perturbations, and provide the first implementation of their algorithm as a variant of our algorithm. On the benchmarks above, we show that whenever a given benchmark admits controllers that give stability guarantees under perturbations, then our lazy algorithm will find a small winning region and can provide stability guarantees similar to those of Dallal et al. without any additional cost.

2   Preliminaries

Given a specification ϕ, the reactive synthesis problem consists in finding a system that satisfies ϕ in an adversarial environment. The problem can be viewed as a game between two players, Player 0 (the system) and Player 1 (the environment), where Player 0 chooses controllable inputs and Player 1 chooses uncontrollable inputs to a given transition function. In this paper we consider synthesis problems for safety specifications: given a transition system that may raise a BAD flag when entering certain states, we check the existence of a function that reads the current state and the values of uncontrollable inputs, and provides valuations of the controllable inputs such that the BAD flag is not raised on any possible execution. We consider systems where the state space is defined by a set L of boolean state variables, also called *latches*. We write $\mathbb{B}$ for the set $\{0, 1\}$. A state of the system is a valuation $q \in \mathbb{B}^L$ of the latches. We will represent sets of states by their characteristic functions of type $\mathbb{B}^L \to \mathbb{B}$, and similarly for sets of transitions etc.

Definition 1. *A **controllable transition system** (or short: controllable system) TS is a 6-tuple $(L, X_u, X_c, \mathcal{R}, BAD, q_0)$, where:*

- *L is a set of state variables for the latches*
- *X_u is a set of uncontrollable input variables*
- *X_c is a set of controllable input variables*
- *$\mathcal{R} : \mathbb{B}^L \times \mathbb{B}^{X_u} \times \mathbb{B}^{X_c} \times \mathbb{B}^{L'} \to \mathbb{B}$ is the transition relation, where $L' = \{l' \mid l \in L\}$ stands for the state variables after the transition*
- *$BAD : \mathbb{B}^L \to \mathbb{B}$ is the set of unsafe states*
- *q_0 is the initial state where all latches are initialized to 0.*

We assume that the transition relation $\mathcal{R}$ of a controllable system is *deterministic* and *total* in its first three arguments, i.e., for every state $q \in \mathbb{B}^L$, uncontrollable input $u \in \mathbb{B}^{X_u}$ and controllable input $c \in \mathbb{B}^{X_c}$ there exists exactly one state $q' \in \mathbb{B}^{L'}$ such that $(q, u, c, q') \in \mathcal{R}$.

In our setting, characteristic functions are usually applied to a fixed vector of variables. Therefore, if $C : \mathbb{B}^L \to \mathbb{B}$ is a characteristic function, we write C as a short-hand for $C(L)$. Characteristic functions of sets of states can also be applied to next-state variables L', in that case we write C' for $C(L')$.

Let $X = \{x_1, \ldots, x_n\}$ be a set of boolean variables, and $Y \subseteq X \setminus \{x_i\}$ for some x_i. For boolean functions $F : \mathbb{B}^X \to \mathbb{B}$ and $f_{x_i} : \mathbb{B}^Y \to \mathbb{B}$, we denote by $F[x_i \leftarrow f_{x_i}]$ the boolean function that substitutes x_i by f_{x_i} in F.

Definition 2. *Given a controllable system $TS = (L, X_u, X_c, \mathcal{R}, BAD, q_0)$, the synthesis problem consists in finding for every $x \in X_c$ a solution function $f_x : \mathbb{B}^L \times \mathbb{B}^{X_u} \to \mathbb{B}$ such that if we replace $\mathcal{R}$ by $\mathcal{R}[x \leftarrow f_x]_{x \in X_c}$, we obtain a safe system, i.e., no state in BAD is reachable.*

If such a solution does not exist, we say the system is unrealizable.

To determine the possible behaviors of a controllable system, two forms of image computation can be used: (i) the *image* of a set of states C is the set of states that are reachable from C in one step, and the *preimage* are those states from which C is reachable in one step—in both cases ignoring who controls the input variables; (ii) the *uncontrollable preimage* of C is the set of states from which the environment can force the next transition to go into C, regardless of the choice of controllable variables. Formally, we define:

Definition 3. *Given a controllable system $TS = (L, X_u, X_c, \mathcal{R}, BAD, q_0)$ and a set of states C, we have:*

- $image(C) = \{q' \in \mathbb{B}^{L'} \mid \exists(q, u, c) \in \mathbb{B}^{L} \times \mathbb{B}^{X_u} \times \mathbb{B}^{X_c} : C(q) \wedge \mathcal{R}(q, u, c, q')\}$.
  We also write this set as $\exists L \; \exists X_u \; \exists X_c \; (C \wedge \mathcal{R})$.
- $preimage(C) = \{q \in \mathbb{B}^{L} \mid \exists(u, c, q') \in \mathbb{B}^{X_u} \times \mathbb{B}^{X_c} \times \mathbb{B}^{L'} : C(q') \wedge \mathcal{R}(q, u, c, q')\}$.
  We also write this set as $\exists X_u \; \exists X_c \; \exists L' \; (C' \wedge \mathcal{R})$.
- $UPRE(C) = \{q \in \mathbb{B}^{L} \mid \exists u \in \mathbb{B}^{X_u} \; \forall c \in \mathbb{B}^{X_c} \; \exists q' \in \mathbb{B}^{L} : C(q') \wedge \mathcal{R}(q, u, c, q')\}$.
  We also write this set as $\exists X_u \; \forall X_c \; \exists L' \; (C' \wedge \mathcal{R})$.

A direct correspondence of the uncontrollable preimage $UPRE$ for forward computation does not exist: if the environment can force the next transition out of a given set of states, in general the states that we reach are not uniquely determined and depend on the choice of the system player.

Efficient symbolic computation. BDDs are a suitable data structure for the efficient representation and manipulation of boolean functions, including all operations needed for computation of $image$, $preimage$, and $UPRE$. Between these three, $preimage$ can be computed most efficiently, while $image$ and $UPRE$ are more expensive—for $image$ not all optimizations that are available for $preimage$ can be used (see Sect. 5), and $UPRE$ contains a quantifier alternation.

3   Existing Approaches

Before we introduce our new approach, we recapitulate three existing approaches and point out their benefits and drawbacks.

Backward fixpoint algorithm. Given a controllable transition system $TS = (L, X_u, X_c, \mathcal{R}, BAD, q_0)$ with $BAD \neq 0$, the standard backward BDD-based algorithm (see e.g. [10]) computes the set of states from which the environment can force the system into unsafe states in a fixed point computation that starts with the unsafe states themselves. To compute a winning region for Player 1, it computes the least fixed-point of $UPRE$ on $BAD : \mu C. \; UPRE(BAD' \vee C')$.

Since safety games are determined, the complement of the computed set is the greatest winning region for Player 0, i.e., all states from which the system can win the game. Thus, this set also represents the most permissive winning strategy for the system player. We note two things regarding this approach:

1. To obtain a winning region, it computes the set of all states that cannot avoid moving into an error state, using the rather expensive $UPRE$ operation.
2. The most permissive winning strategy will not avoid progress towards the error states unless we reach the border of the winning region.

A forward algorithm. [13,14] A forward algorithm is presented by Cassez et al. [14] for the dual problem of solving reachability games, based on the work of Liu and Smolka [13]. The algorithm starts from the initial state and explores all states that are reachable in a forward manner. Whenever a state is visited, the algorithm checks whether it is losing; if it is, the algorithm revisits all reachable states that have a transition to this state and checks if they can avoid moving to a losing state. Although the algorithm is optimal in that it has linear time complexity in the state space, two issues should be taken into account:

1. The algorithm explicitly enumerates states and transitions, which is impractical even for moderate-size systems.
2. A fully symbolic implementation of the algorithm does not exist, and it would have to rely heavily on the expensive forward *image* computation.

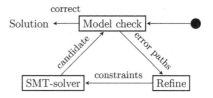

Fig. 1. High-level description of the lazy synthesis algorithm

Lazy Synthesis. [15] Lazy Synthesis interleaves a backwards model checking algorithm that identifies possible error paths with the synthesis of candidate solutions. To this end, the error paths are encoded into a set of constraints, and an SMT solver produces a candidate solution that avoids all known errors. If new error paths are discovered, more constraints are added that exclude them. The procedure terminates once a correct candidate is found (see Fig. 1). The approach works in a more general setting than ours, for systems with multiple components and partial information. When applied to our setting and challenging benchmark problems, the following issues arise:

1. Even though the error paths are encoded as constraints, the representation is such that it explicitly branches over valuations of all input variables, for each step of the error paths. This is clearly impractical for systems that have more than a dozen input variables (which is frequently the case in the classes of problems we target).
2. In each iteration of the main loop a single deterministic candidate is checked. Therefore, many iterations may be needed to discover all error paths.

4   Symbolic Lazy Synthesis Algorithms

In the following, we present symbolic algorithms that are inspired by the lazy synthesis approach and overcome some of its weaknesses to make it suitable for challenging benchmark problems like those from the SYNTCOMP library. We show that in our setting, we can avoid the explicit enumeration of error paths. Furthermore, we can use non-deterministic candidate models that are restricted such that they avoid the known error paths. In this restriction,

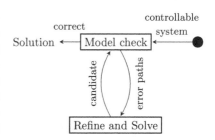

Fig. 2. High-level description of the symbolic lazy synthesis algorithm

we prioritize the removal of transitions that are close to the initial state, which can help us avoid error paths that are not known yet.

4.1 The Basic Algorithm

To explain the algorithm, we need some additional definitions. Fix a controllable system $TS = (L, X_u, X_c, \mathcal{R}, BAD, q_0)$.

An *error level* E_i is a set of states that are on a path from q_0 to BAD, and all states in E_i are reachable from q_0 in i steps. Formally, E_i is a subset of

$$\{q_i \mid \exists (q_0, q_1, \ldots, q_i, \ldots, q_n), q_n \in BAD, \text{ and } \exists (q_j, u, c, q_{j+1}) \in \mathcal{R} \text{ for } 0 \le j < n\}.$$

We call $(E_0, \ldots, E_n)$ a *sequence of error levels* if (i) each E_i is an error level, (ii) each state in each E_i has a transition to a state in E_{i+1}, and (iii) $E_n \subseteq BAD$. Note that the same state can appear in multiple error levels of a sequence, and E_0 contains only q_0.

Given a sequence of error levels $(E_0, \ldots, E_n)$, an *escape* for a transition (q, u, c, q') with $q \in E_i$ and $q' \in E_{i+1}$ is a transition (q, u, c', q'') such that $q'' \notin E_m \ \forall m > i$. We say the transition (q, u, c, q') *matches* the escape (q, u, c', q'').

Given two error levels E_i and E_{i+1}, we denote by RT_i the following set of tuples, representing the "removable" transitions, i.e., all transitions from E_i to E_{i+1} that match an escape:

$$RT_i = \{(q, u, q') \mid q \in E_i, q' \in E_{i+1} \text{ and } \exists (q, u, c, q') \in \mathcal{R} \text{ that has an escape}\}.$$

Overview. Figure 3 sketches the control flow of the algorithm. It starts by model checking the controllable system, without any restriction on the transition relation wrt. the controllable inputs. If unsafe states are reachable, the model checker returns a sequence of error levels. Iterating over all levels, we identify the transitions from the current level for which there exists an escape, and temporarily remove them from the transition relation. Based on the new restrictions on the transition relation, the algorithm then prunes the current error level by removing states that

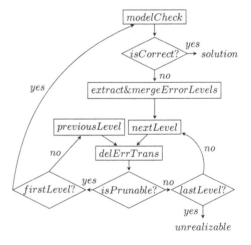

Fig. 3. Control flow of the algorithm

do not have transitions to the next level anymore. Whenever we prune at least one state, we move to the previous level to propagate back this information. If this eventually allows us to prune the first level, i.e., remove the initial state, then this error sequence has been invalidated and the new transition system (with deleted transitions) is sent to the model checker. Otherwise the system is unrealizable. In any following iteration, we accumulate information by merging the new error sequence with the ones we found before, and reset the transition relation before we analyze the error sequence for escapes.

Detailed Description. In more detail, Algorithm 1 describes a symbolic lazy synthesis algorithm. The method takes as input a controllable system and checks if its transition relation can be fixed in a way that error states are avoided. Upon termination, the algorithm returns either *unrealizable*, i.e., the system can not be fixed, or a restricted transition relation that is safe and total. From such a transition relation, a (deterministic) solution for the synthesis problem can be extracted in the same way as for existing algorithms. Therefore, we restrict the description of our algorithm to the computation of the safe transition relation.

LAZYSYNTHESIS: In Line 2, we initialize TR to the unrestricted transition relation $\mathcal{R}$ of the input system and E to the empty sequence, before we enter the main loop. Line 4 uses a model checker to check if the current TR is correct, and returns a sequence of error levels $mcLvls$ if it is not. In more detail, function $ModelCheck(TR)$ starts from the set of error states and uses the *preimage* function (see Definition 3) to iteratively compute a sequence of error levels.[1] It terminates if a level contains the initial state or if it reaches a fixed point. If the initial state was reached, the model checker uses the *image* function to remove from the error levels any state that is not reachable from the initial state.[2] Otherwise, in Line 6 we return the safe transition relation. If TR is not safe yet, Line 7 merges the new error levels with the error levels obtained in previous iterations by letting $E[i] \leftarrow E[i] \vee mcLvls[i]$ for every i. In Line 8 we call $PruneLevels(sys.\mathcal{R}, E)$, which searches for a transition relation that avoids all error paths represented in E, as explained below. If pruning is not successful, in Lines 9–10 we return "$Unrealizable$".

PRUNELEVELS: In the first loop, we call $ResolveLevel(E, i, TR)$ for increasing values of i (Line 4). Resolving a level is explained in detail below; roughly it means that we remove transitions that match an escape, and then remove states from this level that are not on an error path anymore. If $ResolveLevel$ has removed states from the current level, indicated by the return value of $isPrunable$, we check whether we are at the topmost level—if this is the case, we have removed the initial state from the level, which means that we have shown that every path from the initial state along the error sequence can be avoided. If we are not at the topmost level, we decrement i before returning to the start of the loop, in order to propagate the information about removed states to the previous level(s). If $isPrunable$ is false, we instead increment i and continue on the next level of the error sequence.

The first loop terminates either in Line 7, or if we reach the last level. In the latter case, we were not able to remove the initial state from $E[0]$ with the

---

[1] This part is the light-weight backward search: unlike $UPRE$ in the standard backward algorithm, *preimage* does not contain any quantifier alternation.

[2] This is the only place where our algorithm uses *image*, and it is only included to keep the definitions and correctness argument simple - the algorithm also works if the model checker omits this last *image* computation step, see Sect. 5.

Algorithm 1 Lazy Synthesis

1: **procedure** LAZYSYNTHESIS(*ControllableSystem sys*)
2:     $TR \leftarrow sys.\mathcal{R}, \quad E \leftarrow ()$
3:     **while** true **do**
4:         $isCorrect, mcLvls \leftarrow ModelCheck(TR)$
5:         **if** $isCorrect$ **then**
6:             **return** TR
7:         $E \leftarrow mergeLevels(E, mcLvls)$
8:         $isUnrealizable, TR \leftarrow PruneLevels(sys.\mathcal{R}, E)$
9:         **if** $isUnrealizable$ **then**
10:             **return** $Unrealizable$

1: **procedure** PRUNELEVELS(*TransitionRelation TR, ErrorSequence E*)
2:     $i \leftarrow 0$
3:     **while** $i < length(E) - 1$ **do**
4:         $isPrunable, TR, E \leftarrow ResolveLevel(E, i, TR)$
5:         **if** $isPrunable$ **then**
6:             **if** $i == 0$ **then**   // we have removed the initial state from $E[0]$
7:                 **return** *false, TR*
8:             $i \leftarrow i - 1$
9:         **else**
10:             $i \leftarrow i + 1$
11:     **while** $i \geq 1$ **do**   // $i == length(E) - 1$ when we enter the loop
12:         $i \leftarrow i - 1$
13:         $isPrunable, TR, E \leftarrow ResolveLevel(E, i, TR)$
14:     **if** $isPrunable$ **then**   // we have removed the initial state from $E[0]$
15:         **return** *false, TR*
16:     **else** // we could not remove the initial state from $E[0]$
17:         **return** *true*, $\emptyset$

1: **procedure** RESOLVELEVEL(*ErrorSequence E, Int i, TransitionRelation TR*)
2:     $RT \leftarrow (\exists L' \ ((\ \exists X_c \ TR \ ) \wedge \neg E[i+1:n]' \ )) \wedge E[i] \wedge E[i+1]'$
3:     $TR \leftarrow TR \wedge \neg RT$
4:     $AVSet \leftarrow \forall X_u \ (E[i] \ \wedge \exists L'(\ \exists X_c \ TR \wedge \neg E[i+1]' \ ) \ )$
5:     $E[i] \leftarrow E[i] \wedge \neg AVSet$
6:     **return** $AVSet \neq \emptyset, TR, E$

---

local propagation of information during the main loop (that stops if we reach a level that cannot be pruned). To make sure that all information is completely propagated, afterwards we start another loop were we resolve all levels bottom-up, propagating the information about removed states all the way to the top. When we arrive at $E[0]$, we can either remove the initial state now, or we conclude that the system is unrealizable.

RESOLVELEVEL: Line 2 computes the set of transitions that have an escape: $\exists L' \ ((\ \exists X_c \ TR \ ) \wedge \neg E[i+1:n]' \ )$ is the set of all (q, u) for which there exists an escape (q, u, c, q'), and by conjoining $E[i] \wedge E[i+1]'$ we compute all tuples (q, u, q') that represent transitions from $E[i]$ to $E[i+1]$ matching an escape. Line 3 removes the corresponding transitions from the transition relation TR.

Line 4 computes *AvSet* which represents the set of all states such that all their transitions within the error levels match an escape. After removing $AVSet$ from the current level, we return.

Comparison. Compared to Lazy Synthesis (see Fig. 1), the main loop of our algorithm merges the Refine and Solve steps, and instead of computing one deterministic model per iteration, we collect restrictions on the non-deterministic transition relation TR. Keeping TR non-deterministic allows us to find and exclude more error paths per iteration.

Compared to the standard backward fixpoint approach (see Sect. 3), an important difference is that we explore the error paths in a forward analysis starting from the initial state, and avoid progress towards the error states as soon as possible. As a consequence, our algorithm can find solutions that visit only a small subset of the state space. If such solutions exist, our algorithm will find a solution faster and will detect a winning region that is much smaller than the maximal winning region detected by the standard algorithm.

4.2   Correctness of Algorithm 1

Theorem 1 (Soundness). *Every transition relation returned by Algorithm 1 is safe, and total in the first two arguments.*

Proof. The model checker guarantees that the returned transition relation TR is safe, i.e., unsafe states are not reachable. To see that TR is total in the first two arguments, i.e., $\forall q \; \forall u \; \exists c \; \exists q' : (q, u, c, q') \in TR$, observe that this property holds for the initial TR, and is preserved by *ResolveLevels*: lines 2 and 3 ensure that a transition $(q, u, c, q') \in TR$ can only be deleted if $\exists c' \; \exists q'' \neq q' : (q, u, c', q'') \in TR$, i.e., if there exists another transition with the same state q and uncontrollable input u.

To prove completeness of the algorithm, we define formally what it means for an error level to be resolved.

Definition 4 (Resolved). *Given a sequence of error levels $E = (E_0, ..., E_n)$ and a transition relation TR, an error level E_i with $i < n$ is **resolved** with respect to TR if the following conditions hold:*

- $RT_i = \emptyset$
- $\forall q_i \in E_i \setminus BAD : \exists u \; \exists c \; \exists q_{i+1} \in E_{i+1} : (q_i, u, c, q_{i+1}) \in TR$

E_i is unresolved otherwise, and E_n is always resolved.

Informally, E_i is resolved if all transitions from E_i that match an escape have been removed from TR, and every state in E_i can still reach E_{i+1}.

Theorem 2 (Completeness). *If the algorithm returns "Unrealizable", then the controllable system is unrealizable.*

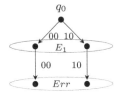
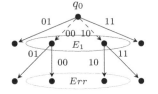

Fig. 4. Error levels from iteration 1   **Fig. 5.** solution for iteration 1

Proof. Observe that if a controllable system is unrealizable, then there exists an error sequence $E = (E_0 = \{q_0\}, E_1, ..., E_n)$ where all levels are resolved and non-empty. Lines 2 and 3 of *ResolveLevel* guarantee that all transitions from E_i to E_{i+1} that match an escape will be deleted, so the only remaining transitions between E_i and E_{i+1} are those that have no escapes. Line 4 computes all states in E_i that have no more transitions to E_{i+1} and line 5 removes these states. Thus, after calling *ResolveLevel*, the current level will be resolved.

However, since *ResolveLevel* may remove states from E_i, the levels E_j with $j < i$ could become *unresolved*. To see that this is not an issue note that before we output *Unrealizable*, we go through the second loop that resolves all levels from n to 0. After execution of this second loop all levels are resolved, and if E_0 still contains q_0, then the controllable system is indeed unrealizable, since from our sequence of error levels we can extract a subsequence of resolved and non-empty error levels.[3]

Theorem 3 (Termination). *Algorithm 1 always terminates.*

Proof. Termination is guaranteed due to the fact that there is a finite number of possible transition relations, and each call to *PruneLevels* either produces a *TR* that is different from all transition relations that we have seen before, or terminates with *isUnrealizable*.

4.3   Illustration of the Algorithm

Figure 4 shows error levels obtained from the model checker. The transitions are labeled with vectors of input bits, where the left bit is uncontrollable and the right bit controllable. The last level is a subset of *BAD*. After the first iteration of the algorithm, the transitions that are dashed in Figure 5 will be deleted. Note that another solution exists where instead we delete the two outgoing transitions from level E_1 to the error level *Err*. This solution can be obtained by a backward algorithm. However, our solution makes all states in E_1 unreachable and thus we detect smaller winning region.

In the second iteration, the model checker uses the restricted transition relation and computes a new sequence of error levels. This sequence is merged with the previous one and the resulting sequence will be resolved as before.

---

[3] It may be a subsequence due to the merging of error levels from different iterations of the main loop.

4.4   Example Problems

We want to highlight the potential benefit of our algorithm on two families of examples.

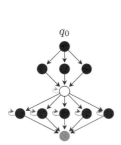

Fig. 6. Example with small solution   **Fig. 7.** Example that is solved fast

First, consider a controllable system where all paths from the initial state to the error states have to go through a bottleneck, e.g., a single state, as depicted in Fig. 6, and assume that Player 0 can force the system not to go beyond this bottleneck. In this case, our algorithm will have a winning region that only includes the states between the initial state and the bottleneck, whereas the standard algorithm may have a much bigger winning region (in the example including all the states in the fourth row). Moreover, the strategy produced by our algorithm will be very simple: if we reach the bottleneck, we force the system to stay there. In contrast, the strategy produced by the standard algorithm will in general be much more complicated, as it has to define the behavior for a much larger number of states.

Second, consider a controllable system where the shortest path between error and initial state is short, but Player 1 can only *force* the system to move towards the error on a long path. Moreover, assume that Player 0 can avoid entering this long path, for example by entering a separated part of the state space like depicted in Fig. 7. In this case, our algorithm will quickly find a simple solution: move to that separate part and stay there. In contrast, the standard algorithm will have to go through many iterations of the backwards fixpoint computation, until finally finding the point where moving into the losing region can be avoided.

5   Optimization

As presented, Algorithm 1 requires the construction of a data structure that represents the full transition relation $\mathcal{R}$, which causes a significant memory consumption. In practice, the size of a BDD that represents the full transition relation can be prohibitive even for moderate-size models.

As the transition relation is deterministic, it can alternatively be represented by a vector of functions, each of which updates one of the state variables. Such a partitioning of the transition relation is an additional computational effort, but it results in a more efficient representation that is necessary to handle large systems. In the following we describe optimizations based on such a representation.

Definition 5. *A **functional controllable system** is a 6-tuple* $TS_f = (L, X_u, X_c, \mathbf{F}, BAD, q_0)$, *where* $\mathbf{F} = (f_1, ..., f_{|L|})$ *with* $f_i : \mathbb{B}^L \times \mathbb{B}^{X_u} \times \mathbb{B}^{X_c} \to \mathbb{B}$ *for all* i, *and all other components are as in Definition 1.*

In a functional system with current state q and inputs u and c, the next-state value of the ith state variable l_i is computed as $f_i(q, u, c)$. Thus, we can compute image and preimage of a set of states C in the following way:

- $image_f(C) = \exists L \ \exists X_u \ \exists X_c \ (\bigwedge_{i=1}^{|L|} l'_i \equiv f_i \wedge C)$
- $preimage_f(C) = \exists L' \ \exists X_u \ \exists X_c \ (\bigwedge_{i=1}^{|L|} l'_i \equiv f_i \wedge C')$

However, computing $\bigwedge_{i=1}^{|L|} l'_i \equiv f_i \wedge C'$ is still very expensive and might be as hard as computing the whole transition relation. To optimize the preimage computation, we instead directly substitute the state variables in the boolean function that represents C by the function that computes their new value:

$$preimage_s(C) = \exists X_u \ \exists X_c \ C[l_i \leftarrow f_i]_{l_i \in L}$$

For the computation of $image(C)$, substitution cannot be used. While alternatives exist (such as using the range function instead [16]), image computation remains much more expensive than preimage computation.

5.1   The Optimized Algorithm

The optimized algorithm takes as input a functional controllable system, and uses the following modified procedures:

OPTIMIZEDLAZYSYNTHESIS: This procedure replaces LAZYSYNTHESIS, with two differences, both in the model checker: the preimage is computed using $preimage_s$, and unreachable states are not removed, in order to avoid image computation. Thus, the error levels are over-approximated.

OPTIMIZEDRESOLVELEVEL: This procedure replaces RESOLVELEVEL and computes RT and $AvSet$ more efficiently. Note that for a given set of states C, the set $pretrans(C) = \{(q, u, c) \in \mathbb{B}^L \times \mathbb{B}^{X_u} \times \mathbb{B}^{X_c} \mid \mathbf{F}(q, u, c) \in C\}$ can efficiently be computed as $C[l_i \leftarrow f_i]_{l_i \in L}$. Based on this, we get the following:
RT: To compute the transitions that can be avoided, we compute the conjunction of the transitions from E_i to E_{i+1} as $pretrans(E[i+1]') \wedge E[i]$ with those transitions that have an escape: $\exists c \ pretrans(\neg E[i+1 : n]') \wedge E[i]$.
AvSet: The states that can avoid all transitions to the lower levels can now be computed as $\forall u \ [\ \exists c \ pretrans(\neg E[i+1 : n]') \wedge E[i] \ ]$.

Generalized Deletion of Transitions. In addition, we consider a variant of our algorithm that uses the following heuristic to speed up computation: whenever we find an escape (q, u, c, q') with $q \in E_i$, then we not only remove all matching transitions that start in E_i, but matching transitions that start anywhere, and lead to a state $q'' \in E_j$ with $j > i$. Thus, we delete more transitions per iteration of the algorithm, all of which are known to lead to an error.

6 Experimental Evaluation

We implemented our algorithm in Python, using the BDD package CUDD [17]. We evaluate our prototype on a family of parameterized benchmarks based on the examples in Sect. 4.4, and on the benchmark set of SYNTCOMP 2017 [12]. We compare two versions of our algorithm (with and without generalized deletion as explained in Sect. 5.1) against a re-implementation of the standard backward approach, in order to have a fair comparison between algorithms that use the same BDD library and programming language. For the SYNTCOMP benchmarks, we additionally compare against the results of the participants in SYNT-COMP 2017. Our implementations of all algorithms include the most important general optimizations for this kind of algorithms, including a functional transition relation and automatic reordering of BDDs (see Jacobs et al. [10]).

6.1 Parameterized Benchmarks

On the parameterized versions of the examples from Sect. 4.4, we observe the expected behaviour:

- for the first example, the winning region found by our algorithm is always about half as big as the winning region for the standard algorithm. Even more notable is the size of the synthesized controller circuit: for example, our solution for an instance with 2^{18} states and 10 input variables has a size of just 9 AND-gates, whereas the solution obtained from the standard algorithm has 800 AND-gates.
- for the second example, we observe that for systems with 15–25 state variables, our algorithm solves the problem in constant time of 0.1s, whereas the solving time increases sharply for the standard algorithm: it uses 1.7s for a system with 15 latches, 92s for 20 latches, and 4194s for 25 latches.

6.2 SYNTCOMP Benchmarks

We compared our algorithm against the standard algorithm on the benchmark set that was used in the safety track of SYNTCOMP 2017, with a timeout of 5000 s on an Intel Xeon processor (E3-1271 v3, 3.6 GHz) and 32 GB RAM.

First, we observe that our algorithms often produce much smaller winning regions: out of the 76 realizable benchmarks that our algorithm without general deletion solved, we found a strictly smaller winning region than the standard backwards algorithm in 28 cases. In 14 cases, the winning region is smaller by a factor of 10^3 or more, in 8 cases by a factor of 10^{20} or more, and in 4 cases by a factor of 10^{30} or more. The biggest difference in winning region size is a factor of 10^{68}. A selection of results for such benchmarks is given in Table 1. Note that these results are for the algorithm without the generalized deletion heuristic; when using the algorithm with generalized deletion, our winning regions are somewhat bigger, but the tendency is the same. Regarding the size of synthesized circuits, the results are mixed: our solutions are often much smaller, but in several cases they are also of bigger or equal size.

Table 1. Comparison of Winning Region Size for Selected Benchmarks

Instance	Standard	Lazy	Difference factor
load_2c_comp_comp5_REAL	$1.08 * 10^{40}$	$5.67 * 10^{13}$	$> 10^{26}$
load_3c_comp_comp4_REAL	$2.39 * 10^{52}$	$1.21 * 10^{18}$	$>10^{44}$
load_3c_comp_comp7_REAL	$4.97 * 10^{86}$	$1.21 * 10^{18}$	$>10^{68}$
ltl2dba_C2-6_comp3_REAL	$2.46 * 10^{35}$	$4.55 * 10^{25}$	$>10^9$
ltl2dba_E4_comp3_REAL	$2.96 * 10^{79}$	$3.74 * 10^{50}$	$>10^{28}$
demo-v10_5_REAL	$1.93 * 10^{25}$	$1.31 * 10^5$	$>10^{20}$
demo-v12_5_REAL	$2.81 * 10^{14}$	$1.64 * 10^4$	$>10^{10}$
demo-v14_5_REAL	$1.23 * 10^{14}$	356	$>10^{11}$
demo-v19_5_REAL	$1.27 * 10^{11}$	305	$>10^8$
demo-v20_5_REAL	$2.31 * 10^{41}$	$3.44 * 10^{10}$	$>10^{30}$
demo-v22_5_REAL	$3.4 * 10^{38}$	$1.71 * 10^{15}$	$>10^{23}$
demo-v23_5_REAL	$1.37 * 10^{12}$	$9.22 * 10^3$	$>10^8$
demo-v24_5_REAL	$3.27 * 10^{63}$	$1.17 * 10^{31}$	$>10^{32}$

Regarding solving time, out of the 234 benchmarks our algorithm without generalized deletion solved 99 before the timeout, and the version with the generalized deletion heuristic solved 116. While the standard algorithm solves a higher number of instances overall (163), for a number of examples the lazy algorithms are faster. In particular, both versions each solve 7 benchmarks that are not solved by the standard algorithm, as shown in Table 2.

Moreover, we compare against the participants of SYNTCOMP 2017: with a timeout of 3600 s, the best single-threaded solver in SYNTCOMP 2017 solved 155 problems, and the virtual best solver (VBS; i.e., a theoretical solver that on each benchmark performs as good as the best participating solver) would have solved 186 instances. If we include our two algorithms with a timeout of 3600 s, the VBS can additionally solve 7 out of the 48 instances that could not be solved by any of the participants of SYNTCOMP before. As our algorithms also solve some instances much faster than the existing algorithms, they would be worthwhile additions to a portfolio solver for SYNTCOMP.

Table 2. Benchmarks solved uniquely by the Lazy algorithm

Instance	Lazy	Generalized deletion	Standard	SYNTCOMP 2017 participants
gb_s2_r3_comp1_UNREAL	38	*TO*	*TO*	Solved by 1
genbuf48c6y	*TO*	3839	*TO*	Solved by 4
ltl2dba_E6_comp4_REAL	2435	*TO*	*TO*	Not solved
ltl2dba_Q4_comp5_REAL	125	304	*TO*	Solved by 1
ltl2dba_U1-6_Comp3_REAL	*TO*	4590	*TO*	Not solved
ltl2dpa_alpha5_Comp2_REAL	*TO*	1880	*TO*	Not solved
ltl2dpa_alpha5_Comp3_REAL	*TO*	2651	*TO*	Not solved
ltl2dpa_E4_comp2_REAL	1081	*TO*	*TO*	Not solved
ltl2dpa_E4_comp4_REAL	2122	*TO*	*TO*	Not solved
ltl2dpa_U14_comp2_REAL	4019	615	*TO*	Not solved
ltl2dpa_U14_comp3_REAL	2605	1681	*TO*	Not solved

7 Synthesis of Resilient Controllers

As mentioned in Sect. 1, our algorithm produces strategies that avoid progress towards the error states as early as possible, which could be useful for generating controllers that are tolerant to faults or perturbations. Dallal et al. [11] have modeled systems with *perturbations*, which are defined essentially as extraordinary transitions where Player 1 chooses values for both the uncontrollable and (a subset of) the controllable inputs. They introduced an algorithm that produces strategies with maximal resilience against such perturbations, defined as the number of perturbations under which the controller can still guarantee not to enter the winning region of Player 1.

The algorithm of Dallal et al. can be seen as a variant of our algorithm, except that it first uses the standard fixpoint algorithm to determine the winning region, and then uses a mixed forward/backward search to find a strategy that makes as little progress towards the losing region as possible. We have implemented this as a variant of our algorithm, providing to our knowledge its first implementation. An evaluation on the SYNTCOMP benchmarks provides interesting insights: only on 6 out of the 234 benchmarks the algorithm can give a guarantee of resilience against one or more perturbations. Moreover, when inspecting the behavior of our lazy algorithms on these benchmarks, we find that for all of them they provide a strictly smaller winning region than the standard algorithm. 5 of the 6 benchmarks appear in Table 1, with winning regions that are smaller by a factor of 10^9 or more. In fact, for these benchmarks our algorithm can give a similar guarantee as the Dallal algorithm, without additional cost. The difference is that we measure the distance to the error states instead of the distance to the losing region (which is not known to us). This leads us to the conjecture that our algorithm performs particularly well on synthesis problems that allow resilient controllers, together with the observation that not many of these appear in the SYNTCOMP benchmark set that we have tested against.

8 Conclusions

We have introduced lazy synthesis algorithms with a novel combination of forward and backward exploration. Our experimental results show that our algorithms find much smaller winning regions in many cases. Moreover, they can solve a number of problems that are intractable for existing synthesis algorithms, both from our own examples and from the SYNTCOMP benchmark set.

In the future, we want to explore how lazy synthesis can be integrated into portfolio solvers and hybrid algorithms. Additionally, we want to further explore the applications of eager strategies in the synthesis of resilient controllers [11,18–20] and connections to lazy algorithms for controllers of cyber-physical systems [21].

Acknowledgments. We thank Bernd Finkbeiner and Martin Zimmermann for fruitful discussions. This work was supported by the German Research Foundation (DFG) under the project ASDPS (JA 2357/2-1).

References

1. Church, A.: Applications of recursive arithmetic to the problem of circuit synthesis. Summ. Summer Inst. Symb. Logic **I**, 3–50 (1957)
2. Büchi, J., Landweber, L.: Solving sequential conditions by finite-state strategies. Trans. Am. Math. Soc. **138**, 295–311 (1969)
3. Pnueli, A., Rosner, R.: On the synthesis of a reactive module. In: POPL, pp. 179–190. ACM Press (1989)
4. Filiot, E., Jin, N., Raskin, J.F.: Antichains and compositional algorithms for LTL synthesis. Form. Methods Syst. Des. **39**(3), 261–296 (2011)
5. Ehlers, R.: Symbolic bounded synthesis. Form. Methods Syst. Des. **40**(2), 232–262 (2012)
6. Sohail, S., Somenzi, F.: Safety first: a two-stage algorithm for the synthesis of reactive systems. STTT **15**(5–6), 433–454 (2013)
7. Finkbeiner, B., Schewe, S.: Bounded synthesis. STTT **15**(5–6), 519–539 (2013)
8. Bloem, R., Könighofer, R., Seidl, M.: SAT-based synthesis methods for safety specs. In: McMillan, K.L., Rival, X. (eds.) VMCAI 2014. LNCS, vol. 8318, pp. 1–20. Springer, Heidelberg (2014). https://doi.org/10.1007/978-3-642-54013-4_1
9. Legg, A., Narodytska, N., Ryzhyk, L.: A SAT-based counterexample guided method for unbounded synthesis. In: Chaudhuri, S., Farzan, A. (eds.) CAV 2016. LNCS, vol. 9780, pp. 364–382. Springer, Cham (2016). https://doi.org/10.1007/978-3-319-41540-6_20
10. Jacobs, S., et al.: The first reactive synthesis competition (SYNTCOMP 2014). STTT **19**(3), 367–390 (2017)
11. Dallal, E., Neider, D., Tabuada, P.: Synthesis of safety controllers robust to unmodeled intermittent disturbances. In: CDC, pp. 7425–7430. IEEE (2016)
12. Jacobs, S., et al.: The 4th reactive synthesis competition (SYNTCOMP 2017): benchmarks, participants & results. In: SYNT@CAV. Volume 260 of EPTCS, pp. 116–143. (2017)
13. Liu, X., Smolka, S.A.: Simple linear-time algorithms for minimal fixed points. In: Larsen, K.G., Skyum, S., Winskel, G. (eds.) ICALP 1998. LNCS, vol. 1443, pp. 53–66. Springer, Heidelberg (1998). https://doi.org/10.1007/BFb0055040

14. Cassez, F., David, A., Fleury, E., Larsen, K.G., Lime, D.: Efficient on-the-fly algorithms for the analysis of timed games. In: Abadi, M., de Alfaro, L. (eds.) CONCUR 2005. LNCS, vol. 3653, pp. 66–80. Springer, Heidelberg (2005). https://doi.org/10.1007/11539452_9

15. Finkbeiner, B., Jacobs, S.: Lazy synthesis. In: Kuncak, V., Rybalchenko, A. (eds.) VMCAI 2012. LNCS, vol. 7148, pp. 219–234. Springer, Heidelberg (2012). https://doi.org/10.1007/978-3-642-27940-9_15

16. Kropf, T.: Introduction to Formal Hardware Verification. Springer Science & Business Media, Berlin (2013)

17. Somenzi, F.: CUDD: CU decision diagram package, release 2.4.0. University of Colorado at Boulder (2009)

18. Neider, D., Weinert, A., Zimmermann, M.: Synthesizing optimally resilient controllers. In: CSL (2018, to appear)

19. Ehlers, R., Topcu, U.: Resilience to intermittent assumption violations in reactive synthesis. In: HSCC, pp. 203–212. ACM (2014)

20. Huang, C., Peled, D.A., Schewe, S., Wang, F.: A game-theoretic foundation for the maximum software resilience against dense errors. IEEE Trans. Softw. Eng. **42**(7), 605–622 (2016)

21. Raman, V., Donzé, A., Sadigh, D., Murray, R.M., Seshia, S.A.: Reactive synthesis from signal temporal logic specifications. In: HSCC, pp. 239–248. ACM (2015)

Modular Verification of Concurrent Programs via Sequential Model Checking

Dan Rasin[1]([✉]), Orna Grumberg[1], and Sharon Shoham[2]

[1] Technion – Israel Institute of Technology, Haifa, Israel
danny.rasin@gmail.com, orna@cs.technion.ac.il
[2] Tel Aviv University, Tel Aviv, Israel
sharon.shoham@gmail.com

Abstract. This work utilizes the plethora of work on verification of sequential programs for the purpose of verifying concurrent programs. We reduce the verification of a concurrent program to a series of verification tasks of sequential programs. Our approach is modular in the sense that each sequential verification task roughly corresponds to the verification of a single thread, with some additional information about the environment in which it operates. Information regarding the environment is gathered during the run of the algorithm, by need. While our approach is general, it specializes on concurrent programs where the threads are structured hierarchically. The idea is to exploit the hierarchy in order to minimize the amount of information that needs to be transferred between threads. To that end, we verify one of the threads, considered "main", as a sequential program. Its verification process initiates queries to its "environment" (which may contain multiple threads). Those queries are answered by sequential verification, if the environment consists of a single thread, or, otherwise, by applying the same hierarchical algorithm on the environment. Our technique is fully automatic, and allows us to use any off-the-shelf sequential model checker. We implemented our technique in a tool called CoMuS and evaluated it against established tools for concurrent verification. Our experiments show that it works particularly well on hierarchically structured programs.

1 Introduction

Verification of concurrent programs is known to be extremely hard. On top of the challenges inherent in verifying sequential programs, it adds the need to consider a high (typically unbounded) number of thread interleavings. An appealing direction is to exploit the modular structure of such programs in verification. Usually, however, a property of the whole system cannot be partitioned into a set of properties that are local to the individual threads. Thus, some knowledge about the interaction of a thread with its environment is required.

In this work we develop a new approach, which utilizes the plethora of work on verification of sequential programs for the purpose of *modularly* verifying the safety of concurrent programs. Our technique automatically reduces the verification of a concurrent program to a series of verification tasks of sequential

© Springer Nature Switzerland AG 2018
S. K. Lahiri and C. Wang (Eds.): ATVA 2018, LNCS 11138, pp. 228–247, 2018.
https://doi.org/10.1007/978-3-030-01090-4_14

programs. This allows us to benefit from any past, as well as future, progress in sequential verification.

Our approach is modular in the sense that each sequential verification task roughly corresponds to the verification of a single thread, with some additional information about the environment in which it operates. This information is *automatically* and *lazily* discovered during the run of the algorithm, when needed.

While our approach is general, it specializes on concurrent programs where the threads are structured hierarchically as it takes a *hierarchical view* of the program. Namely, for the purpose of verification, one of the threads, t_M, is considered "main", and all other threads are considered its "environment". The idea is to exploit the hierarchy in order to minimize the amount of information that needs to be transferred between the verification tasks of different threads.

We first analyze t_M using sequential verification, where, for soundness, all interferences from the environment are abstracted (over-approximated) by a function env_move, which is called by t_M whenever a context switch should be considered. Initially, env_move havocs all shared variables; it is gradually refined during the run of the algorithm. When the sequential model checker discovers a violation of safety in t_M, it also returns a path leading to the violation. The path may include calls to env_move, in which case the violation may be spurious (due to the over-approximation). Therefore, the algorithm initiates *queries* to the environment of t_M whose goal is to check whether *certain* interferences, as observed on the violating path, are feasibles. Whenever an interference turns out to be infeasible, the env_move function is refined to exclude it. Eventually, env_move becomes precise enough to enable full verification of the desired property on the augmented t_M. Alternatively, it can reveal a real counterexample in t_M.

The queries are checked on the environment (that may consist of multiple threads) in the same modular manner. Thus we obtain a *hierarchical modular verification*. Along the algorithm, each thread learns about the next threads in the hierarchy, and is provided with assumptions from former threads in the hierarchy to guide its learning. When the program has a hierarchical structure that is aligned with the verification process, this makes the assumptions simpler and speeds up verification.

Our technique is fully automatic and performs *unbounded verification*, i.e., it can both find bugs and prove safety in concurrent programs even with unbounded executions (e.g., due to loops), as long as the number of threads is fixed. It works on the level of program code and generates standard sequential programs in its intermediate checks. This allows us to use any off-the-shelf sequential model-checker. In particular, we can handle concurrent programs with an infinite state-space, provided that the sequential model checker supports such programs (as is the case in our implementation).

Our experiments show that the approach works particularly well on programs in which the threads are arranged as a chain, $t_1, t_2, \ldots, t_k$, where thread t_i depends only on its immediate successor t_{i+1} in the chain. This induces a natural hierarchical structure in which t_1 is the main thread with environment $t_2, \ldots, t_k$; thread t_2 is the main thread in the environment, and so on. This structure often occurs in concurrent implementations of dynamic programming algorithms.

To summarize, the main contributions of our work are as follows:

- We present a new modular verification approach that reduces the verification of a concurrent program to a series of verification tasks of sequential programs. Any off-the-shelf model checker for sequential programs can thus be used.
- Our approach takes a hierarchical view of the program, where each thread learns about the next threads in the hierarchy, and is provided with assumptions from former threads to guide its learning.
- The needed information on a thread's environment is gathered in the code, automatically and lazily, during the run of the algorithm.
- We implemented our approach and showed that as the number of threads grows, it outperforms existing tools on programs that have a hierarchical structure, such as concurrent implementations of dynamic programming algorithms.

1.1 Related Work

The idea of code transformation to a sequential program appeared in [24,32,33]. However, these works translate the concurrent program to a single nondeterministic sequential program. In contrast, our technique exploits the modular structure of the program.

In the rest of this section, we address unbounded modular techniques for proving safety properties of concurrent programs. Other techniques use bounded model checking, where the bound can address different parameters, such as the number of context switches [19,33], write operations [32] or loop iterations [1, 29,35].

The work most closely related to ours is [16,17]. Their technique uses predicate abstraction of both states and environment transitions (similar to our env_move), as part of an automatic modular verification framework. The technique also iteratively refines this abstraction by checking possible witnesses of errors. However, they treat all threads symmetrically, whereas our approach exploits a hierarchical view of the program. In addition, [16,17] explore abstract single threads using reachability trees, which are inherent to their technique. We, on the other hand, represent threads (augmented with some environment information) as stand-alone C programs. Thus, we can use any off-the-shelf model checker to address the "sequential part" of the verification problem.

The works in [9,12,20] suggest to apply rely-guarantee reasoning for concurrent (or asynchronous) programs, while the different sections of the program can be verified sequentially. However, their technique requires human effort to specify the rely-guarantee conditions, whereas our approach is completely automatic.

[10] suggests a modular algorithm with rely-guarantee reasoning and automatic condition inference. [21] formalizes the algorithm in the framework of

abstract interpretation. However, their algorithm requires finite state systems, and its inferred conditions only refer to changes in global variables. Hence, they fail to prove properties where local variables are necessary for the proof. In our approach, reasoning about local variables is allowed, when we learn that they are necessary for verification. Such variables are then turned into global variables, but their behavior is abstracted, preserving modularity. [6] also tackles the incompetence of modular proofs by exposing local variables as global, according to counterexamples. However, their approach uses BDDs and suits finite state systems. Similar to [16], they treat threads symmetrically. Our approach is applicable to infinite state systems and uses a guided search to derive cross-thread information.

Our queries resemble queries in learning-based compositional verification [5, 25], which are also answered by a model checker. Our hierarchical recursive approach resembles the n-way decomposition handled in [25]. However, these works represent programs, assumptions and specification as LTSs, and although extended to deal with shared memory in [31] these algorithms are suitable for finite state systems.

Several works such as [11,14,28,34], tackle the interleaving explosion problem by performing a thread interleaving reduction. [34] combines partial order reduction [13] with the impact algorithm [22], whereas [28] identifies reducible blocks for compositional verification. These approaches are complementary to ours, as our first step is performing an interleaving reduction (to identify cut-points for env_move calls).

2   Preliminaries

Sequential Programs. A *sequential program* P is defined by a control flow graph whose nodes are a set of program locations L (also called labels), and whose edges E are a subset of $L \times L$. The program has an initial label, denoted $l^{init} \in L$. Each node l is associated with a command $c \in cmds$, denoted $cmd(l)$, which can be an assignment or an if command, as well as havoc, assume and assert (explained below). Intuitively, we think of standard C programs (that may contain loops as well), which can be trivially compiled to such control flow graphs. The program may also include non-recursive functions, which will be handled by inlining.

The program is defined over a set of variables V. Conditions in the program are quantifier-free first-order-logic formulas over V. A special variable pc $\notin V$, ranging over L, indicates the program location. A *state* s of P is a pair (l, σ) where $l \in L$ is the value of pc and σ is a valuation of V. Variables may have unbounded domains, resulting in a potentially infinite state-space. We also assume the existence of a special error state, denoted $\epsilon = (l_\epsilon, \bot)$. We denote by $l(s)$ and $\sigma(s)$ the first and second components (resp.) of a state $s = (l, \sigma)$. Given an initialization formula ϕ_{init} over V, the set of *initial states* consists of all states (l^{init}, σ) where $\sigma \models \phi_{init}$.

For $s = (l, \sigma)$, let $cmd(s) = cmd(l)$. We denote $next(s) = \{s' \mid s' \text{ can be obtained from } s \text{ using } cmd(s)\}$. This set is defined according to the command.

In particular, $s' \in next(s)$ implies that $(l(s), l(s')) \in E$. The definition of $next(s)$ for assignments and if commands is standard. A v=havoc() command assigns a non-deterministic value to the variable v. An assume(b) command is used to disregard any computation in which the condition b does not hold. Formally, if $s = (l, \sigma)$ and $cmd(s)$=assume(b), then $\sigma \vDash b \implies next(s) = \{(l', \sigma)\}$ where $l' \neq l_\epsilon$ is the unique label such that $(l, l') \in E$, and $\sigma \nvDash b \implies next(s) = \emptyset$. An assert($b$) command is defined similarly, except that it moves to the error state if b is violated.

A *computation* ρ of P is a sequence $\rho = s_0 \rightarrow s_1 \rightarrow \ldots \rightarrow s_n$ for some $n \geq 0$ s.t. for every two adjacent states s_i, s_{i+1}: $s_{i+1} \in next(s_i)$. ρ is an *initial computation* in P if it starts from an initial state. ρ is a *reachable computation* in P if there exists an initial computation ρ' for which ρ is the suffix. The *path* of a computation $(l_0, \sigma_0) \rightarrow \ldots \rightarrow (l_n, \sigma_n)$ is the sequence of program locations $l_0, \ldots, l_n$.

Preconditions and Postconditions. Given a condition q over V and an edge $e = (l, l')$, a *precondition* of q w.r.t. e, denoted $pre(e, q)$, is any condition p such that for every state s, if $\sigma(s) \vDash p$ and $l(s) = l$ then there exists $s' \in next(s)$ s.t. $\sigma(s') \vDash q$ and $l(s') = l'$[1]. A precondition extends to a path $\pi = l_0, \ldots, l_n$ in the natural way. The *weakest precondition* of q w.r.t. e (resp., π) is implied by any other precondition, and can be computed in the standard way [8]. We denote it $wp(e, q)$ (resp., $wp(\pi, q)$).

A postcondition of p w.r.t $e = (l, l')$, denoted $post(e, p)$, is any condition q such that if $\sigma(s) \vDash p$, $l(s) = l$ then for every $s' \in next(s)$, if $l(s') = l'$ then $\sigma(s') \vDash q$. Postconditions can also be extended to paths $\pi = l_0, \ldots, l_n$. We use $post(\pi, p)$ to denote a postcondition of condition p w.r.t. path π.

Concurrent Programs A *concurrent program* P. consists of multiple threads $t_1, \ldots, t_m$, where each *thread* t_i has the same syntax as a sequential program over a set of variables V_i and a program location variable $\mathbf{pc}_i$. The threads communicate through shared variables, meaning that generally V_i, V_j are not disjoint for $i \neq j$. A variable is *written* by t_i if it appears on the left hand side of any assignment in t_i. A variable v is *shared* between two threads t_i, t_j if $v \in V_i \cap V_j$. A variable $v \in V_i$ is a *local* variable of t_i if $v \notin V_j$ for every $j \neq i$. Let $V = \bigcup_{i=1}^{m} V_i$. A *state* of P is a pair $(\bar{l}, \sigma)$, where σ is a valuation of V and $\bar{l} = (l_1, \ldots, l_m)$ where l_i is the value of $\mathbf{pc}_i$. We also assume one common error state ϵ. Given an initialization formula ϕ_{init} over V, the set of *initial states* consists of all states $(\bar{l}^{init}, \sigma)$ where $\sigma \vDash \phi_{init}$ and l_i^{init} is the initial label of t_i.

The execution of a concurrent program is interleaving, meaning that exactly one thread performs a command at each step, and the next thread to execute is chosen non-deterministically. We consider a sequentially consistent semantics in which the effect of a single command on the memory is immediate. For $s = (\bar{l}, \sigma)$, let $cmd(s, t_i)$ denote the command of thread t_i at label l_i. We denote $next(s, t_i) = \{s' \mid s' \text{ can be obtained from } s \text{ after } t_i \text{ performs } cmd(s, t_i)\}$. A

---

[1] Note that our definition of a precondition does not require all the successors to satisfy q.

computation ρ of the concurrent program P is a sequence $s_0 \xrightarrow{t^1} s_1 \xrightarrow{t^2} \dots \xrightarrow{t^n} s_n$ s.t. for every two adjacent states s_i, s_{i+1}: $s_{i+1} \in next(s_i, t^{i+1})$. We say that ρ is a computation of thread t in P if $t^j = t$ for every $1 \leq j \leq n$. We define *initial* and *reachable* computations as in the sequential case, but w.r.t. computations of the concurrent program.

We support synchronization operations by modeling them with atomic control commands. For example, `Lock(lock)` is modeled by atomic execution of `assume(lock = false); lock = true`. Since our technique models context switches by explicit calls to `env_move`, we are able to prevent context switches between these commands.

Safety. A computation of a (sequential or concurrent) program is *violating* if it ends in the error state . The computation is *safe* otherwise. A (sequential or concurrent) program is *safe* if it has no initial violating computations. In the case of a sequential program, we refer to the path of a violating computation as a *violating path*.

A *Sequential Model Checker* is a tool which receives a sequential program as input, and checks whether the program is safe. If it is, it returns "SAFE". Otherwise, it returns a *counterexample* in the form of a violating path.

3 Our Methodology

In this section we describe our methodology for verifying safety properties of concurrent programs, given via assertions. The main idea is to use a sequential model checker in order to verify the concurrent program. Our approach handles any (fixed) number of threads. However, for simplicity, we describe our approach for a concurrent program with two threads. The extension to any number of threads can be found in [30].

In the sequel, we fix a concurrent program P with two threads. We refer to one as *the main thread* (t_M) and to the other as *the environment thread* (t_E), with variables V_M and V_E and program location variables pc_M and pc_E, respectively. V_M and V_E might intersect. Let $V = V_M \cup V_E$. Given a state $s = (\bar{l}, \sigma)$, we denote by $l_M(s)$ and $l_E(s)$ the values of pc_M and pc_E, respectively. For simplicity, we assume that safety of P is specified by assertions in t_M (this is not a real restriction of our method).

Our algorithm generates and maintains a sequential program for each thread. Let P_M and P_E be the two sequential programs, with variables $\widehat{V_M} \supseteq V_M$ and $\widehat{V_E} \supseteq V_E$. Each sequential program might include variables of the other thread as well, together with additional auxiliary variables not in V. Our approach is asymmetric, meaning that P_M and P_E have different roles in the algorithm. P_M is based on the code of t_M, and uses a designated function, `env_move`, to abstract computations of t_E. P_E is based on the code of t_E, and is constructed in order to answer specific queries for information required by P_M, specified via assumptions and assertions. The algorithm iteratively applies model checking to each of these programs separately. In each iteration, the code of P_M is gradually modified, as the algorithm learns new information about the environment, and the code of P_E is adapted to answer the query of interest.

In Sect. 4, we first describe the way our algorithm operates on P_M. During the analysis of P_M, information about the environment is retrieved using *environment queries*: Intuitively, an environment query receives two conditions, α and β, and checks whether there exists a reachable computation of t_E in P from α to β. The idea is to perform specific guided queries in t_E, to search for computations that might "help" t_M to reach a violation. If such a computation exists, the environment query returns a formula ψ, which ensures that all states satisfying it can reach β using t_E only. We also require that α and ψ overlap. In order to ensure the reachability of β, the formula ψ might need to address local variables of t_E, as well as pc_E. These variables will then be added to P_M, and may be used for the input of future environment queries. If no such computation of the environment exists, the environment query returns $\psi = FALSE$. Sect. 5 describes how our algorithm answers environment queries. The formal definition follows.

Definition 1 (Environment Query) *An* environment query $Reach_E(\alpha, \beta)$ *receives conditions* α *and* β *over* $V \cup \{pc_E\}$, *and returns a formula* ψ *over* $V \cup \{pc_E\}$ *such that:*

1. *If there exists a computation of* t_E *in* P *that is (1) reachable in* P, *(2) starts from a state* s *s.t.* $s \models \alpha$ *and (3) ends in a state* s' *s.t.* $s' \models \beta$, *then* $\psi \wedge \alpha \not\equiv FALSE$.
2. *If* $\psi \not\equiv FALSE$ *then* $\alpha \wedge \psi \not\equiv FALSE$ *and for every state* s *s.t.* $s \models \psi$, *there exists a computation (not necessarily reachable) of* t_E *in* P *from* s *to some* s' *s.t.* $s' \models \beta$.

Multiple threads. The key ingredients used by our technique are (i) an `env_move` function that is used in P_M to overapproximate finite computations (of any length) of t_E (see Sect. 4), and (ii) a `try_start` function that is used in P_E to overapproximate initial computations of P in order to let P_E simulate non-initial computations of t_E that follow them (see Sect. 5). When P has more than two threads, the environment of t_M consists of multiple threads, hence environment queries are evaluated by a recursive application of the same approach. Since the computations we consider in the environment are not necessarily initial, the main thread of the environment should now include both the `env_move` function and the `try_start` function. For more details see [30].

4   Analyzing the Main Thread

In this section we describe our algorithm for analyzing the main thread of P for the purpose of proving P safe or unsafe (Algorithm 1). Algorithm 1 maintains a sequential program, P_M, over $\widehat{V_M} \supseteq V_M$, which represents the composition of t_M with an abstraction of t_E. The algorithm changes the code of P_M iteratively,

---

Algorithm 1 Algorithm MainThreadCheck

1: **procedure** MAINTHREADCHECK(t_M, t_E, ϕ_{init})
2:     P_M = add **env_move** calls in t_M and initialize **env_move()**
3:     **while** a violating path exists in P_M **do**   // using sequential MC
4:         Let $\pi = l_0, \ldots, l_{n+1}$ be a path violating **assert**(b).
5:         **if** there are no **env_moves** in π **then return** "Real Violation"
6:         let l_k be the label of the last **env_move** call in π
7:         let $\pi_{start} = l_0, \ldots, l_k$ and $\pi_{end} = l_{k+1}, \ldots, l_n$
8:         $\beta = wp(\pi_{end}, \neg b)$ // see (1) in Sect. 4.3
9:         $\alpha = post(\pi_{start}, \phi_{init})$ // see (2) in Sect. 4.3
10:        Let $\psi = Reach_E(\alpha, \beta)$ // environment query for t_E (see Sect. 5)
11:        **if** ψ is *FALSE* **then**
12:            Let $(\alpha', \beta') = Gen_E(\alpha, \beta)$ // see (4) in Sect. 4.3.
13:            $P_M = $ **RefineEnvMove**(P_M, α', β')   // see (4) in Sect. 4.3
14:        **else**   // see (5) in Sect. 4.3
15:            Add **assert**($\neg\psi$) in P_M at new label l' right before l_k
16:    **return** "Program is Safe".

---

by adding new assumptions and assertions, as it learns new information about the environment.

The abstraction of t_E is achieved by introducing a new function, **env_move**. Context switches from t_M to t_E are modeled explicitly by calls to **env_move**. The body of **env_move** changes during the run of Algorithm 1. However, it always has the property that it over-approximates the set of finite (possibly of length zero) computations of t_E in P that are reachable in P. This is formalized as follows:

Definition 2 (Overapproximation) *For a state s_m of P_M (over $\widehat{V_M}$) s.t. $l(s_m)$ is the beginning or the end of **env_move**, we say that s_m matches a state s of P (over V) if (1) s_m and s agree on $\widehat{V_M} \cap V$, i.e. $\sigma(s_m)|_V = \sigma(s)|_{\widehat{V_M}}$, where $\sigma|_U$ is the projection of σ to the variables appearing in U, and (2) if $pc_E \in \widehat{V_M}$, then $\sigma(s_m)(pc_E) = l_E(s)$.*

*We say that **env_move** overapproximates the computations of t_E in P if for every reachable computation $\rho = s \xrightarrow{t_E} \ldots \xrightarrow{t_E} s'$ of t_E in P (possibly of length 0), and for every state s_m s.t. $l(s_m)$ is the beginning of **env_move** and s_m matches s, there exists a computation $\rho_m = s_m \rightarrow \cdots \rightarrow s'_m$ of P_M s.t. (1) ρ_m is a complete execution of **env_move**, i.e., $l(s'_m)$ is the end of **env_move** and for every other state s''_m in ρ_m, $l(s''_m)$ is a label within **env_move**, and (2) s'_m matches s'.*

The code of P_M always consists of the original code of t_M, the body of the **env_move** function (which contains assumptions about the environment), calls to **env_move** that are added at initialization, and new assertions that are added during the algorithm. $\widehat{V_M}$ always consists of V_M, possibly pc_E, some variables of V_E (that are gradually added by need), and some additional auxiliary variables needed for the algorithm (see (4) in Sect. 4.3).

4.1 Initialization

Algorithm 1 starts by constructing the initial version of P_M, based on the code of t_M. To do so, it adds explicit calls to env_move at every location where a context switch needs to be considered in t_M. The latter set of locations is determined by an *interleaving reduction analysis*, which identifies a set of locations, called *cut-points*, such that the original program is safe if and only if all the computations in which context-switches occur only at cut-points are safe.

In addition, the algorithm constructs the initial env_move function which havocs every shared variable of t_E and t_M that is written by t_E. This function will gradually be refined to represent the environment in a more precise way.

```
1   bool claim0 = false , claim1 = false ;
2   bool cs1 = false , cs0 = false ;
3   int turn ;
4   void t0 () {                              14   void t1 () {
5     while ( true ) {                        15     while ( true ) {
6       claim0 = true ;                       16       claim1 = true ;
7       turn = 1;                             17       turn = 0;
8       while ( claim1 && turn != 0) { }      18       while ( claim0 && turn != 1) { }
9       cs0 = true ;                          19       cs1 = true ;
10      // CRITICAL_SECTION                   20       // CRITICAL_SECTION
11      assert (! cs1) ;                      21       cs1 = false ;
12      cs0 = false ;                         22       claim1 = false ;          }}
13      claim0 = false ;         }}
```

Fig. 1. Peterson's mutual exclusion algorithm for two threads $t0$ and $t1$.

Example 3 *We use Peterson's algorithm [26] for mutual exclusion, presented in Fig. 1, as a running example. The algorithm contains a busy-wait loop in both threads, where a thread leaves that loop and enters its critical section only after the* **turn** *variable indicates that it is its turn to enter, or the other thread gave up on its claim to enter the critical section. In order to specify the safety property (mutual exclusion), we use additional variables* **cs0, cs1** *which indicate that* **t0** *and* **t1** *(resp.) are in their critical sections. The safety property is that* $\neg cs0 \lor \neg cs1$ *always holds. It is specified by the* **assert(!cs1)** *command in* **t0** *between lines 9 and 12, where* **cs0** *is* **true**

Assume that t0 was chosen as the main thread and t1 as the environment thread. We generate a sequential program P_0*, based on the code of t0: we add* env_moves *at every cut point, as determined by our interleaving reduction mechanism. The initial* env_move *only havocs all variables of* P_0 *that are written by t1, i.e.,* **claim1, turn, cs1** *(see Fig.4).*

4.2 Iteration of the MainThreadCheck Algorithm

Each iteration of Algorithm 1 starts by applying a sequential model checker to check whether there exists a violating path (that may involve calls to env_move) in P_M (line 3). If not, we conclude that the *concurrent* program is safe (line 16), as the env_move function over-approximates the computations of the environment. If an assertion violation is detected in P_M, the model checker returns a counterexample in the form of a violating path. If there are no env_move calls in the path (line 5), it means that the path represents a genuine violation obtained by a computation of the original main thread, and hence the program is unsafe.

Otherwise, the violation relies on environment moves, and as such it might be spurious. We therefore analyze this counterexample as described in Sect. 4.3. The purpose of the analysis is to check whether t_E indeed enables the environment transitions used along the path. If so, we find "promises of error" for the violated assertion at earlier stages along the path and add them as new assertions in P_M. Intuitively speaking, a "promise of error" is a property ensuring that t_E can make a sequence of steps that will allow t_M to violate its assertion. Such a property may depend on both threads, and hence it is defined over $V \cup \{pc_E\}$ (pc_M is given implicitly by the location of the assertion in P_M). Formally, we have the following definition:

Definition 4 *Let ψ, ψ' be formulas over $V \cup \{pc_E\}$ and let l, l' be labels of t_M. We say that (l, ψ) is a* promise *of (l', ψ') if for every state s of P s.t. $l_M(s) = l$ and $s \vDash \psi$ there exists a computation in P starting from s to a state s' s.t. $l_M(s') = l'$ and $s' \vDash \psi'$.*

If (l, ψ) is a promise of $(l', \neg b)$ and l' has an assert *(b) command, then we say that (l, ψ) is a* promise of error.

Note that the definition is transitive. Specifically, if (l, ψ) is a *promise* of (l', ψ') and (l', ψ') is a promise of error, then (l, ψ) is also a promise of error.

Outcome. Each iteration of Algorithm 1 ends with one of these three scenarios:

1. The algorithm terminates having found a genuine counterexample for P (line 5).
2. The obtained counterexample is found to be spurious since an execution of env_move along the path is proved to be infeasible. The counterexample is eliminated by refining the env_move function (line 13, also see item (4) in the next section).
3. Spuriousness of the counterexample remains undetermined, but a new promise of error is generated before the last env_move call in the violating path. We augment P_M with a new assertion, representing this promise of error (line 15).

4.3   Analyzing a Potentially Spurious Violating Path

Let $\pi = l_0, \ldots, l_{n+1}$ be a violating path of P_M, returned by the sequential model checker in an iteration of Algorithm 1, which is potentially spurious in P, i.e., contains at least one env_move call. Since π is violating, $l_{n+1} = l_e$ and $cmd(l_n) =$ assert (b) for some condition b. Let l_k, for some $0 \le k \le (n-1)$, be the location of the last env_move in π. We perform the following steps, illustrated by Fig.2:

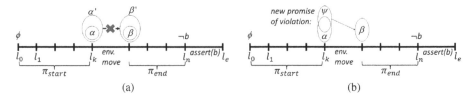

Fig. 2. (a) If $Reach_E(\alpha, \beta) = FALSE$, we search for more general α' and β' which restrict the environment transition; (b) If $Reach_E(\alpha, \beta) = \psi \neq FALSE$, then we know that ψ leads to β and that $\psi \wedge \alpha \neq FALSE$.

```
1  void P0() {
2    assert((!cs1) || claim1);
3    env_move();
4    while (true) {
5      claim0 = true;
6      assert((!cs1) || claim1);
7      env_move();
8      turn = 1;
9      assert((!cs1) ||
             (claim1 && turn != 0));
10     ...
11  }}
```

```
1  void env_move() {
2    bool claim1_copy = claim1;
3    int turn_copy = turn;
4    bool cs1_copy = cs1;
5    claim1 = havoc_bool();
6    turn = havoc_int();
7    cs1 = havoc_bool();
8    if (true) { assume(!cs1 || claim1); }  }
```

Fig. 3. The sequential program P_0 after a few iterations of Algorithm 1.

Fig. 4. The env_move function of P_0: initially (without highlighted lines); and after one refinement (with highlighted lines).

(1) Computing condition after the environment step: We compute (backwards) the weakest precondition of $\neg b$ w.r.t. the path $\pi_{end} = l_{k+1}, \ldots, l_n$ to obtain $\beta = wp(\pi_{end}, \neg b)$ (line 8). Recall that $\neg b$ is necessarily reachable from β along π_{end} in P_M.

(2) Computing condition before the environment step: We compute (forward) a postcondition $\alpha = post(\pi_{start}, \phi_{init})$ starting from ϕ_{init} for the path $\pi_{start} = l_0, \ldots, l_k$ (line 9). To ensure progress, we make sure that if π_{start} ends with a suffix of asserts then $\alpha \implies c$ for every assert(c) command that appears in this suffix (e.g., by conjoining α with c). Recall that α necessarily holds after executing π_{start} in P_M from ϕ_{init}.

(3) Environment query: We compute $\psi = Reach_E(\alpha, \beta)$ (line 10).

Example 5 *Figure 3 presents a prefix of P_M after a few iterations of the algorithm, before the first refinement of env_move (i.e., P_M still uses the initial env_move function). The previous iterations found new promises of error, and augmented P_M with new assertions. Consider the initial conditions from Fig. 1, i.e., $\phi_{init} \triangleq [claim0 = claim1 = cs1 = cs0 = false]$. Assume that our sequential model checker found the violation given by the next path: 2, 3, 4, 5, 6, 7, 8, 9,.*

To check whether the last **env_move** call in line 7 represents a real computation of **t1**, we compute the weakest precondition of the condition $\neg b \triangleq$ **cs1** $\wedge$ ($\neg$**claim1** $\vee$ **turn** $= 0$), taken from the violated assertion in line 9, w.r.t. the path $\pi_{end} = 8,9$. The result is $\beta = wp(\pi_{end}, \neg b) = (\text{\textbf{cs1}} \wedge \neg\text{\textbf{claim1}})$. The computation of $\alpha = post(\pi_{start}, \phi)$ for the path $\pi_{start} = 2,3,4,5,6$ yields $\alpha = (\neg\text{\textbf{cs0}} \wedge \text{\textbf{claim0}} \wedge (\neg\text{\textbf{cs1}} \vee \text{\textbf{claim1}}))$. We then generate an environment query $Reach_E(\alpha, \beta)$.

(4) Refining the **env_move** *function:* If $\psi = FALSE$ (line 11) it means that there is no reachable computation of t_E in P from a state s s.t. $s \models \alpha$ to a state s' s.t. $s' \models \beta$. We apply a generalization procedure $Gen_E(\alpha, \beta)$ that returns α', β' s.t. $\alpha \implies \alpha', \beta \implies \beta'$ and still $Reach_E(\alpha', \beta') = FALSE$ (line 12). To do so, Gen_E iteratively replaces α and/or β with α', β' s.t. $\alpha \implies \alpha', \beta \implies \beta'$ and rechecks $Reach_E(\alpha', \beta')$. For example, if α contains a subformula of the form $\delta_1 \wedge \delta_2$ that appears positively, we attempt to replace it by δ_1 or δ_2 to obtain α'.[2] We then refine **env_move** to eliminate the environment transition from α' to β' (line 13). Fig.2(a) illustrates this step.

The refinement is done by introducing in **env_move**, after the variables are havocked, the command (**if** $(\alpha'(W\_\text{old}))$ **assume**$(\neg\beta')$), where W_old are the values of the variables before they are havocked in **env_move** (these values are copied by **env_move** to allow evaluating α' on the values of the variables before **env_move** is called). The command blocks all computations of **env_move** from α' to β'. Since such computations were proven by the environment query to be infeasible in t_E, we are ensured that **env_move** remains an overapproximation of the computations of t_E.

Example 6 *The call to $Reach_E(\alpha, \beta)$ in Example 5 results in $\psi = FALSE$. Hence, we apply generalization. We obtain two formulas $\alpha' = TRUE, \beta' = \beta$ which indeed satisfy $\alpha \implies \alpha', \beta \implies \beta'$ and $Reach_E(\alpha', \beta') = FALSE$. This means that when t_E is called with $\alpha' = TRUE$, then no computation of t_E reaches a state satisfying $\beta' = \text{cs1} \wedge \neg\text{claim1}$. Fig. 4 presents the* **env_move** *function before and after the refinement step based on (α', β') takes place. The refinement step adds the highlighted line to the initial* **env_move** *function. This line has the constraint* **if (true) assume(!cs1 || claim1)**, *derived from the observation above.*

(5) Adding assertions: If $\psi \neq FALSE$, then for every state satisfying ψ there is a computation of t_E in P to a state satisfying β. Since $\beta = wp(\pi_{end}, \neg b)$, it is guaranteed that this computation can be extended (in t_M) along the path π_{end}, which does not use any environment moves, to reach a state s' that violates the assertion **assert(b)**. This is illustrated in Fig.2(b). We therefore conclude that if ψ is satisfied before the **env_move** at label l_k, a genuine violation can be reached, making $(\hat{l}_k, \psi)$ a promise of error, where $\hat{l}_k$ denotes the label in t_M that corresponds to l_k (the label reached after executing the **env_move** called at label

---

[2] More information about the generalization appears in the optimizations section in [30].

l_k). Therefore, we add a new assertion `assert(`$\neg\psi$`)` right before l_k (line 15). In addition, if ψ includes a variable v that is not in $\widehat{V_M}$ (e.g., `pc`$_E$), then v is added to $\widehat{V_M}$, its declaration (and initialization, if exists) is added to P_M, and `env_move` is extended to havoc v as well (if it is written by t_E).

5   Answering Environment Queries

Recall that an environment query $Reach_E(\alpha, \beta)$ checks whether there exists a reachable computation ρ of t_E in P from a state $s \models \alpha$ to a state $s' \models \beta$. This computation may involve any finite number of steps of t_E, executed without interference of t_M.

If $\alpha \wedge \beta \not\equiv FALSE$, we simply return β, which represents a computation of length zero. Otherwise, we wish to apply a sequential model checker on t_E in order to reveal such computations, or conclude there are none. However, the computation ρ may not be initial, while our sequential model checker can only search for violating paths starting from an initial state. Hence we construct a modified sequential program P_E, based on the code of t_E, which also represents (over-approximates) non-initial, but reachable, computations ρ of t_E in P. For that, we add in P_E calls to a new function, `try_start`, which models the runs of t_M until the start of ρ. The calls to `try_start` are added in all cut-points computed by an interleaving reduction (similar to the one applied to t_M).

The `try_start` *function.* The `try_start` function is responsible for non-deterministically setting the start point of ρ, where context switches to t_M are no longer allowed. This is done by setting a new `start` variable to true (provided that its value is not yet true). We refer to the latter call as the *activation* `try_start`. As long as `start` is false (i.e., prior to the activation call), `try_start` havocs the variables written by t_M. When `start` is set to true, we add an `assume(`α`)` command after the havoc commands as this is the state chosen to start the computation. To handle the case where `pc`$_E$ appears in α, `try_start` receives the original location (in t_E) in which it is called as a parameter, and updates the explicit `pc`$_E$ variable. Whenever `start` is already true, `try_start` immediately exits, ensuring that ρ indeed only uses transitions of t_E.

In P_E, we also add assertions of the form `assert(!start || `$\neg\beta$`)` after every call to `try_start`. Hence, a violating path, if found, reaches `start` $\wedge$ β, i.e., it captures a computation in which α was satisfied (when `start` was set to true), and reached β.

Returning Result. If a violating path is not found, we return $Reach_E(\alpha, \beta) = FALSE$. If a violating path $m_0, \ldots, m_{n+1}$ is found, let m_k be the label of the activation `try_start` for some $0 \leq k \leq (n-1)$. Let π_E be the projection of $m_{k+1}, \ldots, m_{n-1}$ to t_E. We compute the weakest precondition of β w.r.t. the path π_E and obtain $\psi = wp(\pi_E, \beta)$. The computed ψ satisfies the desired requirement: For every state s of P s.t. $s \models wp(\pi_E, \beta)$, there exists a computation ρ of t_E starting from s which follows the path π_E and reaches a state s' satisfying β. Note that ρ might not be reachable, as in the prefix we used an abstraction of t_M. That means that $Reach_E(\alpha, \beta)$ is not "exact" and may return $\psi \neq FALSE$

when there is no reachable computations as required. However, it satisfies the requirements of Definition 1, which is sufficient for soundness and progress. The intuition is that checking the reachability of ψ is done by the main thread.

For an example demonstrating how an environment query is answered see [30].

6 Soundness and Progress

Our algorithm for verifying the concurrent program P terminates when either (i) all the assertions in P_M are proven safe (i.e., neither the original error nor all the new promises of error can be reached in P_M), in which case Algorithm 1 returns "Program is Safe". (ii) a violation of some assertion in P_M, which indicates either the original error or a promise of error, is reached without any env_move calls, in which case Algorithm 1 returns "Real Violation". The following theorem summarizes its soundness[3].

Theorem 1 *If Algorithm 1 returns "Safe" then the concurrent program P has no violating computation; If it returns "Real violation" then P has a violating computation.*

The proof of the first claim shows that our algorithm maintains the overapproximation property of env_move (see Definition 2), from which the claim follows immediately. In the proof of the second claim, we show that the properties of an environment query (see Definition 1) and of promises of errors (Definition 4) are satisfied.

While termination is not guaranteed for programs over infinite domains, the algorithm is ensured to make *progress* in the following sense. Each iteration either refines env_move (step (4) in Sect. 4.3), making it more precise w.r.t. the real environment, or generates new promises of errors at earlier stages along the violating path (step (5) in Sect. 4.3). In the former case, the set of pairs of states (s, s') represented by the start and end states of computations of env_move is strictly decreasing – this set overapproximates the set of pairs of states (s, s') for which t_E has a reachable computation from state s to state s' (see Definition 2). In the latter case, the set of states known to lead to a real violation of safety is strictly increasing. In both cases, the other set remains unchanged.

When the domain of all variables is finite, these two sets are bounded, hence the algorithm is guaranteed to terminate.

7 Experimental Results and Conclusion

Setup. We implemented our algorithm in a prototype tool called CoMuS. The implementation is written in Python 3.5, uses pycparser [2] for parsing and transforming C programs, uses SeaHorn [18] for sequential model checking, and

---

[3] Full proofs appear in https://tinyurl.com/comusfull.

uses Z3 [7] to check logical implications for some optimizations. A description of the optimizations can be found in [30]. CoMuS currently supports only a subset of the syntax of C (see Sect. 2). It does not perform alias analysis and hence has limited pointers support. It also does not support dynamic thread creations, although we support any fixed number of threads.

We compare CoMuS with Threader [27], VVT [15] and UL-CSeq [23], the last two being the top scoring model checkers on the concurrency benchmark among *sound unbounded* tools in SVCOMP'16 and SVCOMP'17 (resp.). On the concurrency benchmark, VVT was 4th overall in SVCOMP'16, and UL-CSeq was 8th overall in SVCOMP'17 [4]. Threader performs modular verification, abstracts each thread separately and uses an interference abstraction for each pair of threads. UL-CSeq performs a reduction to a single non-deterministic sequential program. We used it in its default mode, with CPAChecker [3] as a backend. VVT combines bounded model checking for bug finding with an IC3 [4] based method for full verification.

We ran the experiments on a x86-64 Linux machine, running Ubuntu 16.04 (Xenial) using Intel(R) Xeon(R) CPU E5-2680 v3 @ 2.50GHz with 8GB of RAM.

Experiments. We evaluated the tools using three experiments. One compares the four tools on concurrent programs with a clear hierarchy. The second compares syntactically similar programs with and without hierarchal structure to evaluate the effect of the structure on the verification time. The last one looked at general concurrent programs.

Hierarchically structured programs. For the first experiment, we used three concurrent dynamic-programming algorithms: Sum-Matrix, Pascal-Triangle and Longest-Increasing-Subsequence. The Sum-Matrix programs receive a matrix A as input. For every pair of indexes (i, j), it computes the sum of all elements $A[k, l]$, where $k \geq i$ and $l \geq j$. In their concurrent version, each thread is responsible for the computation of a single row. The Pascal-Triangle programs compute all the binomial coefficients up to a given bound. Each thread computes one row of the triangle, where each element in the row depends on two results of the previous row. The Longest-Increasing-Subsequence programs receive an array, and compute for each index i, the length of the longest increasing subsequence that ends at index i. Each thread is responsible for computing the result for a given index of the array, depending on the result of all prefixes. Both these and the matrix programs are infinite state, as the elements of the array (resp. the matrix) are unbounded inputs.

These algorithms have a natural definition for any finite number of threads. Typically, the verification becomes harder as the number of threads increases. For evaluation, we used programs with an increasing number of threads, and check the influence of the number on the different tools. For each instance, we

---

[4] The same benchmark was used for unbounded sound tools and tools which perform unsound bounded reductions. Bounded tools are typically ranked higher. Our method is unbounded and is able to provide proofs, hence we find the selected tools more suitable for comparison.

use both a safe and an unsafe version. Both versions differ from each other either only by a change of specification, or by a slight modification that introduces a bug.

The chosen programs have two meaningful characteristics: (i) They exhibit non-trivial concurrency. This means that each thread performs a series of computations, and it can advance when the data for each computation is ready, without waiting for the threads it depends on to complete. Consider the Sum-Matrix problem as an example. Assume thread t_i needs to compute the result at some location (i, j), and that each row is computed backwards (from the last cell to the first). The computation exploits the results of thread t_{i+1}. Thread t_i needs to wait for thread t_{i+1} to compute the result for location $(i + 1, j)$. However, t_i does not wait for t_{i+1} to terminate, as it can compute the cell (i, j), while t_{i+1} continues to compute $(i + 1, j - 1)$. (ii) Their data flow graph has a clear chain structure. That is, the threads can be ordered in a chain hierarchy, and each thread only requires information computed by its immediate successor.

| | | Safe | | | | | Unsafe | | | | |
| | | | | | CoMus | | | | | | CoMus | |
class	threads	Threader	VVT	ULCSeq	Time	Seahorn Calls	Threader	VVT	ULCSeq	Time	Seahorn Calls
mat	2	0.18	23.30	13.61	3.53	15	0.20	0.15	8.30	1.53	5
mat	3	0.41	455.13	1194.49	36.85	83	0.42	0.28	Unknown	9.01	22
mat	4	4.82	T/O	T/O	68.46	99	4.58	0.52	Unknown	11.75	25
mat	5	243.81	T/O	T/O	270.69	196	201.63	0.74	T/O	116.59	112
mat	6	T/O	T/O	T/O	3,491.10	772	T/O	1.05	T/O	141.39	118
pas	2	0.67	2.44	6.28	0.65	2	0.24	0.14	3.59	1.45	5
pas	3	7.48	95.11	477.46	15.44	43	5.34	0.70	9.70	18.03	37
pas	4	421.46	689.85	T/O	139.54	142	611.25	3.99	1,073.55	19.33	25
pas	5	T/O	T/O	T/O	T/O	-	T/O	20.95	T/O	110.31	110
long	2	0.43	0.17	13.90	0.67	2	0.22	0.14	3.35	0.50	1
long	3	24.94	6.13	201.23	10.64	29	19.85	0.30	52.93	9.41	25
long	4	T/O	624.00	T/O	96.07	106	T/O	2.56	T/O	110.47	109
long	5	T/O	3,299.94	T/O	552.18	222	T/O	123.09	T/O	619.02	238
Pet	2	10.16	13.38	106.18	17.56	45					

Fig. 5. Run times [secs] for all four tools for verifying concurrent dynamic programs algorithms.

Figure 5 summarizes the results for these programs. The timeout was set to 3600 s. The code of the programs is available at tinyurl.com/comusatva18. We include in the table also our running example, the Peterson algorithm.

The results demonstrate a clear advantage for CoMuS for verification (i.e., for safe programs) as the number of threads increases. This can be attributed to the chain structure that lets CoMuS minimize the amount of information transferred between threads. For falsification, CoMuS is outperformed by VVT's bounded method. However, it still performs significantly better than the two other tools when the number of threads grows.

Hierarchical vs. non-hierarchical programs. The programs used for this evaluation are variants of the "fib_bench" examples of the SV-COMP concurrency benchmark. We compare programs in which the data flow graph has a ring topology, vs. programs in which it has a chain topology. For the ring case, consider a program with threads $t_0, \ldots, t_{n-1}$ and variables $v_0, \ldots, v_{n-1}$. Each thread t_i runs in a loop, and iteratively performs $v_i += v_{(i+1 (mod\ n))}$. The checked property is that v_0 does not surpass an upper bound. The chain case is identical except that for the last thread, t_{n-1}, we break the chain and perform $v_{n-1} += 1$ instead of $v_{n-1} += v_0$. Figure 6 presents the results of this comparison. All the programs in the table are safe and with two loop iterations. The timeout was set to 1200 s.

For the ring case, all tools fail to verify programs with ≥ 4 threads. Threader presents similar results for both ring and chain topologies. VVT benefits from the less dependent chain topology, but still timeouts on > 3 threads. CoMuS, on the other hand, is designed to exploit hierarchy, and benefits significantly from the chain topology, where it verifies all instances. UL-CSeq is excluded from the table as it times-out on the "fib_bench" examples (both in our experiments and in the SV-COMP results).

The reason for CoMuS's different runtime on the chain and ring variants is that for programs that have no clear hierarchy (as in the ring programs), the conditions passed to the environment queries must include information relevant to the caller thread; a manual inspection shows that they typically become more complex. As similar phenomenon happens if the verification order used by CoMuS is not aligned with the hierarchy of the program. For example, switching the verification order of the last two threads in the long_th3_safe example, increases the verification time from 10 to 25 s.

threads	Ring				Chain			
	Threader	VVT	CoMuS		Threader	VVT	CoMuS	
			Time	Seahorn Calls			Time	Seahorn Calls
2	17.70	48.93	8.52	33	11.70	18.47	3.61	16
3	T/O	T/O	126.81	294	T/O	54.51	13.35	42
4	T/O	T/O	T/O	-	T/O	T/O	40.36	88
5	T/O	T/O	T/O	-	T/O	T/O	99.09	151
6	T/O	T/O	T/O	-	T/O	T/O	275.30	247
7	T/O	T/O	T/O	-	T/O	T/O	617.32	368

Fig. 6. Run times [secs] for fib_bench programs with ring topology vs. chain topology.

General concurrent programs. We also evaluated the tools on a partial subset of the SV-COMP concurrency benchmark, whose code is supported by CoMuS. Typically, on these runs CoMuS was outperformed by the other tools. We conclude that even though our method can be applied to programs without a clear hierarchical structure, it is particularly beneficial for programs in which the hierarchy is inherent.

Conclusion. In this work we develop an automatic, modular and hierarchical method for proving or disproving safety of concurrent programs by exploiting model checking for sequential programs. The method can handle infinite-state programs. It is sound and unbounded. We implemented our approach in a prototype tool called CoMuS, which compares favorably with top scoring model checkers on a particular class of problems, as previously characterized. In the future we intend to exploit internal information gathered by the sequential model checker (e.g., SeaHorn) to further speedup our results. We would also like to examine how to apply our approach to other hierarchies (e.g., trees).

Acknowledgment. This publication is part of a project that has received funding from the European Research Council (ERC) under the European Union's Horizon 2020 research and innovation programme (grant agreement No [759102-SVIS]). The research was partially supported by Len Blavatnik and the Blavatnik Family foundation, the Blavatnik Interdisciplinary Cyber Research Center, Tel Aviv University, and the United States-Israel Binational Science Foundation (BSF) grants No. 2016260 and 2012259.

References

1. Alglave, J., Kroening, D., Tautschnig, M.: Partial orders for efficient bounded model checking of concurrent software. In: Computer Aided Verification (CAV) (2013)
2. Bendersky, E.: https://github.com/eliben/pycparser
3. Beyer, D., Keremoglu, M.E.: CPACHECKER: a tool for configurable software verification. In: Gopalakrishnan, G., Qadeer, S. (eds.) CAV 2011. LNCS, vol. 6806, pp. 184–190. Springer, Heidelberg (2011). https://doi.org/10.1007/978-3-642-22110-1_16
4. Bradley, A.R.: SAT-based model checking without unrolling. In: Jhala, R., Schmidt, D. (eds.) VMCAI 2011. LNCS, vol. 6538, pp. 70–87. Springer, Heidelberg (2011). https://doi.org/10.1007/978-3-642-18275-4_7
5. Cobleigh, J.M., Giannakopoulou, D., PǍsǍreanu, C.S.: Learning assumptions for compositional verification. In: Garavel, H., Hatcliff, J. (eds.) TACAS 2003. LNCS, vol. 2619, pp. 331–346. Springer, Heidelberg (2003). https://doi.org/10.1007/3-540-36577-X_24
6. Cohen, A., Namjoshi, K.S.: Local proofs for global safety properties. In: Damm, W., Hermanns, H. (eds.) CAV 2007. LNCS, vol. 4590, pp. 55–67. Springer, Heidelberg (2007). https://doi.org/10.1007/978-3-540-73368-3_9
7. de Moura, L., Bjørner, N.: Z3: an efficient SMT solver. In: Ramakrishnan, C.R., Rehof, J. (eds.) TACAS 2008. LNCS, vol. 4963, pp. 337–340. Springer, Heidelberg (2008). https://doi.org/10.1007/978-3-540-78800-3_24
8. Dijkstra, E.W.: A Discipline of Programming. Prentice-Hall, Upper Saddle River (1976)
9. Flanagan, C., Freund, S.N., Qadeer, S.: Thread-modular verification for shared-memory programs. In: ESOP (2002)
10. Flanagan, C., Qadeer, S.: Thread-modular model checking. In: Ball, T., Rajamani, S.K. (eds.) SPIN 2003. LNCS, vol. 2648, pp. 213–224. Springer, Heidelberg (2003). https://doi.org/10.1007/3-540-44829-2_14
11. Flanagan, C., Qadeer, S.: Transactions for software model checking. Electr. Notes Theor. Comput. Sci. **89**(3), 518–539 (2003)
12. Gavran, I., Niksic, F., Kanade, A., Majumdar, R., Vafeiadis, V.: Rely/guarantee reasoning for asynchronous programs. In: CONCUR (2015)

13. Godefroid, P. (ed.): Partial-Order Methods for the Verification of Concurrent Systems. LNCS, vol. 1032. Springer, Heidelberg (1996). https://doi.org/10.1007/3-540-60761-7
14. Gueta, G., Flanagan, C., Yahav, E., Sagiv, M.: Cartesian partial-order reduction. SPIN'07
15. Günther, H., Laarman, A., Weissenbacher, G.: Vienna verification tool: IC3 for parallel software. In: Chechik, M., Raskin, J.-F. (eds.) TACAS 2016. LNCS, vol. 9636, pp. 954–957. Springer, Heidelberg (2016). https://doi.org/10.1007/978-3-662-49674-9_69
16. Gupta, A., Popeea, C., Rybalchenko, A.: Predicate abstraction and refinement for verifying multi-threaded programs. In: POPL (2011)
17. Gupta, A., Popeea, C., Rybalchenko, A.: Threader: a constraint-based verifier for multi-threaded programs. In: Computer Aided Verification (CAV), pp. 412–417 (2011)
18. Gurfinkel, A., Kahsai, T., Komuravelli, A., Navas, J.A.: The seahorn verification framework. In: Computer Aided Verification (CAV), pp. 343–361 (2015)
19. Lal, A., Reps, T.W.: Reducing concurrent analysis under a context bound to sequential analysis. In: Computer Aided Verification (CAV), pp. 37–51 (2008)
20. Leino, K.R.M., Müller, P.: A Basis for Verifying Multi-threaded Programs. In: Castagna, G. (ed.) ESOP 2009. LNCS, vol. 5502, pp. 378–393. Springer, Heidelberg (2009). https://doi.org/10.1007/978-3-642-00590-9_27
21. Malkis, A., Podelski, A., Rybalchenko, A.: Thread-modular verification is cartesian abstract interpretation. In: Barkaoui, K., Cavalcanti, A., Cerone, A. (eds.) ICTAC 2006. LNCS, vol. 4281, pp. 183–197. Springer, Heidelberg (2006). https://doi.org/10.1007/11921240_13
22. McMillan, K.L.: Lazy abstraction with interpolants. In: Ball, T., Jones, R.B. (eds.) CAV 2006. LNCS, vol. 4144, pp. 123–136. Springer, Heidelberg (2006). https://doi.org/10.1007/11817963_14
23. Nguyen, T.L., Fischer, B., La Torre, S., Parlato, G.: Unbounded lazy-cseq: a lazy sequentialization tool for c programs with unbounded context switches. In: Baier, C., Tinelli, C. (eds.) TACAS 2015. LNCS, vol. 9035, pp. 461–463. Springer, Heidelberg (2015). https://doi.org/10.1007/978-3-662-46681-0_45
24. Nguyen, T.L., Fischer, B., La Torre, S.: and G. Parlato. Lazy sequentialization for the safety verification of unbounded concurrent programs, In ATVA (2016)
25. Pasareanu, C.S., Giannakopoulou, D., Bobaru, M.G., Cobleigh, J.M., Barringer, H.: Learning to divide and conquer: applying the L* algorithm to automate assume-guarantee reasoning. Form. Methods Syst. Des. **32**(3), 175–205 (2008)
26. Peterson, G.L.: Myths about the mutual exclusion problem. Inf. Process. Lett. **12**(3), 115–116 (1981)
27. Popeea, C., Rybalchenko, A.: Threader: a verifier for multi-threaded programs. In: Piterman, N., Smolka, S.A. (eds.) TACAS 2013. LNCS, vol. 7795, pp. 633–636. Springer, Heidelberg (2013). https://doi.org/10.1007/978-3-642-36742-7_51
28. Popeea, C., Rybalchenko, A., Wilhelm, A.: Reduction for compositional verification of multi-threaded programs. In: FMCAD, pp. 187–194 (2014)
29. Rabinovitz, I., Grumberg, O.: Bounded model checking of concurrent programs. In: Etessami, K., Rajamani, S.K. (eds.) CAV 2005. LNCS, vol. 3576, pp. 82–97. Springer, Heidelberg (2005). https://doi.org/10.1007/11513988_9
30. Rasin, D.: Modular verification of concurrent programs via sequential model checking. M.Sc. thesis, Technion – Israel Institute of Technology (2018)

31. Sinha, N., Clarke, E.: SAT-based compositional verification using lazy learning. In: Damm, W., Hermanns, H. (eds.) CAV 2007. LNCS, vol. 4590, pp. 39–54. Springer, Heidelberg (2007). https://doi.org/10.1007/978-3-540-73368-3_8

32. Tomasco, E., Inverso, O., Fischer, B., La Torre, S., Parlato, G.: Verifying concurrent programs by memory unwinding. In: Baier, C., Tinelli, C. (eds.) TACAS 2015. LNCS, vol. 9035, pp. 551–565. Springer, Heidelberg (2015). https://doi.org/10.1007/978-3-662-46681-0_52

33. Tomasco, E., Nguyen, T.L., Inverso, O., Fischer, B., La Torre, S., Parlato, G.: Lazy sequentialization for TSO and PSO via shared memory abstractions. In: FMCAD (2016)

34. Wachter, B., Kroening, D., Ouaknine, J.: Verifying multi-threaded software with impact. In: Formal Methods in Computer-Aided Design, FMCAD, pp. 210–217 (2013)

35. Zheng, M., Edenhofner, J.G., Luo, Z., Gerrard, M.J., Rogers, M.S., Dwyer, M.B., Siegel, S.F.: CIVL: applying a general concurrency verification framework to c/pthreads programs (competition contribution). In: Chechik, M., Raskin, J.-F. (eds.) TACAS 2016. LNCS, vol. 9636, pp. 908–911. Springer, Heidelberg (2016). https://doi.org/10.1007/978-3-662-49674-9_57

Quantifiers on Demand

Arie Gurfinkel[1]([✉]), Sharon Shoham[2], and Yakir Vizel[3]

[1] University of Waterloo, Waterloo, Canada
arie.gurfinkel@uwaterloo.ca
[2] Tel Aviv University, Tel Aviv, Israel
[3] The Technion, Haifa, Israel

Abstract. Automated program verification is a difficult problem. It is undecidable even for transition systems over Linear Integer Arithmetic (LIA). Extending the transition system with theory of Arrays, further complicates the problem by requiring inference and reasoning with universally quantified formulas. In this paper, we present a new algorithm, QUIC3, that extends IC3 to infer universally quantified invariants over the combined theory of LIA and Arrays. Unlike other approaches that use either IC3 or an SMT solver as a black box, QUIC3 carefully manages quantified generalization (to construct quantified invariants) and quantifier instantiation (to detect convergence in the presence of quantifiers). While QUIC3 is not guaranteed to converge, it is guaranteed to make progress by exploring longer and longer executions. We have implemented QUIC3 within the Constrained Horn Clause solver engine of Z3 and experimented with it by applying QUIC3 to verifying a variety of public benchmarks of array manipulating C programs.

1 Introduction

Algorithmic logic-based verification (ALV) is one of the most prominent approaches for automated verification of software. ALV approaches use SAT and SMT solvers to reason about bounded program executions; and generalization techniques, such as interpolation, to lift the reasoning to unbounded executions. In recent years, IC3 [8] (originally proposed for hardware model checking) and its extensions to Constrained Horn Clauses (CHC) over SMT theories [21,24] has emerged as the most dominant ALV technique. The efficiency of the IC3 framework is demonstrated by success of such verification tools as SEAHORN [19].

The IC3 framework has been successfully extended to deal with arithmetic [21], arithmetic and arrays [24], and universal quantifiers [23]. However, no extension supports the *combination* of all three. Extending IC3 to Linear Integer Arithmetic (LIA), Arrays, and Quantifiers is the subject of this paper. Namely, we present a technique to discover universally quantified solutions to CHC over the theories of LIA and Arrays. These solutions correspond to universally quantified inductive invariants of array manipulating programs.

For convenience of presentation, we present our approach over a transition system modelled using the theories of Linear Integer Arithmetic (LIA) and

© Springer Nature Switzerland AG 2018
S. K. Lahiri and C. Wang (Eds.): ATVA 2018, LNCS 11138, pp. 248–266, 2018.
https://doi.org/10.1007/978-3-030-01090-4_15

Arrays, and not the more general, but less intuitive, setting of CHCs. Inductive invariants of such transition systems are typically quantified, which introduces two major challenges: (i) quantifiers tremendously increase the search space for a candidate inductive invariant, and (i) they require deciding satisfiability of quantified formulas – itself an undecidable problem.

Existing ALV techniques for inferring universally quantified arithmetic invariants either restrict the shape of the quantifiers and reduce to quantifier free inference [7,20,29], or guess quantified invariants from bounded executions [1].

In this paper, we introduce QUIC3 – an extension of IC3 [8,21,25] to universally quantified invariants. Rather than fixing the shape of the invariant, or discovering quantifiers as a post-processing phase, QUIC3 computes the necessary quantifiers *on demand* by taking quantifiers into account during the search for invariants. The key ideas are to allow existential quantifiers in proof obligations (or, counterexamples to induction) so that they are *blocked* by universally quantified lemmas, and to extend lemma generalization to add quantifiers.

Generating quantifiers on demand gives more control over the inductiveness checks. These checks (i.e., pushing in IC3) require deciding satisfiability of universally quantified formulas over the combined theory of Arrays and LIA. This is undecidable, and is typically addressed in SMT solvers by *quantifier instantiation* in which a universally quantified formula $\forall x \cdot \varphi(x)$ is approximated by a finite set of ground instances of φ. SMT solvers, such as Z3 [12], employ sophisticated heuristics (e.g., [15]) to find a sufficient set of instantiations. However, the heuristics are only complete in limited situations (recall, the problem is undecidable in general), and it is typical for the solver to return *unknown*, or, even worse, diverge in an infinite set of instantiations.

Instead of using an SMT solver as a black-box, QUIC3 generates and maintains a set of instantiations on demand. This ensures that QUIC3 always makes progress and is never stuck in a single inductiveness check. The generation of instances is driven by the *blocking* phase of IC3 and is supplemented by traditional pattern-based triggers. Generating both universally quantified lemmas and their instantiations on demand, driven by the property, offers additional flexibility compared to the eager quantifier instantiation approach of [7,20,29].

Combining the search for all of the ingredients (quantified and quantifier-free formulas, and instantiations) in a single procedure improves the control over the verification process. For example, even though there is no guarantee of convergence (the problem is, after all, undecidable), we guarantee that QUIC3 makes progress, exploring more of the program, and discovering a counter-example (even the shortest one) if it exists.

While our intended target is program verification, we have implemented QUIC3 in a more general setting of Constrained Horn Clauses (CHC). We build on the Generalized PDR engines [21,25] in Z3. The input is a set of CHC in SMT-LIB format, and the output is a universally quantified inductive invariant, or a counter-example. To evaluate QUIC3, we have used array manipulating C programs from SV-COMP. We show that our implementation is competitive and can automatically discover non-trivial quantified invariants.

In summary, the paper makes the following contributions: (a) extends IC3 framework to support quantifiers; (b) develops quantifier generalization techniques; (c) develops techniques for discovering quantifier instantiations during verification; and (d) reports on our implementation for software verification.

2   Preliminaries

Logic. We consider First Order Logic modulo the combined theory of Linear Integer Arithmetic (LIA) and Arrays. We denote the theory by T and the logic by $FOL(T)$. We assume that the reader is familiar with the basic notions of $FOL(T)$ and provide only a brief description to set the notation. Formulas in $FOL(T)$ are defined over a signature Σ which includes sorts int and array, where sort int is also used as the sort of the array indices and data. We assume that the signature Σ includes equality $(=)$, interpreted functions, predicates, and constants of arithmetic (i.e., the functions $+$, $-$, $*$, the predicates $<$, $\leq$, and the constants 1, 2, etc.) and of arrays (i.e., the functions sel and *store*).

In addition, Σ may be extended with uninterpreted constants. In particular, we assume that Σ includes special *Skolem* uninterpreted constants $SK = \{sk_i\}$ of sort int for i in natural numbers.

We denote by Σ_T the interpreted part of Σ, and by $X \subseteq \Sigma$ the set of uninterpreted constants (e.g., a or sk_i, but not 1). In the sequel we write $\varphi(X)$, and say that φ is defined over X, to denote that φ is defined over signature $\Sigma = \Sigma_T \cup X$. We write $Const(\varphi) \subseteq X$ for the set of all uninterpreted constants that appear in φ. In the rest of the paper, whenever we refer to constants, we only refer to the uninterpreted ones.

We write T for the set of terms of $FOL(T)$, and V for the set of (sorted) variables. We assume that int variables in V are of the form v_i, where i is a natural number. Thus, we can refer to all such variables by their numeric name. For a formula φ, we write $Terms(\varphi) \subseteq T$ and $FVars(\varphi) \subseteq V$ for the terms and free variables of φ, respectively.

A substitution $\sigma : V \to T$ is a partial mapping from V to terms in T that pertains to the sort constraints. We write $dom(\sigma)$ to denote the domain of σ, and $range(\sigma)$ to denote its range. For a formula φ, we write $\varphi\sigma$ for the result of applying substitution σ to φ. Abusing notation, we write $\emptyset$ for an empty substitution, i.e., a substitution σ such that $dom(\sigma) = \emptyset$. Given two substitutions σ_1 and σ_2, we write $(\sigma_1 \mid \sigma_2)$ for a composition of substitutions defined such that: $(\sigma_1 \mid \sigma_2)(x) = \sigma_1(x)$ if $x \in dom(\sigma_1)$, and $\sigma_2(x)$, otherwise. We define a special *Skolem substitution* $sk : V \to T$ such that $sk(v_i) = sk_i$ for $sk_i \in SK$. Given a formula L, we write L_{sk} for Lsk, and given a substitution σ.

We write $abs(U, \varphi) = (\psi, \sigma)$ for an abstraction function that given a set of uninterpreted constants U and a formula φ returns an abstraction ψ of φ in which the constants are replaced by free variables, as well as a substitution σ that records the mapping of variables back to the constants that they abstract. Formally, we require that $abs(U, \varphi) = (\psi, \sigma)$ satisfies the following: $\psi\sigma = \varphi$, $dom(\sigma) = FVars(\psi) \setminus FVars(\varphi)$, and $U \cap Terms(\psi) = \emptyset$. The requirements ensure that *abs* abstracts all uninterpreted constants in U, and σ maps the newly introduced variables back to the constants. Furthermore, we require that for every skolem constant sk_i in U, $abs(U, \varphi)$ abstracts sk_i in φ to v_i in ψ, and accordingly, $\sigma(v_i) = sk_i$. This ensures that applying skolemization, followed by abstraction of SK, reintroduces the same variables and does not result in variable renaming. That is, $abs(SK, \varphi_{sk}) = (\varphi, \_)$.

We write $\forall\varphi$ for a formula obtained from φ by universally quantifying all free variables of φ, and $\exists\varphi$ for a formula obtained by existential quantification, respectively. For convenience, given a set of constants U and a ground formula φ (i.e., a formula where all terms are ground), we write $\exists U \cdot \varphi$ for $\exists\psi$, where $(\psi, \sigma) = abs(U, \varphi)$. We write $\varphi \Rightarrow \psi$ do denote the validity of $\varphi \to \psi$.

Model Based Projection. Given a ground formula φ, a model M of φ, and a set of uninterpreted constants $U \subseteq Const(\varphi)$, (partial, or incomplete) Model Based Projection, MBP, is a function $\text{PMBP}(U, \varphi, M) = (\psi, W)$ such that 1. ψ is a ground monomial (i.e., conjunction of ground literals), 2. $W \subseteq U$ and $Const(\psi) \subseteq Const(\varphi) \setminus (U \setminus W)$, 3. $\psi \Rightarrow (\exists U \setminus W \cdot \varphi)$, 4. $M \models \psi$, 5. PMBP is finite ranging in its third argument: for a fixed U and φ, the set $\{\text{PMBP}(U, \varphi, M) \mid M \models \varphi\}$ is finite. Intuitively, the monomial ψ underapproximates (implies) the result of eliminating the existential quantifiers pertaining to $U \setminus W$ from φ (where quantifier elimination itself may not even be defined). It, therefore, represents one of the ways of satisfying the result of quantifier elimination. The underapproximation ψ is chosen such that it is consistent with the provided model M. In this paper, MBP is used as a way to underapproximate the pre-image of a set of states represented implicitly by some formula.

An MBP is called *complete* if W is always empty. A complete MBP for Linear Arithmetic has been presented in [25] and a partial MBP for the theory of arrays has been presented in [24]. Importantly, in the partial MBP of [24], the remaining set of constants, W, never contains any constant of sort array. We refer the readers to [24, 25] and to [6] for details. A complete MBP underapproximates quantifier elimination relative to a given model. Such an MBP can only exist if the underlying theory admits quantifier elimination. Since the theory of arrays does not admit quantifier elimination it only admits a partial MBP.

In the paper, we further require an MBP to eliminate all the constants of sort array from U, such as the MBP of [24].

Interpolation. Given a ground formula A, and a ground monomial B such that $A \Rightarrow \neg B$, (partial) interpolation, ITP, is a function $\text{PITP}(A, B) = (\varphi, U)$, s.t. 1. φ is a ground clause (i.e., a disjunction of ground literals), 2. $U \subseteq Const(B) \setminus Const(A)$ and $Const(\varphi) \subseteq (Const(A) \cap Const(B)) \cup U$, 3. $A \Rightarrow \forall U \cdot \varphi$, and 4. $\varphi \Rightarrow \neg B$. The set of constants U denotes the constants of φ that exceed the set of shared constants of A and B. An interpolation procedure is complete if for any pair A, B, the returned set U is always empty. The formula φ produced by a complete interpolation procedure is called an *interpolant* of A and B. Note that our definitions admit a trivial partial interpolation procedure defined as $\text{PITP}_{triv}(A, B) = (\neg B, Const(B) \setminus Const(A))$.

Safety problem. We represent transition systems via formulas in $FOL(\mathcal{T})$. The states of the system correspond to structures over a signature $\Sigma = \Sigma_{\mathcal{T}} \cup X$, where X denotes the set of (uninterpreted) constants. The constants in X are used to represent program variables. A *transition system* is a pair $\langle Init(X), Tr(X, X') \rangle$, where *Init* and *Tr* are quantifier-free ground formulas in $FOL(\mathcal{T})$. *Init* represents the initial states of the system and *Tr* represents the transition relation. We write $Tr(X, X')$ to denote that *Tr* is defined over the signature $\Sigma_{\mathcal{T}} \cup X \cup X'$, where X is used to represent the pre-state of a transition, and $X' = \{a' \mid a \in X\}$ is used to represent the post-state. A *safety problem* is a triple $\langle Init(X), Tr(X, X'), Bad(X) \rangle$, where $\langle Init, Tr \rangle$ is a transition system and *Bad* is a quantifier-free ground formula in $FOL(\mathcal{T})$ representing a set of bad states.

The safety problem $\langle Init(X), Tr(X, X'), Bad(X) \rangle$ has a *counterexample of length k* if the following formula is satisfiable:

$$BMC_k(Init, Tr, Bad) = Init(X_0) \wedge \bigwedge_{i=0}^{k-1} Tr(X_i, X_{i+1}) \wedge Bad(X_k),$$

where $X_i = \{a_i \mid a \in X\}$ is a copy of the constants used to represent the state of the system after the execution of i steps. The transition system is *safe* if the safety problem has no counterexample, of any length.

Interpolation sequence and inductive invariants. An *interpolation sequence of length k* for a safety problem $\langle Init(X), Tr(X, X'), Bad(X) \rangle$ is a sequence of formulas $I_1(X), \ldots, I_k(X)$ such that (i) $Init(X) \Rightarrow I_1(X)$, (ii) $I_j(X) \wedge Tr(X, X') \Rightarrow I_{j+1}(X')$ for every $1 \leq j \leq k - 1$, and (iii) $I_k(X) \Rightarrow \neg Bad(X)$. If an interpolation sequence of length k exists, then the transition system has no counterexample of length k. An *inductive invariant* is a formula $Inv(X)$ such that (i) $Init(X) \Rightarrow Inv(X)$, (ii) $Inv(X) \wedge Tr(X, X') \Rightarrow Inv(X')$, and (iii) $Inv(X) \Rightarrow \neg Bad(X)$. If such an inductive invariant exists, then the transition system is safe.

3   Quantified IC3

In this section, we present QUIC3 – a procedure for determining a safety of a transition system by inferring quantified inductive invariants. Given a safety problem, QUIC3 attempts to discover an inductive invariant $Inv(X)$ as a universally-quantified formula of $FOL(\mathcal{T})$ (where quantification is restricted to variables of sort int) or produce a counterexample.

We first present QUIC3 as a set of rules, following the presentation style of [5, 18, 21, 24, 25]. We focus on the data structures, the key differences between QUIC3 and IC3, and soundness of the rules. An imperative procedure based on these rules is presented in Sect. 4. We assume that the reader is familiar with the basics of IC3. Throughout the section, we fix a safety problem $P = \langle Init(X), Tr(X, X'), Bad(X) \rangle$, and assume that *Init*, *Tr* and *Bad* are quantifier free ground formulas. For convenience of presentation, we use the notation $\mathcal{F}(A)$

Input: A safety problem $\langle Init(X), Tr(X, X'), Bad(X) \rangle$.

Assumptions: *Init*, *Tr* and *Bad* are quantifier free.

Data: A POB queue $\mathcal{Q}$, where a POB $c \in \mathcal{Q}$ is a triple $\langle m, \sigma, i \rangle$, m is a
conjunction of literals over X and free variables, σ is a substitution s.t.
$m\sigma$ is ground, and $i \in \mathbb{N}$. A level N. A quantified trace $\mathcal{T} = Q_0, Q_1, \ldots,$
where for every pair $(\ell, \sigma) \in Q_i$, ℓ is a quantifier-free formula over X and
free variables and σ a substitution s.t. $\ell\sigma$ is ground.

Notation: $\mathcal{F}(A) = (A(X) \wedge Tr(X, X')) \vee Init(X')$; $qi(Q) = \{\ell\sigma \mid (\ell, \sigma) \in Q\}$;
$\forall Q = \{\forall \ell \mid (\ell, \sigma) \in Q\}$.

Output: *Safe* or *Cex*

Initially: $\mathcal{Q} = \emptyset$, $N = 0$, $Q_0 = \{(Init, \emptyset)\}$, $\forall i > 0 \cdot Q_i = \emptyset$.

repeat

> **Safe** If there is an $i < N$ s.t. $\forall Q_i \subseteq \forall Q_{i+1}$ **return** *Safe*.
>
> **Cex** If there is an m, σ s.t. $\langle m, \sigma, 0 \rangle \in \mathcal{Q}$ **return** *Cex*.
>
> **Unfold** If $qi(Q_N) \Rightarrow \neg Bad$, then set $N \leftarrow N + 1$.
>
> **Candidate** If for some m, $m \Rightarrow qi(Q_N) \wedge Bad$, then add $\langle m, \emptyset, N \rangle$ to $\mathcal{Q}$.
>
> **Predecessor** If $\langle m, \xi, i + 1 \rangle \in \mathcal{Q}$ and there is a model M s.t.
> $M \models qi(Q_i) \wedge Tr \wedge (m'_{sk})$, add $\langle \psi, \sigma, i \rangle$ to $\mathcal{Q}$, where $(\psi, \sigma) = abs(U, \varphi)$ and
> $(\varphi, U) = \text{PMBP}(X' \cup SK, Tr \wedge m'_{sk}, M)$.
>
> **NewLemma** For $0 \leq i < N$, given a POB $\langle m, \sigma, i + 1 \rangle \in \mathcal{Q}$ s.t.
> $\mathcal{F}(qi(Q_i)) \wedge m'_{sk}$ is unsatisfiable, and $L' = \text{ITP}(\mathcal{F}(qi(Q_i)), m'_{sk})$,
> add (ℓ, σ) to Q_j for $j \leq i + 1$, where $(\ell, \_) = abs(SK, L)$.
>
> **Push** For $0 \leq i < N$ and $((\varphi \vee \psi), \sigma) \in Q_i$, if $(\varphi, \sigma) \notin Q_{i+1}$, $Init \Rightarrow \forall \varphi$ and
> $(\forall \varphi) \wedge \forall Q_i \wedge qi(Q_i) \wedge Tr \Rightarrow \forall \varphi'$, then add (φ, σ) to Q_j, for all $j \leq i + 1$.

until ∞;

Algorithm 1: The rules of QUIC3 procedure.

to denote the formula $(A(X) \wedge Tr(X, X')) \vee Init(X')$ that corresponds to the
forward image of A over the Tr extended by the initial states.

The rules of QUIC3 are shown in Algorithm 1. Similar to IC3, QUIC3 maintains a queue $\mathcal{Q}$ of proof obligations (POBs), and a monotone inductive trace $\mathcal{T}$
of frames containing lemmas at different levels. However, both the proof obligations and the lemmas maintained by QUIC3 are quantified.

Quantified Proof Obligations. Each POB in $\mathcal{Q}$ is a triple $\langle m, \sigma, i \rangle$, where m is a
monomial over X such that $FVars(m)$ are of sort int, σ is a substitution such that
$FVars(m) \subseteq dom(\sigma)$ and $range(\sigma) \subseteq X' \cup SK$, and i is a natural number representing the frame index at which the POB should be either blocked or extended.
The POB $\langle m, \sigma, i \rangle$ expresses an obligation to show that no state satisfying $\exists m$
is reachable in i steps of Tr. The substitution σ records the specific instance of
the free variables in frame $i + 1$ that were abstracted during construction of m.
Whenever the POB is blocked, a universally quantified lemma $\forall \ell$ is generated
in frame i (as a generalization of $\forall \neg m$), and, σ is used to discover the specific
instance of $\forall \ell$ that is necessary to prevent generating the same POB again.

Quantified Inductive Trace. A quantified monotone inductive trace $\mathcal{T}$ is a sequence of sets Q_i. Each Q_i is a set of pairs, where for each pair (ℓ, σ) in Q_i, ℓ is a formula over X, possibly with free variables, such that all free variables $FVars(\ell)$ are of sort int, and σ is a substitution such that $FVars(\ell) \subseteq dom(\sigma)$ and $range(\sigma) \subseteq X' \cup SK$. Intuitively, a pair (ℓ, σ) corresponds to a universally quantified lemma $\forall \ell$ and its ground instance $\ell \sigma$. If ℓ has no free variables, it represents a ground lemma (as in the original IC3). We write $\forall Q_i = \{\forall L \mid (L, \sigma) \in Q_i\}$ for the set of all ground and quantified lemmas in Q_i, and $qi(Q_i) = \{\ell \sigma \mid (\ell, \sigma) \in Q_i\}$ for the set of all instances in Q_i.

QUIC3 maintains that the trace $\mathcal{T}$ is inductive and monotone. That is, it satisfies the following conditions, where N is the size of $\mathcal{T}$:

$$Init \Rightarrow \forall Q_0 \qquad \forall 0 \leq i < N \cdot \forall Q_i \wedge Tr \Rightarrow \forall Q_{i+1} \qquad \forall Q_{i+1} \subseteq \forall Q_i$$

The first two conditions ensure inductiveness and the last ensures syntactic monotonicity. Both are similar to the corresponding conditions in IC3.

The rules. The rules **Safe, Cex, Unfold, Candidate** are essentially the same as their IC3 counterparts. The only exception is that, whenever the lemmas of frame i are required, the instances $qi(Q_i)$ of the quantified lemmas in Q_i are used (instead of $\forall Q_i$). This ensures that the corresponding satisfiability checks are decidable and do not diverge.

Predecessor *rule.* **Predecessor** extends a POB $\langle m, \xi, i+1 \rangle \in \mathcal{Q}$ from frame $i+1$ with a predecessor POB $\langle \psi, \sigma, i \rangle$ at frame i. The precondition to the rule is satisfiability of $qi(Q_i) \wedge Tr \wedge (m'_{sk})$. Note that all free variables in the current POB m are skolemized via the substitution sk (recall that all the free variables are of sort int) and all constants are primed.

Predecessor rule extends the corresponding rule of IC3 in two ways. First, POBs are generated using partial MBP. The $\text{PMBP}(X' \cup SK, Tr \wedge m'_{sk}, M)$ is used to construct a ground monomial φ over $X \cup X' \cup SK$, describing a predecessor of m'_{sk}. Whenever φ contains constants from $X' \cup SK$, these are abstracted by fresh free variables to construct a POB ψ over X. Thus, the newly constructed POB is not ground and its free variables are implicitly existentially quantified. (Since PMBP is guaranteed to eliminate all constants of sort array, the free variables are all of sort int). Second, the **Predecessor** maintains with the POB ψ the substitution σ that corresponds to the inverse of the abstraction used to construct ψ from φ, i.e., $\psi \sigma = \varphi$. It is used to introduce a ground instance that blocks ψ as a predecessor of $\langle m, \xi, i+1 \rangle$ when the POB is blocked (see **NewLemma**).

The soundness of **Predecessor** (in the sense that it does not introduce spurious counterexamples) rests on the fact that every state in the generated POB has a Tr successor in the original POB. This is formalized as follows:

Lemma 1. *Let $\langle m, \xi, i+1 \rangle \in \mathcal{Q}$ and let (ψ, σ, i) be the POB computed by **Predecessor**. Then, $(\exists \psi) \Rightarrow \exists X' \cdot (Tr \wedge \exists m')$.*

Proof. From the definition of **Predecessor**, $(\psi, \sigma) = abs(U, \varphi)$, where $(\varphi, U) = \text{PMBP}(X' \cup SK, Tr \wedge m'_{sk}, M)$. The set $U \subseteq X' \cup SK$ are the constants that were not eliminated by MBP. Then, by properties of PMBP, $\psi\sigma \Rightarrow \exists(X', SK) \setminus U \cdot Tr \wedge m'_{sk}$. Note that $(\exists U \cdot \varphi) = \exists\psi$. By abstracting U in φ and existentially quantifying over the resulting variables in both sides of the implication, we get that $\exists\psi \Rightarrow \exists X', SK \cdot Tr \wedge m'_{sk}$. Since SK does not appear in Tr, the existential quantification distributes over Tr: $\exists X', SK \cdot Tr \wedge m'_{sk} \equiv \exists X' \cdot (Tr \wedge \exists m')$. $\qquad\square$

By induction and Lemma 1, we get that if $\langle\psi, \sigma, i\rangle$ is a POB in $\mathcal{Q}$, then every state satisfying $\exists\psi$ can reach a state in *Bad*.

***NewLemma* rule.** **NewLemma** creates a potentially quantified lemma ℓ and a corresponding instance $\ell\sigma$ to block a quantified POB $\langle m, \sigma, i + 1\rangle$ at level $i + 1$. Note that if ℓ is quantified, then while the instance $\ell\sigma$ is guaranteed to be new at level $i + 1$, the lemma ℓ might already appear in Q_{i+1}. The lemma ℓ is first computed as in IC3, but using a skolemized version of the POB. Second, if any skolem constants remain in the lemma, then they are re-abstracted into the original variables. The corresponding instance of ℓ is determined by the substitution σ of the POB. Note that the instance $\ell\sigma$ is well defined since *abs* abstracts skolem constants back into the variables (of sort int) that introduced them, ensuring that $FVars(\ell) \subseteq dom(\sigma)$. Note further that if ℓ has no free variables, then the substitution σ is redundant and could be replaced by an empty substitution. (In fact, it is always sufficient to project σ to $FVars(\ell)$.)

```
void init_arrray(int [] A, int sz) {
1:  for (int i = 0; i < sz; i++)  A[i] = 0;
2:  j = nd(); assume(0 <= j && j < sz);
3:  assert(A[j] == 0);}
```

Fig. 1. An array manipulating program.

The soundness of **NewLemma** follows form the fact that every lemma (ℓ, σ) that is added to the trace $\mathcal{T}$ keeps the trace inductive. Formally:

Lemma 2. *Let (ℓ, σ) be a quantified lemma added to Q_{i+1} by **NewLemma**. Then, $\mathcal{F}(\forall Q_i) \Rightarrow (\forall\ell')$.*

Proof. ℓ is $abs(SK, L)$, where $L' = \text{ITP}(\mathcal{F}(qi(Q_i)), m'_{sk})$. Therefore, $\mathcal{F}(qi(Q_i)) \wedge \neg L'$ is unsatisfiable. Let Ψ be $\mathcal{F}(\forall Q_i) \wedge (\neg\forall\ell')$, and assume, to the contrary, that Ψ is satisfiable. Since no constants from SK appear in $\mathcal{F}(\forall Q_i)$ and ℓ is $abs(SK, L)$, Ψ is equi-satisfiable to $\mathcal{F}(\forall Q_i) \wedge (\neg L')$. Let M be the corresponding model. Then, in contradiction, $M \models \mathcal{F}(qi(Q_i)) \wedge (\neg L')$. $\qquad\square$

Rules **Predecessor** and **NewLemma** use m'_{sk} that is skolemized with our special skolem substitution where $sk(v_i) = sk_i$. We note that while the skolem constants in m'_{sk} are always a subset of SK and do not overlap with $X \cup X'$, they may overlap the existing skolem constants that appear in the rest of the formula (e.g., if the rest of the formula contains $qi(Q_{i-1})$, where the ground instances result from previously blocked POBs and, therefore, also contain skolem constants). In this sense, our skolemization appears non-standard. However, all the claims in this section only rely on the fact that the range of sk is SK and that SK is disjoint from $X \cup X'$, which holds for sk.

Push *rule.* **Push** is similar to its IC3 counterpart. It propagates a (potentially quantified) lemma to the next frame. The key difference is the use of quantified formulas $\forall Q_i$ (and their instantiations $qi(Q_i)$ in the pre-condition of the rule). Thus, checking applicability of **Push** requires deciding validity of a quantified FOL formula, which is undecidable in general. In practice,, we use a weaker, but decidable, variant of these rules. In particular, we use a finite instantiation strategy to instantiate $\forall Q_i$ in combination with all of the instantiations $qi(Q_i)$ discovered by QUIC3 before theses rules are applied. This ensures progress (i.e., QUIC3 never gets stuck in an application of a rule) at an expense of completeness (some lemmas are not pushed as far as possible, which impedes divergence).

We illustrate the rules on a simple array-manipulating program `init_array` shown in Fig. 1. In the program, `assume` and `assert` stand for the usual assume and assert statements, respectively, and `nd` returns a non-deterministic value. We assume that the program is converted into a safety problem as usual. In this problem, a special variable pc is used to indicate the program counter. The first POB found by **Candidate** is $pc = 3 \wedge \mathsf{sel}(A, j) \neq 0$. Its predecessor, is $pc = 2 \wedge \mathsf{sel}(A, v_0) \neq 0 \wedge 0 \leq v_0 < sz$ and the corresponding substitution is $(v_0 \mapsto j)$. Note that since PMBP could not eliminate j, it was replaced by a free variable. Eventually, this POB is blocked, the lemma that is added is $\forall((pc = 2 \wedge 0 \leq v_0 < sz) \Rightarrow \mathsf{sel}(A, v_0) = 0)$.

$$N \leftarrow 0; Q_0 = \{(Init, \emptyset)\}$$
if $Init \wedge Bad$ **then**
  | **return** CEX
while *(true)* **do**
  | $N \leftarrow N + 1; \quad Q_N \leftarrow \emptyset$
  | **if** Quic3_MakeSafe$(Bad, \emptyset, N) = $ CEX **then**
  | | **return** CEX
  | **if** Quic3_Push$() = $ SAFE **then**
  | | **return** SAFE
  |
end

Fig. 2. Main Procedure (`Quic3_Main`). Wlog, we assume that Bad is a monomial.

Soundness. We conclude this section by showing that applying QUIC3 rules from Algorithm 1 in any order is sound:

Lemma 3. *If* QUIC3 *returns* Cex, *then* P *is not safe (and there exists a counterexample). Otherwise, if* QUIC3 *returns* Safe, *then* P *is safe.*

Proof. The first case follows immediately from Lemma 1. The second case follows from the properties of the inductive trace maintained by QUIC3 that ensure that whenever *Safe* is returned (by **Safe** rule), a safe inductive invariant is obtained. Lemma 2 ensures that these properties are preserved whenever a new quantified lemma is added. Soundness of all other rules follows the same argument as the corresponding rules of IC3.   □

In fact, QUIC3 ensures a stronger soundness guarantee:

Lemma 4. *In every step of* QUIC3, *for every* $k < N$, *the sequence* $\{\forall Q_i\}_{i=1}^{k}$ *is an interpolation sequence of length* k *for* P.

Thus, if QUIC3 reaches $N > k$, then there are no counterexample of length k.

4   Progress and Counterexamples

Safety verification of transition systems described in the theory of LIA and Arrays is undecidable in general. Thus, there is no expectation that QUIC3 always terminates. None-the-less, it is desirable for such a procedure to have strong progress guarantees – the longer it runs, the more executions are explored. In this section, we show how to orchestrate the rules defining QUIC3 (shown in Algorithm 1) into an effective procedure that guarantees progress in exploration and produces a shortest counterexample, if it exists.

Realization of QUIC3. Figure 2 depicts procedure `Quic3_Main` – an instance of QUIC3 where each iteration, starting from $N = 0$, consists of a `Quic3_MakeSafe` phase followed by a `Quic3_Push` phase. The `Quic3_MakeSafe` phase, described in Fig. 3, starts by initializing $\mathcal{Q}$ to the POB $(Bad, \emptyset, N)$ (this is a degenerate application of **Candidate** that is sufficient when *Bad* is a monomial). It then applies **Predecessor** and **NewLemma** iteratively until either a counterexample is found or $\mathcal{Q}$ is emptied. **NewLemma** is preceded by an optional generalization procedure (Line 3) that may introduce additional quantified variables and record the constants that they originated from by extending the substitution ξ. We defer discussion of this procedure to Sect. 5; in the simplest case, it will return the same lemma with the same substitution ξ. At the end of `Quic3_MakeSafe`, the trace $(Q_i)_i$ is an interpolation sequence of length N. The `Quic3_Push` applies **Push** iteratively from frame $i = 1$ to $i = N$. The corresponding satisfiability queries are restricted to use the existing instances of quantified lemmas and a finite set of instantiations pre-determined by heuristically chosen triggers. If, as a result of pushing, two consecutive frames become equal (rule **Safe**), `Quic3_Main` returns *Safe*.

Progress. Recall that we use a *deterministic* skolemization procedure. Namely, for a POB $\langle m, \xi, i \rangle$, in every satisfiability check of the form $qi(Q_{i-1}) \wedge Tr \wedge (m'_{sk})$, the same skolem substitution (defined by $sk(v_i) = sk_i$) is used in m'_{sk}, even if the rest of the formula (i.e., $qi(Q_{i-1})$) changes. The benefit of using a deterministic skolemization procedure is that it ensures that all applications of PMBP in **Predecessor** use exactly the same formula $Tr \wedge m'_{sk}$ and exactly the same set of constants. As a result, the number of predecessors (POBs) generated by applications of **Predecessor** for each POB is bounded by the finite range of PMBP in its third (model) argument:

Input: (Cube m_0, Substitution σ_0, Level i_0)
Data: Queue $\mathcal{Q}$ of triples $\langle m, \sigma, i \rangle$, where m is a cube, σ is a substitution and i is a level

1   $\mathcal{Q} = \emptyset$
    // Apply Candidate rule
2   $\text{Add}(\mathcal{Q}, \langle m_0, \sigma_0, i_0 \rangle)$
3 **while** $\neg\text{Empty}(\mathcal{Q})$ **do**
4     $\langle m, \xi, i \rangle \leftarrow \text{Top}(\mathcal{Q})$
5   **if** $i = 0$ **then**
        // Apply Cex rule; Found a counterexample
6   **return** CEX
7     $M \leftarrow \text{SAT}(qi(Q_{i-1}) \wedge \mathit{Tr} \wedge (m'_{sk}))$
8   **if** $M \neq \bot$ **then**
        // Apply Predecessor rule
9         $(\varphi, U) \leftarrow \text{PMBP}(X' \cup SK, \mathit{Tr} \wedge m'_{sk}, M)$
10       $(\psi, \sigma) \leftarrow abs(U, \varphi)$
11       $\text{Add}(\mathcal{Q}, \langle \psi, \sigma, i - 1 \rangle)$
12   **else**
13       $\text{Remove}(\mathcal{Q}, \langle m, \xi, i \rangle)$
14       $L' \leftarrow \text{ITP}(qi(Q_{i-1} \wedge \mathit{Tr}), m'_{sk})$
        // Abstract all skolem constants
15       $(\ell, \_) \leftarrow abs(SK, L)$
        // Optional quantified generalization (see Sec. 5)
16       $(\ell, \xi) \leftarrow \text{QGen}(\ell, \langle m, \xi, i \rangle)$
        // Apply NewLemma rule
17   **forall** $j \leq i, Q_j \leftarrow Q_j \cup \{(\ell, \xi)\}$
18
19 **end**
20 **return** BLOCKED

Fig. 3. Quic3_MakeSafe procedure of QUIC3.

Lemma 5. *If a deterministic skolemization is used, then for each POB $\langle m, \xi, i \rangle$, the number of POBs generated by applying **Predecessor** on $\langle m, \xi, i \rangle$ is finite.*

Proof. For simplicity, we ignore the application of quantified generalization; the proof extends to handle it as well. After a quantified lemma (ℓ, ξ) is added to Q_{i-1}, every model $M \models qi(Q_{i-1}) \wedge \mathit{Tr} \wedge m'_{sk}$ that is discovered when applying **Predecessor** on $\langle m, \xi, i \rangle$ will be such that $M \models \ell\xi$. Recall that the lemma was generated by a POB $\langle \varphi, \sigma, i - 1 \rangle$ that was blocked since $qi(Q_{i-2}) \wedge \mathit{Tr} \wedge \varphi'_{sk}$ was unsatisfiable, and $(\ell, \_) = abs(SK, L)$ where $L' = \text{ITP}(qi(Q_{i-2} \wedge \mathit{Tr}), \varphi'_{sk})$. Therefore $L \wedge \varphi_{sk} \equiv \bot$. Since abs maps each skolem constant back to the variable that introduced it, we have that the skolems in L are abstracted to the original variables from φ. Hence, $\ell \wedge \varphi \equiv \bot$, which implies that $\ell\xi \wedge \varphi\xi \equiv \bot$. Thus, if $M \models qi(Q_{i-1}) \wedge \mathit{Tr} \wedge m'_{sk}$ then $M \not\models \varphi\xi$. Therefore, $\text{PMBP}(X' \cup SK, \mathit{Tr} \wedge m'_{sk}, M) \neq (\varphi\xi, \_)$. Meaning, once the POB that generated the lemma was blocked, it cannot be rediscovered as a predecessor of $\langle m, \xi, i \rangle$. Since the first two arguments of PMBP are the same in all applications of **Predecessor** on $\langle m, \xi, i \rangle$ (due to the deterministic skolemization), the finite range of PMBP implies that only finitely many predecessors are generated for the POB $\langle m, \xi, i \rangle$.   □

Thus, for any value of N, there is only a finite number of POBs that are added to Q and processed by the rules, resulting in a finite number of rule applications. Moreover, since Quic3_Push restricts the use of quantified lemmas to existing ground instances and a finite instantiation scheme, and since the other rules also use only these instances, all satisfiability queries posed to the solver are of quantifier-free formulas in the combined theories of LIA and Arrays, and as a result guaranteed to terminate. This means that each rule is terminating. Therefore, Quic3_Main always makes progress in the following sense:

Lemma 6. *For every $k \in \mathbb{N}$, Quic3_Main either reaches $N = k$, returns Safe, or finds a counterexample.*

Shortest Counterexamples. Quic3_Main increases N only after an interpolation sequence of length N is obtained, in which case it is guaranteed that no counterexample up to this length exists. Combined with Lemma 6 that ensures progress, this implies that Quic3_Main always find a shortest counterexample, if one exists:

Corollary 1. *If there exists a counterexample, then Quic3_Main is guaranteed to terminate and return a shortest counterexample.*

5   Quantified Generalization

QUIC3 uses quantified POBs to generate quantified lemmas. However, these lemmas are sometimes too specific, hindering convergence. This is addressed by *quantified generalization* (**QGen**), a key part of QUIC3. The QUIC3 rules in Algorithm 1 are extended with the rule **QGen** shown in Algorithm 2, and Quic3_MakeSafe (Fig. 3) is extended with a call to QGen, which implements **QGen**, before a new lemma is added to its corresponding frame.

> **QGen** For $0 \le i < n$ and a lemma $(\ell, \xi) \in Q_{i+1}$, let g be a formula and σ a substitution such that (i) $g\sigma \equiv \ell\xi$, (ii) $FVars(\ell) \subseteq FVars(g)$, and (iii) $\mathcal{F}(qi(Q_i)) \to \forall g'$. Then, add (g, σ) to Q_j for all $0 \le j \le i+1$.
> **Algorithm 2: QGen** rule for Quantified Generalization in QUIC3.

QGen rule. **QGen** generalizes a (potentially quantified) lemma $(\ell, \xi) \in Q_{i+1}$ into a new quantified lemma (g, σ) such that $(\forall g) \to (\forall \ell)$ is valid, i.e., the new lemma g is stronger than ℓ. The new quantified lemma g and a substitution ρ (s.t. $g\rho \equiv \ell$) are constructed by abstracting some terms of ℓ with fresh universally quantified variables. If the new formula $\forall g$ is a valid lemma, i.e., $\mathcal{F}(qi(Q_i)) \to \forall g'$ is valid, then **QGen** adds (g, σ) to Q_j for $0 \le j \le i+1$, where $\sigma = \xi|\rho$. Note that the check ensures that the new lemma maintains the interpolation sequence property of the trace. In the rest of this section, we describe two heuristics to implement **QGen** that we found useful in our benchmarks.

Simple **QGen** abstracts a single term in the input lemma ℓ by introducing one *additional* universally quantified variable to ℓ. In the new lemma g, the new variable v appears only as an index of an array (e.g., $\mathsf{sel}(A, v)$) or as an offset (e.g., $\mathsf{sel}(A, i + v)$). Simple **QGen** considers all sel terms in ℓ and identifies sub-terms t of index terms for which ℓ imposes lower and upper bounds. Each term t is abstracted in turn with bounds used as guards. For example, if ℓ is $0 < sz \rightarrow (\mathsf{sel}(A, 0) = 42)$ and $t = 0$ of $\mathsf{sel}(A, 0)$, then a candidate (g, σ) is $0 \leq v_0 < sz \rightarrow \mathsf{sel}(A, v_0) = 42$, and $\{v_0 \mapsto 0\}$, where v_0 is universally quantified.

Arithmetic **QGen**. Simple **QGen** does not infer correlations neither between abstracted terms nor between index and value terms. For example, it is unable to create a lemma of the form $\forall v \cdot 0 \leq v < sz \rightarrow (\mathsf{sel}(A, v) = exp(v))$, where $exp(v)$ is some linear expression involving v. *Arithmetic* **QGen** addresses this limitation by extracting and generalizing a correlation between interpreted constants in the input lemma ℓ. Arithmetic **QGen** works on lemmas ℓ of the form $(\psi \wedge \phi_0 \wedge \cdots \wedge \phi_{n-1}) \rightarrow \phi_n$, where there is a formula $p(\boldsymbol{v})$ with free variables $\boldsymbol{v}$ and a set of substitutions $\{\sigma_k\}_{k=0}^{n}$ s. t. $\phi_k = p\sigma_k$. For example, ℓ is $((1 < sz) \wedge (\mathsf{sel}(A, 0) = 42)) \rightarrow (\mathsf{sel}(A, 1) = 44)$, where $p(i, j)$ is $\mathsf{sel}(A, i) = j$, σ_0 is $\{i \mapsto 0, j \mapsto 42\}$, and σ_1 is $\{i \mapsto 1, j \mapsto 44\}$. The substitutions can be viewed as *data points* and generalized by a convex hull, denoted ch. For example, $ch(\{\sigma_0, \sigma_1\}) = 0 \leq i \leq 1 \wedge j = 2i + 42$. The lemma ℓ is strengthened by replacing the substitution of ϕ_n with the convex hull by rewriting ℓ into $\forall \boldsymbol{v} \cdot (ch(\{\sigma_1, \ldots, \sigma_n\}) \wedge \psi \wedge \phi_0 \cdots \wedge \phi_{n-1}) \rightarrow p(\boldsymbol{v})$. In our running example, this generates $\forall i, j \cdot (0 \leq i \leq 1 \wedge j = 2i + 42 \wedge 1 < sz) \wedge (\mathsf{sel}(A, 0) = 42)) \rightarrow (\mathsf{sel}(A, i) = j)$. Note that only ϕ_n is generalized, while all other ϕ_k, $0 \leq k < n$, provide the data points. Applying standard generalization might simplify the lemma further by dropping $(\mathsf{sel}(A, 0) = 42)$ and combining $i \leq 1 \wedge 1 < sz$ into $1 < sz$, resulting in $\forall i \cdot (0 \leq i \leq sz) \rightarrow (\mathsf{sel}(A, i) = 2i + 42)$. Note that arithmetic **QGen** applies to arbitrary linear arithmetic terms by replacing the convex hull (ch) with the polyhedral join $(\sqcup)$.

These two generalizations are sufficient for our benchmarks. However, the power of QUIC3 comes from the ability to integrate additional generalizations, as required. For example, arithmetic **QGen** can be extended to consider not only a single lemma, but also mine other existing lemmas for potential data points.

6   Experimental Results

We have implemented QUIC3 within the CHC engine of Z3 [12,22] and evaluated it on array manipulating C programs from SV-COMP [4] and from [13]. We have converted C programs to CHC using SEAHORN [19]. In most of these examples, array bounds are fixed constants. We have manually generalized array bounds to be symbolic to ensure that the problems require quantified invariants. Note, however, that our approach is independent of the value of the array bound (concrete or symbolic). We stress that using SEAHORN prevents us from using the "best CHC encoding" for a given problem, which is unfortunately a common evaluation practice. By using SEAHORN as is, we show how QUIC3 deals with complex realistic intermediate representation. For example, SEAHORN generates constraints supporting memory allocation and pointer arithmetic. This complicates the necessary inductive invariants even for simple examples. While we could have used a problem-specific encoding for specially selected benchmarks, such an encoding does not uniformly extend to all SV-COMP benchmarks.

Experiments were done on a Linux machine with an Intel E3-1240V2 CPU and a timeout of 300 seconds. The source code for QUIC3 is available in the main Z3 repository at https://github.com/Z3Prover/z3. The CHC for all the benchmarks are available at https://github.com/chc-comp/quic3. The results for the safe instances – the most interesting – are shown in Table 1. We compare with the SPACER engine of Z3. SPACER supports arrays, but not quantifiers. As expected, SPACER times out on all of the benchmarks. We emphasize the difference in the number of lemmas discovered by both procedures. Clearly, since QUIC3 discovers quantified lemmas, it generates significantly fewer lemmas than SPACER. Each quantified lemma discovered by QUIC3 represents many ground lemmas that are discovered by SPACER.

As shown in Table 1, QUIC3 times out on some of the instances. This is due to a deficiency of the current implementation of **QGen**. Currently, **QGen** only considers one candidate for abstraction, and generalization fails if that candidate fails. Allowing **QGen** to try several candidates should solve this issue.

Unfortunately, we were unable to compare QUIC3 to other related approaches. To our knowledge, tools that participated in SV-COMP 2018 are not able to discover the necessary quantified invariants and often use unsound (i.e., bounded) inference. The closely related tools, including SAFARI [1], BOOSTER [2], and [13] are no longer available. Based on our understanding of their heuristics, the invariants required in our benchmarks are outside of the templates supported by these heuristics.

7 Related Work

Universally quantified invariants are necessary for verification of systems with unbounded state size (i.e., the size of an individual system state is unbounded) such as array manipulating programs, programs with dynamic memory allocation, and parameterized systems in general. Thus, the problem of universal invariant inference has been a subject of intense research in a variety of areas of automated verification. In this section, we present the related work that is technically closest to ours and is applicable to the area of software verification.

Classical predicate abstraction [3,17] has been adapted to quantified invariants by extending predicates with *skolem* (fresh) variables [14,26]. This is sufficient for discovering complex loop invariants of array manipulating programs similar to the ones used in our experiments. These techniques require a decision procedure for satisfiability of universally quantified formulas, and, significantly

Table 1. Summary of results. TO is timeout; *Depth* is the size of inductive trace; *Lemmas* and *Inv* are the number of lemmas discovered overall and in invariant, respectively.

Benchmark	QUIC				Z3/SPACER	
	Depth	Lemmas	Inv	Time [s]	Depth	Lemmas
Array-init-const	6	24	7	0.14	130	4,483
Array-init-partial	9	45	12	0.34	126	4,224
Array-mono-set	6	25	9	0.22	70	2,436
Array-mono-tuc	6	25	9	0.21	70	2,422
Array-mul-init-tuc	129	8,136	–	TO	131	8,393
Array-nd-2-c-true	6	37	–	TO	39	1,482
Array-reverse	6	21	5	0.18	144	729
Array-shadowinit-tuc	30	252	–	TO	99	5,005
Array-swap	13	136	64	6.38	45	2,700
Array-swap-twice	14	155	–	TO	45	2,991
Sanfoundry-02-tucg	11	89	31	1.57	46	1,986
Sanfoundry-10-tucg	11	71	23	0.67	109	3,245
Sanfoundry-27-tucg	6	24	7	0.14	131	4,568
Std-compMod-tucg	10	120	61	5.48	58	3,871
Std-copy1-tucg	6	33	14	0.33	89	4,035
Std-copy2-tucg	9	65	25	0.77	73	2,751
Std-copy3-tucg	13	109	39	1.86	76	2,806
Std-copy4-tucg	18	217	–	TO	85	3,416
Std-copy5-tucg	19	233	76	5.47	90	3,642
Std-copy6-tucg	22	301	–	TO	97	3,991
Std-copy7-tucg	25	357	–	TO	101	4,321
Std-copy8-tucg	27	430	105	8.05	106	4,581
Benchmark	QUIC3				Z3/SPACER	
	Depth	Lemmas	Inv	Time [s]	Depth	Lemmas
Std-copy9-tucg	31	538	145	14.74	111	5,078
Std-copyInitSum2-tucg	32	511	–	TO	77	2,987
Std-copyInitSum3-tucg	14	127	–	TO	76	3,103
Std-copyInitSum-tucg	9	59	21	0.43	78	3,085
Std-copyInit-tucg	10	69	27	0.59	75	2,851
Std-find-tucg	8	35	7	0.32	105	2,915
Std-init2-tucg	7	29	8	0.14	88	3,662
Std-init3-tucg	7	30	8	0.14	95	4,122
Std-init4-tucg	7	31	8	0.14	94	3,898

(continued)

Table 1. (*continued*)

Benchmark	QUIC				Z3/SPACER	
	Depth	Lemmas	Inv	Time [s]	Depth	Lemmas
Std-init5-tucg	7	32	8	0.14	93	4,152
Std-init6-tucg	7	33	8	0.15	95	4,090
Std-init7-tucg	7	34	8	0.14	100	4,916
Std-init8-tucg	7	35	8	0.15	97	4,604
Std-init9-tucg	7	32	11	0.21	100	4,929
Std-maxInArray-tucg	7	30	9	0.33	132	4,618
Std-minInArray-tucg	7	30	10	0.27	133	4,686
Std-palindrome-tucg	5	14	–	TO	64	1,717
Std-part-orig-tucg	10	83	11	11.59	138	5,035
Std-part-tucg	13	103	41	1.7	132	4,746
Std-sort-N-nd-assert-L	12	100	15	5.02	5	17
Std-vararg-tucg-tt	9	40	10	0.23	133	4,622
Std-vector-diff-tucg	12	112	14	2.94	76	2,964

complicate predicate discovery (e.g., [27]). QUIC3 extends this work to the IC3 framework in which the predicate discovery is automated and quantifier instantiation and instance discovery are carefully managed throughout the procedure.

Recent work [7, 20, 29] studies this problem via the perspective of discovering universally quantified models for CHCs. These works show that fixing the number of expected quantifiers in an invariant is sufficient to approximate quantified invariants by discovering a quantifier free invariant of a more complex system. The complexity comes in a form of transforming linear CHC to non-linear CHC (*linear* refers to the shape of CHC, not the theory of constraints). Unlike predicate abstraction, guessing the predicates apriori is not required. However, both the quantifiers and their instantiations are guessed eagerly based on the syntax of the input problem. In contrast, QUIC3 works directly on linear CHC (i.e., a transition system), and discovers quantifiers and instantiations on demand. Hence, QUIC3 is not limited to a fixed number of quantifiers, and, unlike these techniques, is guaranteed to find the shortest counterexample.

Model-Checking Modulo Theories (MCMT) [16] extends model checking to array manipulating programs and has been used for verifying heap manipulating programs and parameterized systems (e.g., [11]). It uses a combination of quantifier elimination (QELIM) for computing predecessors of *Bad*, satisfiability checking of universally quantified formulas for pruning exploration (and convergence check), and custom generalization heuristics. In comparison, QUIC3 uses MBP instead of QELIM and uses generalizations based on bounded exploration.

SAFARI [1] (and later BOOSTER [2]), that extend MCMT with Lazy Abstraction With Interpolation (LAWI) [28], is closest to QUIC3. As in LAWI, interpolation (in case of SAFARI, for the theory of arrays [10]) is used to construct a quantifier-free proof π of bounded safety. The proof π is generalized by universally quantifying out some terms, and a decision procedure for universally quantified formulas is used to determine convergence. The key differences between SAFARI and QUIC3 are the same as between LAWI and IC3. We refer the reader to [30] for an in-depth comparison. Specifically, `Quic3_MakeSafe` computes an interpolation sequence that can be used for SAFARI. However, unlike SAFARI, QUIC3 does not rely on an external array interpolation procedure. Moreover, in QUIC3, the generalizations are dynamic and the quantifiers are introduced as early as possible, potentially exponentially simplifying the bounded proof. Finally, QUIC3 manages its quantifier instantiations to avoid relying on an external (semi) decision procedure. The acceleration techniques used in BOOSTER are orthogonal to QUIC3 and can be combined in a form of pre-processing.

To our knowledge, UPDR [23] is the only other extension of IC3 to quantified invariants. The key difference is that UPDR focuses on programs specified using the Effectively PRopositional (EPR) fragment of *uninterpreted* first order logic (e.g., without arithmetic) for which quantified satisfiability is decidable. As such, UPDR does not deal with quantifier instantiation and its mechanism for discovering quantifiers is different. UPDR is also limited to abstract counterexamples (i.e., counterexamples to existence of universal inductive invariants, as opposed to counterexamples to safety).

Interestingly, QUIC3 is closely related to algorithms for quantified satisfiability (e.g., [6,9,15]). QUIC3 uses a MBP to construct a complete instantiation, if possible. However, unlike [9,15], the convergence (of `Quic3_MakeSafe`) does not rely on any syntactic feature of the quantified formula.

8 Conclusion

In this paper, we present QUIC3, an extension of IC3 to reasoning about array manipulating programs by discovering quantified inductive invariants. While our extension keeps the basic structure of the IC3 framework, it significantly affects how lemmas and proof obligations are managed and generalized. In particular, guaranteeing progress in the presence of quantifiers requires careful management of the necessary instantiations. Furthermore, discovering quantified lemmas, requires new lemma generalization techniques that are able to infer universally quantified facts based on several examples. Unlike previous works, our generalizations and instantiations are done *on demand* guided by the property and current proof obligations. We have implemented QUIC3 in the CHC engine of Z3 and show that it is competitive for reasoning about C programs.

Acknowledgments. This publication is part of a project that has received funding from the European Research Council (ERC) under the European Union's Horizon 2020 research and innovation programme (grant agreement No [759102-SVIS]). The research was partially supported by Len Blavatnik and the Blavatnik Family foundation, the Blavatnik Interdisciplinary Cyber Research Center, Tel Aviv University, and the United States-Israel Binational Science Foundation (BSF) grants No. 2016260 and 2012259. We acknowledge the support of the Natural Sciences and Engineering Research Council of Canada (NSERC), RGPAS-2017-507912.

References

1. Alberti, F., Bruttomesso, R., Ghilardi, S., Ranise, S., Sharygina, N.: SAFARI: SMT-based abstraction for arrays with interpolants. In: CAV (2012)
2. Alberti, F., Ghilardi, S., Sharygina, N.: Booster: an acceleration-based verification framework for array programs. In: ATVA (2014)
3. Ball, T., Podelski, A., Rajamani, S.K.: Boolean and Cartesian abstraction for model checking C programs. In: TACAS (2001)
4. Beyer, D.: Software verification with validation of results. In: Legay, A., Margaria, T. (eds.) TACAS 2017. LNCS, vol. 10206, pp. 331–349. Springer, Heidelberg (2017). https://doi.org/10.1007/978-3-662-54580-5_20
5. Bjørner, Nikolaj, Gurfinkel, Arie: Property Directed Polyhedral Abstraction. In: D'Souza, Deepak, Lal, Akash, Larsen, Kim Guldstrand (eds.) VMCAI 2015. LNCS, vol. 8931, pp. 263–281. Springer, Heidelberg (2015). https://doi.org/10.1007/978-3-662-46081-8_15
6. Bjørner, N., Janota, M.: Playing with quantified satisfaction. In: LPAR (2015)
7. Bjørner, N., McMillan, K., Rybalchenko, A.: On solving universally quantified horn clauses. In: Logozzo, F., Fähndrich, M. (eds.) SAS 2013. LNCS, vol. 7935, pp. 105–125. Springer, Heidelberg (2013). https://doi.org/10.1007/978-3-642-38856-9_8
8. Bradley, A.R.: SAT-Based Model Checking without Unrolling. In: Jhala, R., Schmidt, D. (eds.) VMCAI 2011. LNCS, vol. 6538, pp. 70–87. Springer, Heidelberg (2011). https://doi.org/10.1007/978-3-642-18275-4_7
9. Bradley, A.R., Manna, Z., Sipma, H.B.: What's decidable about arrays? In: Verification, Model Checking, and Abstract Interpretation (VMCAI) (2006)
10. Bruttomesso, R., Ghilardi, S., Ranise, S.: Quantifier-free interpolation of a theory of arrays. Logical Methods Comput. Sci. 8(2) (2012)
11. Conchon, S., Goel, A., Krstic, S., Mebsout, A., Zaïdi, F.: Invariants for finite instances and beyond. In: FMCAD (2013)
12. de Moura, L., Bjørner, N.: Z3: an efficient SMT solver. In: Ramakrishnan, C.R., Rehof, J. (eds.) TACAS 2008. LNCS, vol. 4963, pp. 337–340. Springer, Heidelberg (2008). https://doi.org/10.1007/978-3-540-78800-3_24
13. Dillig, I., Dillig, T., Aiken, A.: Fluid updates: beyond strong vs. weak updates. In: European Symposium on Programming (ESOP) (2010)
14. Flanagan, C., Qadeer, S.: Predicate abstraction for software verification. In: POPL (2002)
15. Ge, Y., de Moura, L.M.: Complete instantiation for quantified formulas in satisfiability modulo theories. In: Computer Aided Verification (CAV) (2009)
16. Ghilardi, S., Ranise, S.: MCMT: a model checker modulo theories. In: Giesl, J., Hähnle, R. (eds.) IJCAR 2010. LNCS (LNAI), vol. 6173, pp. 22–29. Springer, Heidelberg (2010). https://doi.org/10.1007/978-3-642-14203-1_3
17. Graf, S., Saïdi, H.: Construction of abstract state graphs with PVS. In: CAV'97 (1997)
18. Gurfinkel, A., Ivrii, A.: Pushing to the top. In: FMCAD (2015)

19. Gurfinkel, A., Kahsai, T., Komuravelli, A., Navas, J.A.: The SeaHorn verification framework. In: Computer Aided Verification (CAV) (2015)
20. Gurfinkel, A., Shoham, S., Meshman, Y.: SMT-based verification of parameterized systems. In: FSE (2016)
21. Hoder, K., Bjørner, N.: Generalized property directed reachability. In: Cimatti, A., Sebastiani, R. (eds.) SAT 2012. LNCS, vol. 7317, pp. 157–171. Springer, Heidelberg (2012). https://doi.org/10.1007/978-3-642-31612-8_13
22. Hoder, K., Bjørner, N., de Moura, L.: μZ– an efficient engine for fixed points with constraints. In: Gopalakrishnan, G., Qadeer, S. (eds.) CAV 2011. LNCS, vol. 6806, pp. 457–462. Springer, Heidelberg (2011). https://doi.org/10.1007/978-3-642-22110-1_36
23. Karbyshev, A., Bjørner, N., Itzhaky, S., Rinetzky, N., Shoham, S.: Property-directed inference of universal invariants or proving their absence. In: CAV (2015)
24. Komuravelli, A., Bjørner, N., Gurfinkel, A., McMillan, K.L.: Compositional verification of procedural programs using Horn clauses over integers and arrays. In: FMCAD (2015)
25. Komuravelli, A., Gurfinkel, A., Chaki, S.: SMT-based model checking for recursive programs. Computer Aided Verification (CAV). Springer, Berlin (2014)
26. Lahiri, S.K., Bryant, R.E.: Constructing quantified invariants via predicate abstraction. In: Steffen, B., Levi, G. (eds.) VMCAI 2004. LNCS, vol. 2937, pp. 267–281. Springer, Heidelberg (2004). https://doi.org/10.1007/978-3-540-24622-0_22
27. Lahiri, S.K., Bryant, R.E.: Indexed predicate discovery for unbounded system verification. In: Alur, R., Peled, D.A. (eds.) CAV 2004. LNCS, vol. 3114, pp. 135–147. Springer, Heidelberg (2004). https://doi.org/10.1007/978-3-540-27813-9_11
28. McMillan, K.L.: Lazy abstraction with interpolants. In: Ball, T., Jones, R.B. (eds.) CAV 2006. LNCS, vol. 4144, pp. 123–136. Springer, Heidelberg (2006). https://doi.org/10.1007/11817963_14
29. Monniaux, D., Gonnord, L.: Cell morphing: from array programs to array-free horn clauses. In: Rival, X. (ed.) SAS 2016. LNCS, vol. 9837, pp. 361–382. Springer, Heidelberg (2016). https://doi.org/10.1007/978-3-662-53413-7_18
30. Vizel, Y., Gurfinkel, A.: Interpolating property directed reachability. In: Biere, A., Bloem, R. (eds.) CAV 2014. LNCS, vol. 8559, pp. 260–276. Springer, Cham (2014). https://doi.org/10.1007/978-3-319-08867-9_17

Signal Convolution Logic

Simone Silvetti[1,2]($\boxtimes$), Laura Nenzi[3], Ezio Bartocci[3], and Luca Bortolussi[4]

[1] DIMA, University of Udine, Udine, Italy
[2] Esteco S.p.A., Trieste, Italy
simone.silvetti@gmail.com
[3] TU Wien, Vienna, Austria
{laura.nenzi,ezio.bartocci}@tuwien.ac.at
[4] DMG, University of Trieste, Trieste, Italy
luca@dmi.units.it

Abstract. We introduce a new logic called *Signal Convolution Logic* (SCL) that combines temporal logic with convolutional filters from digital signal processing. SCL enables to reason about the percentage of time a formula is satisfied in a bounded interval. We demonstrate that this new logic is a suitable formalism to effectively express non-functional requirements in Cyber-Physical Systems displaying noisy and irregular behaviours. We define both a qualitative and quantitative semantics for it, providing an efficient monitoring procedure. Finally, we prove SCL at work to monitor the *artificial pancreas* controllers that are employed to automate the delivery of insulin for patients with type-1 diabetes.

1 Introduction

Cyber-Physical Systems (CPS) are engineering, physical and biological systems tightly integrated with networked computational embedded systems monitoring and controlling the physical substratum. The behaviour of CPS is generally modelled as a hybrid system where the flow of continuous variables (representing the state of the physical components) is interleaved with the occurrence of discrete events (representing the switching from one mode to another, where each mode may model a different continuous dynamics). The noise generated by sensors measuring the data plays an important role in the modes switching and it can be captured using a stochastic extension of hybrid systems.

The exhaustive verification for these systems is in general undecidable. The available tools for reachability analysis are based on over-approximation of the possible trajectories and the final reachable set of states may result too coarse (especially for nonlinear dynamics) to be meaningful. A more practical approach is to simulate the system and to monitor both the evolution of the continuous

E.B. and L.N. acknowledge the partial support of the Austrian National Research Network S 11405-N23 (RiSE/SHiNE) of the Austrian Science Fund (FWF). E.B., L.N. and S.S. acknowledge the partial support of the ICT COST Action IC1402 (ARVI).

S. K. Lahiri and C. Wang (Eds.): ATVA 2018, LNCS 11138, pp. 267–283, 2018.
https://doi.org/10.1007/978-3-030-01090-4_16

and discrete state variables with respect to a formal requirement that specifies the expected temporal behaviour (see [4] for a comprehensive survey).

Temporal logics such as Metric Interval Temporal Logic (MITL) [13] and its signal variant, Signal Temporal Logic (STL) [7], are powerful formalisms suitable to specify in a concise way complex temporal properties. In particular, STL enables to reason about real-time properties of components that exhibit both discrete and continuous dynamics. The Boolean semantics of STL decides whether a signal is correct or not w.r.t. a given specification. However, since a CPS model approximates the real system, the Boolean semantics is not always suitable to reason about its behaviour, because it is not tolerant to approximation errors or to uncertainty.

More recently, several notions of quantitative semantics (also called robustness) [7,9,14] have been introduced to overcome this limitation. These semantics enrich the expressiveness of Boolean semantics, passing from a Boolean concept of satisfaction (yes/no) to a (continuous) degree of satisfaction. This allows us to quantify "how much" (w.r.t. a given notion of distance) a specific trajectory of the simulated system satisfies a given requirement. A typical example is the notion of robustness introduced by Fainekos et al. in [9], where the binary satisfaction relation is replaced with a quantitative robustness degree function. The positive or negative sign of the robustness value indicates whether the formula is respectively satisfied or violated. This notion of quantitative semantics is typically exploited in the falsification analysis [1,4,8,16] to systematically generate counterexamples by searching, for example, the sequence of inputs that would minimise the robustness towards the violation of the requirement. On the other hand, the maximisation of the robustness can be employed to tune the parameters of the system [2–4,6] to obtain a better resilience. A more thorough discussion on other quantitative semantics will be provided in Sect. 2.

Motivating Challenges. Despite STL is a powerful specification language, it does not come without limitations. An important type of properties that STL cannot express are the non-functional requirements related to the percentage of time certain events happen. The globally and eventually operators of STL can only check if a condition is true for all time instants or in at least one time instant, respectively. There are many real situations where these conditions are too strict, where it could be interesting to describe a property that is in the middle between eventually and always. Consider for instance a medical CPS, e.g., a device measuring glucose level in the blood to release insulin in diabetic patients. In this scenario, we need to check if glucose level is above (or below) a given threshold for a certain amount of time, to detect critical settings. Short periods under Hyperglycemia (high level of glucose) are not dangerous for the patient. An unhealthy scenario is when the patient remains under Hyperglycemia for more than 3 h during the day, i.e., for 12.5% of 24 h (see Fig. 1 left). This property cannot be specified by STL. A second issue is that often such measurements are noisy, and measurement errors or short random fluctuations due to environmental factors can easily violate (or induce the satisfaction) of a property. One way to approach this problem is to filter the signal to reduce the impact of noise,

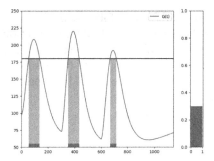 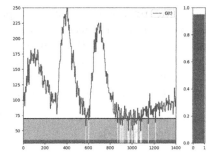

Fig. 1. (**left**) A graphical representation of the property $\phi : G(t) \geq 180$ for at least 12.5% in [0,24 h], meaning that the concentration of glucose has to be greater than 180 for at least 3h in 24h. (**right**) A graphical representation of the property $\psi : G(t) > 70$ for at least 95% in [0,24h]. The bars represents the percentage.

This requires a signal pre-processing phase, which may however alter the signal introducing spurious behaviours. Another possibility, instead is to ask that the property is true for at least 95% of operating time, rather than for 100% of time, this requirements can be seen as a relaxed globally condition (see Fig. 1 right). Finally, there are situations in which the relevance of events may change if they happen at different instants in a time window. For instance, while measuring glucose level in blood, it is more dangerous if the glucose level is high just before meal, that means "the risk becomes greater as we move away from the previous meal and approach the next meal". To capture this, one could give different weights if the formula is satisfied or not at the end or in the middle of a time interval, i.e., considering inhomogeneous temporal satisfaction of a formula. This is also not possible in STL.

Contributions. In this paper, we introduce a new logic based on a new temporal operator, $\langle k_T, p \rangle \phi$, that we call *the convolution operator*, which overcomes these limitations. It depends on a non-linear kernel function k_T, and requests that the convolution between the kernel and the signal (i.e., the satisfaction of ϕ) is above a given threshold p. This operator allows us to specify queries about the fraction of time a certain property is satisfied, possibly weighting unevenly the satisfaction in a given time interval T, e.g., allowing to distinguish traces that satisfy a property in specific parts of T. We provide a Boolean semantics, and then define a quantitative semantics, proving its soundness and correctness with respect to the former. Similarly to STL, our definition of quantitative semantics permits to quantify the maximum allowed uniform translation of the signals preserving the true value of the formula. We also show that SCL is strictly more expressive than $STL(\Diamond, \Box)$ (the fragment of STL which considers only eventually $\Diamond$ and globally $\Box$ operators) and then we provide the monitoring algorithms for both semantics. Finally, we show SCL at work to monitor the behaviour of an artificial pancreas device releasing insulin in patients affected by type-I diabetes.

Paper structure. The rest of the paper is organized as follows. In Sect. 2 we discuss the related work. Section 3 provides the necessary preliminaries. Section 4 presents the syntax and the semantics of SCL and discuss its expressiveness. In Sect. 5, we describe our monitoring algorithm and in Sect. 6 we show an application of SCL for monitoring an insulin releasing device in diabetic patients. Finally, we draw final remarks in Sect. 7.

2   Related Work

The first quantitative semantics, introduced by Fainekos et al. [9] and then used by Donze et al. [7] for STL, is based on the notion of *spatial robustness*. Their approach replaces the binary satisfaction relation with a function returning a real-value representing the distance from the unsatisfiability set in terms of the uniform norm. In [7] the authors consider also the displacement of a signal in the time domain (temporal robustness). These semantics, since are related with the uniform-norm, are very sensitive to glitches (i.e., sporadic peaks in the signals due to measurement errors).

To overcome this limitation Rodionova et al. [14] proposed a quantitative semantics based on filtering. More specifically they provide a quantitative semantics for the *positive normal form* fragment of STL which measures the number of times a formula it is satisfied within an interval associating with different types of kernels. However, restricting the quantitative semantics to the positive normal form gives up the duality property between the eventually and the globally operators, and the correctness property, which instead are both kept in our approach. Furthermore, their work is just theoretical and there is no discussion on how to efficiently evaluate such a properties.

In [1], Akazaki et al. have extended the syntax of STL by introducing averaged temporal operators. Their quantitative semantics expresses the preference that a specific requirement occurs as earlier as possible or for as long as possible, in a given time range. Such time inhomogeneity can be evaluated only in the quantitative semantics (i.e. the new operators, at the Boolean level, are equal to the classic STL temporal operators). Furthermore, the new operators force separations of two robustness (positive and negative) and it is lost also in this case the correctness property.

An alternative way to tackle the noise of a signal is to consider explicitly their stochasticity. Recently, there has been a great effort to define several stochastic extensions of STL, such as Stochastic Signal Temporal Logic (StSTL) [12], Probabilistic Signal Temporal Logic (PrSTL) [15] and Chance Constrained Temporal Logic (C2TL) [11]. The type of quantification is intrinsically different, while the probabilistic operators quantify on the signal values, our convolutional operator quantifies over the time in which the nested formula is satisfied. Furthermore, all these approaches rely on the use of probabilistic atomic predicates that need to be quantified over the probability distribution of a model (usually a subset of samples). As such, they need computationally expensive procedures to be analyzed. Our logic, instead, operates directly on the single trace, without the

Table 1. Different kind of kernels.

Kernel	Expression
Constant ($\mathtt{flat}(x)$)	$\mathbf{1}(x)/(T_1 - T_0)$
Exponential ($\mathtt{exp}[\alpha](x)$)	$\exp(\alpha x)/\int_T \exp(\alpha \tau)d\tau$
Gaussian ($\mathtt{gauss}[\mu,\sigma](x)$)	$\exp((x-\mu)^2)/\sigma^2)/\int_T \exp((x-\mu)^2)/\sigma^2)d\tau$

need of any probabilistic operator, in this respect being closer to digital signal processing.

3 Background

In this section, we introduce the notions needed later in the paper: signals, kernels, and convolution.

Definition 1 (Signal). *A signal $s : T \to S$ is a function from an interval $T \subseteq \mathbb{R}$ to a subset S of $\mathbb{R}^n$, $n < +\infty$. Let us denote with $\mathcal{D}(T; S)$ a generic set of signals.*

When $S = \{0, 1\}$, we talk of Boolean signals. In this paper, we consider piecewise constant signals, represented by a sequence of time-stamps and values. Different interpolation schemes (e.g. piecewise linear signals) can be treated similarly as well.

Definition 2 (Bounded Kernel). *Let be $T \subset \mathbb{R}$ a closed interval. We call bounded kernel a function $k_T \colon \mathbb{R} \to \mathbb{R}$ such that:*

$$\int_T k_T(\tau)d\tau = 1 \quad and \quad \forall t \in T, \, k_T(t) > 0. \tag{1}$$

Several examples of kernels are shown in Table 1. We call T the time window of the bounded kernel k_T, which will be used as a convolution [1] operator, defined as:

$$(k_T * f)(t) = \int_{t+T} k_T(\tau - t)f(\tau)d\tau$$

We also write $k_T(t) * f(t)$ in place of $(k_T * f)(t)$.

In the rest of the paper, we assume that the function f is always a Boolean function: $f \colon \mathbb{R} \to \{0, 1\}$. This implies that $\forall t \in \mathbb{R}$, $(k_T * f)(t) \in [0, 1]$, i.e. the convolution kernel will assume a value in $[0, 1]$ This value can be interpreted as a sort of *measure* of how long the function f is true in $t + T$. In fact, the kernel induces a measure on the time line, giving different importance of the time instants contained in its time window T. As an example, suppose we are interested in designing a system to make an output signal f as true as possible

---

[1] This operation is in fact a cross-correlation, but here we use the same convention of the deep learning community and call it convolution.

in a time window T (i.e., maximizing $k_T * f$). Using a non-constant kernel k_T will put more effort in making f true in the temporal regions of T where the value of the kernel k_T is higher. More formally, the analytical interpretation of the convolution is simply the expectation value of f in a specific interval $t + T$ w.r.t. the measure $k_T(dx)$ induced by the kernel. In Fig. 2 (a) we show some example of different convolution operators on the same signal.

4   Signal Convolution Logic

In this section, we present the syntax and semantics of SCL, in particular of the new convolutional operator $\langle k_T, p \rangle$, discussing also its soundness and correctness, and finally comment on the expressiveness of the logic.

Syntax and Semantics. The atomic predicates of SCL are inequalities on a set of real-valued variables, i.e. of the form $\mu(\boldsymbol{s}):=[g(\boldsymbol{s}) \geq 0]$, where $g : \mathcal{S} \to \mathbb{R}$ is a continuous function, $\boldsymbol{s} \in \mathcal{S}$ and consequently $\mu : \mathcal{S} \to \{\top, \bot\}$. The well formed formulas $\mathcal{L}_{\text{SCL}}$ of SCL are defined by the following grammar:

$$\phi := \bot \mid \top \mid \mu \mid \neg\phi \mid \phi \vee \phi \mid \langle k_T, p \rangle \, \phi, \tag{2}$$

where μ are atomic predicates as defined above, k_T is a bounded kernel and $p \in [0,1]$. SCL introduces the novel convolutional operator $\langle k_T, p \rangle \phi$ (more precise, a family of them) defined parametrically w.r.t. a kernel k_T and a threshold p. This operator specifies the probability of ϕ being true in T, computed w.r.t. the probability measure $k_T(ds)$ of T, the choice of different types of kernel k will give rise to different kind of operators (e.g. a constant kernel will measure the fraction of time ϕ is true in T, while an exponentially decreasing kernel will concentrate the focus on the initial part of T). As usual, we interpret the SCL formulas over signals.

Before describing the semantics, we give a couple of examples of properties. Considering again the glucose scenario presented in Sect. 1. The properties in Fig. 1 are specified in SCL as $\phi : \langle \text{flat}_{[0,24h]}, 0.125 \rangle \, G(t) \geq 180$, $\psi : \langle \text{flat}_{[0,24h]}, 0.95 \rangle \, G(t) \geq 70$. We can use instead an exponential increasing kernel to described the more dangerous situation of high glucose closed to the next meal, e.g. $\psi : \langle \text{exp}_{[0,8h]}, 0.95 \rangle \, G(t) \geq 180$.

We introduce now the Boolean and quantitative semantics. As the temporal operators $\langle k_T, p \rangle$ are time-bounded, time-bounded signals are sufficient to assess the truth of every formula. In the following, we denote with $\mathcal{T}(\phi)$ the minimal duration of a signal allowing a formula ϕ to be always evaluated. $\mathcal{T}(\phi)$ is computed as customary by structural recursion.

Definition 3 (Boolean Semantics). *Given a signal $\boldsymbol{s} \in \mathcal{D}(\mathcal{T}; \mathcal{S})$, the Boolean semantics $\chi \colon \mathcal{D}(\mathcal{T}; \mathcal{S}) \times \mathcal{T} \times \mathcal{L}_{\text{SCL}} \to \{0,1\}$ is defined recursively by:*

$$\chi(\boldsymbol{s}, t, \mu) = 1 \iff \mu(\boldsymbol{s}(t)) = \top \text{ where } \mu(X) \equiv [g(X) \geq 0] \tag{3a}$$

$$\chi(\boldsymbol{s}, t, \neg\phi) = 1 \iff \chi(\boldsymbol{s}, t, \phi) = 0 \tag{3b}$$

$$\chi(\boldsymbol{s}, t, \phi_1 \vee \phi_2) = \max(\chi(\boldsymbol{s}, t, \phi_1), \chi(\boldsymbol{s}, t, \phi_2)) \tag{3c}$$

$$\chi(\boldsymbol{s}, t, \langle k_T, p \rangle \phi) = 1 \iff k_T(t) * \chi(\boldsymbol{s}, t, \phi) \geq p \tag{3d}$$

Moreover, we let $\chi(\boldsymbol{s}, \phi) = 1 \iff \chi(\boldsymbol{s}, 0, \phi) = 1.$

The atomic propositions μ are inequalities over the signal's variables. The semantics of negation and conjunction are the same as classical temporal logics. The semantics of $\langle k_T, p \rangle \phi$ requires to compute the convolution of k_T with the truth value $\chi(\boldsymbol{s}, t, \phi)$ of the formula ϕ as a function of time, seen as a Boolean signal, and compare it with the threshold p.

An example of the Boolean semantics can be found in Fig. 2 (**left - bottom**) where four horizontal bars visually represent the validity of $\psi = \langle k_{[0,0.5]}, 0.5 \rangle (s > 0)$, for 4 different kernels k (one for each bar). We can see that the the only kernel for which $\chi(s, \psi) = 1$ is the exponential increasing one $k = \texttt{exp}[3]$.

Definition 4 (Quantitative semantics). *The quantitative semantics* $\rho :$ $\mathcal{D}(\mathcal{T}; \mathcal{S}) \times \mathcal{T} \times \mathcal{L}_{SCL} \to \mathbb{R}$ *is defined as follows:*

$$\rho(\boldsymbol{s}, t, \top) = +\infty \tag{4a}$$

$$\rho(\boldsymbol{s}, t, \mu) = g(\boldsymbol{s}(t)) \text{ where } g \text{ is such that } \mu(X) \equiv [g(X) \geq 0] \tag{4b}$$

$$\rho(\boldsymbol{s}, t, \neg\phi) = -\rho(\phi, \boldsymbol{s}, t) \tag{4c}$$

$$\rho(\boldsymbol{s}, t, \phi_1 \vee \phi_2) = \max(\rho(\phi_1, \boldsymbol{s}, t), \rho(\phi_2, \boldsymbol{s}, t)) \tag{4d}$$

$$\rho(\boldsymbol{s}, t, \langle k_T, p \rangle \phi) = \max\{r \in \mathbb{R} \mid k_T(t) * [\rho(\boldsymbol{s}, t, \phi) > r] \geq p\} \tag{4e}$$

Moreover, we let $\rho(\boldsymbol{s}, \varphi) := \rho(\boldsymbol{s}, 0, \varphi).$

where $[\rho(\boldsymbol{s}, t, \phi) > r]$ is a function of t such that $[\rho(\boldsymbol{s}, t, \phi) > r] = 1$ if $\rho(\boldsymbol{s}, t, \phi) > r$, 0 otherwise. Intuitively the quantitative semantics of a formula ϕ w.r.t. a primary signal $\boldsymbol{s}$ describes the maximum allowed uniform translation of the secondary signals $g(\boldsymbol{s}) = (g_1(\boldsymbol{s}), \dots, g_{n(\phi)}(\boldsymbol{s}))$ in ϕ preserving the truth value of ϕ. Stated otherwise, a robustness of r for ϕ means that all signals $\boldsymbol{s}'$ such that $\|g(\boldsymbol{s}') - g(\boldsymbol{s})\|_\infty \leq r$ will result in the same truth value for ϕ: $\chi(\boldsymbol{s}, t, \phi) = \chi(\boldsymbol{s}', t, \phi)$. Fig. 2(b) shows this geometric concept visually. Let us consider the formula $\phi = \langle k_{[0,3]}, 0.3 \rangle (s > 0)$, k a flat kernel. A signal $s(t)$ satisfies the formula if it is greater than zero for at most the 30% of the time interval $T = [0, 3]$. The robustness value corresponds to how much we can translate $s(t)$ s.t. the formula is still true, i.e. r s.t. $s(t) - r$ still satisfies ϕ. In the figure, we can see that $r = 0.535$. The formal justification of it is rooted in the correctness theorem (Theorem 2).

Soundness and Correctness. We turn now to discuss soundness and correctness of the quantitative semantics with respect to the Boolean one. The proofs of the theorems can be found in the on-line version of the paper on arXiv.

Theorem 1 (Soundness Property). *The quantitative semantics is sound with respect to the Boolean semantics, than means:*

$$\rho(\boldsymbol{s}, t, \phi) > 0 \implies (\boldsymbol{s}, t) \models \phi \qquad and \qquad \rho(\boldsymbol{s}, t, \phi) < 0 \implies (\boldsymbol{s}, t) \not\models \phi$$

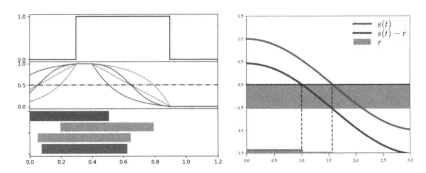

Fig. 2. (left - top) A Boolean signal $s(t)$ TRUE in $[0.3, 0.9]$ and FALSE outside. **(left - middle)** Convolution of the kernel function $(\exp[3]_{[0,0.5]} * s)(t)$ (blue), $(\exp[-3]_{[0,0.5]} * s)(t)$ (orange), $(\mathtt{flat}_{[0,0.5]} * s)(t)$ (green) and $(\mathtt{gauss}_{[0,0.5]} * s)(t)$ (red) with the signal above in the time windows. The horizontal threshold is set to 0.5. **(left - bottom)** The 4 horizontal bars show when $\chi(s, \psi, t) = 1$, with $\psi = \langle k_{[0,0.05]}, 0.5 \rangle (s > 0)$, i.e when $(k_{[0,0.5]} * s)(t) > 0.5$. **(right)** Example of quantitative semantics of SCL. A signal $s(t)$ satisfies the formula $\phi = \langle k_{[0,3]}, 0.3 \rangle (s > 0)$, with k a flat kernel, if it is greater than zero for at most the 30% of the time interval $T = [0, 3]$. The robustness value corresponds to how much we can translate $s(t)$ s.t. the formula is still true, i.e. $\rho(s, \phi) = r$ s.t. $s(t) - r$ still satisfies ϕ, (red line). In the figure we can see that $\rho(s, \phi) = 0.535$.

Definition 5. *Consider a SCL formula ϕ with atomic predicates $\mu_i := [g_i(X) \geq 0]$, $i \leq n$, and signals $s_1, s_2 \in \mathcal{D}(\mathcal{T}; \mathcal{S})$. We define*

$$\|s_1 - s_2\|_\phi := \max_{i \leq n} \max_{t \in \mathcal{T}(\phi)} |g_i(s_1(t)) - g_i(s_2(t))|$$

Theorem 2 (Correctness Property). *The quantitative semantics ρ satisfies the correctness property with respect to the Boolean semantics if and only if, for each formula ϕ, it holds:*

$$\forall s_1, s_2 \in \mathcal{D}(\mathcal{T}; \mathcal{S}), \|s_1 - s_2\|_\phi < \rho(s_1, t, \phi) \Rightarrow \chi(s_1, t, \phi) = \chi(s_2, t, \phi)$$

Expressiveness. We show that SCL is more expressive than the fragment of STL composed of the logical connectivities and the eventually $\Diamond$ and globally $\Box$ temporal operators, i.e., $STL(\Diamond, \Box)$.

First of all, globally is easily definable in SCL. Take any kernel k_T, and observe that $\Box_T \phi \equiv \langle k_T, 1 \rangle \phi$, as $\langle k_T, 1 \rangle \phi$ holds only if ϕ is true in the whole interval T. This holds provided that we restrict ourselves to Boolean signals of finite variation, as for [13], which are changing truth value a finite amount of times and are never true or false in isolated points: in this way we do not have to care what happens in sets of zero measure. With a similar restriction in mind, we can define the eventually, provided we can check that $k_T(t) * \chi(s, t, \phi) > 0$.

To see how this is possible, start from the fundamental equation $k_T(t) * \chi(s, t, \neg\phi) = 1 - k_T(t) * \chi(s, t, \phi)$. By applying 3d and 3b we easily get $\chi(s, t, \neg\langle k_T, 1 - p \rangle \neg\phi) = 1 \iff k_T(t) * \chi(s, t, \neg\phi) < 1 - p \iff k_T(t) * \chi(s, t, \phi) > p$. For compactness we write $\langle k_T, p \rangle^* = \neg\langle k_T, 1 - p \rangle \neg$, and thus define the eventually modality as $\Diamond_T\phi \equiv \langle k_T, 0\rangle^*\phi$. By definition, this is the dual operator of $\Box_T$. Furthermore, consider the uniform kernel $\texttt{flat}_T$: a property of the form $\langle \texttt{flat}_T, 0.5\rangle\phi$, requesting ϕ to hold at least half of the time interval T, cannot be expressed in STL, showing that SCL is more expressive than STL($\Diamond, \Box$).

Note that defining a new quantitative semantics has an intrinsic limitation. Even if the robustness can help the system design or the falsification process by guiding the underline optimization, it cannot be used at a syntactic level. It means that we cannot write logical formulas which predicate about the property. For example, we cannot specify behaviors as *the property has to be satisfied in at least the 50% of interval I*, but we can only measure the percentage of time the properties has been verified. Furthermore, lifting filtering and percentage at the syntactic level has other important two advantages. First, it preserves duality of eventually and globally operator, meaning that we are not forced to restrict our definition to positive formulae, as in [14], or to present two separate robustness measures as in [1]. Second, it permits to introduce a quantitative semantics which quantifies the robustness with respect to signal values instead of the percentage values and that satisfies the correctness property.

5   Monitoring Algorithm

In this section, we present the monitoring algorithms to evaluate the convolution operators $\langle k_T, p\rangle\phi$. For all the other operators we can rely on established algorithms as [13] for Boolean monitoring and [7] for the quantitative one.

Boolean Monitoring. We provide an efficient monitor algorithm for the Boolean semantics of SCL formulas. Consider an SCL formula $\langle k_{[T_0,T_1]}, p\rangle\phi$ and a signal s. We are interested in computing $\chi(s, t, \langle k_{[T_0,T_1]}, p\rangle\phi) = [H(t) - p \geq 0]$, as a function of t, where H is the following convolution function

$$H(t) = k_T(t) * \chi(s, t, \phi) = \int_{t+T} k_T(\tau - t)\chi(s, \tau, \phi)d\tau \tag{5}$$

It follows that the efficient monitoring of the Boolean semantics of SCL is linked to the efficient evaluation of $H(t) - p$, which is possible if $H(t + \delta)$ can be computed by reusing the value of $H(t)$ previously stored. To see how to proceed, assume the signal $\chi(s, t, \phi)$ to be *unitary*, namely that it is true in a single interval of time, say from time u_0 to time u_1, and false elsewhere. We remark that is always possible to decompose a signal in unitary signals, see [13].

In this case, it easily follows that the convolution with the kernel will be non-zero only if the interval $[u_0, u_1]$ intersects the convolution window $t + T$. Inspecting Fig. 3, we can see that sliding the convolution window forward of a small time δ corresponds to sliding the positive interval of the signal $[u_0, u_1]$ of δ time units backwards with respect to the kernel window. In case $[u_0, u_1]$ is fully contained into $t + T$, by making δ infinitesimal and invoking the fundamental theorem of calculus, we can compute the derivative of $H(t)$ with respect to time

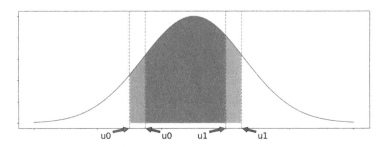

Fig. 3. Sketch of the general monitoring algorithm. The green arrows represents $[u_0, u_1]$ in the constitutional window at time t, the red arrows instead represents the same interval at time $t + \delta$ (backwards translation).

as $\frac{d}{dt}H(t) = k_T(u_0 - t) - k_T(u_1 - t)$. By taking care of cases in which the overlap is only partial, we can derive a general formula for the derivative:

$$\frac{d}{dt}H(t) = k_T(u_0 - (t + T_0))I\{u_0 \in t + T\} - k_T(u_1 - (t + T_1))I\{u_1 \in t + T\}, \quad (6)$$

where I is the indicator function, i.e. $I\{u_i \in t + T\} = 1$ if $u_i \in t + T$ and zero otherwise. This equation can be seen as a differential equation that can be integrated with respect to time by standard ODE solvers (taking care of discontinuities, e.g. by stopping and restarting the integration at boundary times when the signal changes truth value), returning the value of the convolution for each time t. The initial value is $H(0)$, that has to be computed integrating explicitly the kernel (or setting it to zero if $u_0 \geq T_1$). If the signal $\chi(\boldsymbol{s}, t, \phi)$ is not unitary, we have to add a term like the right hand side of 6 in the ODE of $H(t)$ for each unitary component (positive interval) in the signal. We use also a root finding algorithm integrated in the ODE solver to detect when the property will be true or false, i.e. when $H(t)$ will be above or below the threshold p.

    The time-complexity of the algorithm for the convolution operator is proportional to the computational cost of numerically integrating the differential equation above. Using a solver with constant step size δ, the complexity is proportional to the number of integration steps, times the number N_U of unitary components in the input signal, i.e. $O(N_U(T_s/\delta))$. A more detailed description of the algorithm can be found in the on-line version of the paper on arXiv.

Quantitative Monitoring. In this paper, we follow a simple approach to monitor it: we run the Boolean monitor for different values of r and t in a grid, using a coarse grid for r, and compute at each point of such grid the value $H(t, r) = k_T(t) * [\rho(\boldsymbol{s}, t, \phi) > r] - p$. Relying on the fact that $H(t, r)$ is monotonically decreasing in r, we can find the correct value of r, for each fixed t, by running a bisection search starting from the unique values r_k and r_{k+1} in the grid such that $H(t, r)$ changes sign, i.e. such that $H(t, r_k) < 0 < H(t, r_{k+1})$. The bounds of the r grid are set depending on the bounds of the signal, and may be expanded (or contracted) during the computation if needed. Consider that the robustness can assumes only a finite number of values because of the finite values assumed by the piecewise-constant inputs signals. A more efficient procedure for quantitative monitoring is in the top list of our future work, and it can be obtained by exploring only a portion of such a grid, combining the method with the Boolean monitor based on ODEs, and alternating steps in which we advance time from t to $t + h$ (fixing r_t to its exact value at time t), by integrating ODEs and computing $H(t + h, r_t)$, and steps in which we adjust the value of r_t at time $t + h$ by locally increasing or decreasing its value (depending if $H(t + h, r_t)$ is negative or positive), finding r_{t+h} such that $H(t + h, r_{t+h}) = 0$.

6   Case Study: Artificial Pancreas

In this example, we show how SCL can be useful in the specification and monitoring of the Artificial Pancreas (AP) systems. The AP is a closed-loop system of insulin-glucose for the treatment of Type-1 diabetes (T1D), which is a chronic disease caused by the inability of the pancreas to secrete insulin, an hormone essential to regulate the blood glucose level. In the AP system, a Continuous Glucose Monitor (CGM) detects the blood glucose levels and a pump delivers insulin through injection regulated by a software-based controller.

The efficient design of control systems to automate the delivery of insulin is still an open challenge for many reasons. Many activities are still under control of the patient, e.g., increasing insulin delivery at meal times (meal bolus), and decreasing it during physical activity. A complete automatic control includes several risks for the patient. High level of glucose (hyperglycemia) implies ketacidosis and low level (hypoglycemia) can be fatal leading to death. The AP controller must tolerate many unpredictable events such as pump failures, sensor noise, meals and physical activity.

AP Controller Falsification via SMT solver [18] and robustness of STL [5] has been recently proposed. In particular, [5] formulates a series of STL properties testing insulin-glucose regulatory system. Here we show the advantages of using SCL for this task.

PID Controller. Consider a system/process which takes as input a function $u(t)$ and produces as output a function $y(t)$. A PID controller is a simple closed-loop system aimed to maintain the output value $y(t)$ as close as possible to a set point sp. It continuously monitors the error function, i.e., $e(t) = sp - y(t)$ and defines the input of the systems accordingly to $u(t) = K_p \cdot e(t) + K_i \cdot \int_0^t e(s)ds + K_d \cdot \frac{d}{dt}e(t)$. The *proportional* ($K_p$), *integral* ($K_i$) and *derivative* ($K_d$) parameters uniquely define the PID controller and have to be calibrated in order to achieve a proper behavior.

System. PID controllers have been successfully used to control the automatic infusion of insulin in AP. In [18], for example, different PID have been synthesized to control the glucose level for the well studied Hovorka model [10]:

$$\frac{d}{dt}G(t) = F(G(t), u(t), \Theta), \tag{7}$$

where the output $G(t)$ represents the glucose concentration in blood and the input $u(t)$ is the infusion rate of bolus insulin which has to be controlled. The vector $\Theta = (dg1, dg2, dg3, T_1, T_2)$ are the control parameters which define the quantity of carbohydrates $(dg1, dg2, dg3)$ assumed during the three daily meals and the inter-times between each of them T_1 and T_2. Clearly a PID controller for Eq. (7) has to guarantee that under different values of the control parameters Θ the glucose level remains in the *safe region* $G(t) \in [70, 180]$. In [18], four different PID controllers that satisfy the safe requirement, have been discovered by leveraging SMT solver under the assumption that the inter-times T_1 and T_2 are both fixed to 300 minutes (5 hrs) and that $(dg1, dg2, dg3) \in (\mathcal{N}(40, 10), \mathcal{N}(90, 10), \mathcal{N}(60, 10))$, which correspond to the average quantity of carbohydrates contained in breakfast, lunch and dinner[2]. Here, we consider the PID controller C_1 which has been synthesized by fixing the glucose setting point sp to $110\,mg/dl$ and maximizing the probability to remain in the safe region, provided a distribution of the control parameter Θ as explained before. We consider now some properties which can be useful to check expected or anomalous behaviors of an AP controller.

Hypoglycemia and Hyperglycemia. Consider the following informal specifications: *never during the day the level of glucose goes under 70 mg/dl*, and *never during the day the level of glucose goes above 180 mg/dl*, which technically mean that the patient is never under Hypoglycemia or Hyperglycemia, respectively. These behaviours can be formalized with the two **STL** formulas $\phi_{STL}^{HO} = \Box_{[0,24h]}G(t) \geq 70$ and $\psi_{STL}^{HR} = \Box_{[0,24h]}G(t) \leq 180$. The problem of STL is that it does not distinguish if these two conditions are violated for a second, few minutes or even hours. It only says those events happen. Here we propose stricter requirements described by the two following SCL formulas $\phi_{SCL}^{HO} = \langle \mathbf{flat}_{[0,24h]}, 0.95 \rangle\, G(t) \geq 70$ for the Hypoglycemia regime, and $\phi_{SCL}^{HR} = \langle \mathbf{flat}_{[0,24h]}, 0.95 \rangle\, G(t) \leq 180$ for the Hyperglycemia regime. We are imposing not that globally in a day the hypoglycemia and the hyperglycemia event never occur, but that these conditions persist for at least 95% of the day (i.e., 110 minutes). We will show above in a small test case how this requirement can be useful.

Prolongated Conditions. As already mentioned in the motivating example, the most dangerous conditions arise when Hypoglycemia or Hyperglycemia last for a prolongated period of the day. In this context a typical condition is the **Prolongated Hyperglycemia** which happens if the total time under hyperglycemia (i.e., $G(t) \geq 180$) exceed the 70% of the day, or the **Prolongated Severe Hyperglycemia** when the level of glucose is above $300\,mg/dl$ for at least 3 hrs in a day. The importance of these two conditions has been explained in [17], however the authors cannot formalized them in STL. On the contrary, SCL is perfectly suited to describe these conditions as shown by the following two formulas: $\phi_{SCL}^{PHR} = \langle \mathbf{flat}_{[0,24h]}, 0.7 \rangle\, G(t) \geq 180$ and $\phi_{SCL}^{PSHR} = \langle \mathbf{flat}_{[0,24h]}, 0.125 \rangle\, G(t) \geq 300$. Here we use flat kernels to mean that the period of a day where the patient is under Hyperglycemia or Severe Hyper-

---

[2] $\mathcal{N}(\mu, \sigma^2)$ is the Gaussian distribution with mean μ and variance σ^2.

glycemia does not count to the evaluation of the Boolean semantics. Clearly, an hyperglycemia regime in different times of the day can count differently. In order to capture this "preference" we can use non-constant kernels.

Inhomogeneous time conditions. Consider the case of monitoring Hyperglycemia during the day. Even if avoiding that regime during the entire day is always a best practice, there may be periods of the day where avoiding it is more important than others. We imagine the case to avoid hyperglycemia with a particular focus on the period close to the first meal. We can express this requirement considering the following SCL formula: $\phi_{SCL(Gauss)}^{PHR} = \langle \text{gauss}[0.03, 0.1]_{[0,24h]}, 0.07 \rangle \, G(t) \geq 180$. Thanks to an decreasing kernel, indeed, the same quantity of time under hyperglycemia which is close to zero counts more than the same quantity far from it.

Correctness of the insulin delivery. During the Hypoglycemia regime the insulin should not be provided. The SCL formula: $\square_{[0,24h]}(\langle \text{flat}_{[0,10min]}, 0.95 \rangle \, G(t) \leq 70 \rightarrow \langle \text{flat}_{[0,10min]}, 0.90 \rangle \, I(t) \leq 0)$ states that if during the next 10 minutes the patient is in Hypoglycemia for at least the 95% of the time then the delivering insulin pump is shut off (i.e., $I(t) \leq 0$) for at least the 90% of the time. This is the "cumulative" version of the STL property $\square_{[0,24h]}(G(t) \leq 70 \rightarrow I(t) \leq 0)$ which says that in hypoglycemia regime no insulin should be delivered. During the Hyperglycemia regime the insulin should be provided as soon as possible. The property SCL formula: $\square_{[0,24h]}(G(t) \geq 300 \rightarrow \langle \exp[-1]_{[0,10min]}, 0.9 \rangle \, I(t) \geq k)$ says that if we are in severe Hyperglycemia regime (i.e., $G(t) \geq 300$) the delivered insulin should be higher than k for at least the 90% of the following 10 minutes. We use a negative exponential kernel to express (at the robustness level) the preference of having a higher value of delivered insulin as soon as possible.

Test Case: falsification. As a first example we show how SCL logic can be effectively used for falsification. The AP control system has to guarantee that the level of glucose remains in a safe region, as explained before. The falsification approach consists in identifying the control parameters (Θ^*) which force the system to violate the requirements, i.e., to escape from the safe region. The standard approach consists in minimizing the robustness of suited temporal logic formulas which express the aforementioned requirements, e.g. $\phi_{SCL}^{HR}, \phi_{SCL}^{HO}$. In this case the minimization of the STL robustness forces the identification of the control parameters which causes the generation of trajectories with a maximum displacement under the threshold 70 or above 180. To show differences among the STL and SCL logics, we consider the PID C_1 + Hovorka model and perform a random sampling exploration among its input parameters. At each sampling we calculate the robustness of the STL formulas ϕ_{STL}^{HO} and the SCL formula ϕ_{SCL}^{HO} and separately store the minimum robustness value. For this minimum value, we estimate the maximum displacement with respect to the hypoglycemia and hyperglycemia thresholds and the maximum time spent violating the hypoglycemia and hyperglycemia thresholds. Fig. 4(left, middle) shows the trajectory with minimum robustness. We can see that the trajectory which minimizes the robustness of the STL formula has an higher value of the displacement from the hypoglycemia (13) and hyperglycemia (98) thresholds than SCL trajectory (which are 11 and 49 respectively). On the contrary, the trajectory which minimizes the robustness of the SCL formula remains under hypoglycemia (for 309 min) and hyperglycemia (for 171 min) longer than the STL trajectory (189 min and 118 min, respectively). These results show how the convolutional operator and its quantitative semantics can be useful in a falsification procedure. This is particularly evident in the Hyperglycemia case (Fig. 4 (middle)) where the falsification of the SCL Hyperglycemia formula ϕ_{SCL}^{HR} shows two subintervals where the level of glucose is above the threshold. In order to show the effect of non-homogeneous kernel, we perform the previous experiment, with the same setting, for properties ϕ_{SCL}^{PHR} and $\phi_{SCL(Gauss)}^{PHR}$. From the results (Fig. 4 (right)) is evident how the Gaussian kernel of property $\phi_{SCL(Gauss)}^{PHR}$ forces the glucose to be higher of the hyperglycemia threshold just before the first meal ($t \in [0, 200]$) and ignores for example the last meal ($t \geq 600$).

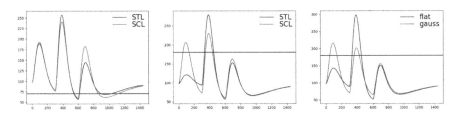

Fig. 4. (left),(middle) The solution of the SCL formula falsification (red line) maximize the time under Hypoglycemia (left) and Hyperglycemia (right), whereas the solution of the STL formula falsification (blue line) maximizes the displacement w.r.t the predicate thresholds. **(right)** Solution of the falsification for the SCL properties ϕ_{SCL}^{PHR} (blue line) and $\phi_{SCL(Gauss)}^{PHR}$ (red line) which implement **flat** and **gaussian** kernel, respectively.

Test Case: noise robustness. Now we compare the sensitivity to noise of SCL and STL formulae. We consider three degrees of hypoglycemia $h_k(t) = \{G \leq k\}$, where $k \in \{55, 60, 65, 70\}$ and estimate the probability that the Hovorka model controlled by the usual PID C_1 (i.e., PID C_1 + Hovorka Model) satisfies the STL formulas $\phi_{STL}^k = \Diamond_{[0,24h]} h_k$ and the SCL formulas $\phi_{SCL}^k = \langle \mathtt{flat}_{[0,24h]}, 0.03 \rangle h_k$ under the usual distribution assumption for the control parameters Θ. The results are reported in column "noise free" of Table 2. Afterwards, we consider a noisy outcome of the same model by adding a Gaussian noise, i.e., $\epsilon \in \mathcal{N}(0, 5)$, to the generated glucose trajectory. We estimate the probability that this noisy system satisfies the STL and SCL formulas above, see column "with noise" of Table 2. The noise correspond to the disturbance of the original signals which can occur, for example, during the measurement process.

As shown in Table 2, the probability estimation of the STL formulas changes drastically with the addition of noise (the addition of noise forces all the trajectory to satisfy the STL formula). On the contrary, the SCL formulas ϕ_{SCL}^k are

Table 2. Results of the falsification test case. The performance of STL and SCL formulas verified on the PID C_1 + Hovorka model with noise and noise free are compared. The STL formula on the noisy model is uninformative.

	Noise free				With noise			
	h_{55}	h_{60}	h_{65}	h_{70}	h_{55}	h_{60}	h_{65}	h_{70}
$\Diamond_{[0,24h]}$	0.00	0.19	0.81	1.00	0.98	1.00	1.00	1.00
$\langle \text{flat}_{[0,24]}, 0.03 \rangle$	0.00	0.00	0.20	0.91	0.00	0.02	0.77	1.00

more stable under noise and can be even used to approximate the probability of the STL formulas on the noise-free model. To better asses this, we checked how much the STL formula ϕ^k_{STL} and the SCL formula ϕ^k_{SCL}, evaluated in the noisy model, agree with the STL formula ϕ^k_{STL} evaluated in the noise-free model, by computing their truth value on 2000 samples, each time choosing a random threshold $k \in [50, 80]$. The score for STL is 56%, while SCL agrees on 78% of the cases.

7   Conclusion

We have introduced SCL, a novel specification language that employs signal processing operations to reason about temporal behavioural patterns. The key idea is the definition of a family of modal operators which compute the convolution of a kernel with the signal and check the obtained value against a threshold. Our case study on monitoring glucose level in artificial pancreas demonstrates how SCL empowers the classical temporal logic operators (i.e., such as *finally* and *globally*) with noise filtering capabilities, and enable us to express temporal properties with soft time bounds and with non symmetric treatment of time instants in a unified way.

The convolution operator of SCL can be seen as a syntactic bridge between temporal logic and digital signal processing, trying to combine the advantages of both these two worlds. This point of view can be explored further, bringing into the monitoring algorithms of SCL tools from frequency analysis of signals. Future work includes the release of a Python library, and the design of efficient monitoring algorithms also for the quantitative semantics. Finally, we also plan to develop online monitoring algorithms for real-time systems using hardware dedicated architecture such as field-programmable gate array (FPGA) and digital signal processor (DSP).

References

1. Akazaki, Takumi, Hasuo, Ichiro: Time robustness in MTL and expressivity in hybrid system falsification. In: Kroening, Daniel, Păsăreanu, Corina S. (eds.) CAV 2015. LNCS, vol. 9207, pp. 356–374. Springer, Cham (2015). https://doi.org/10.1007/978-3-319-21668-3_21

2. Bartocci, E., Bortolussi, L., Nenzi, L.: A temporal logic approach to modular design of synthetic biological circuits. In: Proceedings of CMSB, pp. 164–177. Springer, Berlin (2013)

3. Bartocci, E., Bortolussi, L., Nenzi, L., Sanguinetti, G.: System design of stochastic models using robustness of temporal properties. Theor. Comput. Sci. **587**, 3–25 (2015)

4. Bartocci, Ezio, Deshmukh, Jyotirmoy, Donzé, Alexandre, Fainekos, Georgios, Maler, Oded, Ničković, Dejan, Sankaranarayanan, Sriram: Specification-based monitoring of cyber-physical systems: a survey on theory, tools and applications. In: Bartocci, Ezio, Falcone, Yliès (eds.) Lectures on Runtime Verification. LNCS, vol. 10457, pp. 135–175. Springer, Cham (2018). https://doi.org/10.1007/978-3-319-75632-5_5

5. Cameron, Fraser, Fainekos, Georgios, Maahs, David M., Sankaranarayanan, Sriram: Towards a verified artificial pancreas: challenges and solutions for runtime verification. In: Bartocci, Ezio, Majumdar, Rupak (eds.) RV 2015. LNCS, vol. 9333, pp. 3–17. Springer, Cham (2015). https://doi.org/10.1007/978-3-319-23820-3_1

6. Donzé, Alexandre: Breach, a toolbox for verification and parameter synthesis of hybrid systems. In: Touili, Tayssir, Cook, Byron, Jackson, Paul (eds.) CAV 2010. LNCS, vol. 6174, pp. 167–170. Springer, Heidelberg (2010). https://doi.org/10.1007/978-3-642-14295-6_17

7. Donzé, Alexandre, Maler, Oded: Robust satisfaction of temporal logic over real-valued signals. In: Chatterjee, Krishnendu, Henzinger, Thomas A. (eds.) FOR-MATS 2010. LNCS, vol. 6246, pp. 92–106. Springer, Heidelberg (2010). https://doi.org/10.1007/978-3-642-15297-9_9

8. Fainekos, G.E., Sankaranarayanan, S., Ueda, K., Yazarel, H.: Verification of automotive control applications using S-TaLiRo. In: Proceedings of ACC. IEEE (2012)

9. Fainekos, G.E., Pappas, G.J.: Robustness of temporal logic specifications for continuous-time signals. Theor. Comput. Sci. **410**(42), 4262–4291 (2009)

10. Hovorka, R., Canonico, V., Chassin, L.J., Haueter, U., Massi-Benedetti, M., Federici, M.O., Pieber, T.R., Schaller, H.C., Schaupp, L., Vering, T.: Nonlinear model predictive control of glucose concentration in subjects with type 1 diabetes. Physiol. Meas. **25**(4), 905 (2004)

11. Jha, S., Raman, V., Sadigh, D., Seshia, S.A.: Safe autonomy under perception uncertainty using chance-constrained temporal logic. J. Autom. Reason. **60**(1), 43–62 (2018)

12. Li, J., Nuzzo, P., Sangiovanni-Vincentelli, A., Xi, Y., Li, D.: Stochastic contracts for cyber-physical system design under probabilistic requirements. In: Proceedings of MEMOCODE, pp. 5–14. ACM (2017)

13. Maler, Oded, Nickovic, Dejan: Monitoring temporal properties of continuous signals. In: Lakhnech, Yassine, Yovine, Sergio (eds.) FORMATS/FTRTFT -2004. LNCS, vol. 3253, pp. 152–166. Springer, Heidelberg (2004). https://doi.org/10.1007/978-3-540-30206-3_12

14. Rodionova, A., Bartocci, E., Ničković, D., Grosu, R.: Temporal logic as filtering. In: Proceedings of HSCC 2016, pp. 11–20. ACM (2016)

15. Sadigh, D., Kapoor, A.: Safe control under uncertainty with probabilistic signal temporal logic. In: Robotics: Science and Systems XII, University of Michigan, Ann Arbor, Michigan, USA, June 18 - June 22, 2016 (2016)

16. Sankaranarayanan, S., Fainekos, G.: Falsification of temporal properties of hybrid systems using the cross-entropy method. In: Proc. of HSCC. pp. 125–134 (2012)
17. Sankaranarayanan, S., Kumar, S.A., Cameron, F., Bequette, B.W., Fainekos, G., Maahs, D.M.: Model-based falsification of an artificial pancreas control system. SIGBED Rev. **14**(2), 24–33 (2017). Mar
18. Shmarov, F., Paoletti, N., Bartocci, E., Lin, S., Smolka, S.A., Zuliani, P.: SMT-based synthesis of safe and robust PID controllers for stochastic hybrid systems. In: Proceedings of HVC, pp. 131–146 (2017)

Efficient Symbolic Representation of Convex Polyhedra in High-Dimensional Spaces

Bernard Boigelot and Isabelle Mainz[(✉)]

Institut Montefiore, B28, Université de Liège, 4000 Liège, Belgium
{Bernard.Boigelot,Isabelle.Mainz}@uliege.be

Abstract. This work is aimed at developing an efficient data structure for representing symbolically convex polyhedra. We introduce an original data structure, the *Decomposed Convex Polyhedron (DCP)*, that is closed under intersection and linear transformations, and allows to check inclusion, equality, and emptiness. The main feature of DCPs lies in their ability to represent concisely polyhedra that can be expressed as combinations of simpler sets, which can overcome combinatorial explosion in high dimensional spaces. DCPs also have the advantage of being reducible into a canonical form, which makes them efficient for representing simple sets constructed by long sequences of manipulations, such as those handled by state-space exploration tools. Their practical efficiency has been evaluated with the help of a prototype implementation, with promising results.

1 Introduction

Convex polyhedra, i.e., the subsets of $\mathbb{R}^n$ defined by finite conjunctions of linear constraints, are extensively used in many areas of computer science. Among their many applications, convex polyhedra are employed in optimization theory and in particular linear programming [23], constraint programming, Satisfiability Modulo Theories (SMT) solving [10], abstract interpretation, for which they are one of the most used numerical abstract domains [12,13], and computer-aided verification [5,15,19].

Our motivation for studying convex polyhedra is to use them for representing the reachable sets produced during symbolic state-space exploration of linear hybrid systems and temporal automata [1,7,9,18]. For this application, one needs a data structure that is closed under intersection and linear transformations, in order to be able to compute the image of sets by the transition relation of the system under analysis. Furthermore, it should be possible to decide inclusion, equality, and emptiness of represented sets, in order to detect that a fixed point has been reached, as well as for comparing the reachability set against the safety property of interest. Our choice is to aim for an exact symbolic representation, in the sense that it should both rely only on exact arithmetic, and not over- or under-approximate the represented sets.

© Springer Nature Switzerland AG 2018
S. K. Lahiri and C. Wang (Eds.): ATVA 2018, LNCS 11138, pp. 284–299, 2018.
https://doi.org/10.1007/978-3-030-01090-4_17

Existing solutions to this problem have several drawbacks. Representations based on logical formulas are notoriously difficult to simplify. This makes them inefficient for handling simple sets constructed by long sequences of manipulations, such as those produced by state-space exploration procedures.

Another well known representation is the double description method [11, 22], used by most popular software libraries for handling convex polyhedra, such as cdd [16], PolyLib [21], NewPolka [20], and PPL [4]. This technique consists in jointly describing a polyhedron by two different geometric representations: a constraint system, expressing the polyhedron as the set of solutions of a finite conjunction of linear constraints, and a generator system, defining the polyhedron as the convex-conical combination of a finite set of vertices and extremal rays. These two representations are equivalent, in the sense that each of them can be reconstructed from the other. However, keeping both of them makes it possible to speed up some operations, such as removing their redundant elements. The major drawback of the double description method is that it suffers from combinatorial explosion in high dimensional spaces. For instance, the n-cube $[0, 1]^n$ is characterized by $2n$ constraints, but its generator system contains 2^n vertices, which leads to a representation that grows exponentially with n.

From a mathematical point of view, the geometrical structure of a convex polyhedron is precisely described by its face lattice, which corresponds to a partial ordering of its faces. The double description method can actually be seen as an explicit representation of the non trivial top and bottom layers of this face lattice. Another strategy is to keep a representation of the whole face lattice of polyhedra, which has the advantage of providing complete information about the adjacency relation between their faces. This information makes it possible, in particular, to remove redundant constraints and elements of the generator system in polynomial time [3].

A data structure that explicitly represents the face lattice is the Real Vector Automaton, whose expressive power goes beyond first-order additive arithmetic of mixed integer and real variables [8]. When it represents a convex polyhedron, an RVA is essentially a deterministic decision graph for determining which face contains a given point. RVA have the advantage of being easily reducible to a minimal canonical form, which makes the representation of a set independent from its construction history. Nevertheless, their size grows linearly with the coefficients of linear constraints, and they suffer from the same combinatorial explosion as the double description method. The former drawback is alleviated by the Implicit Real Vector Automaton (IRVA) [14] and the Convex Polyhedron Decision Diagram (CPDD)[7], in which parts of the decision graph are encoded by more efficient algebraic structures.

Our goal is to make CPDDs efficient in high dimensional spaces. In order to deal with the combinatorial explosion of the generator system, a decomposition mechanism for convex polyhedra has been proposed in [17]. The approach consists in partitioning syntactically the variables involved in the linear constraints into independent subsets. Roughly speaking, convex polyhedra are decomposed into Cartesian products of simpler ones defined over disjoint subsets of variables.

This procedure has the disadvantage of being unable to handle efficiently constraints that jointly involve many variables, which makes it ill-suited for our intended applications. During the reachability analysis of timed automata for instance, applying a time-step operation to a polyhedron will generally produce constraints linking together all clock variables, making decomposition unfeasible.

The contributions of this work are twofold. First, by keeping an explicit representation of the face lattice of polyhedra, we obtain a significant advantage over the double description method, leading in particular to a more efficient implementation of the projection operation. Second, we tackle the combinatorial explosion in high dimensional spaces by introducing a novel decomposition mechanism. As opposed to the purely syntactic approach of [17], this mechanism is not affected by non-singular linear transformations, which significantly broadens its applicability. The resulting data structure, the Decomposed Convex Polyhedron (DCP), admits an easily computable canonical form, which simplifies comparison operations and leads to concise representations of simple sets constructed in a complex way. DCPs share the same advantages as CPDDs, such as offering a simple decision procedure for checking which face of a convex polyhedron contains a given point.

The rest of this paper is organized as follows. Section 2 recalls basic concepts and the principles of the double description method. Section 3 introduces DCPs, starting from CPDDs and enhancing them with a decomposition mechanism. Section 4 discusses the implementation of operations over DCPs. Section 5 assesses the practical efficiency of our proposed data structure with the help of a prototype implementation.

2   Preliminaries

2.1   Basics

A *convex polyhedron* P is defined as the set of solutions of a finite conjunction of linear constraints, i.e., $P = \{x \in \mathbb{R}^n \mid \bigwedge_{i=1}^k a_i.x \#_i b_i\}$ where, for all i, $a_i \in \mathbb{Z}^n$, $b_i \in \mathbb{Z}$, and $\#_i \in \{\leq, <\}$. Such polyhedra can either be bounded or unbounded, as well as topologically closed or not[1]. We denote by $\overline{P}$ the topological closure of P, that is, the set $\overline{P} = \{x \in \mathbb{R}^n \mid \bigwedge_{i=1}^k a_i.x \leq b_i\}$.

Given a constraint $a_i.x \#_i b_i$, a point $v \in \mathbb{R}^n$ *satisfies* this constraint if $a_i.v \#_i b_i$, and *saturates* it if $a_i.v = b_i$. Constraints of the form $a_i.x \leq b_i$ are called *closed*, or *non-strict*, and constraints of the form $a_i.x < b_i$ are called *open*, or *strict*. The *dimension* of a convex polyhedron P, noted dim P, is the dimension of its affine hull, i.e the smallest affine space that contains P. The *lineality space* lin P of P is the largest vector space L such that $P + L = P$, where $+$ denotes the Minkowski sum.

A closed convex polyhedron $\overline{P}$ can be represented as a finite intersection of halfspaces by its *constraint system* $\mathcal{H} = \{a_i.x \leq b_i\}$. Alternatively, $\overline{P}$ can be expressed in terms of a *generator set* $\mathcal{G} = (V, R)$, where $V, R \in \mathbb{Q}^n$ are finite sets

---

[1] They are also known as NNC (Not Necessarily Closed) polyhedra, or copolyhedra.

of (respectively) *vertices* and *extremal rays*. One then has $P = \{\sum_{i=1}^{p} \lambda_i v_i + \sum_{i=1}^{q} \mu_i r_i\}$, where $V = \{v_1, \ldots, v_p\}$, $R = \{r_1, \ldots, r_q\}$, $\lambda_i, \mu_i \geq 0$ for all i, and $\sum_{i=1}^{p} \lambda_i = 1$. The pair $(\mathcal{H}, \mathcal{G})$ forms the *double description* of $\overline{P}$ [11,22].

2.2 Face Lattice of a Polyhedron

With respect to a polyhedron P, a linear inequality $c.x \leq \delta$ is said to be *valid* if it is satisfied by all $x \in \overline{P}$. A *face* of P is any set F such that $F = \overline{P} \cap \{x \mid c.x = \delta\}$, where $c.x \leq \delta$ is valid. Note that from the valid inequalities $0.x \leq 0$ and $0.x \leq 1$, we get that $\overline{P}$ and the empty set $\emptyset$ are both faces of P. These two faces are said to be *trivial*. Note that a face is itself a polyhedron; the *dimension* of a face is its dimension as a polyhedron. The faces of dimension 0, 1, and $\dim P - 1$ are respectively called *vertices*, *edges*, and *facets*. Remark that the intersection of any set of faces of P is itself a face of P.

A *partial order* $\preceq$ over a set S is a binary relation that is reflexive, anti-symmetric and transitive. We then say that $(S, \preceq)$, or simply S if the partial order is clear from the context, is a *partially ordered set*. A partially ordered set S is a *lattice* if every two elements $x, y \in S$ admit a unique minimal upper bound in S, called the *join* $x \sqcup y$, and a unique maximal lower bound in S, called the *meet* $x \sqcap y$.

The set $\mathcal{F}'(P)$ of nonempty faces of P is partially ordered by set inclusion. However, this set does not necessarily contain a minimum element, hence we define the smallest face of P as the intersection $F_0 = \cap_{F \in \mathcal{F}'(P)} F$ of all its nonempty faces. The set $\mathcal{F}(P) = \{F_0\} \cup \mathcal{F}'(P)$ is a finite lattice under set inclusion, called the *face lattice* of P.

For $F, G \in \mathcal{F}(P)$, the face $F \sqcup G = \cap\{H \in \mathcal{F}(P) \mid F \cup G \subseteq H\}$, is the smallest one containing both F and G. Similarly, the face $F \sqcap G = F \cap G$ is the largest one contained in both F and G. Furthermore, we say that F is an *ascendant* of G, or equivalently that G is a *descendant* of F, if $F \subset G$. We use the terms *direct ascendant* and *direct descendant* if there does not exist $H \in \mathcal{F}(P)$ such that $F \subset H \subset G$.

2.3 Canonical Representation of Convex Polyhedra

In the double description $(\mathcal{H}, \mathcal{G})$ of a closed convex polyhedron $\overline{P}$, the constraint system $\mathcal{H}$ and the generator system $\mathcal{G}$ admit minimal forms, meaning that no element can be removed from them without affecting $\overline{P}$.

Under two hypotheses, the minimal forms of $\mathcal{H}$ and $\mathcal{G}$ are unique for a given $\overline{P}$, which implies that $(\mathcal{H}, \mathcal{G})$ can then provide a canonical representation of $\overline{P}$. The first hypothesis is to have a *fully dimensional* polyhedron, meaning that $\overline{P} \subseteq \mathbb{R}^n$ is such that $\dim \overline{P} = n$. If $\overline{P}$ is not fully dimensional, then it can be expressed as the image $\overline{P} = A\overline{Q} + b$ of a fully dimensional polyhedron $\overline{Q} \subset \mathbb{R}^m$ of smaller dimension $m < n$ by a linear transformation (A, b), with $A \in \mathbb{Z}^{n \times m}$ and $b \in \mathbb{Q}^n$. This transformation can be made canonical by Gaussian elimination.

The second hypothesis is to have a polyhedron $\overline{P}$ with a lineality space of dimension 0. If this condition is not satisfied, then $\overline{P}$ can be expressed as a sum

$\overline{P} = \overline{Q} + L$, where $\operatorname{lin} \overline{Q} = 0$, $L = \operatorname{lin} \overline{P}$, and $\dim \overline{P} = \dim \overline{Q} + \dim L$. The vector space L can be described canonically by applying Gaussian elimination to one of its bases.

Consider a polyhedron $\overline{P}$ that satisfies both hypotheses, for which the double description $(\mathcal{H}, \mathcal{G})$ has been made minimal. This means that all redundant constraints have been removed from $\mathcal{H}$, hence the saturated form of each constraint in $\mathcal{H}$ is a facet. More generally, each face of $\overline{P}$ corresponds to a subset of saturated constraints in $\mathcal{H}$. Similarly, the vertices of $\mathcal{G}$ correspond to the minimal non-trivial faces of $\overline{P}$. If $\overline{P}$ is bounded, then $\mathcal{G}$ does not contain extremal rays, and the double description $(\mathcal{H}, \mathcal{G})$ exactly contains the minimal and maximal non-trivial elements of the face lattice of $\overline{P}$. If $\overline{P}$ is unbounded, the extremal rays of $\mathcal{G}$ can be computed from the direct descendants of the vertices.

3   Decomposed Convex Polyhedra

We now present our proposed data structure, by first introducing the principles of CPDDs, and then enhancing them with a decomposition mechanism.

3.1   Convex Polyhedron Decision Diagram

A *Convex Polyhedron Decision Diagram* (CPDD) [7] representing a convex polyhedron P is a directed acyclic graph (Q, T, q_0) such that:

- Q is a finite set of *nodes*. Each node $q \in Q$ corresponds to a face of P, and is labeled by the constraints of P that are saturated by that face. (In the special case where q represents the empty face, all constraints are considered to be saturated.) Moreover, q is associated with a binary *polarity* that is true if each constraint that is saturated by q is an open constraint of P, and false otherwise. This polarity is used for representing the strictness of constraints; the representations of P and $\overline{P}$ only differ in the polarity of their nodes.
- $q_0 \in Q$ is an *initial node*, representing the unique minimal element of the face lattice of P.
- $T \subseteq Q \times Q$ is a transition relation corresponding to the inclusion relation between faces, removing the edges that are redundant by transitivity. An edge $(q_1, q_2) \in T$ is labeled by the constraints that are saturated in q_1 but not in q_2.

An example of a CPDD is given in Fig. 1. This data structure can be seen as a deterministic decision graph for determining which face of P contains a given point $v \in \mathbb{R}^n$. This operation consists in starting from the initial node, and then following edges labeled by constraints satisfied by v. The procedure ends either upon reaching a node q labeled by constraints saturated by v, in which case q represents the face of P containing v, and the polarity of q indicates whether v belongs to P, or when no outgoing edge can be followed from the current node, corresponding to $v \notin P$. Note that if several paths can be followed

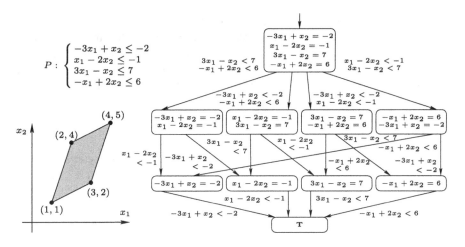

Fig. 1. Example of CPDD.

from a given node, one of them can be chosen arbitrarily without the need for backtracking, since for every pair of nodes q_1, $q_2 \in Q$, all paths linking q_1 to q_2 are labeled with the same constraints. Intuitively, a CPDD can be understood as a compact representation of a deterministic finite automaton accepting the points of a convex polyhedron [7, 8].

3.2   Decomposition of Convex Polyhedra

Like the double description method, CPDDs suffer from combinatorial explosion in high dimensional spaces. For instance, a simple polyhedron such as the n-cube $[0, 1]^n$ has 2^n vertices, which makes its representation grow exponentially with the dimension n.

In this example, each constraint involves a single variable. In order to check whether a given point $\boldsymbol{p} = (p_1, \ldots, p_n)$ belongs to the cube, one can separately check that each p_i is inside $[0, 1]$. This essentially amounts to decomposing the n-cube into a Cartesian product of intervals, that can be processed individually. This idea is developed in [17], which shows how to determine syntactically blocks of variables that can be considered independently from each other.

This approach is however not sufficient for handling the reachable sets computed by state-space exploration tools. In particular, the analysis of timed automata often produces constraints that involve all variables, expressing that they share an identical rate of variation with time. Another example is given by the polyhedron in Fig. 1, which depicts a typical region obtained during the state-space exploration of a linear hybrid system.

In this latter example, one notices however that the polyhedron can become decomposable into a Cartesian product of two intervals by expressing it in a different coordinate system, for instance the one defined by the basis $\{(2, 1), (1, 3)\}$.

The idea behind our improved decomposition scheme is to detect whether a suitable coordinate system exists, that makes the polyhedron decomposable into a Cartesian product of simpler ones. The main advantage of this strategy over a purely syntactic one is that the decomposability property of polyhedra remains unaffected by changes of coordinate system, or equivalently, by non-singular linear transformations (cf. Sect. 4.2).

We define a *decomposition* of a finite set of vectors $S \subset \mathbb{R}^n$ as a partition of S into blocks, such that:

– If a block B contains at least two elements, then each of them can be written as a linear combination of the other ones. Formally, if $B = \{b_1, \ldots, b_k\}$ with $k \geq 2$, then

$$\forall i \in [1, k] : \exists \beta_1 \ldots, \beta_k \in \mathbb{R}^n : \; b_i = \sum_{j \in [1,k],\, j \neq i} \beta_j b_j.$$

– For each block B, there does not exist a non-zero linear combination of the elements of B that can be written as a linear combination of the elements of the other blocks. Formally, if $B = \{b_1, \ldots, b_k\}$, then

$$\sum_{b_i \in B} \beta_i b_i = \sum_{b_i' \in S \setminus B} \beta_i' b_i' \; \Rightarrow \; \sum_{b_i \in B} \beta_i b_i = 0.$$

Intuitively, a decomposition of a set of vectors partitions this set into blocks that are linearly independent from each other. For example, the set $\{(1,1,1), (1,1,2), (-2,-2,-2), (1,-1,0), (0,1,1)\}$ admits the decomposition $\{\{(1,1,1), (-2,-2,-2)\}, \{(1,1,2), (1,-1,0), (0,1,1)\}\}$.

If P_1 and P_2 are two partitions of a set S, then P_1 is *finer* than P_2 (or, equivalently, P_2 is *coarser* than P_1) if every block of P_1 is a subset of some block of P_2. This notion generalizes to decompositions as follows.

Proposition 1. *If D_1 and D_2 are decompositions of a set S, then the partition*

$$D = D_1 \cap D_2 = \{B_i \cap B_j' \mid B_i \cap B_j' \neq \emptyset \; \wedge \; B_i \in D_1, \, B_j' \in D_2\}$$

is itself a decomposition.

This property naturally leads to a notion of *finest decomposition* of a set, obtained by computing the intersection of all its decompositions. This finest decomposition is, by definition, unique.

The finest decomposition of a given set S can be computed by an incremental procedure that considers successively all vectors v in S. At each step, one checks whether v can be expressed as a linear combination of the vectors that have already been dealt with. In the positive case, the blocks containing these vectors have to be merged into a single one, to which the vector v is added. Otherwise, a new block is created, containing only v.

We are now ready to apply our notion of decomposition to polyhedra. The *canonical decomposition* of a convex polyhedron $P \subseteq \mathbb{R}^n$ is defined as the finest

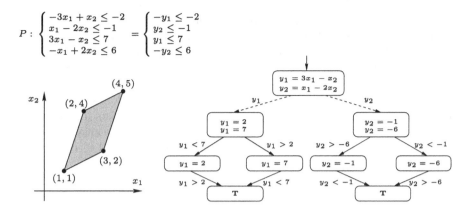

$$P: \begin{cases} -3x_1 + x_2 \leq -2 \\ x_1 - 2x_2 \leq -1 \\ 3x_1 - x_2 \leq 7 \\ -x_1 + 2x_2 \leq 6 \end{cases} = \begin{cases} -y_1 \leq -2 \\ y_2 \leq -1 \\ y_1 \leq 7 \\ -y_2 \leq 6 \end{cases}$$

Fig. 2. Example of DCP.

decomposition of the set of normal vectors of its bounding hyperplanes, that is, of the set $\{a_1, \ldots, a_k\}$ where $P = \{x \in \mathbb{R}^n \mid \bigwedge_{i=1}^k a_i.x \#_i b_i\}$.

Let $D = \{B_1, \ldots, B_k\}$ be the canonical decomposition of P. In order to express P in a coordinate system in which it can be decomposed into a Cartesian product of simpler polyhedra, one builds a new basis of $\mathbb{R}^n$ by computing individual bases for the blocks $B_1, \ldots, B_k$, and then taking their union. The next step is to perform a coordinate change by expressing the constraints of P in terms of this new basis. This operation will turn a constraint $a_i.x \#_i b_i$ into $a_i'.x \#_i b_i'$, in which the components of a_i' are all zero, except for the ones provided by the basis of the block B_j containing a_i. In other words, if B_j contains up to d linearly independent vectors, then the constraint $a_i'.x \#_i b_i'$ will only involve d variables. The change of coordinates induced by the canonical decomposition of P is the one that maximizes the possibility of separating syntactically the variables.

3.3 Decomposed Convex Polyhedron

A *Decomposed Convex Polyhedron* representing a polyhedron $P \subseteq \mathbb{R}^n$ is a tuple (A, b, q_0, C), where

- (A, b) with $A \in \mathbb{Z}^{n \times m}$ and $b \in \mathbb{Q}^n$ is a linear transformation such that $P = A\,Q + b$, where $Q \in \mathbb{R}^m$ is a fully dimensional polyhedron (cf. Sect. 2.3).
- q_0 is an initial node labeled with the canonical decomposition D of Q, and its associated change of coordinates.
- C is a finite set of CPPDs, each of them being associated to an element of D. One thus has $|C| = |D|$. The transition from q_0 to an element of C is called a *decomposition branch*. Each decomposition branch is labeled by its corresponding variables in the new coordinate system.

An example of DCP is given in Fig. 2. In this example, the represented polyhedron is fully dimensional, thus the transformation (A, b) can be chosen as the identity relation, which we do not depict for clarity sake. Decomposition branches are denoted by dashed edges. The set of normal vectors of the constraints is $\{(-3,1),(1,-2),(3,-1),(-1,2)\}$, the canonical decomposition of which is $\{\{(-3,1),(3,-1)\},\{(1,-2),(-1,2)\}\}$. The basis of $\mathbb{R}^2$ induced by this decomposition is $\{(3,-1),(1,-2)\}$.

In order to determine whether a given point $v \in \mathbb{R}^n$ belongs to a polyhedron P represented by a DCP (A,b,q_0,C), the first step consists in computing $v' \in \mathbb{R}^m$ such that $v = Av'+b$. If no such vector exists, then the answer is negative. Otherwise, the coordinate change associated to q_0 is applied to v', yielding vectors $y_1,\dots y_k$ such that $k = |C|$ and $\dim v' = \dim y_1 + \cdots + \dim y_k$. One then runs the point location procedure described in Sect. 3.1 for one y_i in each of the k decomposition branches, all of which have to succeed in order to conclude that v belongs to P. Determining which face of P contains v amounts to combining together the faces reached in each decomposition branch. For example, in Fig. 2, the point $v = (2,1.5)$ is found to belong to the universal (bottom) node in the branch labeled by y_1, and to the node $y_2 = -1$ in the one labeled by y_2. The corresponding face of P is thus $x_1 - 2x_2 = -1$.

Finally, it is worth mentioning that in the case of a polyhedron with a lineality space of non-zero dimension d, our decomposition strategy will produce d trivial decomposition branches, associated to the universal set. Such branches do not have to be explicitly constructed and can be omitted in an actual implementation of the data structure.

4   Operations

4.1   Intersection

We now discuss the computation of operations over convex polyhedra represented by DCPs, starting with the intersection $P_1 \cap P_2$ of two given polyhedra P_1 and P_2. These polyhedra may define different decompositions. We go around this problem by proceeding incrementally, starting from P_1 and successively intersecting the polyhedron with each constraint of P_2.

Dealing with Decompositions. In order to intersect a polyhedron P with a constraint $c.x \# \delta$, the first step consists in inserting c in the current decomposition of P, following the procedure outlined in Sect. 3.2. If c is placed in a single existing branch, or in a newly created one, then the intersection can be computed locally over the CPDD associated to this branch. Otherwise, if several decomposition blocks become merged, then a single CPDD corresponding to the Cartesian product of their associated branches first needs to be constructed. The intersection operation is then computed over this CPDD, leaving the other decomposition branches untouched. Then, after having intersected a CPDD with a constraint, the result is inspected in order to detect whether it is further decomposable. This is achieved by applying the procedure of Sect. 3.2 to its system of constraints. A final step is to check whether the resulting polyhedron is fully dimensional, which amounts to inspecting the bottom component of the CPDD of the branch affected by the intersection. Depending on the outcome of this operation, it may be needed to adapt the linear transformation of the DCP.

CPDD Intersection. The intersection of a polyhedron P represented by a CPDD with a constraint $c.x \# \delta$ is computed by means of a coloring procedure, consisting in labeling the nodes of the CPDD with a color that indicates how they are affected by the operation.

Recall that the CPDD nodes correspond to the faces of P. The coloring scheme uses the colors Green, Red, Blue, and Yellow. A face F is colored Red if $\forall x \in F : c.x \geq \delta \wedge \exists x \in F : c.x > \delta$ (no point in F satisfies the open form of the constraint), Green if $\forall x \in F : c.x \leq \delta \wedge \exists x \in F : c.x < \delta$ (all points in F satisfy the closed form of the constraint), Blue if $\forall x \in F : c.x = \delta$ (all points in F saturate the constraint), and Yellow if $\exists x, y \in F : c.x < \delta \wedge c.y > \delta$ (some points in F satisfy the constraint, and some others do not).

The color of all nodes can be computed by first coloring the minimal non-trivial faces of P, and then propagating this information through its face lattice. Consider for instance the case of a face F that has a direct ascendant F_1 labeled Green, and another one F_2 labeled Red. Thus, there exist $x_1 \in F_1$ such that $c.x_1 < \delta$ and $x_2 \in F_2$ such that $c.x_2 > \delta$. Since $F_1 \cup F_2 \subseteq F$, the face F must be colored Yellow.

Similar propagation rules are easily obtained for all cases, except for a technical difficulty arising when P is unbounded. In such a case it is possible for a face G to have a single direct ascendant F. In order to determine the color of G from the color of F, one then needs to take into account a direction d from F to G, defined as a vector satisfying $\forall x' \in G : \exists x \in F, \lambda \geq 0 : x' = x + \lambda d$. This direction will be colored Green if it is compatible with the constraint $(c.d < 0)$, Red if it is not $(c.d > 0)$, and Blue if it saturates it $(c.d = 0)$. It will then be considered as an additional ascendant of G. Intuitively, this direction simulates a face F' with the same dimension as F, located infinitely far away from F in the same direction as G.

After all nodes have been colored, a CPDD representing the result of the intersection is obtained as follows. All Green and Blue nodes remain unchanged, since they represent faces that satisfy $c.x \leq \delta$. Similarly, Red nodes disappear, since all points of their associated face violate the constraint. Yellow faces F are split into two new faces: A first one $F_1 = F \cap \{x \mid c.x \leq \delta\}$ with the same dimension as F, and another one $F_2 = F \cap \{x \mid c.x = \delta\}$ of smaller dimension. Note that F_1 is associated with the same set of saturated constraints as F, and can thus be considered as being a modified copy of F.

After having computed all the faces of the resulting polyhedron, it remains to restore the inclusion relation between them. For the nodes left untouched by the intersection operation, such as Green and Blue ones, this information can simply be copied from the original CPDD. For Yellow nodes, an additional step needs to be performed. Consider two Yellow nodes F and G such that F is a direct ascendant of G. The nodes F and G will respectively be split into F_1, F_2, and G_1, G_2, where F_2 (resp. G_2) is a direct ascendant of F_1 (resp. G_1). In this situation, one has $F_2 \subset G_2$, hence an edge needs to be added linking F_2 to G_2. A similar phenomenon occurs when a Blue face F has a Green direct descendant G, that has a Yellow direct descendant H. The node H is split into H_1 and H_2 with $\dim H_2 < \dim H_1$. In this case, one has $F \subset H_2$, hence an edge must be added between those nodes. These two situations are illustrated in Fig. 3 (added edges are in bold).

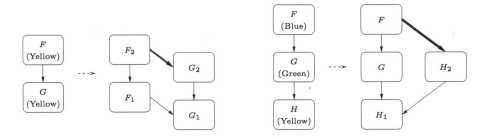

Fig. 3. Restoring the inclusion relation between faces.

A pseudocode version of the CPDD intersection algorithm is sketched in Fig. 4.

Implementation Issues. In our implementation, the coloring procedure is implemented lazily, meaning that it only considers the nodes that will potentially be present in the resulting CPDD. In particular, the descendants of a Red node will not be explored, except if they are reached by another path. When several decomposition branches need to be merged upon processing a new constraint, the CPDD representing their Cartesian product is not explicitly constructed but computed on-the-fly, which helps keeping the memory used by the procedure under control. Finally, we keep a canonical double representation of the maximal and non-trivial minimal faces of polyhedra within their respective nodes of their face lattice. This information makes it possible to speed up the computation of the color of minimal faces, as well as the check for full dimensionality.

4.2 Linear Transformations

We now address the problem of computing the image of a convex polyhedron $P \subseteq \mathbb{R}^n$ represented by a DCP by an affine transformation $\pi : x \mapsto Ax + b$, with $A \in \mathbb{Q}^{n \times n}$ and $b \in \mathbb{Q}^n$.

There are two cases to consider. First, if A is a non-singular matrix, then applying the transformation amounts to expressing P in a new coordinate system. The decomposition of P and the structure of its face lattice are thus left unchanged, and the operation can be implemented by translating the constraints

```
Color(node N, constraint C):
   if N is minimal:
     compute N.color from the saturated constraints of N
   else:
     S = set of colors of the direct ascendants of N
     if S == { Green } or S == { Green, Blue }: N.color = Green
     if S == { Red } or S == { Red, Blue }: N.color = Red
     if S == { Blue}: N.color = Blue
     if Yellow in S: N.color = Yellow
     if Green in S and Red in S: N.color = Yellow

SplitYellowNodes(node N, constraint C):
   if N.color == Yellow:
     add new node N2 and new edge from N2 to N
   for all direct ascendants M of N:
     if M.color == Yellow:
        add new edge from M to N2
     if M.color == Green:
        for all direct ascendants L of M:
           if L.color == Blue:
             add new edge from L to N2

Intersect(CPDD P, constraint C):
   for all N:
     N.color = undefined
   FIFO Queue Q = { }
   Q.put(P.initialNode)
   while not IsEmpty(Q):
     Node N = Q.get()
     if N.color == undefined:
        Color(N, C)
        if N.color != Red or MinimalNonTrivial(N):
           for all direct descendants M of N:
              Q.put(M)
   Q.put(P.initialNode)
   while not IsEmpty(Q)
     Node N = Q.get()
     SplitYellowNodes(N, C)
     for all direct descendants M of N:
        Q.put(M)
   CheckFullDimensionality(P)
```

Fig. 4. CPDD intersection algorithm.

of P in the new coordinate system, and then updating the labels of the nodes and edges of the DCP accordingly.

If on the other hand A is singular, then the transformation represents a *projection*, mapping P into a polyhedron $P' = \pi(P)$ such that $\dim P' = \operatorname{rank}(A)$, hence $\dim P' < \dim P$. It is well known that P' is itself a convex polyhedron, and that for each face F' of P', there exists a face F of P such that $\pi(F) = F'$. Moreover, the face lattice of P' shares the same structure as the one of P.

W.l.o.g., we assume $\mathrm{rank}(A) = n - 1$, since any projection can easily be expressed as a sequence of projections that satisfy this hypothesis. The first step of the computation consists in checking whether the decomposition of the DCP can be preserved. This is done by computing a *direction* for the projection, defined as a vector d that satisfies $Ad = 0$. This intuitively means that two points that only differ in a multiple of this direction are projected identically. In the current decomposition, all the branches that are not orthogonal to d (i.e., containing a vector a such that $a.d \neq 0$) must be merged together. The projection is then applied separately to the CPDD associated to each branch.

Consider a CPDD representing a polyhedron $P \subseteq \mathbb{R}^n$. The computation of its projection by π proceeds bottom-up in its face lattice, as opposed to the intersection operation that was carried out in top-down order. We start by projecting the trivial face of dimension n (corresponding to the whole polyhedron P). This projection yields the trivial face $P' = \pi(P)$, of dimension $n - 1$.

The next step consists in projecting the following two layers, that is, the facets of P (of dimension $n - 1$), and their direct ascendants (of dimension $n - 2$). The projection $\pi(F)$ of a facet F of P may either be of dimension $n - 1$ or $n - 2$. In the former case, it corresponds to the unique trivial face of dimension $n - 1$ of P'. In the latter, the set $\pi(F)$ needs to be explicitly computed.

The projection $\pi(F)$ of a face F of P such that $\dim F = n - 2$ can either be a face of P' (of dimension $n - 2$ or $n - 3$), or it will not be a face of P'. These situations are distinguished by performing Fourier-Motzkin elimination. This is illustrated in Fig. 5, the two parts of which show a vertex (of dimension 0) that respectively remains as a face of P', or vanishes after projecting out x_2.

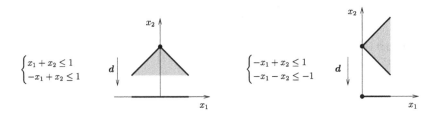

Fig. 5. Effect of Fourier-Motzkin projection.

The major difference with the double description method [11,22] is that we only apply Fourier-Motzkin elimination to the constraints that intersect at the face of interest, which are readily determined using the adjacency relation represented in the face lattice. This is the key to the efficiency of our procedure.

After having projected the first two non-trivial layers, it remains to compute the projection of the other faces. Since the face lattice of P' matches the one of P, this is simply done by following the structure of this lattice in bottom up order, computing each face as the meet (thus, the intersection), of its direct descendants. The resulting representation of P' is, by construction, free from redundancy in its constraint and generator systems.

Finally, the computation of the projection of a DCP is followed by a cleanup step aimed at detecting further decompositions and checking full dimensionality. This step is identical to the last operation of the intersection algorithm presented in Fig. 4.

5   Experimental Results

In order to assess the advantages of DCPs against other solutions for dealing with convex polyhedra, we have implemented a prototype tool that builds the minimal DCP representing a polyhedron given by its set of constraints. Unsurprisingly, other tools based on the double description method do not come with benchmarks containing problems expressed in high dimensional spaces. Our first idea was to construct a set of examples composed of polyhedra that are decomposable by design. Our implementation handles them in an exponentially faster way than the other tools that we have considered, but this was expected since these examples were specifically tailored to our decomposition mechanism.

Obtaining instances of realistic problems related to the state-space exploration of hybrid systems, which was the main motivation for this work, is not easy since to the best of our knowledge, no existing tool can handle high-dimensional problems. We therefore turned to the domain of SMT solving, for which extensive benchmarks of problems involving a large number of variables are available. Our approach consisted in running the SMT prover veriT [10] on the verification problem `uart-9.base`[2] from the QF_LRA benchmark of the SMT-LIB library [6]. During its operation, the SMT prover generates systems of linear inequalities that are checked for satisfiability by an external simplex procedure. We replaced this procedure by an explicit construction of a DCP representing the corresponding convex polyhedron.

The results of this experimental evaluation are summarized in Fig. 6. We compare the execution time (in seconds) of our prototype implementation against cdd [16] and PPL [4], which are based on the double description method with some clever optimizations, as well as lrs [2], which implements the reverse search algorithm for computing the vertices of polyhedra. The experiments were carried out on a computer equipped with a i7-970 processor running at 3.2 GHz, with turbo boost disabled. Timeout was set at one hour. The indices 1, 50, 100, ... of the instances correspond to the steps at which these problems were produced by veriT (selected arbitrarily), and not to the increasing value of some parameter. In this setting, the results show that our approach (DCP) compares quite favorably against the other tools.

---

[2] The test cases are available at http://www.montefiore.ulg.ac.be/~boigelot/research/ atva2018-case-study.tgz.

Problem	#Var.	#Constr.	DCP	PPL	cdd	lrs
dump-1	80	171	0.036	0.019	0.157	0.041
dump-50	129	402	0.091	0.158	1.306	0.240
dump-100	141	482	0.111	1006.717	2.014	0.350
dump-150	153	561	0.123	timeout	2.066	0.490
dump-200	166	639	0.148	timeout	4.458	0.650
dump-250	171	732	0.163	timeout	5.401	0.899

Fig. 6. Experimental results (times in s).

6   Conclusions

This paper introduces a new data structure, the Decomposed Convex Polyhedron (DCP), for representing symbolically convex polyhedra in $\mathbb{R}^n$. This data structure is based on an explicit representation of the whole face lattice of polyhedra, including complete adjacency information between its faces, which makes some operations (such as projection) more efficient. It is able to scale up to high dimensional spaces thanks to a novel decomposition mechanism that is not affected by changes of coordinates. DCPs have been evaluated experimentally with a prototype implementation. On an SMT solving case study related to software verification, they perform better than other existing tools for handling convex polyhedra.

Future work will focus on implementing additional operations on DCPs, such as the time-elapse operator needed for exploring the state-space of linear hybrid systems, and on improving our prototype with some optimization mechanisms borrowed from other tools. The practical cost of operations performed over DCPs also needs to be thoroughly evaluated in the scope of a more detailed case study.

Acknowledgment. The authors wish to thank Pascal Fontaine and Laurent Poirrier for their precious help in obtaining relevant benchmarks.

References

1. Alur, R., Dill, D.L.: A theory of timed automata. Theor. Comput. Sci. **126**(2), 183–235 (1994)
2. Avis, D.: A revised implementation of the reverse search vertex enumeration algorithm. Polytopes – Combinatorics and Computation, pp. 177–198. Birkhäuser, Basel (2000)
3. Bachem, A., Grötschel, M.: Characterizations of adjacency of faces of polyhedra. Mathematical Programming at Oberwolfach, pp. 1–22. Springer, Berlin (1981)
4. Bagnara, R., Hill, P.M., Zaffanella, E.: The Parma Polyhedra Library: Toward a complete set of numerical abstractions for the analysis and verification of hardware and software systems. Sci. Comput. Program. **72**(1–2), 3–21 (2008)
5. Bagnara, R., Hill, P.M., Zaffanella, E.: Applications of polyhedral computations to the analysis and verification of hardware and software systems. Theor. Comput. Sci. **410**(46), 4672–4691 (2009)

6. Barrett, C., Stump, A., Tinelli, C.: The SMT-LIB Standard: Version 2.0. In: Proceedings of the SMT'10 (2010)
7. Boigelot, B., Herbreteau, F., Mainz, I.: Acceleration of affine hybrid transformations. In: Cassez, F., Raskin, J.-F. (eds.) ATVA 2014. LNCS, vol. 8837, pp. 31–46. Springer, Cham (2014). https://doi.org/10.1007/978-3-319-11936-6_4
8. Boigelot, B., Jodogne, S., Wolper, P.: An effective decision procedure for linear arithmetic over the integers and reals. ACM Trans. Comput. Log. 6(3), 614–633 (2005)
9. Bournez, O., Maler, O., Pnueli, A.: Orthogonal polyhedra: Representation and computation. In: Vaandrager, F.W., van Schuppen, J.H. (eds.) HSCC'1999. LNCS, vol. 1569, pp. 46–60. Springer, Heidelberg (1999). https://doi.org/10.1007/3-540-48983-5_8
10. Bouton, T., Caminha B. de Oliveira, D., Déharbe, D., Fontaine, P.: veriT: an open, trustable and efficient SMT-solver. In: Schmidt, R.A. (ed.) CADE 2009. LNCS (LNAI), vol. 5663, pp. 151–156. Springer, Heidelberg (2009). https://doi.org/10.1007/978-3-642-02959-2_12
11. Chernikova, N.: Algorithm for finding a general formula for the non-negative solutions of a system of linear inequalities. USSR Comput. Math. Math. Phys. 5(2), 228–233 (1965)
12. Cousot, P., Cousot, R.: Abstract interpretation: A unified lattice model for static analysis of programs by construction or approximation of fixpoints. In: Proceedings of the POPL'77. pp. 238–252. ACM Press (1977)
13. Cousot, P., Halbwachs, N.: Automatic discovery of linear restraints among variables of a program. In: Proceedings of the POPL'78. pp. 84–96. ACM (1978)
14. Degbomont, J.F.: Implicit Real-Vector Automata. Ph.D. thesis, Université de Liège (2013)
15. Frehse, G.: PHAVer: algorithmic verification of hybrid systems past HyTech. Int. J. Softw. Tools Technol. Transf. 10(3), 263–279 (2008)
16. Fukuda, K.: cdd. https://www.inf.ethz.ch/personal/fukudak/cdd_home/
17. Singh, G., Püschel, M., Vechev, M.: Fast polyhedra abstract domain. In: Proceedings of the POPL'17, pp. 46–59. ACM (2017)
18. Halbwachs, N., Proy, Y.-E., Raymond, P.: Verification of linear hybrid systems by means of convex approximations. In: Le Charlier, B. (ed.) SAS 1994. LNCS, vol. 864, pp. 223–237. Springer, Heidelberg (1994). https://doi.org/10.1007/3-540-58485-4_43
19. Halbwachs, N., Proy, Y.E., Roumanoff, P.: Verification of real-time systems using linear relation analysis. Form. Methods Syst. Des. 11(2), 157–185 (1997)
20. Jeannet, B., Miné, A.: Apron: A library of numerical abstract domains for static analysis. In: Bouajjani, A., Maler, O. (eds.) CAV 2009. LNCS, vol. 5643, pp. 661–667. Springer, Heidelberg (2009). https://doi.org/10.1007/978-3-642-02658-4_52
21. Le Verge, H., Wilde, D.: PolyLib. http://www.irisa.fr/polylib/
22. Motzkin, T.S., Raiffa, H., Thompson, G.L., Thrall, R.M.: The Double Description Method, pp. 51–74. Princeton University Press, Princeton (1953)
23. Schrijver, A.: Theory of Linear and Integer Programming. Wiley, New York (1999)

Accelerated Model Checking of Parametric Markov Chains

Paul Gainer, Ernst Moritz Hahn$^{(\boxtimes)}$, and Sven Schewe

University of Liverpool, Liverpool, UK
{p.gainer,e.m.hahn,sven.schewe}@liverpool.ac.uk

Abstract. Parametric Markov chains occur quite naturally in various applications: they can be used for a conservative analysis of probabilistic systems (no matter how the parameter is chosen, the system works to specification); they can be used to find optimal settings for a parameter; they can be used to visualise the influence of system parameters; and they can be used to make it easy to adjust the analysis for the case that parameters change. Unfortunately, these advancements come at a cost: parametric model checking is—or rather was—often slow. To make the analysis of parametric Markov models scale, we need three ingredients: clever algorithms, the right data structure, and good engineering. Clever algorithms are often the main (or sole) selling point; and we face the trouble that this paper focuses on – the latter ingredients to efficient model checking. Consequently, our easiest claim to fame is in the speedup we have often realised when comparing to the state of the art.

1 Introduction

The analysis of parametric Markov models is a young and growing field of research. As not only the research direction but also the term 'parametric Markov models' is attractive, it has been used for various generalisations of traditional Markov models. We use Markov chains, where the parameter is used to determine the probabilities and rewards, such that we can reason about the likelihood of obtaining simple temporal properties like safety and reachability as well as standard reward functions, such as long-run average.

What we do *not* intend to do in this paper is to use parameters to change the size of the system or the shape of the Markov chain. (The latter can, of course, be encoded by using parameters to assign a probability of 0 to an edge, effectively removing it. This would, however, come at the cost of efficiency and is not what we want to use the parameters for.)

Using parameters to describe the probabilities of transitions is not quite as easy as it sounds: even when parameters appear in a simple way, like 'p' or '$1-p$', the terms that represent the likelihood of obtaining a temporal property or an expected reward can quickly become quite intricate. One ends up with rational functions. We make a virtue of necessity by using this as a motivation to allow for using rational functions of the occurring parameters to represent the probabilities and payoffs.

S. K. Lahiri and C. Wang (Eds.): ATVA 2018, LNCS 11138, pp. 300–316, 2018.
https://doi.org/10.1007/978-3-030-01090-4_18

To allow for an efficient analysis of such complex parametrised systems, we have taken a look at different strategies for the evaluations of—parametric and non-parametric—Markov chains, and considered their suitability for our purposes. We found the stepwise elimination of vertices from a model to be the most attractive approach to port.

Broadly speaking, this approach works like the transformation from finite automata to regular expressions: a vertex is removed, and the new structure has all successors of this state as—potentially new—successors of the predecessors of this vertex. In the transformation from finite automata to regular expressions, one changes the expressions on the edges, while we adjust the probabilities and, if applicable, the rewards on the edges.

When using this approach with explicit probabilities and rewards, one ends up with a Directed Acyclic Graph (DAG) structure in the evaluation. This DAG structure has been exploited to reduce the cost of re-calculating the probabilities for simple temporal properties or expected rewards, and it proves that it also integrates nicely into our framework, where the probabilities and rewards are provided as rational functions. In fact it integrates so naturally that it seems surprising in hindsight that it has not been discovered earlier.

The natural connection occurs when choosing a similar data structure to represent the rational functions that represent the probabilities and rewards. To make full use of the DAG structure that comes with the elimination, we represent these functions in the form of arithmetic circuits—which are essentially DAGs. We have integrated the resulting representation organically in a small extension of ePMC, and tested it on a range of case studies. We have obtained a speed-up of a hefty factor of 20 to 120 when compared to storing functions in terms of coprime numerator and denominator polynomials.

Related work. For (discrete-time) Markov chains (MCs), Daws [6] has devised a language-theoretic approach to solve this problem. In this approach, the transition probabilities are considered as letters of an alphabet. Thus, the model can be viewed as a finite automaton. Then, based on the state elimination method [22], a regular expression that describes the language of such an automaton is calculated. In a post-processing step, this regular expression is recursively evaluated, resulting in a rational function over the parameters of the model. One of the authors has been involved in extending and tuning this method [16] so as to operate with rational functions, which are stored as coprime numerator and denominator polynomials rather than with regular expressions.

The process of computing a function that describes properties (like reachability probabilities or long-run average rewards) that depend on model parameters is often costly. However, once the function has been obtained, it can very efficiently be evaluated for given parameter instantiations. Because of this, parametric model checking of Markov models has also attracted attention in the area of runtime verification, where the acceptable time to obtain values is limited [3,11].

Other works in the area are centred around deciding the validity of boolean formulas depending on the parameter range using SMT solvers or extending these techniques to models that involve nondeterminism [5,7,14,27].

As an example for a para-
metric model, consider Fig. 1.
Knuth and Yao [24] have shown
how a six-sided dice can be
simulated by repeatedly tossing a coin. The idea is to build
a Markov chain with transition probabilities of only 0.5
or 1. Borrowing a model from
the PRISM website, we have
extended this example to a
biased dice, simulated by tossing a biased coin. With probability x we see heads, while
with probability $1 - x$ we see
tails. This way, we move around
in the Markov chain until we
obtain a result.

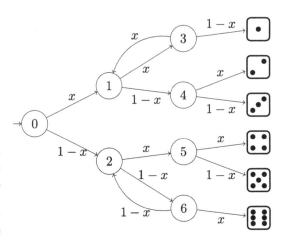

Fig. 1. Simulating a biased dice by a biased coin.

Organisation of the paper. After formalising our setting in Sect. 2, we
describe how we exploit DAGs in the representation of rational functions, and
exploit them using synergies with the DAG-style state elimination technique, in
Sect. 3. We then describe how to expand this technique to determine long-run
average rewards in Sect. 4. In Sect. 5, we evaluate our approach on a range of
benchmarks, and discuss the results briefly in Sect. 6.

2   Preliminaries

2.1   Parametric Markov Chains with State Rewards

Let $V = \{v_1, \ldots, v_n\}$ denote a set of variables over $\mathbb{R}$. A *polynomial g* over V is
a sum of monomials

$$g(v_1, \ldots, v_n) = \sum_{i_1, \ldots, i_n} a_{i_1, \ldots, i_n} v_1^{i_1} \ldots v_n^{i_n},$$

where each $i_j \in \mathbb{N}$ and each $a_{i_1}, \ldots, i_n \in \mathbb{R}$. A *rational function f* over a set of
variables V is a fraction $f(v_1, \ldots, v_n) = \frac{f_1(v_1, \ldots, v_n)}{f_2(v_1, \ldots, v_n)}$ of two polynomials f_1, f_2
over V. We denote the set of rational functions from V to $\mathbb{R}$ by $\mathcal{F}_V$.

Definition 1. *A* parametric Markov chain *(PMC) is a tuple* $\mathcal{D} = (\mathcal{S}, \overline{s}, \mathbf{P}, V)$,
*where $\mathcal{S}$ is a finite set of states, $\overline{s}$ is the initial state, $V = \{v_1, \ldots, v_n\}$ is a
finite set of parameters, and $\mathbf{P}$ is the probability matrix $\mathbf{P} \colon \mathcal{S} \times \mathcal{S} \to \mathcal{F}_V$. A
path ω of a PMC $\mathcal{D} = (\mathcal{S}, \overline{s}, \mathbf{P}, V)$ is a non-empty finite, or infinite, sequence
$s_0, s_1, s_2, \ldots$ where $s_i \in \mathcal{S}$ and $\mathbf{P}(s_i, s_{i+1}) > 0$ for $i \geq 0$. We let Ω denote the
set of infinite paths. With Pr_s, we denote the parametric probability measure
over Ω assuming that we start in state s, with $\mathsf{pr} = \mathsf{pr}_{\overline{s}}$. We use Exp_s, Exp to*

Algorithm 1 Parametric Reachability Probability for PMCs

1: **procedure** STATEELIMINATION($\mathcal{D}, \mathcal{B}$)
2:     **requires:** A PMC $\mathcal{D} = (\mathcal{S}, \bar{s}, \mathbf{P}, V)$ and set of target states $\mathcal{B} \subseteq \mathcal{S}$, where reach$_D(\bar{s}, s)$ holds for all $s \in \mathcal{S}$.
3:     $E \leftarrow \mathcal{S}$
4:     **while** $E \neq \emptyset$ **do**
5:         $s_e \leftarrow$ choose(E)
6:         $E \leftarrow E \setminus \{s_e\}$
7:         **for all** $s \in$ post$_{\mathcal{D}}(s_e)$ **do**
8:             $\mathbf{P}(s_e, s) \leftarrow \mathbf{P}(s_e, s)/(1 - \mathbf{P}(s_e, s_e))$
9:         **end for**
10:        $\mathbf{P}(s_e, s_e) \leftarrow 0$
11:        **for all** $(s_1, s_2) \in$ pre$_{\mathcal{D}}(s_e) \times$ post$_{\mathcal{D}}(s_e)$ **do**
12:            $\mathbf{P}(s_1, s_2) \leftarrow \mathbf{P}(s_1, s_2) + \mathbf{P}(s_1, s_e)\mathbf{P}(s_e, s_2)$
13:        **end for**
14:        **if** $s_e \neq \bar{s} \wedge s_e \notin \mathcal{B} \wedge$ post$_{\mathcal{D}}(s_e) \neq \emptyset$ **then**
15:            Eliminate($\mathcal{D}, s_e$) // *remove s_e and incident transitions from $\mathcal{D}$*
16:        **end if**
17:    **end while**
18:    **return** $\sum_{s \in \mathcal{B}} \mathbf{P}(\bar{s}, s)$
19: **end procedure**

---

denote according expectations. With $X(\mathcal{D})_{s,i} \colon \Omega \to \mathcal{S}$, $X(\mathcal{D})_{s,i}(s_0, s_1, \ldots) = s_i$ we denote the random variable expressing the state occupied at step $i \geq 0$, and let $X(\mathcal{D})_i = X(\mathcal{D})_{\bar{s},i}$.

Definition 2. *Given a PMC $\mathcal{D} = (\mathcal{S}, \bar{s}, \mathbf{P}, V)$, the underlying graph of $\mathcal{D}$ is given by $\mathcal{G}_{\mathcal{D}} = (\mathcal{S}, E)$ where $E = \{(s, s') \mid \mathbf{P}(s, s') > 0\}$. A bottom strongly connected component (BSCC) is a set $A \subseteq \mathcal{S}$ such that in the underlying graph each state $s_1 \in A$ can reach each state $s_2 \in A$ and there is no $s_3 \in \mathcal{S} \setminus A$ reachable from s_1.*

Given a state s, we denote the set of all immediate predecessors and successors of s in the underlying graph of $\mathcal{D}$ by pre$_{\mathcal{D}}(s)$ and post$_{\mathcal{D}}(s)$, respectively, excluding s itself. We write reach$_D(s, s')$ if s' is reachable from s in the underlying graph of D.

Given a PMC $\mathcal{D} = (\mathcal{S}, \bar{s}, \mathbf{P}, V)$ we are interested in computing the function that represents the probability of reaching some set of target states $\mathcal{B} \subset \mathcal{S}$.

$$\text{Reach}(\mathcal{D}, \mathcal{B}) = \Pr\left[\exists i \geq 0.X(\mathcal{D})_{\bar{s},i} \in \mathcal{B}\right]$$

Our base algorithm to obtain this value is described in Algorithm 1. A state $s_e \in \mathcal{S}$ is selected, and then eliminated by considering each pair $(s_1, s_2) \in$ pre$_{\mathcal{D}}(s_e) \times$ post$_{\mathcal{D}}(s_e)$ and updating the existing probability $\mathbf{P}(s_1, s_2)$ by the probability of reaching s_2 from s_1 via s_e. Heuristics to determine the order in which states are chosen for elimination by the choose function are discussed in Sect. 5.5.

Definition 3. *A parametric reward function for a PMC $\mathcal{D} = (\mathcal{S}, \bar{s}, \mathbf{P}, V)$ is a function $r \colon \mathcal{S} \to \mathcal{F}_V$.*

The reward function labels states in $\mathcal{D}$ with a rational function over V that corresponds to the reward that is gained if that state is visited. Given a PMC $\mathcal{D} = (\mathcal{S}, \bar{s}, \mathbf{P}, V)$ and a reward function $r \colon \mathcal{S} \to \mathcal{F}_V$, we are interested in the *parametric expected accumulated reward* defined as

$$\mathsf{Acc}(\mathcal{D}, r) = \mathsf{Exp}\left[\sum_{i=0}^{\infty} r(X(\mathcal{D}))_{\bar{s},i}\right]$$

or a variation [25], the *parametric expected accumulated reachability reward* given $\mathcal{B} \subseteq \mathcal{S}$ defined as

$$\mathsf{Acc}(\mathcal{D}, r, \mathcal{B}) = \mathsf{Exp}\left[\sum_{i=0}^{\{j \mid X(\mathcal{D})_{\bar{s},j} \in \mathcal{B}\}} r(X(\mathcal{D}))_{\bar{s},i}\right].$$

This can, however, be transformed to the former.

Algorithm 1 can be extended to compute the parametric expected accumulated reward. In addition to updating the probability matrix for each predecessor and successor pair, we also update the reward function as follows:

$$r(s_1) \leftarrow r(s_1) + \mathbf{P}(s_1, s_e)\frac{\mathbf{P}(s_e, s_e)}{1 - \mathbf{P}(s_e, s_e)}r(s_e).$$

The updated value for $r(s_1)$ reflects the reward that would be accumulated if a transition would be taken from s_1 to s_e, where the expected number of self-loops would be $\frac{\mathbf{P}(s_e,s_e)}{1-\mathbf{P}(s_e,s_e)}$. Upon termination, the algorithm returns the value $r(\bar{s})$.

3   Representing Formulas Using Directed Acyclic Graphs

In existing tools for parametric model checking of Markov models, rational functions have traditionally been represented in the form $f(v_1, \ldots, v_n) = \frac{f_1(v_1, \ldots, v_n)}{f_2(v_1, \ldots, v_n)}$, where $f_1(v_1, \ldots, v_n)$ and $f_2(v_1, \ldots, v_n)$ [8,15,26] are coprime. As a result, for some cases the representations of such functions are very short. Often, during the state elimination phase, large common factors can be cancelled out, such that one can operate with relatively small functions throughout the whole algorithm. There are, however, many cases without—or with very few—large common factors. The nominator-denominator representations then become larger and larger during the analysis. In this case, the analysis is slowed down severely, mostly by the time taken for the cancellation of common factors. Cancelling out such factors is non-trivial, and indeed a research area in itself. In addition, if formulas become large, this can also lead to out-of-memory problems.

To overcome this issue, we propose the representation of rational functions by arithmetic circuits. These arithmetic circuits are directed acyclic graphs (DAG).

Terminal nodes are labelled with either a variable of the set of parameters V, or with a rational number. Non-final nodes are labelled with a function to be applied on the nodes it has edges to. In our setting, we require two unary functions, additive inverse and multiplicative inverse, and two binary functions, addition and multiplication. All functions used are represented using a single DAG, and a function is represented by a reference to a node of this common DAG.

This representation has two advantages. Firstly, all operations are practically constant time: to apply an operator on two functions, one simply introduces a new node labelled with the according operator, with edges pointing to the two nodes to connect. In particular, we do not have to use expensive methods to cancel out common factors. Secondly, because we are using a DAG and not a tree, common sub-expressions can be shared between different formulas, which is not possible when representing rational functions in terms of two polynomials represented as a list of monomials.

For illustration, let us consider the example from Fig. 1. We analyse the probability that the final result is ⚃. This probability can be described by the function

$$\frac{-x^2 + 2x - 1}{x - 2}.$$

In our DAG-based representation, we would represent the function as in Fig. 2;

When operating with arithmetic circuits, there are a number of ways to reduce their memory footprint, which will, however, lead to a higher running time. The simplest one is that, while creating a new node to represent a function, it might turn out that there already exists a node with exactly the same operator, and exactly the same operand. In this case, it is better to drop the newly created node and use a reference to the existing node to counter the growth of the DAG. In case we use hash maps for the lookup, we can also still keep the overhead close to constant time. Another optimisation is to use simple algebraic equivalences. This includes computing the values of constant functions. E.g. instead of creating a node representing $2+3$ we introduce a new terminal node labelled 5, and if we are about the create a new node for $y + x$ but we already have a node for $x + y$ we reuse this node instead. We also take the additive and multiplicate neutral elements into account (rather than creating a new node for $0 + x$, we return the one for x, and the like). Another optimisation method is to evaluate functions of the DAG at random points and then to identify functions if the result of this evaluation is the same. Using the Schwartz-Zippel

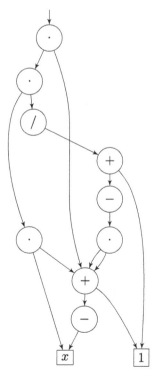

Fig. 2. Probability of rolling ⚃.

Lemma [9, 29, 30], we can then bound the probability that we mistakenly identify two nodes although they do not represent the same function. We can again minimise the overheads incurred by this method by using hash maps.

Arithmetic circuits sometimes become very large, consisting of millions of nodes. This way, they cannot serve as a concise, human-readable description of the analysis result. Compared to performing a non-parametric analysis, it is however often still beneficial to obtain a function representation in this form. Even for large dags, obtaining evaluating parameter instantiations is very fast, and linear in the number of DAG nodes. This is useful in particular if a large number of points is required, for instance for plotting a graph. In this case, results can be obtained much faster than using non-parametric model checking, as demonstrated in Sect. 5. In particular, for any instantiation, values can be obtained in the same, predictable, time. This is quite in contrast to value iteration, where the number of iterations required to obtain a certain precision varies with the concrete values of parameters.

For this reason, parametric model checking is particularly useful for online model checking or runtime verification [3]. Here, one can precompute the DAG before running the actual system, while concrete values can be instantiated at runtime, with a running time that can be precisely calculated offline. Using arithmetic circuits expands the range of systems for which this method is applicable. Evaluation of parameter instantiations can be performed using exact arithmetic or floating-point arithmetic. From our experience, the quality of the floating-point results using DAGs is often better than the one using the representation of rational functions as coprime numerator and denominator, which has been used so far in known implementations. The reason is that, in the latter approach, one often runs into numerical problems such as cancellation, which often forces the use of expensive exact arithmetic to be used for evaluation. The DAG-based method seems to be more robust against such problems.

It has recently come noted by the verification community that the usual way in which value iteration is implemented is not safe, and solutions have already been proposed [1]. While this solves the problem, it requires more complex algorithms and leads to increased model checking time. In case arithmetic circuits are used, it is easy to obtain conservative upper and lower bounds for parameter instantiations. One only has to use interval arithmetic and provide implementations for the basic operations used (addition, multiplication, additive and multiplicative inverse). The increase in the time to evaluate functions is small. In our experiments, the largest interval diameter we have obtained is around 10^{-13}.

4   Computation of Fractional Long-Run Average Values

Consider a PMC $\mathcal{D} = (\mathcal{S}, \bar{s}, \mathbf{P}, V)$ together with two reward functions $r_u \colon \mathcal{S} \to \mathcal{F}_V$ and $r_l \colon \mathcal{S} \to \mathcal{F}_V$. The problem we are interested in is computing the value *fractional long-run average reward* [2, 10]

$$\mathsf{LRA}(\mathcal{D}, r_u, r_l, s) = \mathsf{Exp}\left[\lim_{n \to \infty} \frac{\sum_{i=0}^{n} r_u(X(\mathcal{D})_{s,i})}{\sum_{i=0}^{n} r_l(X(\mathcal{D})_{s,i})}\right], \mathsf{LRA}(\mathcal{D}, r_u, r_l) = \mathsf{LRA}(\mathcal{D}, r_u, r_l, \bar{s}).$$

In a simple case, $r_l(\cdot) = 1$, which means that we compute the *long-run average reward*

$$\mathsf{Exp}\left[\lim_{n\to\infty}\frac{1}{n+1}\sum_{i=0}^{n} r_u(X(\mathcal{D})_{s,i})\right],$$

where each step is assumed to take the same amount of time. Solution methods for this property has been implemented (but to the best of our confidence, not been published) for parametric models in PRISM and Storm. The fractional long-run average reward is more general and allows to express values like the average energy usage per task performed more easily. Given a reward structure $r: S \to \mathcal{F}_V$, we define the *recurrence reward* as

$$\mathsf{Return}(\mathcal{D}, r, s) = \mathsf{Exp}\left[\sum_{i=0}^{\min\{j|X(\mathcal{D})_{s,j}=s\wedge j>0\}} r(X(\mathcal{D})_{s,i})\right], \mathsf{Return}(\mathcal{D}, r) = \mathsf{Return}(\mathcal{D}, r, \bar{s}).$$

It is known [4] that this value is the same for all states of a BSCC. Furthermore, for $r_l(\cdot) = 1$ we have

$$\frac{\mathsf{Return}(\mathcal{D}, r_u, s)}{\mathsf{Return}(\mathcal{D}, r_l, s)} = \mathsf{LRA}(\mathcal{D}, r_u, r_l, s),$$

which immediately extends to the general case.

In Sect. 2, we have discussed how state elimination can be used to obtain values for the expected accumulated reward values. For this, we have repeatedly eliminated states so as to bring the PMC of interest into a form in which reward values can be obtained in a trivial way. It is easy to see that the transformations for the expected accumulated rewards also maintains the recurrence rewards. After having handled each state of our model, we have two possible outcomes (Fig. 3).

In the simpler case, the remaining model consists of the initial state $\bar{s}$ with a self-loop with probability one and $r_u = u_{\bar{s}}$, $r_l = l_{\bar{s}}$. In this case, we have $\mathsf{LRA}(\mathcal{D}, r_u, r_l) = \frac{u_{\bar{s}}}{l_{\bar{s}}}$. In the other case, the remaining model consists of the initial state $\bar{s}$ which has a probability of p_i to move to one of the other n remaining states s_i , $i = 1, \ldots, n$, which all have a self-loop with probability one and $r_u(s_i) = u_i$, $r_l(s_i) = l_i$. In this case, we have $\mathsf{LRA}(\mathcal{D}, r_u, r_l) = \sum_{i=1,\ldots,n} p_i\frac{u_i}{l_i}$.

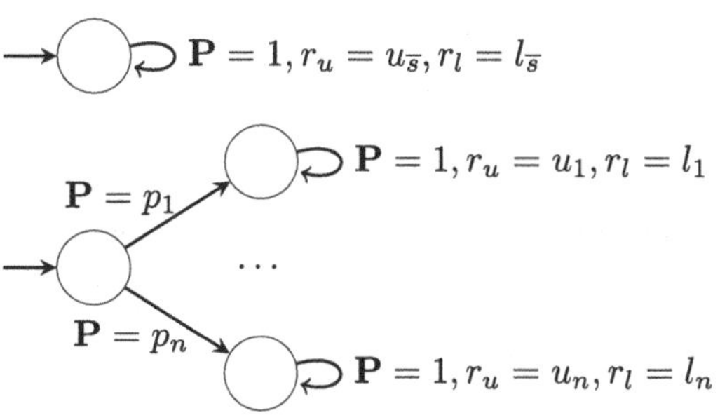

Fig. 3. Computation of long-run average values.

5   Experiments

We now consider four case studies that illustrate the efficiency and scalability of our approach. Three models [21,23,28] are taken from the PRISM benchmark suite[1], and the last is taken from the authors' work on synchronisation protocols [12,13]. All experiments were conducted on a PC with an Intel Core i7-2600 (tm) processor at 3.4 GHz, equipped with 16 GB of RAM, and running Ubuntu 16.04. For each case study we compare the performance times obtained for model analysis when using the parametric engine of the model checker ePMC [17][2], using either polynomial fractions or DAGs to represent the functions corresponding to transition probabilities and state rewards. Basically, the DAG is implemented as an array of 64-bit integers. Functions are represented as indices to this array. 4 bits describe the type of the node. For terminal nodes, the remaining bits denote the parameter or number used. For non-terminal nodes, 2×30 bits are used to refer to the operands within the DAG. We also compare our results to those obtained using the parametric engine of PRISM [26], and the parametric and sampling engines of Storm [8][3].

Given a parametric model, and a set of valuations for its parameters, we are interested in the total time taken to check some property of interest for every valuation for the parameters. Since our primary concern is the efficiency of multiple evaluations of an existing model, we omit model construction times and restrict our analysis to the total time taken for the evaluation of all parameter valuations. For the parametric engines of ePMC, PRISM, and Storm, we record the total time taken for both state elimination and the evaluation of the resulting function for all parameter valuations. For the sparse engine of Storm, we record the total time taken for value iteration, using default settings to determine convergence. For Storm, we set the precision to 10^{-10} rather than the default of 10^{-6}. This had a very minor influence on the runtime, and allowed a better comparison to ePMC, the results of which have a precision of $< 10^{-13}$.

5.1   Crowds Protocol

The Crowds protocol [28] provides anonymity for a crowd consisting of N Internet users, of whom M are dishonest, by hiding their communication via random routing, where there are R different path reformulates. The model is a PMC parametrised by $B = \frac{M}{M+N}$, the probability that a member of the crowd is untrustworthy, and P, the probability that a member sends a package to a randomly selected receiver. With probability $1 - P$ the packet is directly delivered to the receiver. The property of interest is the probability that the untrustworthy members observe the sender more than they observe others.

Table 1 shows the performance statistics for different values of N and R, where each entry shows the total time taken to check all pairwise combinations of

---

[1] http://www.prismmodelchecker.org/benchmarks/.
[2] http://iscasmc.ios.ac.cn/?p=1241, https://github.com/liyi-david/ePMC.
[3] http://www.stormchecker.org/.

Table 1. Performance statistics for crowds protocol.

N	R	States	Trans.	PRISM	ePMC	ePMC(D)	ePMC(DS)	Storm(P)	Storm(S)
5	3	1198	2038	722	737	13	13	681	26
5	5	8653	14953	745	806	15	15	723	64
5	7	37291	65011	818	900	19	17	735	153
10	3	6563	15143	732	771	15	14	690	26
10	5	111294	261444	1146	910	23	16	712	63
10	7	990601	2351961	–T–	–T–	103	42	737	159
15	3	19228	55948	761	825	16	16	703	26
15	5	592060	1754860	–T–	–M–	42	28	709	64
15	7	8968096	26875216	–M–	–M–	–M–	–M–	777	174
20	3	42318	148578	814	805	15	14	709	26
20	5	2061951	7374951	–M–	–M–	108	90	720	67

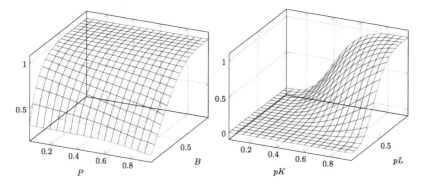

Fig. 4. Upper crowds protocol (L). Bounded retransmission protocol (R).

values for B, P taken from $0.002, 0.004, \ldots, 0.998$. There is a substantial increase in the performance of ePMC when using non-simplified DAGs (ePMC(D)), and using DAGs (ePMC(DS)) simplified by evaluating random points (cf. Sect. 3), instead of polynomial fractions (ePMC) to represent functions. Here, ePMC clearly outperforms the parametric engines of both PRISM and Storm. In some instances, ePMC turns out to be the fastest choice, while the sampling engine of Storm proves to be faster for other instances. Processes that exceeded the time limit of one hour are indicated by –T–, and processes that ran out of memory are indicated by –M–. In Fig. 4 (left) we plot the results for $N = 5$ and $R = 7$.

5.2 Bounded Retransmission Protocol

The bounded retransmission protocol [21] divides a file, which is to be transmitted, into N chunks. For each chunk, there are at most MAX retransmissions over two lossy channels K and L that send data and acknowledgements, respectively. The model is a PMC parametrised by pK and pL, the reliability of the chan-

Table 2. Performance statistics for bounded retransmission protocol.

N	MAX	States	Trans.	PRISM	ePMC	ePMC(D)	ePMC(DS)	Storm(P)	Storm(S)
64	4	4139	5543	1029	1016	36	38	991	160
64	5	4972	6695	1145	1118	36	33	1021	188
256	4	16427	22055	–M–	–M–	48	40	3332	403
256	5	19756	26663	–M–	–M–	35	15	–T–	318
512	4	32811	44071	–M–	–M–	29	19	–T–	491
512	5	39468	53287	–M–	–M–	28	23	–T–	596

nels. We are interested in the probability that the sender reports an unsuccessful transmission after more than 8 chunks have been sent successfully.

The performance statistics for different values of N and MAX are shown in Table 2, where each entry shows the total time taken to check all pairwise combinations of values for pK, pL taken from $0.002, 0.004, \ldots, 0.998$. Here, ePMC with DAGs again has the best performance: the running time remains approximately constant when using this data structure, even for much larger problem instances. In contrast, the running time for both engines of Storm scale linearly. Both the parametric engine of PRISM and ePMC with polynomial fraction representation, run out of memory for all larger problem instances.

Figure 4 (right) plots the results obtained for $N = 256$ and $MAX = 4$. As we see the probability of interest first increases with increasing channel reliability, but then decreases again. The reason is that, on the one hand, if the channel reliability is low, then we do not send many chunks successfully. On the other hand, if the channel reliability is high, then it is unlikely that the transmission will fail in the end.

5.3   Cyclic Polling Server

This cyclic server polling model [23] is a model of a network, described as a continuous-time Markov chain. There are two parameters, μ and γ. The model consists of one server and N clients. When a client is idle, then a new job arrives at this client with a rate of μ/N. The server 'polls' the clients in a cyclic manner. At each point of time, it observes a single client. If there is a job waiting for a given client, the server servers its job (provided there is one) with a rate of μ. When the client it observes is idle, then the server moves on to observe the next client with a rate of γ. Even though our method targets discrete-time models, we can handle this model by computing the embedded DTMC.

In this case study, we consider the probability that, in the long run, Station 1 is idle. That is, the expected limit average of the time that Station 1, or, due to symmetry, any other station, is idle. We compute this long-run average value using the method described in Sect. 4. Probabilities are displayed as a function of the parameters in Fig. 5, and Table 3 shows how the various tools perform on this benchmark. With increasing γ the likelihood that Station 1 is idle increases: if we increase γ, then the server will more quickly find stations to be served. As

Table 3. Performance statistics for cyclic polling server.

N	States	Trans.	PRISM	ePMC	ePMC(D)	ePMC(DS)	Storm(P)	Storm(S)
4	96	272	1166	888	14	14	953	50
5	240	800	–T–	–T–	28	25	–T–	121
6	576	2208	3550	–T–	108	102	–T–	305
7	1344	5824	1399	–T–	759	736	–T–	801
8	3072	14848	1052	–T–	–T–	–T–	–T–	1991
9	6912	36864	–T–	–T–	–M–	–M–	–T–	–T–

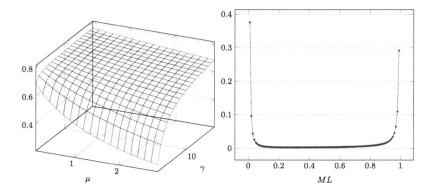

Fig. 5. Cyclic polling server (L). Synchronisation model (R).

the long-run average idle time only depends on the rate between μ and γ, the likelihood that Station 1 is idle falls with increasing μ.

For the current configuration, classic parametric model checking does not seem to be advantageous. Using our DAG-based implementation, however, is much more efficient than classic parametric model checking, but it is space consuming. With the chosen number of parameter instantiations, our method does not quite compete with non-parametric model checking.

5.4 Oscillator Synchronisation

The models of [12,13] encode the behaviour of a population of N coupled nodes in a network. Each node has a clock that progresses, cyclically, through a range of discrete values $1, \ldots, T$. At the end of each clock cycle a node transmits a message to other nodes in the network. Nodes that receive this message adjust their clocks to more closely match those of the firing node. The model is a PMC, parametrised by the likelihood ML that a firing message is lost in the communication medium. The property of interest is the expected power consumption of the network (in Watt-hours) to reach a state, where the clocks of all nodes are synchronised.

Table 4. Performance statistics for synchronisation model.

N	T	States	Trans.	PRISM	ePMC	ePMC(D)	ePMC(DS)	Storm(P)	Storm(S)
4	6	218	508	280	304	6	4	6	20
4	7	351	822	302	399	7	4	6	28
4	8	535	1257	542	1520	9	5	13	37
5	6	449	1179	354	499	10	5	11	39
5	7	799	2094	1694	–T–	11	6	34	60
5	8	1333	3533	–T–	–T–	17	8	137	90
6	6	841	2491	1070	–T–	12	7	48	74
6	7	1639	4820	–T–	–T–	19	8	239	130
6	8	2971	8871	–T–	–T–	33	10	2311	211

Table 4 shows the results for different values of N and T, where each entry shows the total time taken to check all values of ML taken from $10^{-5}, 2 \cdot 10^{-5}, \ldots, 1 - 10^{-5}$.

Figure 5 (right) plots the results obtained for $N = 6$ and $T = 8$. For extremal values of ML, the network is expected to use much more energy to synchronise, because the expected time required for this to occur increases. Very high values of ML result in nearly all firing messages being lost, and hence nodes cannot communicate well enough to coordinate, while very low values of ML lead to perpetually asynchronous states for the network, an artefact of the discreteness of the clock values [12].

In this case study, the DAG-based method, in particular with random points evaluation, performs best, followed by the sampling-based method of Storm. We note that the time required for each value iteration is relatively high, while the cost of evaluating a point for the DAG-based method is quite low. Therefore, the advantage of our approach would have been even more pronounced, if we had evaluated more instantiations in the experiments above. The method of choice thus depends mostly on whether such a high number of instantiations is required.

We have performed value iteration with a (local) precision of 10^{-10} for Storm. This does, however, not guarantee any global precision [1]. Obtaining guaranteed results using value iteration is relatively expensive while, as discussed in Sect. 3, extending our approach to obtain conservative guarantees is relatively simple—and inexpensive—to achieve by using basic interval arithmetic.

5.5   Heuristics

An important consideration when performing state elimination is the order, in which different states are eliminated from the graph. Using different elimination orders to evaluate the same model can result in functions, whose representations (nominator-denominator or DAGs) vary greatly in size, and hence also in the corresponding memory footprint and analysis time. Heuristics for efficient

Table 5. Performance statistics for different heuristics.

Model		Elimination Heuristic					
		NumNew	MinProd	TargetBFS	Random	BFS	ReverseBFS
Crowds	$(N = 10,\ R = 5)$	19	103	5	14	22	6
BRP	$(N = 512,\ MAX = 5)$	4	11	4	–M–	5	4
Cyclic	$(N = 7)$	7	9	8	8	8	8
Synch	$(N = 6, T = 8)$	18	18	17	19	18	17

state elimination have been studied in automata theory, to obtain shorter regular expressions from finite-state automata [18,19], and in graph theory, for efficient peeling of a probabilistic network [20]. We employ the following heuristics, consisting of both existing schemes taken from the literature, and novel schemes that prove to be effective for some models.

- NumNew: each state is weighted by the number of new transitions that are introduced to the model when that state is eliminated. That is, we consider each predecessor-successor pair for that state, and add one to the weight if the transition from the predecessor to the successor was not already defined in the underlying graph before state elimination. States with the lowest weight are eliminated first. The aim here is to minimise the total number of transitions as elimination progresses.
- MinProd: similarly to NumNew, we consider each predecessor-successor pair. However, one is added to the weight irrespective of whether that transition already existed in the underlying graph. Again states with the lowest weight are considered first.
- TargetBFS: states are eliminated in the order in which they are discovered when conducting a breadth-first search backwards from the target states.
- Random: a state is selected uniformly at random for elimination from the set of remaining states.
- BFS: states are eliminated in the order in which they are discovered when conducting a breadth-first search from the initial state(s) of the model.
- ReverseBFS: similar to BFS, except states are eliminated in reverse order.

In Table 5, we compare the different heuristics described. We have applied each of them for each considered model, and provide the time in seconds required for medium-sized instances. As seen, it turns out that TargetBFS is in general a good choice. In one case, however, NumNew turns out to be faster.

6   Conclusion and Future Work

We have implemented an approach for the evaluation of parametric Markov chains that exploits the synergies of using DAGs in a state-elimination based analysis and using DAGs in an encoding of rational functions as arithmetic circuits. Our experimental evaluation suggests that these two approaches integrated so seamlessly that they often sprovide a notable speedup. The nicest observation is that this seems so natural in hindsight that it is almost more surprising that this has not been attempted before than that it works so well. We therefore hope to have discovered one of these simple and natural approaches that will stand the test of time.

The next step in exploiting our approach could be an integration into applications. One of the applications we have in mind is to use it in the context of parameter extraction, which we expect to work similar to Model extraction, for online Model checking. The growing knowledge of the model can be used to refine or adjust the parameters in this application. Our application can help to provide the speed required to make the approach scale, and to keep the analysis and, if required, the visualisation[4] of the effect of the learnt parameters (and the confidence area around them) efficient.

We also note that interval arithmetic could be used to evaluate *boxes*— hyperrectangles $[a_1, b_1] \times \cdots [a_n, b_n]$ of parameter ranges—so as to obtain bounds on the lower and upper values taken by any occurring function value in the box. This approach could be used instead of using SMT solvers (as in [7,14]) to decide PCTL properties. A similar approach to avoid using SMT solvers has been proposed [27], which is however not based on computing a function depending on the parameters but on value iteration. We assume that the DAG-based approach will perform better when a high coverage of the parameter space is required.

It would also be straightforward to parallelise evaluation of points using SIMD approaches such as GPGPU.

References

1. Baier, C., Klein, J., Leuschner, L., Parker, D., Wunderlich, S.: Ensuring the reliability of your model checker: interval iteration for Markov decision processes. In: Majumdar, R., Kunčak, V. (eds.) CAV 2017. LNCS, vol. 10426, pp. 160–180. Springer, Cham (2017). https://doi.org/10.1007/978-3-319-63387-9_8
2. Bloem, R., et al.: Synthesizing robust systems. Acta Inf. **51**(3–4), 193–220 (2014)
3. Calinescu, R., Ghezzi, C., Kwiatkowska, M., Mirandola, R.: Self-adaptive software needs quantitative verification at runtime. CACM **55**(9), 69–77 (2012)
4. Cox, D.R.: Renewal Theory. Methuen & Co., Ltd, London (1967)
5. Cubuktepe, M., et al.: Sequential convex programming for the efficient verification of parametric MDPs. In: Legay, A., Margaria, T. (eds.) TACAS 2017. LNCS, vol. 10206, pp. 133–150. Springer, Heidelberg (2017). https://doi.org/10.1007/978-3-662-54580-5_8
6. Daws, C.: Symbolic and parametric model checking of discrete-time Markov chains. In: Liu, Z., Araki, K. (eds.) ICTAC 2004. LNCS, vol. 3407, pp. 280–294. Springer, Heidelberg (2005). https://doi.org/10.1007/978-3-540-31862-0_21
7. Jovanović, A., Kwiatkowska, M.: Parameter synthesis for probabilistic timed automata using stochastic game abstractions. In: Ouaknine, J., Potapov, I., Worrell, J. (eds.) RP 2014. LNCS, vol. 8762, pp. 176–189. Springer, Cham (2014). https://doi.org/10.1007/978-3-319-11439-2_14

---

[4] We obtain the probablities and expected rewards as functions of the parameters. This can be visualised, just as we have visualised this in Sect. 5.

8. Dehnert, C., Junges, S., Katoen, J.-P., Volk, M.: A storm is coming: a modern probabilistic model checker. In: Majumdar, R., Kunčak, V. (eds.) CAV 2017. LNCS, vol. 10427, pp. 592–600. Springer, Cham (2017). https://doi.org/10.1007/978-3-319-63390-9_31

9. DeMillo, R.A., Lipton, R.J.: A probabilistic remark on algebraic program testing. Inf. Process. Lett. **7**, 193–195 (1978)

10. von Essen, C., Jobstmann, B.: Synthesizing systems with optimal average-case behavior for ratio objectives. In: iWIGP, pp. 17–32 (2011)

11. Filieri, A., Ghezzi, C., Tamburrelli, G.: Run-time efficient probabilistic model checking. In: ICSE, pp. 341–350. ACM (2011)

12. Gainer, P., Linker, S., Dixon, C., Hustadt, U., Fisher, M.: Investigating parametric influence on discrete synchronisation protocols using quantitative model checking. In: Bertrand, N., Bortolussi, L. (eds.) QEST 2017. LNCS, vol. 10503, pp. 224–239. Springer, Cham (2017). https://doi.org/10.1007/978-3-319-66335-7_14

13. Gainer, P., Linker, S., Dixon, C., Hustadt, U., Fisher, M.: The power of synchronisation: formal analysis of power consumption in networks of pulse-coupled oscillators. arXiv preprint arXiv:1709.04385 (2017)

14. Hahn, E.M., Han, T., Zhang, L.: Synthesis for PCTL in parametric Markov decision processes. In: Bobaru, M., Havelund, K., Holzmann, G.J., Joshi, R. (eds.) NFM 2011. LNCS, vol. 6617, pp. 146–161. Springer, Heidelberg (2011). https://doi.org/10.1007/978-3-642-20398-5_12

15. Hahn, E.M., Hermanns, H., Wachter, B., Zhang, L.: PARAM: a model checker for parametric Markov models. In: Touili, T., Cook, B., Jackson, P. (eds.) CAV 2010. LNCS, vol. 6174, pp. 660–664. Springer, Heidelberg (2010). https://doi.org/10.1007/978-3-642-14295-6_56

16. Hahn, E.M., Hermanns, H., Zhang, L.: Probabilistic reachability for parametric Markov models. STTT **13**(1), 3–19 (2011)

17. Hahn, E.M., Li, Y., Schewe, S., Turrini, A., Zhang, L.: ISCASMC: a web-based probabilistic model checker. In: Jones, C., Pihlajasaari, P., Sun, J. (eds.) FM 2014. LNCS, vol. 8442, pp. 312–317. Springer, Cham (2014). https://doi.org/10.1007/978-3-319-06410-9_22

18. Han, Y.S.: State elimination heuristics for short regular expressions. FI **128**(4), 445–462 (2013)

19. Han, Y.S., Wood, D.: Obtaining shorter regular expressions from finite-state automata. TCS **370**(1–3), 110–120 (2007)

20. Harbron, C.: Heuristic algorithms for finding inexpensive elimination schemes. SC **5**(4), 275–287 (1995)

21. Helmink, L., Sellink, M.P.A., Vaandrager, F.W.: Proof-checking a data link protocol. In: TYPES, pp. 127–165. Springer, Berlin (1993)

22. Hopcroft, J.E.: Introduction to Automata Theory, Languages, and Computation. Pearson Education India (2008)

23. Ibe, O.C., Trivedi, K.S.: Stochastic Petri net models of polling systems. J-SAC **8**(9), 1649–1657 (1990)

24. Knuth, D., Yao, A.: The complexity of nonuniform random number generation. Algorithms and Complexity: New Directions and Recent Results. Academic Press, Orlando (1976)

25. Kwiatkowska, M., Norman, G., Parker, D.: Stochastic model checking. In: Bernardo, M., Hillston, J. (eds.) SFM 2007. LNCS, vol. 4486, pp. 220–270. Springer, Heidelberg (2007). https://doi.org/10.1007/978-3-540-72522-0_6

26. Kwiatkowska, M., Norman, G., Parker, D.: PRISM 4.0: verification of probabilistic real-time systems. In: Gopalakrishnan, G., Qadeer, S. (eds.) CAV 2011. LNCS, vol. 6806, pp. 585–591. Springer, Heidelberg (2011). https://doi.org/10.1007/978-3-642-22110-1_47

27. Quatmann, T., Dehnert, C., Jansen, N., Junges, S., Katoen, J.-P.: Parameter synthesis for Markov models: faster than ever. In: Artho, C., Legay, A., Peled, D. (eds.) ATVA 2016. LNCS, vol. 9938, pp. 50–67. Springer, Cham (2016). https://doi.org/10.1007/978-3-319-46520-3_4

28. Reiter, M.K., Rubin, A.D.: Crowds: anonymity for web transactions. TISSEC **1**(1), 66–92 (1998)

29. Schwartz, J.T.: Fast probabilistic algorithms for verification of polynomial identities. J. ACM **27**(4), 701–717 (1980)

30. Zippel, R.: Probabilistic algorithms for sparse polynomials. In: Ng, E.W. (ed.) Symbolic and Algebraic Computation. LNCS, vol. 72, pp. 216–226. Springer, Heidelberg (1979). https://doi.org/10.1007/3-540-09519-5_73

Continuous-Time Markov Decisions Based on Partial Exploration

Pranav Ashok[1], Yuliya Butkova[2], Holger Hermanns[2], and Jan Křetínský[1(✉)]

[1] Technical University of Munich, Munich, Germany
{ashok,jan.kretinsky}@in.tum.de
[2] Saarland University, Saarbrücken, Germany
{butkova,hermanns}@cs.uni-saarland.de

Abstract. We provide a framework for speeding up algorithms for time-bounded reachability analysis of continuous-time Markov decision processes. The principle is to find a small, but almost equivalent *subsystem* of the original system and only analyse the subsystem. Candidates for the subsystem are identified through simulations and iteratively enlarged until runs are represented in the subsystem with high enough probability. The framework is thus dual to that of abstraction refinement. We instantiate the framework in several ways with several traditional algorithms and experimentally confirm orders-of-magnitude speed ups in many cases.

1 Introduction

Continuous-time Markov decision processes (CTMDP) [Ber95, Sen99, Fei04] are the natural real-time extension of (discrete-time) Markov decision processes (MDP). They can likewise be viewed as non-deterministic extensions of continuous-time Markov chains (CTMC). As such, CTMDP feature probabilistic and non-deterministic behaviour as well as random time delays governed by exponential probability distributions. Prominent application areas of CTMDP include operations research [BDF81, Fei04], power management and scheduling [QQP01], networked, distributed systems [HHK00, GGL03], as well as epidemic and population processes [Lef81]. Moreover, CTMDPs are the core semantic model underlying formalisms such as generalised stochastic Petri nets, Markovian stochastic activity networks, and interactive Markov chains [EHKZ13].

A large variety of properties can be expressed using logics such as CSL [ASSB96]. Apart from classical techniques from the MDP context, the analysis of such properties relies fundamentally on the problem of time-bounded

This research was supported in part by Deutsche Forschungsgemeinschaft (DFG) through the TUM International Graduate School of Science and Engineering (IGSSE) project 10.06 *PARSEC*, the ERC through Advanced Grant 695614 (POWVER), the Czech Science Foundation grant No. 18-11193S, and the DFG project 383882557 *Statistical Unbounded Verification*.

ⓒ Springer Nature Switzerland AG 2018
S. K. Lahiri and C. Wang (Eds.): ATVA 2018, LNCS 11138, pp. 317–334, 2018.
https://doi.org/10.1007/978-3-030-01090-4_19

reachability (TBR), i.e. *what is the maximal/minimal probability to reach a given state within a given time bound.* Since this is the cornerstone of the analysis, a manifold of algorithms have been proposed for TBR [BHHK04,BFK+09,NZ10, FRSZ11,BS11,HH13,BHHK15]. While the algorithmic approaches are diverse, relying on uniformisation and various forms of discretization, they are mostly back-propagating the values computed, i.e. in the form of value iteration.

Not surprisingly, all these algorithms naturally process the state space of the CTMDP in its entirety. In this work we instead suggest a framework that enables TBR analysis with guaranteed precision while often exploring only a small, property-dependent part of the state space. Similar ideas have appeared for (discrete-time) MDPs and unbounded reachability [BCC+14] or mean payoff [ACD+17]. These techniques are based on *asynchronous* value-iteration approaches, originally proposed in the probabilistic planning world, such as bounded real-time dynamic programming (BRTDP) [MLG05]. Intuitively, the back-propagation of values (value iteration steps) are not performed on all states in each iteration (synchronously), but always only the "interesting" ones are considered (asynchronously); in order to bound the error in this approach, one needs to compute both an under- and an over-approximation of the actual value.

In other words, the main idea is to keep track of (under- and over-)approximation of the value when accepting that we have no information about the values attained in certain states. Yet if we can determine that these states are reached with very low probability, their effect on the actual value is provably negligible and thus the lack of knowledge only slightly increases the difference between the under- and over-approximations. To achieve this effect, the algorithm of [BCC+14] alternates between two steps: (i) simulating a run of the MDP using a (hopefully good) scheduler, and (ii) performing the standard value iteration steps on the states visited by this run.

It turns out that this idea cannot be transferred to the continuous-time setting easily. In technical terms, the main issue is that the value iteration in this context takes the form of synchronous back-propagation, which when implemented in an asynchronous fashion results in memory requirements that tend to dominate the memory savings expectable due to partial exploration.

Therefore, we twist the above approach and present a yet simpler algorithmic strategy in this paper. Namely, our approach alternates between several simulation steps, and a subsequent run of TBR analysis only focussed on the already explored subsystem, instead of the entire state space. If the distance between under- and over-approximating values is small enough, we can terminate; otherwise, running more simulations extends the considered state subspace, thereby improving the precision in the next round. If the underlying TBR analysis provides an optimal scheduler along with the value of time-bounded reachability, then our solution as well provides the optimal scheduler for the TBR problem on the given CTMDP.

There are thus two largely independent components to the framework, namely (i) a heuristic how to explore the system via simulation, and (ii) an algorithm to solve time-bounded reachability on CTMDP. The latter is here instantiated with some of the classic algorithms mentioned above, namely the first discretization-based algorithm [NZ10] and the two most competitive improvements over it [BS11,BHHK15], based on uniformisation and untimed analysis. The former basically boils down to constructing a scheduler resolving the nondeterminism effectively. We instantiate this exploration heuristics in two ways. Firstly, we consider a scheduler returned by the most recent run of the respective TBR algorithm, assuming this to yield a close-to-optimal scheduler, so as to visit the most important parts of the state space, relative to the property in question. Secondly, since this scheduler may not be available when working with TBR algorithms that return only the value, we also employ a scheduler resolving choices uniformly. Although the latter may look very straightforward, it turns out to already speed up the original algorithm considerably in many cases. This is rooted in the fact that that scheduler best represents the available knowledge, since the uniform distribution is the one with maximimal entropy.

Depending on the model and the property under study, different ratios of the state space entirety need to be explored to achieve the desired precision. Furthermore, our approach is able to exploit that the reachability objective is of certain forms, in stark contrast to the classic algorithm that needs to perform the same computation irrespective of the concrete set of target states. Still, the approach we propose will naturally profit from future improvements in effectiveness of classic TBR analysis.

We summarize our contribution as follows:

- We introduce a framework to speed up TBR algorithms for CTMDP and instantiate it in several ways. It is based on a partial, simulation-based exploration of the state space spanned by a model.
- We demonstrate its effectiveness in combination with several classic algorithms, obtaining orders of magnitude speed ups in many experiments. We also illustrate the limitations of this approach on cases where the state space needs to be explored almost in its entirety.
- We conclude that our framework is a generic add-on to arbitrary TBR algorithms, often saving considerably more work than introduced by its overhead.

2 Preliminaries

In this section, we introduce some central notions. A *probability distribution* on a finite set X is a mapping $\rho : X \rightarrow [0, 1]$, such that $\sum_{x \in X} \rho(x) = 1$. $\mathcal{D}(X)$ denotes the set of all probability distributions on X.

Definition 1. *A* continuous-time Markov decision process *(CTMDP) is a tuple* $\mathcal{M} = (s_{init}, S, Act, \mathbf{R}, G)$ *where* S *is a finite set of* states, s_{init} *is the initial state,* Act *is a finite set of* actions, $\mathbf{R} : S \times Act \times S \rightarrow \mathbb{R}_{\geq 0}$ *is a rate matrix and* $G \subseteq S$ *is a set of* goal *states.*

For a state $s \in S$ we define the set of *enabled actions* $Act(s)$ as follows: $Act(s) = \{\alpha \in Act \mid \exists s' \in S : \mathbf{R}(s, \alpha, s') > 0\}$. States s' for which $\mathbf{R}(s, \alpha, s') > 0$

form the set of *successor states of s via* α, denoted as $\mathrm{Succ}(s, \alpha)$. W.l.o.g.
we require that all sets $\mathrm{Act}(s)$ and $\mathrm{Succ}(s, \alpha)$ are non-empty. A state s, s.t.
$\forall \alpha \in \mathrm{Act}(s) : \mathrm{Succ}(s, \alpha) = \{s\}$ is called *absorbing*.

For a given state s and action $\alpha \in \mathrm{Act}(s)$, we denote by $\lambda(s, \alpha) = \sum_{s'} \mathbf{R}(s, \alpha, s')$ the *exit rate* of α in s and $\Delta(s, \alpha, s') = \mathbf{R}(s, \alpha, s')/\lambda(s, \alpha)$.

An example CTMDP is depicted in Fig. 1a. Here states are depicted in circles
and are labelled with numbers from 0 to 5. The goal state G is marked with a
double circle. Dashed transitions represent available actions, e.g. state 1 has two
enabled actions α and β. A solid transition labelled with a number denotes the
rate, e.g. $\mathbf{R}(1, \beta, G) = 1.1$, therefore there is a solid transition from state 1 via
action β to state G with rate 1.1. If there is only one enabled action for a state,
we only show the rates of the transition via this action and omit the action itself.
For example, state 0 has only 1 enabled action (lets say α) and therefore it only
has outgoing solid transition with rate $1.1 = \mathbf{R}(0, \alpha, 1)$.

The system starts in the initial state $s_0 = s_{\mathrm{init}}$.
While being in a state s_0, the system picks an action
$\alpha_0 \in \mathrm{Act}(s)$. When an action is picked the CTMDP
resides in s_0 for the amount of time t_0 which is sampled from exponential distribution with parameter
$\lambda(s_0, \alpha_0)$. Later in this paper we refer to this as
residence time in a state. After t_0 time units the
system transitions into one of the successor states
$s_1 \in \mathrm{Succ}(s_0, \alpha_0)$ selected randomly with distribution $\Delta(s_0, \alpha_0, \cdot)$. After this transition the process
is repeated from state s_1 forming an *infinite path*
$\rho = s_0 \xrightarrow{\alpha_0, t_0} s_1 \xrightarrow{\alpha_1, t_1} s_2 \ldots$. A finite prefix of an infinite path is called a *(finite) path*. We will use $\rho\!\downarrow$
to denote the last state of a finite path ρ. We will
denote the set of all finite paths in a CTMDP with
$Paths^*$, and the set of all infinite paths with $Paths$.

CTMDPs pick actions with the help of *sched-*
ulers. A scheduler is a measurable[1] function π :

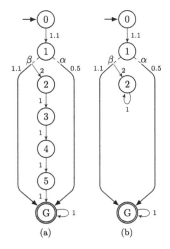

Fig. 1. Example CTMDPs.

$Paths^* \times \mathbb{R}_{\geqslant 0} \to \mathcal{D}(\mathrm{Act})$ such that $\pi(\rho, t) \in \mathrm{Act}(\rho\!\downarrow)$. Being in a state s at
time point t the CTMDP samples an action from $\pi(\rho, t)$, where ρ is the path
that the system took to arrive in s. We denote the set of all schedulers with Π.

Fixing a scheduler π in a CTMDP $\mathcal{M}$, the unique probability measure $\mathrm{Pr}_\pi^{\mathcal{M}}$
over the space of all infinite paths can be obtained [Neu10], denoted also by Pr_π
when $\mathcal{M}$ is clear from context.

Optimal Time-Bounded Reachability
Let $\mathcal{M} = (s_{\mathrm{init}}, S, \mathrm{Act}, \mathbf{R}, G)$ be a CTMDP, $s \in S$, $T \in \mathbb{R}_{\geqslant 0}$ a time bound, and
$\mathrm{opt} \in \{\sup, \inf\}$. The *optimal (time-bounded) reachability probability* (or *value*)
of state s in $\mathcal{M}$ is defined as follows:

$$\mathrm{val}_{\mathcal{M}}^s(T) := \mathrm{opt}_{\pi \in \Pi} \, \mathrm{Pr}_\pi^{\mathcal{M}} \left[\Diamond^{\leqslant T} G \right],$$

---

[1] Measurable with respect to the standard σ-algebra on the set of paths [NZ10].

where $\Diamond^{\leq T} G = \{s_0 \xrightarrow{\alpha_0, t_0} s_1 \xrightarrow{\alpha_1, t_1} s_2 \ldots \mid s_0 = s \wedge \exists i : s_i \in G \wedge \sum_{j=0}^{i-1} t_j \leq T\}$ is
the set of paths starting from s and reaching G before T.

The *optimal (time-bounded) reachability probability* (or *value*) of $\mathcal{M}$ is
defined as $\mathrm{val}_{\mathcal{M}}(T) = \mathrm{val}_{\mathcal{M}}^{s_{\mathrm{init}}}(T)$. A scheduler that achieves optimum for
$\mathrm{val}_{\mathcal{M}}(T)$ is the *optimal scheduler*. A scheduler that achieves value v, such that
$||v - \mathrm{val}_{\mathcal{M}}(T)||_{\infty} < \varepsilon$ is called ε-*optimal*.

3   Algorithm

In this work we target CTMDPs that have large state spaces, but only a small
subset of those states is actually contributing significantly to the reachability
probability.

Consider, for example, the *polling system*
represented schematically in Fig. 2. Here two
stations store continuously arriving tasks in a
queue. Tasks are to be processed by a server. If
the task is processed successfully it is removed
from the queue, otherwise it is returned back
into the queue. State space of the CTMDP
$\mathcal{M}$ modelling this polling system is a tuple
(q_1, q_2, s), where q_i is the amount of tasks in
queue i and s is a state of the server (could be
e. g. *processing task*, *awaiting task*, etc.).

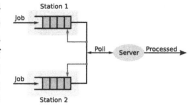

Fig. 2. Schematic representation
of polling system

One of the possible questions could be, for example, *what is the maximum
probability of both queues to be full after a certain time point*. This corresponds to
goal states being of the form (N, N, s), where N is the maximal queue capacity
and s – any state of the server. Given that both queues are initially empty, all
the paths reaching goal states have to visit states $(q_1, q_2, \cdot)$, where $q_i = [0..N]$.
However, for similar questions, for example, *what is the maximum probability
of the first queue to be full after a certain time point*, the situation changes.
Here goal states are of the form (N, q_2, s), where $q_2 = 0..N$ and s – any state
of the server. The scheduler that only extracts tasks from the second queue is
the fastest to fill the first one and is therefore the optimal one. The set of states
that are most likely visited when following this scheduler are those states where
the size of the second queue is small. This naturally depends on the rates of
task arrival and processing. Assuming that the size of the queue rarely exceeds
2 tasks, all the states $(\cdot, q_2, \cdot)$, where $q_2 = 3..N$ do not affect the reachability
probability too much.

As a more concrete example, consider the CTMDP of Fig. 1a. Here all the
states in the center have exit rate 1 and form a long chain. Due to the length of
this chain the probability to reach the goal state via these states within time 2
is very small. In fact, the maximum probability to reach the target state within
2 time units in the CTMDP on the left and the one on the right are exactly the
same and equal 0.4584. Thus, on this CTMDP, 40% of the state space can be
reduced without any effect on the reachability value.

Classical model checking algorithms do not take into account any information about the property and perform exhaustive state-space exploration. Given that only a subset of states is relevant to the reachability value, these algorithms may perform many unnecessary computations.

Our Solution

Throughout this section we work with a CTMDP $\mathcal{M} = (s_{\text{init}}, S, \text{Act}, \mathbf{R}, G)$ and a time bound $T \in \mathbb{R}_{\geq 0}$.

The main contribution of this paper is a simple framework for solving the time-bounded reachability objective in CTMDPs without considering their whole state-space. This framework in presented in Algorithm 1. The algorithm involves the following major steps:

Algorithm 1 SUBSPACETBR

Input: CTMDP $\mathcal{M} = (s_{\text{init}}, S, \text{Act}, \mathbf{R}, G)$, time bound T, precision ε
Output: $(\ell, u) \in [0, 1]^2$ such that $\ell \leqslant \text{val}(T) \leqslant u$ and $u - \ell < \varepsilon$ and
$\qquad \varepsilon-$ optimal scheduler π for $\text{val}_{\mathcal{M}}(T)$

1: **if** $s_{\text{init}} \in G$ **then return** $(1, 1)$, and an arbitrary scheduler $\pi \in \Pi$
2: $\ell = 0, u = 1$
3: $\pi_{\text{sim}} = \pi_{\text{uniform}}$
4: $S' = \{s_{\text{init}}\}$
5: **while** $u - \ell \geqslant \varepsilon$ **do**
6: $\qquad S' = S' \cup \text{GETRELEVANTSUBSET}(\mathcal{M}, T, \pi_{\text{sim}})$
7: $\qquad \underline{\mathcal{M}} = \text{lower}(\mathcal{M}, S'), \overline{\mathcal{M}} = \text{upper}(\mathcal{M}, S')$
8: $\qquad \ell = \text{val}_{\underline{\mathcal{M}}}(T), u = \text{val}_{\overline{\mathcal{M}}}(T)$
9: $\qquad \overline{\pi}_{\text{opt}} \leftarrow$ optimal scheduler for $\text{val}_{\overline{\mathcal{M}}}(T)$, $\underline{\pi}_{\text{opt}} \leftarrow$ optimal scheduler for $\text{val}_{\underline{\mathcal{M}}}(T)$
10: $\qquad \pi_{\text{sim}} = \text{CHOOSESCHEDULER}(\pi_{\text{uniform}}, \overline{\pi}_{\text{opt}})$ // choose a scheduler for simulations
11: $\forall t \in [0, T], \forall s \in S' : \pi(s, t) = \overline{\pi}_{\text{opt}}(s, t)$
12: $\forall t \in [0, T], \forall s \in S \setminus S' : \pi(s, t) \leftarrow$ any $\alpha \in \text{Act}(s)$ // extend optimal scheduler to S
13: **return** $(\ell, u), \pi$

Step 1 A "relevant subset" of the state-space $S' \subseteq S$ is computed (line 6).
Step 2 Using this subset, CTMDPs $\underline{\mathcal{M}}$ and $\overline{\mathcal{M}}$ are constructed (line 7). We define functions $\text{upper}(\mathcal{M}, S')$ and $\text{lower}(\mathcal{M}, S')$ later in this section.
Step 3 The reachability values of $\underline{\mathcal{M}}$ and $\overline{\mathcal{M}}$ are under- and over-approximations of the reachability value $\text{val}_{\mathcal{M}}(T)$. The values are computed in line 8 along with the optimal schedulers in line 9.
Step 4 Scheduler π_{sim}, used for obtaining the relevant subset, is selected at line 10.
Step 5 If the two approximations are sufficiently close, i.e. $\text{val}_{\overline{\mathcal{M}}}(T) - \text{val}_{\underline{\mathcal{M}}}(T) < \varepsilon$, $\left[\text{val}_{\underline{\mathcal{M}}}(T), \text{val}_{\overline{\mathcal{M}}}(T)\right]$ is the interval in which the actual reachability value lies. The algorithm is stopped and this interval along with the ε-optimal scheduler are returned. If not, the algorithm repeats from line 6, growing the relevant subset in each iteration.

Algorithm 2 GetRelevantSubset$(\mathcal{M}, T, \pi_{\mathtt{sim}})$

Input: CTMDP $\mathcal{M} = (s_{\mathrm{init}}, S, \mathrm{Act}, \mathbf{R}, G)$, time bound T, a scheduler $\pi_{\mathtt{sim}}$
Parameters: $n_{\mathrm{sim}} \in \mathbb{N}$
Output: $S' \subseteq S$

1: **for** $(i = 0;\ i < n_{\mathrm{sim}};\ i = i + 1)$ **do**
2:     $\rho = s_{\mathrm{init}},\ t = 0$
3:     **while** $t < T$ **and** $\rho{\downarrow} \notin G$ **do**
4:         $s = \rho{\downarrow}$
5:         Sample action α from distribution $\mathcal{D}(\mathrm{Act}(s)) = \pi_{\mathtt{sim}}(\rho, 0)$
6:         Sample t' from exponential distribution with parameter $\lambda(s, \alpha)$
7:         Sample a successor s' of s with distribution $\Delta(s, \alpha, \cdot)$.
8:         $\rho = \rho \xrightarrow{t'} s',\ t = t + t'$
9:     add all states of ρ to S'

In the following section, we elucidate these steps and discuss several instantiations and variations of this framework.

3.1   Step 1: Obtaining the Relevant Subset

The main challenge of the approach is to extract a relatively small *representative* set $S' \subseteq S$, for which $\mathrm{val}_{\overline{\mathcal{M}}}(T)$ and $\mathrm{val}_{\underline{\mathcal{M}}}(T)$ are close to the value $\mathrm{val}_{\mathcal{M}}(T)$ of the original model. If this is possible, then instead of computing the probability of reaching goal in $\mathcal{M}$, we can compute the same in $\overline{\mathcal{M}}$ and $\underline{\mathcal{M}}$ to get an ε-width interval in which the actual value is guaranteed to lie. If the sizes of $\overline{\mathcal{M}}$ and $\underline{\mathcal{M}}$ are relatively small, then the computation is generally much faster.

In this work we propose a heuristics for selecting the relevant subset based on simulations. Simulation of continuous-time Markov chains (CTMDPs with singleton set $\mathrm{Act}(s)$ for all states) is a widely used approach that performs very well in many practical cases. It is based on sampling a path of the model according to its probability space. Namely, upon entering a state s the residence time is sampled from the exponential distribution and then the successor state s' is sampled randomly from the distribution $\Delta(s, \alpha, s')$. Here α is the only action available in state s. The process is repeated from state s' until a goal state is reached or the cumulative time over this path exceeds the time-bound.

However this approach only works for fully stochastic processes, which is not the case for arbitrary CTMDPs due to the presence of multiple available actions. In order to make the process fully stochastic one has to fix a scheduler that decides which actions are to be selected during the run of a CTMDP.

Our heuristic is presented in Algorithm 2. It takes as input the CTMDP, time bound and a scheduler $\pi_{\mathtt{sim}}$. The algorithms performs n_{sim} simulations and outputs all the states visited during the execution. Here $n_{\mathrm{sim}} \in \mathbb{N}$ is a parameter of the algorithm. Each simulation run starts in the initial state. At first an action is sampled from $\mathcal{D}(\mathrm{Act}(s)) = \pi_{\mathtt{sim}}(\rho, 0)$ and then the simulation proceeds in the same way as described above for CTMCs by sampling residence times and successor states. Notice that even though time-point 0 is used for the scheduler, this does not affect the correctness of the approach, since it is only used as a heuristic to sample the subspace. In fact, one could instantiate GETRELEVANTSUBSET with an arbitrary heuristic (e. g. from artificial intelligence domain, or one that is more targeted towards a specific model). Correctness of the lower and upper bounds will not be affected by this. However, termination of the algorithm cannot be ensured for any arbitrary heuristic. Indeed, one has to make sure that the bounds will eventually converge to the value.

Example 1. Consider the CTMDP from Fig. 3a. Figure 3b, c show two possible sampled paths. The path in 3c reaches the target within the given time-bound and the path in 3b times out before reaching the goal state. The relevant subset is thus all the states visited during the two simulations.

3.2   Step 2: Under- and Over-Approximating CTMDP

We will now explain line 7 of Algorithm 1. Here we obtain two CTMDPs, such that the value of $\underline{\mathcal{M}}$ is a guaranteed lower bound, and the value of $\overline{\mathcal{M}}$ is a guaranteed upper bound on the value of $\mathcal{M}$.

Let $S' \subseteq S$ be the subset of states obtained in line 6. We are interested in extracting some information regarding the reachability value of $\mathcal{M}$ from this subset. In order to do this, we consider two cases. (i) A pessimistic case, where all the unexplored states are non-goal states and absorbing (or *sink states*); and (ii) an optimistic case, where all the unexplored states are indeed goals. It is easy to see that the "pessimistic" CTMDP $\underline{\mathcal{M}}$ will have a smaller (or equal) value than the original CTMDP, which in turn will have a value smaller (or equal) than the "optimistic" CTMDP $\overline{\mathcal{M}}$. Notice that for the reachability value the goal states can also be made absorbing and this will not change the value[2]. Before we define the two CTMDPs formally, we illustrate the construction on an example. Note that the fringe "one-step outside" of the relevant subset is still a part of the considered sub-CTMDPs.

Example 2. Let S' be the state space of the CTMDP from Fig. 3a explored in Example 1. Figure 4a depicts the sub-CTMDP obtained by restricting the state space of the original model to S'. Figure 4b, c demonstrate how the "pessimistic" and "optimistic" CTMDPs can be obtained. All the states that are not part of S' are made absorbing for the "pessimistic" CTMDP Fig. 4b and are made goal states for the "optimistic" CTMDP Fig. 4c.

Formally, we define methods $\mathsf{lower}(\mathcal{M}, S')$ and $\mathsf{upper}(\mathcal{M}, S')$ that return the pessimistic and optimistic CTMDP, respectively. The $\mathsf{lower}(\mathcal{M}, S')$ method returns a CTMDP $\underline{\mathcal{M}} = (s_{\mathrm{init}}, \widetilde{S}, \mathrm{Act}, \widetilde{\mathbf{R}}, G)$, where $\widetilde{S} = S' \cup \mathrm{Succ}(S')$, and $\forall s', s'' \in \widetilde{S}$:

$$\widetilde{\mathbf{R}}[s', \alpha, s''] = \begin{cases} \mathbf{R}[s', \alpha, s''] & \text{if } s' \in S' \\ \lambda & \text{if } s' \notin S', s'' = s' \\ 0 & \text{otherwise,} \end{cases}$$

---

[2] This is due to the fact that for the reachability value, only what happens before the first arrival to the goal matters, and everything that happens afterwards is irrelevant.

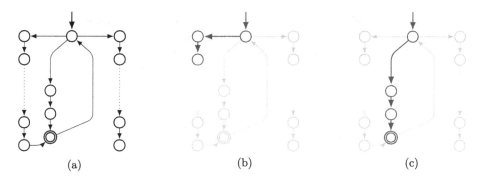

Fig. 3. A simple CTMDP is presented in (a) with rates and action labels ignored. (b) shows a sampled run which ends on running out of time while exploring the left-most branch. (c) shows a simulation which ends on discovering a target state.

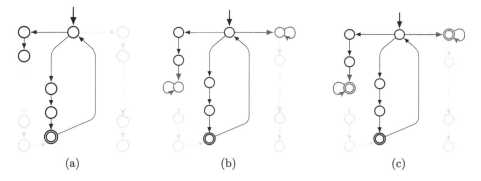

Fig. 4. (a) depicts the relevant subset obtained at line 6 of Algorithm 1. (b, c) show the addition of successors (in highlight) of the states at the fringe. In (b), the appended states are made absorbing by adding a self-loop of rate $\overline{\lambda}$. Meanwhile in (c), the newly added states are made goals.

where $\overline{\lambda}$ is the maximum exit rate in $\mathcal{M}$. And the method $\mathsf{upper}(\mathcal{M}, S')$ returns CTMDP $\overline{\mathcal{M}} = (s_{\mathrm{init}}, \widetilde{S}, \mathrm{Act}, \widetilde{\mathbf{R}}, \overline{G})$, where $\overline{G} = G \cup (\widetilde{S} \setminus S')$, and state space $\widetilde{S}$ and the rate matrix $\widetilde{\mathbf{R}}$ are the same as for $\mathsf{lower}(\mathcal{M}, S')$.

Since many states are absorbing now large parts of the state space may become unreachable, namely all the states that are not in $\widetilde{S}$.

Lemma 1. $\mathrm{val}_{\underline{\mathcal{M}}}(T) \leqslant \mathrm{val}_{\mathcal{M}}(T) \leqslant \mathrm{val}_{\overline{\mathcal{M}}}(T)$

3.3 Step 3: Computing the Reachability Value

Algorithm 1 requires computing the reachability values for CTMDPs $\underline{\mathcal{M}}$ and $\overline{\mathcal{M}}$ (line 9). This can be done by any algorithm for reachability analysis, e. g. [BHHK15, NZ10, HH13, BS11, FRSZ11, BHHK04] which approximate the value up to an arbitrary precision ε. These algorithms usually also compute the ε-optimal scheduler along with the approximation of the reachability value. In the following we will use interchangeably the notions of the value and its ε-approximation, as well as an optimal scheduler and an ε-optimal scheduler.

Notice that some of the algorithms mentioned above compute optimal reachability value only w. r. t. a subclass of schedulers, rather than the full class Π. In this case the result of Algorithm 1 will be the optimal reachability value with respect to this subclass and not class Π.

3.4   Step 4: The Choice of Scheduler $\pi_{\texttt{sim}}$

At line 10 of Algorithm 1 the scheduler $\pi_{\texttt{sim}}$ is selected that is used in the subsequent iteration for refining the relevant subset of states. We propose two ways of instantiating the function CHOOSESCHEDULER($\pi_{\texttt{uniform}}, \overline{\pi}_{\texttt{opt}}$), one with the uniform scheduler $\pi_{\texttt{uniform}}$, and another with the scheduler $\overline{\pi}_{\texttt{opt}}$. Depending on the model, its goal and the time bound one of the options may deliver smaller relevant subset than another:

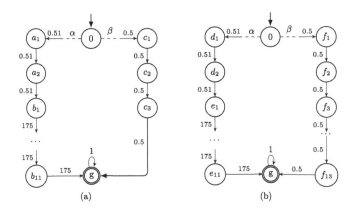

(a)   (b)

Fig. 5. An example of a CTMDP where the uniform scheduler delivers possibly smaller relevant subset than the optimal scheduler (a), and vice versa (b).

Example 3. Consider, the CTMDP in Fig. 5a and the time bound 3.0. Assuming that the goal state has not yet been sampled from the right and left chains, action α delivers higher reachability value than action β. For example, if states a_1 to a_2 are sampled from the chain on the left and c_1 to c_2 from the chain on the right, the reachability value of the respective over-approximating CTMDP when choosing action β is 0.1987 and when choosing action α is 0.1911. And this situation persists also when states $b_1 - b_{10}$ are sampled due to high exit rates of the respective transitions. However if state b_{11} is sampled, the reachability value when following α becomes 0.1906. Only at this moment the optimal behaviour is to choose action β. However, when following the uniform scheduler, there is a chance that the whole chain on the right is explored before any of the states b_i are visited. If the precision $\varepsilon = 0.01$, then at the moment the goal state is reached via the right chain and at least states a_1 to a_2 are sampled on the left, the algorithm has converged. Thus using the uniform scheduler SUBSPACETBR may in fact explore fewer states than when using the optimal one.

Naturally, there are situation when following the optimal scheduler is the best one can do. For example, in the CTMDP in Fig. 5b it is enough to explore only state f_1 on the right to realise that action β is sub-optimal. From this moment on only action α is chosen for simulations, which is in fact the best way to proceed. At the moment the goal state is reached the algorithm has converged for precision 0.01.

One of the main advantages of the uniform scheduler is that it does not require too much memory and is simple to implement. Moreover, since some algorithms to compute time-bounded reachability probability do not provide an optimal scheduler in the classical way as defined in Sect. 2 ([BHHK15]), the use of π_{uniform} may be the only option. In spite of its simplicity, in many cases this scheduler generates very succinct state spaces, as we will show in Sect. 4.

Using the uniform scheduler is beneficial in those cases when, for example, different actions of the same state have exit rates that differ drastically, e. g. by an order of magnitude. If the goal state is reachable via actions with high rates, choosing an action with low rate leads to higher residence times (due to properties of the exponential distribution) and therefore fewer states will be reachable within the time bound, compared to choosing an action with a high exit rate. In this case using the uniform scheduler may lead to larger sub-space, compared to using the optimal scheduler. However, the experiments show this difference is typically negligible.

The drawback of the uniform scheduler is that the probability of it choosing each action is positive. Thus it will choose also those actions that are clearly suboptimal and could be omitted during the simulations. The uniform scheduler π_{uniform} does not take this information into account while the scheduler $\overline{\pi}_{\text{opt}}$ does. The latter is optimal on the sub-CTMDP obtained during the previous iterations. This scheduler will thus pick only those actions that look most promising to be optimal. Using this scheduler may induce smaller sampled state space than the one generated by π_{uniform}, as we also show in Sect. 4.

Notice that it is possible to alternate between using π_{uniform} and $\overline{\pi}_{\text{opt}}$ at different iterations of Algorithm 1, for instance, when $\overline{\pi}_{\text{opt}}$ is costly to obtain or simulate. However, in our experiments, we always choose either one of the two, with the exception for the first iteration when only the uniform scheduler is available.

3.5   Step 5: Termination and Optimal Schedulers

The algorithm runs as long as the values of $\underline{\mathcal{M}}$ and $\overline{\mathcal{M}}$, as computed in Step 3 are not sufficiently close. It terminates when the difference becomes less than ε. The scheduler π_{opt} obtained in line 9 is ε-optimal for $\underline{\mathcal{M}}$ since it is obtained by running a standard TBR algorithm on $\underline{\mathcal{M}}$. From this scheduler one can obtain ε-optimal scheduler π for $\mathcal{M}$ itself by choosing the same actions as π_{opt} on the relevant subset of states (S' in Algorithm 1) and any arbitrary action on other states.

Lemma 2. *Scheduler π computed by Algorithm 1 is ε-optimal.*

Theorem 1. *Algorithm 1 converges almost surely.*

On any CTMDP, if $\pi_{\text{sim}} = \pi_{\text{uniform}}$, Algorithm 1 will, in the worst case, eventually explore the whole CTMDP. In such a situation, $\underline{\mathcal{M}}$ and $\overline{\mathcal{M}}$ will be the same as $\mathcal{M}$. The algorithm would then terminate since the condition on line 5 would be falsified. If $\pi_{\text{sim}} = \overline{\pi}_{\text{opt}}$, the system is continuously driven to the fringe as long as the condition on line 5 holds. This is because all unexplored states act as goal states in the upper-bound model. Such a scheduler will eventually explore the state-space reachable by the optimal scheduler on the original model and leave out those parts that are only reachable with suboptimal decisions.

4   Experiments

The framework described in Sect. 3 was evaluated against 5 different benchmarks available in the MAPA[3] language [TKvdPS12]:

Fault Tolerant Work Station Cluster (ftwc-n) [HHK00]: models two networks of n workstations each. Each network is interconnected by a switch. The switches communicate via a backbone. All the components may fail and can be repaired only one at a time. The system starts in a fully functioning state and a state is goal if in both networks either all the workstations or the switch are broken.

Google File System (gfs-n) [HCH+02,GGL03]: in this benchmark files are split into chunks, each maintained by one of n chunk servers. We fix the number of chunks a server may store to 5000 and the total number of chunks to 10000. The GFS starts in the state where for one of the chunks no replica is stored and the target is to have at least 3 copies of the chunk available.

Polling System (ps-j-k-g): We consider the variation of the polling system case [GHH+13,TvdPS13], that consists of j stations and one server. Incoming requests of j types are buffered in queues of size k each, until they are processed by the server and delivered to their station. The system starts in a state with all the queues being nearly full. We consider 2 goal conditions: (i) all the queues are empty (g=all) and (ii) one of the queues is empty (g=one).

Erlang Stages (erlang-k-r): this is a synthetic model with known characteristics [ZN10]. It has two different paths to reach the goal state: a fast but risky path or a slow but sure path. The slow path is an Erlang chain of length k and rate r.

Stochastic Job Scheduling (sjs-m-j) [BDF81]: models a multiprocessor architecture running a sequence of independent jobs. It consists of m identical processors and j jobs. As goal we define the states with all jobs completed;

---

[3] Translated to explicit state format by the tool Scoop [Tim11].

Our algorithm is implemented as an extension to PRISM [KNP11] and we use IMCA [GHKN12] in order to solve the sub-CTMDPs ($\mathcal{M}$ and $\overline{\mathcal{M}}$). We would like to remark, however, that the performance of our algorithm can be improved by using a better toolchain than our PRISM-IMCA setup (see [ABHK18, Appendix A.2]).

In order to instantiate our framework, we need to describe how we perform Steps 1 and 3 (Sect. 3). Recall from Sect. 3.1 that we proposed two different schedulers to be used as the simulating scheduler $\pi_{\mathtt{sim}}$: the uniform scheduler $\pi_{\mathtt{uniform}}$ and the optimal scheduler $\overline{\pi}_{\mathtt{opt}}$ obtained by solving $\overline{\mathcal{M}}$.

For Step 3, we select three algorithms for time-bounded reachability analysis: the first discretisation-based algorithm [NZ10] (D), and the two most competitive algorithms according to the comparison performed in [BHHK15], namely the adaptive version of discretization [BS11] (A) and the uniformisation-based [BHHK15] (U). SUBSPACETBR instantiated with these algorithms and with $\pi_{\mathtt{sim}} = \pi_{\mathtt{uniform}}$ is referred to with $D_{\mathtt{uni}}$, $A_{\mathtt{uni}}$ and $U_{\mathtt{uni}}$ respectively. For $\pi_{\mathtt{sim}} = \overline{\pi}_{\mathtt{opt}}$, the instantiations are referred to as $D_{\mathtt{opt}}$, $A_{\mathtt{opt}}$ and $U_{\mathtt{opt}}$. Since U does not provide the scheduler in a classical form as defined in Sect. 2, we omit $U_{\mathtt{opt}}$. We also omit experiments on $D_{\mathtt{opt}}$ as our experience with D and $D_{\mathtt{uni}}$ suggested that $D_{\mathtt{opt}}$ would also run out of time on most experiments.

We compare the performance of the instantiated algorithms with their originals, implemented in IMCA. We set the precision parameter for SUBSPACETBR and the original algorithms in IMCA to 0.01. Indicators such as the median model checking time (excluding the time taken to load the model into memory) and explored state-space are measured.

Table 1. An overview of the experimental results along with the state-space sizes. Runtime (in seconds) for the various algorithms are presented. '-' indicates a timeout (1800 s). $U_{\mathtt{uni}}$, $A_{\mathtt{uni}}$ and $A_{\mathtt{opt}}$ perform quite well on erlang, gfs and ftwc while only $A_{\mathtt{opt}}$ is better than U and A on the ps-one family of models. ps-4-8-all and sjs are hard instances for both $\pi_{\mathtt{uniform}}$ and $\overline{\pi}_{\mathtt{opt}}$. D times out on all benchmarks except on sjs due to its small state-space.

Benchmark	States	U	$U_{\mathtt{uni}}$	A	$A_{\mathtt{uni}}$	$A_{\mathtt{opt}}$	D	$D_{\mathtt{uni}}$
erlang-10^6-10	1,000k	71	1	4	1	1	-	299
gfs-120	1,479k	-	2	-	2	2	-	-
ftwc-128	597k	251	10	114	11	15	-	-
ps-4-24-one	7,562k	507	-	171	-	105	-	-
ps-4-8-all	119k	1,475	-	826	-	-	-	-
sjs-2-9	18k	6	99	2	139	-	1,199	-

Tables 1 and 2 summarize the main results of our experiments. Table 1 reports the runtime of the algorithms on several benchmarks, while Table 2 reports on the state-space complexity. Here the last column refers to the smallest relevant

Table 2. For each benchmark, we report (i) the size of the state-space; (ii) total states explored by our instantiations of SUBSPACETBR; (iii) size of the final over-approximating sub-CTMDP $\overline{\mathcal{M}}$; and (iv) size of the relevant subset returned by the greedy search of Sect. 4.1. We use ps-4-4-one and sjs-2-7 instead of larger models in their respective families as running the greedy search is a highly computation-intensive task.

Benchmark	States	Explored		Size of last $\overline{\mathcal{M}}$	Post greedy reduction
		by π_{sim}	%		
erlang-10^6-10	1,000k	559	0.06	561	496
gfs-120	1,479k	105	0.01	200	85
ftwc-128	597k	296	0.05	858	253
sjs-2-7	2k	2,537	93.86	2,704	1,543
ps-4-4-one	10k	697	6.63	2,040	696
ps-4-8-all	119k	-	-	-	-
ps-4-24-one	7,562k	23,309	0.31	-	-

subset of $\overline{\mathcal{M}}$ that we can obtain with reasonable effort. This subset is computed by running the greedy algorithm described in Sect. 4.1 on $\overline{\mathcal{M}}$. It attempts to reduce more states of the explored subset without sacrificing the precision too much. We run the greedy algorithm with a precision of $\varepsilon/10$, where ε is the precision used in SUBSPACETBR.

We recall that our framework is targeted towards models which contain a small subset of valuable states. We can categorize the models into three classes:

Easy with Uniform Scheduler $(\pi_{\text{sim}} = \pi_{\text{uniform}})$. Surprisingly enough, the uniform scheduler performs well on many instances, for example erlang, gfs and ftwc. For erlang and gfs, it was sufficient to explore a few hundred states no matter how the parameter which increased the state-space was changed (see description of the models above). Here the running time of the instantiations of our framework outperformed the original algorithms due to the fact that less than 1% of the state-space is sufficient to approximate the reachability value up to precision 0.01.

Easy with Optimal Scheduler $(\pi_{\text{sim}} = \overline{\pi}_{\text{opt}})$. Predictably, there are cases in which uniform scheduler does not provide good results. For example consider the case of ps-4-24-one. Here the goal condition requires that one of the queues be empty. An action in this benchmark determines the queue from which the task to be processed is picked. Choosing tasks uniformly from different queues, not surprisingly, leads to larger explored state spaces and longer runtimes. Notice that all the instantiations that use uniform scheduler run out of time on this instance. On the other hand, targeted exploration with the most promising scheduler (column A_{opt}) performs even better than the original algorithm A, finishing within 105 s compared to 171 s and exploring only 0.31% of the state space.

Hard Instances. Naturally there are instances where it is not possible to find a small sub-CTMDP that preserves the properties of interest. For example in ps-4-8-all, the system is started with all queues being nearly full and the property queried requires all of the queues in the polling system to be empty. As discussed in the beginning of Sect. 3, most of the states of the model have to be explored in order to reach the goal state. In this model there is simply no small sub-CTMDP that preserves the reachability probabilities. As expected, all instantiations timed out and nearly all the states had to be explored. The situation is similar with sjs. We identified (using the greedy algorithm in Sect. 4.1) that on some small instances of this model, only 30% to 40% of the state-space can be sacrificed.

Explored State Space and Running Time. In general, as we have mentioned in Sect. 3, the problem is heavily dependent not only on the structure of the model, but also on the specified time-bound and the goal set. Increasing the time-bound for erlang, for example, leads to higher probability to explore fully the states of the Erlang chain. This in turn affects the optimal scheduler and for some time-bounds no small sub-CTMDP preserving the value exists.

Naturally, whenever the algorithm explored only a small fraction of the state space, the running time was usually also smaller than the running time of the respective original algorithm. The performance of our framework is heavily dependent on the parameter n_{sim}. This is due to the fact that computation of the reachability value is an expensive operation when performed many times even on small models. Usually in our experiments the amount of simulations was in the order of several thousands. For more details please refer to [ABHK18, Appendix A.2].

4.1   Smallest Sub-CTMDP

In this section, we provide an argument that in the cases where our techniques do not perform well, the reason is not a poor choice of the relevant subsets, but rather that in such cases there are no small subsets which can be removed, at least not such that can be easily obtained. An ideal brute-force method to ascertain this would be to enumerate all subsets of the state space, make the states of the subset absorbing $(\underline{\mathcal{M}})$ or goal $(\overline{\mathcal{M}})$ and then to check whether the difference in values of $\underline{\mathcal{M}}$ and $\overline{\mathcal{M}}$ is ε-close only for small subsets. Unfortunately, this is computationally infeasible. As an alternative, we now suggest a greedy algorithm which we use to search for the largest subset of states one could remove in reasonable time.

The idea is to systematically pick states and observe their effect on the value when they are made absorbing $(\underline{\mathcal{M}}(s))$ or goal $(\overline{\mathcal{M}}(s))$. If a state does not influence the value of the original CTMDP too much, then $\delta(s) = \text{val}_{\overline{\mathcal{M}}(s)}(T) - \text{val}_{\underline{\mathcal{M}}(s)}(T)$ would be small. We first sort all the states in ascending order according to the value $\delta(s)$. And then iteratively build $\underline{\mathcal{M}}$ and $\overline{\mathcal{M}}$ by greedily picking states in this order and making them absorbing (for $\underline{\mathcal{M}}$) and goal (for $\overline{\mathcal{M}}$). The process is repeated until $\mathrm{val}_{\overline{\mathcal{M}}}(T) - \mathrm{val}_{\underline{\mathcal{M}}}(T)$ exceeds ε.

The results of running this algorithm is presented in the right-most column of Table 2. The comparison of the last two columns of the table shows that the portion of the state space our heuristic explored is of the same order of magnitude as what can be obtained with high computational effort. Consequently, this suggests that the surprising choice of the simple uniform scheduler is not poor, but typically indeed achieves the desired degree of reduction.

5   Conclusion

We have introduced a framework for time-bounded reachability analysis of CTMDPs. This framework allows us to run arbitrary algorithms from the literature on a subspace of the original system and thus obtain the result faster, while not compromising its precision beyond a given ε. The subspace is iteratively identified using simulations. In contrast to the standard algorithms, the amount of computation needed reflects not only the model, but also the property to be checked.

The experimental results have revealed that the models often have a small subset which is sufficient for the analysis, and thus our framework speeds up all three considered algorithms. For the exploration, already the uninformed uniform scheduler proves efficient in many settings. However, the more informed scheduler, fed back from the analysis tools, may provide yet better results. In cases where our technique explores the whole state space, our conjecture, confirmed by the preliminary results using the greedy algorithm, is that these models actually do not posses any small relevant subset of states and cannot be exploited by this approach.

This work is agnostic of the structure of the models. Given that states are typically given by a valuation of variables, the corresponding structure could be further utilized in the search for the small relevant subset. A step in this direction could follow the ideas of [PBU13], where discrete-time Markov chains are simulated, the simulations used to infer invariants for the visited states, and then the invariants used to identify a subspace of the original system, which is finally analyzed. An extension of this approach to a non-deterministic and continuous setting could speed up the subspace-identification part of our approach and thus decrease our overhead. Another way to speed up this process is to quickly obtain good schedulers (with no guarantees), e.g. [BBB+17], use them to identify the subspace faster and only then apply a guaranteed algorithm.

References

[ABHK18] Ashok, P., Butkova, Y., Hermanns, H., Křetínský, J.: Continuous-Time Markov Decisions Based on Partial Exploration. ArXiv e-prints (2018). https://arxiv.org/abs/1807.09641

[ACD+17] Ashok, P., Chatterjee, K., Daca, P., Kretínský, J., Meggendorfer, T.: Value iteration for long-run average reward in Markov decision processes. In: CAV (2017)

[ASSB96] Aziz, A., Sanwal, K., Singhal, V., Brayton, R.K.: Verifying continuous time Markov chains. In: CAV (1996)

[BBB+17] Bartocci, E., Bortolussi, L., Brázdil, T., Milios, D., Sanguinetti, G.: Policy learning in continuous-time Markov decision processes using gaussian processes. Perform. Eval. **116**, 84–100 (2017)

[BCC+14] Brázdil, T., et al.: Verification of Markov decision processes using learning algorithms. In: ATVA (2014)

[BDF81] Bruno, J.L., Downey, P.J., Frederickson, G.N.: Sequencing tasks with exponential service times to minimize the expected flow time or makespan. J. ACM **28**(1), 100–113 (1981)

[Ber95] Bertsekas, D.P.: Dynamic Programming and Optimal Control, vol. II. Athena Scientific (1995)

[BFK+09] Brázdil, T., Forejt, V., Krčál, J., Křetínský, J., Kučera, A.: Continuous-time stochastic games with time-bounded reachability. In: FSTTCS (2009)

[BHHK04] Baier, C., Haverkort, B.R., Hermanns, H., Katoen, J.: Efficient computation of time-bounded reachability probabilities in uniform continuous-time Markov decision processes. In: TACAS (2004)

[BHHK15] Butkova, Y., Hatefi, H., Hermanns, H., Krcál, J.: Optimal continuous time Markov decisions. In: ATVA (2015)

[BS11] Buchholz, P., Schulz, I.: Numerical analysis of continuous time Markov decision processes over finite horizons. Comput. OR **38**(3), 651–659 (2011)

[EHKZ13] Eisentraut, C., Hermanns, H., Katoen, J., Zhang, L.: A semantics for every GSPN. In: Petri Nets (2013)

[Fei04] Feinberg, E.A.: Continuous time discounted jump Markov decision processes: a discrete-event approach. Math. Oper. Res. **29**(3), 492–524 (2004)

[FRSZ11] Fearnley, J., Rabe, M., Schewe, S., Zhang, L.: Efficient approximation of optimal control for continuous-time Markov games. In: FSTTCS (2011)

[GGL03] Ghemawat, S., Gobioff, H., Leung, S.: The google file system. In: SOSP (2003)

[GHH+13] Guck, D., Hatefi, H., Hermanns, H., Katoen, J., Timmer, M.: Modelling, reduction and analysis of Markov automata. In: QEST (2013)

[GHKN12] Guck, D., Han, T., Katoen, J., Neuhäußer, M.R.: Quantitative timed analysis of interactive Markov chains. In: NFM (2012)

[HCH+02] Haverkort, B.R., Cloth, L., Hermanns, H., Katoen, J., Baier, C.: Model checking performability properties. In: DSN (2002)

[HH13] Hatefi, H., Hermanns, H.: Improving time bounded reachability computations in interactive Markov chains. In: FSEN (2013)

[HHK00] Haverkort, B.R., Hermanns, H., Katoen, J.: On the use of model checking techniques for dependability evaluation. In: SRDS'00 (2000)

[KNP11] Kwiatkowska, M., Norman, G., Parker, D.: PRISM 4.0: verification of probabilistic real-time systems. In: Gopalakrishnan, G., Qadeer, S. (eds.) CAV 2011. LNCS, vol. 6806, pp. 585–591. Springer, Heidelberg (2011). https://doi.org/10.1007/978-3-642-22110-1_47

[Lef81] Lefèvre, C.: Optimal control of a birth and death epidemic process. Oper. Res. **29**(5), 971–982 (1981)

[MLG05] McMahan, H.B., Likhachev, M., Gordon, G.J.: Bounded real-time dynamic programming: RTDP with monotone upper bounds and performance guarantees. In: ICML (2005)

[Neu10] Neuhäußer, M.R.: Model checking nondeterministic and randomly timed systems. Ph.D. thesis, RWTH Aachen University (2010)

[NZ10] Neuhäußer, M.R., Zhang, L.: Time-bounded reachability probabilities in continuous-time Markov decision processes. In: QEST (2010)

[PBU13] Pavese, E., Braberman, V.A., Uchitel, S.: Automated reliability estimation over partial systematic explorations. In: ICSE, pp. 602–611 (2013)

[QQP01] Qiu, Q., Qu, Q., Pedram, M.: Stochastic modeling of a power-managed system-construction and optimization. IEEE Trans. CAD Integr. Circuits Syst. **20**(10), 1200–1217 (2001)

[Sen99] Sennott, L.I.: Stochastic Dynamic Programming and the Control of Queueing Systems. Wiley-Interscience, New York (1999)

[Tim11] Timmer, M.: Scoop: a tool for symbolic optimisations of probabilistic processes. In: QEST (2011)

[TKvdPS12] Timmer, M., Katoen, J.-P., van de Pol, J., Stoelinga, M.I.A.: Efficient modelling and generation of Markov automata. In: Koutny, M., Ulidowski, I. (eds.) CONCUR 2012. LNCS, vol. 7454, pp. 364–379. Springer, Heidelberg (2012). https://doi.org/10.1007/978-3-642-32940-1_26

[TvdPS13] Timmer, M., van de Pol, J., Stoelinga, M.I.A.: Confluence reduction for Markov automata. In: Braberman, V., Fribourg, L. (eds.) FORMATS 2013. LNCS, vol. 8053, pp. 243–257. Springer, Heidelberg (2013). https://doi.org/10.1007/978-3-642-40229-6_17

[ZN10] Zhang, L., Neuhäußer, M.R.: Model checking interactive Markov chains. In: Esparza, J., Majumdar, R. (eds.) TACAS 2010. LNCS, vol. 6015, pp. 53–68. Springer, Heidelberg (2010). https://doi.org/10.1007/978-3-642-12002-2_5

A Fragment of Linear Temporal Logic for Universal Very Weak Automata

Keerthi Adabala[(✉)] and Rüdiger Ehlers

University of Bremen, Bremen, Germany
adabala@uni-bremen.de

Abstract. Many temporal specifications used in practical model checking can be represented as universal very weak automata (UVW). They are structurally simple and their states can be labeled by simple temporal logic formulas that they represent. For complex temporal properties, it can be hard to understand why a trace violates a property, so when employing UVWs in model checking, this information helps with interpreting the trace. At the same time, the simple structure of UVWs helps the model checker with finding short traces.

While a translation from computation tree logic (CTL) with only universal path quantifiers to UVWs has been described in earlier work, complex temporal properties that define sequences of allowed events along computations of a system are easier to describe in linear temporal logic (LTL). However, no direct translation from LTL to UVWs with little blow-up is known.

In this paper, we define a fragment of LTL that gives rise to a simple and efficient translation from it to UVW. The logic contains the most common shapes of safety and liveness properties, including all nestings of "Until"-subformulas. We give a translation from this fragment to UVWs that only has an exponential blow-up in the worst case, which we show to be unavoidable. We demonstrate that the simple shape of UVWs helps with understanding counter-examples in a case study.

1 Introduction

Complex reactive systems often have complex specifications. To obtain a sufficient degree of quality assurance, a model of the system can be verified against the specification. Automata-based model checking is a classical approach in this context, as it permits the specification to be written in a powerful logic such as linear temporal logic (LTL, [1]), which is then translated to an automaton for the verification process [2].

Whenever the system to be verified is found to violate the specification, a model checker can compute a (lasso-shaped) *counter-example trace* [2,3]. Such traces are often lengthy and the problem of explaining why the system behaves

---

This work was supported by DFG grant EH 481/1-1 and the Institutional Strategy of the University of Bremen, funded by the German Excellence Initiative.

S. K. Lahiri and C. Wang (Eds.): ATVA 2018, LNCS 11138, pp. 335–351, 2018.
https://doi.org/10.1007/978-3-030-01090-4_20

in the way observed in the trace has received some attention in the literature [4,5]. However, finding out why the behavior actually violates the property is also difficult [5]. While the trace includes a run of the automaton built from the specification, the various optimizations in the translation process from the specification to the automaton normally lead to a loss of structure. Hence, the run of the automaton does not give rise to an easy interpretation of the reason for the violation of the specification written by a system engineer. When not optimizing an automaton, it frequently becomes huge, which translates to a higher computational workload and can also lead to longer counter-example traces.

These observations give rise to the question if we can help a model checker with finding easy to interpret counter-example traces by employing very structured, but still small automata in the verification process. We present an approach for this purpose in this paper that is based on *universal very weak ω-automata*. Maidl [6] showed that this automaton class captures exactly the specifications that are representable both in linear temporal logic (LTL) and computation tree logic (CTL), where in the latter case only universal path quantifiers are used. Universal very weak automata (UVWs) expose the sequences of events that must not lead to errors, deadlocks or livelocks. They can be decomposed into a finite number of so-called *simple chains* that represent these sequences of events. There are multiple reasons for why this makes them interesting for counter-example trace generation:

1. Whenever a property is violated, we can search for counter-example traces for all simple chains. The information for which of these chains a violation can be found is helpful for pinpointing the error.
2. Counter-example traces for different simple chains can have different lengths, so the shortest one can be reported to the system engineer.
3. Along a trace, a UVW run can move to a different state only few times. These state changes represent points in time in which interesting events happen, so they can be highlighted to the engineer.
4. Every state in a UVW can be labeled by a relatively simple temporal logic formula that the state represents, and no two states in a minimized automaton are labeled in the same way, which eases the interpretation of a trace by the engineer.

So for those specification parts that can be represented as universal very weak automata, employing them for model checking the specification part simplifies debugging the model and hence speeds up the iterations of model and specification refinement that are characteristic for a model-based system development process.

Despite their nice properties, universal very weak automata are not well-studied. It is for example currently unknown how much blow-up is unavoidable when translating from LTL to UVW. Earlier work [7] contained a translation construction, but it requires the input to be represented as a deterministic Büchi automaton, which implies at least a doubly-exponential translation time and potentially large automata. Furthermore, the construction computes the UVW in an iterative way, which further increases the computation times.

To counter this problem, we provide a characterization of a subset of linear temporal logic (LTL) that permits an efficient translation to universal very weak automata in this paper. This characterization is given in the form of a context-free grammar and captures, for example, all possible nestings of the *Until*-operator of LTL. We provide a translation procedure from formulas in the grammar to UVW. All states in the resulting UVWs represent languages of Boolean combinations of subformulas in the LTL specification. While we do employ simulation-based state minimization techniques, they are used in a way in which they do not invalidate the temporal logic state labeling in the UVW case. At the same time, no two states represent the same LTL (sub-)formulas, which can happen for minimally-sized classical Büchi automata, which are normally used in model checking. Hence, the state information in counter-example traces produced by a model checker is easy to interpret.

We demonstrate in a case study (using the model checker `spin` [8]) that the structure of the specification UVWs helps with finding the root cause of a specification violation. Since our LTL fragment covers the majority of specification shapes found in the literature, our construction is applicable in many application contexts.

1.1 Related Work

Translating properties from linear temporal logic (LTL) to automata is a classical topic in the formal methods literature as it is a required step for automata-based model checking (or reactive synthesis). When translating to non-deterministic Büchi automata, an exponential blow-up cannot be avoided [9], but by applying *simulation-based minimization* of the resulting automaton, automata sizes can be substantially reduced in practice [3, 10]. Since model checking problems generally become easier when employing small automata, they are normally preferred. It has been noted, however, that the efficiency of model checking is also influenced by the *shape* of the specification automata. In particular, automata that delay the first visit to an accepting state have been found to lead to better model checking efficiency [3].

Another special automaton shape are *very weak* ω-automata. In such automata, all loops are self-loops, and universal very weak automata (UVW) have been identified as the automaton class that exactly characterizes the word languages that can be represented in LTL and for which the containment of all paths in a computation tree in the language can also be represented by a formula in computation tree logic (CTL) using only universal path quantifiers [6] (abbreviated as ACTL). This fragment is interesting as it unifies the two commonly used specification logics and because UVWs can be decomposed for distributed model checking, as we show in Sect. 2. While Maidl gave a construction to translate from ACTL to UVW whenever possible, the subset of LTL for which she gave a translation to UVW is highly restrictive and does not even allow to express $a \, \mathcal{U} \, b$ (a holds until b holds at least once). Effectively, her approach requires the specification engineer to encode the structure of a UVW into the logical specification. The grammar that we define in the next section does not have this restriction and allows arbitrary nestings of $\mathcal{U}$ operators. It also includes Maidl's LTL subset as a special case.

All of the automata translations discussed so far compute automata that can have a very complicated structure and that are hard to interpret. For example, one of the classical approaches to translating from LTL to Büchi automata involves *de-alternation* [11], which introduces *breakpoints* into the automaton structure. The main alternative translation appraoch involves *de-generalizing* generalized Büchi automata [12], which introduces a similar automaton structure. Subsequent automaton minimization steps [10] lead to additional incoherence between the automaton structure and the original specification. As a consequence, observing a run of an automaton does not help to explain *why* a trace satisfies a specification or not.

To solve this issue, Basin et al. [5] defined a calculus for *annotating* a counter-example obtained from a model checker (which has a lasso shape) with an explanation why it violates a given LTL property. Their approach is only applicable after a lasso has been computed, and there is no guarantee that the model checker picks a lassos that has an easy to explain reason for violating the specification. While short lassos make this more likely, their length is still influenced by the structure of the specification automaton. Asking for a counter-example trace of the form uv^ω with $|u| + |v|$ as short as possible would solve this problem, but approximating the minimal attainable length $|u| + |v|$ by any factor has been shown to be NP-hard [13], unlike finding shortest lassos.

In the approach that we present in this paper, we solve this problem by computing automata that have a simple structure and whose states are labeled by the LTL property that the state represents. The automata can be decomposed so that a model checker that searches for short lassos also searches for lassos that have an easy explanation.

2   Preliminaries

An ω-word automaton over some finite alphabet Σ (which we assume to be 2^{AP} for some set AP for the scope of this paper) is a tuple $\mathcal{A} = (Q, \delta, Q_0, \mathcal{F})$ with the finite set of states Q, the transition relation $\delta \subseteq Q \times \Sigma \times Q$, the set of initial states $Q_0 \subseteq Q$, and the acceptance condition $\mathcal{F} \subseteq Q$.

Given a word $w = w_0 w_1 \ldots \in \Sigma^\omega$, we say that $\mathcal{A}$ induces an *infinite run* $\pi = \pi_0 \pi_1 \ldots \in Q^\omega$ if $\pi_0 \in Q_0$ and for all $i \in \mathbb{N}$, we have $(\pi_i, w_i, \pi_{i+1}) \in \delta$. For the scope of this paper, we are only interested in infinite runs.

Word automata come in different types. In this paper, we will consider two types, namely *non-deterministic Büchi automata* (NBA) and *universal very weak automata* (UVW). For the former, we say that the automaton accepts a word w if there exists a run π induced by it and $\mathcal{A}$ along which states in $\mathcal{F}$ occur infinitely often. For a universal very weak automaton $\mathcal{A}$, we say that it accepts a word w if for *all* infinite runs π induced by $\mathcal{A}$ and w, we have that states in $\mathcal{F}$ appear only

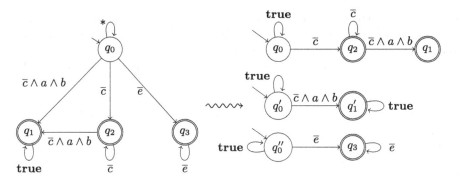

Fig. 1. A UVW and its decomposition into simple UVW chains for the property of $G((a \rightarrow b)\,\mathcal{U}\,c) \wedge GF(d\,\mathcal{U}\,e)$

finitely often along π. For an automaton to be a UVW, its states furthermore need to be ranked, i.e., there exists a ranking function $r : Q \rightarrow \mathbb{N}$ such that for every $q \in Q$ and $q' \in Q$, if there exists a $x \in \Sigma$ with $(q, x, q') \in \delta$ then $r(q') < r(q)$ or $q = q'$. Intuitively, this means that all loops in the automaton are self-loops (as visualized in Fig. 1). Due to the existence of a ranking function, the acceptance of a word basically boils down to stating that no infinite run should eventually get stuck in a state $q \in \mathcal{F}$. We call $\mathcal{F}$ the set of *rejecting states* in case of UVWs, and the set of *accepting* states for NBAs. The language of an automaton $\mathcal{A}$, denoted as $\mathcal{L}(\mathcal{A})$, is defined to be the set of words accepted by $\mathcal{A}$.

If the set AP is suitable for modeling the current state of a system to be verified, ω-word automata over the alphabet $\Sigma = 2^{AP}$ serve as an (internal) representation of a specification for model checking. They are however cumbersome to write, so a temporal logic such as linear temporal logic (LTL, [1]) typically serves as specification language used by system engineers, with the aim to automatically translate LTL properties to automata. LTL enriches Boolean logic by the addition of the *next* (X), *until* ($\mathcal{U}$), *weak until* ($\mathcal{W}$), *release* ($\mathcal{R}$), *globally* (G), and *finally* (F) operators, and a formal definition of the logic and its semantics can be found in [1]. We say that an automaton is equivalent to an LTL formula if the set of words over 2^{AP} that are models of the LTL formula is the same as the language of the automaton. A finite word over the character set 2^{AP} is a bad prefix for some LTL formula ψ if it cannot be extended to a word that satisfies the formula. A good prefix of some LTL formula ψ is a finite word all of whose infinite extensions satisfy the LTL formula. A specification for which all words that violate it have a bad prefix is called a *safety specification*. A specification without bad prefixes is called a *liveness specification*.

In the following, we use subsets of atomic propositions and their characteristic (Boolean) functions interchangeably. A transition (q_1, t, q_2) for some Boolean formula t represents transitions from a state q_1 to q_2 for all $x \in \Sigma$ that satisfy t. The $\bot$ symbol henceforth represents an invalid Boolean formula – applying any operation to it yields $\bot$ again. We also use these notations in figures depicting automata, where states are given as circles, states in $\mathcal{F}$ are doubly-circled, and transitions are depicted by arrows that are labeled by Boolean formulas t. When depicting UVWs, we furthermore draw them in a way that their ranking functions become apparent, e.g., by letting all non-self-loop transitions lead to the right or down.

In the verification literature, non-deterministic Büchi automata are often used to represent a set of traces that a system to be verified should *not* permit and hence represent the complement of a specification. By switching from non-deterministic to universal branching (as common in the literature on ACTL ∩ LTL [6,14]), we avoid this complementation in reasoning, as UVWs accept all traces that *do* satisfy the specification. The complement of a specification representable as a UVW can be represented as a nondeterministic Büchi automaton (with exactly the same automaton tuple elements).

A UVW $\mathcal{A}$ can be decomposed into multiple sub-automata $\mathcal{A}_1, \ldots, \mathcal{A}_n$ (for some $n \in \mathbb{N}$), where each sub-automaton represents one path through $\mathcal{A}$, as shown in Fig. 1. We call these paths *simple chains*, and formally, the intersection of their languages is the language of $\mathcal{A}$, i.e., we have $\mathcal{L}(\mathcal{A}_1) \cap \mathcal{L}(\mathcal{A}_2) \cap \ldots \cap \mathcal{L}(\mathcal{A}_n) = \mathcal{L}(\mathcal{A})$.

3   A Temporal Logic for Universal Very Weak Automata

In this section, we give a context-free grammar that captures a subclass of LTL formulas and a translation from this subclass to UVWs. Without loss of generality, we assume that occurrences of the negation operator in front of temporal operators have already been pushed inwards, just like in the *negation normal form* [2] of LTL. Negation operators located in front of pure Boolean sub-formulas do not have to be pushed inwards. The grammar for UVWs has the following components:

$$\chi ::= p \mid \neg\chi \mid \chi \wedge \chi \mid \chi \vee \chi \mid \textbf{true} \mid \textbf{false}$$
$$\psi ::= \chi \mid \psi \vee \psi \mid \mathsf{F}\psi \mid \phi\,\mathcal{U}\,\psi$$
$$\phi ::= \psi \mid \phi \wedge \phi \mid \phi \vee \phi \mid \mathsf{G}\phi \mid \mathsf{X}\phi \mid \psi\,\mathcal{R}\,\phi \mid (b \wedge \phi)\,\mathcal{U}\,(\neg b \wedge \phi) \mid (b \wedge \phi)\,\mathcal{W}\,(\neg b \wedge \phi)$$

In this grammar, p denotes an atomic proposition and b is a Boolean formula without temporal operators. Such formulas are accepted by the nonterminal χ. Note that in the last two rules for ϕ, we assume that the Boolean formula b is the same for both occurrences.

The acceptance of an LTL formula by the top-level nonterminal ϕ indicates that the LTL formula can be translated to a UVW, as we show below. The nonterminal ψ represents subformulas for which *quitting points* can be detected, which are defined as follows:

Definition 1. *Let f be an LTL formula with (strict) subformulas S for some set of propositions* AP. *A prefix word $w = w_0 \ldots w_n \in (2^{\mathsf{AP}})^*$ is called a* quitting point *if there exists a Boolean combination f' of subformulas from S such that for all words $u = w_0 \ldots w_{n-1} w_n u_{n+1} u_{n+2} \ldots \in \Sigma^\omega$, we have $u \models f$ if and only if $w_n u_{n+1} u_{n+2} \ldots \models f'$.*

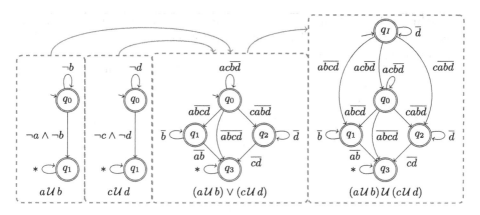

Fig. 2. Building a UVW for the LTL formula $f = (a \mathcal{U} b) \mathcal{U} (c \mathcal{U} d)$ in a step-by-step way from the UVW for the subformulas. Rejecting states are doubly-circled.

Quitting points intuitively represent prefix words for some LTL formula for which the top-level formula does not need to be monitored in order to find out if a word satisfies the formula after the point has been reached. For example, for the LTL formula $f = (a \mathcal{U} b) \mathcal{U} c$, any prefix word that ends with a character that includes c is such a quitting point, as after a c is seen along a trace, the outer-level obligation encoded in f is satisfied. However, when a quitting point has been reached, this does not necessarily mean that the satisfaction of the LTL formula is already established. For example, for $f = (a \mathcal{U} b) \mathcal{U} c$, the prefix word $\{a\}\{a,c\}$ is a quitting point, but the remainder of the word still has to satisfy $a \mathcal{U} b$ for f to be satisfied along the complete trace.

In the grammar given above, ψ has been carefully defined to only contain subformulas for which quitting points can be detected without recall for the history of the prefix word observed earlier. This enables us to construct UVWs for a specification with liveness objectives. Take for example the specification $f = (a \mathcal{U} b) \mathcal{U} (c \mathcal{U} d)$. The sub-formula $(a \mathcal{U} b)$ has all words ending with b as quitting points, whereas the second sub-formula has all words ending with d as quitting points. We can implement a translation to a UVW by adding one UVW state for each until-subformula $f^1 \mathcal{U} f^2$ such that at least one run stays in this state until a quitting point has been seen, and until that is the case, the run branches to a state representing that $f^1 \vee f^2$ should hold. The overall translation is depicted in Fig. 2. Note that a disjunction of two sub-formulas that enable history-free detection of quitting points has this property again, which we use in the translation.

The (recursive) TRANSLATE function that builds on this idea is given in Algorithm 1. The function takes an LTL formula and returns a pair consisting of a UVW for the LTL formula and a Boolean formula that encodes the set of characters with which quitting point prefixes for the LTL formulas end. For our implementation that we evaluate in Sect. 5, we cache the results of calls to TRANSLATE on an LTL subformula in case it occurs multiple times for the input

Algorithm 1 Translation procedure from an LTL subformula to a UVW and the characters that indicate that a quitting point has been just seen.

1: **function** TRANSLATE(f)
2:     **if** $f = t$ for some subformula t without temporal operators **then**
3:         $\mathcal{A} \leftarrow (\{q_0, q_1\}, \{(q_0, \neg t, q_1), (q_1, \mathbf{true}, q_1)\}, \{q_0\}, \{q_1\})$
4:         **return** $(\mathcal{A}, t)$
5:     **if** $f = f^1 \wedge f^2$ **then**
6:         $((Q^1, \delta^1, Q_0^1, \mathcal{F}^1), X^1) \leftarrow$ TRANSLATE(f_1)
7:         $((Q^2, \delta^2, Q_0^2, \mathcal{F}^2), X^2) \leftarrow$ TRANSLATE(f_2)
8:         $\mathcal{A} \leftarrow (Q^1 \uplus Q^2, \delta^1 \cup \delta^2, Q_0^1 \cup Q_0^2, \mathcal{F}^0 \cup \mathcal{F}^1)$
9:         **return** $(\mathcal{A}, \bot)$
10:    **if** $f = f^1 \vee f^2$ **then**
11:        $(\mathcal{A}^1, X^1) \leftarrow$ TRANSLATE(f_1), $(\mathcal{A}^2, X^2) \leftarrow$ TRANSLATE(f_2)
12:        **return** $(\mathcal{A}, X^1 \vee X^2)$, where $\mathcal{A}$ is the product of $\mathcal{A}^1$ and $\mathcal{A}^2$, where every state is rejecting for which both factor states are rejecting.
13:    **if** $f = f^1 \mathcal{U} f^2$ **then**
14:        $((Q^1, \delta^1, Q_0^1, \mathcal{F}^1), X^1) \leftarrow$ TRANSLATE($f_1 \vee f_2$)
15:        $((Q^2, \delta^2, Q_0^2, \mathcal{F}^2), X^2) \leftarrow$ TRANSLATE(f_2)
16:        $\mathcal{A} \leftarrow (Q^1 \uplus Q^2 \uplus \{q_0\}, \{(q_0, x, q_1) \mid \exists q_0^1 \in Q_0^1, (q_0^1, x, q_1) \in \delta^1, x \not\models X^2\} \cup \{(q_0, x, q_1) \mid \exists q_0^2 \in Q_0^2, (q_0^2, x, q_1) \in \delta^2, x \models X^2\} \cup \{(q_0, x, q_0) \mid x \not\models X^2\}, \{q_0\}, \mathcal{F}^0 \cup \mathcal{F}^1 \cup \{q_0\})$
17:        **return** $(\mathcal{A}, X^2)$
18:    **if** $f = f^2 \mathcal{R} f^1$ **then**
19:        $((Q^1, \delta^1, Q_0^1, \mathcal{F}^1), X^1) \leftarrow$ TRANSLATE($f_1 \vee f_2$)
20:        $((Q^2, \delta^2, Q_0^2, \mathcal{F}^2), X^2) \leftarrow$ TRANSLATE(f_2)
21:        $\mathcal{A} \leftarrow (Q^1 \uplus Q^2 \uplus \{q_0\}, \{(q_0, x, q_1) \mid \exists q_0^1 \in Q_0^1, (q_0^1, x, q_1) \in \delta^1\} \cup \{(q_0, x, q_1) \mid \exists q_0^2 \in Q_0^2, (q_0^2, x, q_1) \in \delta^2, x \models X^2\} \cup \{(q_0, x, q_0) \mid x \not\models X^2\}, \{q_0\}, \mathcal{F}^0 \cup \mathcal{F}^1 \cup \{q_0\})$
22:        **return** $(\mathcal{A}, \bot)$
23:    **if** $f = \mathsf{X} f^1$ **then**
24:        $((Q^1, \delta^1, Q_0^1, \mathcal{F}^1), X^1) \leftarrow$ TRANSLATE(f^1)
25:        $\mathcal{A} \leftarrow (Q^1 \cup \{q_0\}, \delta^1 \cup \{(q_0, \mathbf{true}, q_1) \mid q^1 \in Q_0^1\}, \{q_0\}, \mathcal{F}^1)$
26:        **return** $(\mathcal{A}, \bot)$
27:    **if** $f = (b \wedge f^1) \mathcal{U} (\neg b \wedge f^2)$ or $f = (b \wedge f^1) \mathcal{W} (\neg b \wedge f^2)$ **then**
28:        $((Q^1, \delta^1, Q_0^1, \mathcal{F}^1), X^1) \leftarrow$ TRANSLATE(f^1)
29:        $((Q^2, \delta^2, Q_0^2, \mathcal{F}^2), X^2) \leftarrow$ TRANSLATE(f^2)
30:        $\mathcal{A} \leftarrow (Q^1 \uplus Q^2 \uplus \{q_0\}, \{(q_0, x \wedge b, q_1) \mid \exists q_0^1 \in Q_0^1, (q_0^1, x, q_1) \in \delta^1\} \cup \{(q_0, x \wedge \neg b, q_1) \mid \exists q_0^2 \in Q_0^2, (q_0^2, x, q_1) \in \delta^2\} \cup \{(q_0, b, q_0)\}, \{q_0\}, \mathcal{F}^0 \cup \mathcal{F}^1 \cup K)$ for $K = \{q_0\}$ if $f = (b \wedge f^1) \mathcal{U} (\neg b \wedge f^2)$ and $K = \emptyset$ otherwise
31:        **return** $(\mathcal{A}, \bot)$

---

formula. The number of generated UVW nodes is then at most exponential in the size of the formula (as every node generated by the algorithm can be labeled by an LTL formula for its language, which is always a disjunction of subterms present in the original LTL formula). The algorithm does not show the implementations of the G and F operators, as they are special cases of the other operators (using the equivalences $\mathsf{G} f \equiv \mathbf{true} \, \mathcal{R} \, f$ and $\mathsf{F} f \equiv \mathbf{true} \, \mathcal{U} \, f$).

The construction is mostly straight-forward. For the disjunction case, we have to build a product automaton, which can lead to some blow-up.

Theorem 1. *Algorithm 1 computes a correct UVW for a given LTL formula under the assumption that the LTL formula is accepted by the grammar given in Sect. 3.*

Proof. Before we start with the main part of the proof, we need to show that for every subformula $f^1 \mathcal{U} f^2$ and $f^2 \mathcal{R} f^1$ in an overall LTL formula that is accepted by the nonterminal φ, we have that TRANSLATE(f^2) returns a UVW with exactly a single initial state. Since both of these temporal operators require that the operand f^2 is accepted by the ψ nonterminal, we only have to prove this for all subformulas accepted by this non-termininal. For all non-temporal subformulas, this sub-claim is true, as the UVW computed have exactly two states each, where only one is initial. This case forms our induction basis. For the disjunction case ($\psi :: = \psi \vee \psi$), the claim is also true as when taking the product of two UVW with one initial state each, the product also has only one initial state. Finally, the part of Algorithm 1 for the $\phi \mathcal{U} \psi$ and $\psi \mathcal{R} \phi$ cases all return UVWs with one initial state each.

Similarly, it can also be shown that for every subformula accepted by the ψ nonterminal, the second element of the tuple returned by TRANSLATE is never $\bot$, which we use for the proof.

Now to the main part of the proof. We prove the claim by induction on the structure of the LTL formula, where we use the induction hypothesis that for every subformula f, TRANSLATE(f) returns a pair $(\mathcal{A}, X)$ consisting of

1. a UVW $\mathcal{A}$ for f and
2. a subset $X \subseteq \Sigma$ such that
   (a) every prefix word ending with a letter from the subset is a quitting point,
   (b) X characterizes the one-letter prefix words that are good prefixes for f,
   (c) every word that is a model of f has to contain a character from X, and
   (d) for every prefix word $w_0 \ldots w_n \in \Sigma^*$ that is a good prefix of f, we have that $w_n \in X$ and $w_1 \ldots w_n$ is a good prefix for f as well.
   We also call X the set of *quitting characters* henceforth.

In this definition and henceforth, we treat character sets and LTL formulas that are free of temporal operators and that characterize such sets interchangeably. We still use $\bot$ to symbolize that no set/no Boolean function is provided.

Induction Basis: The only case in which TRANSLATE(f) does not recurse is when f is free of temporal operators. By the LTL semantics, the returned UVW should reject exactly the words not starting with a character that satisfies f. The UVW returned by the function has exactly two states. The non-initial one rejects all words. The initial one has a transition to the non-initial one that is taken whenever the first character of an input word does *not* satisfy f. Whenever this happens, the word is rejected as a run then visits the second non-initial state that is rejecting and self-loops on all characters. This implements exactly the semantics of an LTL formula that is free of temporal operators.

The quitting characters returned along with the UVW are exactly the set of characters satisfying f (or, more precisely, for which exactly the words starting with one of them satisfy f), which is a valid set of quitting characters for f (by its definition).

Induction Step: We do a case split on the type of operator and assume that for the f^1 and f^2 sub-formulas, recursive calls to TRANSLATE yielded the UVWs $\mathcal{A}^1$ and $\mathcal{A}^2$ along with the quitting character sets X^1 and X^2, respectively.

– **Case $f^1 \wedge f^2$:** In this case, the resulting UVW should accept a word if and only if both of the UVWs for f^1 and f^2 accept a word. So all runs of both of them must accept a word. Under the inductive hypothesis that the UVWs returned by the calls to TRANSLATE(f^1) and TRANSLATE(f^2) are correct, this is achieved by merging the two UVWs into one and taking the initial states of both of them as new initial state set. The set of quitting characters is $\bot$, which means "does not apply" and is – by definition – a safe return value.

– **Case $f^1 \vee f^2$:** In this case, the resulting UVW should accept a word if and only if one of the UVWs for f^1 and f^2 accept the word. This case uses a product construction, where given the UVWs $\mathcal{A}^1 = (Q^1, \delta^1, Q^1_0, \mathcal{F}^1)$ and $\mathcal{A}^2 = (Q^2, \delta^2, Q^2_0, \mathcal{F}^2)$, the product UVW $\mathcal{A} = (Q, \delta, Q_0, \mathcal{F})$ with the following components is computed:
  - $Q = Q^1 \times Q^2$
  - $\delta = \{((q^1, q'^1), x, (q^2, q'^2)) \in Q \times \Sigma \times Q \mid (q^1, x, q^2) \in \delta^1, (q'^1, x, q'^2) \in \delta^2\}$
  - $Q_0 = Q^1_0 \times Q^2_0$
  - $\mathcal{F} = \mathcal{F}^1 \times \mathcal{F}^2$

  Let a word be given that is accepted by, w.l.o.g., $\mathcal{A}^1$. Then, every trace of $\mathcal{A}^1$ visits rejecting states only finitely often. All runs in $\mathcal{A}$ simulate runs of $\mathcal{A}^1$ and $\mathcal{A}^2$ in parallel. Since $\mathcal{F} = \mathcal{F}^1 \times \mathcal{F}^2$, we know that a run for $\mathcal{A}$ then also only visits rejecting states finitely often.

  On the other hand, let a word be rejected by both $\mathcal{A}^1$ and $\mathcal{A}^2$. Then there exist rejecting runs for both $\mathcal{A}^1$ and $\mathcal{A}^2$, and by the construction of $\mathcal{A}$, the product of these rejecting runs is a run of $\mathcal{A}$. Since both rejecting runs eventually get stuck in rejecting states, the product run in $\mathcal{A}$ also eventually gets stuck in a state in $\mathcal{F}^1 \times \mathcal{F}^2 = \mathcal{F}$, and hence is rejecting as well. Thus, the word is rejected by $\mathcal{A}$ as well.

  If furthermore a character set $X \subseteq \Sigma$ is returned by the TRANSLATE function for both f^1 and f^2 (i.e., not the $\bot$ element is returned), then the function definition declares its own returned character set to be the union of the character sets for f^1 and f^2. By the inductive hypothesis, any word starting with a character in the union of the characters satisfies one of f^1 and f^2. Likewise, every word without characters in this union is, by the inductive hypothesis, rejected by both $\mathcal{A}^1$ and $\mathcal{A}^2$. The same argument can be made for the conditions 2.(a) and 2.(d) of the inductive hypothesis given above.

– **Case $f^1 \, \mathcal{U} \, f^2$:** We assume that X^2 has the properties stated in the inductive hypothesis. By the definition, a word can only be a model of $f^1 \, \mathcal{U} \, f^2$ if eventually, a character from X^2 occurs in the word. The construction from Algorithm 1 for this case generates an initial state that is not left until such a character is read. Before the occurrence of this character, the outgoing transitions of the state are taken, which model the transitions leaving the initial states of a UVW for $f^1 \vee f^2$.

So see why this construction is correct, let a word be given that satisfies $f^1 \mathcal{U} f^2$, where at positions 0 to j, f^1 is satisfied and at position $j + 1$, f^2 is satisfied. Let, without loss of generality, j be the least possible such index. A character from X^2 may first occur at a position $j' \geq j$ (it cannot occur earlier because otherwise j would not be the earliest possible such index). From positions 0 to j, the word surely satisfies $f^1 \vee f^2$ as it satisfies f^1. At position $j + 1$ it satisfies f^2. In between positions j and j' in the word, we however now also know that f^2 is satisfied from there by the inductive hypothesis for X^2: by it, the word from position j onwards is a good prefix for f^2, and every suffix of this good prefix is a good prefix as well (except for the empty suffix). This includes the words from positions $j + 1$, $j + 2$, ..., until the character from X^2 occurs along the trace.

Note that the UVW generated for $f^1 \mathcal{U} f^2$ also does not accept too many words, as it enforces $f^1 \mathcal{U} f^2$ to hold until a letter has been seen that guarantees that f^2 is met. If $f^1 \vee f^2$ is always satisfied before this point, this implies that $f^1 \mathcal{U} f^2$ holds at the beginning of the word as well.

The algorithm returns X^2 as the set of quitting characters. This is correct as

1. no word not containing a character in X^2 can satisfy $f^1 \mathcal{U} f^2$
2. If a word satisfies $f^1 \mathcal{U} f^2$ from the first character, then it also satisfies $f^1 \mathcal{U} f^2$ from the second character onwards if f^2 is only satisfied later. If f^2 is satisfied from the first character onwards, then by the inductive hypothesis, the suffix of the word satisfies it as well (as otherwise X^2 would need to be $\bot$).

- **Case $f^1 \mathcal{R} f^2$**: This case is analogous to the $f^1 \mathcal{U} f^2$ case, except that $\bot$ is returned as quitting character set (which is always safe).

- **Case $X f^1$**: In this case, a new UVW is generated that has one initial state from which all initial states of the UVW for f^1 are reached unconditionally. This implements exactly that the first character of a (suffix) trace is ignored. The algorithm returns $\bot$ as quitting character set, which is a safe choice.

- **Cases $(\alpha \wedge \phi) \mathcal{U} (\neg \alpha \wedge \phi)$ and $(\alpha \wedge \phi) \mathcal{W} (\neg \alpha \wedge \phi)$**: These special cases are similar to the $f^1 \mathcal{U} f^2$ and $f^1 \mathcal{R} f^2$ cases above, except that quitting character sets are not needed for determining whether at least one run should stay in the initial state added to $\mathcal{A}^1$ and $\mathcal{A}^2$ by the construction. Instead, the b condition is used to detect when every run should leave the added state. As quitting character set, the TRANSLATE function returns $\bot$ in this case, which is always safe.

The termination of the algorithm for every possible LTL formula follows from the fact that the algorithm only recurses on disjunctions of sub-formulas that are present in the original LTL specification and it always recurses into strict subformulas. Note that this observation also shows that the computed automata have a number of states that is at most exponential in the length of the LTL formula. Cichon et al. [9] showed that the smallest non-deterministic Büchi automata for

LTL formulas of the shape $\bigwedge_{1 \leq i \leq n} F p_1$ need a number of states that is exponential in n in general. Since the negation of these LTL formulas are accepted by the grammar given above, it follows that an exponential blow-up for translating LTL formulas in our grammar to UVWs is unavoidable (as every UVW for a specification is also a non-deterministic Büchi word automaton for the complement language).

After constructing a UVW with the procedure from Algorithm 1, it makes sense to minimize it. Unlike in the general Büchi automaton case [10], in UVWs it is always sound to merge states with the same language. The only case in which this would be unsound is if both states lie in the same strongly connecting component, which cannot happen in UVWs. When merging UVW states, we can simply reroute all transitions to a higher-ranked state to the lower-ranked states (for some arbitrary valid ranking function). In addition we merge states that are reachable using the same prefix words, and if for some pair of states q_1 and q_2, we have that q_1 has a language that is a subset of the language of q_2, but whenever q_2 is reached for some prefix trace, so is q_1, we remove q_2 (if q_1 and q_2 are not reachable from each other). For simplicity, we approximate language inclusion by fair simulation [10].

4   Discussion

Before looking into how UVWs can simplify the debugging process of models in the next section, we want to discuss the merits and drawbacks of the grammar and construction given in the preceding section.

The grammar that we defined in the preceding section does not support the use of the $\wedge$ operator for the nonterminal ψ. This is a necessity. For example, the property $\phi = a \, \mathcal{U} \, (b \wedge (c \, \mathcal{U} \, d))$ cannot be represented as a UVW. When building a state in which the UVW waits for $(b \wedge (c \, \mathcal{U} \, d))$ to hold and checks for a to hold along the way, we cannot predict when the state should be left. If the character $\{a, b, c\}$ occurs, then the next character could be $\{a\}$ (so that a UVW run has to stay in the state), but the next character could also be $\{c\}$ (and then we would have just observed a good prefix for the LTL formula). We verified that indeed no UVW for this LTL formula exists by using the tool `ltl2dstar` to translate it to a single-pair deterministic Rabin automaton, and then applying the test from [14] (implemented as part of the `bassist` reactive synthesis tool [7]).

The UVWs computed by the construction from the previous section can be labeled by temporal logic formulas that they represent. For example, Fig. 1 shows a UVW for the LTL property $\psi = G((a \rightarrow b) \mathcal{U} \, c) \wedge GF(d \, \mathcal{U} \, e)$ that we computed with our approach. The states can be labeled by

$$
\begin{aligned}
&- \; q_0 \equiv \psi, && - \; q_2 \equiv (a \rightarrow b) \, \mathcal{U} \, c, \\
&- \; q_1 \equiv \textbf{true}, && - \; q_3 \equiv F(d \, \mathcal{U} \, e),
\end{aligned}
$$

which explains how the individual states contribute to the encoding of the LTL property. Our implementation of Algorithm 1 computes such a labelling automatically by keeping track of for which subformula a sub-UVW was computed.

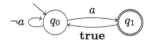

Fig. 3. A (minimally-sized) nondeterministic Büchi automaton for the language $\mathsf{GF}a$. All states represent the same language.

The later automaton minimization steps do not lead to a loss of this information, and since in UVWs, two states that represent the same language can always be merged, there is always only one state for each subformula, which makes them easy to understand. This is not the case for (non-deterministic) Büchi automata. Figure 3 shows an example nondeterministic Büchi automaton with two states that represent the same language. In fact, all Büchi automata that encode the same LTL formula have this property.

5 Case Studies and Experiments

5.1 LTL to UVW Translation

We implemented the translation from LTL to UVWs in Python. All experiments reported in the following were conducted on a computer with an Intel Core i5-7200U CPU and 16 GB of memory while using **spin** version 6.4.7 and **spot** [15] version 2.4.1 under the Ubuntu 16.04 LTS operating system. From the formal verification framework **spot**, we only use the **ltl2tgba** [15] tool for translating LTL properties to (non-deterministic) Büchi automata. In many cases the automata computed by our construction and by **spot** (for the negation of the respective specification) are very similar, but our construction always guarantees that the output is a very weak automaton. For example, **spot** does not translate the negation of the LTL property $\psi = \mathsf{G}(a \vee \mathsf{X}b)$ to a very weak automaton, even though there exists an equivalent UVW for ψ.

As a first experiment, we tested how many of the properties that Blahoudek et al. [3] compiled for a study are accepted by the grammar that we define in this paper. Out of the 134 unique properties, 77 can be translated to UVWs, as we found out using the construction from [14]. Of these, 74 are accepted by our grammar, and their translation to UVWs took 257 milliseconds of computation time in total. Out of the remaining three properties, one is equivalent to **true** and the other two differ only in the names of the atomic propositions.

5.2 Case Study

The *General Inter-Orb Protocol (GIOP)* is a key component in the Common Object Request Broker Architecture (CORBA). Kamel and Leue [16] gave a model and specifications for this protocol. One of the specifications that they give for this model is quite convoluted, and we chose it as main benchmark, as it can be translated to a non-trivial UVW. The property is as follows:

$$\psi = \mathsf{G}(\mathsf{F}r \rightarrow (\mathsf{G}((s \wedge \mathsf{F}r) \rightarrow (\bar{r}\,\mathcal{U}\,p))$$
$$\wedge\,\mathsf{G}((s \wedge \mathsf{F}r) \rightarrow ((\bar{p} \wedge \bar{r})\,\mathcal{U}\,(r \vee ((p \wedge \bar{r})\,\mathcal{U}\,(r \vee (\bar{p}\,\mathcal{U}\,r)))))))$$

It is neither a pure safety property, nor a pure liveness property. Proposition s represents that a user sends a request, p represents that a server processes a request, and r represents that a user receives a reply. Intuitively, the formula states that if a user sends a request and eventually a reply message is received, that particular request was served exactly once in case of successful processing by the server or at most once in case of unsuccessful processing. So in any case, the same request should not be served and processed twice by the server.

The original model by Kamel and Leue is too large to model check it against the specification with spin and 16 GB of memory. To demonstrate how the simple shape of UVWs helps with understanding counter-example traces, we injected an error into the model, so that the model checker spin can compute a counter-example trace within the memory limit.

We use spin's exhaustive verification algorithm. The ltl2tgba tool of spot translates the (negation of the) LTL specification above to a Büchi automaton comprising of 6 states (which happens to be very weak). When trying to verify the GIOP model with this automaton as specification, spin generates an error trace of length 526 in 3.4 s using 893 Mbytes of memory. The error trace is quite long and hence hard to inspect. While the trace involves only few state changes in the specification automaton, due to the absence of a labelling of the states with the LTL properties that they represent, interpreting the trace is difficult.

The same experiment when executed with a UVW constructed with the algorithm presented in this paper leads to an error trace of length 524 in 1.71 s using a total memory of 510 Mbytes. Figure 4 shows the full UVW computed for the LTL property given above. It can be decomposed into 6 simple chains, which are highlighted by different colors. The smallest chain comprises of just two states, whereas the longest one has five states. When running spin for all simple chains (and the model) separately, we first of all observe that spin finds counter-example traces for all chains except for the chains along $q_0 \rightarrow T$ and $q_0 \rightarrow q_2 \rightarrow T$, for which the verification process ran out of memory (in 59.9 and 77 s, respectively). Out of remaining four, for two chains a trace of length 526 was computed by spin in 3.69 and 4.0 s. For the other two, traces of length 455 were computed in 5.24 and 2.16 s, respectively.

We analyze one of the traces of length 455, as they are shorter and hence easier to understand. We show the values of the variables s, r, and p in the characters of the counter-example trace in Fig. 5 along with the UVW chain. The UVW states are labeled by the following LTL formulas:

$- q_0 \equiv \psi$ $- q_5 \equiv \mathsf{G}\neg r \vee (\neg p\,\mathcal{U}\,r)$

$- q_4 \equiv \mathsf{G}\neg r \vee ((p \wedge \neg r)\mathcal{U}(r \vee (\neg p\,\mathcal{U}\,r)))$ $- q_2 \equiv \mathsf{G}\neg r$

Only those characters that lead to a state change in the UVW chain are shown. Restricting our attention to these characters gives us a summary of the error trace. The labelling shows that from state q_4, the trace character $s\overline{p}\overline{r}$ leads to the second disjunct of q_4 to only be satisfiable if $\neg p\,\mathcal{U}\,r$ holds in the future. The following two highlighted characters then successively lead to the violation of every disjunct of the remaining obligation. We can also see that the s variable has a **true** value in all cases, which implies that user requests are sent more than once, or that the sending process does not leave the "just sent" state along the trace. After a request is sent in character t_1, it is processed twice in t_2 and t_3, which is the cause for the violation – an absorbing rejecting state is reached immediately afterwards. With this analysis of the cause of the error, we could now further inspect the trace to find the parts of the execution leading towards the double processing of the request.

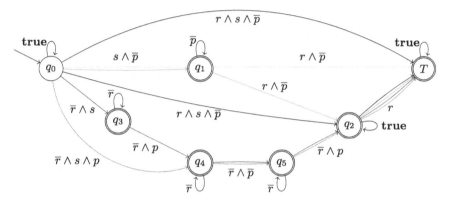

Fig. 4. UVW computed from our construction for the first case study. Each decomposed chain is highlighted with different color coding.

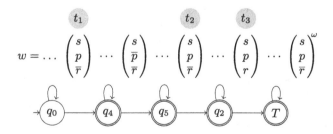

Fig. 5. Error trace analysis with a single chain of the UVW decomposition.

6   Conclusion

We defined a context-free grammar for a subset of LTL and a translation from specifications accepted by this grammar to universal very weak automata. The key technical contribution was the definition of *quitting points* for LTL properties, which we exploited to give a grammar that covers the vast majority of the properties that are translatable to UVWs from an LTL property database compiled by Blahoudek et al. [3]. Furthermore, our grammar contains all possible nestings of the LTL *Until* operator. All states in the UVWs computed by our construction are automatically labeled by LTL formulas that they represent, and even when applying classical simulation-based state reduction techniques, this information is not lost. We demonstrated using a short case study how the favourable properties of UVWs can be used to simplify a model debugging process. For space reasons, more thorough experiments are left for future work.

We believe that UVWs are also a useful automaton model for many other applications in the domain of formal methods. For instance, the translation presented in this paper is useful for *reactive synthesis*, where very large specifications need to be processed. Using UVWs to represent the specifications enables the use of *anti-chains* [17] as data structure for solving synthesis games without the introduction of counters that are normally used in *bounded synthesis* [18] for full LTL, which has the potential to substantially improve synthesis times.

References

1. Pnueli, A.: The temporal logic of programs. In: Proceedings of the 18th IEEE FOCS, pp. 46–57 (1977)
2. Clarke, E.M., Grumberg, O., Peled, D.: Model Checking. MIT Press, Cambridge (1999)
3. Blahoudek, F., Duret-Lutz, A., Kretínský, M., Strejcek, J.: Is there a best Büchi automaton for explicit model checking? In: SPIN Symposium, pp. 68–76 (2014)
4. Beer, I., Ben-David, S., Chockler, H., Orni, A., Trefler, R.J.: Explaining counterexamples using causality. Form. Methods Syst. Des. **40**(1), 20–40 (2012)
5. Basin, D., Bhatt, B.N., Traytel, D.: Optimal proofs for linear temporal logic on lasso words. In: 16th International Symposium on Automated Technology for Verification and Analysis (ATVA 2018) (2018)
6. Maidl, M.: The common fragment of CTL and LTL. In: Proceedings of the 41st Annual Symposium on Foundations of Computer Science (FOCS), pp. 643–652 (2000)
7. Ehlers, R.: ACTL ∩ LTL synthesis. In: Madhusudan, P., Seshia, Sanjit A. (eds.) CAV 2012. LNCS, vol. 7358, pp. 39–54. Springer, Heidelberg (2012). https://doi.org/10.1007/978-3-642-31424-7_9
8. Holzmann, G.J.: The SPIN Model Checker - Primer and Reference Manual. Addison-Wesley, Menlo Park (2004)
9. Cichon, J., Czubak, A., Jasinski, A.: Minimal Büchi automata for certain classes of LTL formulas. In: Fourth International Conference on Dependability of Computer Systems, (DepCos-RELCOMEX), pp. 17–24 (2009)
10. Gurumurthy, S., Bloem, R., Somenzi, F.: Fair simulation minimization. In: Brinksma, E., Larsen, K.G. (eds.) CAV 2002. LNCS, vol. 2404, pp. 610–623. Springer, Heidelberg (2002). https://doi.org/10.1007/3-540-45657-0_51
11. Vardi, M.Y.: Nontraditional applications of automata theory. In: Hagiya, M., Mitchell, J.C. (eds.) TACS 1994. LNCS, vol. 789, pp. 575–597. Springer, Heidelberg (1994). https://doi.org/10.1007/3-540-57887-0_116

12. Gerth, R., Peled, D.A., Vardi, M.Y., Wolper, P.: Simple on-the-fly automatic verification of linear temporal logic. In: Protocol Specification, Testing and Verification XV, pp. 3–18 (1995)
13. Ehlers, R.: Short witnesses and accepting lassos in ω-automata. In: Dediu, A.-H., Fernau, H., Martín-Vide, C. (eds.) LATA 2010. LNCS, vol. 6031, pp. 261–272. Springer, Heidelberg (2010). https://doi.org/10.1007/978-3-642-13089-2_22
14. Bojańczyk, M.: The common fragment of ACTL and LTL. In: Amadio, R. (ed.) FoSSaCS 2008. LNCS, vol. 4962, pp. 172–185. Springer, Heidelberg (2008). https://doi.org/10.1007/978-3-540-78499-9_13
15. Duret-Lutz, A.: LTL translation improvements in Spot 1.0. Int. J. Crit. Comput. Based Syst. 5(1/2), 31–54 (2014)
16. Kamel, M., Leue, S.: Validation of a remote object invocation and object migration in CORBA GIOP using Promela/Spin. In: International SPIN Workshop (1998)
17. Filiot, E., Jin, N., Raskin, J.: Antichains and compositional algorithms for LTL synthesis. Form. Methods Syst. Des. 39(3), 261–296 (2011)
18. Finkbeiner, B., Schewe, S.: Bounded synthesis. STTT 15(5–6), 519–539 (2013)

Quadratic Word Equations with Length Constraints, Counter Systems, and Presburger Arithmetic with Divisibility

Anthony W. Lin[1($\boxtimes$)] and Rupak Majumdar[2]

[1] Oxford University, Oxford, UK
antlin@cs.ox.ac.uk
[2] Max Planck Institute for Software Systems, Kaiserslautern, Germany

Abstract. Word equations are a crucial element in the theoretical foundation of constraint solving over strings. A word equation relates two words over string variables and constants. Its solution amounts to a function mapping variables to constant strings that equate the left and right hand sides of the equation. While the problem of solving word equations is decidable, the decidability of the problem of solving a word equation with a length constraint (i.e., a constraint relating the lengths of words in the word equation) has remained a long-standing open problem. We focus on the subclass of quadratic word equations, i.e., in which each variable occurs at most twice. We first show that the length abstractions of solutions to quadratic word equations are in general not Presburger-definable. We then describe a class of counter systems with Presburger transition relations which capture the length abstraction of a quadratic word equation with regular constraints. We provide an encoding of the effect of a simple loop of the counter systems in the existential theory of Presburger Arithmetic with divisibility (PAD). Since PAD is decidable, we get a decision procedure for quadratic words equations with length constraints for which the associated counter system is *flat* (i.e., all nodes belong to at most one cycle). In particular, we show a decidability result (in fact, also an NP algorithm with a PAD oracle) for a recently proposed NP-complete fragment of word equations called regular-oriented word equations, when augmented with length constraints. Decidability holds when the constraints are extended with regular constraints with a 1-weak control structure.

1 Introduction

Reasoning about strings is a fundamental problem in computer science and mathematics. The first order theory over strings and concatenation is undecidable. A seminal result by Makanin [24] (see also [11,15]) shows that the satisfiability problem for the *existential fragment* is decidable, by giving an algorithm for the satisfiability of *word equations*. A word equation $L = R$ consists of two words L and R over an alphabet of constants and variables. It is satisfiable if there is a

S. K. Lahiri and C. Wang (Eds.): ATVA 2018, LNCS 11138, pp. 352–369, 2018.
https://doi.org/10.1007/978-3-030-01090-4_21

mapping σ from the variables to strings over the constants such that $\sigma(L)$ and $\sigma(R)$ are syntactically identical.

An original motivation for studying word equations was to show undecidability of Hilbert's 10th problem (see, e.g., [26]). While Makanin's later result shows that word equations could not, by themselves, show undecidability, Matiyasevich in 1968 considered an extension of word equations with *length constraints* as a possible route to showing undecidability of Hilbert's 10th problem [26]. A length constraint constrains the solution of a word equation by requiring a linear relation to hold on the lengths of words in a solution σ (e.g., $|x| = |y|$, where $|\cdot|$ denotes the string-length function). The decidability of word equations with length constraints remains open.

In recent years, reasoning about strings with length constraints has found renewed interest through applications in program verification and reasoning about security vulnerabilities. The focus of most research has been on developing practical string solvers (cf. [1,5,6,14,16,21,28,31–33]). These solvers are sound but make no claims of completeness. Relatively few results are known about the decidability status of strings with length and other constraints (see [9] for an overview of the results in this area). The main idea in most existing decidability results is the encoding of length constraints into Presburger arithmetic [1,9,13,22]. However, as we shall see in this paper, the length abstraction of a word equation (i.e. the set of possible lengths of variables in its solutions) need not be Presburger definable.

In this paper, we consider the case of *quadratic* word equations, in which each variable can appear at most twice [12,19], together with length constraints and *regular constraints* (conjunctions $\bigwedge_{i=1}^{n} x \in L_i$ of assertions that the variable x must be assigned a string in the regular language L_i for each i). For quadratic word equations, there is a simpler decision procedure (called the Nielsen transform or Levi's method) based on a non-deterministic proof tree construction. The technique can be extended to handle regular constraints [12]. However, we show that already for this class (even for a simple equation like $xaby = yabx$, where x, y are variables and a, b are constants), the length abstraction need not be Presburger-definable. Thus, techniques based on Presburger encodings are not sufficient to prove decidability.

Our first observation in this paper is a connection between the problem of quadratic word equations with length constraints and a class of counter systems with Presburger transitions. Informally, the counter system has control states corresponding to the nodes of the proof tree constructed by Levi's method, and a counter standing for the length each word variable. Each step of Levi's method may decrease at most one counter. Thus, from any initial state, the counter system terminates. We show that the set of initial counter values which can lead to a successful leaf (i.e., one containing the trivial equation $\epsilon = \epsilon$) is precisely the length abstraction of the word equation.

Our second observation is that the reachability relation for a simple loop of the counter system can be encoded in the existential theory of Presburger arithmetic with divisibility ($\mathcal{PAD}$). The encoding is non-trivial in the presence of regular constraints, and depends on structural results on semilinear sets. As $\mathcal{PAD}$ is decidable [18,23], we obtain a technique to symbolically represent the reachability relation for *flat* counter systems, in which each node belongs to at most one loop.

Moreover, the same encoding shows decidability for word equations with length constraints, provided the proof tree is associated with flat counter systems. In particular, we show that the class of *regular-oriented* word equations, introduced by [10], have flat proof trees. Thus, the satisfiability problem for quadratic regular-oriented word equations with length constraints is decidable (and in NEXP[1]).

While our decidability result is for a simple subclass, this class is already non-trivial without length and regular constraints: satisfiability of regular-oriented word equations is NP-complete [10]. Our result generalizes previous decidability results [9]. Moreover, we believe that the techniques in this paper — the connection between acceleration and word equations, and the use of existential Presburger with divisibility — can pave the way to more sophisticated decision procedures based on counter system acceleration.

2   Preliminaries

General notation: Let $\mathbb{N} = \mathbb{Z}_{\geq 0}$ be the set of all natural numbers. For integers $i \leq j$, we use $[i,j]$ to denote the set $\{i, i+1, \ldots, j-1, j\}$ of integers. If $i \in \mathbb{N}$, let $[i]$ denote $[0,i]$. We use $\preceq$ to denote the component-wise ordering on $\mathbb{N}^k$, i.e., $(x_1, \ldots, x_k) \preceq (y_1, \ldots, y_k)$ iff $x_i \leq y_i$ for all $i \in [1,k]$. If $\bar{x} \preceq \bar{y}$ and $\bar{x} \neq \bar{y}$, we write $\bar{x} \prec \bar{y}$.

If S is a set, we use S^* to denote the set of all finite sequences, or *words*, $\gamma = s_1 \ldots s_n$ over S. The length $|\gamma|$ of γ is n. The empty sequence is denoted by ϵ. Notice that S^* forms a monoid with the concatenation operator $\cdot$. If γ' is a prefix of γ, we write $\gamma' \preceq \gamma$. Additionally, if $\gamma' \neq \gamma$ (i.e. a strict prefix of γ), we write $\gamma' \prec \gamma$. Note that the operator $\preceq$ is overloaded here, but the meaning should be clear from the context.

Words and automata: We assume basic familiarity with word combinatorics and automata theory. Fix a (finite) alphabet A. For each finite word $w := w_1 \ldots w_n \in A^*$, we write $w[i,j]$, where $1 \leq i \leq j \leq n$, to denote the segment $w_i \ldots w_j$.

Two words x and y are *conjugates* if there exist words u and v such that $x = uv$ and $y = vu$. Equivalently, $x = \text{cyc}^k(y)$ for some k and for the *cyclic permutation* operation $\text{cyc} : A^* \to A^*$, defined as $\text{cyc}(\epsilon) = \epsilon$, and $\text{cyc}(a \cdot w) = w \cdot a$ for $a \in A$ and $w \in A^*$.

Given a *nondeterministic finite automaton (NFA)* $\mathcal{A} := (A, Q, \Delta, q_0, q_F)$, a *run* of $\mathcal{A}$ on w is a function $\rho : \mathbb{N} \to Q$ with $\rho(0) = q_0$ that obeys the transition relation Δ. We may also denote the run ρ by the word $\rho(0) \cdots \rho(n)$ over the

---

[1]   In fact, it is a NP algorithm with an oracle access to $\mathcal{PAD}$. The best complexity bound for the latter is NEXP and NP-hardness [18].

alphabet Q. The run ρ is said to be *accepting* if $\rho(n) = q_F$, in which case we say that the word w is *accepted* by $\mathcal{A}$. The language $\mathcal{L}(\mathcal{A})$ of $\mathcal{A}$ is the set of words in A^* accepted by $\mathcal{A}$. In the sequel, for $p, q \in Q$ we will write $\mathcal{A}_{p,q}$ to denote the NFA $\mathcal{A}$ with initial state replaced by p and final state replaced by q.

Word equations: Let A be a (finite) alphabet of constants and V a set of variables; we assume $A \cap V = \emptyset$. A *word equation* E is an expression of the form $L = R$, where $(L, R) \in (A \cup V)^* \times (A \cup V)^*$. A system of word equations is a nonempty set $\{L_1 = R_1, L_2 = R_2, \ldots, L_k = R_k\}$ of word equations. The length of a system of word equations is the length $\sum_{i=1}^{k}(|L_i| + |R_i|)$. A system is called *quadratic* if each variable occurs at most twice in all. A *solution* to a system of word equations is a homomorphism $\sigma : (A \cup V)^* \to A^*$ which maps each $a \in A$ to itself that equates the l.h.s. and r.h.s. of each equation, i.e., $\sigma(L_i) = \sigma(R_i)$ for each $i = 1, \ldots, k$.

For each variable $x \in V$, we shall use $|x|$ to denote a formal variable that stands for the length of variable x, i.e., for any solution σ, the formal variable $|x|$ takes the value $|\sigma(x)|$. Let L_V be the set $\{|x| \mid x \in V\}$. A *length constraint* is a formula in Presburger arithmetic whose free variables are in L_V.

A *solution* to a system of word equations with a length constraint $\Phi(|x_1|, \ldots, |x_n|)$ is a homomorphism $\sigma : (A \cup V)^* \to A^*$ which maps each $a \in A$ to itself such that $\sigma(L_i) = \sigma(R_i)$ for each $i = 1, \ldots, k$ and moreover $\Phi(|\sigma(x_1)|, \ldots, |\sigma(x_n)|)$ holds. That is, the homomorphism maps each variable to a word in A^* such that each word equation is satisfied, and the lengths of these words satisfy the length constraint.

The *satisfiability problem* for word equations with length constraints asks, given a system of word equations and a length constraint, whether it has a solution.

We also consider the extension of the problem with regular constraints. For a system of word equations, a variable $x \in V$, and a regular language $\mathcal{L} \subseteq A^*$, a *regular constraint* $x \in \mathcal{L}$ imposes the additional restriction that any solution σ must satisfy $\sigma(x) \in \mathcal{L}$. Given a system of word equations, a length constraint, and a set of regular constraints, the satisfiability problem asks if there is a solution satisfying the word equation, the length constraints, as well as the regular constraints.

In the sequel, for clarity of exposition, we restrict our discussion to a system consisting of a single word equation.

Linear arithmetic with divisibility: Let $\mathcal{P}$ be a first-order language with equality, with binary relation symbol $\leq$, and with terms being linear polynomials with integer coefficients. We write $f(x)$, $g(x)$, etc., for terms in integer variables $x = x_1, \ldots, x_n$. Atomic formulas in Presburger arithmetic have the form $f(x) \leq g(x)$ or $f(x) = g(x)$. The language $\mathcal{PAD}$ of *Presburger arithmetic with divisibility* extends the language $\mathcal{P}$ with a binary relation $|$ (for divides). An atomic formula has the form $f(x) \leq g(x)$ or $f(x) = g(x)$ or $f(x)|g(x)$, where $f(x)$ and $g(x)$ are linear polynomials with integer coefficients. The full first order theory of $\mathcal{PAD}$ is undecidable, but the existential fragment is decidable [18,23].

Note that the divisibility predicate $x|y$ is *not* expressible in Presburger arithmetic: a simple way to see this is that $\{(x, y) \in \mathbb{N}^2 \mid x|y\}$ is not a semi-linear set.

Counter systems: In this paper, we specifically use the term "counter systems" to mean counter systems with Presburger transition relations (e.g. see [3]). These more general transition relations can be simulated by standard Minsky's counter machines, but they are more useful for coming up with decidable subclasses of counter systems. A *counter system* $\mathcal{C}$ is a tuple (X, Q, Δ), where $X = \{x_1, \ldots, x_m\}$ is a finite set of counters, Q is a finite set of control states, and Δ is a finite set of transitions of the form $(q, \Phi(\bar{x}, \bar{x}'), q')$, where $q, q' \in Q$ and Φ is a Presburger formula with free variables $x_1, \ldots, x_m, x_1', \ldots, x_m'$. A *configuration* of $\mathcal{C}$ is a tuple $(q, \mathbf{v}) \in Q \times \mathbb{N}^m$.

The semantics of counter systems is given as a transition system. A *transition system* is a tuple $\mathfrak{S} := \langle S; \rightarrow \rangle$, where S is a set of *configurations* and $\rightarrow \subseteq S \times S$ is a binary relation over S. A *path* in $\mathfrak{S}$ is a sequence $s_0 \rightarrow \cdots \rightarrow s_n$ of configurations $s_0, \ldots, s_n \in S$. If $S' \subseteq S$, let $pre^*(S')$ denote the set of $s \in S$ such that $s \rightarrow^* s'$ for some $s' \in S'$. We might write $pre^*_{\rightarrow}(S')$ to disambiguate the transition system.

A counter system $\mathcal{C}$ generates the transition system $\mathfrak{S}_{\mathcal{C}} = \langle S; \rightarrow \rangle$, where S is the set of all configurations of $\mathcal{C}$, and $(q, \mathbf{V}) \rightarrow (q', \mathbf{V}')$ if there exists a transition $(q, \Phi(\bar{x}, \bar{x}'), q') \in \Delta$ such that $\Phi(\mathbf{v}, \mathbf{v}')$ is true.

In the sequel, we will be needing the notion of flat counter systems [3,4,7,20]. Given a counter system $\mathcal{C} = (X, Q, \Delta)$, the *control structure* of $\mathcal{C}$ is an edge-labeled directed graph $G = (V, E)$ with the set $V = Q$ of nodes and the set $E = \Delta$. The counter system $\mathcal{C}$ is *flat* if each node $v \in V$ is contained in at most one simple cycle.

3   Solving Quadratic Word Equations

We start by recalling a simple textbook recipe (Nielsen transformation, a.k.a., Levi's Method) [11,19] for solving quadratic word equations, both for the cases with and without regular constraints. We then discuss the length abstractions of solutions to quadratic word equations, and provide a natural example that is not Presburger-definable.

3.1   Nielsen Transformation

We will define a rewriting relation $E \Rightarrow E'$ between quadratic word equations E, E'. Let E be an equation of the form $\alpha w_1 = \beta w_2$ with $w_1, w_2 \in (A \cup V)^*$ and $\alpha, \beta \in A \cup V$. Then, there are several possible E':

- *Rules for erasing an empty prefix variable.* These rules can be applied if $\alpha \in V$ (symmetrically, $\beta \in V$). We nondeterministically guess that α be the empty word ϵ, i.e., E' is $(w_1 = \beta w_2)[\epsilon/\alpha]$. The symmetric case of $\beta \in V$ is similar.
- *Rules for removing a nonempty prefix.* These rules are applicable if each of α and β is either a constant or a variable that we nondeterministically guess to be a nonempty word. There are several cases:

(P1) $\alpha \equiv \beta$ (syntactic equality). In this case, E' is $w_1 = w_2$.

(P2) $\alpha \in A$ and $\beta \in V$. In this case, E' is $w_1[\alpha\beta/\beta] = \beta(w_2[\alpha\beta/\beta])$. In the sequel, to avoid notational clutter we will write $\beta w_2[\alpha\beta/\beta]$ instead of $\beta(w_2[\alpha\beta/\beta])$.

(P3) $\alpha \in V$ and $\beta \in A$. In this case, E' is $\alpha(w_1[\beta\alpha/\alpha]) = w_2[\beta\alpha/\alpha]$.

(P4) $\alpha, \beta \in V$. In this case, we nondeterministically guess if $\alpha \preceq \beta$ or $\beta \preceq \alpha$. In the former case, the equation E' is $w_1[\alpha\beta/\beta] = \beta(w_2[\alpha\beta/\beta])$. In the latter case, the equation E' is E' is $\alpha(w_1[\beta\alpha/\alpha]) = w_2[\beta\alpha/\alpha]$.

Note that the transformation keeps an equation quadratic.

Proposition 1. *E is solvable iff* $E \Rightarrow^* (\epsilon = \epsilon)$. *Furthermore, checking if E is solvable is in PSPACE.*

See [11] for a proof. Roughly speaking, the proof uses the fact that each step either decreases the size of the equation, or the length of a length-minimal solution. It runs in PSPACE because each rewriting does not increase the size of the equation.

3.2 Handling Regular Constraints

Nielsen transformation easily extends to quadratic word equations with regular constraints (e.g. see [12]). We assume that a regular constraint $x \in \mathcal{L}$ is given as an NFA $\mathcal{A}_{p,q}$ representing $\mathcal{L}$. If q_0 and q_F are the initial and final states (respectively) of an NFA $\mathcal{A}$, we can be more explicit and write $\mathcal{A}_{q_0,q_F}$ instead of $\mathcal{A}$.

Our rewriting relation $\Rightarrow$ now works over a pair consisting of an equation E and a set S of regular constraints over variables in E. Let E be an equation of the form $\alpha w_1 = \beta w_2$ with $w_1, w_2 \in (A \cup V)^*$ and $\alpha, \beta \in A \cup V$. We now define $(E, S) \Rightarrow (E', S')$ by extending the pervious definition of $\Rightarrow$ without regular constraints. Firstly, we make sure that S is satisfiable by a standard automata-theoretic algorithm, which can be done in PSPACE. In particular, it has to be the case that $E \Rightarrow E'$ and additionally do the following:

- *Rules for erasing an empty prefix variable* α. When applied, ensure that each regular constraint $\alpha \in \mathcal{L}$ in S satisfies $\epsilon \in \mathcal{L}$. Define S' as S minus all regular constraints of the form $\alpha \in \mathcal{L}$.
- *Rules for removing a nonempty prefix.* For (P1), we set S' to be S minus all constraints of the form $\alpha \in \mathcal{L}$ if α is a variable. For (P2)–(P4), assume that E' is $w_1[\alpha\beta/\beta] = \beta(w_2[\alpha\beta/\beta])$; the other case is symmetric. For each regular constraint $\beta \in \mathcal{L}(\mathcal{A}_{p,q})$, we nondeterministically guess a state r, and add $\alpha \in \mathcal{L}(\mathcal{A}_{p,r})$ and $\beta \in \mathcal{L}(\mathcal{A}_{r,q})$ to S'. In the case when $\alpha \in A$, we could immediately perform the check $\alpha \in \mathcal{L}(\mathcal{A}_{p,r})$: a positive outcome implies removing this constraint from S', while on a negative outcome our algorithm simply fails on this branch. For any variable y that is distinct from β, we add all regular constraints $y \in L$ in S to S'. If α still occurs in E', add regular constraints $\alpha \in L$ in S to S'. If S' is unsatisfiable, fail on this this branch.

Proposition 2. (E, S) *is solvable iff* $(E, S) \Rightarrow^* (\epsilon = \epsilon, \emptyset)$. *Furthermore, checking if* (E, S) *is solvable is in PSPACE.*

Note that this is still a PSPACE algorithm because it never creates a new NFA or adds new states to existing NFA in the regular constraints, but rather adds a regular constraint $x \in \mathcal{L}(\mathcal{A}_{p,q})$ to a variable x, where $\mathcal{A}$ is an NFA that is already in the regular constraint.

3.3 Generating All Solutions Using Nielsen Transformation

One result that we will need in this paper is that Nielsen transformation is able to *generate all solutions* of quadratic word equations with regular constraints. To clarify this, we extend the definition of $\Rightarrow$ so that each a configuration E or (E, S) in the graph of $\Rightarrow$ is also annotated by an assignment σ of the variables in E to concrete strings. We write $E_1[\sigma_1] \Rightarrow E_2[\sigma_2]$ if $E_1 \Rightarrow E_2$ and σ_2 is the modification from σ_1 according to the operation used to obtain E_2 from E_1. Observe that the domain of σ_2 is a subset of the domain of σ_1; in fact, some rules (e.g., erasing an empty prefix variable) could remove a variable in the prefix in E_1 from σ_1. The following example illustrates how $\Rightarrow$ works with this extra annotated assignment. Suppose that $\sigma_1(x) = ab$ and $\sigma_1(y) = abab$ and $E_1 := xy = yx$ and E_2 is obtained from E_1 using rule (P4), i.e., substitute xy for y. In this case, $\sigma_2(x) = \sigma_2(y) = \sigma_1(x) = ab$. Observe that $E_2[\sigma_2] \Rightarrow E_3[\sigma_3] \Rightarrow E_4[\sigma_4]$, where $E_3 := E_2$, $\sigma_3(x) = ab$, $\sigma_3(y) = \epsilon$, $E_4 := x = x$, and $\sigma_4(x) = ab$. The definition for the case with regular constraints is identical.

Proposition 3. $(E, S)[\sigma] \rightarrow^* (\epsilon = \epsilon, \emptyset)[\sigma']$ *where* σ' *has the empty domain iff* σ *is a solution of* (E, S).

This proposition immediately follows from the proof of correctness of Nielsen transformation for quadratic word equations (cf. [11]).

3.4 Length Abstractions and Semilinearity

Given a quadratic word equation E with constants A and variables $V = \{x_1, \ldots, x_k\}$, its *length abstraction* is defined as follows

$$\text{LEN}(E) = \{(|\sigma(x_1)|, \ldots, |\sigma(x_k)|) : \sigma \text{ is a solution to } E\},$$

namely the set of tuples of numbers corresponding to lengths of solutions to E.

Example 1. Consider the quadratic equation $E := xaby = yz$, where $V = \{x, y, z\}$ and A contains at least two letters a and b. We will show that its length abstraction $\text{LEN}(E)$ can be captured by the Presburger formula $|z| = |x| + 2$. Observe that each $(n_x, n_y, n_z) \in \text{LEN}(E)$ must satisfy $n_z = n_x + 2$ by a length argument on E. Conversely, we will show that each triple $(n_x, n_y, n_z) \in \mathbb{N}^3$ satisfying $n_z = n_x + 2$ must be in $\text{LEN}(E)$. To this end, we will define a solution σ to E such that $(|\sigma(x)|, |\sigma(y)|, |\sigma(z)|) = (n_x, n_y, n_z)$. Consider $\sigma(x) = a^{n_x}$.

Then, for some $q \in \mathbb{N}$ and $r \in [n_x + 1]$, we have $n_y = q(n_x + 2) + r$. Let w be a prefix of $\sigma(x)ab$ of length r. Therefore, for some v, we have $wv = \sigma(x)ab$. Define $\sigma(y) = (\sigma(x)ab)^q w$. We then have $\sigma(x)ab\sigma(y) = \sigma(y)vw$. Thus, setting $\sigma(z) = vw$ gives us a satisfying assignment for E which satisfies the desired length constraint. □

However, it turns out that Presburger Arithmetic is not sufficient for capturing length abstractions of quadratic word equations.

Theorem 1. *There is a quadratic word equation whose length abstraction is not Presburger-definable.*

To this end, we show that the length abstraction of $xaby = yabx$, where $a, b \in A$ and $x, y \in V$, is not Presburger definable.

Lemma 1. *The length abstraction* $\mathrm{LEN}(xaby = yabx)$ *coincides with tuples* $(|x|, |y|)$ *of numbers satisfying the expression* $\varphi(|x|, |y|)$ *defined as:*

$$|x| = |y| \vee (|x| = 0 \wedge |y| \equiv 0 \pmod 2) \vee (|y| = 0 \wedge |x| \equiv 0 \pmod 2)$$
$$\vee\, (|x|, |y| > 0 \wedge \gcd(|x| + 2, |y| + 2) > 1)$$

Observe that this would imply non-Presburger-definability: for otherwise, since the first three disjuncts are Presburger-definable, the last disjunct would also be Presburger-definable, which is not the case since the property that two numbers are relatively prime is not Presburger-definable. Let us prove this lemma. Let $S = \mathrm{LEN}(xaby = yabx)$. We first show that given any numbers n_x, n_y satisfying $\varphi(n_x, n_y)$, there are solutions σ to $xaby = yabx$ with $|\sigma(x)| = n_x$ and $|\sigma(y)| = n_y$. If they satisfy the first disjunct in φ (i.e., $n_x = n_y$), then set $\sigma(x) = \sigma(y)$ to an arbitrary word $w \in A^{n_x}$. If they satisfy the second disjunct, then $aby = yab$ and so set $\sigma(x) = \epsilon$ and $\sigma(y) \in (ab)^*$. The same goes with the third disjunct, symmetrically. For the fourth disjunct (assuming the first three disjuncts are false), let $d = \gcd(n_x + 2, n_y + 2)$. Define $\sigma(x), \sigma(y) \in (a^{d-1}b)^*(a^{d-2})$ so that $|\sigma(\alpha)| = n_\alpha$ for $\alpha \in V$. It follows that $\sigma(x)ab\sigma(y) = \sigma(y)ab\sigma(x)$.

We now prove the converse. So, we are given a solution σ to $xaby = yabx$ and let $u := \sigma(x)$, $v := \sigma(y)$. Assume to the contrary that $\varphi(|u|, |v|)$ is false and that u and v are the shortest such solutions. We have several cases to consider:

- $u = v$. Then, $|u| = |v|$, contradicting that $\varphi(|u|, |v|)$ is false.
- $u = \epsilon$. Then, $abv = vab$ and so $v \in (ab)^*$, which implies that $|v| \equiv 0 \pmod 2$. Contradicting that $\varphi(|u|, |v|)$ is false.
- $v = \epsilon$. Same as previous item and that $|u| \equiv 0 \pmod 2$.
- $|u| > |v| > 0$. Since $\varphi(|u|, |v|)$ is false, we have $\gcd(|u| + 2, |v| + 2) = 1$. It cannot be the case that $|u| = |v| + 1$ since then, comparing prefixes of $uabv = vabu$, the letter at position $|u| + 2$ would be b on l.h.s. and a on r.h.s., which is a contradiction. Therefore $|u| \geq |v| + 2$. Let $u' = u[|v| + 3, |u|]$, i.e., u but with its prefix of length $|v| + 2$ removed. By Nielsen transformation, we have $u'abv = vabu'$. It cannot be the case that $u' = \epsilon$; for, otherwise, $abv = vab$ implies $v \in (ab)^*$ and so $u = vab$, implying that 2 divides both

$|u| + 2$ and $|v| + 2$, contradicting that $\gcd(|u| + 2, |v| + 2) = 1$. Therefore, $|u'| > 0$. Since $\gcd(|u'| + 2, |v| + 2) = \gcd(|u| + 2, |v| + 2) = 1$, we have a shorter solution to $xaby = yabx$, contradicting minimality.
- $|v| > |u| > 0$. Same as previous item.

4   Reduction to Counter Systems

In this section, we will provide an algorithm for computing a counter system from (E, S), where E is a quadratic word equation and S is a set of regular constraints. We will first describe this algorithm for the case without regular constraints, after which we show the extension to the case with regular constraints.

Given the quadratic word equation E, we show how to compute a counter system $\mathcal{C}(E) = (X, Q, \Delta)$ such that the following theorem holds.

Theorem 2. *The length abstraction of E coincides with*

$$\{v \in \mathbb{N}^{|V|} \mid (E, v) \in pre^*_{\mathcal{C}(E)}(\{\epsilon = \epsilon\} \times \mathbb{N}^{|V|})\}$$

Before defining $\mathcal{C}(E)$, we define some notation. Define the following formulas:

- $\mathtt{ID}(\bar{x}, \bar{x}') := \bigwedge_{x \in \bar{x}} x' = x$
- $\mathtt{SUB}_{y,z}(\bar{x}, \bar{x}') := z \le y \wedge y' = y - z \wedge \bigwedge_{x \in \bar{x}, x \neq y} x' = x$
- $\mathtt{DEC}_y(\bar{x}, \bar{x}') := y > 0 \wedge y' = y - 1 \wedge \bigwedge_{x \in \bar{x}, x \neq y} x' = x$

Note that the $\neq$ symbol in the guard of $\bigwedge$ denotes syntactic equality (i.e. not equality in Preburger Arithmetic). We omit mention of the free variables $\bar{x}$ and $\bar{x}'$ when they are clear from the context.

We now define the counter system. Given a quadratic word equation E with constants A and variables V, we define a counter system $\mathcal{C}(E) = (X, Q, \Delta)$ as follows. The counters X will be precisely all variables that appear in E, i.e., $X := V$. The control states are precisely all equations E' that can be rewritten from E using Nielsen transformation, i.e., $Q := \{E' : E \Rightarrow^* E'\}$. The set Q is finite (at most exponential in $|E|$) as per our discussion in the previous section.

We now define the transition relation Δ. We use $\bar{x}$ to enumerate V in some order. Given $E_1 \Rightarrow E_2$ with $E_1, E_2 \in Q$, we then add the transition $(E_1, \Phi(\bar{x}, \bar{x}'), E_2)$, where Φ is defined as follows:

- If $E_1 \Rightarrow E_2$ applies a rule for erasing an empty prefix variable $y \in \bar{x}$, then $\Phi := y = 0 \wedge \mathtt{ID}$.
- If $E_1 \Rightarrow E_2$ applies a rule for removing a nonempty prefix:
  - If (P1) is applied, then $\Phi = \mathtt{ID}$.
  - If (P2) is applied, then $\Phi = \mathtt{DEC}_\beta$.
  - If (P3) is applied, then $\Phi = \mathtt{DEC}_\alpha$.
  - If (P4) is applied and $\alpha \preceq \beta$, then $\Phi = \mathtt{SUB}_{\beta,\alpha}$. If $\beta \preceq \alpha$, then $\Phi = \mathtt{SUB}_{\alpha,\beta}$.

Observe that if $(E_1, \mathbf{v}_1) \to (E_2, \mathbf{v}_2)$, then $|E_1| \leq |E_2|$ and $\mathbf{v}_1 \preceq \mathbf{v}_2$. In addition, if $\mathbf{v}_1 = \mathbf{v}_2$, then $|E_1| < |E_2|$. This implies the following lemma.

Lemma 2. *The counter system* $\mathcal{C}(E)$ *terminates from every configuration* $(E_0, \mathbf{v}_0)$.

The proof of Theorem 2 immediately follows from Proposition 3 that Nielsen transformation generates all solutions.

Extension to the case with regular constraints: In this extension, we will only need to assert that the counter values belong to the length abstractions of the regular constraints, which are effectively semilinear due to Parikh's Theorem [27]. Given a quadratic word equation E with a set S of regular constraints, we define the counter system $\mathcal{C}(E, S) = (X, Q, \Delta)$ as follows. Let $\mathcal{C}(E) = (X_1, Q_1, \Delta_1)$ be the counter system from the previous paragraph, obtained by ignoring the regular constraints. We define $X = X_1$. Let Q be the finite set of all configurations reachable from (E, S), i.e., $Q = \{(E', S') : (E, S) \Rightarrow^* (E', S')\}$. Given $(E_1, S_1) \Rightarrow (E_2, S_2)$, we add the transition $((E_1, S_2), \Phi(\bar{x}, \bar{x}'), (E_2, S_2))$ as follows. Suppose that $(E_1, \Phi'(\bar{x}, \bar{x}'), E_2)$ was added to Δ_1 by $E_1 \Rightarrow E_2$. Then,

$$\Phi := \Phi' \wedge \bigwedge_{x \in \bar{x}} \left(x \in \text{LEN}(\bigcap_{(x \in L) \in S} L) \wedge x' \in \text{LEN}(\bigcap_{(x \in L) \in S'} L) \right).$$

The size of the NFA for $\bigcap_{(x \in L) \in S} L$ is exponential in the number of constraints of the form $(x \in L)$ in S (of which there are polynomially many). The constraint $x \in \text{LEN}(L)$ is well-known to be effectively semilinear [27]. In fact, using the algorithm of Chrobak-Martinez [8,25,29], we can compute in polynomial time two finite sets A, A' of integers and an integer b such that, for each $n \in \mathbb{N}$, $n \in U := A \cup (A' + b\mathbb{N})$ is true iff $n \in \text{LEN}(L)$. Note that U is a finite union of arithmetic progressions (with period 0 and/or b). In fact, each number $a \in A \cup A'$ (resp. the number b) is at most quadratic in the size of the NFA, and so it is a polynomial [2] size even when they are written in unary. Therefore, treating U as an existential Presburger formula $\varphi(x)$ with one free variable (an existential quantifier is needed to guess the coefficient n such that $x = a_i + bn$ for some i), the resulting Φ' is a polynomial-sized existential Presburger formula.

Theorem 3. *The length abstraction of* (E, S) *coincides with*

$$\{v \in \mathbb{N}^{|V|} \mid ((E, S), v) \in pre^*_{\mathcal{C}(E,S)}(\{(\epsilon = \epsilon, \emptyset)\} \times \mathbb{N}^{|V|})\}$$

As for the case without regular constraints, the proof of Theorem 2 immediately follows from Proposition 3 that Nielsen transformation generates all solutions.

---

[2] Note that we mean polynomial in the size of the NFA, which can be exponential in $|S|$.

5   Decidability via Linear Arithmetic with Divisibility

5.1   Accelerating a 1-Variable-Reducing Cycle

Consider a counter system $\mathcal{C} = (X, Q, \Delta)$ with $Q = \{q_0, \dots, q_{n-1}\}$, such that for some $y \in X$ the transition relation Δ consists of precisely the following transition $(q_i, \Phi_i, q_{i+1 \pmod n})$, for each $i \in [n-1]$, and each Φ_i is either $\mathtt{SUB}_{y,z}$ (with z a variable distinct from y) or $\mathtt{DEC}_y$. Such a counter system is said to be a *1-variable-reducing cycle*.

Lemma 3. *There exists a polynomial-time algorithm which given a 1-variable-reducing cycle $\mathcal{C} = (X, Q, \Delta)$ and two states $p, q \in Q$ computes an formula $\varphi_{p,q}(\bar{x}, \bar{x}')$ in existential Presburger arithmetic with divisibility such that $(p, \mathbf{v}) \rightarrow_{\mathcal{C}}^* (q, \mathbf{w})$ iff $\varphi_{p,q}(\mathbf{v}, \mathbf{w})$ is satisfiable.*

This lemma can be seen as a special case of the acceleration lemma for flat parametric counter automata [7] (where all variables other than y are treated as parameters). However, its proof is in fact quite simple. Without loss of generality, we assume that $q = q_0$ and $p = q_i$, for some $i \in \mathbb{N}$. Any path $(q_0, \mathbf{v}) \rightarrow_{\mathcal{C}}^* (q_i, \mathbf{w})$ can be decomposed into the cycle $(q_0, \mathbf{v}) \rightarrow^* (q_0, \mathbf{v}')$ and the simple path $(q_0, \mathbf{w}_0) \rightarrow \cdots \rightarrow (q_i, \mathbf{w}_i)$ of length i. Therefore, the reachability relation $(q_0, \mathbf{x}) \rightarrow_{\mathcal{C}}^* (q_i, \mathbf{y})$ can be expressed as

$$\exists \mathbf{z}_0, \cdots, \mathbf{z}_{i-1} : \varphi_{q_0, q_0}(\mathbf{x}, \mathbf{z}_0) \wedge \Phi_0(\mathbf{z}_0, \mathbf{z}_1) \wedge \cdots \wedge \Phi_{i-1}(\mathbf{z}_{i-1}, \mathbf{y}).$$

Thus, it suffices to show that $\varphi_{q_0, q_0}(\mathbf{x}, \mathbf{x}')$ is expressible in $\mathcal{PAD}$. Consider a linear expression $M = a_0 + \sum_{x \in X \setminus \{y\}} a_x x$, where a_0 is the number of instructions i in the cycle such that $\Phi_i = \mathtt{DEC}_y$ and a_x is the number of instructions i such that $\Phi_i = \mathtt{SUB}_{y,x}$. Each time around the cycle, y decreases by M. Thus, for some $n \in \mathbb{N}$ we have $y' = y - nM$, or equivalently

$$nM = y - y'$$

The formula φ_{q_0, q_0} can be defined as follows:

$$\varphi_{q_0, q_0} := M \mid (y - y') \wedge y' \le y \wedge \bigwedge_{x \in X \setminus \{y\}} x' = x.$$

Handling unary Presburger guards: Recalling our reduction for the case with regular constraints from Sect. 4 reveals that we also need unary Presburger guards on the counters. We will show how to extend Lemma 3 to handle such guards. As we will see shortly, we will need a bit of the theory of semilinear sets.

As before, our counter system $\mathcal{C} = (X, Q, \Delta)$ has $Q = \{q_0, \dots, q_{n-1}\}$, and the control structure is a simple cycle of length n, i.e., the transitions in Δ are precisely $(q_i, \Phi_i, q_{i+1 \pmod n})$ for some Presburger formula $\Phi_i(\bar{x}, \bar{x}')$, for each $i \in [n-1]$. We say that $\mathcal{C}$ is *1-variable-reducing with unary Presburger guards* if there exists a counter $y \in X$ such that each Φ_i is of the form $\theta_i \wedge \psi_i$, where θ_i is either $\mathtt{SUB}_{y,z}$ (with z a variable distinct from y) or $\mathtt{DEC}_y$, and ψ_i is a conjunction of formulas of the form $x \in A_i \cup (A_i' + b\mathbb{N})$, where both A_i and A_i' are finite sets of natural numbers and $x \in X$. For each counter $x \in X$, we use $\psi_{i,x}$ to denote the set of conjuncts in ψ_i that refers to the counter x.

Lemma 4. *There exists a polynomial-time algorithm which given a 1-variable-reducing cycle with unary Presburger guards $\mathcal{C} = (X, Q, \Delta)$ and two states $p, q \in Q$ computes an formula $\lambda_{p,q}(\bar{x}, \bar{x}')$ in existential Presburger arithmetic with divisibility such that $(p, \mathbf{v}) \to_{\mathcal{C}}^* (q, \mathbf{w})$ iff $\lambda_{p,q}(\mathbf{v}, \mathbf{w})$ is satisfiable.*

Unlike Lemma 3, this lemma does not immediately follow from the results of [7] on flat parametric counter automata. To prove this, let us first take the formula $\varphi_{p,q}(\bar{x}, \bar{x}')$ from Lemma 3 applied to $\mathcal{C}'$, which is obtained from $\mathcal{C}$ by first removing the unary Presburger guards. We can insert these unary Presburger guards to $\varphi_{p,q}$, but this is not enough because we need to make sure that all "intermediate" values of y have to also satisfy the Presburger guards corresponding to y on that control state. More precisely, let the counter decrement in θ_i be α_i (which can either be a variable x distinct from y or 1). Write $f(\bar{x}) = \sum_{i=0}^{n-1} \alpha_i$. Then, we can write

$$\lambda_{q_0,q_0} := \bar{x}' = \bar{x} \vee \left(\varphi_{q_0,q_0} \wedge \bigwedge_{i=0}^{n-1} \psi_i(\bar{x}) \wedge \eta_{q_0,q_0} \right)$$

$$\eta_{q_0,q_0} := \forall k : y' + (k+1)f(\bar{x}) \leq y \longrightarrow$$
$$\left(\bigwedge_{i=0}^{n-1} \bigwedge_{(\alpha_i \in A \cup A' + b\mathbb{N}) \in \psi_{i,y}} y' + kf(\bar{x}) + \alpha_i \in A \cup (A' + b\mathbb{N}) \right)$$

Owing to the constraint φ_{q_0,q_0}, the premise $y' + (k+1)f(\bar{x}) \leq y$ in η_{q_0,q_0} could have been rewritten to $y' + (k+1)f(\bar{x}) = y$. As we shall soon see, the former will be more useful for completing our proof of Lemma 4. The formula λ_{q_0,q_0} is a correct expression that captures the reachability relation $(q_0, \mathbf{w}) \to_{\mathcal{C}}^* (q_0, \mathbf{w}')$, but the problem is that it has a universal quantifier and therefore is not a formula of existential Presburger arithmetic with divisibility. To fix this problem, we will need to exploit the semilinear structure of unary Presburger guards. To this end, we first notice that, by taking the big conjunction over i and the big conjunction over α_i out, the formula η_{q_0,q_0} is equivalent to:

$$\eta_{q_0,q_0} \equiv \bigwedge_{i=0}^{n-1} \bigwedge_{(\alpha_i \in A \cup A' + b\mathbb{N}) \in \psi_{i,y}} \forall k : y' + (k+1)f(\bar{x}) \leq y \longrightarrow$$
$$(y' + kf(\bar{x}) + \alpha_i \in A \cup (A' + b\mathbb{N}))$$

Therefore, it suffices to rewrite each conjunct $C(\bar{x}) := \forall k : y' + (k+1)f(\bar{x}) \leq y \longrightarrow (y' + kf(\bar{x}) + \alpha_i \in A \cup (A' + b\mathbb{N}))$ as an existential Presburger formula, for each i and constraint $(\alpha_i \in A \cup A' + b\mathbb{N})$. To this end, let $a := \max A$ and let N denote $|A'|$. We claim that φ_{q_0,q_0} entails

$$C(\bar{x}) \Leftrightarrow \bigwedge_{i=0}^{a} y' + (i+1)f(\bar{x}) \le y \to y' + if(\bar{x}) + \alpha_i \in A \cup (A' + b\mathbb{N})$$

$$\wedge \bigwedge_{i=a+1}^{a+N+1} y' + (i+1)f(\bar{x}) \le y \to y' + if(\bar{x}) + \alpha_i \in A' + b\mathbb{N}.$$

Simply put, we distinguish the cases when $y' + if(\bar{x}) + \alpha_i$ is "small" (i.e., less than the maximum threshold that can keep this number in an arithmetic progression with 0 period), and when this number is "big" (i.e. must be in an arithmetic progression with a nonzero period). To prove this equivalence, it suffices to show that if $y' + kf(\bar{x}) + \alpha_i \notin A \cup (A' + b\mathbb{N})$ with $k > a+N+1$ and $y' + (k+1)f(\bar{x}) \le y$ (i.e. $y' + kf(\bar{x}) + \alpha_i \le y$ since $y' = y + hf(\bar{x})$ for some h because of φ_{q_0, q_0}), then we can find $k' \le a + N + 1$ such that $y' + k'f(\bar{x}) + \alpha_i \notin A \cup (A' + b\mathbb{N})$. Suppose to the contrary that such k' does not exist. Then, since there are $N+1$ numbers in between $a + 1$ and $a + N + 1$, by pigeonhole principle there is an arithmetic progression $a' + b\mathbb{N}$ and two different numbers $a+1 \le j_1 < j_2 \le a+N+1$ such that $y' + j_h f(\bar{x}) + \alpha_i \in a' + b\mathbb{N}$, for $h = 1, 2$. Let $d := (j_2 - j_1)$. Note that $df(\bar{x})$ denotes the difference between $y' + j_1 f(\bar{x}) + \alpha_i$ and $y' + j_2 f(\bar{x}) + \alpha_i$, and this difference is of the form mb, for some positive integer m. We now find a number $j \in [a+1, a+N]$ with $j + qd = k$ for some positive integer q. Since $y' + jf(\bar{x}) + \alpha_i \in a'' + b\mathbb{N}$ for some $a'' \in A'$, it must be the case that $y' + (j + qd)f(\bar{x}) + \alpha_i \in a'' + b\mathbb{N}$ for $q \in \mathbb{N}$, contradicting that $y' + kf(\bar{x}) + \alpha_i \notin A \cup (A' + b\mathbb{N})$.

We have proven correctness, and what remains is to analyse the size of the formula λ_{q_0, q_0}. To this end, it suffices to show that each formula $C(\bar{x})$ is of polynomial size. This is in fact the case since there are at most polynomially many numbers in A and A' and that the size of all numbers in $A \cup A' \cup \{b\}$ are of polynomial size even when they are written in unary.

5.2   An Extension to Flat Control Structures and an Acceleration Scheme

The following generalisation to flat control structures is an easy corollary of Lemmas 3 and 4.

Theorem 4. *There exists a polynomial-time algorithm which, given a flat Presburger counter system $\mathcal{C} = (X, Q, \Delta)$, each of whose simple cycle is 1-variable-reducing with unary Presburger guards and two states $p, q \in Q$, computes an formula $\lambda_{p,q}(\bar{x}, \bar{x}')$ in existential Presburger with divisibility such that $(p, \mathbf{v}) \to_{\mathcal{C}}^* (q, \mathbf{w})$ iff $\lambda_{p,q}(\mathbf{v}, \mathbf{w})$ is satisfiable.*

Indeed, to prove this theorem, we can simply use Lemma 4 to accelerate all cycles and the fact that transition relations expressed in existential Presburger with divisibility is closed under composition.

5.3   Application to Word Equations with Length Constraints

Theorem 4 gives rise to a simple and sound (but not complete) technique for solving quadratic word equations with length constraints: given a quadratic word equation (E, S) with regular constraints, if the counter system $\mathcal{C}(E, S)$ is flat, each of whose simple cycle is 1-variable-reducing with unary Presburger guards, then apply the decision procedure from Theorem 4. In this section, we show completeness of this method for the class of regular-oriented word equations recently defined in [10], which can be extended with regular constraints given as 1-weak NFA [2]. A word equation is *regular* if each variable $x \in V$ occurs at most once on each side of the equation. Observe that $xy = yx$ is regular, but $xxyy = zz$ is not. It is easy to see that a regular word equation is quadratic. A word equation $L = R$ is said to be *oriented* if there is a total ordering $<$ on V such that the occurrences of variables on each side of the equation preserve $<$, i.e., if $w = L$ or $w = R$ and $w = w_1 \alpha w_2 \beta w_3$ for some $w_1, w_2, w_3 \in (A \cup V)^*$ and $\alpha, \beta \in V$, then $\alpha < \beta$. Observe that $xy = yz$ (i.e. that x and z are conjugates) is oriented, but $xy = yx$ is not oriented. It was shown in [10] that the satisfiability for regular-oriented word equations is NP-hard. We show satisfiability for this class with length constraints is decidable.

Theorem 5. *The satisfiability problem of regular-oriented word equations with length constraints is decidable in nondeterministic exponential time.*

This decidability (in fact, an NP upper bound) for the *strictly regular-ordered* subcase, in which each variable occurs precisely once on each side, was proven in [9]. For this subcase, it was shown that Presburger Arithmetic is sufficient, but the decidability for the general class of regular-oriented word equations with length constraints remained open. Theorem 5 shows the problem is decidable.

We start with a simple lemma that $\Rightarrow$ preserves regular-orientedness. Its proof can be found in the full version.

Lemma 5. *If $E \Rightarrow E'$ and E is regular-oriented, then E' is also regular-oriented.*

Next, we show a bound on the lengths of cycles and paths of the counter system associated with a regular-oriented word equation.

Lemma 6. *Given a regular-oriented word equation E, the counter system $\mathcal{C}(E)$ is flat. Moreover, the length of each simple cycle (resp. path) in the control structure of $\mathcal{C}(E)$ is of length $O(|E|)$ (resp. $O(|E|^2)$).*

Let $E := L = R$. We first show that the length of a simple cycle in the control structure of $\mathcal{C}(E)$ is of length at most $N = \max\{|L|, |R|\} - 1$. Given a simple cycle $E_0 \Rightarrow E_1 \Rightarrow \cdots \Rightarrow E_n$ with $n > 0$ (i.e. $E_0 = E_n$ and $E_i \neq E_j$ for all $0 \le i < j < n$), it has to be the case that each rewriting in this cycle applies one of the (P2)–(P4) rules since the other rules reduce the size of the equation. We have $|E_0| = |E_1| = \cdots = |E_n|$. Let $E_i := L_i = R_i$ with $L_i = \alpha_i w_i$ and $R_i = \beta_i w_i'$. Let us assume that E_1 be $w_0[\alpha_0 \beta_0 / \beta_0] = \beta_0 w_0'[\alpha_0 \beta_0 / \beta_0]$; the case with E_1 be $\alpha_0 w_0 [\beta_0 \alpha_0 / \alpha_0] = w_0' [\beta_0 \alpha_0 / \alpha_0]$ will be easily seen to be symmetric. This assumption implies that β_0 is a variable y, and that $L_0 = uyv$ for some words $u, v \in (A \cup V)^*$ (for, otherwise, $|E_1| < |E_0|$ because of regularity of E). Furthermore, it follows that, for each $i \in [n-1]$, E_{i+1} is $w_i[\alpha_i y/] = y w_i'$ and $\beta_i = y$, i.e., the counter system $\mathcal{C}(E)$ applies either $\mathtt{SUB}_{y,x}$ (in the case when $x = \alpha_i$) or $\mathtt{DEC}_y$ (in the case when $\alpha_i \in A$). For, otherwise, taking a minimal $i \in [1, n-1]$ with E_{i+1} being $\alpha_i w_i [y\alpha_i/\alpha_i] = w_i'[y\alpha_i/\alpha_i]$ for some variable $x = \alpha_i$ shows that E_i is of the form $x...y... = y...x...$ (since $|E_{i+1}| = |E_i|$) contradicting that E_i is oriented. Consequently, we have

- $R_i = R_j$ for all i, j, and
- $L_i = \mathrm{cyc}^i(u)yv$ for all $i \in [n]$

implying that the length of the cycle is at most $|L_0| - 1 \le |L| - 1$.

Consider the control structure $\mathcal{C}(E)$ as a dag of SCCs. In this dag, each edge from one SCC to the next is size-reducing. Therefore, the maximal length of a path in this dag is $|E|$. Therefore, since the maximal path of each SCC is N (from the above analysis), the maximal length of a simple path in the control structure is at most N^2.

Handling regular constraints: First, we note that the length abstraction of regular-oriented word equations with regular constraints is already not Presburger-definable in general (see full version for proof):

Proposition 4. *The regular-oriented word equation $xy = yz$ over the alphabet $\{a, b, \#\}$, together with regular constraints $x, y \in \#(a+b)^*$ has non-Presburger-definable length abstraction.*

It is difficult to extend Theorem 5 to the case with regular constraints because they may introduce nestings of cycles (which breaks the flat control structure) even for regular-oriented word equation. However, we can show that restricting to regular constraints given by *1-weak NFA* [2] (i.e. a dag of SCCs, each with at most one state) preserves the flat control structure. A 1-weak regular constraint is of the form $x \in L$ where L is accepted by a 1-weak NFA. The class of 1-weak automata is in fact quite powerful, e.g., when considered as recognisers of languages of ω-words, they capture the subclass of LTL with operators **F** and **G** [2]. They have also been used to obtain a decidable extension of infinite-state concurrent systems in term rewriting systems, e.g., see [17,30]. Note that the regular constraint in Proposition 4 is accepted by a 1-weak NFA: the NFA has two states q_0 and q_1, and transitions $q_0 \xrightarrow{\#} q_1$ and $q_1 \xrightarrow{a,b} q_1$, where q_0 is an initial state and q_1 a final state.

Theorem 6. *The satisfiability problem of regular-oriented word equations with 1-weak regular constraints and length constraints is solvable in nondeterministic double exponential time (2NEXP).*

Let us prove this theorem. Suppose E is a regular-oriented word equation with the set S of 1-weak regular constraints. Let $\mathcal{C}(E, S) = (X, Q, \Delta)$ be the corresponding counter system. Let $M(S)$ denote the maximum number of states ranging over all NFA in S.

Lemma 7. *The counter system $\mathcal{C}(E, S)$ is flat. Moreover, the length of each simple cycle in the control structure of $\mathcal{C}(E, S)$ is of length $O(|E|)$, while the length of each simple path is of length $O(|E|^2|V||S|M(S)^3)$.*

By virtue of Theorem 4, this lemma implies decidability of Theorem 6, but it does NOT imply the nondeterministic exponential time upper bound since each unary Presburger guard in $\mathcal{C}(E)$ will be of the form $x \in \text{LEN}(\bigcap_{(x \in L) \in S} L)$. Even though we know that $|S|$ is always of a polynomial size, their intersection requires performing a product automata construction, which will result in an NFA of an exponential size. Therefore, we obtain a nondeterministic double exponential time complexity upper bound (2NEXP), instead of NEXP as for the case without regular constraints. The proof of Lemma 7 can be found in the full version.

Remark 1. Our proof of Theorem 6 does not extend to the case when we allow *generalised flat* NFA (i.e. after mapping all the letters in A to a new symbol '?', the control structure of the NFA is flat) in the regular constraints. This is because a simple cycle involving two or more states will result in a counter system that is no longer flat.

6   Future Work

One research direction is to study extensions of our techniques to deal with the class of regular (but not necessarily oriented) word equations with length constraints. We believe that this is a key subproblem of the general class of quadratic word equations with length constraints. We also conjecture that the length abstractions of general quadratic word equations can be effectively captured by existential Presburger with divisibility.

Acknowledgment. We thank Jatin Arora, Dmitry Chistikov, Volker Diekert, Matthew Hague, Artur Jeż, Philipp Rümmer, and James Worrell for the helpful discussions. This research was partially funded by the ERC Starting Grant AV-SMP (grant agreement no. 759969) and the ERC Synergy Grant IMPACT (grant agreement no. 610150).

References

1. Abdulla, P.A., Atig, M.F., Chen, Y.-F., Holík, L., Rezine, A., Rümmer, P., Stenman, J.: String constraints for verification. In: Biere, A., Bloem, R. (eds.) CAV 2014. LNCS, vol. 8559, pp. 150–166. Springer, Cham (2014). https://doi.org/10.1007/978-3-319-08867-9_10
2. Babiak, T., Rehák, V., Strejcek, J.: Almost linear Büchi automata. Mathematical Structures in Computer Science **22**(2), 203–235 (2012)
3. Bardin, S., Finkel, A., Leroux, J., Petrucci, L.: FAST: acceleration from theory to practice. STTT **10**(5), 401–424 (2008)
4. Bardin, S., Finkel, A., Leroux, J., Schnoebelen, P.: Flat acceleration in symbolic model checking. In: Peled, D.A., Tsay, Y.-K. (eds.) ATVA 2005. LNCS, vol. 3707, pp. 474–488. Springer, Heidelberg (2005). https://doi.org/10.1007/11562948_35

5. Berzish, M., Ganesh, V., Zheng, Y.: Z3str3: a string solver with theory-aware heuristics. In: FMCAD, pages 55–59. (2017)
6. Bjørner, N., Tillmann, N., Voronkov, A.: Path feasibility analysis for string-manipulating programs. In: Kowalewski, S., Philippou, A. (eds.) TACAS 2009. LNCS, vol. 5505, pp. 307–321. Springer, Heidelberg (2009). https://doi.org/10.1007/978-3-642-00768-2_27
7. Bozga, M., Iosif, R., Lakhnech, Y.: Flat parametric counter automata. Fundam. Inform. **91**(2), 275–303 (2009)
8. Chrobak, M.: Finite automata and unary languages. Theor. Comput. Sci. **47**(3), 149–158 (1986)
9. Day, J.D., et al.: The Satisfiability of Extended Word Equations: The Boundary Between Decidability and Undecidability. CoRR, abs/1802.00523 (2018)
10. Day, J.D., Manea, F., Nowotka, D.: The hardness of solving simple word equations. In: MFCS, pp. 18:1–18:14 (2017)
11. Diekert, V.: Makanin's algorithm. In: Lothaire, M.(ed.) Algebraic Combinatorics on Words, Volume 90 of Encyclopedia of Mathematics and its Applications, Chapter 12, pp. 387–442. Cambridge University Press, Cambridge (2002)
12. Diekert, V., Robson, J.M.: Quadratic word equations. In: Jewels are Forever, Contributions on Theoretical Computer Science in Honor of Arto Salomaa, pp. 314–326. (1999)
13. Ganesh, V., Minnes, M., Solar-Lezama, A., Rinard, M.: Word equations with length constraints: what's decidable? In: Biere, A., Nahir, A., Vos, T. (eds.) HVC 2012. LNCS, vol. 7857, pp. 209–226. Springer, Heidelberg (2013). https://doi.org/10.1007/978-3-642-39611-3_21
14. Holík, L., Janku, P., Lin, A.W., Rümmer, P., Vojnar, T.: String constraints with concatenation and transducers solved efficiently. PACMPL, 2(POPL):4:1–4:32 (2018)
15. Jéz, A.: Recompression: a simple and powerful technique for word equations. In: STACS 2013, LIPIcs, vol. 20, pp. 233–244 (2013)
16. Kiezun, A.: HAMPI: A solver for word equations over strings, regular expressions, and context-free grammars. ACM Trans. Softw. Eng. Methodol. **21**(4), 25 (2012)
17. Kretínský, M., Rehák, V., Strejcek, J.: Reachability is decidable for weakly extended process rewrite systems. Inf. Comput. **207**(6), 671–680 (2009)
18. Lechner, A., Ouaknine, J., Worrell, J.: On the complexity of linear arithmetic with divisibility. In: LICS 15: Logic in Computer Science. IEEE (2015)
19. Lentin, A.: Equations dans les Monoides Libres. Gauthier-Villars, Paris (1972)
20. Leroux, J., Sutre, G.: Flat counter automata almost everywhere! In: Software Verification: Infinite-State Model Checking and Static Program Analysis, 19.02.2006–24.02.2006 (2006)
21. Liang, T., Reynolds, A., Tinelli, C., Barrett, C., Deters, M.: A DPLL(T) theory solver for a theory of strings and regular expressions. In: Biere, A., Bloem, R. (eds.) CAV 2014. LNCS, vol. 8559, pp. 646–662. Springer, Cham (2014). https://doi.org/10.1007/978-3-319-08867-9_43
22. Lin, A.W., Barceló, P.: String solving with word equations and transducers: towards a logic for analysing mutation XSS. In: POPL, pp. 123–136 (2016)
23. Lipshitz, L.: The Diophantine problem for addition and divisibility. Trans. Am. Math. Soc. **235**, 271–283 (1976)
24. Makanin, G.S.: The problem of solvability of equations in a free semigroup. Sb. Math. **32**(2), 129–198 (1977)
25. Martinez, A.: Efficient computation of regular expressions from unary NFAs. In: DFCS, pp. 174–187 (2002)

26. Matiyasevich, Y.: A connection between systems of words-and-lengths equations and Hilbertc tenth problem. Zap. Nauchnykh Semin. POMI **8**, 132–144 (1968)
27. Parikh, R.: On context-free languages. J. ACM **13**(4), 570–581 (1966)
28. Saxena, P., Akhawe, D., Hanna, S., Mao, F., McCamant, S., Song, D., et al.: A symbolic execution framework for JavaScript. In: S&P, pp. 513–528 (2010)
29. To, A.W.: Unary finite automata vs. arithmetic progressions. Inf. Process. Lett. **109**(17), 1010–1014 (2009)
30. To, A.W., Libkin, L.: Algorithmic metatheorems for decidable LTL model checking over infinite systems. In: Ong, L. (ed.) FoSSaCS 2010. LNCS, vol. 6014, pp. 221–236. Springer, Heidelberg (2010). https://doi.org/10.1007/978-3-642-12032-9_16
31. Trinh, M., Chu, D., Jaffar, J.: S3: a symbolic string solver for vulnerability detection in web applications. In: CCS, pp. 1232–1243. (2014)
32. Wang, H.-E., Tsai, T.-L., Lin, C.-H., Yu, F., Jiang, J.-H.R.: String analysis via automata manipulation with logic circuit representation. In: Chaudhuri, S., Farzan, A. (eds.) CAV 2016. LNCS, vol. 9779, pp. 241–260. Springer, Cham (2016). https://doi.org/10.1007/978-3-319-41528-4_13
33. Yu, F., Alkhalaf, M., Bultan, T., Ibarra, O.H.: Automata-based symbolic string analysis for vulnerability detection. Form. Methods Syst. Des. **44**(1), 44–70 (2014)

Round-Bounded Control of
Parameterized Systems

Benedikt Bollig[1]([⊠]), Mathieu Lehaut[2], and Nathalie Sznajder[2]

[1] CNRS, LSV & ENS Paris-Saclay, Université Paris-Saclay, Cachan, France
bollig@lsv.ens-cachan.fr
[2] Sorbonne Université, CNRS, LIP6, 75005 Paris, France
mathieu.lehaut@lip6.fr, nathalie.sznajder@lip6.fr

Abstract. We consider systems with unboundedly many processes that communicate through shared memory. In that context, simple verification questions have a high complexity or, in the case of pushdown processes, are even undecidable. Good algorithmic properties are recovered under round-bounded verification, which restricts the system behavior to a bounded number of round-robin schedules. In this paper, we extend this approach to a game-based setting. This allows one to solve synthesis and control problems and constitutes a further step towards a theory of languages over infinite alphabets.

1 Introduction

Ad-hoc networks, mobile networks, cache-coherence protocols, robot swarms, and distributed algorithms have (at least) one thing in common: They are referred to as *parameterized* systems, as they are usually designed to work for *any* number of processes. The last few years have seen a multitude of approaches to parameterized verification, which aims to ensure that a system is correct no matter how many processes are involved. We refer to [15] for an overview.

Now, the above-mentioned applications are usually part of an open world, i.e., they are embedded into an environment that is not completely under the control of a system. Think of scheduling problems, in which an unspecified number of jobs have to be assigned to (a fixed number of) resources with limited capacity. The arrival of a job and its characteristics are typically not under the control of the scheduler. However, most available verification techniques are only suitable for closed systems: A system is correct if *some* or *every* possible behavior satisfies the correctness criterion, depending on whether one considers reachability or, respectively, linear-time objectives.

This paper is a step towards a theory of synthesis and *control*, which provides a more fine-grained way to reason about parameterized systems. Our system model is essentially that from [24], but defined in a way that reveals similarities with data automata/class-memory automata, a certain automata model over infinite alphabets [8,9]. Actually, we consider *parameterized pushdown systems*, as each process has a dedicated stack to model recursion. A parameterized

---

Partly supported by ANR FREDDA (ANR-17-CE40-0013).

S. K. Lahiri and C. Wang (Eds.): ATVA 2018, LNCS 11138, pp. 370–386, 2018.
https://doi.org/10.1007/978-3-030-01090-4_22

pushdown system distinguishes between a finite-state *global process* (sometimes referred to as a *global store* or *leader process*) and a *local process*. The global process can spawn new local processes. Thus, while a system configuration contains only one global state, the number of instantiations of local processes is unbounded. Moreover, when a local process takes a transition, it is allowed to read, and modify, the global store.

So far so good. Now, it is well-known that reachability is undecidable as soon as two pushdown processes communicate through shared memory. And even when local processes are finite-state, the problem is at least as hard as reachability in Petri nets [9]. This led La Torre, Madhusudan, and Parlato to consider round-bounded verification of parameterized systems, which restricts system executions to a bounded number of round-robin schedules [24]. Not only did they show that reachability drops to PSPACE, but the corresponding fixed-point computation also turned out to be practically feasible. Moreover, they give a sound method (i.e., a sufficient criterion) for proving that all reachable states can already be reached within a bounded number of round-robin schedules. This is done using a game that is different from the one we introduce here. Actually, we extend their model by adding the possibility to distinguish, in parameterized pushdown automata, between controllable global states and uncontrollable ones.

The classical reachability problem then turns into a reachability objective in an infinite-state game. As our main result, it is shown that the winner of such a game can be computed, though in (inherently) non-elementary time. Our proof makes a detour via games on multi-pushdown systems, which are undecidable in general but decidable under a bound on the number of *phases*, each restricting the number of pop operations to a dedicated stack [5,29]. Note that round-robin schedules maintain processes in a queue fashion. However, bounding the number of rounds allows us to store both the states of a local process as well as its stack contents in a configuration of a multi-pushdown system. It is worth noting that multi-pushdown systems have been employed in [23], too, to solve seemingly different verification problems involving queues.

Related Work. As already mentioned, there is a large body of literature on parameterized verification, mostly focusing on closed systems (e.g., [2,4,14,15]).

Infinite-state games have been extensively studied over vector addition systems with states (VASS) (e.g., [3,7,10,12,19]). However, reachability is already undecidable for simple subclasses of VASS games, unless coverability objectives are considered. Unfortunately, the latter do not allow us to require that *all* local processes terminate in a final state. Interestingly, tight links between VASS/energy games and games played on infinite domains have recently been established [16].

Underapproximate verification goes back to Qadeer and Rehof [27]. In the realm of multi-threaded recursive programs, they restricted the number of control switches between different threads. The number of processes, however, was considered to be fixed. Another kind of bounded verification of *parameterized* systems with thread creation was studied in [6]. Contrary to our restriction, the order in which processes evolve may vary from round to round.

We believe that our results will fertilize *synthesis* of parameterized systems [18] and more classical questions whose theoretical foundations go back to the 50s and Church's synthesis problem. Let us cite Brütsch and Thomas, who observed a lack of approaches to synthesis over infinite alphabets [11]: "It is remarkable, however, that a different kind of 'infinite extension' of the Büchi-Landweber Theorem has not been addressed in the literature, namely the case where the input alphabet over which ω-sequences are formed is infinite." Indeed, an execution of a parameterized system can be considered as a sequence of letters, each containing the process identifier of the process involved in performing the corresponding action. Recall that our model of parameterized systems is largely inspired by data automata/class-memory automata [8,9], which were originally defined as language acceptors over infinite alphabets. The automata studied in [11] are quite different. Since synthesis problems are often reduced to game-theoretic questions, our work can be considered as an orthogonal step towards a theory of synthesis over infinite alphabets.

Outline. We define parameterized pushdown systems in Sect. 2, where we also recall known results on reachability questions. The control problem is addressed in Sect. 3, and we conclude in Sect. 4. Missing proof details can be found at the following link: https://hal.archives-ouvertes.fr/hal-01849206.

2   Reachability in Parameterized Systems

We start with some preliminary definitions.

Words. Let Σ be a (possibly infinite) set. A *word* w over Σ is a finite or (countably) infinite sequence $a_0 a_1 a_2 \dots$ of elements $a_i \in \Sigma$. Let Σ^* denote the set of finite words over Σ, Σ^ω the set of infinite words, and $\Sigma^\infty = \Sigma^* \cup \Sigma^\omega$. Given $w \in \Sigma^\infty$, we denote by $|w|$ the *length* of w, i.e., $|w| = n$ if $w = a_0 \dots a_{n-1} \in \Sigma^*$, and $|w| = \omega$ if $w \in \Sigma^\omega$. In particular, the length $|\varepsilon|$ of the empty word ε is 0.

Transition Systems. A *transition system* is a triple $\mathcal{T} = (V, E, v_{\text{in}})$ such that V is a (possibly infinite) set of *nodes*, $E \subseteq V \times V$ is the *transition relation*, and $v_{\text{in}} \in V$ is the initial node. For $(u, v) \in E$, we call v a *successor* of u.

A *partial run* of $\mathcal{T}$ is a non-empty, finite or infinite sequence $\rho = v_0 v_1 v_2 \dots \in V^\infty$ such that, for all $0 < i < |\rho|$, v_i is a successor of v_{i-1}. If, in addition, we have $v_0 = v_{\text{in}}$, then we call ρ a *run*. A (partial) run from u to v is a finite (partial) run of the form $u \dots v$. In particular, u is a partial run (of length 1) from u to u.

2.1   Parameterized Pushdown Systems

We consider parameterized systems in which processes may be created dynamically. Every process can manipulate a stack as well as its *local* state. Information shared by all the processes is modeled in terms of a *global* state.

Definition 1. *A parameterized pushdown system (PPS) is given by a tuple* $\mathcal{P} = (S, L, \Gamma, s_{\text{in}}, \ell_{\text{in}}, \Delta, F_{\text{glob}}, F_{\text{loc}})$ *where*

- S is the finite set of global states, including the initial global state s_{in},
- L is the finite set of local states, including the initial local state ℓ_{in},
- Γ is the finite stack alphabet,
- $\Delta \subseteq (S \times L) \times (Act \times \Gamma) \times (S \times L)$ is the transition relation with $Act = \{\text{push}, \text{pop}, \text{int}\}$ (where int stands for internal), and
- $F_{\text{glob}} \subseteq S$ and $F_{\text{loc}} \subseteq L$ are the sets of accepting global states and accepting local states, respectively. We assume that $s_{\text{in}} \notin F_{\text{glob}}$.

A configuration of $\mathcal{P}$ is a tuple $c = (s, (\ell_1, \gamma_1), \ldots, (\ell_k, \gamma_k))$ where $k \in \mathbb{N}$ (possibly $k = 0$), $s \in S$ is the current global state, and, for each $p \in \{1, \ldots, k\}$, $\ell_p \in L$ and $\gamma_p \in \Gamma^*$ are respectively the local state and stack content of process p. We let $C_{\mathcal{P}}$ denote the set of configurations of $\mathcal{P}$. The initial configuration is (s_{in}) and a configuration $c = (s, (\ell_1, \gamma_1), \ldots, (\ell_k, \gamma_k))$ is final if $s \in F_{\text{glob}}$ and $\{\ell_1, \ldots, \ell_k\} \subseteq F_{\text{loc}}$. The size $|c|$ of a configuration c is the number k of processes in c.

The semantics of a PPS $\mathcal{P}$ is defined as a transition system $\llbracket \mathcal{P} \rrbracket = (V, E, v_{\text{in}})$ where $V = C_{\mathcal{P}}$, $v_{\text{in}} = (s_{\text{in}})$, and the transition relation is $E = \bigcup_{p \geq 1} E_p$ with E_p defining the transitions of process p. Actually, E_p contains two types of transitions. The first type corresponds to the activity of a process that has already been created. Formally, for two configurations $(s, (\ell_1, \gamma_1), \ldots, (\ell_k, \gamma_k))$ and $(s', (\ell'_1, \gamma'_1), \ldots, (\ell'_k, \gamma'_k))$ of size $k \geq 1$,

$$((s, (\ell_1, \gamma_1), \ldots, (\ell_k, \gamma_k)), (s', (\ell'_1, \gamma'_1), \ldots, (\ell'_k, \gamma'_k))) \in E_p$$

if and only if $p \leq k$ and there are $op \in Act$ and $A \in \Gamma$ such that

- $((s, \ell_p), (op, A), (s', \ell'_p)) \in \Delta$,
- $\ell_q = \ell'_q$ and $\gamma_q = \gamma'_q$ for all $q \in \{1, \ldots, k\} \setminus \{p\}$, and
- one of the following holds: (i) $op = \text{push}$ and $\gamma'_p = A \cdot \gamma_p$, (ii) $op = \text{pop}$ and $\gamma_p = A \cdot \gamma'_p$, or (iii) $op = \text{int}$ and $\gamma_p = \gamma'_p$ (in which case A is meaningless).

Note that the topmost stack symbol can be found at the leftmost position of γ_p.

The second type of transition is when a new process joins the system. For a configuration $(s, (\ell_1, \gamma_1), \ldots, (\ell_k, \gamma_k))$ of size $k \geq 0$,

$$((s, (\ell_1, \gamma_1), \ldots, (\ell_k, \gamma_k)), (s', (\ell_1, \gamma_1), \ldots, (\ell_k, \gamma_k), (\ell_{k+1}, \gamma_{k+1}))) \in E_p$$

if and only if $p = k + 1$ and there are $op \in Act$ and $A \in \Gamma$ such that $((s, \ell_{\text{in}}), (op, A), (s', \ell_{k+1})) \in \Delta$ and one of the following holds: (i) $op = \text{push}$ and $\gamma_{k+1} = A$, or (ii) $op = \text{int}$ and $\gamma_{k+1} = \varepsilon$.

A run of $\mathcal{P}$ is a run of the transition system $\llbracket \mathcal{P} \rrbracket$. A finite run of $\mathcal{P}$ is accepting if it ends in a final configuration.

Similarly, we define a parameterized finite-state system (PFS), which is a PPS without stacks. That is, a PFS is a tuple $\mathcal{P} = (S, L, s_{\text{in}}, \ell_{\text{in}}, \Delta, F_{\text{glob}}, F_{\text{loc}})$ where $\Delta \subseteq (S \times L) \times (S \times L)$ and the rest is defined as in PPS. Configurations in $C_{\mathcal{P}}$ are tuples $c = (s, \ell_1, \ldots, \ell_k)$ with $k \geq 0$. The semantics of $\mathcal{P}$ is $\llbracket \mathcal{P} \rrbracket = (C_{\mathcal{P}}, E, (s_{\text{in}}))$ with $E = \bigcup_{p \geq 1} E_p$ defined as follows:

$$((s, \ell_1, \ldots, \ell_k), (s', \ell'_1, \ldots, \ell'_k)) \in E_p$$

if and only if $p \leq k$, $((s, \ell_p), (s', \ell'_p)) \in \Delta$, and $\ell_q = \ell'_q$ for all $q \neq p$, and

$$((s, \ell_1, \ldots, \ell_k), (s', \ell_1, \ldots, \ell_k, \ell_{k+1})) \in E_p$$

if and only if $p = k + 1$ and $((s, \ell_{in}), (s', \ell_{k+1})) \in \Delta$. The notions of runs and accepting runs are defined accordingly.

Reachability Problems. Consider Table 1. The problem PPS-REACHABILITY (respectively, PFS-REACHABILITY) consists in deciding if, in a given PPS (respectively, PFS), there is an accepting run, starting in the initial configuration.

In the general case, these problems are already known and we recall here the results. The first is folklore (cf. also [28]), as two stacks are already sufficient to simulate a Turing machine. For the second, we observe that parameterized systems without stacks are essentially Petri nets (cf. [9]).

Theorem 1. PPS-REACHABILITY *is undecidable, while* PFS-REACHABILITY *is decidable (and as hard as Petri-net reachability).*

2.2   Round-Bounded Behaviors

To regain decidability in the case of PPS, we restrict ourselves to runs that are *round-bounded*, a notion introduced in [24]. Intuitively, during a *round*, the first process will do any number of transitions (possibly 0), then the second process will do any number of transitions, and so on. Once process $p + 1$ has started performing transitions, process p cannot act again in this round. A run is then said to be *B-round bounded* if it uses at most B rounds. Formally, given a natural number $B \geq 1$ and a PPS $\mathcal{P} = (S, L, \Gamma, s_{in}, \ell_{in}, \Delta, F_{glob}, F_{loc})$, we define the *bounded semantics* of $\mathcal{P}$ as the transition system $[\![\mathcal{P}]\!]^B = (V^B, E^B, v_{in}^B)$ where

- nodes are *enhanced configurations* of the form $v = (c, p, r)$ with $c \in C_{\mathcal{P}}$ a configuration, say, of size k, $p \in \{0, \ldots, k\}$ represents the last process that made a transition (or 0 if it is not yet defined), and $r \in \{1, \ldots, B\}$ is the number of the current round,
- the initial node is $v_{in}^B = ((s_{in}), 0, 1)$, and
- there is an edge between (c, p, r) and (c', p', r') if, in $[\![\mathcal{P}]\!] = (V, E, v_{in})$, there is an edge (c, c') in $E_{p'}$ and either
  - $p' \geq p$ and $r' = r$, or
  - $p' < p$, $r < B$, and $r' = r + 1$.

The bounded semantics of a PFS is defined accordingly.

A *B-run* (or simply *run* if B is understood) of $\mathcal{P}$ is a run of $[\![\mathcal{P}]\!]^B$. A *B-run* is *accepting* if it is finite and ends in a node (c, p, r) where c is a final configuration.

Consider the problems on the right-hand side of Table 1 (note that B is encoded in unary). Deciding the existence of an accepting B-run is PSPACE-complete for both PPS and PFS.

Table 1. Reachability Problems

PPS-REACHABILITY	PPS-REACHABILITY^{rb}
I: PPS $\mathcal{P}$	**I:** PPS $\mathcal{P}$; $B \geq 1$ (given in unary)
Q: Is there an accepting run of $\mathcal{P}$?	**Q:** Is there an accepting B-run of $\mathcal{P}$?

PFS-REACHABILITY	PFS-REACHABILITY^{rb}
I: PFS $\mathcal{P}$	**I:** PFS $\mathcal{P}$; $B \geq 1$ (given in unary)
Q: Is there an accepting run of $\mathcal{P}$?	**Q:** Is there an accepting B-run of $\mathcal{P}$?

Theorem 2. PPS-REACHABILITY^{rb} and PFS-REACHABILITY^{rb} are *PSPACE-complete.*

The rest of this section is devoted to the proof of this theorem. Actually, we prove that PPS-REACHABILITY^{rb} is in PSPACE and PFS-REACHABILITY^{rb} is PSPACE-hard. The upper bound has already been stated in [24], the lower bound in [25], for a similar model. For the sake of completeness, we give proofs for both bounds.

PPS-Reachability^{rb} is in PSPACE. We give an (N)PSPACE algorithm solving the problem PPS-REACHABILITY^{rb} using a slight variant of the notion of interfaces as described in [24]. Let $\mathcal{P} = (S, L, \Gamma, s_{\mathsf{in}}, \ell_{\mathsf{in}}, \Delta, F_{\mathsf{glob}}, F_{\mathsf{loc}})$ be a PPS and $B \geq 1$ be the maximal number of rounds.

An interface for a single process is a triple $\mathcal{I} = [t, (s_1, \ldots, s_B), (s'_1, \ldots, s'_B)] \in \{1, \ldots, B\} \times S^B \times S^B$ satisfying the following conditions:

1. For all $1 \leq i < t$, we have $s_i = s'_i$.
2. There are local states $\ell_{t-1}, \ldots, \ell_B$ and stack contents $\gamma_{t-1}, \ldots, \gamma_B$ such that (i) for all $t \leq i \leq B$ there is a finite partial run in $[\![\mathcal{P}]\!]$ from $c_i = (s_i, (\ell_{i-1}, \gamma_{i-1}))$ to $c'_i = (s'_i, (\ell_i, \gamma_i))$, (ii) this run has length at least two (i.e., it performs at least one transition) if $i = t$, and (iii) ℓ_{t-1} is the initial local state, $\gamma_{t-1} = \varepsilon$, and ℓ_B is an accepting local state.

We refer to the first B-tuple of $\mathcal{I}$ as $\mathcal{I}^\ell$ and to the second B-tuple as $\mathcal{I}^r$. The natural number t is the starting round and is referred to as $t_{\mathcal{I}}$. We say that an interface $\mathcal{I}_1$ is *compatible* with an interface $\mathcal{I}_2$ if $t_{\mathcal{I}_1} \leq t_{\mathcal{I}_2}$ and $\mathcal{I}_1^r = \mathcal{I}_2^\ell$.

Intuitively, an interface represents the possibility of a computation of a single process during a run of the PPS. Global states are the only piece of information needed to be able to coordinate between different processes, since a process cannot access the local content of another one. Moreover, when a process is created, it takes the last position in a round. The starting round t of each interface is needed to check that the order of the processes respects the order of their creation. In other words, interfaces can be viewed as the skeleton of a run of $\mathcal{P}$. This is formalised in the following lemma, which is illustrated in Fig. 1.

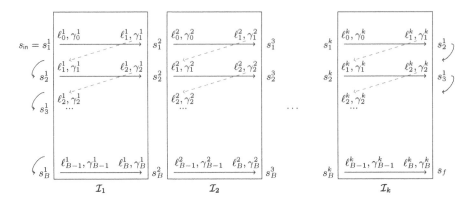

Fig. 1. A run as the composition of compatible interfaces; all starting rounds are 1

Lemma 1. *There is an accepting B-run of $\mathcal{P}$ if and only if there are k interfaces $\mathcal{I}_1, \ldots, \mathcal{I}_k$ for $k \geq 1$ verifying the following conditions:*

- *For all $1 < i \leq k$, $\mathcal{I}_{i-1}$ is compatible with $\mathcal{I}_i$.*
- *Let $\mathcal{I}_1^\ell = (s_1, \ldots, s_B)$ and $\mathcal{I}_k^r = (s_1', \ldots, s_B')$. Then, s_1 is the initial global state s_{in}, s_B' is an accepting global state, and $s_j = s_{j-1}'$ for all $1 < j \leq B$.*

Given $\mathcal{I} = [t, (s_1, \ldots, s_B), (s_1', \ldots, s_B')]$, one can check in polynomial time whether $\mathcal{I}$ is an interface. To do this, we check the emptiness of a pushdown automaton that simulates the actions of $\mathcal{P}$ on a single process and has special transitions to change the global state from s_j' to s_{j+1}. As non-emptiness of a pushdown automaton can be checked in polynomial time [17], so can the validity of a given interface.

The algorithm to solve PPS-REACHABILITY^{rb} first guesses an interface $\mathcal{I}_1$ for the first process, and stores $t_{\mathcal{I}_1}$, $\mathcal{I}_1^\ell$, and $\mathcal{I}_1^r$. Then, it guesses an interface $\mathcal{I}_2$ for the second process, checks that it is compatible by comparing $t_{\mathcal{I}_2}$ and $\mathcal{I}_2^\ell$ with the previously stored $t_{\mathcal{I}_1}$ and $\mathcal{I}_1^r$, and then replaces $\mathcal{I}_1^r$ by $\mathcal{I}_2^r$ and $t_{\mathcal{I}_1}$ by $t_{\mathcal{I}_2}$ (so only $\mathcal{I}_1^\ell$, $t_{\mathcal{I}_2}$, and $\mathcal{I}_2^r$ are stored). We continue guessing compatible interfaces, storing at each step i the values of $\mathcal{I}_1^\ell$, $t_{\mathcal{I}_i}$, and $\mathcal{I}_i^r$. Eventually, the algorithm guesses that the last process has been reached. At that point, there are two halves of interfaces stored in memory: the left interface $\mathcal{I}_1^\ell = (s_1, \ldots, s_B)$ of the first process, and the right interface $\mathcal{I}_k^r = (s_1', \ldots, s_B')$ of the last process. We accept if, for all $i \in \{1, \ldots, B-1\}$, we have that $s_i' = s_{i+1}$, $s_1 = s_{\mathrm{in}}$, and $s_B' \in F_{\mathrm{glob}}$. By Lemma 1, there is an accepting B-run of $\mathcal{P}$.

PFS-Reachability^{rb} is PSPACE-hard. This can be shown by a reduction from the non-emptiness of the intersection of a collection of finite automata $\mathcal{A}_1, \ldots, \mathcal{A}_n$, which is PSPACE-complete [21]. The bound B on the number of rounds will be n. We construct a PFS that non-deterministically guesses a word w in the first round. Moreover, in round i, it will check that w is accepted by $\mathcal{A}_i$. To do this, each process simulates one transition of $\mathcal{A}_i$ on one letter of w. That is, the number of processes is $|w|$. Each process performs exactly one action each round, and, to ensure that the word w is the same for each $\mathcal{A}_i$, stores the corresponding letter in its local state. The global state stores the state of the currently simulated automaton.

3   Round-Bounded Control of Parameterized Systems

We will extend parameterized pushdown systems to a game-based setting with the aim of modeling systems with a centralized control that are embedded into an uncontrollable environment.

3.1   Parameterized Pushdown Games

Games. A *game* is given by an *arena*, i.e., a transition system $\mathcal{G} = (V, E, v_{\mathsf{in}})$ where $V = V_0 \uplus V_1$ is partitioned into the set of states controlled by Player 0 and Player 1, respectively, along with a winning condition $\mathcal{W} \subseteq V^{\infty}$.

A *play* of $\mathcal{G}$ is a run of the underlying transition system. A play is *maximal* if it is infinite, or ends in a node that has no successor. A maximal play is *winning* for Player 0 if it is in $\mathcal{W}$, otherwise it is winning for Player 1.

We will be concerned with two winning conditions: A *reachability condition* is given by a set of nodes $\mathcal{F} \subseteq V$. It induces the set $\mathcal{W}_{\mathcal{F}} = \{\rho = v_0 v_1 v_2 \ldots \in V^{\infty} \mid v_i \in \mathcal{F} \text{ for some } 0 \leq i < |\rho|\}$. A *parity condition* is given by a ranking function $\alpha : V \to Col$ where $Col \subseteq \mathbb{N}$ is a finite set of colors. It induces the set $\mathcal{W}_{\alpha} = \{\rho \in V^{\omega} \mid \min(\mathrm{Inf}_{\alpha}(\rho)) \text{ is even}\}$ with $\mathrm{Inf}_{\alpha}(v_0 v_1 v_2 \ldots) = \{m \in Col \mid m \text{ appears infinitely often in } \alpha(v_0)\alpha(v_1)\alpha(v_2)\ldots\}$. I.e., $\mathcal{W}_{\alpha}$ contains an infinite run if and only if the minimal color seen infinitely often is even.

Let $j \in \{0, 1\}$. A *strategy* for Player j is a partial mapping $f_j : V^* V_j \to V$ such that, for all $w \in V^*$ and $v \in V_j$, the following hold: if $f_j(wv)$ is defined, then $(v, f_j(wv)) \in E$; otherwise, v has no successor.

Fix strategies f_0 and f_1 for Players 0 and 1, respectively. An (f_0, f_1)-*play* of $\mathcal{G}$ is a maximal play $\rho = v_0 v_1 v_2 \ldots$ such that, for all $0 < i < |\rho|$ and $j \in \{0, 1\}$, if $v_{i-1} \in V_j$, then $f_j(v_0 \ldots v_{i-1}) = v_i$.

We say that f_j is *winning* if, for all strategies f_{1-j}, the unique maximal (f_0, f_1)-play is winning for Player j. A game is *determined* if either Player 0 has a winning strategy, or Player 1 has a winning strategy. Furthermore, we say that f_j is *memoryless* if, for all $w, w' \in V^*$ and $v \in V_j$, we have $f_j(wv) = f_j(w'v)$, i.e., the strategy only depends on the last node.

Theorem 3 (cf. [13,33]). *Games with a parity winning condition are determined, and if Player j has a winning strategy, then Player j has a winning memoryless strategy.*

Parameterized Pushdown Games. We now introduce the special case of games played on the infinite transition system induced by a round-bounded PPS.

A round-bounded parameterized pushdown game is described by a PPS $\mathcal{P} = (S, L, \Gamma, s_{\mathsf{in}}, \ell_{\mathsf{in}}, \Delta, F_{\mathsf{glob}}, F_{\mathsf{loc}})$ together with a partition $S = S_0 \uplus S_1$. For a bound

$B \geq 1$, the *B-round-bounded parameterized pushdown game* induced by $\mathcal{P}$ is the game $\mathcal{G}_{\mathcal{P}}^B$ given by the transition system $[\![\mathcal{P}]\!]^B = (V^B, E^B, v_{\text{in}}^B)$ where a node $v = (c, p, r) \in V^B$ with $c = (s, (\ell_1, \gamma_1), \ldots, (\ell_k, \gamma_k))$ belongs to Player j if $s \in S_j$. We consider the reachability winning condition $\mathcal{W}_{\mathcal{F}}$ given by $\mathcal{F} = \{(c, p, r) \in V^B \mid c$ is a final configuration of $\mathcal{P}\}$. Since a reachability game can be easily transformed into a parity game, Theorem 3 implies that $\mathcal{G}_{\mathcal{P}}^B$ is determined.

Parameterized games on PFS are defined similarly as for PPS. Note that, without a bound on the number of rounds, games on PFS are already undecidable, which is shown by an easy adaptation of the undecidability proof for VASS games [1]. Therefore, we only define control for round-bounded games:

CONTROL^{rb}

I: PPS $\mathcal{P} = (S_0 \uplus S_1, L, \Gamma, s_{\text{in}}, \ell_{\text{in}}, \Delta, F_{\text{glob}}, F_{\text{loc}})$; $B \geq 1$

Q: Does Player 0 have a winning strategy in $\mathcal{G}_{\mathcal{P}}^B$?

We are now ready to present our main result, which is shown in the remainder of this section:

Theorem 4. CONTROL^{rb} *is decidable, and inherently non-elementary.*

3.2   Upper Bound

Decidability of CONTROL^{rb} comes from decidability of games on phase-bounded multi-pushdown systems (short: multi-pushdown games), which were first studied in [29] and rely on the phase-bounded multi-pushdown automata from [22].

Multi-pushdown Games. Intuitively, a *phase* is a sequence of actions in a run during which only one fixed "active" stack can be read (i.e., either make a pop transition or a zero-test transition), but push and internal transitions are unrestricted. There are no other constraints on the number of transitions or the order of the transitions done during a phase.

Definition 2. *A* multi-pushdown system (MPS) *is a tuple* $\mathcal{M} = (\kappa, N, S_0 \uplus S_1, \Gamma, \Delta, s_{\text{in}}, \alpha)$ *where the natural number* $\kappa \geq 1$ *is the* phase bound, $N \in \mathbb{N}$ *is the number of stacks,* $S = S_0 \uplus S_1$ *is the partitioned finite set of states,* Γ *is the finite stack alphabet,* $\Delta \subseteq S \times Act_{\text{zero}} \times \{1, \ldots, N\} \times \Gamma \times S$ *is the transition relation where* $Act_{\text{zero}} = \{\text{push}, \text{pop}, \text{int}, \text{zero}\}$, $s_{\text{in}} \in S$ *is the initial state, and* $\alpha : S \to Col$ *with* $Col \subseteq \mathbb{N}$ *a finite set is the* ranking function.

The associated game $\mathcal{G}_{\mathcal{M}}$ is then played on the transition system $[\![\mathcal{M}]\!] = (V = V_0 \uplus V_1, E, v_{\text{in}})$ defined as follows.

A node $v \in V$ is of the form $v = (s, \gamma_1, \ldots, \gamma_N, st, ph)$ where $s \in S$, $\gamma_\sigma \in \Gamma^*$ is the content of stack σ, and $st \in \{0, \ldots, N\}$ and $ph \in \{1, \ldots, \kappa\}$ are used to keep track of the current active stack (0 when it is undefined) and the current phase, respectively. For $j \in \{0, 1\}$, we let $V_j = \{(s, \gamma_1, \ldots, \gamma_N, st, ph) \in V \mid s \in S_j\}$.

Given nodes $v = (s, \gamma_1, \ldots, \gamma_N, st, ph) \in V$ and $v' = (s', \gamma_1', \ldots, \gamma_N', st', ph') \in V$, we have an edge $(v, v') \in E$ if and only if there exist $op \in Act_{\mathsf{zero}}$, $\sigma \in \{1, \ldots, N\}$, and $A \in \Gamma$ such that $(s, op, \sigma, A, s') \in \Delta$ and the following hold:

- $\gamma_\tau = \gamma_\tau'$ for all $\tau \neq \sigma$,
- $\gamma_\sigma = \gamma_\sigma'$ if $op = \mathsf{int}$, $\gamma_\sigma' = A \cdot \gamma_\sigma$ if $op = \mathsf{push}$, $\gamma_\sigma = A \cdot \gamma_\sigma'$ if $op = \mathsf{pop}$, and $\gamma_\sigma = \gamma_\sigma' = \varepsilon$ if $op = \mathsf{zero}$,
- if $op \in \{\mathsf{int}, \mathsf{push}\}$, then $st = st'$ and $ph = ph'$ (the active stack and, hence, the phase do not change),
- if $op \in \{\mathsf{pop}, \mathsf{zero}\}$, then either $st = 0$, $st' = \sigma$, and $ph = ph' = 1$ (this is the first time a current stack is defined), or $st = \sigma$, $st' = \sigma$, and $ph = ph'$ (the stack σ corresponds to the current active stack), or $st \neq \sigma$, $ph < \kappa$, $st' = \sigma$, and $ph' = ph + 1$ (stack σ is not the active stack so that a new phase starts).

The initial node is $v_{\mathsf{in}} = (s_{\mathsf{in}}, \varepsilon, \ldots, \varepsilon, 0, 1)$. The winning condition of $\mathcal{G}_\mathcal{M}$ is a parity condition given by $\bar{\alpha} : V \to Col$ where, for $v = (s, \gamma_1, \ldots, \gamma_N, st, ph)$, we let $\bar{\alpha}(v) = \alpha(s)$.

The control problem for MPS, denoted by $\mathrm{CONTROL}^{\mathrm{MPS}}$, is defined as follows: Given an MPS $\mathcal{M}$, does Player 0 have a winning strategy in $\mathcal{G}_\mathcal{M}$?

Theorem 5 ([5,29])**.** $\mathrm{CONTROL}^{\mathrm{MPS}}$ *is decidable, and is non-elementary in the number of phases.*

The upper bound was first shown in [29] by adopting the technique from [32], which reduces pushdown games to games played on finite-state arenas. On the other hand, [5] proceeds by induction on the number of phases, reducing a $(\kappa+1)$-phase game to a κ-phase game. Similarly, we could try a direct proof of our Theorem 4 by induction on the number of rounds. However, this proof would be very technical and essentially reduce round-bounded parameterized systems to multi-pushdown systems. Therefore, we proceed by reduction to multi-pushdown games, providing a modular proof with clearly separated parts.

From Parameterized Pushdown Games to Multi-pushdown Games. We reduce $\mathrm{CONTROL}^{\mathrm{rb}}$ to $\mathrm{CONTROL}^{\mathrm{MPS}}$. Let $\mathcal{P} = (S, L, \Gamma, s_{\mathsf{in}}, \ell_{\mathsf{in}}, \Delta, F_{\mathsf{glob}}, F_{\mathsf{loc}})$, with $S = S_0 \uplus S_1$, be a PPS and $B \geq 1$. We will build an MPS $\mathcal{M}$ such that Player 0 has a winning strategy in $\mathcal{G}_\mathcal{P}^B$ if and only if Player 0 has a winning strategy in $\mathcal{G}_\mathcal{M}$. In the following, given $s \in S$, we let $pl(s) \in \{0, 1\}$ denote the player associated with s, i.e., $pl(s) = 0$ if and only if $s \in S_0$.

The main idea of the reduction is to represent a configuration

$$(s, (\ell_1, \boxed{\uparrow \gamma_1}), \ldots, (\ell_{p-1}, \boxed{\uparrow \gamma_{p-1}}), (\ell_p, \boxed{\uparrow \gamma_p}), (\ell_{p+1}, \boxed{\uparrow \gamma_{p+1}}), \ldots, (\ell_k, \boxed{\uparrow \gamma_k}), p, r)$$

of $\mathcal{G}_\mathcal{P}^B$ as a configuration in $\mathcal{G}_\mathcal{M}$ of the form depicted in Fig. 2.

Component $j \in \{0, 1\}$ of the global state denotes the current player (which, by default, is $pl(s)$). We explain f_1 and f_2 further below.

The process p that has moved last is considered as the *active* process whose local state ℓ_p is kept in the global state of $\mathcal{G}_\mathcal{M}$ along with s, and whose stack

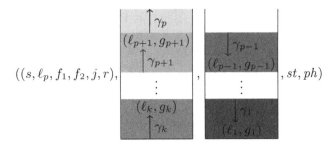

Fig. 2. Encoding of a configuration in $\mathcal{G}_{\mathcal{P}}^{B}$ by a configuration in $\mathcal{G}_{\mathcal{M}}$

contents γ_p is accessible on stack 1 (in the correct order). This allows the multi-pushdown game to simulate transitions of process p, modifying its local state and stack contents accordingly (see *Basic Transitions* in the formalization below).

If a player decides to take a transition for some process $p' > p$, she will store ℓ_p on stack 2 and shift the contents of stack 1 onto stack 2 until she retrieves the local state $\ell_{p'}$ of p' along with its stack contents $\gamma_{p'}$ (see Fig. 3 and *Transitions for Process Change* in the formalization of $\mathcal{M}$).

If, on the other hand, the player decides to take a transition for some process $p' < p$, then she stores ℓ_p on stack 1 and shifts the contents of stack 2 onto stack 1 to recover the local state $\ell_{p'}$ and stack contents $\gamma_{p'}$ (see Fig. 4 and *Transitions for Round Change*). This may imply two phase switches, one to shift stack symbols from 2 to 1, and another one to continue simulating the current process on stack 1. However, $2B - 1$ phases are sufficient to simulate B rounds.

There are a few subtleties: First, at any time, we need to know whether the current configuration of $\mathcal{G}_{\mathcal{M}}$ corresponds to a final configuration in $\mathcal{G}_{\mathcal{P}}^{B}$. To this aim, the state component $(s, \ell_p, f_1, f_2, j, r)$ of $\mathcal{M}$ contains the flags $f_1, f_2 \in \{\checkmark, \bm{\mathsf{X}}\}$ where, as an invariant, we maintain $f_1 = \checkmark$ if and only if $\{\ell_{p+1}, \dots, \ell_k\} \subseteq F_{\mathsf{loc}}$ and $f_2 = \checkmark$ if and only if $\{\ell_1, \dots, \ell_{p-1}\} \subseteq F_{\mathsf{loc}}$. Thus, Player 0 wins in $\mathcal{G}_{\mathcal{M}}$ as soon as she reaches a configuration with global state $(s, \ell, f_1, f_2, j, r)$ such that $s \in F_{\mathsf{glob}}$, $\ell \in F_{\mathsf{loc}}$, and $f_1 = f_2 = \checkmark$. To faithfully maintain the invariant, every local state ℓ_q that is pushed on one of the two stacks, comes with an additional flag $g_q \in \{\checkmark, \bm{\mathsf{X}}\}$, which is $\checkmark$ if and only if all local states *strictly below* on the stack are contained in F_{loc}. It is then possible to keep track of a property of *all* local states on a given stack simply by inspecting and locally updating the topmost stack symbols.

Second, one single transition in $\mathcal{P}$ is potentially simulated by several transitions in $\mathcal{M}$ in terms of the gadgets given in Figs. 3 and 4. The problem here is that once Player j commits to taking a transition by entering a gadget, she is not allowed to get stuck. To ensure progress, there are transitions from inside a gadget to a state win_{1-j} that is winning for Player $1 - j$.

Third, suppose that, in a non-final configuration of $\mathcal{G}_{\mathcal{P}}^{B}$, it is Player 1's turn, but no transition is available. Then, Player 1 wins the play. But how can Player 1 prove in $\mathcal{G}_{\mathcal{M}}$ that no transition is available in the original game $\mathcal{G}_{\mathcal{P}}^{B}$? Actually, he will give the control to Player 0, who will eventually get stuck and, therefore, lose (cf. transitions for *Change of Player* below).

Let us define the MPS $\mathcal{M} = (\kappa, N, S' = S'_0 \uplus S'_1, \Gamma', \Delta', s'_{in}, \alpha)$ formally. We let $\kappa = 2B - 1$, $N = 2$ (the number of stacks), and $\Gamma' = \Gamma \uplus (L \times \{\checkmark, \boldsymbol{X}\})$.

States. The set of states is $S' = \{s'_{in}\} \uplus S_{sim} \uplus \{win_0, win_1\} \uplus \mathfrak{J}$ where s'_{in} is the initial state. Moreover, $S_{sim} = S \times L \times \{\checkmark, \boldsymbol{X}\}^2 \times \{0, 1\} \times \{1, \dots, B\}$. A state $(s, \ell, f_1, f_2, j, r) \in S_{sim}$ stores the global state s and the local state ℓ of the last process p that executed a transition. The third and forth component f_1 and f_2 tell us whether all processes $p' > p$ and, respectively, $p' < p$ of the current configuration are in a local final state (indicated by $\checkmark$). Then, j denotes the player that is about to play (usually, we have $j = pl(s)$, but there will be deviations). Finally, r is the current round that is simulated. Recall that $(s, \ell, f_1, f_2, j, r)$ represents a final configuration if and only if $s \in F_{glob}$, $\ell \in F_{loc}$, and $f_1 = f_2 = \checkmark$. Let $\mathfrak{F} \subseteq S_{sim}$ be the set of such states. The states win_0 and win_1 are self-explanatory. Finally, we use several intermediate states, contained in $\mathfrak{J}$, which will be determined below along with the transitions.

The partition $S' = S'_0 \uplus S'_1$ is defined as follows: First, we have $s'_{in} \in S'_{pl(s_{in})}$. Concerning states from S_{sim}, we let $(s, \ell, f_1, f_2, j, r) \in S'_j$. The states win_0 and win_1 both belong to Player 0 (but this does not really matter). Membership of intermediate states is defined below. The ranking function α maps win_0 to 0, and everything else to 1. In fact, we only need a reachability objective and use the parity condition to a very limited extent.

Initial Transitions. For all transitions $(s_{in}, \ell_{in}) \xrightarrow{(op, A)} (s', \ell')$ in $\mathcal{P}$, we introduce, in $\mathcal{M}$, a transition $s'_{in} \xrightarrow{(op, 1, A)} (s', \ell', \checkmark, \checkmark, pl(s'), 1)$.

Final Transitions. For all states $(s, \ell, f_1, f_2, j, r) \in \mathfrak{F}$, we will have a transition $(s, \ell, f_1, f_2, j, r) \xrightarrow{int} win_0$ (we omit the stack symbol, as it is meaningless), which will be the only transition outgoing from $(s, \ell, f_1, f_2, j, r)$. Moreover, $win_0 \xrightarrow{int} win_0$ and $win_1 \xrightarrow{int} win_1$.

Basic Transitions. We now define the transitions of $\mathcal{M}$ simulating transitions of $\mathcal{P}$ that do not change the process. For all $(s, \ell, f_1, f_2, j, r) \in S_{sim} \setminus \mathfrak{F}$ and transitions $(s, \ell) \xrightarrow{(op, A)} (s', \ell')$ from Δ (in $\mathcal{P}$), the MPS $\mathcal{M}$ has a transition $(s, \ell, f_1, f_2, j, r) \xrightarrow{(op, 1, A)} (s', \ell', f_1, f_2, pl(s'), r)$.

Transitions for Process Change. For all $(s, \ell, f_1, f_2, j, r) \in S_{sim} \setminus \mathfrak{F}$, we introduce, in $\mathcal{M}$, the gadget given in Fig. 3. As we move to another process, the current local state ℓ is pushed on stack 2, along with flag f_2, which tells us whether, henceforth, all states on stack 2 *below* the new stack symbol are local accepting states. Afterwards, the value of f_2 kept in the global state has to be updated, depending on whether $\ell \in F_{loc}$ or not. Actually, maintaining the value of f_2 is done in terms of additional (but finitely many) states. For the sake of readability, however, we rather consider that f_2 is a variable and use $upd(f_2, \ell)$ to update its value. We continue shifting the contents of stack 1 onto stack 2 (updating f_2 when retrieving a local state). Now, there are two possibilities. We may eventually pop

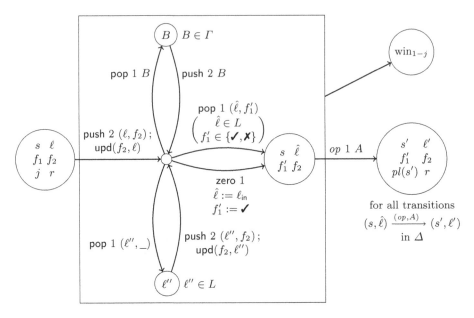

Fig. 3. Change from process p to some process $p' > p$ (staying in the same round). All intermediate states belong to Player j; from every intermediate state, there is an outgoing internal transition to win_{1-j}. Moreover, $\text{upd}(f_2, \bar{\ell})$ stands for the update rule IF $(f_2 = \checkmark \wedge \bar{\ell} \in F_{\text{loc}})$ THEN $f_2 := \checkmark$ ELSE $f_2 := \times$

a new current local state $\hat{\ell}$ and then simulate the transition of the corresponding existing process. Or, when there are no more symbols on stack 1, we create a new process.

Transitions for Round Change. For all $(s, \ell, f_1, f_2, j, r) \in S_{\text{sim}} \setminus \mathfrak{F}$ such that $r < B$, we introduce, in $\mathcal{M}$, the gadget given in Fig. 4. It is similar to the previous gadget. However, we now shift symbols from stack 2 onto stack 1 and have to update f_1 accordingly.

Change of Player. When Player 1 thinks he does not have an outgoing transition (in $\mathcal{P}$), he can give the token to Player 0. That is, for all $(s, \ell, f_1, f_2, 1, r) \in S_{\text{sim}} \setminus \mathfrak{F}$, we introduce the transition $(s, \ell, f_1, f_2, 1, r) \xrightarrow{\text{int}} (s, \ell, f_1, f_2, 0, r)$.

Lemma 2 *Player 0 has a winning strategy in $\mathcal{G}_\mathcal{M}$ if and only if Player 0 has a winning strategy in $\mathcal{G}_\mathcal{P}^B$.*

3.3 Lower Bound

Our lower-bound proof is inspired by [5], but we reduce from the satisfiability problem for first-order formulas on finite words, which is known to be non-elementary [30]. Note that the lower bound already holds for PFS.

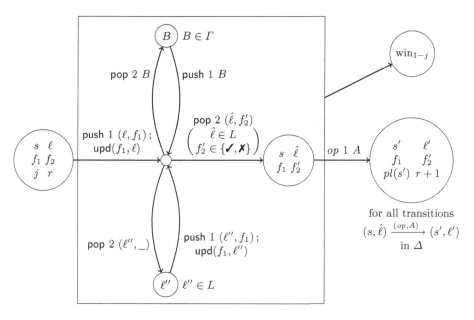

Fig. 4. Go from a process p to some process $p' < p$ (involving a round change). All intermediate states belong to Player j; from every intermediate state, there is an outgoing internal transition to win_{1-j}. Moreover, $upd(f_1, \bar{\ell})$ stands for the update rule IF $(f_1 = \checkmark \land \bar{\ell} \in F_{loc})$ THEN $f_1 := \checkmark$ ELSE $f_1 := \times$

Let Var be a countably infinite set of variables and Σ a finite alphabet. Formulas φ are built by the grammar $\varphi ::= a(x) \mid x < y \mid \neg(x < y) \mid \varphi \lor \varphi \mid \varphi \land \varphi \mid \exists x.\varphi \mid \forall x.\varphi$ where $x, y \in$ Var and $a \in \Sigma$.

Let $w = a_0 \dots a_{n-1} \in \Sigma^*$ be a word. Variables are interpreted as positions of w, so a valuation is a (partial) function $\nu : \text{Var} \to \{0, \dots, n-1\}$. The satisfaction relation is defined as follows. We let $w, \nu \models a(x)$ if and only if $a_{\nu(x)} = a$. Moreover, $w, \nu \models x < y$ if and only if $\nu(x) < \nu(y)$. Quantification, negation, disjunction, and conjunction are defined as usual. We refer to [31] for details. A formula φ without free variables is *satisfiable* if there is a word w such that $w, \emptyset \models \varphi$. We suppose that φ is given in prenex normal form.

We build a PFS-based round-bounded game that is winning for Player 0 if and only if φ is satisfiable. In the first round of the game, Player 0 chooses a word w by creating a different process for each letter of w, each of them holding the corresponding letter in its local state. To prove that w is indeed a model of φ, the following rounds are devoted to the valuation of the variables appearing in φ, $\nu(x) = i$ being represented by memorizing the variable x in the local state of the ith process. If x appears in the scope of a universal quantifier, the choice of the process is made by Player 1, otherwise it is made by Player 0. The last round is used to check the valuation of the variables. To this end, the players will inductively choose a subformula to check, until they reach an atomic proposition: If the subformula is a disjunction $\varphi_1 \lor \varphi_2$, Player 0 chooses either φ_1 or φ_2; if it is

384 B. Bollig et al.

a conjunction, Player 1 chooses the next subformula. Finally, to verify whether $a(x)$ is satisfied, we check that there is a process with letter a and variable x in its local state. For $x < y$, we check that the process with x in its local state is eventually followed by a distinct process with y in its local state. This check is done during the same round, which guarantees that the positions corresponding to x and y are in the correct order. The number of states needed and the number of rounds are linearly bounded in the length of the formula.

4 Conclusion

We extended the verification of round-bounded parameterized systems to a game-based setting, which allows us to model an uncontrollable environment. It would be interesting to consider game-based extensions for the setting from [6], too. Moreover, as games constitute an important approach to verifying branching-time properties (e.g., [26]), our results may be used for branching-time model checking of parameterized systems (using a variant of data logics [20] and a reduction of the model-checking problem to a parameterized pushdown game).

References

1. Abdulla, P.A., Bouajjani, A., d'Orso, J.: Deciding monotonic games. In: Baaz, M., Makowsky, J.A. (eds.) CSL 2003. LNCS, vol. 2803, pp. 1–14. Springer, Heidelberg (2003). https://doi.org/10.1007/978-3-540-45220-1_1
2. Abdulla, P.A., Delzanno, G.: Parameterized verification. Int. J. Softw. Tools Technol. Transf. **18**(5), 469–473 (2016)
3. Abdulla, P.A., Mayr, R., Sangnier, A., Sproston, J.: Solving parity games on integer vectors. In: D'Argenio, P.R., Melgratti, H. (eds.) CONCUR 2013. LNCS, vol. 8052, pp. 106–120. Springer, Heidelberg (2013). https://doi.org/10.1007/978-3-642-40184-8_9
4. Aminof, B., Jacobs, S., Khalimov, A., Rubin, S.: Parameterized model checking of token-passing systems. In: McMillan, K.L., Rival, X. (eds.) VMCAI 2014. LNCS, vol. 8318, pp. 262–281. Springer, Heidelberg (2014). https://doi.org/10.1007/978-3-642-54013-4_15
5. Atig, M.F., Bouajjani, A., Narayan Kumar, K., Saivasan, P.: Parity games on bounded phase multi-pushdown systems. In: El Abbadi, A., Garbinato, B. (eds.) NETYS 2017. LNCS, vol. 10299, pp. 272–287. Springer, Cham (2017). https://doi.org/10.1007/978-3-319-59647-1_21
6. Atig, M.F., Bouajjani, A., Qadeer, S.: Context-bounded analysis for concurrent programs with dynamic creation of threads. Log. Methods Comput. Sci. **7**(4) (2011)
7. Bérard, B., Haddad, S., Sassolas, M., Sznajder, N.: Concurrent games on VASS with inhibition. In: Koutny, M., Ulidowski, I. (eds.) CONCUR 2012. LNCS, vol. 7454, pp. 39–52. Springer, Heidelberg (2012). https://doi.org/10.1007/978-3-642-32940-1_5
8. Björklund, H., Schwentick, T.: On notions of regularity for data languages. Theor. Comput. Sci. **411**(4–5), 702–715 (2010)

9. Bojańczyk, M., David, C., Muscholl, A., Schwentick, T., Segoufin, L.: Two-variable logic on data words. ACM Trans. Comput. Log. **12**(4), 27 (2011)
10. Brázdil, T., Jančar, P., Kučera, A.: Reachability games on extended vector addition systems with states. In: Abramsky, S., Gavoille, C., Kirchner, C., Meyer auf der Heide, F., Spirakis, P.G. (eds.) ICALP 2010. LNCS, vol. 6199, pp. 478–489. Springer, Heidelberg (2010). https://doi.org/10.1007/978-3-642-14162-1_40
11. Brütsch, B., Thomas, W.: Playing games in the Baire space. In: Proceedings Cassting Workshop on Games for the Synthesis of Complex Systems and 3rd International Workshop on Synthesis of Complex Parameters, Volume 220 of EPTCS, pp. 13–25 (2016)
12. Courtois, J.-B., Schmitz, S.: Alternating vector addition systems with states. In: Csuhaj-Varjú, E., Dietzfelbinger, M., Ésik, Z. (eds.) MFCS 2014. LNCS, vol. 8634, pp. 220–231. Springer, Heidelberg (2014). https://doi.org/10.1007/978-3-662-44522-8_19
13. Emerson, E.A., Jutla, C.S.: Tree automata, mu-calculus and determinacy. In: Proceedings of FOCS 1991, pp. 368–377. IEEE Computer Society (1991)
14. Emerson, E.A., Namjoshi, K.S.: On reasoning about rings. Int. J. Found. Comput. Sci. **14**(4), 527–550 (2003)
15. Esparza, J.: Keeping a crowd safe: on the complexity of parameterized verification. In: STACS 2014, Volume 25 of Leibniz International Proceedings in Informatics, pp. 1–10. Leibniz-Zentrum für Informatik (2014)
16. Figueira, D., Praveen, M.: Playing with repetitions in data words using energy games. In: Proceedings of LICS 2018, pp. 404–413. ACM (2018)
17. Hopcroft, J.E., Motwani, R., Rotwani, Ullman, J.D.: Introduction to Automata Theory, Languages and Computability, 2nd edn. Addison-Wesley Longman Publishing Company Inc., (2000)
18. Jacobs, S., Bloem, R.: Parameterized synthesis. Log. Methods Comput. Sci. **10**(1) (2014)
19. Jančar, P.: On reachability-related games on vector addition systems with states. In: Bojańczyk, M., Lasota, S., Potapov, I. (eds.) RP 2015. LNCS, vol. 9328, pp. 50–62. Springer, Cham (2015). https://doi.org/10.1007/978-3-319-24537-9_6
20. Kara, A.: Logics on data words: expressivity, satisfiability, model checking. Ph.D. thesis, Technical University of Dortmund (2016)
21. Kozen, D.: Lower bounds for natural proof systems. In: Proceedings of SFCS 1977, pp. 254–266. IEEE Computer Society (1977)
22. La Torre, S., Madhusudan, P., Parlato, G.: A robust class of context-sensitive languages. In: LICS 2007, pp. 161–170. IEEE Computer Society Press (2007)
23. La Torre, S., Madhusudan, P., Parlato, G.: Context-bounded analysis of concurrent queue systems. In: Ramakrishnan, C.R., Rehof, J. (eds.) TACAS 2008. LNCS, vol. 4963, pp. 299–314. Springer, Heidelberg (2008). https://doi.org/10.1007/978-3-540-78800-3_21
24. La Torre, S., Madhusudan, P., Parlato, G.: Model-checking parameterized concurrent programs using linear interfaces. In: Touili, T., Cook, B., Jackson, P. (eds.) CAV 2010. LNCS, vol. 6174, pp. 629–644. Springer, Heidelberg (2010). https://doi.org/10.1007/978-3-642-14295-6_54
25. La Torre, S., Madhusudan, P., Parlato, G.: Model-checking parameterized concurrent programs using linear interfaces. Technical Report 2142/15410, University of Illinois (2010). Available at http://hdl.handle.net/2142/15410
26. Lange, M., Stirling, C.: Model checking games for branching time logics. J. Log. Comput. **12**(4), 623–639 (2002)

27. Qadeer, S., Rehof, J.: Context-bounded model checking of concurrent software. In: Halbwachs, N., Zuck, L.D. (eds.) TACAS 2005. LNCS, vol. 3440, pp. 93–107. Springer, Heidelberg (2005). https://doi.org/10.1007/978-3-540-31980-1_7

28. Ramalingam, G.: Context-sensitive synchronization-sensitive analysis is undecidable. ACM Trans. Program. Lang. Syst. **22**(2), 416–430 (2000)

29. Seth, A.: Games on multi-stack pushdown systems. In: Artemov, S., Nerode, A. (eds.) LFCS 2009. LNCS, vol. 5407, pp. 395–408. Springer, Heidelberg (2008). https://doi.org/10.1007/978-3-540-92687-0_27

30. Stockmeyer, L.J.: The Complexity of Decision Problems in Automata Theory and Logic. Ph.D. thesis, MIT (1974)

31. Thomas, Wolfgang: Languages, automata, and logic. In: Rozenberg, Grzegorz, Salomaa, Arto (eds.) Handbook of Formal Languages, pp. 389–455. Springer, Heidelberg (1997). https://doi.org/10.1007/978-3-642-59126-6_7

32. Walukiewicz, I.: Pushdown processes: games and model-checking. Inf. Comput. **164**(2), 234–263 (2001)

33. Zielonka, W.: Infinite games on finitely coloured graphs with applications to automata on infinite trees. TCS **200**(1–2), 135–183 (1998)

PSense: Automatic Sensitivity Analysis for Probabilistic Programs

Zixin Huang$^{(\boxtimes)}$, Zhenbang Wang, and Sasa Misailovic

University of Illinois at Urbana-Champaign, Urbana, IL 61801, USA
{zixinh2,zw11,misailo}@illinois.edu

Abstract. PSense is a novel system for sensitivity analysis of probabilistic programs. It computes the impact that a noise in the values of the parameters of the prior distributions and the data have on the program's result. PSense relates the program executions with and without noise using a developer-provided *sensitivity metric*. PSense calculates the impact as a set of symbolic functions of each noise variable and supports various non-linear sensitivity metrics. Our evaluation on 66 programs from the literature and five common sensitivity metrics demonstrates the effectiveness of PSense.

1 Introduction

Probabilistic programing offers a promise of user-friendly and efficient probabilistic inference. Recently, researchers proposed various probabilistic languages and frameworks, e.g., [10–12,19,24,27]. A typical probabilistic program has the following structure: a developer first specifies the initial assumptions about the random variables as *prior* distributions. Then the developer specifies the *model* by writing the code that relates these variables selecting those whose values have been observed. Finally, the developer specifies the query that asks how this evidence changes the distribution of some of the unobserved (latent) variables, i.e., their *posterior* distribution.

In many applications, both the choices of the prior parameters and the observed data points are *uncertain*, i.e., the used values may diverge from the true ones. Understanding the *sensitivity* of the posterior distributions to the perturbations of the input parameters is one of the key questions in probabilistic modeling. Mapping the sources of sensitivity can help the developer in debugging the probabilistic program and updating it to improve its robustness.

Sensitivity analysis has a rich history in engineering and statistics [15,22] and has also been previously studied in the context of probabilistic models in machine learning [5,7,17,25]. While useful, these techniques are typically sampling-based (providing only sensitivity estimates) or work for a limited subset of discrete models. However, sensitivity in probabilistic programming has not been studied extensively. Recently, Barthe et al. proposed a logic for reasoning about the expected sensitivity of probabilistic programs [4]. While sound, this approach requires a developer to prove properties using a proof assistant, supports only

© Springer Nature Switzerland AG 2018
S. K. Lahiri and C. Wang (Eds.): ATVA 2018, LNCS 11138, pp. 387–403, 2018.
https://doi.org/10.1007/978-3-030-01090-4_23

expectation distance and presets results for only a few examples. Like similar techniques for deterministic programs [8], its reliance on linearity of noise propagation may result in coarse over-approximations of non-linear operations.

Key Challenges. Key challenges for an effective probabilistic sensitivity analysis include (1) automation that aims to maintain both soundness and precision and (2) ability to work with non-linear programs and sensitivity metrics. Solving these challenges can help with understanding and improving robustness of probabilistic programs.

Our Work. PSense is a system for automatic sensitivity analysis of probabilistic programs. For each parameter in a probabilistic program, the analysis answers the question: *if the parameter/data value is changed by some value ε, how much does the posterior distribution change?* The analysis is fully symbolic and exact: it produces the distance expression that is valid for all legal values of ε. It uses a developer-specified sensitivity metric that quantifies the change in the posterior distributions between the programs with and without the noise. In this paper we present analysis with five classical metrics from statistics: two versions of expectation distance, Kolmogorov-Smirnov statistic, Total variation distance, and Kullback-Leibler divergence.

PSense can also answer sensitivity-related *optimization queries*. First, it can compute the numerical value of the maximum posterior distance given that ε is in some range. More interestingly, for a given acceptable threshold of difference between the posterior distributions, PSense can compute the maximum and minimum values of ε that satisfy the threshold.

PSense operates on imperative probabilistic programs with mixed discrete and continuous random variables, written in the PSI language [10]. PSI also comes with a powerful symbolic solver for exact probabilistic inference. One of the key insights behind PSense's design is that the sensitivity analysis can directly leverage PSI's inference. However, we also identified that PSI's analysis alone is not sufficient: (1) the expressions for distribution distance cannot be easily simplified by PSI's solver and (2) PSI does not support optimization queries. We therefore formulated these (non-linear and non-convex) queries and solved symbolically with Mathematica computer algebra system [2]. PSense workflow demonstrates the synergistic usage of symbolic solvers, guided by the domain-specific information. PSense is open-source software, available at http://psense.info.

In addition to the exact sensitivity analysis, PSense also supports an approximate analysis via a sampling-based backend. PSense translates the sensitivity analysis queries into WebPPL programs. WebPPL [13] is a probabilistic language with support for approximate MCMC inference. This way, PSense implements a common empirical approach for estimating sensitivity in probabilistic models.

Results. We evaluated PSense on a set of 66 probabilistic programs from the literature. We ran the sensitivity analysis for five metrics and 357 parameters per metric. Both the programs and the metrics are challenging: the programs have both discrete and continuous variables and many metrics are non-linear.

The results show that (1) PSense, applied on all sensitivity metrics, successfully computed the exact sensitivity for the majority of analyzed parameters and data points, with a typical analysis being well under a minute; (2) PSense's optimization is also effective in computing the maximum noise that keeps the posterior difference below an acceptable threshold; (3) PSense's exact symbolic analysis is often significantly more precise than the sampling-based approach. Jointly, these results demonstrate that symbolic analysis is a solid foundation for automatic and precise sensitivity analysis.

Contributions. The paper makes the following contributions:

⋆ **System for Automated Sensitivity:** To the best of our knowledge, PSense is the first automated system for exact symbolic analysis of sensitivity in probabilistic programs.

⋆ **Symbolic Analysis and Optimization:** We present PSense's global sensitivity analysis, which solves queries exactly, by building on the capabilities of PSI and Mathematica symbolic engines. We also present how to formulate and solve sensitivity-related optimization queries.

⋆ **Evaluation:** We evaluated PSense on 66 probabilistic programs from the literature, with a total of 357 parameter analyses. The experiments show the effectiveness and efficiency of PSense in analyzing sensitivity and solving optimization problems for various sensitivity metrics. We also show that PSense's symbolic analysis is often significantly more precise than sampling.

2   Examples

We demonstrate the capabilities of PSense through two representative examples. The first example shows the analysis of a simple discrete program. The second shows the analysis of stochastic gradient descent algorithm.

2.1   Sensitivity Analysis of Discrete Programs

Figure 1 presents a program that flips three coins. Each coin toss is a "head" (1) or a "tail" (0). The first three statements simulate tossing three independent coins. The variable D sums up the outcomes. While the value of D is not known, the developer includes the condition that at least two heads were observed (but not for which coins). We want to know the posterior probability that the coin toss A resulted in a "head", given this evidence.

```
def main(){
  A:=flip(0.5);
  B:=flip(0.5);
  C:=flip(0.5);
  D:=A+B+C;
  observe(D>=2);
  return A;
}
```

Fig. 1. Example

Problem Definition. The program has three constant parameters for the Bernoulli distributions assigned to A, B, and C. Different values of the parameters will give different posterior distributions. We are interested in the question: *what happens to the posterior distribution if we perturb the parameter of the prior distribution?*

To estimate the change in the output distribution, we can add noise to each of our prior `flip(0.5)`. In particular, PSense interprets the first statement as `A:=flip(0.5+eps)`, where the variable `eps` represents this noise. The noise may have any legal value, such that the flip probability is between 0.0 and 1.0.

Sensitivity Results. PSense first computes the posterior distribution of the variable `A`, which is a function of the noise variable `eps`. Then it compares it to the distribution of the program without noise using a sensitivity metrics. PSense can compute several built-in metrics of sensitivity, defined in Sect. 3.

For instance, the Expectation distance has been defined in [4] as the absolute difference between $\mathbb{E}[\mathtt{main}_{eps}]$ and $\mathbb{E}[\mathtt{main}]$ the expectations of the program's output distributions with and without noise: $D_{Exp} =\mid \mathbb{E}[\mathtt{main}_{eps}] - \mathbb{E}[\mathtt{main}] \mid$. After changing the parameter of the first `flip` statement, PSense produces the symbolic expression of this distance: `(3*Abs[eps])/(4*(1+eps))`. It also calculates the range of legal values for `eps`, which is $[-0.5, 0.5]$. PSense can successfully obtain the symbolic expressions for all other metrics and parameters.

Other Queries. PSense can perform several additional analyses:

- It can find the maximum value of the Expectation distance with respect to the noise `eps` within e.g., $\pm 10\%$ of the original parameter value. PSense formulates and solves an optimization problem, which in this case returns that the maximum value of the Expectation distance is approximately 0.0395, when `eps` is -0.05. One can similarly obtain the maximum absolute `eps` subject to the bound on the sensitivity metric.
- It analyzes whether the distance grows linearly as the noise `eps` increases. Interestingly, even for this a simple example, the Expectation distance is not linear, because `eps` appeared in the denominator. This is due to the rescaling of the posterior caused by the `observe` statement. In the version of the program without the `observe` statement, the Expectation distance is linear.

2.2 Sensitivity Analysis of Stochastic Gradient Descent

We now turn to a more complicated example, which implements a stochastic gradient descent (SGD) algorithm, in Fig. 2. It is derived from the algorithm analyzed in [4], applied to the linear regression scenario (as in [1]).

The variables x and y are two arrays that store the observed data. We fit a simple linear regression model $y_i = w_1 + w_2 x_i$. We first set the parameters w_1 and w_2 to some initial values. Then we use the gradient descent algorithm to adjust the parameters in order to minimize the error of the current fit. To make the model simpler, we set w_1 to a concrete initial value and assume w_2 follows the uniform distribution. We set the learning rate a to 0.01. In each iteration we adjust the value of w_1 and w_2 so that the square error in the prediction moves against the gradient and towards the minimum. Finally we want to find how much does the choice of the initial value of w_2 affect the precision. Therefore, we return the distribution of w_2 after multiple iterations of the algorithm – in this experiment, between 1 and 10 (the iteration count must be fixed, which is a limitation of the underlying PSI solver). With more iterations, the value of w_2 approaches 2.0, as expected.

Find Sensitivity with PSense. We want to find out how the output distribution of $w2$ changes if we perturb the parameters of the prior distribution. We add noise *eps* to each parameter in `uniform(0,1)`. PSense can output the results for different metrics, including expectation distance, KL divergence and total variation distance.

Figure 3 presents the change of the expectation distance subject to the fixed noise in the lower bound of the uniform distribution (w2.lower) and the upper bound of the uniform distribution (w2.upper) in the prior of $w2$. The Y-axis shows the maximum expectation distance after each iteration on the X-axis. The solid line is produced by the symbolic backend,

```
def main(){
  x := [1.4,1.8,3.3,4.3,4.8,6.0,
        7.5,8.1,9.0,10.2];
  y := [2.2,4.0,6.1,8.6,10.2,12.4,
        15.1,15.8,18.4,20.0];
  w1 := 0;
  w2 := uniform(0, 1);
  a := 0.01;
  for t in [0..8]{
    i := t;
    xi := x[i];
    yi := y[i];
    w1 = w1-a*2*(w1+w2*xi-yi);
    w2 = w2-a*2*(xi*(w1+w2*xi-yi));
  }
  return w2;
}
```

Fig. 2. Sample SGD program

while the dashed lines are generated by the sampling backend. The function for w2.lower and w2.upper for the symbolic backend are the same (and mark them as just w2). The results indicate that the noise in the prior has little effect on the output distribution after several iterations of the algorithm. The plot also illustrates the imprecision of the sampling backend: the computed sensitivities significantly differ in several iterations.

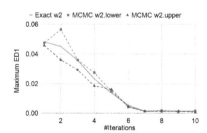

Fig. 3. Analysis of SGD

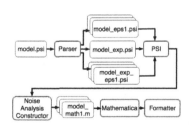

Fig. 4. PSense workflow

3   PSense System

Figure 4 presents the overview of the PSense workflow. PSense accepts programs written in the PSI language (Sect. 3.1). A developer also provides the sensitivity metrics that characterize parameter sensitivities (Sect. 3.2).

PSense supports two backends: Symbolic and Sampling. The symbolic backend first leverages PSI's analysis to get the distribution expression for the modified program. Then, it compiles the results from the programs with and without noise, and computes the sensitivity metric and other queries. PSense builds its query solver on top of Mathematica (Sect. 3.3). The sampling backend translates the programs into WebPPL, and instructs it to run the programs with and without noise for a specific number of times (Sect. 3.4).

As its output, PSense creates a table that presents the sensitivity of the program result to the change of each parameter/observation. The sensitivity is either a symbolic expression for symbolic backend, or an estimate and its variance for the sampling backend.

$n \in \mathbb{Z}$ $\qquad$ $bop \in \{+, -, *, /, \hat{}\}$ $\quad$ $lop \in \{\&\&, ||\}$ $\quad$ $cop \in \{==, \neq, <, >, \leq, \geq\}$

$r \in \mathbb{R}$ $\qquad$ $\mathrm{Dist} \in \{\texttt{Bernoulli}, \texttt{Gaussian}, \texttt{Uniform}, \dots\}$

$x \in \mathrm{Var}$ $\qquad$ $p \in \mathrm{Prog} \rightarrow \mathrm{Func}^+$

$a \in \mathrm{ArrVar}$ $\qquad$ $f \in \mathrm{Func} \rightarrow \texttt{def}\ Id(Var^*)\ \{\texttt{Stmt; return}\ Var^*\}$

$se \in \mathrm{Expr} \rightarrow$ $\quad$ $n\ |\ r\ |\ x\ |\ ?x\ |\ a\texttt{[Expr]}\ |\ \mathrm{Dist}(\mathrm{Expr}^+)\ |\ f(\mathrm{Expr}^*)\ |$
$\mathrm{Expr}\ bop\ \mathrm{Expr}\ |\ \mathrm{Expr}\ cop\ \mathrm{Expr}\ |\ \mathrm{Expr}\ lop\ \mathrm{Expr}$

$s \in \mathrm{Stmt} \rightarrow$ $\quad$ $x := \mathrm{Expr}\ |\ a := \texttt{array}(\mathrm{Expr})\ |\ x = \mathrm{Expr}\ |\ a\texttt{[Expr]} = \mathrm{Expr}\ |$
$\texttt{observe}\ \mathrm{Expr}\ |\ \texttt{assert}\ \mathrm{Expr}\ |\ \texttt{skip}\ |\ \mathrm{Stmt; Stmt}\ |$
$\texttt{if}\ \mathrm{Expr}\ \{\mathrm{Stmt}\}\ \texttt{else}\ \{\mathrm{Stmt}\}\ |\ \texttt{for}\ x\ \texttt{in}\ [\mathrm{Expr} .. \mathrm{Expr})\ \{\mathrm{Stmt}\}$

Fig. 5. PSI language syntax [10]

3.1 Language

Figure 5 presents the syntax of PSI programs. Overall, it is a simple imperative language with scalar and array variables, conditionals, bounded for-loops (each loop can be unrolled as a sequence of conditional statements) and function calls. The language supports various discrete and continuous distributions. To sample from a distribution, a user assigns the distribution expression to a variable. The observe statement conditions on the expressions of random variables. PSense supports the following distributions: Bernoulli, Uniform, Binomial, Geometric, Poisson (discrete), Normal, Uniform, Exponential, Beta, Gamma, Laplace, Cauchy, Pareto, Student's t, Weibull, and Rayleigh (continuous).

PSI has the ability to symbolically analyze probabilistic programs with *uncertain variables*. They may take any value and do not have a specified distribution. Uncertain variables in PSI are specified as arguments of the main function. PSense uses uncertain variables to represent noise.

3.2 Sensitivity Metrics

To compare the distributions, PSense uses a developer-selected metric. PSense currently supports several standard metrics for continuous and discrete distributions. Let P be a cumulative distribution function over the support Ω. For probabilistic programs, we denote the distribution represented by the noisy program as $P_{\texttt{maineps}} = P[\texttt{main} \mid \texttt{eps}]$ and the distribution represented by the original program (without noise) as $P_{\texttt{main}} = P[\texttt{main} \mid \texttt{eps} = 0]$. We present the metrics for discrete distributions:

* **(ED1)** Expectation distance: $D_{\text{ED1}} = |\mathbb{E}_{X \sim \texttt{main}}[X] - \mathbb{E}_{Y \sim \texttt{maineps}}[Y]|$, which was defined in [4].
* **(ED2)** Expectation distance (alternative): $D_{\text{ED2}} = \mathbb{E}[|X - Y|]$, where $X \sim \texttt{main}, Y \sim \texttt{maineps}$; It is a more natural definition of distance, generalizing absolute distance, but harder to compute (as it is not easy to decompose).
* **(KS)** Kolmogorov-Smirnov statistic: $D_{\text{KS}} = \sup_{\omega \in \Omega} |P_{\texttt{main}}(\omega) - P_{\texttt{maineps}}(\omega)|$.
* **(TVD)** Total variation distance: $D_{\text{TVD}} = \frac{1}{2} \sum_{\omega \in \Omega} |P_{\texttt{main}}(\omega) - P_{\texttt{maineps}}(\omega)|$.
* **(KL)** Kullback-Leibler divergence: $D_{\text{KL}} = \sum_{\omega \in \Omega} P_{\texttt{maineps}}(\omega) \log \frac{P_{\texttt{maineps}}(\omega)}{P_{\texttt{main}}(\omega)}$.

The metrics for continuous distributions are defined analogously, replacing sums with the corresponding integrals. The metrics provide several computational challenges, such as (1) integrations in ED2, TVD, and KL, (2) mathematical optimization in KS, and (3) non-linearity in ED2, KS, and KL.

3.3 PSense Symbolic Analysis

Algorithm 1 presents the pseudo-code of PSense's analysis algorithm. The symbolic analysis goes through several stages and synergistically leverages the capabilities of PSI and Mathematica. We describe each stage below.

Identifying Noisy Parameters. PSense's front end identifies all parameters that are used inside the distribution expressions (such as `flip(0.5)` in the first example) and observations (such as `observe(D>=2)` in the same example). For each of these parameters, PSense generates a probabilistic program that expresses uncertainty about the value of the parameter. PSense leverages the uncertain variables, such as `eps`, to generate legal PSI programs with noise.

Computing Posterior Distribution with Noise. For each program with uncertain variables, PSI computes symbolic distribution expressions (both probability mass/density and cumulative distribution functions) parameterized by the uncertain variables. PSI can work with programs that have discrete or continuous distributions. Many of PSI's simplification and integration rules can operate on programs with uncertain variables and produce posterior distributions that fully solve integrals/summations. In the analysis of while loops (which are unrolled up to some constant, after which a status assertion will fail), the dependence of the iteration count on `eps` will be reflected through the probability of failure, which will also be a function of `eps`.

Both PSense and PSI analyses keep track of the legal parameter values for the distribution parameters. Based on this, PSense can then automatically determine the legal bounds of the noise variables. For instance, for `flip(0.7+eps)`, the computed distribution expression will specify that the variable `eps` should be between -0.7 and 0.3 (because the parameter of Bernoulli is between 0 and 1).

Algorithm 1 PSense Algorithm

INPUT : Program Π, Sensitivity Metric M
OUTPUT : Sensitivity Table $T : Param \rightarrow Expr \times Bool$

1: **procedure** PSENSE
2:     $P \leftarrow IdentifyParams(\Pi)$
3:     $d \leftarrow PSI(\Pi)$
4:     **for** $p \in P$ **do**
5:         $\Pi' \leftarrow transformProgram(\Pi, p)$
6:         $d_\varepsilon \leftarrow PSI(\Pi')$
7:         $s \leftarrow distrSupport(d_\varepsilon)$
8:         $\Delta_0 \leftarrow M(d, d_\varepsilon)$
9:         $\Delta \leftarrow MathematicaSimplify(\Delta_0, s)$
10:        **if** $(doApproximate \wedge hasIntegral(\Delta))$ **then**
11:            $\Delta \leftarrow approximateIntegral(\Delta, s)$
12:        **end if**
13:        $l \leftarrow isLinear(\Delta, s)$
14:        $T[p] \leftarrow (\Delta, l)$
15:    **end for**
16: **return** T
17: **end procedure**

Computing Sensitivity Metrics. In general, one can define the computation of the sensitivity as a product program that has two calls to `main` with and without noise, however we optimize the analysis to skip the computation of the posterior for the original program (without noise), since we can obtain it by substituting `eps` with zero. After computing the distribution expression for one program with PSI, PSense calls Mathematica to compute and simplify the expression of the sensitivity metric. Some metrics, such as KS and ED2 may take advantage of the support Ω of the distribution, to successfully simplify the expression. PSense implements a support computation as Mathematica code.

To address these challenges, we combine the solving mechanisms from Mathematica and PSI. Our experience is that Mathematica has a more powerful simplification engine (when it scales) and has capabilities to perform symbolic and numerical optimization and interpolation, which are out of the scope of PSI.

To support the symbolic analysis and provide an additional context to the user, we implemented several procedures that check for various properties of the functions of the noise variable `eps`:

– **Linearity Check:** We have two linearity checks. The exact version checks the standard property from calculus, that the derivative of the function is a non-zero constant with respect to `eps`. An alternative approximate version searches for the upper and lower linear coefficients that tightly bound the function (as tangents that touch it). If the distance between these lines is within a specified tolerance, PSense reports approximate linearity.

- **Convexity/Concavity Check:** For this check, we also implement the test in Mathematica based on the standard definition from calculus: a function of a variable `eps` is convex (resp. concave) if the second derivative is non-negative (resp. negative) for all legal values of `eps`. To establish this property, we set the appropriate inequalities and query Mathematica to find counterexamples. PSense returns if the expression is in any of these categories.
- **Distribution support:** A distribution support is a set of values for which the distribution mass/density function is non-zero. Knowing support is critical for efficient computation of sums and integrals that appear in the distance expressions, especially for optimization problems and for the optional approximate integration. Surprisingly, solving for support in Mathematica is not straightforward. Among several alternatives, we found that the most effective one was the built-in function `FunctionDomain[f]`, which returns the interval on which the function `f` is defined. To use it, we redefine the query to check the domain of a fractional function that is defined only when `dist[eps]` is non-negative.
- **Numerical Integration:** The analysis of continuous distributions may produce complicated (potentially multidimensional) integrals. Since not all integrals have a closed-form, PSense implements numerical approximation that evaluates integrals that PSI/Mathematica could not solve. The numerical integration can be optionally selected by the user. The approximation creates a hypercube of the parameter values and samples the values of `eps` and the other variables at the regular boundaries. It uses the distribution support computed by PSense's analysis and relies on the user to set up the lower/upper integration bounds.

Properties. Soundness of the technique follows from the soundness of the underlying solvers: given the legal intervals for the uncertain variables, both PSI and Mathematica do sound simplification of mathematical expressions; In addition, PSense's analyses for determining distribution support, linearity and convexity are derived from the standard mathematical definitions. The time complexity of the analysis is determined by the underlying inference (which is #P for discrete programs) and algebraic simplifications.

Global vs. Local Sensitivity. In the present analysis, the value of `eps` is bound only by the legality range and can assume any value. This therefore enables us to conduct *a global* sensitivity analysis, which asks a question, whether some property about the distribution holds for *all* values of `eps`. This is in contrast to *a local* sensitivity analysis, which assumes that `eps` is a constant small perturbation around an input x_0, e.g., $x_0 - 0.1$ and $x_0 + 0.1$. Computing the local analysis follows directly from the result of the global analysis.

Our approach can, in principle, also analyze multiple uncertain variables in parallel (*multi-parameter* sensitivity analysis). While PSense algorithm would apply to this setting, we note that when selecting all variables as noisy, the current solvers would not be able to apply effective simplification on such expressions (unless most of noise variables are 0).

3.4 Sampling-Based Sensitivity Algorithm

We also implemented a sampling backend as an approximate alternative to the exact symbolic analysis. For a concrete numerical value of noise (e.g., 1%, 5%, or 10% of the original value), the sampling backend translates the program with and without noise to WebPPL, a popular probabilistic language with an approximate MCMC backend and runs its inference. The translation between PSI and WebPPL is mostly straightforward, except for the loops, which are translated as recursions. The translated program calls the two functions, `main` and `maineps`, which are the translated functions, and `eps` is a constant:

```
var sensitivity = function() {
    var eps = 0.01;
    var r1 = main();
    var r2 = maineps(eps);
    return sensitivity_metric(r1, r2);
}
var dist = Infer({method: 'MCMC', samples: 1000},  sensitivity);
```

While the sampling-based sensitivity analysis will typically work for a wider variety of probabilistic programs than the symbolic analysis, it has at least three important limitations: (1) it may produce imprecise results, especially when `eps` is small and therefore a user cannot rely on it soundness, and (2) it works only for concrete values of `eps`, and cannot express global properties (for all `eps`), and (3) it cannot be used in the optimization queries we describe next.

4   Optimization

PSense can leverage the results from the symbolic analysis to formulate and solve sensitivity-related optimization problems.

Maximum Acceptable Perturbation. This optimization problem seeks the answer to the question: *What is the maximum absolute noise of the input such that the distance between the output distributions does not exceed a provided constant?* A user provides an acceptable threshold τ on the distribution distance of their choice. We then leverage PSense analysis (Sect. 3) to get the symbolic expression for the distribution distance $\Delta(\varepsilon)$ for a noise variable ε. We define the optimization problem as follows:

$$
\begin{aligned}
\textit{Maximize:} \quad & |\varepsilon| \\
\textit{Constraints:} \quad & 0 \le \Delta(\varepsilon) \le \tau \\
& \text{LEGALITYCHECKS}(\varepsilon) \\
\textit{Variable:} \quad & \varepsilon \in \text{DOMAIN}
\end{aligned}
$$

The optimization problem maximizes the absolute value of ε subject to the constraint given by the distance expression. In general, a distance expression Δ

may have multiple branches (expressed as `Boole` functions). In such cases, we break Δ into non-overlapping branch components and make sure all of them are within the bound τ. We also support a non-symmetric optimization problem that independently maximizes ε and $-\varepsilon$ to get more precise bounds.

As already mentioned, PSense keeps track of the legal values of the distribution parameters for each standard distribution. These checks typically have the form $a \leq \varepsilon \leq b$. It is possible for a variable to have multiple such (sub)intervals, which we add all to the optimization problem. Finally, ε's domain may be either reals or integers. While most parameters are real (e.g., for Bernoulli and Gaussian), integer noise exists in distributions such as uniform for integers (upper and lower bounds) or negative binomial (first parameter).

The optimization problem is univariate, but the constraint on Δ can be non-linear. We use Mathematica's function `Maximize[]`, which symbolically solves optimization problems, producing the infinite-precision value for ε. In addition, PSense runs an auxiliary convexity check, which can indicate whether the found optimum is global one (if the function is convex, then a local maximum is also the global maximum).

Optimization for Local Sensitivity. We can similarly formulate the local-sensitivity query: *What is the maximum distance between the output distributions when the input noise is within an interval $[x_0 - \sigma, x_0 + \sigma]$?* ($x_0$ is the original value, and the constant σ is a radius of the ball around it). The optimization problem is formulated similarly as the previous one. The optimization objective is to maximize $\Delta(\varepsilon)$, subject to the constraint $\varepsilon \in [-\sigma, \sigma]$ and legality checks for ε. If $\Delta(\varepsilon)$ has multiple terms, we solve for each and combine. For this problem, we also use Mathematica's `Maximize[]` to compute the (exact) symbolic solution.

5   Evaluation

Our evaluation focuses on the following research questions:

* **RQ1:** Is PSense effective in computing the sensitivity of the parameters of prior distributions?
* **RQ2:** Is PSense effective in computing the sensitivity of the observations?
* **RQ3:** Is PSense effective in finding maximum allowed parameter sensitivity subject to the bound on the final noise?
* **RQ4:** How does the precision of PSense symbolic approach compare to a sampling-based sensitivity analysis?

Benchmarks. We evaluated PSense on three sets of programs: (1) 21 benchmark programs from the PSI paper [10], (2) a subset of the programs from the book *Probabilistic Models of Cognition* [14] that we translated into PSI, and (3) three code examples from [4]: SGD that we specialized for regression, one-dimensional population dynamics, and path coupling.

Table 1 presents the statistics of the benchmark programs. In addition to the total number of programs and the constant parameters that can be changed, it also presents the number of statements that specify prior distributions per benchmark, the number of observation statements, and the number of lines of code. Note that even when a probabilistic program has only a few lines of code, they still represent complicated probabilistic models that can be challenging for automated analyses.

Table 1. Benchmark statistics

#Progs	66
#Params	357
#Priors/Prog	min: 1
	avg: 4.6
	max: 16
#Observe/Prog	min: 0
	avg: 0.77
	max: 10
#LOC	min: 3
	avg: 16.8
	max: 76

Setup. We analyzed the programs with five sensitivity metrics defined in Sect. 3.2. We set the timeout for computing the individual metric to 10 min. We performed the experiments on Xeon CPU E5-2687W (3.00GHz) with 64GB RAM, running Ubuntu 16.04.

Table 2. Sensitivity to perturbation of priors

Metric	Discrete					Continuous				
	OK	Fail	T/O	N/A	Time (s)	OK	Fail	T/O	N/A	Time (s)
ED1	94	44	5	25	4.47±2.08	49	30	39	20	9.84±2.62
ED2	136	1	6	25	18.7±6.82	39	0	79	20	115±30.0
KS	142	2	24	0	27.1±7.90	38	19	81	0	81.3±23.6
TVD	127	7	34	0	19.1±6.58	55*	16	67	0	87.9±26.9
KL	128	17	23	0	23.1±6.18	32*	17	89	0	114±28.0

5.1 Sensitivity to Perturbation of Priors

We computed the sensitivity of the result to the change in each prior parameter. Table 2 presents the counts of the outcomes of parameter sensitivity, separately for discrete and continuous/mixed programs. The first column presents the metrics from Sect. 3.2. Column "OK" counts the cases for which PSense successfully computed the symbolic noise expression (we denote * if we applied approximate integration). Column "Fail" counts the cases for which PSense was unable to compute the result automatically; we discuss the reasons below. Column "T/O" counts the cases that did not complete within the timeout. Column "N/A" counts cases for which the metrics cannot be applied (e.g., when the program returns a tuple). Finally, Column "Time" presents the average time and standard deviation of the analysis runs.

The results show that PSense can be effective in producing sensitivity information for many benchmark programs. For discrete programs, we analyze all programs fully symbolically and provide exact difference expressions. In addition, for all these programs, we were able to compute the linearity and the maximum input noise that corresponds to the pre-specified output noise in the case of KS distribution distance. For continuous programs, PSense can compute the expectation and KS distances exactly, but for TVD and KL, the majority of the integrals do not have the closed form, and therefore we instructed PSense to compute the approximate integrals.

Table 3. Sensitivity to perturbations of observed data

Metric	Discrete					Continuous				
	OK	Fail	T/O	N/A	Time (s)	OK	Fail	T/O	N/A	Time (s)
ED1	6	19	1	6	0.45±0.31	6	5	6	2	5.07±3.20
ED2	25	0	1	6	7.58±7.15	8	0	9	2	39.4±23.6
KS	28	0	4	0	4.27±2.46	9	1	9	0	3.22±2.60
TVD	28	0	4	0	3.61±1.94	11*	1	7	0	56.5±35.6
KL	9	20	3	0	22.7±16.1	3*	1	15	0	1.34±0.83

Some of the PSense analyses failed to produce the results. We manually inspected these programs. For expectation distance, all failures are due to expectation expressions that have multiple cases. For instance, one case when eps $>=$ 0 and another when eps $<$ 0. We currently do not support the sensitivity of such composite expressions, but plan to do so in the future. For KS distance, the failures were due to the internal exceptions in PSI (problems computing results) or in Mathematica's Maximize (returns "Indeterminate"). For TVD/KL, the failures happen when PSense cannot find the distribution support. For continuous distributions, Mathematica's numerical integration (NIntegrate) can result in 0 in the denominator or raise an "Infinity, or Indeterminate" exception. In some cases, we cannot apply the computation – e.g., expectation distances ED1 and ED2 are not defined when the program returns a tuple.

The execution time consists of three components: (1) the time to do PSI analysis, (2) the time to determine the distribution support, and (3) the time to compute the sensitivity metric. Out of those, our current computation of the distribution support takes about 20 s (for most programs), while the computation of the sensitivity metric takes between 4 s (ED2) and 20 s (KL). Continuous distributions typically take more time, since the analysis needs to solve complicated integrals or optimizations (e.g., ED2, KS), in contrast to the discrete cases, which only have finite sums. For continuous TVD and KL, the time of approximate integration is proportional to the number of points for which the integrals are numerically computed. Finally, complex integrals cause more timeouts for continuous programs.

5.2 Sensitivity to Perturbations of Observed Data

Similarly, we ran PSense to add a noise variable to the expressions within each observation statement. Table 3 presents the counts of observation sensitivity analyses (one for each observe statement) and their outcomes, separately for discrete and continuous/mixed programs. The columns have the same meaning as for Table 2. We identify the same trends for the ability of PSense to analyze sensitivity as in the case of the prior distributions in Sect. 5.1 for the majority of metrics. The exceptions are ED1 and KL (discrete cases), where the sensitivity expressions are more likely to be discontinuous or nonlinear because noise variables in observations result in more complicated constraints.

5.3 Solving Optimization Problem

We also present the results of solving the optimization problem, which seeks the maximum absolute value of the noise variable, subject to the bound on the program's final distance. We set the maximum acceptable program threshold to 10% of the true distance. We analyzed only the programs for which PSense (Sects. 5.1 and 5.2) gave an "OK" status. We only optimized the exact symbolic expressions, therefore skipping TVD and KL distances for continuous programs.

Table 3 presents the counts of problems that were successfully solved. The columns of the table have the same meaning as in the previous sections. The results show that many of the problems can be successfully (and exactly) solved by the Mathematica backend that PSense calls. For the several cases that failed to produce the result, Mathematica was not able to generate initial points that satisfy the inequality or the solution failed to converge, typically for programs with discrete variables, which resolve to plateaus in optimization. Only a small fraction of analyses experienced timeout, indicating that the current symbolic techniques are effective in solving a variety of problems.

Table 4. PSense results for solving optimization problems

Metric	Discrete					Continuous				
	OK	Fail	T/O	N/A	Time (s)	OK	Fail	T/O	N/A	Time (s)
ED1	99	0	1	31	3.11±1.81	54	0	1	22	7.26±2.25
ED2	160	1	0	31	14.7±5.43	42	3	2	22	94.7±25.0
KS	138	23	9	0	163±12.4	25	7	15	0	105±29.6
TVD	148	7	0	0	5.72±2.51	-	-	-	-	-
KL	113	21	3	0	13.4±4.46	-	-	-	-	-

5.4 Comparison with Sampling Sensitivity Analysis

Finally, we compared the results and the execution times of PSense compared to estimating sensitivity using the sampling (WebPPL-based) backend. We set the

Table 5. Symbolic vs. sampling algorithm for expectation distances

Metric	Total	Diff. (>1-stderr)	Diff. (>2-stderr)	Time Symbolic	Time Sampling
ED1	86	57 (66%)	35 (41%)	0.45±0.027	0.29±0.002
ED2	78	62 (79%)	44 (56%)	0.21±0.003	0.29±0.002

value of the noise variable to 10% of the original value and run 1000 simulations. Since the sampling backend has to operate only on the concrete values of noise variables, we evaluated symbolic analysis too with the specific noise value. We selected only the programs for which PSI returned that `Pr[error]` (probability of error state) is zero. For each analysis run, we checked if there exists a significant difference between the exact symbolic sensitivity and approximate sensitivity from the simulation by running a statistical t-test with one ($p = 0.32$) and two standard errors ($p = 0.05$).

Table 5 presents the comparison. Column "Total" presents the total number of sensitivity analyses run. Column "Different" presents the number of simulation runs that were significantly different from the exact result, according to the t-test. This backend therefore complements PSense's symbolic analysis. Columns "Time Symbolic" and "Time Sampling" present the average execution times in seconds for the two analyses. Since both analyses operate with a particular numerical value for the noise variable, the run time is much shorter than for the previous analyses that considered the symbolic noise variable. The results show that for a substantial fraction (41% of ED1 analyses and 57% of ED2 analyses), sampling produced a sensitivity estimate that is more than two standard errors away from the exact sensitivity. The trend is even more visible with one standard error distance (66% and 79% of the analyses have a significantly different result). Both indicate that sampling-based analysis is imprecise (for a similar execution time).

6   Related Work

Probabilistic Programming Systems. Recent years have seen a significant interest in probabilistic programming languages [10–12,19,20,27]. A developer who wants to check the sensitivity of their models needs to manually modify the programs for every parameter, and since most languages support only approximate inference, the analysis is only valid for concrete values or distribution of noise. In comparison, the goal of PSense is to fully automate the sensitivity analysis and present exact results via symbolic analysis.

Researchers have also looked into various static analyses that compute safe upper bounds of the probabilities of assertions in the program executions, e.g., [3, 9,16,21,23,26]. We anticipate that the future advances in static analysis and appropriate abstractions, as well as principled combinations of analysis with sampling [20] will improve the scalability of PSense and related analyses.

Comparison with PSI and Mathematica. While PSense leverages PSI's core analysis, PSI alone cannot identify locations of noise variables, compute the distance, run optimization for computing KS distance and other optimization and linearity/continuity queries. PSI's engine cannot solve various integrals arising from TVD and KL. On the other hand, Mathematica is limited when simplifying arbitrary program state expressions [10]. PSense builds on and reformulates the problems hard for PSI as more efficiently computable Mathematica queries and computes hints, e.g., distribution supports, to make the analysis feasible.

Sensitivity Analyses. Sensitivity techniques from machine learning [5–7,17,25] are typically numeric and mainly analyze local sensitivity. For instance, Darwiche and Chan present a framework for testing individual discrete-only parameters of Belief networks [6] and later present how to extend the analysis for multiple parameters and capture their interactions [7]. Like [6], PSense focuses on individual parameters, but can analyze both discrete and continuous distributions. Recently, Llerena et al. [18] present an analysis of perturbed Markov Decision Processes, but only analyze models of systems and do not analyze program code. Barthe et al. presented a logic for reasoning about probabilistic program sensitivity [4]. Unlike PSense, it is manual, requiring a developer to prove properties using a proof assistant, but it supports overapproximation. In contrast, PSense is fully automated and computes various non-linear sensitivity metrics.

7   Conclusion

We presented PSense, a system for automatic sensitivity analysis of probabilistic programs to the perturbations in the prior parameters and data. PSense leverages symbolic algebra techniques to compute the exact sensitivity expressions and solve optimization queries. The evaluation on 66 programs and 357 parameters shows that PSense can compute the exact sensitivity expressions for many existing problems. PSense demonstrates that symbolic analysis can be a solid foundation for automatic and precise sensitivity analysis of probabilistic programs.

Acknowledgments. We thank the anonymous reviewers for the useful comments on the previous versions of this work. This research was supported in part by NSF Grants No. CCF 17-03637 and CCF 16-29431.

References

1. Wikipedia: SGD. https://en.wikipedia.org/wiki/Stochastic_gradient_descent
2. Mathematica (2015). https://www.wolfram.com/mathematica/
3. Albarghouthi, A., D'Antoni, L., Drews, S., Nori, A.: Fairsquare: probabilistic verification of program fairness. In: OOPSLA (2017)
4. Barthe, G., Espitau, T., Grégoire, B., Hsu, J., Strub, P.: Proving expected sensitivity of probabilistic programs. In: POPL (2018)

5. Borgonovo, E., Plischke, E.: Sensitivity analysis: a review of recent advances. Eur. J. Oper. Res. **248**(3), 869–887 (2016)
6. Chan, H., Darwiche, A.: When do numbers really matter? J. Artif. Intell. Res. **17**, 265–287 (2002)
7. Chan, H., Darwiche, A.: Sensitivity analysis in Bayesian networks: from single to multiple parameters. In: UAI (2004)
8. Chaudhuri, S., Gulwani, S., Lublinerman, R., Navidpour, S.: Proving programs robust. In: FSE (2011)
9. Filieri, A., Păsăreanu, C., Visser, W.: Reliability analysis in symbolic pathfinder. In: ICSE (2013)
10. Gehr, T., Misailovic, S., Vechev, M.: PSI: exact symbolic inference for probabilistic programs. In: CAV (2016)
11. Gelman, A., Lee, D., Guo, J.: Stan: a probabilistic programming language for Bayesian inference and optimization. J. Educ. Behav. Stats. **40**, 530–543 (2015)
12. Goodman, N., Mansinghka, V., Roy, D., Bonawitz, K., Tenenbaum, J.: Church: a language for generative models. In: UAI (2008)
13. Goodman, N., Stuhlmüller, A.: The design and implementation of probabilistic programming languages (2014)
14. Goodman, N., Tenenbaum, J.: Probabilistic Models of Cognition. https://probmods.org/
15. Gustafson, P., Srinivasan, C., Wasserman, L.: Local sensitivity analysis. Bayesian Stat. **5**, 197–210 (1996)
16. Holtzen, S., Millstein, T., Broeck, G.: Probabilistic program abstractions. In: UAI (2017)
17. Iooss, B., Saltelli, A.: Introduction to sensitivity analysis. Handbook of Uncertainty Quantification, pp. 1–20. Springer, Cham (2016)
18. Llerena, Y., Su, G., Rosenblum, D.: Probabilistic model checking of perturbed mdps with applications to cloud computing. In: FSE (2017)
19. Mansinghka, V., Selsam, D., Perov, Y.: Venture: a higher-order probabilistic programming platform with programmable inference. *ArXiv* arXiv:1404.0099 (2014)
20. Narayanan, P., Carette, J., Romano, W., Shan, C., Zinkov, R.: Probabilistic inference by program transformation in hakaru. In: FLOPS (2016)
21. Olmedo, F., Kaminski, B., Katoen, J., Matheja, C.: Reasoning about recursive probabilistic programs. In: LICS (2016)
22. Saltelli, A., et al.: Global sensitivity analysis: the primer (2008)
23. Sankaranarayanan, S., Chakarov, A., Gulwani, S.: Static analysis for probabilistic programs: inferring whole program properties from finitel many paths. In: PLDI 2013
24. Tran, D., Kucukelbir, A., Dieng, A., Rudolph, M., Liang, D., Blei, D.: Edward: a library for probabilistic modeling, inference, and criticism. arXiv:1610.09787 (2016)
25. van der Gaag, L., Renooij, S., Coupé, V.: Sensitivity analysis of probabilistic networks. Advances in Probabilistic Graphical Models, pp. 103–124. Springer, Berlin (2007)
26. Wang, D., Hoffmann, J., Reps, T.: PMAF: an algebraic framework for static analysis of probabilistic programs. In: PLDI (2018)
27. Wood, F., van de Meent, J., Mansinghka, V.: A new approach to probabilistic programming inference. In: AISTATS (2014)

Information Leakage in Arbiter Protocols

Nestan Tsiskaridze[1(✉)], Lucas Bang[2], Joseph McMahan[1], Tevfik Bultan[1],
and Timothy Sherwood[1]

[1] University of California, Santa Barbara 93106, USA
{nestan,jmcmahan,bultan,sherwood}@cs.ucsb.edu
[2] Harvey Mudd College, Claremont, CA 91711, USA
bang@cs.hmc.edu

Abstract. Resource sharing while preserving privacy is an increasingly important problem due to a wide-scale adoption of cloud computing. Under multitenancy, it is common to have multiple mutually distrustful "processes" (e.g. cores, threads, etc.) running on the same system simultaneously. This paper explores a new approach for automatically identifying and quantifying the information leakage in protocols that arbitrate utilization of shared resources between processes. Our approach is based on symbolic execution of arbiter protocols to extract constraints relating adversary observations to victim requests, then using model counting constraint solvers to quantify the information leaked. We present enumerative and optimized methods of exact model counting, and apply our methods to a set of nine different arbiter protocols, quantifying their leakage under different scenarios and allowing for informed comparison.

Keywords: Arbiter protocols · Quantitative information flow
Model counting · Symbolic execution

1   Introduction

Many of the computer systems we use today have access to secret information, confidentiality of which should not be compromised. In program analysis, methods of *secure information flow* (SIF) are dedicated to tracking the propagation of sensitive information through a program. SIF methods aim to produce a binary answer: *yes,* there is an information leak, or *no,* there is not, and have seen success in verifying anonymity protocols [13], firewall protocols [3], and network security protocols [7]. However, a binary answer to information leakage is not sufficient in general, due to cost of establishing strict non-interference, side-channels

This material is based on research sponsored by DARPA under the agreement number FA8750-15-2-0087 and the National Science Foundation under Grants No. 1740352, 1730309, 1717779, 1563935. The U.S. Government is authorized to reproduce and distribute reprints for Governmental purposes notwithstanding any copyright notation thereon. The views and conclusions contained herein are those of the authors and should not be interpreted as necessarily representing the official policies or endorsements, either expressed or implied, of DARPA or the U.S. Government.

S. K. Lahiri and C. Wang (Eds.): ATVA 2018, LNCS 11138, pp. 404–421, 2018.
https://doi.org/10.1007/978-3-030-01090-4_24

that may leak information through non-functional properties of a system, or due to application semantics that require some information leakage (for example, a password checker always leaks information by reporting if the input matched the secret password). Hence, the general question about information flow in a computer system is not *if* information leaks, but *how much* information leaks? This "how much" question led to the development of *Quantitative Information Flow* (QIF) techniques, which provide a foundational framework for measuring information leakage [25].

In this paper, we present a QIF technique for assessment and comparison of information leakage among resource sharing protocols. Various arbiter protocols have been developed for coordinating processes that share common resources [11]. An arbiter takes resource requests and grants access to the resource based on its policy. We assume that the requests made by one process should not be revealed to another process. In an ideal situation no process should reveal any information to another process unless it is intentional. In reality, many designs need to leak some degree of information to meet other design goals. We demonstrate that using the QIF technique we present one can determine and compare the *amount* of information leakage for different arbiter protocols.

Previous work on information flow properties of protocols has been limited. The techniques we present in this paper introduce a new dimension in protocol analysis, and provide a new way to classify protocols with respect to the amount of information they leak. Interestingly, as our experiments demonstrate, reducing information leakage can conflict with other desirable properties of protocols. For example, improving resource usage or fairness in a given protocol could increase the amount of information leaked.

Our approach is based on symbolic execution and constraint model counting techniques and can handle randomized protocols. Given a protocol specification, we extend symbolic execution to extract constraints characterizing relationships between the secret and the adversary-observable events. With model counting constraint solvers, we quantify the amount of information leaked, in terms of entropy, by observable events. We present a novel, efficient and exact model counting technique for a class of constraints extracted during QIF analysis of arbiter protocols.

The rest of the paper is organized as follows. Section 2 discusses different arbiter protocols to be analyzed; Sect. 3 explains our method of computing leakage of the protocols. Section 4 contains our optimized method of constraint counting, vastly improving performance of the analysis. Section 5 gives our experimental results, Sect. 6 discusses related work, and Sect. 7 concludes.

2   Arbiter Protocols

We model synchronous arbiter protocols as a multi-process, multi-round model with n processes and k rounds. Each process i in each round j sends the arbiter a request bit for a shared resource (R_{ij}, where if the bit is one the process is requesting the resource), and receives a grant bit (G_{ij}, where if the bit is one the request is granted) as a response from the arbiter. The basic arbiter protocol architecture is shown in Fig. 1. In the protocols we analyze only one process can be granted access to the shared resource in each round. The basic problem is whether an adversary process can infer the sequence of request bits of another process from the grant bits that adversary receives, and to what extent.

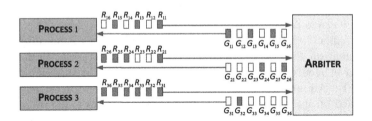

Fig. 1. Arbiter protocol model. Shaded box depicts a bit set to one, white – to zero. Number of processes is 3, rounds 6.

Example. Consider an arbiter protocol that resolves simultaneous requests for the same resource by giving access to the process with the minimum process ID, (e.g. the PRIORITY procedure in Fig. 2, also depicted in Fig. 1). Suppose an adversary controls Process 2 and targets a victim Process 1. If Process 2 requests access to the resource and does not get the access granted, it is so because the Process 1 has also requested access during the same arbitration round. On the other hand, if Process 2 is granted the access, it must be the case that Process 1 did not request in that round. Consequently, Process 2 can fully infer the request pattern of Process 1. Now suppose the adversary controls Process 3, makes a request, and does not get the access granted. Then the attacker can infer that either Process 1 or Process 2 or both have requested, but cannot distinguish among these cases based on its own response from the arbiter, thereby learning only partial information. In fact, the best strategy for the adversary is to keep requesting in each round, as Process 3 in Fig. 1. One expects that resolving resource-request races randomly (e.g. the RANDOM procedure in Fig. 2) should not allow one process to infer the request pattern of another process from its own pattern of access grants.

For more complex protocols, it becomes difficult to manually reason about the information flow properties. In this paper, we give automatic techniques for quantifying the amount of information that can be gained from an arbiter protocol by any process about any other process.

We categorize arbiter protocols based on three characteristics: (I) how the concurrent requests are resolved; (II) whether the protocols are stateful or stateless; and (III) whether the processes are stateful or stateless.

We say a protocol (or a process) is *stateless* if access grants (respectively requests) made at each round are independent from those of the previous rounds; and is *stateful* otherwise. Among the stateful process behaviors, we consider the one in which every process holds each initiated request without interruption across the rounds until the arbiter grants access to this process, after which the process is unconstrained on when to initiate a new request.

We resolve concurrent request in three ways: (i) based on a predefined static priority, (ii) based on a dynamically-defined priority, or (iii) randomly. We define a static priority based on the process IDs—the lower a process ID, the higher its priority. Dynamic priorities are defined in, and by, the stateful protocols where the priority of a process at the current round depends on the requests and grants for all processes made at the previous rounds. Concurrences are resolved randomly either in a uniformly-distributed random or a weighted random manner. Handling random components in symbolic analysis is a challenging task on its own. We introduce our approach for extending the quantitative symbolic analysis to support symbolic random components in the arbiter protocols in Sect. 3.3.

Below, we present various arbiter protocols and discuss how to quantify their information flow properties using our automated approach. We give pseudocode of arbiter protocols for a single round. Let $P = \{P_1, P_2, \ldots, P_n\}$ be a list of processes communicating with an arbiter. In a single round, the arbiter receives a list of requests from these processes $R = \{R_1, R_2, \ldots, R_n\}$ for a shared resource, and returns a grant response to each of the processes, $G = \{G_1, G_2, \ldots, G_n\}$. The requests R_i and grants G_i are modeled to take Boolean values: $\top$ if the request (respectively, grant) is instantiated (respectively, granted), and $\bot$ otherwise.

Stateless arbiters. A *priority-based arbiter* (PRIORITY) and a *randomized arbiter* (RANDOM) are stateless arbiters which differ by how they resolve concurrent requests when multiple processes place a request within the same round.

(1) The PRIORITY arbiter resolves concurrent requests based on a predefined *static priority*, always granting access to the process with the highest priority. Without loss of generality, we assume the order $P_1 \succ P_2 \succ \cdots \succ P_n$ on the processes and say that P_1 has the highest priority and P_n the lowest.

(2) The RANDOM arbiter resolves concurrent requests randomly. Pseudocode for a single round of these protocols is shown in Fig. 2. ISRACE(R) routine returns *true* if and only if multiple processes request concurrently. PICK-RND(R) randomly selects a process, among those racing, with equal probability. If a single process requests, FINDREQ(R) returns the ID of this process, and returns NULL when no process requests.

Stateful arbiters. This category includes a *round robin arbiter* (ROUND ROBIN), a *lottery-based arbiter* (LOTTERY), a *first-come-first-serve-based arbiter* (FCFS), and a *longest-idle-based arbiter* (LONGESTIDLE) as shown in Figs. 3, 4 and 5. The concurrences are resolved with a *dynamic priority* order on the processes based on the history of the previous rounds.

(3) The ROUNDROBIN arbiter grants access to processes in a circular order by passing around a token incremented at each round: if a process with an ID equal to the value of the token has requested access in a given round the arbiter grants access to this process, otherwise the arbiter does not grant access to any process and moves to the next round with the incremented token. When the token reaches the last process ID it resets to the first one.

Procedure PRIORITY
Input: $R[1..n]$ an array of requests
Output: $G[1..n]$ an array of responses
 1: $G \leftarrow (\bot, \ldots, \bot)$
 2: **for** $i \leftarrow 1$ **to** n **do**
 3:     **if** $R[i] = \top$ **then**
 4:         $G[i] \leftarrow \top$
 5:         **break**
 6:     **end if**
 7: **end for**
 8: **return** G

Procedure RANDOM
Input: $R[1..n]$ an array of requests
Output: $G[1..n]$ an array of responses
 1: $G \leftarrow (\bot, \ldots, \bot)$
 2: **if** ISRACE(R) **then**
 3:     $G[\text{PICKRND}(R)] \leftarrow \top$
 4: **else**
 5:     $pid \leftarrow \text{FINDREQ}(R)$
 6:     **if** $pid \neq$ NULL **then**
 7:         $G[pid] \leftarrow \top$
 8:     **end if**
 9: **end if**
10: **return** G

Fig. 2. Priority and random arbiters.

(4) ROUNDROBINSKIP is a variant of the round robin protocol that never passes a round without a grant when there is a requesting process. The routine FINDFIRST(R, tkn) returns an ID of the first requesting process it finds starting from the token and following in a circular manner by skipping over the idle processes that made no request in a given round; if no process made a request in the round—the routine returns NULL.

Global: tkn

Procedure ROUNDROBIN
Input: $R[1..n]$ an array of requests
Output: $G[1..n]$ an array of responses
 1: $G \leftarrow (\bot, \ldots, \bot)$
 2: **if** $tkn = n + 1$ **then** $tkn \leftarrow 1$
 3: **end if**
 4: **if** $R[tkn]$ **then**
 5:     $G[tkn] \leftarrow \top$
 6: **end if**
 7: $tkn \leftarrow tkn + 1$
 8: **return** G

Global: tkn

Procedure ROUNDROBINSKIP
Input: $R[1..n]$ an array of requests
Output: $G[1..n]$ an array of responses
 1: $G \leftarrow (\bot, \ldots, \bot)$
 2: **if** $tkn = n + 1$ **then** $tkn \leftarrow 1$
 3: **end if**
 4: $pid = \text{FINDFIRST}(R, tkn)$
 5: **if** $pid \neq$ NULL **then**
 6:     $G[pid] \leftarrow \top$
 7:     $tkn \leftarrow pid + 1$
 8: **end if**
 9: **return** G

Fig. 3. Round robin and round robin skip arbiters.

(5) The LOTTERY arbiter selects a process in a weighted-random manner. In contrast with the RANDOM arbiter, it counts the wait-times of the processes that have been waiting for the access to be granted and resolves concurrent requests by probabilistically prioritizing processes with longer waiting time. $W = (W_1, \ldots, W_n)$ is a list of wait-times of each process. PICKRND(W) selects a process among the racing ones in a weighted-random manner.

Global: $W[1..n]$ an array of wait-times
Procedure LOTTERY
Input: $R[1..n]$ an array of requests
Output: $G[1..n]$ an array of responses
1: $G \leftarrow (\bot, \ldots, \bot)$
2: **for** $i \leftarrow 1$ **to** n **do**
3:      **if** $R[i] = \top$ **then**
4:          $W[i] \leftarrow W[i] + 1$
5:      **else**
6:          $W[i] \leftarrow 0$
7:      **end if**
8: **end for**
9: **if** ISRACE(R) **then**
10:      $pid \leftarrow$ PICKRND(W)
11: **else**
12:      $pid \leftarrow$ FINDREQ(R)
13: **end if**
14: **if** $pid \neq$ NULL **then**
15:      $G[pid] \leftarrow \top$
16:      $W[pid] \leftarrow 0$
17: **end if**
18: **return** G

Fig. 4. Lottery arbiter.

(6) The FCFS (first-come-first-served) arbiter resolves concurrent requests by considering wait-times of the processes W. The ALLMAX(W) routine returns the IDs of the processes with the maximal wait-time. If multiple processes have been waiting for the permission grant for the same number of rounds, PICKONE() breaks ties. We consider two approaches for PICKONE(): based on the static priority where the process with the lowest ID gets access, and uniformly random.

(7) The LONGESTIDLE arbiter does the opposite to the FCFS in the sense that it prioritizes processes by length of idle time. $I = (I_1, \ldots, I_n)$ is a list of idle-times of each process. Ties are broken in the same manner as in FCFS.

3   Information Leakage in Arbiter Protocols

We consider a system, which accepts a public input (also referred as the low security input) L, a secret input (or the so-called private, high-security input) H, and produces an observable output O. The model includes an *adversary*, the *malicious user* $\mathcal{A}$. The adversary invokes the system with the input L and observes the output O. $\mathcal{A}$ does not have direct access to the secret H, but would like to learn its value. Before invoking the system, $\mathcal{A}$ has some initial uncertainty about the value of H, while after observing O, some amount of information is leaked, thereby reducing $\mathcal{A}$'s uncertainty about H.

In our model, we consider three types of processes (1) an adversary controlled process, denoted by $P_{\mathcal{A}}$, (2) a process belonging to the victim, denoted by $P_{\mathcal{V}}$ ($P_{\mathcal{V}} \neq P_{\mathcal{A}}$), and (3) a benign process introduced as additional unpredictable behavior to the system. The adversary can observe only permission responses issued by the arbiter on his/her requests, denoted by $R_{\mathcal{A}} = \{R_{\mathcal{A}1}, R_{\mathcal{A}2}, \ldots, R_{\mathcal{A}k}\}$, with the aim to gain as much information as possible on the permission requests of the victim's process $R_{\mathcal{V}} = \{R_{\mathcal{V}1}, R_{\mathcal{V}2}, \ldots, R_{\mathcal{V}k}\}$. We consider the secret $H = R_{\mathcal{V}}$ to be the list of permission requests of the victim process. The low security input to the system $L = R_{\mathcal{A}}$ is the adversary-controlled

Global: $W[1..n]$ an array of wait-times	**Global:** $I[1..n]$ an array of idle-times
Procedure FCFS	**Procedure** LONGESTIDLE
Input: $R[1..n]$ an array of requests	**Input:** $R[1..n]$ an array of requests
Output: $G[1..n]$ an array of responses	**Output:** $G[1..n]$ an array of responses

```
 1: G ← (⊥, ..., ⊥)                      1: G ← (⊥, ..., ⊥)
 2: for i ← 1 to n do                    2: for i ← 1 to n do
 3:     if R[i] = ⊤ then                 3:     if R[i] = ⊥ then
 4:         W[i] ← W[i] + 1              4:         I[i] ← I[i] + 1
 5:     else                             5:     end if
 6:         W[i] ← 0                     6: end for
 7:     end if                           7: if ISRACE(R) then
 8: end for                              8:     pid ← PICKONE(ALLMAX(I))
 9: if ISRACE(R) then                    9: else
10:     pid ← PICKONE(ALLMAX(W))        10:     pid ← FINDREQ(R)
11: else                                11: end if
12:     pid ← FINDREQ(R)                12: if pid ≠ NULL then
13: end if                              13:     G[pid] ← ⊤
14: if pid ≠ NULL then                  14:     I[pid] ← 0
15:     G[pid] ← ⊤                      15: end if
16:     W[pid] ← 0                      16: return G
17: end if
18: return G
```

Fig. 5. First come first serve and longest idle priority arbiters.

data—the permission requests placed by the adversary process. The corresponding permission grants received by the adversary on his/her own requests, denoted by $G_{\mathcal{A}} = \{G_{\mathcal{A}1}, G_{\mathcal{A}2}, \ldots, G_{\mathcal{A}k}\}$, are the data observed by the adversary $O = G_{\mathcal{A}}$ (referred as the *observations*).

In this work, we quantify and compare the amount of maximal expected leakage the adversary can obtain for arbiter protocols presented in Sect. 2 considering possible choices of $P_{\mathcal{A}}$ and $P_{\mathcal{V}}$. This is a QIF analysis problem through the *main channel*, when the adversary observes the direct output of the system (i.e. his/her own access grant pattern). If the adversary can also observe nonfunctional aspects of the system behavior (e.g. the time it takes to respond to a request, or the power consumed) through a *side channel*, then one would also take those observations into account to quantify the information leakage through such side-channels.

3.1 Quantifying Information Leakage Using Entropy

Intuitively, the amount of information gained by the adversary is the difference between the initial uncertainty about the secret and the remaining uncertainty [25]. The field of QIF formalizes this intuitive statement by casting the problem in the language of *information theory*. Information theory uses the concept of *entropy* for the purpose of measuring the amount of information that can be transmitted over a channel, measuring information transmission in *bits of entropy*. Then, information entropy is used as a measurement of *uncertainty*.

We briefly define relevant information entropy measures here. Given a random variable X with a finite domain $\mathcal{X}$, and a variable Z that indexes the probabilities of X to take values $x \in \mathcal{X}$, denoted as $P(X = x \mid Z = z)$, the *information entropy* of X, denoted as $\mathcal{H}(X \mid Z = z)$, is given by

$$\mathcal{H}(X \mid Z = z) = \sum_{x \in \mathcal{X}} P(X = x \mid Z = z) \log_2 \frac{1}{P(X = x \mid Z = z)} \tag{1}$$

Let $\mathcal{Z}$ be the domain of Z. Given another random variable Y, over the domain $\mathcal{Y}$, and a conditional probabilities $P(X = x \mid Y = y, Z = z)$, also indexed by Z, the *conditional Shannon entropy of X given knowledge of Y indexed by Z* is

$$\mathcal{H}(X \mid Y, Z = z) = \sum_{y \in \mathcal{Y}} P(Y = y \mid Z = z) \mathcal{H}(X \mid Y = y, Z = z), \text{ where} \tag{2}$$

$$\mathcal{H}(X \mid Y = y, Z = z) = \sum_{x \in \mathcal{X}} P(X = x \mid Y = y, Z = z) \log_2 \frac{1}{P(X = x \mid Y = y, Z = z)} \tag{3}$$

We are interested in the maximal amount of information about X that could be learned given the knowledge of Y, as this describes the worst case leakage scenario. For this, we use *conditional Shannon entropy* and compute the maximal amount of the expected information gain as the difference of the initial uncertainty about X and the uncertainty after acquiring the knowledge of Y

$$\mathcal{I}(X, Y, Z) = \max_{z \in \mathcal{Z}} (\mathcal{H}(X \mid Z = z) - \mathcal{H}(X \mid Y, Z = z)) \tag{4}$$

In the context of QIF, we consider the public input L to be the *index* variable indexing probability distributions of the secret input H and the output O, with H and O being *random variables*. Thus, the above notations correspond to $Z = L$, $X = H$ and $Y = O$. A value of the input L along with the corresponding observation of the output O defines an *event* in the analysis.

To compute the expected maximal amount of information leaked, we need:

(i) **Initial uncertainty** the adversary has about the secret, $\mathcal{H}_{init}(H \mid L = l)$, for each of his/her inputs before making observations. This is computed following the Formula (1) using the initial probability distribution of the secret $P(H = h \mid L = l)$ conditioned by the adversary's inputs;

(ii) **Expected remaining uncertainty** about the secret, $\mathcal{H}_{fin}(H \mid O, L = l)$, over all observations the adversary can make after he/she provides an input l, computed as in (2): $\sum_{\omega \in \Omega} P(O = \omega \mid L = l) \mathcal{H}(H \mid O = \omega, L = l)$, where Ω is the domain of O, $P(O = \omega \mid L = l)$ is the probability of the adversary observing ω given the input l, and $\mathcal{H}(H \mid O = \omega, L = l)$ is the uncertainty about the secret given the event (ω, l), the latter computed using (3) and the probabilities of the secret conditioned by this event $P(H = h \mid O = \omega, L = l)$;

(iii) Then $\mathcal{I}(H, O, L) = \max(\mathcal{H}_{init}(H \mid L = l) - \mathcal{H}_{fin}(H \mid O, L = l))$ is the
expected maximal amount of information leaked, as defined in (4).

These definitions formalize our intuition that the information leaked is the
maximal difference between the uncertainty about the secret before and after
making an observation. The value of the adversary's input L for which the maximal leakage is obtained defines the best strategy for the adversary to follow in
order to obtain the maximal information leakage on H.

3.2 Extracting Observation Constraints with Symbolic Execution

Symbolic execution is a technique that extracts path constraints from a system
by executing it on *symbolic* inputs, as opposed to concrete input values. It can
be used to extract a set of path constraints characterizing all possible execution
paths of the system (typically up to an execution depth bound).

We adopt and extend symbolic execution techniques to automatically extract
constraints that relate secret values with observations that an adversary can
make. Traditional symbolic execution does not focus on extracting constraints
on observations that can be made by an adversary, such as timing or power
measurements, or constraints on resources that can be shared with adversarial processes. To formalize this concept, we introduce *event constraints* of the
protocol as defined below.

Let $\phi(H, L)$ be a path constraint returned by a traditional symbolic execution tool. Consider the set of observations Ω for the observable O. In practice
multiple execution paths may map to the same observation. We assume, however, that each execution path maps to a single observation. To express this,
we define a function $\mathcal{O}$, where $\mathcal{O}(\phi(H, L))$ is the observation that the execution
path constraint $\phi(H, L)$ maps to. Then, we extend each path constraint $\phi(H, L)$
into an *event constraint* $\mathbb{C}_\phi(H, O, L)$ to pair it with the observation it yields to:

$$\mathbb{C}_\phi(H, O, L) : (O = \omega) \wedge \phi(H, L), \quad \text{where} \quad \mathcal{O}(\phi(H, L)) = \omega \tag{5}$$

The disjunction of all event constraints with the the same observation ω,
characterizes ω by a constraint $\mathbb{C}_\omega(H, O, L)$ that holds if and only if the observation ω occurs, and can be written in the form:

$$\mathbb{C}_\omega(H, O, L) = \bigvee_{\mathcal{O}(\phi(H,L))=\omega} \wedge (O = \omega) \phi(H, L) \tag{6}$$

We define a *characteristic constraint* $\mathbb{C}(H, O, L)$ for the protocol as the constraint that describes all possible events:

$$\mathbb{C}(H, O, L) : \bigvee_{\omega \in \Omega} \mathbb{C}_\omega(H, O, L). \tag{7}$$

Example. Let us use the PRIORITY arbiter as a running example. For a
single round $\Omega = \{\top, \bot\}$. We give the characteristic constraint for a single
round of a three-process PRIORITY arbiter where $P_A = P_2$ below:

$\mathbb{C} = \mathbb{C}_\top \vee \mathbb{C}_\perp$:

$((O = \top) \wedge (R_1 = \perp \wedge R_2 = \top)) \vee$
$\vee ((O = \perp) \wedge (R_1 = \top \vee (R_1 = \perp \wedge R_2 = \perp \wedge R_3 = \top) \vee (R_1 = \perp \wedge R_2 = \perp \wedge R_3 = \perp))$

3.3 Extension for the Symbolic Analysis of Random Components

Handling random components in symbolic analysis is a challenging task on its own. The first work on supporting random instances in symbolic execution has been introduced recently [18]. We propose a technique simulating randomness of symbolic variables that is well-fitted for quantitative analysis and is simpler. Since our approach is based on computing probabilities of protocol behaviors (i.e. the probabilities of the protocol following corresponding execution paths), we should take into account the distribution of random variables occurring in this protocol, and thus, in the path constraints. If a path constraint contains a random variable R, the probability of triggering that path depends on the probability of R taking specific values defined by the path.

To incorporate the probability distribution of R into the computation of the probabilities of the execution paths, we introduce a fresh symbolic integer variable sym_R and implement the PICKRAND() procedure in a way that it simulates the desired random generator behavior and extends path constraints to reflect the relation between sym_R and R as follows: each value r of R leads to multiple values of sym_R representing the weight of r in the probability distribution of R. Let R take values in $(R_1, \ldots, R_n)$ with probability weights $\boldsymbol{W} = (W_1, \ldots, W_n)$, each $W_i \in \mathbb{Z}^+$. PICKRND() takes $\boldsymbol{W}$ for input and returns a value of R selected in a weighted-random manner in accord with $\boldsymbol{W}$. For each W_i, we define a *domain interval* $\mathcal{D}(W_i)$ of the length W_i as

$$\mathcal{D}(W_i) = \begin{cases} [1, W_i], & i = 1 \\ \left(\sum_{j=1}^{i-1} W_j, \sum_{j=1}^{i} W_j \right], & 1 < i \leq n \end{cases} \tag{8}$$

We restrict sym_R to take values in non-empty domain intervals by instrumenting the code with the implementation of PICKRND() as given in Fig. 6. If all domain intervals are empty, we set $sym\_R = \text{NULL}$.

3.4 Computing Event Probabilities with Model Counting

In order to compute information leakage, we need to compute the probabilities given in (2) and (3). We compute the probability of an event by counting the number of values that satisfy the observation constraint (i.e., the number of solutions to the observation constraint) that corresponds to that event. To formalize this, we will use the following notations. Given an ordered set of variables $\boldsymbol{V}$ and an ordered subset $\boldsymbol{V}' \subseteq \boldsymbol{V}$, we define *a partial assignment* on $\boldsymbol{V}'$ as a mapping $\boldsymbol{V}' \mapsto \boldsymbol{v}$, where $\boldsymbol{v}$ is an assignment on all variables in $\boldsymbol{V}'$. Given a constraint $\Psi(\boldsymbol{V})$, we denote by $\Psi(\boldsymbol{V}) \mid_{\boldsymbol{V}' \mapsto \boldsymbol{v}}$ the result of assigning and propagating the

---

Global: sym_R a symbolic integer variable
Procedure PICKRND
Input: $\boldsymbol{W}[1..n]$ an array of weights
Output: id an ID of a randomly selected value R_{id}
1: **for** $id \leftarrow 1$ **to** $id \leq n$ **do**
2:     **if** $\boldsymbol{W}[id] > 0$ and $sym\_R \in \mathcal{D}(\boldsymbol{W}[id])$ **then**
3:         **return** id
4:     **end if**
5: **end for**
6: **return** NULL

Fig. 6. Selecting a value from a domain with a weighted-random distribution.

values $\boldsymbol{v}$ to the variables $\boldsymbol{V}'$ in Ψ. We denote by $\#\Psi(\boldsymbol{V}) \mid_{\boldsymbol{V}' \mapsto \boldsymbol{v}}$ the number of solutions to $\Psi(\boldsymbol{V}) \mid_{\boldsymbol{V}' \mapsto \boldsymbol{v}}$ over the free variables.

Then the probabilities in (2) and (3) are computed using model counting on observation constraints as follows:

$$P(O = \omega | L = l) = \frac{\#\mathbb{C}(H,O,L) \mid_{(O,L) \mapsto (\omega,l)}}{\#\mathbb{C}(H,O,L) \mid_{(L) \mapsto (l)}} \tag{9}$$

$$P(H = h \mid O = \omega, L = l) = \frac{\#\mathbb{C}(H,O,L) \mid_{(H,O,L) \mapsto (h,\omega,l)}}{\#\mathbb{C}(H,O,L) \mid_{(O,L) \mapsto (\omega,l)}} \tag{10}$$

Example. In Table 1, we give the probability and entropy computations for the PRIORITY arbiter when $P_{\mathcal{A}} = P_2$ and $P_{\mathcal{V}} = P_1$. We follow the computation steps described in Sect. 3.1 using (1)–(4) for the entropy calculations and (9), (10) for the probabilities.

Table 1. Probability and entropy computations for the PRIORITY arbiter. Adversary controls P_2. Victim's process is P_1. $\mathbb{C}$ is the characteristic constraint for PRIORITY.

r_2	0				1			
g_2	0		1		0		1	
r_1	0	1	0	1	0	1	0	1
$\#\mathbb{C} \mid_{(R_1,G_2,R_2) \mapsto (r_1,g_2,r_2)}$	2	2	0	0	0	2	2	0
$\#\mathbb{C} \mid_{(G_2,R_2) \mapsto (g_2,r_2)}$	4		0		2		2	
$\#\mathbb{C} \mid_{(R_2) \mapsto (r_2)}$	4				4			
$P(R_1 = r_1 \mid R_2 = r_2)$	$P(0\mid0)=1/2$ $P(1\mid0)=1/2$				$P(0\mid1)=1/2$ $P(1\mid1)=1/2$			
$\mathcal{H}_{init}(R_1 \mid R_2 = r_2)$	1				1			
$P(R_1 = r_1 \mid G_2 = g_2, R_2 = r_2)$	1/2	1/2	0	0	0	1	1	0
$\mathcal{H}(R_1 \mid G_2 = g_2, R_2 = r_2)$	1		0		0		0	
$P(G_2 = g_2 \mid R_2 = r_2)$	1		0		1/2		1/2	
$\mathcal{H}_{fin}(R_1 \mid G_2, R_2 = r_2)$	1				0			
$\Delta\mathcal{H}$	0				1			
$max(\Delta\mathcal{H})$	1							

4   Model Counter for Arbiter Protocol Constraints

We observed that constraints extracted with the symbolic execution of the arbiter protocols were, on one hand, large—especially for those with random components as the randomization increases the variety of behaviours of the protocols, with over five million distinguished protocol behaviours for 6 rounds.

On the other hand, we observed that the constraints extracted from arbiter protocols can be characterized by a common structure. We define a grammar representing this structure, as described in Fig. 7, and refer to its language as a *range constraint language*, denoted by $\mathcal{L}_{\mathcal{RC}}$. In the context of the constraints extracted with the extended symbolic execution: $\mathcal{B}$ stands for the Boolean variables representing each process's requests in each round and corresponding arbiter responses, and $\mathcal{I}$ for the integer variables, one per round, responsible for random components of the protocols. For deterministic protocols the domain of $\mathcal{I}$ is empty. An atomic constraint C in this grammar represents a single event constraint $\mathbb{C}_\phi(H,O,L)$ (defined in (5)) extracted with the extended symbolic execution. Variables representing arbiter responses are always present in an atomic constraint. Consequently, the atomic constraints have disjoint sets of solutions.

$$
\begin{aligned}
\mathcal{C} &\rightarrow \mathcal{C} \wedge \mathcal{C} \mid \mathcal{R} \\
\mathcal{R} &\rightarrow \mathcal{B} = \top \mid \mathcal{B} = \bot \mid \mathcal{I} \in [a,b]
\end{aligned}
$$

Fig. 7. Range constraint grammar. $\mathcal{B}$ ranges over Boolean, $\mathcal{I}$ over integer variables.

We need to compute $\#\mathbb{C}(H,O,L) \mid_{(H,O,L) \mapsto (h,\omega,l)}$ for each tuple (h,ω,l). Based on the above observation on event constraints in $\mathcal{L}_{\mathcal{RC}}$, we built an efficient exact model counter which is linear in time in the size of the input constraint. The model counting is performed during parsing of the constraint and uses only as much space as required to store the final counts. We give a pseudocode for our model counter in Fig. 8, where $\text{TUPLES}(\mathbb{C}_\phi, P_\mathcal{A}, P_\mathcal{V})$ returns a set of all tuples (h,ω,l) of the partial assignments $(R_\mathcal{V}, G_\mathcal{A}, R_\mathcal{A}) \mapsto (h,\omega,l)$ of $\mathbb{C}_\phi$.

Given $P_\mathcal{V}$ and $P_\mathcal{A}$, each $\mathbb{C}_\phi$ determines values (h,ω,l) for (H,O,L), thus contributes to model counting for the tuple (h,ω,l). We define a *free variable* in an atomic constraint $\mathbb{C}_\phi$ to be a Boolean variable from the domain of $\mathcal{B}$ as a variable (i) distinguished from $R_\mathcal{V}$ and $R_\mathcal{A}$; and (ii) not appearing in $\mathbb{C}_\phi$. An event constraint $\mathbb{C}_\phi$ in $\mathbb{C}$ contributes towards the model-counting of multiple tuples (equally, with the same number of models s) when any of the variables $R_\mathcal{V}$ and $R_\mathcal{A}$ is absent in $\mathbb{C}_\phi$. The number of models, s, depends only on the number of free variables and the ranges on the integer variables in $\mathbb{C}_\phi$.

5   Experiments

To test our framework, we conduct quantification experiments on nine different arbiter protocols discussed in Sect. 2, considering both stateless and stateful

---

Global: S a data structure for storing model counts
Procedure $\mathcal{L}_{\mathcal{RC}}$_MODELCOUNTER
Input: $\mathbb{C}$ a characteristic constraint, $P_\mathcal{V}$ victim's process, $P_\mathcal{A}$ adversary's process
Output: Model counts stored in S
 1: **for each** $\mathbb{C}_\phi$ **in** $\mathbb{C}$ **do**   ▷ Also, by construction $\mathbb{C}_\phi \in \mathcal{L}_{\mathcal{RC}}$
 2:     $m \leftarrow \#\text{FREEVARS}(\mathbb{C}_\phi, P_\mathcal{V}, P_\mathcal{A})$
 3:     $s \leftarrow 2^m$
 4:     **for each** $(r \in [a, b])$ **in** I **do**
 5:         $s \leftarrow (b - a + 1) \times s$
 6:     **end for**
 7:     **for each tuple** (h, ω, l) **in** $\text{TUPLES}(\mathbb{C}_\phi, P_\mathcal{V}, P_\mathcal{A})$ **do**
 8:         $S[(h, \omega, l)] \leftarrow S[(h, \omega, l)] + s$
 9:     **end for**
10: **end for**

Fig. 8. Model counter for range constraints.

processes. Each experiment involves a single arbiter protocol, three processes, and rounds from one to six. We compute the maximum expected information leakage the adversary can learn about the victim process, and determine the position of the victim-adversary processes for which the arbiter leaks the most.

Our current implementation requires specification of each arbiter protocol in Java. We use SPF (Symbolic Java Pathfinder) [23], a well-established symbolic execution tool to analyze Java bytecode, to extract characteristic constraints for the arbiter protocols, as discussed in Sect. 3.2. Then, we perform model counting as explained in Sects. 3.4 and 4. Based on the distribution of these counts, we calculate the information leakage according to Sect. 3.1.

We perform model counting with two methods: an enumerative counting method $\mathcal{EC}$ (Sect. 3.4), and our faster range-constraint counting method $\mathcal{RC}$ (Sect. 4). The former provides us a slow method serving as a ground truth, the latter an optimized method for higher numbers of rounds when the exponential blowup makes enumerative counting infeasible. Table 2 shows the execution time, in seconds, for $\mathcal{EC}$ vs $\mathcal{RC}$ methods. $\mathcal{RC}$ ranges from 1.4x faster to $2,647$x faster, with an average speedup of 250x (excluding time outs for $\mathcal{EC}$).

Figure 9 shows the results of our experiments, executed on a 128 GB RAM machine. The protocols are given in two groups: one with stateless processes, one of stateful processes. The leakage for each protocol is shown for each arrangement of $(victim, adversary)$ process IDs and six rounds of data; six horizontal lines in each bar delineate the information learned up through that round. The full bar is the information learned in six rounds; the lowest line is the information learned in the first round. The worst-case leakage of each protocol across all process pairs, for each round, is shown in Fig. 10, which illustrates interesting trends and groupings among the protocols.

The variety of interesting subtleties in the results are more than we can discuss here, but we note a few points. The arrangement $(1, 2)$ is the best scenario

Table 2. Max leakage (in bits) and execution time (in seconds) for leakage computation with the Range-constraint Counting ($\mathcal{RC}$) vs Enumerative Counting ($\mathcal{EC}$) methods. A timeout of 20 min (1200 s) was used. '-' indicates a timeout; (S) – stateful processes; (R) – resolving wait-time and idle-time concurrences randomly.

Protocol	1 Round			2 Rounds			3 Rounds			4 Rounds			5 Rounds			6 Rounds		
	$max\ bit$	$\mathcal{RC}\ sec$	$\mathcal{EC}\ sec$	$max\ bit$	$\mathcal{RC}\ sec$	$\mathcal{EC}\ sec$	$max\ bit$	$\mathcal{RC}\ sec$	$\mathcal{EC}\ sec$	$max\ bit$	$\mathcal{RC}\ sec$	$\mathcal{EC}\ sec$	$max\ bit$	$\mathcal{RC}\ sec$	$\mathcal{EC}\ sec$	$max\ bit$	$\mathcal{RC}\ sec$	$\mathcal{EC}\ sec$
PRIORITY	1.00	0.1	0.3	2.00	0.2	0.7	3.00	0.2	10.2	4.00	0.3	346.4	5.00	0.5	-	6.00	1.5	-
ROUNDROBIN	0.00	0.2	0.4	0.00	0.1	0.3	0.00	0.2	1.2	0.00	0.3	10.3	0.00	0.3	225.0	0.00	0.8	-
ROUNDROBINSKIP	1.00	0.2	0.3	1.16	0.2	0.6	1.57	0.1	10.3	1.97	0.3	337.9	2.32	0.5	-	2.71	1.5	-
FCFS	1.00	0.2	0.3	1.27	0.2	1.2	1.86	0.4	53.2	2.16	0.7	-	2.71	4.8	-	3.02	44.1	-
LONGESTIDLE	1.00	0.1	0.3	1.55	0.2	1.0	2.10	0.3	53.7	2.66	0.8	-	3.22	5.1	-	3.78	45.7	-
FCFS_R	0.13	0.1	3.2	0.27	0.3	11.5	0.45	0.5	439.1	0.64	4.9	-	0.83	74.3	-	1.02	1121.1	-
LONGESTIDLE_R	0.05	0.1	2.7	0.21	0.1	10.0	0.40	0.4	241.8	0.58	1.9	-	0.76	19.5	-	0.92	200.3	-
LOTTERY	0.05	0.2	2.7	0.09	0.2	13.2	0.13	0.5	399.7	0.17	4.2	-	0.21	65.2	-	0.25	981.2	-
RANDOM	0.05	0.1	4.8	0.10	0.2	10.6	0.15	0.5	372.2	0.20	4.2	-	0.24	66.2	-	0.29	983.1	-
PRIORITY_S	1.00	0.1	0.3	2.00	0.2	0.9	3.00	0.3	18.9	4.00	0.4	-	5.00	0.8	-	6.00	4.4	-
ROUNDROBIN_S	0.00	0.1	0.3	0.00	0.2	0.5	0.00	0.3	5.2	0.00	0.3	260.8	0.00	0.4	-	0.00	1.2	-
ROUNDROBINSKIP_S	1.00	0.2	0.4	1.07	0.1	1.1	1.33	0.2	17.6	1.53	0.4	979.5	1.64	0.8	-	1.81	3.2	-
FCFS_S	1.00	0.1	0.4	1.16	0.1	1.0	1.41	0.3	32.4	1.67	0.4	-	1.83	1.2	-	2.06	6.4	-
LONGESTIDLE_S	1.00	0.2	0.4	1.55	0.2	1.2	2.14	0.3	36.7	2.78	0.4	-	3.47	1.3	-	4.20	6.6	-
FCFS_RS	0.13	0.2	4.3	0.25	0.1	17.3	0.41	0.4	283.2	0.55	1.3	-	0.70	9.5	-	0.84	79.2	-
LONGESTIDLE_RS	0.05	0.2	4.1	0.14	0.2	15.7	0.31	0.3	184.0	0.35	0.6	-	0.43	3.1	-	0.48	20.5	-
LOTTERY_S	0.05	0.2	4.6	0.06	0.3	22.1	0.06	0.4	312.6	0.07	1.2	-	0.08	10.2	-	0.09	88.2	-
RANDOM_S	0.05	0.1	2.9	0.06	0.2	18.8	0.08	0.3	290.8	0.09	1.3	-	0.10	10.2	-	0.11	88.9	-

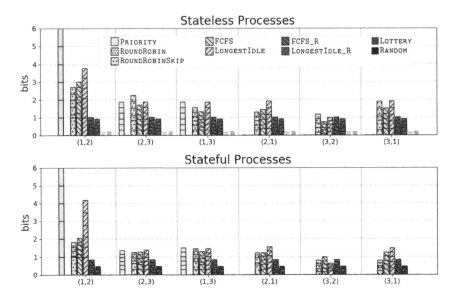

Fig. 9. Computed leakage for each protocol for 1–6 rounds, given for each (*victim, adversary*) process pair. Cumulative leakage is shown for 6 rounds.

for the attacker, as he/she directly follows the victim and no other processes cause noise. The PRIORITY arbiter leaks the most for this arrangement, but leaks less for (2, 3) and (1, 3), and does not leak for other arrangements. The ROUNDROBIN protocol leaks no information in any arrangement, but it is inefficient with respect to resource usage since it wastes cycles where the resource is not utilized. Introducing a simple optimization in the ROUNDROBINSKIP protocol improves resource usage, but introduces leakage. The random protocols (LOTTERY and RANDOM) have low leakage, but they are non-deterministic protocols in how they award resources which can lead to unfair resource allocation. Introducing randomness to other algorithms, like FCFS and LONGESTIDLE improve their leakage characteristics (again, at the expense of non-determinism). Typically, the stateful process version of each protocol leaks slightly less than the stateless version, as processes have less freedom in choosing their requests which means that there is less amount of information (entropy) to leak.

6 Related Work

Arbiter protocols have been studied intensively for effectiveness and fairness ([11] gives a brief survey). Various arbitration techniques have been proposed and compared in providing fairness and efficiency for shared-resource access management. More recent work has been focusing on privacy aspects of the arbitration, covert channel and timing side channel information leakage, including quantitative leakage analysis and channel capacity evaluations [4,9,14,24]. However,

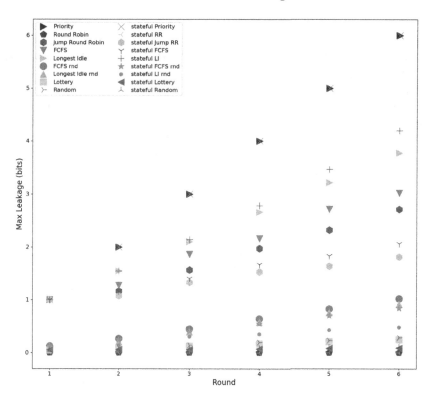

Fig. 10. Worst-case leakage of each protocol as a function of the round number.

these approaches are either manual, or consider a fixed number of processes and rounds, or focus on deterministic arbiters.

We make use of concepts from foundational and theoretical works in quantitative information flow [25] and combine them with symbolic execution and model counting techniques to automatically quantify security vulnerabilities in protocols. There are other model counting techniques that handle constraints with different levels of expressiveness [1,17], and they can be integrated with the quantitative information flow analysis we present in this paper. Quantitative measurement of information leakage in programs has been an active area of research [2,6,15,26]. Most previous works quantify the leakage in a single run of the program given a concrete value of low input. There have been recent works for performing automatic QIF for programs using symbolic execution [20,21], bounded model checking [12] , and graph theoretic methods [19], or random sampling [5], as well as in detecting and quantifying information flow and timing side channels at the hardware design and specification level [8,10]. Multi-run analyses based on input enumeration [16] and symbolic approaches [22] have also been proposed for side-channel attack synthesis.

7   Conclusion

Contention for shared resources will only grow with time as we become increasingly reliant on multi-tenant, cloud systems. Isolation and privacy preservation are of the utmost importance in these systems, but virtual machines and OS guards cannot always prevent information from crossing from one domain to another. Adversaries can use information leakages to extrapolate privileged information that needs to remain secure. The novel QIF analysis technique in this paper combines and extends symbolic execution and model counting techniques providing protocol designers and users a new dimension in assessment and comparison of protocols in terms of the amount of information leaked over time.

References

1. Aydin, A., Bang, L., Bultan, T.: Automata-based model counting for string constraints. In: Kroening, D., Păsăreanu, C.S. (eds.) CAV 2015, Part I. LNCS, vol. 9206, pp. 255–272. Springer, Cham (2015). https://doi.org/10.1007/978-3-319-21690-4_15
2. Backes, M., Kopf, B., Rybalchenko, A.: Automatic discovery and quantification of information leaks. In: Proceedings of the 30th IEEE Symposium on Security and Privacy, SP 2009, Washington, DC, USA (2009)
3. Backes, M., Pfitzmann, B.: Computational probabilistic noninterference. Int. J. Inf. Sec. **3**(1), 42–60 (2004)
4. Cabuk, S., Brodley, C.E., Shields, C.: IP covert channel detection. ACM Trans. Inf. Syst. Secur. **12**(4), 22:1–22:29 (2009)
5. Chothia, T., Kawamoto, Y., Novakovic, C.: Leakwatch: estimating information leakage from java programs. In: Proceedings of 19th European Symposium on Research in Computer Security, Computer Security - ESORICS 2014 (2014)
6. Clark, D., Hunt, S., Malacaria, P.: A static analysis for quantifying information flow in a simple imperative language. J. Comput. Secur. **15**(3), 321–371 (2007)
7. Ensafi, R., Park, J.C., Kapur, D., Crandall, J.R.: Idle port scanning and noninterference analysis of network protocol stacks using model checking. In: 19th USENIX Security Symposium, Washington, DC, USA (2010)
8. Ferraiuolo, A., Hua, W., Myers, A.C., Suh, G.E.: Secure information flow verification with mutable dependent types. In: Proceedings of the 54th Annual Design Automation Conference, DAC 2017 (2017)
9. Gong, X., Kiyavash, A.: Quantifying the information leakage in timing side channels in deterministic work-conserving schedulers. IEEE/ACM Trans. Netw. **24**(3), 1841–1852 (2016)
10. Guo, S., Wu, M., Wang, C.: Symbolic execution of programmable logic controller code. In: ESEC/SIGSOFT FSE (2017)
11. Gupta, J., Goel, N.: Efficient bus arbitration protocol for SoC design. In: 2015 International Conference on Smart Technologies and Management for Computing, Communication, Controls, Energy and Materials (ICSTM) (2015)
12. Heusser, J., Malacaria, P.: Quantifying information leaks in software. In: Twenty-Sixth Annual Computer Security Applications Conference, ACSAC 2010, Austin, Texas, USA, 6–10 December 2010, pp. 261–269 (2010)
13. Hughes, D.J.D., Shmatikov, V.: Information hiding, anonymity and privacy: a modular approach. J. Comput. Secur. **12**(1), 3–36 (2004)

14. Kadloor, S., Kiyavash, N.: Delay optimal policies offer very little privacy. In: Proceedings of the IEEE INFOCOM 2013, Turin, Italy (2013)
15. Klebanov, V., Manthey, N., Muise, C.: SAT-based analysis and quantification of information flow in programs. In: Joshi, K., Siegle, M., Stoelinga, M., D'Argenio, P.R. (eds.) QEST 2013. LNCS, vol. 8054. Springer, Heidelberg (2013). https://doi.org/10.1007/978-3-642-40196-1_16
16. Köpf, B., Basin, D.A.: An information-theoretic model for adaptive side-channel attacks. In: Proceedings of the ACM Conference on Computer and Communications Security, CCS 2007, Alexandria, Virginia, USA (2007)
17. De Loera, J.A., Hemmecke, R., Tauzer, J., Yoshida, R.: Effective lattice point counting in rational convex polytopes. J. Symb. Comput. **38**(4), 1273–1302 (2004)
18. Malacaria, P., Khouzani, M.H.R., Pasareanu, C.S., Phan, Q.S., Luckow, K.: Symbolic side-channel analysis for probabilistic programs. IACR Cryptology ePrint Archive, 2018, p. 329 (2018)
19. McCamant, S., Ernst, M.D.: Quantitative information flow as network flow capacity. In: Proceedings of the ACM SIGPLAN 2008 Conference on Programming Language Design and Implementation, Tucson, AZ, USA (2008)
20. Phan, Q.S., Bang, L., Pasareanu, C.S., Malacaria, P., Bultan, T.: Synthesis of adaptive side-channel attacks. In: 30th IEEE Computer Security Foundations Symposium, CSF 2017, Santa Barbara, CA, USA (2017)
21. Phan, Q.-S., Malacaria, P., Tkachuk, O., Pasareanu, C.S.: Symbolic quantitative information flow. ACM SIGSOFT Softw. Eng. Notes **37**(6), 1–5 (2012)
22. Păsăreanu, C.S., Phan, Q.S., Malacaria, P.: Multi-run side-channel analysis using Symbolic Execution and Max-SMT. In: 29th IEEE Computer Security Foundations Symposium, CSF 2016, Washington, DC, USA (2016)
23. Păsăreanu, C.S., Visser, W., Bushnell, D., Geldenhuys, J., Mehlitz, P., Rungta, N.: Symbolic PathFinder: integrating symbolic execution with model checking for Java bytecode analysis. ASE **20**, 391 (2013)
24. Sellke, S.H., Wang, C.C., Shroff, N.E., Bagchi, S.: Capacity bounds on timing channels with bounded service times. In: 2007 IEEE International Symposium on Information Theory, pp. 981–985 (2007)
25. Smith, G.: On the foundations of quantitative information flow. In: Proceedings of the 12th International Conference on Foundations of Software Science and Computational Structures (FOSSACS), pp. 288–302 (2009)
26. Wang, C., Patrick, S.: Security by compilation: an automated approach to comprehensive side-channel resistance. ACM SIGLOG News **4**(2), 76–89 (2017)

Neural State Classification for Hybrid Systems

Dung Phan[1], Nicola Paoletti[1], Timothy Zhang[1], Radu Grosu[2],
Scott A. Smolka[1(✉)], and Scott D. Stoller[1]

[1] Department of Computer Science, Stony Brook University,
Stony Brook, NY, USA
sas@cs.stonybrook.edu

[2] Department of Computer Engineering, Technische Universitat Wien,
Vienna, Austria

Abstract. We introduce the *State Classification Problem* (SCP) for hybrid systems, and present *Neural State Classification* (NSC) as an efficient solution technique. SCP generalizes the model checking problem as it entails classifying each state s of a hybrid automaton as either positive or negative, depending on whether or not s satisfies a given time-bounded reachability specification. This is an interesting problem in its own right, which NSC solves using machine-learning techniques, Deep Neural Networks in particular. State classifiers produced by NSC tend to be very efficient (run in constant time and space), but may be subject to classification errors. To quantify and mitigate such errors, our approach comprises: (i) techniques for certifying, with statistical guarantees, that an NSC classifier meets given accuracy levels; (ii) tuning techniques, including a novel technique based on *adversarial sampling*, that can virtually eliminate false negatives (positive states classified as negative), thereby making the classifier more conservative. We have applied NSC to six nonlinear hybrid system benchmarks, achieving an accuracy of 99.25% to 99.98%, and a false-negative rate of 0.0033 to 0, which we further reduced to 0.0015 to 0 after tuning the classifier. We believe that this level of accuracy is acceptable in many practical applications, and that these results demonstrate the promise of the NSC approach.

1 Introduction

Model checking of hybrid systems is usually expressed in terms of the following reachability problem for hybrid automata (HA): given an HA $\mathcal{M}$, a set of initial states I, and a set of unsafe states U, determine whether there exists a trajectory of $\mathcal{M}$ starting in an initial state and ending in an unsafe state. The time-bounded version of this problem considers trajectories that are within a given time bound T. It has been shown that reachability problems and time-bounded reachability

This material is based on work supported in part by AFOSR Grant FA9550-14-1-0261, NSF Grants CPS-1446832, IIS-1447549, CNS-1445770, CNS-1421893, and CCF-1414078, FWF-NFN RiSE Award, and ONR Grant N00014-15-1-2208.

© Springer Nature Switzerland AG 2018
S. K. Lahiri and C. Wang (Eds.): ATVA 2018, LNCS 11138, pp. 422–440, 2018.
https://doi.org/10.1007/978-3-030-01090-4_25

problems for HA are undecidable [16], except for some fairly restrictive classes of HA [7,16]. HA model checkers cope with this undecidability by providing approximate answers to reachability [13].

This paper introduces the *State Classification Problem* (SCP), a generalization of the model checking problem for hybrid systems. Let $\mathbb{B} = \{0,1\}$ be the set of Boolean values. Given an HA $\mathcal{M}$ with state space S, time bound T, and set of unsafe states $U \subset S$, the SCP problem is to find a function $F^* : S \to \mathbb{B}$ such that for all $s \in S$, $F^*(s) = 1$ if it is possible for $\mathcal{M}$, starting in s, to reach a state in U within time T; $F^*(s) = 0$ otherwise. A state $s \in S$ is called *positive* if $F^*(s) = 1$. Otherwise, s is *negative*. We call such a function a *state classifier*.

SCP generalizes the model checking problem. Model checking, in the context of SCP, is simply the problem of determining whether there exists a positive state in the set of initial states. Its intent is not to classify all states in S.

Classifying the states of a complex system is an interesting problem in its own right. State classification is also useful in at least two other contexts. First, due to random disturbances, a hybrid system may restart in a random state outside the initial region, and we may wish to check the system's safety from that state. Secondly, a classifier can be used for *online model checking* [27], where in the process of monitoring a system's behavior, one would like to determine, in real-time, the fate of the system going forward from the current (non-initial) state.

This paper shows how deep neural networks (DNNs) can be used for state classification, an approach we refer to as *Neural State Classification* (NSC). An NSC classifier is subject to *false positives* (FPs) – a state s is deemed positive when it is actually negative, and, more importantly, *false negatives* (FNs) – s is deemed negative when it is actually positive.

A well-trained NSC classifier offers high accuracy, runs in constant time (approximately 1 ms, in our experiments), and takes constant space (e.g., a DNN with l hidden layers and n neurons only requires functions of dimension $l \cdot n$ for its encoding). This makes NSC classifiers very appealing for applications such as online model checking, a type of analysis subject to strict time and space constraints. NSC classifiers can also be used in runtime verification applications where a low probability of FNs is acceptable, e.g., performance-related system monitoring.

Our approach can also classify states of *parametric* HA by simply encoding each parameter as an additional input to the classifier. This makes NSC more powerful than state-of-the-art hybrid system reachability tools that have little or no support for parametric analysis [12,13]. In particular, we can train a classifier that classifies states of any instance of the parameterized HA, even instances with parameter values not seen during training.

NSC-based classification can be lifted from states to (convex) sets of states by applying output-range estimation [30]. Such techniques can be used to compute safe bounds for the given state region.

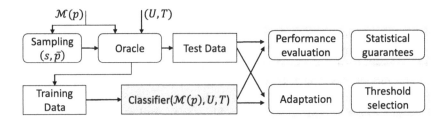

Fig. 1. Overview of the NSC approach.

The NSC method is summarized in Fig. 1. We train the state classifier using supervised learning, where the training examples are derived by sampling the state and parameter spaces according to some distribution. Reachability values for the examples are computed by invoking an oracle, i.e., an hybrid system model checker [13] or a simulator when the system is deterministic.

We consider three sampling strategies: *uniform*, where every state is equiprobable, *balanced*, which seeks to improve accuracy by drawing a balanced number of positive and negative states, and *dynamics-aware*, which assigns to each state the estimated probability that the state is visited in any time-bounded evolution of the system. The choice of sampling strategy depends on the intended application of NSC. For example, in the case of online model checking, dynamics-aware sampling may be the most appropriate. For balanced sampling, we introduce a method to generate arbitrarily large sets of positive samples based on constructing and simulating reverse HAs.

NSC is not limited to DNN-based classifiers. We demonstrate that other machine-learning models for classification, such as support vector machines (SVMs) and binary decision trees (BDTs), also provide powerful solution techniques.

Given the impossibility of training machine-learning models with guaranteed accuracy w.r.t. the true input distribution, we evaluate a trained state classifier by estimating its accuracy, false-positive rate, and false-negative rate (together with their confidence intervals) on a test dataset of fresh samples. This allows us to quantify how well the classifier extrapolates to unseen states, i.e., the probability that it correctly predicts reachability for any state.

Inspired by statistical model checking [24], we also provide statistical guarantees through sequential hypothesis testing to certify (up to some confidence level) that the classifier meets prescribed accuracy levels on unseen data. Note that the systems we consider are *nonprobabilistic*. The statistical guarantees we provide are for the probability that the classifier makes the correct prediction. In contrast, the aim of *probabilistic model checking* [22] and *statistical model checking* [24] is to compute the probability that a probabilistic system satisfies a given correctness property. Relatedly, the focus of neural network (NN) verification [11,18,21] is on proving properties of an NN's output rather than the NN's accuracy.

We also consider two tuning methods that can reduce and virtually eliminate false negatives: a new method called *falsification-guided adaptation* that iteratively re-trains the classifier with false negatives found through adversarial sampling; and *threshold selection*, which adjusts the NN's classification threshold to favor FPs over FNs.

Our experimental results demonstrate the feasibility and promise of our approach, evaluated on six nonlinear hybrid system benchmarks. We consider shallow (1 hidden layer) and deep (3 hidden layers) NNs with sigmoid and ReLU activation functions. Our techniques achieve a prediction accuracy of 99.25% to 99.98% and a false-negative rate of 0.0033 to 0, taking into account the best classifier for each of the six models, with DNNs yielding superior accuracy than shallow NNs, SVMs, and BDTs. We believe that such a range for the FN rate is acceptable in many practical applications, and we show how this can be further improved through tuning of the classifiers.

In summary, our main contributions are the following:

- We introduce the State Classification Problem for hybrid systems.
- We develop the Neural State Classification method for solving the SCP, including techniques for sampling, establishing statistical guarantees on a classifier's accuracy, and reducing its FN rate.
- We introduce a new technique for constructing the *reverse HA* of a given HA, for a general class of HAs, and use reverse HAs to generate balanced training datasets.
- We introduce a *falsification-guided adaptation algorithm* for eliminating FNs, thereby producing conservative state classifiers.
- We provide an extensive evaluation on six nonlinear hybrid system models.

2   Problem Formulation

We introduce the problem of learning a state classifier for a hybrid automaton and a bounded reachability property. First, we define these terms.

Definition 1 (Hybrid automaton). A *hybrid automaton* (HA) is a tuple $\mathcal{M} = (Loc, Var, Init, Flow, Trans, Inv)$, where Loc is a finite set of discrete *locations* (or modes); $Var = \{x_1, \ldots, x_n\}$ is a set of continuous *variables*, evaluated over a *continuous domain* $X \subseteq \mathbb{R}^n$; $Init \subseteq S(\mathcal{M})$ is the set of *initial states*, where $S(\mathcal{M}) = Loc \times X$ is the *state space* of $\mathcal{M}$; $Flow : Loc \to (X \to X)$ is the *flow* function, defining the continuous dynamics at each location; $Trans$ is the *transition relation*, consisting of tuples of the form (l, g, v, l'), where $l, l' \in Loc$ are *source and target locations*, respectively, $g \subseteq X$ is the *guard*, and $v : X \to X$ is the *reset*; $Inv : Loc \to 2^X$ is the *invariant* at each location.

We also consider *parameterized* HA in which the flow, guard, reset and invariant may have parameters whose values are constant throughout an execution. We treat parameters as continuous variables with flow equal to zero and identity reset map.

The behavior of an HA $\mathcal{M}$ can be described in terms of its trajectories. A trajectory may start from any state; it does not need to start from an initial state. For time bound $T \in \mathbb{R}^{\geq 0}$, let $\mathbb{T} = [0, T] \subseteq \mathbb{R}^{\geq 0}$ be the time domain.

Definition 2 (Trajectory [3]). For HA $\mathcal{M} = (Loc, Var, Init, Flow, Trans, Inv)$, time domain $\mathbb{T} = [0, T]$, let $\rho : \mathbb{T} \to S(\mathcal{M})$ be a function mapping time instants into states of $\mathcal{M}$. For $t \in \mathbb{T}$, let $\rho(t) = (l(t), \mathbf{x}(t))$ be the state at time t, with $l(t)$ being the location and $\mathbf{x}(t)$ the vector of continuous variables. Let $(\xi_i)_{i=0,\dots,k} \in \mathbb{T}^{k+1}$ be the ordered sequence of time points where mode jumps happen, i.e., such that $\xi_0 = 0$, $\xi_k = T$, and for all $i = 0, \dots, k-1$ and for all $t \in [\xi_i, \xi_{i+1})$, $l(t) = l(\xi_i)$. Then, ρ is a *trajectory* of $\mathcal{M}$ if it is consistent with the invariants: $\forall t \in \mathbb{T}. \ \mathbf{x}(t) \in Inv(l(t))$; flows: $\forall t \in \mathbb{T}. \ \dot{\mathbf{x}}(t) = Flow(l(t))(\mathbf{x}(t))$; and transition relation: $\forall i < k. \ \exists (l(\xi_i), g, v, l(\xi_{i+1})) \in Trans. \ \mathbf{x}(\xi_{i+1}^-) \in g \wedge \mathbf{x}(\xi_{i+1}) = v(\mathbf{x}(\xi_{i+1}^-))$.

Definition 3 (Time-bounded reachability). Given an HA $\mathcal{M}$, set of states $U \subseteq S(\mathcal{M})$, state $s \in S(\mathcal{M})$, and time bound T, decide whether there exists a trajectory ρ of $\mathcal{M}$ starting from s and $t \in [0, T]$ such that $\rho(t) \in U$, denoted $\mathcal{M} \models \mathsf{Reach}(U, s, T)$.

Definition 4 (Positive and negative states). Given an HA $\mathcal{M}$, set of states $U \subseteq S(\mathcal{M})$, called *unsafe states*, and time bound T, a state $s \in S(\mathcal{M})$ is called *positive* if $\mathcal{M} \models \mathsf{Reach}(U, s, T)$, i.e., an unsafe state is reachable from s within time T. Otherwise, s is called *negative*.

We will use the term *positive (negative) region* for $\mathcal{M}$'s set of positive (negative) states.

Definition 5 (State classification problem). Given an HA $\mathcal{M}$, set of states $U \subseteq S(\mathcal{M})$, and time bound T, find a function $F^* : S(\mathcal{M}) \to \mathbb{B}$ such that $F^*(s) = \mathcal{M} \models \mathsf{Reach}(U, s, T)$ for all $s \in S(\mathcal{M})$.

It is easy to see that the model checking problem for hybrid systems can be expressed as an SCP in which the domain of F^* is the set of initial states *Init*, instead of the whole state space. SCP is therefore a generalization of the model checking problem.

Sample sets are used by NSC to learn state classifiers and to evaluate their performance. Unsafe states are trivially positive (for any T), so we exclude them from the sampling domain. Each sample consists of a state s and Boolean b which is the answer to the reachability problem starting from state s. We call $(s, 1)$ a *positive sample* and $(s, 0)$ a *negative sample*. Both kinds of samples are generally needed for adequately learning a classifier.

Definition 6 (Sample set). For model $\mathcal{M}$, set of states $U \subseteq S(\mathcal{M})$, and time bound T, a *sample set* is any finite set $\{(s, b) \in (S(\mathcal{M}) \setminus U) \times \mathbb{B} \mid b = (\mathcal{M} \models \mathsf{Reach}(U, s, T))\}$.

The derivation of an NSC classifier reduces to a *supervised learning problem*, specifically, a binary classification problem. Given a sample set D called the *training set*, NSC approximates the exact state classifier F^* in Definition 5 by learning a total function $F : (S(\mathcal{M}) \setminus U) \to \mathbb{B}$ from D.

Learning F typically corresponds to finding values of F's parameters that minimize some measure of discrepancy between F and the training set D. We do not require that the learned function agree with the D on every state that appears in D, because this can lead to over-fitting to D and hence poor generalization to other states.

To evaluate the performance of F, we use three standard metrics: *accuracy* P_A, i.e, the probability that F produces the correct prediction; the probability of *false positives*, P_{FP}; and the probability of *false negatives*, P_{FN}. In safety-critical applications, achieving a low FN rate is typically more important than achieving a low FP rate. Precisely computing these probabilities is, in general, infeasible. We therefore compute an empirical accuracy measure, false-positive rate, and false-negative rate over a *test set* $\mathcal{D}'$ containing n fresh samples not appearing in the training set as follows:

$$\hat{P}_A = \frac{1}{n} \sum_{(s,b) \in D'} \mathbf{1}_{F(s)=b} \;, \quad \hat{P}_{FP} = \frac{1}{n} \sum_{(s,b) \in D'} \mathbf{1}_{F(s) \wedge \neg b} \;, \quad \hat{P}_{FN} = \frac{1}{n} \sum_{(s,b) \in D'} \mathbf{1}_{\neg F(s) \wedge b} \quad (1)$$

where $\mathbf{1}$ is the indicator function. We obtain statistically sound bounds for these probabilities through the Clopper-Pearson method for deriving precise confidence intervals.

3   Neural State Classification

This section introduces the main components of the NSC approach.

3.1   Neural Networks for Classification

NSC uses *feedforward* neural networks, a type of neural network with one-way connections from input to output layers [23]. NSC uses both *shallow* NNs, with one hidden layer and one output layer, and *deep* NNs, with multiple hidden layers. Additional background on NNs is provided in an extended version of this paper [26].

An NN defines a real-valued function $F(\mathrm{x})$. When using an NN for classification, a *classification threshold* θ is specified, and an input vector x is classified as positive if $F(\mathrm{x}) \geq \theta$, and as negative otherwise.

The theoretical justification for using NNs to solve the SCP is the following. In [17], it is shown that shallow feedforward NNs are universal approximators; i.e., with appropriate parameters, they can approximate any Borel-measurable function arbitrarily well with a finite number of neurons (and just one hidden layer). Under mild assumptions, this also applies to the true state classifier F^* of the SCP (Definition 5). A proof of this claim is given in [26] . Arbitrarily high precision might not be achievable in practice, as it would require significantly large training sets and numbers of neurons, and a precise learning algorithm. Nevertheless, NNs are extremely powerful.

3.2   Oracles

Given a state (sample) s of an HA M, an NSC *oracle* is a procedure for labeling s; i.e., for deciding whether $M \models \mathsf{Reach}(U, s, T)$. NSC utilizes the following oracles.

Reachability checker. For nonlinear HA, NSC uses dReal [13], an SMT solver that supports bounded model checking of such HA. dReal provides sound unsatisfiability proofs, but satisfiability is approximated up to a user-defined precision (δ-satisfiability). The oracle first attempts to verify that s is negative by checking $M \models \mathsf{Reach}(U, s, T)$ for unsatisfiability. If this instance is instead δ-sat, the oracle attempts to prove the unsatisfiability of $M \models \neg\mathsf{Reach}(U, s, T)$, which would imply that s is positive. The latter instance can also be δ-sat, meaning that this oracle cannot make a decision about s. This situation never occurred in our evaluation and can be made less likely by choosing a small δ. If it did occur, our plan would be to conservatively mark the state as positive. The oracle requires an upper bound on the number of discrete jumps to be considered. It supports HAs with Lipschitz continuous dynamics and hyperrectangular continuous domains (i.e., defined as the product of closed intervals), and allows trigonometric and other non-polynomial functions in the initial conditions, guards, invariants, and resets.

Simulator. For deterministic systems, we implemented a simulator based on MATLAB's ode45 variable-step ODE solver. To check reachability, we employ the solver's event-detection method to catch relevant zero-crossing events (i.e., reaching U).

Backwards simulator. The backwards simulator is not an oracle per se, but, as described in Sect. 3.3, is central to one of our sampling methods. We first construct the reverse HA according to Definition 7, which is more general than the one for rectangular HAs given in [16]. We use dot-notation to indicate members of a tuple, and lift resets v to sets of states; i.e., $v(X') = \{v(\mathsf{x}) \mid \mathsf{x} \in X'\}$.

Definition 7 (Reverse HA). Given an HA M, its *reverse HA* $\overleftarrow{M}$ is an HA such that the modes, continuous variables, and invariants are the same as for M, the flows are reversed, i.e., $\forall (l, \mathsf{x}) \in S(M)$, $\overleftarrow{M}.Flow(l)(\mathsf{x}) = -M.Flow(l)(\mathsf{x})$, and for each transition $(l, g, v, l') \in M.Trans$, the corresponding transition $(l', \overleftarrow{g}, \overleftarrow{v}, l) \in \overleftarrow{M}.Trans$ must be such that $\overleftarrow{g} = v(g)$ and $\overleftarrow{v}$ is the inverse of v if v is injective; otherwise, $\overleftarrow{v}$ updates the continuous state x to any value in the set $\overleftarrow{v}(\mathsf{x}) = \{\mathsf{x}' \mid \mathsf{x}' \in g \wedge v(\mathsf{x}') = \mathsf{x}\}$.[1]

Although every HA admits a reverse counterpart according to Definition 7, it is clearly impractical to find a reverse reset function $\overleftarrow{v}(\mathsf{x})$ if v is a one-way function. For an example of reversible HA with non-injective reset functions, see the HA and reverse HA in [26, Appendix D.4].

---

[1] Technically, for v non-injective, $\overleftarrow{v}$ is in general a nondeterministic reset: $\overleftarrow{v} : X \to 2^X$.

Note that a deterministic HA may admit a nondeterministic reverse HA. Since we classify all states in the state space, we assume that $\mathcal{M}$ and $\overset{\leftarrow}{\mathcal{M}}$ can be initialized to any state. We next define the notion of a reverse trajectory $\overset{\leftarrow}{\rho}$, which intuitively is obtained by running ρ backwards, starting from ρ's last state and ending with its first state.

Definition 8 (Reverse trajectory). For HA $\mathcal{M}$, time domain $\mathbb{T} = [0, T]$, trajectory ρ with its corresponding sequence of switching time points $(\xi_i)_{i=0,\ldots,k} \in \mathbb{T}^{k+1}$, the *reverse trajectory* $\overset{\leftarrow}{\rho} = (l(t), \mathbf{x}(t))$ of ρ and its corresponding sequence of switching time points $\left(\overset{\leftarrow}{\xi}_i\right)_{i=0,\ldots,k} \in \mathbb{T}^{k+1}$ are such that for $i = 0, \ldots, k$, $\overset{\leftarrow}{\xi}_i = T - \xi_{k-i}$, and $\forall i < k, \overset{\leftarrow}{\rho}.l(\overset{\leftarrow}{\xi}_i) = \rho.l(\xi_{k-i-1}) \wedge \forall t \in [\overset{\leftarrow}{\xi}_i, \overset{\leftarrow}{\xi}_{i+1}), \overset{\leftarrow}{\rho}.l(t) = \overset{\leftarrow}{\rho}.l(\overset{\leftarrow}{\xi}_i) \wedge \overset{\leftarrow}{\rho}.\mathbf{x}(t) = \rho.\mathbf{x}(T - t).$

Theorem 1. *For an HA $\mathcal{M}$ that admits a reverse HA $\overset{\leftarrow}{\mathcal{M}}$, every trajectory ρ of $\mathcal{M}$ is reversible, i.e., the reverse trajectory $\overset{\leftarrow}{\rho}$ of ρ is a trajectory of $\overset{\leftarrow}{\mathcal{M}}$, and every trajectory $\overset{\leftarrow}{\rho}$ of $\overset{\leftarrow}{\mathcal{M}}$ is forward-feasible, i.e., the reverse trajectory ρ of $\overset{\leftarrow}{\rho}$ is a trajectory of $\mathcal{M}$.*

Proof. See [26, Appendix A.2].

Given an unsafe state $u \in U$ of an HA $\mathcal{M}$ that admits a reverse HA $\overset{\leftarrow}{\mathcal{M}}$, Theorem 1 allows one to find a positive state $s \in S(\mathcal{M}) \setminus U$ from which u can be reached within time T. The method works by simulating multiple trajectories of $\overset{\leftarrow}{\mathcal{M}}$ starting in u and up to time T. In particular, we explore the reverse trajectories from u through an isotropic random walk, i.e., by choosing uniformly at random, at each step of the simulation, the next transition from those available.

3.3   Generation of Training Data and Test Data

We present three sampling methods for generation of training data and test data. Let $\bar{X}$ denote the continuous component of $S(\mathcal{M}) \setminus U$, i.e., without the automaton's location. Recall that model parameters, when present, are expressed as (constant) continuous state variables. They can be sampled independently from the other state variables using appropriate distributions, possibly different from those described below.

Uniform Sampling. When the union of mode invariants covers $\bar{X}$, the algorithm first uniformly samples a continuous state x from $\bar{X}$ and then samples a mode m whose invariant is consistent with x (i.e, $x \in Inv(m)$). When the union of mode invariants does not cover $\bar{X}$, we first uniformly sample the mode m and then a continuous state $x \in Inv(m)$. For simplicity, we restrict attention to cases where the region to be sampled is rectangular, although we could use algorithms for uniform sampling of convex polytopes [20]. We use the reachability checker or the simulator (for deterministic systems) to label the sampled states.

Balanced Sampling. In systems where the unsafe states U are a small part of the overall state space, a uniform sampling strategy produces imbalanced datasets with insufficient positive samples, causing the learned classifier to have relatively low accuracy. For such systems, we generate balanced datasets with equal numbers of negative and positive samples as follows. Negative samples are obtained by uniformly sampling states from $S(\mathcal{M}) \setminus U$ and invoking the reachability checker on those states. In this case, the oracle only needs to verify that the sampled state is negative, i.e., to check that $\mathcal{M} \models \mathsf{Reach}(U, s, T)$ is unsatisfiable. For deterministic systems, the simulator is used instead. Positive samples are obtained by uniformly sampling unsafe states u from U and invoking the backwards simulator from u.

Dynamics-Aware Sampling. This technique generates datasets according to a state distribution expected in a deployed system. It does this by estimating the probability that a state is visited in a trajectory starting from the initial region Init within time T', where $T' > T$. This is accomplished by uniformly sampling states from Init and performing a random exploration of the trajectories from those states up to time T'. The resulting distribution, called *dynamics-aware state distribution*, is estimated from the multiset of states encountered in those trajectories. In our experiments, we estimate a discrete distribution, but other kinds of distributions (e.g., smooth kernel or piecewise-linear) are also supported. The reachability checker or simulator is used to label states sampled from the resulting distribution. This method typically yields highly unbalanced datasets, and thus should not be applied on its own to generate training data.

3.4 Statistical Guarantees with Sequential Hypothesis Testing

Given the infeasibility of training machine-learning models with guaranteed accuracy on unseen data[2], we provide statistical guarantees *a posteriori*, i.e., after training. Inspired by statistical approaches to model checking [24], we employ hypothesis testing to certify that our classifiers meet prescribed levels of accuracy, and FN/FP rates.

We provide guarantees of the form $P_\mathsf{A} \geq \theta_\mathsf{A}$ (i.e., the true accuracy value is above θ_A), $P_\mathsf{FN} \leq \theta_\mathsf{FN}$ and $P_\mathsf{FP} \leq \theta_\mathsf{FP}$ (i.e., the true rate of FNs and FPs are below θ_FN and θ_FP, respectively). Being based on hypothesis testing, such guarantees are precise up to arbitrary error bounds $\alpha, \beta \in (0, 1)$, such that the probability of Type-I errors (i.e., of accepting $P_x < \theta_x$ when $P_x \geq \theta_x$, where $x \in \{\mathsf{A}, \mathsf{FN}, \mathsf{FP}\}$) is bounded by α, and the probability of Type-II errors (i.e., of accepting $P_x \geq \theta_x$ when $P_x < \theta_x$) is bounded by β. The pair (α, β) is known as the *strength* of the test.

To ensure both error bounds simultaneously, the original test $P_x \geq \theta_x$ vs $P_x < \theta_x$ is relaxed by introducing a small indifference region, i.e., we test the hypothesis $H_0 : P_x \geq \theta_x + \delta$ against $H_1 : P_x \leq \theta_x - \delta$ for some $\delta > 0$. We use Wald's sequential probability ratio test (SPRT) to provide the above guarantees. SPRT has the important advantage that it does not require a prescribed number

---

[2] Statistical learning theory [29] provides statistical bounds on the generalization error of learn models, but these bounds are very conservative and thus of little use in practice. We use these bounds, however, in the proof of Theorem 2.

of samples to accept one of the two hypotheses, but the decision is made if the available samples provide sufficient evidence. Details of the SPRT can be found in [26, Appendix B].

Note that in statistical model checking, SPRT is used to verify that a probabilistic system satisfies a given property with probability above/below a given threshold. In contrast, in NSC, SPRT is used to verify that the probability of the classifier producing the correct prediction meets a given threshold.

3.5   Reducing the False Negative Rate

We discuss strategies to reduce the rate of FNs, the most serious errors from a safety-critical perspective. *Threshold selection* is a simple, yet effective method, which is based on tuning the classification threshold θ of the NN classifier (see Sect. 3.1). Decreasing θ reduces the number of FNs but may increase the number of FPs and thereby reduce overall accuracy. We evaluate the trade-off between accuracy and FNs in Sect. 4.2.

Another way to reduce the FN rate is to re-train the classifier with unseen FN samples found in the test stage. For this purpose, we devised a whitebox *falsification-guided adaptation algorithm* that, at each iteration, systematically searches for FNs using *adversarial sampling*; i.e., by solving an optimization problem that seeks to maximize the disagreement between predicted and true reachability values. The optimization problem exploits the knowledge it possesses of the function computed by the NN classifier (whitebox approach). FNs found in this way are used to retrain the classifier. The algorithm iterates until the falsifier cannot find any more FNs.

This approach can be viewed as the dual of counterexample-guided abstraction refinement [9]. CEGAR starts from an abstract model that represents an over-approximation of the system dynamics, and uses counterexamples (FPs) to refine the model, thereby reducing the FP rate. Our approach starts from an under-approximation of the positive region (i.e., the set of states leading to a violation) and uses counterexamples (FNs) to make this region more conservative, reducing the FN rate.

We show that under some assumptions about the performance of the classifier and the falsifier, our algorithm converges to an empty set of FNs. Although it may be difficult in practice to guarantee that these assumptions are satisfied, we also show in Sect. 4.2 that our algorithm performs reasonably well in practice.

For a state s, let $F(s) \in [0, 1]$ and $b(s) \in \{0, 1\}$ be the NN prediction and true reachability value, respectively. Let FN_k denote the true set of false negatives (i.e., all states s such that $b(s) = 1$ and $F(s) < \theta$) at the k-th iteration of the adaptation algorithm, and let $\hat{FN}_k$ denote the finite subset of FN_k found by the falsifier. The cumulative set of training samples at the k-th iteration of the algorithm is denoted $D_k = D \cup \bigcup_{i=1}^{k} \hat{FN}_k$, where D is the set of samples for the initial training of the classifier.

Assumption 1. *At each iteration k, the classifier correctly predicts positive training samples, i.e., $\forall s \in D_k$. $b(s) = 1 \implies F(s) \geq \theta$, and is such that the FP rate w.r.t. training samples is no larger than the FP rate w.r.t. unseen samples.*

Assumption 2. *At each iteration k, the falsifier can always find an FN when it exists, i.e., $FN_k \neq \emptyset \iff \hat{FN}_k \neq \emptyset$.*

Theorem 2. *Under Assumptions 1–2, the adaptation algorithm converges to an empty set of FNs with high probability, i.e., for all $\eta \in (0, 1)$, $\Pr(\lim_{k \to \infty} FN_k = \emptyset) \geq 1 - \eta$.*

Proof. See [26, Appendix A.3].

We developed a falsifier that uses a genetic algorithm (GA) [25], a nonlinear optimization method for finding multiple global (sub-)optima. In our case, we indeed have multiple solutions because FN samples are found at the decision boundaries of the classifier, separating the predicted positive and negative regions. Due to the real-valued state space, each set FN_k is either empty or infinite.

FN states have $F(s) - b(s) < -\theta$, while FPs are such that $F(s) - b(s) \geq \theta$. By maximizing the absolute discrepancy $|F(s) - b(s)|$, we can identify both FNs and FPs, where only the former are kept for retraining. Specifically, the GA minimizes the objective function $o(s) = 1/(8 \cdot (F(s) - b(s))^2)$ which, for default threshold $\theta = 0.5$, gives a proportionally higher penalty to correctly predicted states ($0.5 \leq o(s) \leq \infty$) than wrong predictions ($0.125 \leq o(s) \leq 0.5$). We retrain the network with all FN candidates found by the GA, not just the optima.

4   Experimental Evaluation

We evaluated our NSC approach on six hybrid-system case studies: a model of the spiking neuron action potential [8], the classic inverted pendulum on a cart, a quadcopter system [15], a cruise controller [8], a powertrain model [19], and a helicopter model [2]. These case studies represent a broad spectrum of hybrid systems and varying degrees of complexity (deterministic, nondeterministic, nonlinear dynamics including trig functions, 2–29 variables, 1–6 modes, 1–11 transitions). Detailed descriptions of the case studies are given in [26, Appendix A.3].

For all case studies, NSC neural networks were learned using MATLAB's `train` function, with the Levenberg-Marquardt backpropagation algorithm optimizing the mean square error loss function, and the Nguyen-Widrow initialization method for the NN layers. With this setup, we achieved better performance than more standard approaches such as minimizing binary cross entropy using stochastic gradient methods. Training is very fast, taking 2–19 s for a training dataset with 20,000 samples.

We evaluated the following types of classifiers: sigmoid DNNs (**DNN-S**) with 3 hidden layers of 10 neurons each, with the Tan-Sigmoid activation function for the hidden layers and the Log-Sigmoid activation function for the output layer; shallow NNs (**SNN**), with the same activation functions as **DNN-S** but with one hidden layer of 20 neurons; ReLU DNNs (**DNN-R**), with 3 hidden layers of 10 neurons each, the rectified linear unit (ReLU) activation function for the hidden layers, and the softmax function for the output layer; support vector machines with radial kernel (**SVM**); binary decision trees (**BDT**); and a simple classifier that returns the label of the nearest neighbor in the training set (**NBOR**). We also obtained results for DNN ensembles that combine the predictions of multiple DNNs through majority voting. As expected, ensembles outperformed all of the other classifiers. Due to space limitations, these results are omitted.

We learned the classifiers from relatively small datasets, using training sets of 20 K samples and test sets of 10 K samples, except where noted otherwise. Larger training sets significantly improved classifier performance for only two of the case studies; see Fig. 2. Unless otherwise specified, training and test sets are drawn from the same distribution. The NN architecture (numbers of layers and neurons) was chosen empirically. To avoid overfitting, we did not tune the architecture to optimize the performance for our data. We systematically evaluated other architectures (see [26, Appendix E]), but found no alternatives with consistently better performance than our default configuration of 3 layers and 10 neurons. We also experimented with 1D Convolutional Neural Networks (CNNs), but they performed worse than the DNN architectures.

In the following, when clear from the context, we omit the modifier "empirical" when referring to accuracy, FN, and FP rates over a test dataset (as opposed to the true accuracy over the state distribution).

4.1 Performance Evaluation

Table 1 shows empirical accuracy and FN rate for all classifiers and case studies, using uniform and balanced sampling. We obtain very high classification accuracy for neuron, pendulum, quadcopter and cruise. For these case studies, DNN-based classifiers registered the best performance, with accuracy values ranging between 99.48% and 99.98% and FN rates between 0.24% and 0%. Only a minor performance degradation is observed for the shallow neural network **SNN**, with accuracy in the range 98.89–99.85%.

In contrast, the accuracy for the helicopter and powertrain models is poor if we use only 20 K training samples. These models are indeed particularly challenging, owing to their high dimensionality (helicopter) and highly nonlinear dynamics (powertrain). Larger training sets provide considerable improvement in accuracy and FN rate, as shown in Fig. 2. For helicopter, accuracy jumps from 98.49% (20 K samples) to 99.92% (1 M

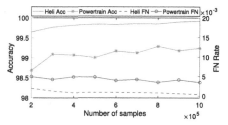

Fig. 2. Performance of DNN-S classifier on helicopter and powertrain models with varying numbers of training samples (uniform sampling).

samples), and the FN rate decreases from 0.84% (20 K) to 0.04% (1 M). For powertrain, accuracy increases from 96.68% (20 K) to 99.25% (1 M), and the FN rate decreases from 1.28% (20 K) to 0.33% (1 M).

In general, we found that the NN-based classifiers have superior accuracy compared to support vector machines and binary decision trees. As expected, the nearest-neighbor method demonstrated poor prediction capabilities. No single sampling method provides a clear advantage over the others in terms of accuracy, most likely because training and test sets are drawn from the same distribution.

Dynamics-aware state distribution. To evaluate the behavior of the classifiers with the dynamics-aware state distribution (introduced in Sect. 3.3), we generate training data with a combination of dynamics-aware sampling and either uniform or balanced sampling, because dynamics-aware sampling alone yields unbalanced datasets unsuitable for training. Test data consists exclusively of dynamics-aware samples.

Table 1. Empirical accuracy (Acc) and FN rate of the state classifiers for each case study, classifier type, and sampling method. Values are in percentages. For each measure and sampling method, the best result is highlighted in bold. False positives and confidence intervals are reported in Tables 5 and 6 of the Appendix provided in [26].

	Neuron Acc	FN	Pendulum Acc	FN	Quadcopter Acc	FN	Cruise Acc	FN	Powertrain Acc	FN	Helicopter Acc	FN	
DNN-S	**99.81**	**0.1**	**99.98**	**0**	99.83	0.1	99.95	0.01	**96.68**	1.28	**98.49**	**0.84**	Uniform
DNN-R	99.52	0.29	99.93	0.04	**99.89**	**0.06**	**99.98**	**0**	96.21	**1.08**	98	0.96	
SNN	99.17	0.43	99.81	0	99.85	0.08	99.84	0.15	96.02	1.37	97.69	1.25	
SVM	98.73	0.75	99.84	0	97.33	0.69	99.88	0.1	92.26	3.48	95.58	2.42	
BDT	99.3	0.37	99.6	0.17	99.52	0.2	99.84	0.08	95.59	2.19	80.07	9.8	
NBOR	97.03	1.22	99.69	0.14	99.53	0.25	99.49	0.33	71.44	14.51	67.39	16.98	

	Acc	FN	Acc	FN	Acc	FN	Acc	FN	Acc	FN	Acc	FN	
DNN-S	**99.83**	**0.12**	**99.89**	**0**	**99.82**	0.04	99.94	**0**	**97.2**	**0.86**	**98.24**	**0.79**	Balanced
DNN-R	99.48	0.24	99.63	0.01	99.67	0.09	**99.95**	**0**	96.07	1.24	97.91	1.2	
SNN	98.89	0.69	99.2	0	99.49	**0.01**	99.6	0	95.21	1.79	97.58	1.16	
SVM	98.63	0.78	99.37	0	96.93	0.2	99.61	0	91.84	3.3	95.36	1.85	
BDT	99.07	0.45	99.46	0.05	99.36	0.22	99.9	0.03	95.86	2.4	79.03	10.26	
NBOR	96.95	1.62	99.51	0.04	99.11	0.56	99.47	0.11	71.33	13.99	65.18	17.48	

Table 2 shows that the classifiers yield accuracy values comparable to those of Table 1 (compiled with balanced and uniform distributions) for all case studies. We see that the powertrain model attains 100% accuracy, indicating that its dynamics-aware distribution favors states that are easy enough for the DNN to classify correctly.

Table 2. Empirical accuracy of DNN-S classifiers tested on 10 K dynamics-aware samples and trained with 20 K samples. Each row corresponds to a different training distribution. **Unif+Dyn-aware** and **Bal+Dyn-aware** were obtained by combining 10 K uniform/balanced samples with 10 K dynamics-aware samples. In parenthesis is the accuracy difference with the corresponding classifier from Table 1

	Neuron	Pendulum	Quadcopter	Cruise	Helicopter	Powertrain
Unif+Dyn-aware	99.91 (+0.1)	99.93 (−0.05)	99.84 (+0.01)	99.14 (−0.81)	98.77 (+0.28)	100 (+3.32)
Bal+Dyn-aware	99.8 (−0.03)	99.88 (−0.01)	99.79 (−0.03)	99.35 (−0.59)	98.46 (+0.22)	100 (+2.8)

Parametric analysis. We show that NSC works effectively for parametric systems, being able to classify states in models with parameter values not seen during training. We derive parametric versions of the neuron model by turning constants a, b, c, d, I (see [26, Appendix D.1]) into parameters uniformly distributed in the $\pm 50\%$ interval around their default value.

Table 3. Empirical accuracy $(\hat{P}_A)$ and FN rate $(\hat{P}_{FN})$ for DNN-S classifier for neuron model with increasing number of parameters.

	Num. of parameters				
	1	2	3	4	5
$\hat{P}_A$	99.8	99.7	97.9	98.1	97.8
$\hat{P}_{FN}$	0.2	0.2	1.6	1.3	1.5

Table 3 shows the accuracy and FN rates for DNN-S, trained with 110 K samples for models with increasing numbers of parameters, which are increasingly long prefixes of the sequence a, b, c, d, I. We achieve very high accuracy ($\geq 99.7\%$) for up to two parameters. For three to five parameters, the accuracy decreases but stays relatively high (around 98%), suggesting that larger training sets are required for these cases. Indeed the input space grows exponentially in the number of parameters, while we kept the size of the training set constant.

Statistical guarantees. We use SPRT (Sect. 3.4) to provide statistical guarantees for four case studies, each trained with 20 K balanced samples. See Table 4. We assess two properties certifying that the *true* (not empirical) accuracy and FNs meet given performance levels: $P_A \geq 99.7\%$, and $P_{FN} \leq 0.2\%$. We omit the

Table 4. Statistical guarantees based on the SPRT. Samples were generated using balanced sampling. In parenthesis are the number of samples required to reach the decision. Parameters of the test are $\alpha = \beta = 0.01$ and $\delta = 0.001$. Thresholds are $\theta_A = 99.7\%$ and $\theta_{FN} = 0.2\%$.

	Neuron		Pendulum		Quadcopter		Cruise	
	$P_A \geq \theta_A$	$P_{FN} \leq \theta_{FN}$	$P_A \geq \theta_A$	$P_{FN} \leq \theta_{FN}$	$P_A \geq \theta_A$	$P_{FN} \leq \theta_{FN}$	$P_A \geq \theta_A$	$P_{FN} \leq \theta_{FN}$
DNN-S	✓ (5800)	✓ (2900)	✓ (2300)	✓ (2300)	✓ (4400)	✓ (2300)	✓ (3000)	✓ (2300)
DNN-R	✗ (3600)	✗ (8600)	✓ (15500)	✓ (4000)	✗ (1400)	✓ (7300)	✓ (3000)	✓ (2300)
SNN	✗ (700)	✗ (1000)	✗ (2900)	✓ (2300)	✗ (1500)	✓ (3400)	✗ (3600)	✓ (2300)
SVM	✗ (400)	✗ (600)	✗ (6600)	✓ (2300)	✗ (200)	✗ (5300)	✗ (3400)	✓ (2300)
BDT	✗ (1700)	✗ (3300)	✗ (6300)	✓ (15000)	✗ (800)	✗ (1100)	✓ (2700)	✓ (2900)
NBOR	✗ (300)	✗ (300)	✗ (28500)	✓ (2900)	✗ (1000)	✗ (1300)	✗ (3400)	✗ (2300)

helicopter and powertrain models from this assessment, because performance results for these models are clearly outside the desired levels when only 20 K samples are used for training.

The only classifier that guarantees these performance levels for all case studies is the sigmoid DNN. We also observe that a small number of samples suffices to obtain statistical guarantees with the given strength: only 3 out of 48 tests needed more than 10 K samples to reach a decision.

4.2   Reducing the False Negative Rate

Falsification-guided adaptation. We evaluate the benefits of adaptation by incrementally adapting the trained NNs with false negative samples (see Sect. 3.5). At each iteration, we run our GA-based falsifier to find FN samples, which are then used to adapt the DNN. The adaptation loop terminates when the falsifier cannot find a FN.

We employ MATLAB's `adapt` function with gradient descent learning algorithm and learning rates of 0.0005 for neuron and 0.003 for quadcopter, helicopter, and powertrain. For neuron and quadcopter, we use DNN-S classifiers trained with 20 K balanced samples. We use DNN-S trained with 1 M balanced samples for helicopter, and DNN-S trained with 1 M uniform samples for powertrain, because these classifiers have the best accuracy before adaptation. To measure adaptation performances, we test the DNNs on 10 K samples after each iteration of adaptation. Figure 3 shows how accuracy, FNs and FPs of the classifier evolve at each adaptation step. For the neuron, quadcopter, and helicopter case studies, our falsification-guided adaptation algorithm works well to eliminate the FN rate at the cost of a slight increase in the FP rate after only 5–10 iterations. In these case studies, the number of FNs found by the falsifier decreases quickly from hundreds or thousands to zero. For powertrain, the number of FNs found by the falsifier stays almost constant at about 70 on average at each iteration. After 150 iterations, FN rate of the powertrain DNN decreases slowly from 0.33% to 0.15%.

Figure 4 visualizes the effects of adaptation on the **DNN-S** classifier for the neuron case study. Figure 4 (a) shows the prediction of the DNN after training

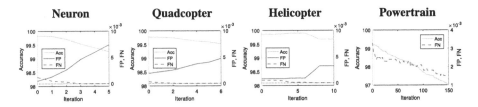

Fig. 3. Impact of incremental adaptation on empirical accuracy, FN and FP rates. FP-rate curve for powertrain is omitted to allow using a scale that shows the decreasing trend of the FN rate. The FP rate for powertrain increases from 0.48% to 2.89%.

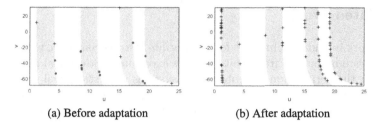

(a) Before adaptation   (b) After adaptation

Fig. 4. Effects of adaptation on the DNN-S for the neuron case study. The white region is the predicted negative region. The yellow region is the predicted positive region. Red dots are FN samples. Crosses are FP samples.

with 20 K samples. Figure 4 (b) shows the prediction of the DNN after adaptation. We see that adaptation expands the predicted positive region to enclose all previous FN samples, i.e., they are correctly re-classified as positive. The enlarged positive region also means the adapted DNN is more conservative, producing more FPs as shown in Fig. 4 (b).

Threshold selection. We show that threshold selection can considerably reduce the FN rate. Figure 5 shows the effect of threshold selection on accuracy, FN rate, and FP rate for classifier **DNN-S** trained with uniform sampling (20 K samples for neuron and quadcopter, 1 M samples for helicoper and powertrain). Pendulum and cruise control case studies are excluded as they have low FN rate ($\leq 0.01\%$) prior to threshold selection.

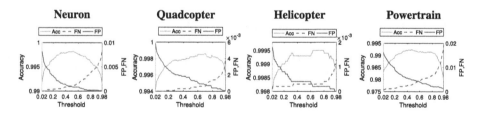

Fig. 5. Impact of classification threshold on empirical accuracy, FN rate, and FP rate.

For the neuron case study, selecting $\theta = 0.32$ reduces the FN rate from 10^{-3} to $5 \cdot 10^{-4}$, with an accuracy loss of only 0.02%. With $\theta = 0.06$, we obtain a zero FN rate and a minor accuracy loss of 0.37%. For quadcopter, selecting $\theta = 0.28$ decreases the FN rate from $4 \cdot 10^{-4}$ to 10^{-4}, with an accuracy loss of just 0.02%. Selecting $\theta = 0.16$ yields zero FN rate and accuracy loss of just 0.12%. For helicopter, selecting $\theta = 0.33$ reduces the FN rate from $3 \cdot 10^{-4}$ to $2 \cdot 10^{-4}$, with an *accuracy gain* of 0.01%. For powertrain, $\theta = 0.34$ yields a good trade-off between FN rate reduction (from $3.3 \cdot 10^{-3}$ to $2.1 \cdot 10^{-3}$) and accuracy loss (0.1%).

5   Related Work

Related work includes techniques for *simulation-based verification*, which enables rigorous system analysis from finitely many executions. Statistical model checking [24] for the verification of probabilistic systems with statistical guarantees is an example of this form of verification. Simulation is also used for falsification and reachability analysis of hybrid systems [1,2]. Our NSC approach also simulates system executions (when the system is deterministic), but for the purpose of learning a state classifier.

Other applications of *machine learning in verification* include parameter synthesis of stochastic systems [5], techniques for inferring temporal logic specifications from examples [4], synthesis of invariants for program verification [14,28], and reachability checking of Markov decision processes [6].

For safety-critical applications, *verification of NNs* has become a very active area, with a focus on the derivation of adversarial inputs (i.e., those that induce incorrect predictions). Most such approaches rely on SMT-based techniques [11,18,21], while sampling-based methods are used in [10] for the analysis of NN components "in the loop" with cyber-physical system models. Similarly, our adaptation method systematically searches for adversarial inputs (FNs) to render the classifier more conservative. A related problem is that of range estimation [30], i.e., computing safe and tight enclosures for the predictions of an NN over a (convex) input region. Such methods could be used to extend NSC classification to sets of states.

6   Conclusions

We have introduced the state classification problem for hybrid systems and offered a highly efficient solution based on neural state classification. NSC features high accuracy and low false-negative rates, while including techniques for virtually eliminating such errors and for certifying an NSC classifier's performance with statistical guarantees. Plans for future work include considering more expressive temporal properties and extending our approach to stochastic hybrid systems.

References

1. Annpureddy, Y., Liu, C., Fainekos, G., Sankaranarayanan, S.: S-TaLiRo: a tool for temporal logic falsification for hybrid systems. In: Abdulla, P.A., Leino, K.R.M. (eds.) TACAS 2011. LNCS, vol. 6605, pp. 254–257. Springer, Heidelberg (2011). https://doi.org/10.1007/978-3-642-19835-9_21
2. Bak, S., Duggirala, P.S.: Rigorous simulation-based analysis of linear hybrid systems. In: Legay, A., Margaria, T. (eds.) TACAS 2017. LNCS, vol. 10205, pp. 555–572. Springer, Heidelberg (2017). https://doi.org/10.1007/978-3-662-54577-5_32
3. Bak, S., et al.: Hybrid automata: from verification to implementation. Int. J. Softw. Tools Technol. Transf. 1–18 (2017)

4. Bartocci, E., Bortolussi, L., Sanguinetti, G.: Data-driven statistical learning of temporal logic properties. In: Legay, A., Bozga, M. (eds.) FORMATS 2014. LNCS, vol. 8711, pp. 23–37. Springer, Cham (2014). https://doi.org/10.1007/978-3-319-10512-3_3

5. Bortolussi, L., Silvetti, S.: Bayesian statistical parameter synthesis for linear temporal properties of stochastic models. In: Beyer, D., Huisman, M. (eds.) TACAS 2018. LNCS, vol. 10806, pp. 396–413. Springer, Cham (2018). https://doi.org/10.1007/978-3-319-89963-3_23

6. Brázdil, T., et al.: Verification of Markov decision processes using learning algorithms. In: Cassez, F., Raskin, J.-F. (eds.) ATVA 2014. LNCS, vol. 8837, pp. 98–114. Springer, Cham (2014). https://doi.org/10.1007/978-3-319-11936-6_8

7. Brihaye, T., Doyen, L., Geeraerts, G., Ouaknine, J., Raskin, J.-F., Worrell, J.: On reachability for hybrid automata over bounded time. In: Aceto, L., Henzinger, M., Sgall, J. (eds.) ICALP 2011. LNCS, vol. 6756, pp. 416–427. Springer, Heidelberg (2011). https://doi.org/10.1007/978-3-642-22012-8_33

8. Chen, X., Schupp, S., Makhlouf, I.B., Ábrahám, E., Frehse, G., Kowalewski, S.: A benchmark suite for hybrid systems reachability analysis. In: Havelund, K., Holzmann, G., Joshi, R. (eds.) NFM 2015. LNCS, vol. 9058, pp. 408–414. Springer, Cham (2015). https://doi.org/10.1007/978-3-319-17524-9_29

9. Clarke, E., Grumberg, O., Jha, S., Lu, Y., Veith, H.: Counterexample-guided abstraction refinement. In: Emerson, E.A., Sistla, A.P. (eds.) CAV 2000. LNCS, vol. 1855, pp. 154–169. Springer, Heidelberg (2000). https://doi.org/10.1007/10722167_15

10. Dreossi, T., Donzé, A., Seshia, S.A.: Compositional falsification of cyber-physical systems with machine learning components. In: Barrett, C., Davies, M., Kahsai, T. (eds.) NFM 2017. LNCS, vol. 10227, pp. 357–372. Springer, Cham (2017). https://doi.org/10.1007/978-3-319-57288-8_26

11. Ehlers, R.: Formal verification of piece-wise linear feed-forward neural networks. In: D'Souza, D., Narayan Kumar, K. (eds.) ATVA 2017. LNCS, vol. 10482, pp. 269–286. Springer, Cham (2017). https://doi.org/10.1007/978-3-319-68167-2_19

12. Frehse, G., et al.: SpaceEx: scalable verification of hybrid systems. In: Gopalakrishnan, G., Qadeer, S. (eds.) CAV 2011. LNCS, vol. 6806, pp. 379–395. Springer, Heidelberg (2011). https://doi.org/10.1007/978-3-642-22110-1_30

13. Gao, S., Kong, S., Clarke, E.M.: dReal: an SMT solver for nonlinear theories over the reals. In: Bonacina, M.P. (ed.) CADE 2013. LNCS (LNAI), vol. 7898, pp. 208–214. Springer, Heidelberg (2013). https://doi.org/10.1007/978-3-642-38574-2_14

14. Garg, P.: Learning invariants using decision trees and implication counterexamples. ACM Sigplan Not. **51**(1), 499–512 (2016)

15. Gibiansky, A.: Quadcopter dynamics and simulation (2012). http://andrew.gibiansky.com/blog/physics/quadcopter-dynamics/

16. Henzinger, T.A., et al.: What's decidable about hybrid automata? In: STOC, pp. 373–382. ACM Press (1995)

17. Hornik, K., Stinchcombe, M., White, H.: Multilayer feedforward networks are universal approximators. Neural Netw. **2**(5), 359–366 (1989)

18. Huang, X., Kwiatkowska, M., Wang, S., Wu, M.: Safety verification of deep neural networks. In: Majumdar, R., Kunčak, V. (eds.) CAV 2017. LNCS, vol. 10426, pp. 3–29. Springer, Cham (2017). https://doi.org/10.1007/978-3-319-63387-9_1

19. Jin, X., et al.: Powertrain control verification benchmark. In: HSCC, pp. 253–262. ACM Press (2014)

20. Kannan, R., Lovász, L., Simonovits, M.: Random walks and an $o^*(n^5)$ volume algorithm for convex bodies. Random Struct. Algorithms **11**(1), 1–50 (1997)

21. Katz, G., Barrett, C., Dill, D.L., Julian, K., Kochenderfer, M.J.: Reluplex: an efficient SMT solver for verifying deep neural networks. In: Majumdar, R., Kunčak, V. (eds.) CAV 2017. LNCS, vol. 10426, pp. 97–117. Springer, Cham (2017). https://doi.org/10.1007/978-3-319-63387-9_5

22. Kwiatkowska, M., Norman, G., Parker, D.: Stochastic model checking. In: Bernardo, M., Hillston, J. (eds.) SFM 2007. LNCS, vol. 4486, pp. 220–270. Springer, Heidelberg (2007). https://doi.org/10.1007/978-3-540-72522-0_6

23. LeCun, Y., Bengio, Y., Hinton, G.: Deep learning. Nature **521**(7553), 436 (2015)

24. Legay, A., Delahaye, B., Bensalem, S.: Statistical model checking: an overview. In: Barringer, H., et al. (eds.) RV 2010. LNCS, vol. 6418, pp. 122–135. Springer, Heidelberg (2010). https://doi.org/10.1007/978-3-642-16612-9_11

25. Mitchell, M.: An Introduction to Genetic Algorithms. MIT press, Cambridge (1998)

26. Phan, D., Paoletti, N., Zhang, T., Grosu, R., Smolka, S.A., Stoller, S.D.: Neural state classification for hybrid systems. arXiv:1807.09901 (2018)

27. Sen, K., Roşu, G., Agha, G.: Online efficient predictive safety analysis of multithreaded programs. In: Jensen, K., Podelski, A. (eds.) TACAS 2004. LNCS, vol. 2988, pp. 123–138. Springer, Heidelberg (2004). https://doi.org/10.1007/978-3-540-24730-2_9

28. Sharma, R., Gupta, S., Hariharan, B., Aiken, A., Liang, P., Nori, A.V.: A data driven approach for algebraic loop invariants. In: Felleisen, M., Gardner, P. (eds.) ESOP 2013. LNCS, vol. 7792, pp. 574–592. Springer, Heidelberg (2013). https://doi.org/10.1007/978-3-642-37036-6_31

29. Vapnik, V.: The Nature of Statistical Learning Theory. Springer, New York (2013)

30. Xiang, W., Tran, H.D., Johnson, T.T.: Output reachable set estimation and verification for multi-layer neural networks. arXiv:1708.03322 (2017)

Bounded Synthesis of Reactive Programs

Carsten Gerstacker$^{(\boxtimes)}$, Felix Klein, and Bernd Finkbeiner

Reactive Systems Group, Saarland University, Saarbrücken, Germany
{gerstacker,fklein,finkbeiner}@cs.uni-saarland.de

Abstract. Most algorithms for the synthesis of reactive systems focus on the construction of finite-state machines rather than actual programs. This often leads to badly structured, unreadable code. In this paper, we present a bounded synthesis approach that automatically constructs, from a given specification in linear-time temporal logic (LTL), a program in Madhusudan's simple imperative language for reactive programs. We develop and compare two principal approaches for the reduction of the synthesis problem to a Boolean constraint satisfaction problem. The first reduction is based on a generalization of bounded synthesis to two-way alternating automata, the second reduction is based on a direct encoding of the program syntax in the constraint system. We report on preliminary experience with a prototype implementation, which indicates that the direct encoding outperforms the automata approach.

1   Introduction

In reactive synthesis, we automatically construct a reactive system, such as the controller of a cyberphysical system, that is guaranteed to satisfy a given specification. The study of the synthesis problem, known also as Church's problem [1], dates back to the 1950s and has, especially in recent years, attracted a lot of attention from both theory and practice. There is a growing number of both tools (cf. [2–5]) and success stories, such as the synthesis of an arbiter for the AMBA AHB bus, an open industrial standard for the on-chip communication and management of functional blocks in system-on-a-chip (SoC) designs [6].

The practical use of the synthesis tools has, however, so far been limited. A serious criticism is that, compared to code produced by a human programmer, the code produced by the currently available synthesis tools is usually badly structured and, quite simply, unreadable. The reason is that the synthesis tools do not actually synthesize *programs*, but rather much simpler computational models, such as *finite state machines*. As a result, the synthesized code lacks control structures, such as *while* loops, and symbolic operations on program *variables*: everything is flattened out into a huge state graph.

A significant step towards better implementations has been the *bounded synthesis* [7] approach, where the number of states of the synthesized implementation is bounded by a constant. This can be used to construct finite state machines

Supported by the European Research Council (ERC) Grant OSARES (No. 683300) and by the Saarbrücken Graduate School of Computer Science.

© Springer Nature Switzerland AG 2018
S. K. Lahiri and C. Wang (Eds.): ATVA 2018, LNCS 11138, pp. 441–457, 2018.
https://doi.org/10.1007/978-3-030-01090-4_26

with a *minimal* number of states. Bounded synthesis has also been extended with other structural measures, such as the number of cycles [8]. Bounded synthesis reduces the synthesis problem to a constraint satisfaction problem: the existence of an implementation of bounded size is expressed as a set of Boolean constraints, which can subsequently be solved by a SAT or QBF solver [9]. Bounded synthesis has proven highly effective in finding finite state machines with a *simple* structure. However, existing methods based on bounded synthesis do not make use of syntactical program constructs like loops or variables. The situation is different in the synthesis of sequential programs, where programs have long been studied as the target of synthesis algorithms [10–14]. In particular, in *syntax-guided synthesis* [10], the output of the synthesis algorithm is constrained to programs whose syntax conforms to a given grammar. A first theoretical step in this direction for reactive systems was proposed by Madhusudan [15]. Madhusudan defines a small imperative programming language and shows that the existence of a program in this language with a fixed set of Boolean variables is decidable. For this purpose, the specification is translated into an alternating two-way tree automaton that reads in the syntax tree of a program, simulates its behavior, and accepts all programs whose behavior satisfies the specification. Because the set of variables is fixed in advance, the approach can be used to synthesize programs with a minimal number of variables. However, unlike bounded synthesis, this does not lead to programs that are minimial in other ways, such as the number of states or cycles.

In this paper, we present the first bounded synthesis approach for reactive programs. As in standard bounded synthesis [7], we reduce the synthesis problem to a constraint satisfaction problem. The challenge is to find a constraint system that encodes the existence of a program that satisfies the specification, and that, at the same time, can be solved efficiently. We develop and compare two principal methods. The first method is inspired by Madhusudan's construction in that we also build a two-way tree automaton that recognizes the correct programs. The key difficulty here is that the standard bounded synthesis approach does not work with two-way automata, let alone the alternating two-way automata produced in Madhusudan's construction. We first give a new automata construction that produces universal, instead of alternating, two-way automata. We then generalize bounded synthesis to work on arbitrary graphs, including the run graphs of two-way automata. The second method follows the original bounded synthesis approach more closely. Rather than simulating the execution of the program in the automaton, we encode the existence of both the program and its run graph in the constraint system. The correctness of the synthesized program is ensured, as in the original approach, with a universal (one-way) automaton derived from the specification. Both methods allow us to compute programs that satisfy the given specification and that are minimal in measures such as the size of the program. The two approaches compute the exact same reactive programs, but differ, conceptually, in how much work is done via an automata-theoretic construction vs. in the constraint solving. In the first approach, the verification of the synthesized program is done by the automaton, in the second approach by the constraint solving. Which approach is better? While no method has a clear theoretical advantage over the other, our experiments with a prototype implementation indicate a strong advantage for the second approach.

2 Preliminaries

We denote the Boolean values $\{0,1\}$ by $\mathbb{B}$. The set of non-negative integers is denoted by $\mathbb{N}$ and for $a \in \mathbb{N}$ the set $\{0,1,\ldots,a\}$ is denoted by $[a]$. An *alphabet* Σ is a non-empty finite set of symbols. The elements of an alphabet are called letters. A *infinite word* α over an alphabet Σ is a infinite concatenation $\alpha = \alpha_0\alpha_1\ldots$ of letters of Σ. The set of infinite words is denoted by Σ^ω. With $\alpha_n \in \Sigma$ we access the n-th letter of the word. For an infinite word $\alpha \in \Sigma^\omega$ we define with $\mathrm{Inf}(\alpha)$ the set of states that appear infinitely often in α. A subset of Σ^ω is a *language over infinite words*.

2.1 Implementations

Implementations are arbitrary input-deterministic reactive systems. We fix the finite input and output alphabet $\mathcal{I}$ and $\mathcal{O}$, respectively. A *Mealy machine* is a tuple $\mathcal{M} = (\mathcal{I}, \mathcal{O}, M, m_0, \tau, o)$ where $\mathcal{I}$ is an input-alphabet, $\mathcal{O}$ is an output-alphabet, M is a finite set of states, $m_0 \in M$ is an initial state, $\tau : M \times 2^\mathcal{I} \to M$ is a transition function and $o : M \times 2^\mathcal{I} \to 2^\mathcal{O}$ is an output function. A *system path* over an infinite input sequence $\alpha^\mathcal{I}$ is the sequence $m_0 m_1 \ldots \in M^\omega$ such that $\forall i \in \mathbb{N} : \tau(m_i, \alpha_i^\mathcal{I}) = m_{i+1}$. The thereby produced infinite output sequence is defined as $\alpha^\mathcal{O} = \alpha_0^\mathcal{O} \alpha_1^\mathcal{O} \ldots \in (2^\mathcal{O})^\omega$, where every element has to match the output function, i.e., $\forall i \in \mathbb{N} : \alpha_i^\mathcal{O} = o(m_i, \alpha_i^\mathcal{I})$. We say a Mealy machine $\mathcal{M}$ produces a word $\alpha = (\alpha_0^\mathcal{I} \cup \alpha_0^\mathcal{O})(\alpha_1^\mathcal{I} \cup \alpha_1^\mathcal{O}) \ldots \in (2^{\mathcal{I} \cup \mathcal{O}})^\omega$, iff the output $\alpha^\mathcal{O}$ is produced for input $\alpha^\mathcal{I}$. We refer to the set of all producible words as the language of $\mathcal{M}$, denoted by $\mathcal{L}(\mathcal{M}) \subseteq (2^{\mathcal{I} \cup \mathcal{O}})^\omega$.

A more succinct representation of implementations are *programs*. The programs we are working with are imperative reactive programs over a fixed set of Boolean variables B and fixed input/output arities $N_\mathcal{I}/N_\mathcal{O}$. Our approach builds upon [15] and we use the same syntax and semantics. Let $b \in B$ be a variable and both $\vec{b_\mathcal{I}}$ and $\vec{b_\mathcal{O}}$ be vectors over multiple variables of size $N_\mathcal{I}$ and $N_\mathcal{O}$, respectively. The syntax is defined with the following grammar

$$\langle stmt \rangle ::= \langle stmt \rangle ; \langle stmt \rangle \mid \mathbf{skip} \mid b := \langle expr \rangle \mid \mathbf{input}\ \vec{b_\mathcal{I}} \mid \mathbf{output}\ \vec{b_\mathcal{O}}$$
$$\mid\ \mathbf{if}(\langle expr \rangle)\,\mathbf{then}\,\{\langle stmt \rangle\}\,\mathbf{else}\,\{\langle stmt \rangle\} \mid \mathbf{while}(\langle expr \rangle)\{\langle stmt \rangle\}$$
$$\langle expr \rangle ::= b \mid \mathbf{tt} \mid \mathbf{ff} \mid (\langle expr \rangle \vee \langle expr \rangle) \mid (\neg \langle expr \rangle)$$

The semantics are the natural one. Our programs start with an initial variable valuation we define to be 0 for all variables. The program then interacts with the environment by the means of input and output statements, i.e., for a vector over Boolean variables $\vec{b}$ the statement "$\mathbf{input}\ \vec{b}$" takes an input in $\{0,1\}^{N_\mathcal{I}}$ from the environment and updates the values of $\vec{b}$. The statement "$\mathbf{output}\ \vec{b}$"

```
while(tt) {
    input (r1, r2);
    if(r1) then {
        r2 = ff
    } else {
        skip
    };
    output (r1, r2)
}
```

Fig. 1. Example-Code

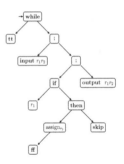

Fig. 2. Example-Program-Tree

outputs the values stored in $\vec{b}$, that is an output in $\{0,1\}^{N_{\mathcal{O}}}$. Therefor a program with input/output arity $N_{\mathcal{I}}/N_{\mathcal{O}}$ requires at least $max(N_{\mathcal{I}}, N_{\mathcal{O}})$ many variables, i.e., $|B| \geq max(N_{\mathcal{I}}, N_{\mathcal{O}})$. Between two input and output statements the program can internally do any number of steps and manipulate the variables using assignments, conditionals and loops. Note that programs are input-deterministic, i.e., a program maps an infinite input sequence $\alpha^{\mathcal{I}} \in (\{0,1\}^{N_{\mathcal{I}}})^{\omega}$ to an infinite output sequence $\alpha^{\mathcal{O}} \in (\{0,1\}^{N_{\mathcal{O}}})^{\omega}$ and we say a program can produce a word $\alpha = (\alpha_0^{\mathcal{I}}\alpha_0^{\mathcal{O}})(\alpha_1^{\mathcal{I}}\alpha_1^{\mathcal{O}})\ldots \in (\{0,1\}^{N_{\mathcal{I}}+N_{\mathcal{O}}})^{\omega}$, iff it maps $\alpha^{\mathcal{I}}$ to $\alpha^{\mathcal{O}}$. We define the language of $\mathcal{T}$, denoted by $\mathcal{L}(\mathcal{T})$, as the set of all producible words. We assume programs to alternate between input and output statements.

We represent our programs as Σ-*labeled binary trees*, i.e., a tuple (T, τ) where $T \subseteq \{L, R\}^*$ is a finite and prefix closed set of nodes and $\tau : T \to \Sigma$ is a labeling function. Based on the defined syntax, we fix the set of labels as

$$\Sigma_P = \{\neg, \vee, ; , \mathbf{if}, \mathbf{then}, \mathbf{while}\} \cup B \cup \{assign_b \mid b \in B\}$$

$$\cup \{\mathbf{input}\ \vec{b} \mid \vec{b} \in B^{N_{\mathcal{I}}}\} \cup \{\mathbf{output}\ \vec{b} \mid \vec{b} \in B^{N_{\mathcal{O}}}\}.$$

We refer to Σ_P-labeled binary trees as *program trees*. If a node has only one subtree we define it to be a the left subtree. Note that our program trees do therefore not contain nodes with only a right subtree. For example, Fig. 1 depicts an arbitrary program and Fig. 2 the corresponding program tree.

We express the current variable valuation as a function $s : B \to \mathbb{B}$. We update variables $\vec{b} \in B^n$ with new values $\vec{v} \in \mathbb{B}^n$ using the following notation:

$$s[\vec{b}/\vec{v}](x) = \begin{cases} v_i & \text{if } b_i = x, \text{for all } i \\ s(x) & \text{otherwise} \end{cases}$$

2.2   Automata

We define *alternating automata over infinite words* as usual, that is a tuple $A = (\Sigma, Q, q_0, \delta, Acc)$ where Σ is a finite alphabet, Q is a finite set of states,

$q_0 \in Q$ is an initial state, $\delta : Q \times \Sigma \rightarrow \mathbb{B}^+(Q)$ is a transition function and $Acc \subseteq Q^\omega$ is an acceptance condition.

The *Büchi acceptance condition* BÜCHI(F) on a set of states $F \subseteq Q$ is defined as BÜCHI(F) = $\{q_0 q_1 \ldots \in Q^\omega \mid \text{Inf}(\alpha) \cap F \neq \emptyset\}$ and F is called the set of accepting states. The *co-Büchi acceptance condition* COBÜCHI(F) on a set of states $F \subseteq Q$ is defined as COBÜCHI(F) = $\{q_0 q_1 \ldots \in Q^\omega \mid \text{Inf}(\alpha) \cap F = \emptyset\}$, where F is called the set of rejecting states. To express combinations of Büchi and co-Büchi expressions we use the *Streett acceptance condition*. Formally, STREETT(F) on a set of tuples $F = \{(A_i, G_i)\}_{i \in [k]} \subseteq Q \times Q$ is defined as STREETT(F) = $\{q_0 q_1 \ldots \in Q^\omega \mid \forall i \in [k] : \text{Inf}(\alpha) \cap A_i \neq \emptyset \implies \text{Inf}(\alpha) \cap G_i \neq \emptyset\}$. A run with a Streett condition is intuitively accepted, iff for all tuples (A_i, G_i), the set A_i is hit only finitely often or the set G_i is hit infinitely often.

Two-way alternating tree automata are tuple $(\Sigma, P, p_0, \delta_L, \delta_R, \delta_{LR}, \delta_\emptyset, Acc)$, where Σ is an input alphabet, P is a finite set of states, $p_0 \in P$ is an initial state, Acc is an acceptance condition, and δ are transition functions of type $\delta_S : P \times \Sigma \times (S \cup \{D\}) \rightarrow \mathbb{B}^+(P \times (S \cup \{U\}))$, for $S \in \{L, R, LR, \emptyset\}$. We introduce $\mu : T \times \{L, R, U\} \rightarrow T \times \{L, R, D\}$ as a function to map states and directions to move in, to the reached states and the matching incoming directions.

$$\mu(t, L) = (t \cdot L, D) \qquad \mu(t.L, U) = (t, L)$$
$$\mu(t, R) = (t \cdot R, D) \qquad \mu(t.R, U) = (t, R)$$

We consider specifications given in linear time-temporal logic (*LTL*). Such specifications can be translated into non-deterministic Büchi automata or dually into an universal co-Büchi automata as shown in [16]. For an arbitrary specification we denote by A_{spec} and $\overline{A}_{spec}$ the corresponding non-deterministic Büchi and universal co-Büchi automaton, respectively.

3   Automata Construction

We have already argued that programs, as a more succinct representation of implementations, are highly desirable. However, in contrast to Mealy machines, which only dependent on the current state and map an input to a corresponding output, in programs such a direct mapping is not possible. Instead, programs need to be simulated, variables to be altered, expressions to be evaluated and an output statement to be traversed until we produce the corresponding output to the received input. These steps not only depend on the current position in the program but additionally also on the valuation of all variables.

We build upon Madhusudans reactive program synthesis approach [15] were program synthesis is solved by means of two-way alternating Büchi tree automata walking up and down over program trees while keeping track of the current valuation and the state of a given Büchi specification automaton, which is simulated by the input/output produced by traversing the program tree. The automaton accepts a program tree whenever the simulated specification automaton accepts the provided input/output. The constructed automaton, we will further refer to as $\mathcal{A}$, is intersected with two other constructed automata which enforce syntactically correctness and reactivity of the synthesized program, respectively. Then a reactive and syntactically correct program is synthesized by means of an emptiness check of the obtained automaton, involving an exponential blowup to eliminate two-wayness and alternation.

3.1   Two-Way Universal Co-Büchi Tree Automaton

We construct a two-way *non-deterministic* Büchi tree automaton $\mathcal{B}$ that is equivalent to $\mathcal{A}$ by using deterministic evaluation of Boolean expressions. We construct $\mathcal{B}$ without an exponential blowup in the state space. We then complement $\mathcal{B}$ into a two-way universal co-Büchi tree automaton convenient for the bounded synthesis approach.

The two-way alternating Büchi tree automaton $\mathcal{A}$ uses universal choices only in relation to Boolean expression evaluation. For example, for **if, while** and *assign$_b$*-statements a Boolean evaluation is needed. In this cases it nondeterministically guesses whether the expression evaluates to 0 or 1 and then universally sends one copy into the Boolean expression, which evaluates to *true* iff the expression evaluates to the expected value, and one copy to continue the corresponding normal execution. The copy evaluating the Boolean expression walks only downwards and since the subtree corresponding to the Boolean expression is finite, this copy terminates to either *true* or *false* after finitely many steps. Instead of using both non-deterministic and universal choices, we evaluate the Boolean subtree deterministically in finitely many steps and then continue the normal execution based on the result of the evaluation.

Note that we not only remove all universal choices but additionally all unnecessary sources of non-determinism. Therefore, besides traversing input- and output-labels, that introduce unavoidable non-determinism, our program simulation is deterministic.

Our automaton $\mathcal{B}$ with the set of states

$$P_{exec} = S \times Q_{spec} \times \mathbb{B}^{N_{\mathcal{I}}} \times \{inp, out\} \times \mathbb{B}$$

$$P_{expr}^{\mathcal{B}} = S \times Q_{spec} \times \mathbb{B}^{N_{\mathcal{I}}} \times \{inp, out\} \times \{\top, \bot\}$$

$$P^{\mathcal{B}} = P_{expr}^{\mathcal{B}} \cup P_{exec}$$

and initial state $p_0^{\mathcal{B}} = (s_0, q_0, i_0, inp, 0)$, is defined with the transitions shown in Fig. 3, where $s \in S$ is a variable valuation, $q \in Q_{spec}$ the state of the simulated specification automaton, $i \in \mathbb{B}^{N_{\mathcal{I}}}$ the last received input, $m \in \{inp, out\}$ a flag to ensure alternation between inputs and outputs, $r \in \{\top, \bot\}$ the result of a Boolean evaluation and $t \in \{0, 1\}$ a flag for the Büchi condition, which ensures that the specification automaton is simulated for infinite steps and is only set to 1 for a single simulation step after an output statement. We express states corresponding to Boolean evaluations and program execution as $(s, q, i, m, r) \in P_{expr}^{\mathcal{B}}$ and $(s, q, i, m, t) \in P_{exec}^{\mathcal{B}}$, respectively.

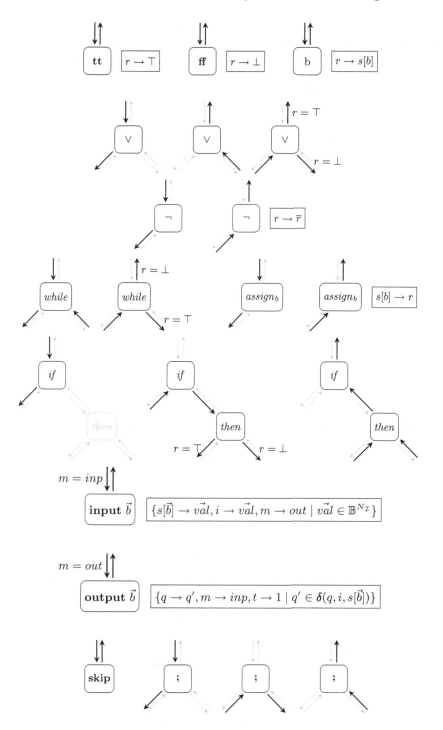

Fig. 3. Semantics of the constructed two-way automata

The notation reads as follows: If the automaton enters a node with one of the black incoming edges, it can move in the direction of the black outgoing edges, while updating his state corresponding to the annotated update expression, depicted by an enclosing rectangle. Additionally, the automaton needs to fulfill the conditions annotated to the edges it traverses. To express non-determinism we use sets of update expressions, such that each expression represents one possible successor. All state values not contained in the update expression stay the same, except t which is set to 0. When changing from Boolean evaluation to program execution, we copy s, q, i, m and vice versa.

The set of accepting states is defined as

$$F^{\mathcal{B}} = \big\{(s, q, i, m, 1) \mid q \in F_{spec}\big\}$$

A formal construction of $\mathcal{B}$ is given in the full version of the paper [17, 18]. Note that $\mathcal{B}$ behaves similar to $\mathcal{A}$ during normal execution and that only Boolean evaluation was altered. Therefore, the state spaces of the automata only differ in the states corresponding to Boolean evaluation and especially the sets of accepting states $F^{\mathcal{A}}$ and $F^{\mathcal{B}}$ are equivalent. Therefore, we can prove the equivalence by showing that both automata visit the same sequences of accepting states and thus accept the same program trees.

Theorem 1 ([17,18]). $\mathcal{L}(\mathcal{A}) = \mathcal{L}(\mathcal{B})$

We now complement the constructed two-way non-deterministic Büchi automaton into a two-way universal co-Büchi automaton. From this point onwards, we refer with $\mathcal{B}$ to the two-way universal co-Büchi automaton.

Since $\mathcal{A}$ accepts precisely the programs that fail the specification and interact infinitely often with the environment, the complement now only accepts programs that do satisfy the specification or interact finitely often with the environment. We fix the remaining misbehavior by enforcing syntactical correctness and reactiveness.

3.2   Guarantee Syntactical Correctness

Due to the fact that $\mathcal{B}$ was designed to correctly simulate programs of our defined syntax and transitions were only defined for syntax-valid statements, $\mathcal{B}$ implicitly rejects programs that are syntactically invalid. But such programs are only then rejected when their syntactically incorrect statements are traversed in the simulation, therefore $\mathcal{B}$ does not check for syntactically correct subtrees that are unreachable. It is now arguable whether the syntax check is necessary in practice. One could expect programs to be syntactically correct in total and this expectation is in general well-argued. On the other hand, we do perform bounded synthesis, i.e., we search for implementations with a bound on the implementation size and then increment this bound until a valid implementation is found. It is easy to see that programs with unreachable parts can be represented by smaller programs with the same behavior simply by removing unreachable statements. Therefore, with an incremental search one first finds the smallest and thus syntactically correct programs.

3.3 Guarantee Reactiveness

It now remains to guarantee reactiveness of the programs accepted by $\mathcal{B}$. For that purpose, we introduce a two-way universal Büchi automaton $\mathcal{B}_{reactive}$, which only accepts program trees that are reactive. This automaton is designed with the exact same states and transitions as $\mathcal{B}$ but with another acceptance condition. The intersection of $\mathcal{B}$ and $\mathcal{B}_{reactive}$ then yields a two-way universal Streett automaton $\mathcal{B}'$. We construct $\mathcal{B}_{reactive}$ with the set of accepting states:

$$F_{reactive}^{\mathcal{B}} = \big\{(s, q, i, m, 1) \mid \forall s, q, i, m\big\}$$

$\mathcal{B}_{reactive}$ accepts a program tree, iff it produces infinitely many outputs on all possible executions. Due to the alternation between input and output statements the program reacts infinitely often with its environment, i.e., it is reactive.

Formally, $\mathcal{B}'$ is the tuple $(\Sigma_P, P^{\mathcal{B}}, \delta_L^{\mathcal{B}}, \delta_R^{\mathcal{B}}, \delta_{LR}^{\mathcal{B}}, \delta_{\emptyset}^{\mathcal{B}}, \mathrm{STREETT}(F^{\mathcal{B}'}))$, where

$$F^{\mathcal{B}'} = \big\{(F^{\mathcal{B}}, \emptyset), (P^{\mathcal{B}}, F_{reactive}^{\mathcal{B}})\big\}.$$

Lemma 1. $\mathcal{L}(\mathcal{B}') = \mathcal{L}(\mathcal{B}) \cap \mathcal{L}(\mathcal{B}_{reactive})$.

Proof. Besides the acceptance condition, all three automata are equivalent. The tuples of the Streett condition $(F^{\mathcal{B}}, \emptyset)$ and $(P^{\mathcal{B}}, F_{reactive}^{\mathcal{B}})$ express the co-Büchi and Büchi condition of $\mathcal{B}$ and $\mathcal{B}_{reactive}$, respectively.   □

We capture the complete construction by the following theorem.

Theorem 2. *Let B be a finite set of Boolean variables and φ a specification given as LTL-formula. The constructed two-way universal Streett automaton $\mathcal{B}'$ accepts program trees over B that satisfy the specification.*

4 Bounded Synthesis

In this section, we generalize the bounded synthesis approach towards arbitrary universal automata and then apply it to the constructed two-way automaton to synthesize bounded programs.

We fix Q to be a finite set of states. A run graph is a tuple $\mathcal{G} = (V, v_0, E, f)$, where V is a finite set of vertices, v_0 is an initial vertex, $E \subseteq V \times V$ is a set of directed edges and $f : V \to Q$ is a labeling function. A path $\pi = \pi_0 \pi_1 \ldots \in V^{\omega}$ is *contained* in $\mathcal{G}$, denoted by $\pi \in \mathcal{G}$, iff $\forall i \in \mathbb{N} : (\pi_i, \pi_{i+1}) \in E$ and $\pi_0 = v_0$, i.e., a path in the graph starting in the initial vertex. We denote with $f(\pi) = f(\pi_0) f(\pi_1) \ldots \in Q^{\omega}$ the application of f on every node in the path, i.e., a projection to an infinite sequence of states. We call a vertex v *unreachable*, iff there exists no path $\pi \in \mathcal{G}$ containing v. Let $Acc \subseteq Q^{\omega}$ be an acceptance condition. We say $\mathcal{G}$ *satisfies Acc*, iff every path of $\mathcal{G}$ satisfies the acceptance condition, i.e., $\forall \pi \in \mathcal{G} : f(\pi) \in Acc$.

Run graphs are used to express all possible runs of a universal automaton on some implementation. This is usually done for universal word automata on

Mealy machines, but we need a generalized version to later utilize it for two-way universal tree automata on program trees. Let $\Sigma = 2^{\mathcal{I} \cup \mathcal{O}}$. We define a run graph $\mathcal{G}_{\mathcal{M}}^A = (V, v_0, E, f)$ of a universal word automaton $A = (\Sigma, Q, q_0, \delta, Acc)$ on a Mealy machine $\mathcal{M} = (\mathcal{I}, \mathcal{O}, M, m_0, \tau, o)$ as an instantiation of the given definition, where

- $V = Q \times M$,
- $v_0 = (q_0, m_0)$,
- $E = \{((q, m), (q', m')) \mid \exists in \in 2^{\mathcal{I}}, out \in 2^{\mathcal{O}} :$
  $\tau(m, in) = m' \wedge o(m, in) = out \wedge q' \in \delta(q, in \cup out)\}$ and
- $f(q, m) = q$.

Since the run graph contains all infinite runs of A on words producible by $\mathcal{M}$, A *accepts* $\mathcal{M}$, iff all runs in $\mathcal{G}_{\mathcal{M}}^A$ are accepting, i.e., $\mathcal{G}_{\mathcal{M}}^A$ satisfies Acc.

For some bound $c \in \mathbb{N}$ we denote $\{0, 1, \ldots, c\}$ by D_c. For a run graph $\mathcal{G} = (V, v_0, E, f)$ and a bound $c \in \mathbb{N}$ a c-bounded annotation function on $\mathcal{G}$ is a function $\lambda : V \to D_c$. An annotation comparison relation of arity n is a family of relations $\rhd = (\rhd_0, \rhd_1, \ldots, \rhd_{n-1}) \in (2^{Q \times D_c \times D_c})^n$. We refer to $\rhd_i \subseteq Q \times D_c \times D_c$ as basic comparison relations for $i \in [n]$. We denote the arity with $|\rhd| = n$. We write $\lambda(v) \rhd_i \lambda(v')$ for $(f(v), \lambda(v), \lambda(v')) \in \rhd_i$ and for comparison relations of arity $|\rhd| = 1$ we omit the index.

We say a path $\pi \in \mathcal{G}$ *satisfies* a comparison relation $\rhd$ with arity $|\rhd| = n$, denoted by $\pi \models \rhd$, iff for every basic comparison relation there exists an annotation function that annotates every node with a value such that the annotated number for all consecutive nodes in the path satisfy the basic comparison relation, i.e., $\forall i \in [n] : \exists \lambda : \forall j \in \mathbb{N} : \lambda(\pi_j) \rhd_i \lambda(\pi_{j+1})$. For an acceptance condition $Acc \subseteq Q^\omega$ we say a comparison relation $\rhd$ *expresses* Acc, iff all paths in $\mathcal{G}$ satisfy the relation if and only if the path satisfies the acceptance condition, i.e., $\forall \pi \in \mathcal{G} : \pi \models \rhd \leftrightarrow f(\pi) \in Acc$. A c-bounded annotation function λ on $\mathcal{G} = (V, v_0, E, f)$ is *valid* for a basic annotation comparison relation $\rhd \subseteq Q \times D_c \times D_c$, iff for all reachable $v, v' \in V : (v, v') \in E \to \lambda(v) \rhd \lambda(v')$.

We use the following annotation comparison relations to express Büchi, co-Büchi and Streett acceptance conditions.

- Let $F \subseteq Q$ and $Acc = \text{BÜCHI}(F)$. Then $\rhd_B^F$ is defined as

$$\lambda(v) \rhd_B^F \lambda(v') = \begin{cases} true & \text{if } f(v) \in F \\ \lambda(v) > \lambda(v') & \text{if } f(v) \notin F \end{cases}$$

- Let $F \subseteq Q$ and $Acc = \text{CO-BÜCHI}(F)$. Then $\rhd_C^F$ is defined as

$$\lambda(v) \rhd_C^F \lambda(v') = \begin{cases} \lambda(v) > \lambda(v') & \text{if } f(v) \in F \\ \lambda(v) \geq \lambda(v') & \text{if } f(v) \notin F \end{cases}$$

– Let $F = \{(A_i, G_i)\}_{i \in [k]} \subseteq 2^{Q \times Q}$ and $Acc = \mathrm{STREETT}(F)$. Then $\triangleright_S^F = (\triangleright_S^{F,0}, \triangleright_S^{F,1}, \dots, \triangleright_S^{F,k-1})$ is defined as

$$\lambda(v) \triangleright_S^{F,i} \lambda(v') = \begin{cases} true & \text{if } f(v) \in G_i \\ \lambda(v) > \lambda(v') & \text{if } f(v) \in A_i \wedge f(v) \notin G_i \\ \lambda(v) \geq \lambda(v') & \text{if } f(v) \notin A_i \cup G_i \end{cases}$$

Note that $|\triangleright_B^F| = |\triangleright_C^F| = 1$ and $|\triangleright_S^F| = k$.

Theorem 3 ([7,19]). *Let F be a set, the acceptance condition of A be expressed by $\triangleright_X^F$ with $X \in \{B, C, S\}$, $c \in \mathbb{N}$ a bound and $\mathcal{G}_\mathcal{M}^A$ the run graph of A on $\mathcal{M}$.*

If and only if, there exists a valid c-bounded annotation function λ_i on $\mathcal{G}_\mathcal{M}^A$ for each basic comparison relation $\triangleright_i$, then $\mathcal{G}_\mathcal{M}^A$ satisfies Acc.

4.1 General Bounded Synthesis

In Theorem 3 we saw that the acceptance of a Mealy machine $\mathcal{M}$ by a universal automata A can be expressed by the existence of an annotation comparison relation. To do the same for two-way automata on program trees, we generalize this theorem towards arbitrary run graphs.

Let $\mathcal{A} = (\Sigma_P, P, p_0, \delta_L, \delta_R, \delta_{LR}, \delta_\emptyset, Acc)$ be a two-way universal tree automaton and $\mathcal{T} = (T, \tau)$ a program tree. We define the run graph of $\mathcal{A}$ on $\mathcal{T}$ as $\mathcal{G}_\mathcal{T}^A = (V, v_0, E, f)$, where

– $V = P \times T \times \{L, R, D\}$,
– $v_0 = (p_0, \epsilon, D)$,
– $E = \{((p, t, d), (p', t', d')) \mid \exists d'' \in \{L, R, U\} : \mu(t, d'') = (t', d') \wedge (p', d'') \in \delta_t(p, \tau(t), d)\}$ and
– $f(p, t, d) = p$.

For the generalized encoding, we use the same construction for the annotation comparison relation as presented in [19] for Street acceptance conditions, which conveniently suffices for the general run graphs. Büchi and co-Büchi then follow as special cases.

Lemma 2 ([17,18]). *For a Streett acceptance condition $Acc = Streett(F)$ with set of tuples of states $F \subseteq 2^{Q \times Q}$ and a run graph $\mathcal{G} = (V, v_0, E, f)$:*

If $\mathcal{G}$ satisfies Acc, then there exists a valid $|V|$-bounded annotation function λ for each basic comparison relation in $\triangleright_S^F$.

Theorem 4. *Let $\mathcal{G} = (V, v_0, E, f)$ be a run graph, $Acc \subseteq Q^\omega$ a Büchi, co-Büchi or Streett acceptance condition expressed by the relation $\triangleright_X$ for $X \in \{B, C, S\}$.*

There exists a valid $|V|$-bounded annotation function λ_i on $\mathcal{G}$ for each basic comparison relation $\triangleright_i$, if and only if $\mathcal{G}$ satisfies Acc.

Proof. " $\Rightarrow$ " : Let $\mathcal{G}$, Acc, $\triangleright$ with arity $|\triangleright| = n$ and c be given and λ_i be a valid c-bounded annotation comparison relation on $\mathcal{G}$ for $\triangleright_i$ for all $i \in [n]$. Let $\pi = \pi_0 \pi_1 \dots \in \mathcal{G}$ be an arbitrary path in $\mathcal{G}$ and $i \in [n]$. Since λ_i is a valid annotation function, $\lambda_i(\pi_0) \triangleright_i \lambda_i(\pi_1) \triangleright_i \dots$ holds and therefore $\pi \models \triangleright$. Since $\triangleright$ expresses Acc it follows that $f(\pi) \in Acc$, i.e., $\mathcal{G}$ satisfies Acc.

" $\Leftarrow$ " : Lemma 2. $\qquad\square$

4.2   General Encoding

We showed that the run graph satisfies an acceptance condition Acc, iff the implementation is accepted by the automaton. We also proved that the satisfaction of Acc by a run graph can be expressed by the existence of valid annotation functions.

We encode these constraints in SAT. The valid implementation can then be extracted from the satisfied encoding. Note that in our definition of program trees the structure was implicitly expressed by the nodes and for the encoding we need to express them explicitly. Therefore, the structure of the tree is encoded with successor functions L and R, expressing the left and right child of a node, respectively. We encode the program tree and the annotation function as uninterpreted functions as explained in the following. We introduce the following variables for arbitrary two-way automata $\mathcal{A}$, program trees $\mathcal{T}$, bounds c and annotation comparison relations $\triangleright$:

- τ_t encodes label l of t with $\log(|\Sigma|)$ many variables, notated as $\tau_t \equiv l$
- L_t iff t has left child (implicitly the next program state $t+1$)
- R_t encodes right the child of $t \in T$ with $\log(|T|)$ many variables
- $\lambda^{\mathbb{B}}_{p,t,d}$ iff state (p,t,d) is reachable in the run graph
- $\lambda^{\#}_{i,p,t,d}$ encodes the i-th annotation of state (p,t,d) with $\log(c)$ many variables. We omit the index i in the encoding

The SAT formula $\Phi^{\mathcal{A},\triangleright}_{\mathcal{T}}$ consists of the following constraints:

- The initial state is reachable and all annotations fulfill the given bound:

$$\lambda^{\mathbb{B}}_{p_0,t_0,D} \wedge \bigwedge_{\substack{p \in P, \\ t \in T, \\ d \in \{L,R,D\}}} \lambda^{\#}_{p,t,d} \leq c$$

- Bounded synthesis encoding

$$\bigwedge_{\substack{p \in P, \\ t \in T, \\ d \in D}} \lambda^{\mathbb{B}}_{p,t,d} \rightarrow \bigwedge_{\sigma \in \Sigma} (\tau_t \equiv \sigma) \rightarrow \bigwedge_{\substack{(p',d'') \in \delta(p,\sigma,d), \\ t' \in T, \\ (\varphi,d') \in \mu'(t,d'',t')}} \varphi \rightarrow \lambda^{\mathbb{B}}_{p',t',d'} \wedge \lambda^{\#}_{p,t,d} \triangleright \lambda^{\#}_{p',t',d'}$$

$\mu' : T \times D' \times T \rightarrow [\mathbb{B}(L_t, R_t) \times D]$ returns a list of pairs (φ,d'), where formula φ enforces the tree structure needed to reach p',t',d'.

The encoding checks whether universal properties in the run graph hold. Note that we need to additionally forbid walking up from the root node, which is omitted here.

Theorem 5. *Given a two-way universal tree automaton $\mathcal{A}$ with a Büchi, co-Büchi or Streett acceptance condition Acc expressed by $\triangleright$ and a bound $c \in \mathbb{N}$. The constraint system $\Phi^{\mathcal{A},\triangleright}_{\mathcal{T}}$ is satisfiable, iff there is a program tree $\mathcal{T}$ with size $|\mathcal{T}| \leq \lfloor c/|\mathcal{A}| \rfloor$ that is accepted by $\mathcal{A}$.*

Proof. " $\Rightarrow$ " : Let $\mathcal{T}$ be accepted by $\mathcal{A}$, then with Theorem 4 there exists a valid annotation function λ_i on $\mathcal{G}$ for each $i \in [|\triangleright|]$. Let λ_i be represented by $\lambda_i^{\#}$ and $\lambda_i^{\mathcal{B}}$ be *true* for all reachable states in the run graph $\mathcal{G}$. Then $\Phi_{\mathcal{T}}^{\mathcal{A},\triangleright}$ is satisfied.

" $\Leftarrow$ " : Let $\Phi_{\mathcal{T}}^{\mathcal{A},\triangleright}$ be satisfied. Then there exists a valid annotation function λ_i encoded by $\lambda_i^{\#}$ for each $i \in [|\triangleright|]$ (set $\lambda_i(v) = 0$ for all unreachable states v, i.e., where $\lambda_i^{\#}(v)$ is *false*) that satisfies the encoding. With Theorem 4 the acceptance of $\mathcal{T}$ by $\mathcal{A}$ follows. $\square$

Utilizing this theorem, we now can by means of the encoding $\Phi_S^{\mathcal{B}'}$ synthesize program trees accepted by $\mathcal{B}'$, i.e., precisely those program trees, which correspond to reactive programs that satisfy the given specification the automaton was constructed with.

Corollary 1. *The SAT encoding $\Phi_S^{\mathcal{B}'}$ is satisfiable, if and only if there exists a program tree $\mathcal{T}$ with size $|\mathcal{T}| \leq \lfloor c/|\mathcal{B}'| \rfloor$ accepted by $\mathcal{B}'$.*

Size of construction The automaton can be constructed of size $O(2^{|B|+|\varphi|})$, i.e., for a fixed set of Boolean variables the automaton is linear in the size of the specification automaton or exponential in the size of the specification formula. The constructed constraint system $\Phi_S^{\mathcal{B}'}$ is of size $O(|T| \cdot |\delta| \cdot |\Sigma_P|)$ with x many variables, where $x \in O(|T| \cdot (|T| + |\Sigma_P| + |Q| \cdot log(|Q| \cdot |T|)))$. Note that $|\Sigma_P| \in O(|B|^{N_I + N_O})$ grows polynomial in the number of variables for fixed input/output arities.

5   Two-Wayless Encoding

Next, we sketch the second encoding that avoids the detour via universal two-way automata. To this end, we alter the construction in that input- and output-labels collapse to a single *InOut*-label with semantics as follows

$$\boxed{\textbf{InOut}} \quad \boxed{\{\vec{i} \rightarrow \vec{val}, q \rightarrow q' \mid \vec{val} \in \mathbb{B}^{N_I}, q' \in \delta(q, \vec{i}, s[\vec{o}])\}}$$

where we use output variables $\vec{o}$ and input variables $\vec{i}$ that correspond to inputs and outputs of the system, respectively. In a nutshell, our new encoding consists of four parts:

1. The first part guesses the program and ensures syntactical correctness.
2. The second part simulates the program for every possible input from every reachable *InOut*-labeled state until it again reaches the next *InOut*-labeled state. Note that every such simulation trace is deterministic once the input, read at the initial *InOut*-labeled state, has been fixed.

Table 1. Comparison of the general and the two-wayless encoding.

SPECIFICATION	STATES	ADDITIONAL VARIABLES	$|\mathcal{B}'|$	TWO-WAY ENCODING	TWO-WAYLESS ENCODING
$in \leftrightarrow out$	6	0	16	00 m 16 s	00 m 02 s
$in \leftrightarrow \bigcirc out$	9	1	64	11 m 29 s	08 m 34 s
Latch	10	0	64	>120 m	08 m 07 s
2-bit arbiter	10	0	128	66 m 48 s	14 m 18 s

3. The third part extracts a simplified transition structure from the resulting execution graph, that consists of direct input labeled transitions from one *InOut*-labeled state to the next one and output labeled states.
4. In the last part, this structure is then verified by a run graph construction that must satisfy the specification, given as universal co-Büchi automaton. To this end, we couple inputs on the edges with the outputs of the successor state to preserve the Mealy semantics of the program.

The first part utilizes a similar structure as used for the previous encoding and thus is skipped for convenience here. To simulate the program in the second part, we introduce the notion of a *valuation* $v \in \mathcal{V}$, where

$$\mathcal{V} = P \times \mathbb{B}^{B \setminus \mathcal{I}} \times \{L, R, U\} \times \mathbb{B}$$

captures the current program state, the current values of all non-input variables, the current direction, and the result of the evaluation of the last Boolean expression, respectively. The simulation of the program is then expressed by a finite execution graph, in which, after fixing a inputs $\vec{i} \in 2^{\mathcal{I}}$, every valuation points to a successor valuation. This successor valuation is unique, except for *InOut*-labeled states, whose successor depends on the next input to be read. The deterministic evaluation follows from the rules of Fig. 3 and selects a unique successor for every configuration, accordingly.

In part three, this expression graph then is compressed into a simplified transition structure. To this end, we need for every input and *InOut*-labeled starting valuation, the target *InOut*-labeled valuation that is reached as a result of the deterministic evaluation. In other words, we require to find a shortcut from every such valuation to the next one. We use an inductive chain of constraints to determine this shortcut efficiently. Remember that we only know the unique successor of every valuation which only allows to make one step forward at a time. Hence, we can store for every valuation and input a second shortcut successor, using an additional set of variables, constrained as follows: if the evaluated successor is *InOut*-labeled, then the shortcut successor must be the same as the evaluated one. Otherwise, it is the same as the shortcut successor of the successor valuation, leading to the desired inductive definition. Furthermore, to ensure a proper induction base, we use an additional ranking on the valuations that bounds the number of steps between two *InOut* labeled valuations. This annotation is realized in a similar fashion as in the previously presented encoding.

Table 2. Synthesized implementations for the two-wayless encoding.

$in \leftrightarrow out$	$in \leftrightarrow \bigcirc out$	latch	2-bit arbiter
```while(tt) { out = in; InOut } ```	```while(tt) { out = var; var = in; InOut } ```	```while (tt) { if (upd) { out = in } else { skip }; InOut } ```	```while (tt) { g0 = g1; g1 = not g1; InOut } ```

With these shortcuts at hand, we then can extract the simplified transition structure, which is verified using a standard run graph encoding as used for classical bounded synthesis. Furthermore, we use an over-approximation to bound the size of the structure and use a reachability annotation that allows the solver to reduce the constraints to those parts as required by the selected solution. The size can, however, also be bound using an explicit bound that is set manually.

Using this separation into four independent steps allows to keep the encoding compact in size, and results in the previously promised performance improvements presented in the next section.

6   Experimental Results

Table 1 compares the general encoding of Sect. 4.1 and the two-wayless encoding of Sect. 5 on a selection of standard benchmarks. The table contains the of number of states of the program's syntax tree, the number of additional variables, i.e., variables that are not designated to handle inputs and outputs, the size of the two-way universal Streett automaton, created for the general encoding, and the solving times for both encodings. Table 2 shows the results in terms of the synthesized program trees for the two-wayless encoding. The experiments indicate a strong advantage of the second approach.

7   Conclusions

We introduced a generalized approach to bounded synthesis that is applicable whenever all possible runs of a universal automaton on the possibly produced input/output words of an input-deterministic implementation can be expressed by a run graph. The acceptance of an implementation can then be expressed by the existence of valid annotation functions for an annotation comparison relation that expresses the acceptance of the automaton for Büchi, co-Büchi and Streett acceptance conditions. The existence of valid annotation functions for a run graph is encoded as a SAT query that is satisfiable if and only if there exists an implementation satisfying a given bound that is accepted by the automaton.

For LTL specifications, we constructed a two-way universal Streett automaton which accepts reactive programs that satisfy the specification. We then constructed a run graph that represents all possible runs and applied the generalized bounded synthesis approach. Next, we constructed a SAT query that guesses a reactive program of bounded size as well as valid annotation functions that witnesses the correctness of the synthesized program.

Finally, we merged the previous transformations into an extended encoding that simulates the program directly via the constraint solver. We evaluated both encodings with the clear result that the encoding avoiding the explicit run graph construction for two-way automata wins in the evaluation.

References

1. Church, A.: Application of recursive arithmetic to the problem of circuit synthesis. J. Symb. Log. **28**(4), 289–290 (1963)
2. Jobstmann, B., Galler, S., Weiglhofer, M., Bloem, R.: Anzu: a tool for property synthesis. In: Damm, W., Hermanns, H. (eds.) CAV 2007. LNCS, vol. 4590, pp. 258–262. Springer, Heidelberg (2007). https://doi.org/10.1007/978-3-540-73368-3_29
3. Ehlers, R.: Unbeast: symbolic bounded synthesis. In: Abdulla, P.A., Leino, K.R.M. (eds.) TACAS 2011. LNCS, vol. 6605, pp. 272–275. Springer, Heidelberg (2011). https://doi.org/10.1007/978-3-642-19835-9_25
4. Bohy, A., Bruyère, V., Filiot, E., Jin, N., Raskin, J.-F.: Acacia+, a tool for LTL synthesis. In: Madhusudan, P., Seshia, S.A. (eds.) CAV 2012. LNCS, vol. 7358, pp. 652–657. Springer, Heidelberg (2012). https://doi.org/10.1007/978-3-642-31424-7_45
5. Faymonville, P., Finkbeiner, B., Tentrup, L.: BoSy: an experimentation framework for bounded synthesis. [20] 325–332
6. Bloem, R., Galler, S.J., Jobstmann, B., Piterman, N., Pnueli, A., Weiglhofer, M., et al.: Interactive presentation: automatic hardware synthesis from specifications: a case study. In: Lauwereins, R., Madsen, J. (eds.) DATE, pp. 1188–1193. Nice, France, EDA Consortium, San Jose, CA, USA (2007)
7. Finkbeiner, B., Schewe, S.: Bounded synthesis. STTT **15**(5–6), 519–539 (2013)
8. Finkbeiner, B., Klein, F.: Bounded cycle synthesis. In: Chaudhuri, S., Farzan, A. (eds.) CAV 2016. LNCS, vol. 9779, pp. 118–135. Springer, Cham (2016). https://doi.org/10.1007/978-3-319-41528-4_7
9. Faymonville, P., Finkbeiner, B., Rabe, M.N., Tentrup, L.: Encodings of bounded synthesis. In: Legay, A., Margaria, T. (eds.) TACAS 2017. LNCS, vol. 10205, pp. 354–370. Springer, Heidelberg (2017). https://doi.org/10.1007/978-3-662-54577-5_20
10. Alur, R., et al.: Syntax-guided synthesis. In: FMCAD, pp. 1–8. Portland, OR, USA, IEEE (2013)
11. Gulwani, S.: Automating string processing in spreadsheets using input-output examples. In: Ball, T., Sagiv, M. (eds.) POPL, pp. 317–330. Austin, TX, USA, ACM (2011)

12. Osera, P., Zdancewic, S.: Type-and-example-directed program synthesis. In: Grove, D., Blackburn, S. (eds.) PLDI, pp. 619–630. Portland, OR, USA, ACM (2015)
13. Solar-Lezama, A.: Program sketching. STTT **15**(5–6), 475–495 (2013)
14. Vechev, M.T., Yahav, E., Yorsh, G.: Abstraction-guided synthesis of synchronization. STTT **15**(5–6), 413–431 (2013)
15. Madhusudan, P.: Synthesizing reactive programs. In: Bezem, M., (ed.) CSL, Bergen, Norway. Volume 12 of LIPIcs, pp. 428–442. Schloss Dagstuhl (2011)
16. Vardi, M.Y., Wolper, P.: Reasoning about infinite computations. Inf. Comput. **115**(1), 1–37 (1994)
17. Gerstacker, C.: Bounded Synthesis of Reactive Programs, Bachelor's Thesis (2017)
18. Gerstacker, C., Klein, F., Finkbeiner, B.: Bounded synthesis of reactive programs. CoRR 1807.09047 (2018)
19. Khalimov, A., Bloem, R.: Bounded Synthesis for Streett, Rabin, and CTL*. [20] 333–352
20. Majumdar, R., Kunčak, V. (eds.): CAV 2017. LNCS, vol. 10427. Springer, Cham (2017). https://doi.org/10.1007/978-3-319-63390-9

Maximum Realizability for Linear Temporal Logic Specifications

Rayna Dimitrova[1(✉)], Mahsa Ghasemi[2], and Ufuk Topcu[2]

[1] University of Leicester, Leicester, UK
rd307@leicester.ac.uk
[2] University of Texas at Austin, Austin, USA

Abstract. Automatic synthesis from linear temporal logic (LTL) specifications is widely used in robotic motion planning and control of autonomous systems. A common specification pattern in such applications consists of an LTL formula describing the requirements on the behaviour of the system, together with a set of additional desirable properties. We study the synthesis problem in settings where the overall specification is unrealizable, more precisely, when some of the desirable properties have to be (temporarily) violated in order to satisfy the system's objective. We provide a quantitative semantics of sets of safety specifications, and use it to formalize the "best-effort" satisfaction of such *soft* specifications while satisfying the *hard* LTL specification. We propose an algorithm for synthesizing implementations that are optimal with respect to this quantitative semantics. Our method builds upon the idea of bounded synthesis, and we develop a MaxSAT encoding which allows for maximizing the quantitative satisfaction of the soft specifications. We evaluate our algorithm on scenarios from robotics and power distribution networks.

1 Introduction

Automatic synthesis from temporal logic specifications is increasingly becoming a viable alternative for system design in a number of domains such as control and robotics. The main advantage of synthesis is that it allows the system designer to focus on *what* the system should do, rather than on *how* it should do it. Thus, the main challenge becomes providing the right specification of the system's required behaviour. While significantly easier than developing a system at a lower level, specification design is on its own a difficult and error-prone task. For example, in the case of systems operating in a complex adversarial environment, such as robots, the specification might be over-constrained, and as a result unrealizable, due to failure to account for some of the behaviours of the environment. In other cases, the designer might have several alternative specifications in mind, possibly

R. Dimitrova—This work was done while the author was at The University of Texas at Austin.

This work was supported in part by AFRL grants UTC 17-S8401-10-C1 and FA8650-15-C-2546, and ONR grant N000141613165.

© Springer Nature Switzerland AG 2018
S. K. Lahiri and C. Wang (Eds.): ATVA 2018, LNCS 11138, pp. 458–475, 2018.
https://doi.org/10.1007/978-3-030-01090-4_27

with some preferences, and wants to know what the best realizable combination of requirements is. For instance, a temporary violation of a safety requirement might be acceptable, if it is necessary to achieve an important goal. In such cases it is desirable that, when the specification is unrealizable, the synthesis procedure provides a "best-effort" implementation either according to some user-given criteria, or according to the semantics of the specification language.

The challenges of specification design motivate the need to develop synthesis methods for the *maximum realizability problem*, where the input to the synthesis tool consists of a *hard specification* which *must* be satisfied by the system, and *soft specifications* which describe other desired, possibly prioritized properties.

A key ingredient of the formulation of the maximum realizability problem is a quantitative semantics of the soft requirements. We focus on soft specifications of the form $\Box \varphi_1, \ldots, \Box \varphi_n$, where each φ_i is a safety LTL formula, and consider a quantitative semantics typically used in the context of robustness. The quantitative semantics accounts for how often each φ_i is satisfied. In particular, we consider truth values corresponding to φ_i being satisfied at every point of an execution, being violated only finitely many times, being both violated and satisfied infinitely often, or being continuously violated from some point on. Based on this semantics, we define the numerical value of a conjunction $\Box \varphi_1 \wedge \ldots \wedge \Box \varphi_n$ of soft specifications in a given implementation. We propose a method for synthesizing an implementation that maximizes this value.

Our approach to maximum realizability is based on the bounded synthesis technique. Bounded synthesis is able to synthesize implementations by leveraging the power of SAT (or QBF, or SMT) solvers. Since maximum realizability is an optimization problem, we reduce its bounded version to maximum satisfiability (MaxSAT). More precisely, we encode the bounded maximum realizability problem with hard and soft specifications as a partial weighted MaxSAT problem, where hard specifications are captured by hard clauses in the MaxSAT formulation, and the weights of soft clauses encode the quantitative semantics of soft specifications. By adjusting these weights our approach can easily capture different quantitative semantics. Although the formulation encodes the bounded maximum realizability problem (where the maximum size of the implementation is fixed), by providing a bound on the size of the optimal implementation, we establish the completeness of our synthesis method. The existence of such completeness bound is guaranteed by considering quantitative semantics in which the values of soft specifications can be themselves encoded by LTL formulas.

We have applied the proposed synthesis method to examples from two domains where considering combinations of hard and soft specifications is natural and often unavoidable. For example, such a combination of specifications arises in power networks where generators of limited capacity have to power a set of vital and non-vital loads, whose total demand may exceed the capacity of the generators. Another example is robotic navigation, where due to the adversarial nature of the environment in which robots operate, safety requirements might prevent a system from achieving its goal, or a large number of tasks of different nature might not necessarily be consistent when posed together.

Related work. Maximum realizability and several closely related problems have attracted significant attention in recent years. Planning over a finite horizon with prioritized safety requirements was studied in [20], where the goal is to synthesize a least-violating control strategy. A similar problem for infinite-horizon temporal logic planning was studied in [12], which seeks to revise an inconsistent specification, minimizing the cost of revision with respect to costs for atomic propositions provided by the specifier. [14] describes a method for computing optimal plans for co-safe LTL specifications, where optimality is again with respect to the cost of violating each atomic proposition, which is provided by the designer. All of these approaches are developed for the planning setting, where there is no adversarial environment, and thus they are able to reduce the problem to the computation of an optimal path in a graph. The case of probabilistic environments was considered in [15]. In contrast, in our work we seek to maximize the satisfaction of the given specification against the worst-case behaviour of the environment.

The problem setting that is the closest to ours is that of [19]. The authors of [19] study a maximum realizability problem in which the specification is a conjunction of a *must* (or *hard*, in our terms) LTL specification, and a number of weighted *desirable* (or *soft*, in our terms) specifications of the form $\Box\,\varphi$, where φ is an arbitrary LTL formula. When φ is not a safety property it is first strengthened to a safety formula before applying the synthesis procedure, which then weakens the result to a mean-payoff term. Thus, while [19] considers a broader class of soft specifications than we do, when φ is not a safety property there is no clear relationship between $\Box\,\varphi$ and the resulting mean-payoff term. When applied to multiple soft specifications, the method from [19] combines the corresponding mean-payoff terms in a weighted sum, and synthesizes an implementation optimizing the value of this sum. Thus, it is not possible to determine to what extent the individual desirable specifications are satisfied without inspecting the synthesized implementation. In contrast, in our maximum realizability procedure each satisfaction value is characterized as an LTL formula, which is useful for explainability and providing feedback to the designer.

To the best of our knowledge, our work is the first to employ MaxSAT in the context of reactive synthesis. MaxSAT has been used in [11] for preference-based planning. However, since maximum realizability is concerned with reactive systems, it requires a fundamentally different approach than planning.

Two other main research directions related to maximum realizability are *quantitative synthesis* and *specification debugging*. There are two predominant flavours of quantitative synthesis problems studied in the literature. In the first one (cf. [4]), the goal is to generate an implementation that maximizes the value of a mean-payoff objective, while possibly satisfying some ω-regular specification. In the second setting (cf. [1,18]), the system requirements are formalized in a multi-valued temporal logic. The synthesis methods in these works, however, do not solve directly the corresponding optimization problem, but instead check for the existence of an implementation whose value is in a given set. The optimization problem can then be reduced to a sequence of such queries.

An optimal synthesis problem for an ordered sequence of prioritized ω-regular properties was studied in [2], where the classical fixpoint-based game-solving algorithms are extended to a quantitative setting. The main difference in our work is that we allow for incomparable soft specifications each with a number of prioritized relaxations, for which the equivalent set of preference-ordered combinations would be of size exponential in the number of soft specifications. Our MaxSAT formulation avoids considering explicitly these combinations.

In specification debugging there is a lot of research dedicated to finding good explanations for the unsatisfiability or unrealizability of temporal specifications [6], and more generally to the analysis of specifications [5,9]. Our approach to maximum realizability can prove useful for specification analysis, since instead of simply providing an optimal value, it computes an optimal relaxation of the given specification in the form of another LTL formula.

2 Maximum Realizability Problem

We first give an overview of linear-time temporal logic (LTL) and the corresponding synthesis problem, which asks to synthesize an implementation, in the form of a transition system, that satisfies an LTL formula given as input.

Then, we proceed by providing a quantitative semantics for a class of LTL formulas, and the definition of the corresponding maximum realizability problem.

2.1 Specifications, Transition Systems, and the Synthesis Problem

Linear-time temporal logic (LTL) is a standard specification language for formalizing requirements on the behaviour of reactive systems. Given a finite set $\mathcal{P}$ of atomic propositions, the set of LTL formulas is generated by the grammar $\varphi := p \mid true \mid false \mid \neg\varphi \mid \varphi_1 \wedge \varphi_2 \mid \varphi_1 \vee \varphi_2 \mid \bigcirc\varphi \mid \varphi_1 \mathcal{U} \varphi_2 \mid \varphi_1 \mathcal{R} \varphi_2$, where $p \in \mathcal{P}$ is an atomic proposition, $\bigcirc$ is the *next* operator, $\mathcal{U}$ is the *until* operator, and $\mathcal{R}$ is the *release* operator. As usual, we define the derived operators *finally*: $\Diamond\varphi = true \,\mathcal{U}\, \varphi$ and *globally*: $\square\varphi = false \,\mathcal{R}\, \varphi$. Every LTL formula can be converted to an equivalent one in negation normal form (NNF), where negations appear only in front of atomic propositions. Thus, we consider only formulas in NNF.

Let $\Sigma = 2^{\mathcal{P}}$ be the finite alphabet consisting of the valuations of the propositions $\mathcal{P}$. A letter $\sigma \in \Sigma$ is interpreted as the valuation that assigns value true to all $p \in \sigma$ and false to all $p \in \mathcal{P} \setminus \sigma$. LTL formulas are interpreted over infinite words $w \in \Sigma^\omega$. If a word $w \in \Sigma^\omega$ satisfies an LTL formula φ, we write $w \models \varphi$. The definition of the semantics of LTL can be found for instance in [3]. We denote with $|\varphi|$ the length of φ, and with $\mathsf{subf}(\varphi)$ the set of its subformulas.

A *safety LTL formula* φ is an LTL formula such that for each $w \in \Sigma^\omega$ with $w \not\models \varphi$ there exists $u \in \Sigma^*$ such that for all $v \in \Sigma^\omega$ it holds that $u \cdot v \not\models \varphi$ (u is called a *bad prefix* for φ). A class of safety LTL formulas is the class of *syntactically safe* LTL formulas, which contain no occurrences of $\mathcal{U}$ in their NNF.

In the rest of the paper we assume that the set $\mathcal{P}$ of atomic propositions is partitioned into disjoint sets of *input* propositions $\mathcal{I}$ and *output* propositions $\mathcal{O}$.

A *transition system* over a set of input propositions $\mathcal{I}$ and a set of output propositions $\mathcal{O}$ is a tuple $\mathcal{T} = (S, s_0, \tau)$, where S is a set of states, s_0 is the initial state, and the transition function $\tau : S \times 2^{\mathcal{I}} \to S \times 2^{\mathcal{O}}$ maps a state s and a valuation $\sigma_I \in 2^{\mathcal{I}}$ of the input propositions to a successor state s' and a valuation $\sigma_O \in 2^{\mathcal{O}}$ to the output propositions. Let $\mathcal{P} = \mathcal{I} \cup \mathcal{O}$ be the set of all propositions. For $\sigma \in \Sigma = 2^{\mathcal{P}}$ we denote $\sigma \cap \mathcal{I}$ by σ_I, and $\sigma \cap \mathcal{O}$ by σ_O.

If the set S is finite, then $\mathcal{T}$ is a finite-state transition system. In this case we define the size $|\mathcal{T}|$ of $\mathcal{T}$ to be the number of its states, i.e., $|\mathcal{T}| \overset{\text{def}}{=} |S|$.

An *execution* of $\mathcal{T}$ is an infinite sequence $s_0, (\sigma_{I0} \cup \sigma_{O0}), s_1, (\sigma_{I1} \cup \sigma_{O1}), s_2 \ldots$ such that s_0 is the initial state, and $(s_{i+1}, \sigma_{Oi}) = \tau(s_i, \sigma_{Ii})$ for every $i \geq 0$. The corresponding sequence $(\sigma_{I0} \cup \sigma_{O0}), (\sigma_{I1} \cup \sigma_{O1}), \ldots \in \Sigma^{\omega}$ is called a trace. We denote with $\mathsf{Traces}(\mathcal{T})$ the set of all traces of a transition system $\mathcal{T}$.

We say that a transition system $\mathcal{T}$ satisfies an LTL formula φ over atomic propositions $\mathcal{P} = \mathcal{I} \cup \mathcal{O}$, denoted $\mathcal{T} \models \varphi$, if $w \models \varphi$ for every $w \in \mathsf{Traces}(\mathcal{T})$.

The *realizability problem for LTL* is to determine whether for a given LTL formula φ there exists a transition system $\mathcal{T}$ that satisfies φ. The *LTL synthesis problem* asks to construct such a transition system if one exists.

Often, the specification is a combination of multiple requirements, which might not be realizable in conjunction. In such a case, in addition to reporting the unrealizability to the system designer, we would like the synthesis procedure to construct an implementation that satisfies the specification "as much as possible". Such implementation is particularly useful in the case where some of the requirements describe desirable but not necessarily essential properties of the system. To determine what "as much as possible" formally means, a quantitative semantics of the specification language is necessary. In the next subsection we provide such semantics for a fragment of LTL. The quantitative interpretation is based on the standard semantics of LTL formulas of the form $\Box \varphi$.

2.2 Quantitative Semantics of Soft Safety Specifications

Let $\Box \varphi_1, \ldots, \Box \varphi_n$ be LTL specifications, where each φ_i is a safety LTL formula. In order to formalize the maximal satisfaction of $\Box \varphi_1 \wedge \ldots \wedge \Box \varphi_n$, we first give a quantitative semantics of formulas of the form $\Box \varphi$.

Quantitative semantics of safety specifications. For an LTL formula of the form $\Box \varphi$ and a transition system $\mathcal{T}$, we define *the value* $val(\mathcal{T}, \Box \varphi)$ of $\Box \varphi$ in $\mathcal{T}$ as

$$val(\mathcal{T}, \Box \varphi) \overset{\text{def}}{=} \begin{cases} (1,1,1) & \text{if } \mathcal{T} \models \Box \varphi, \\ (1,1,0) & \text{if } \mathcal{T} \not\models \Box \varphi \text{ and } \mathcal{T} \models \Diamond \Box \varphi, \\ (1,0,0) & \text{if } \mathcal{T} \not\models \Box \varphi \text{ and } \mathcal{T} \not\models \Diamond \Box \varphi, \text{ and } \mathcal{T} \models \Box \Diamond \varphi, \\ (0,0,0) & \text{if } \mathcal{T} \not\models \Box \varphi, \text{ and } \mathcal{T} \not\models \Diamond \Box \varphi, \text{ and } \mathcal{T} \not\models \Box \Diamond \varphi. \end{cases}$$

Thus, the value of $\Box \varphi$ in a transition system $\mathcal{T}$ is a vector $(v_1, v_2, v_3) \in \{0,1\}^3$, where the value $(1,1,1)$ corresponds to the *true* value in the classical semantics of LTL. When $\mathcal{T} \not\models \Box\varphi$, the values $(1,1,0)$, $(1,0,0)$ and $(0,0,0)$ capture the extent to which φ holds or not along the traces of $\mathcal{T}$. For example, if $val(\mathcal{T},\Box\varphi) = (1,0,0)$, then φ holds infinitely often on each trace of $\mathcal{T}$, but there exists a trace of $\mathcal{T}$ on which φ is violated infinitely often. When $val(\mathcal{T},\Box\varphi) = (0,0,0)$, then on some trace of $\mathcal{T}$, φ holds for at most finitely many positions.

Note that by the definition of val, if $val(\mathcal{T},\Box\varphi) = (v_1, v_2, v_3)$, then (1) $v_1 = 1$ iff $\mathcal{T} \models \Box\Diamond\varphi$, (2) $v_2 = 1$ iff $\mathcal{T} \models \Diamond\Box\varphi$, and (3) $v_3 = 1$ iff $\mathcal{T} \models \Box\varphi$. Thus, the lexicographic ordering on $\{0,1\}^3$ captures the preference of one transition system over another with respect to the quantitative satisfaction of $\Box\varphi$.

Example 1. Suppose that we want to synthesize a transition system representing a navigation strategy for a robot working at a restaurant. We require that the robot must serve the VIP area infinitely often, formalized in LTL as $\Box\Diamond$ *vip_area*. We also desire that the robot never enters the staff's office, formalized as $\Box\neg$*office*. Now, suppose that initially the key to the VIP area is in the office. Thus, in order to satisfy $\Box\Diamond$ *vip_area*, the robot must violate $\Box\neg$*office*. A strategy in which the office is entered only once, and satisfies $\Diamond\Box\neg$*office*, is preferable to one which enters the office over and over again, and only satisfies $\Box\Diamond\neg$*office*. Thus, we want to synthesize a strategy $\mathcal{T}$ maximizing $val(\mathcal{T},\Box\neg$*office*$)$.

In order to compare implementations with respect to their satisfaction of a conjunction $\Box\varphi_1 \wedge \ldots \wedge \Box\varphi_n$ of several safety specifications, we will extend the above definition. We consider the case when the specifier has not expressed any preference for the individual conjuncts. Consider the following example.

Example 2. We consider again the restaurant robot, now with two soft specifications. The soft specification $\Box(\textit{req1} \rightarrow \bigcirc \textit{table1})$ requires that each request by Table 1 is served immediately at the next time instance. Similarly, $\Box(\textit{req2} \rightarrow \bigcirc \textit{table2})$, requires the same for table number 2. Since the robot cannot be at both tables simultaneously, formalized as the hard specification $\Box(\neg\textit{table1} \vee \neg\textit{table2})$, the conjunction of these requirements is unrealizable. Unless the two tables have priorities, it is preferable to satisfy each of $\textit{req1} \rightarrow \bigcirc \textit{table1}$ and $\textit{req2} \rightarrow \bigcirc \textit{table2}$ infinitely often, rather than serve one and the same table all the time.

Quantitative semantics of conjunctions. To capture the idea illustrated in Example 2, we define a value function, which, intuitively, gives higher values to transition systems in which a fewer number of soft specifications have low values. Formally, let *the value of* $\Box\varphi_1 \wedge \ldots \wedge \Box\varphi_n$ *in* $\mathcal{T}$ be

$$val(\mathcal{T},\Box\varphi_1 \wedge \ldots \wedge \Box\varphi_n) \overset{\text{def}}{=} \left(\sum_{i=1}^{n} v_{i,1}, \sum_{i=1}^{n} v_{i,2}, \sum_{i=1}^{n} v_{i,3} \right),$$

where $val(\mathcal{T},\Box\varphi_i) = (v_{i,1}, v_{i,2}, v_{i,3})$ for $i \in \{1, \ldots, n\}$. To compare transition systems according to these values, we use lexicographic ordering on $\{0, \ldots, n\}^3$.

Example 3. For the specifications in Example 2, the above value function assigns value $(2,0,0)$ to a system satisfying $\Box\Diamond(\textit{req1} \rightarrow \bigcirc \textit{table1})$ and $\Box\Diamond(\textit{req2} \rightarrow$

$\bigcirc$ table2), but neither of $\Diamond \Box (req1 \rightarrow \bigcirc table1)$ and $\Diamond \Box (req2 \rightarrow \bigcirc table2)$. It assigns the smaller value $(1, 1, 1)$ to an implementation that gives priority to Table 1 and satisfies $\Box (req1 \rightarrow \bigcirc table1)$ but not $\Box \Diamond (req2 \rightarrow \bigcirc table2)$.

According to the above definition, a transition system that satisfies all soft requirements to some extent is considered better in the lexicographic ordering than a transition system that satisfies one of them and violates all the others. We could instead inverse the order of the sums in the triple, thus giving preference to satisfying some soft specification, over having some lower level of satisfaction over all of them. The next example illustrates the differences between the two variations.

Example 4. For the two soft specifications from Example 2, reversing the order of the sums in the definition of $val(\mathcal{T}, \Box \varphi_1 \wedge \ldots \wedge \Box \varphi_n)$ results in giving the higher value $(1, 1, 1)$ to a transition system that satisfies $\Box (req1 \rightarrow \bigcirc table1)$ but not $\Box \Diamond (req2 \rightarrow \bigcirc table2)$, and the lower value $(0, 0, 2)$ to the one that guarantees only $\Box \Diamond (req1 \rightarrow \bigcirc table1)$ and $\Box \Diamond (req2 \rightarrow \bigcirc table2)$. The most suitable ordering usually depends on the specific application.

In [7] we discuss generalizations of the framework, where the user provides a set of relaxations for each of the soft specifications, and possibly a priority ordering among the soft specifications, or numerical weights.

2.3 Maximum Realizability

Using the definition of quantitative satisfaction of soft safety specifications, we now define the maximum realizability problem, which asks to synthesize a transition system that satisfies a given *hard* LTL specification, and is optimal with respect to the satisfaction of a conjunction of *soft* safety specifications.

Maximum realizability problem: Given an LTL formula φ and formulas $\Box \varphi_1, \ldots, \Box \varphi_n$, where each φ_i is a safety LTL formula, the maximum realizability problem asks to determine if there exists a transition system $\mathcal{T}$ such that $\mathcal{T} \models \varphi$, and if the answer is positive, to synthesize a transition system $\mathcal{T}$ such that $\mathcal{T} \models \varphi$, and such that for every transition system $\mathcal{T}'$ with $\mathcal{T}' \models \varphi$ it holds that $val(\mathcal{T}, \Box \varphi_1 \wedge \ldots \wedge \Box \varphi_n) \geq val(\mathcal{T}', \Box \varphi_1 \wedge \ldots \wedge \Box \varphi_n)$.

Bounded maximum realizability problem: Given an LTL formula φ and formulas $\Box \varphi_1, \ldots, \Box \varphi_n$, where each φ_i is a safety LTL formula, and a bound $b \in \mathbb{N}_{>0}$, the bounded maximum realizability problem asks to determine if there exists a transition system $\mathcal{T}$ with $|\mathcal{T}| \leq b$ such that $\mathcal{T} \models \varphi$, and if the answer is positive, to synthesize a transition system $\mathcal{T}$ such that $\mathcal{T} \models \varphi$, $|\mathcal{T}| \leq b$ and such that for every transition system $\mathcal{T}'$ with $\mathcal{T}' \models \varphi$ and $|\mathcal{T}'| \leq b$, it holds that $val(\mathcal{T}, \Box \varphi_1 \wedge \ldots \wedge \Box \varphi_n) \geq val(\mathcal{T}', \Box \varphi_1 \wedge \ldots \wedge \Box \varphi_n)$.

3   Preliminaries

In this section we recall bounded synthesis, introduced in [17], and in particular the approach based on reduction to SAT. We begin with the necessary preliminaries from automata theory, and the notion of annotated transition systems.

3.1 Bounded Synthesis

A *Büchi automaton* over a finite alphabet Σ is a tuple $\mathcal{A} = (Q, q_0, \delta, F)$, where Q is a finite set of states, q_0 is the initial state, $\delta \subseteq Q \times \Sigma \times Q$ is the transition relation, and $F \subseteq Q$ is a subset of the set of states. A run of $\mathcal{A}$ on an infinite word $w = \sigma_0 \sigma_1 \ldots \in \Sigma^\omega$ is an infinite sequence $q_0, q_1, \ldots$ of states, where q_0 is the initial state and for every $i \geq 0$ it holds that $(q_i, \sigma_i, q_{i+1}) \in \delta$.

A run of a Büchi automaton is accepting if it contains infinitely many occurrences of states in F. A *co-Büchi automaton* $\mathcal{A} = (Q, q_0, \delta, F)$ differs from a Büchi automaton in the accepting condition: a run of a co-Büchi automaton is accepting if it contains only *finitely many* occurrences of states in F. For a Büchi automaton the states in F are called *accepting states*, while for a co-Büchi automaton they are called *rejecting states*. A *nondeterministic* automaton $\mathcal{A}$ accepts a word $w \in \Sigma^\omega$ if *some* run of $\mathcal{A}$ on w is accepting. A *universal* automaton $\mathcal{A}$ accepts a word $w \in \Sigma^\omega$ if *every* run of $\mathcal{A}$ on w is accepting.

The *run graph* of a universal automaton $\mathcal{A} = (Q, q_0, \delta, F)$ on a transition system $\mathcal{T} = (S, s_0, \tau)$ is the unique graph $G = (V, E)$ with set of nodes $V = S \times Q$ and set of labelled edges $E \subseteq V \times \Sigma \times V$ such that $((s, q), \sigma, (s', q')) \in E$ iff $(q, \sigma, q') \in \delta$ and $\tau(s, \sigma \cap \mathcal{I}) = (s', \sigma \cap \mathcal{O})$. That is, G is the product of $\mathcal{A}$ and $\mathcal{T}$.

A run graph of a universal Büchi (resp. co-Büchi) automaton is accepting if every infinite path $(s_0, q_0), (s_1, q_1), \ldots$ contains infinitely (resp. finitely) many occurrences of states q_i in F. A transition system $\mathcal{T}$ is accepted by a universal automaton $\mathcal{A}$ if the unique run graph of $\mathcal{A}$ on $\mathcal{T}$ is accepting. We denote with $\mathcal{L}(\mathcal{A})$ the set of transition systems accepted by $\mathcal{A}$.

The bounded synthesis approach is based on the fact that for every LTL formula φ one can construct a universal co-Büchi automaton $\mathcal{A}_\varphi$ with at most $2^{O(|\varphi|)}$ states such that $\mathcal{T} \in \mathcal{L}(\mathcal{A}_\varphi)$ iff $\mathcal{T} \models \varphi$ for every transition system $\mathcal{T}$ [13].

An *annotation* of a transition system $\mathcal{T} = (S, s_0, \tau)$ with respect to a universal co-Büchi automaton $\mathcal{A} = (Q, q_0, \delta, F)$ is a function $\lambda : S \times Q \rightarrow \mathbb{N} \cup \{\bot\}$ that maps nodes of the run graph of $\mathcal{A}$ on $\mathcal{T}$ to the set $\mathbb{N} \cup \{\bot\}$. Intuitively, such an annotation is valid if every node (s, q) that is reachable from the node (s_0, q_0) is annotated with a natural number, which is an upper bound on the number of rejecting states visited on any path from (s_0, q_0) to (s, q).

Formally, an annotation $\lambda : S \times Q \rightarrow \mathbb{N} \cup \{\bot\}$ is *valid* if

- $\lambda(s_0, q_0) \neq \bot$, i.e., the pair of initial states is labelled with a number, and
- whenever $\lambda(s, q) \neq \bot$, then for every edge $((s, q), \sigma, (s', q'))$ in the run graph of $\mathcal{A}$ on $\mathcal{T}$ we have that (s', q') is annotated with a number (i.e., $\lambda(s', q') \neq \bot$), such that $\lambda(s', q') \geq \lambda(s, q)$, and if $q' \in F$, then $\lambda(s', q') > \lambda(s, q)$.

Valid annotations of finite-state systems correspond to accepting run graphs. An annotation λ is *c-bounded* if $\lambda(s, q) \in \{0, \ldots, c\} \cup \{\bot\}$ for all $s \in S$ and $q \in Q$.

The synthesis method proposed in [10,17] employs the following result in order to reduce the bounded synthesis problem to checking the satisfiability of propositional formulas: A transition system $\mathcal{T}$ is accepted by a universal co-Büchi automaton $\mathcal{A} = (Q, q_0, \delta, F)$ iff there exists a $(|\mathcal{T}| \cdot |F|)$-bounded valid annotation for $\mathcal{T}$ and $\mathcal{A}$. One can estimate a bound on the size of the transition system, which allows to reduce the synthesis problem to its bounded version. Namely, if there exists a transition system that satisfies an LTL formula φ, then there exists a transition system satisfying φ with at most $\left(2^{(|\mathsf{subf}(\varphi)|+\log|\varphi|)}\right)!^2$ states.

Let $\mathcal{A} = (Q, q_0, \delta, F)$ be a universal co-Büchi automaton for the LTL formula φ. Given a bound b on the size of the sought transition system $\mathcal{T}$, the bounded synthesis problem can be encoded as a satisfiability problem with the following sets of propositional variables and constraints.

Variables: The variables represent the sought transition system $\mathcal{T}$, and the sought valid annotation λ of the run graph of $\mathcal{A}$ on $\mathcal{T}$. A transition system with b states $S = \{1, \ldots, b\}$ is represented by Boolean variables $\tau_{s,\sigma_I,s'}$ and o_{s,σ_I} for every $s, s' \in S$, $\sigma_I \in 2^{\mathcal{I}}$, and output proposition $o \in \mathcal{O}$. The variable $\tau_{s,\sigma_I,s'}$ encodes the existence of transition from s to s' on input σ_I, and the variable o_{s,σ_I} encodes o being true in the output from state s on input σ_I.

The annotation λ is represented by the following variables. For each $s \in S$ and $q \in Q$, there is a Boolean variable $\lambda_{s,q}^{\mathbb{B}}$ and a vector $\lambda_{s,q}^{\mathbb{N}}$ of $\log(b \cdot |F|)$ Boolean variables: the variable $\lambda_{s,q}^{\mathbb{B}}$ encodes the reachability of (s,q) from the initial node (s_0, q_0) in the corresponding run graph, and the vector of variables $\lambda_{s,q}^{\mathbb{N}}$ represents the bound for the node (s,q). The constraints are as follows.

Constraints for input-enabled $\mathcal{T}$: $C_\tau \overset{\text{def}}{=} \bigwedge_{s \in S} \bigwedge_{\sigma_I \in 2^{\mathcal{I}}} \bigvee_{s' \in S} \tau_{s,\sigma_I,s'}$.

Constraints for valid annotation:

$$C_\lambda \overset{\text{def}}{=} \lambda_{s_0,q_0}^{\mathbb{B}} \wedge$$

$$\bigwedge_{q,q' \in Q} \bigwedge_{s,s' \in S} \bigwedge_{\sigma_I \in 2^{\mathcal{I}}} \left(\left(\lambda_{s,q}^{\mathbb{B}} \wedge \delta_{s,q,\sigma_I,q'} \wedge \tau_{s,\sigma_I,s'} \right) \to \mathsf{succ}_\lambda(s,q,s',q') \right),$$

where $\delta_{s,q,\sigma_I,q'}$ is a formula over the variables o_{s,σ_I} that characterizes the transitions in $\mathcal{A}$ between q and q' on labels consistent with σ_I, and $\mathsf{succ}_\lambda(s,q,s',q')$ is a formula over the annotation variables such that $\mathsf{succ}_\lambda(s,q,s',q') \overset{\text{def}}{=} (\lambda_{s',q'}^{\mathbb{B}} \wedge (\lambda_{s',q'}^{\mathbb{N}} > \lambda_{s,q}^{\mathbb{N}}))$ if $q' \in F$, and $\mathsf{succ}_\lambda(s,q,s',q') \overset{\text{def}}{=} (\lambda_{s',q'}^{\mathbb{B}} \wedge (\lambda_{s',q'}^{\mathbb{N}} \geq \lambda_{s,q}^{\mathbb{N}}))$ if $q' \notin F$.

3.2 Maximum Satisfiability (MaxSAT)

While the bounded synthesis problem can be encoded into SAT, for the synthesis of a transition system that satisfies a set of soft specifications "as much as possible", we need to solve an optimization problem. To this end, we reduce the bounded maximum realizability problem to a *partial weighted MaxSAT problem*.

MaxSAT is a Boolean optimization problem. A MaxSAT instance is a conjunction of clauses, each of which is a disjunction of literals, where a literal is a Boolean variable or its negation. The objective in MaxSAT is to compute a variable assignment that maximizes the number of satisfied clauses. In *weighted MaxSAT*, each clause is associated with a positive numerical weight and the objective is now to maximize the sum of the weights of the satisfied clauses. In *partial weighted MaxSAT*, there are two types of clauses, namely *hard* and *soft* clauses, where only the soft clauses have weights. A solution to a partial weighted

MaxSAT formula is a variable assignment satisfying all the hard clauses. An optimal solution additionally maximizes the sum of the weights of the soft clauses.

In the encoding in the next section we use hard clauses for the hard specification, and soft clauses to capture the soft specifications in the maximum realizability problem. The weights for the soft clauses will encode the lexicographic ordering on values of conjunctions of soft specifications.

4 From Maximum Realizability to MaxSAT

We now describe the proposed MaxSAT-based approach to maximum realizability. First, we establish an upper bound on the minimal size of an implementation that satisfies a given LTL specification φ and maximizes the satisfaction of a conjunction of the soft specifications $\Box\varphi_1, \ldots, \Box\varphi_n$ according to the value function defined in Sect. 2.2. This bound can be used to reduce the maximum realizability problem to its bounded version, which we encode as a MaxSAT problem.

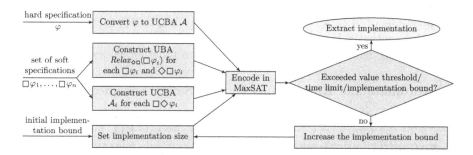

Fig. 1. Schematic overview of the maximum realizability procedure.

4.1 Bounded Maximum Realizability

To establish an upper bound on the minimal (in terms of size) optimal implementation, we make use of an important property of the function *val* defined in Sect. 2.2. Namely, the property that for each of the possible values of $\Box\varphi_1 \wedge \ldots \wedge \Box\varphi_n$ there is a corresponding LTL formula that encodes this value in the classical LTL semantics, as we formally state in the next lemma.

Lemma 1. *For every transition system $\mathcal{T}$ and soft safety specifications $\Box\varphi_1, \ldots, \Box\varphi_n$, if $val(\mathcal{T}, \Box\varphi_1 \wedge \ldots \wedge \Box\varphi_n) = v$, then there exists an LTL formula ψ_v where*

(1) $\psi_v = \varphi'_1 \wedge \ldots \wedge \varphi'_n$, where $\varphi'_i \in \{\Box\varphi_i, \Diamond\Box\varphi_i, \Box\Diamond\varphi_i, true\}$ for $i = 1, \ldots, n$,
(2) $\mathcal{T} \models \psi_v$, and for every $\mathcal{T}'$, if $\mathcal{T}' \models \psi_v$, then $val(\mathcal{T}', \Box\varphi_1 \wedge \ldots \wedge \Box\varphi_n) \geq v$.

The following theorem is a consequence of Lemma 1.

Theorem 1. *Given an LTL specification φ and soft safety specifications $\Box\varphi_1, \ldots, \Box\varphi_n$, if there exists a transition system $\mathcal{T} \models \varphi$, then there exists $\mathcal{T}^*$ such that*

(1) $val(\mathcal{T}^*, \Box\varphi_1 \wedge \ldots \wedge \Box\varphi_n) \geq val(\mathcal{T}, \Box\varphi_1 \wedge \ldots \wedge \Box\varphi_n)$ for all $\mathcal{T}$ with $\mathcal{T} \models \varphi$,
(2) $\mathcal{T}^* \models \varphi$ and $|\mathcal{T}^*| \leq \left((2^{(b+\log b)})!\right)^2$,

where $b = \max\{|\mathsf{subf}(\varphi \wedge \varphi_1' \wedge \ldots \wedge \varphi_n')| \mid \forall i : \varphi_i' \in \{\Box\varphi_i, \Diamond\Box\varphi_i, \Box\Diamond\varphi_i\}\}$.

Lemma 1 immediately provides a naive synthesis procedure, which searches for an optimal implementation by enumerating possible ψ_v formulas and solving the corresponding realizability questions. The total number of these formulas is 4^n, where n is the number of soft specifications. The approach that we propose avoids this rapid growth, by reducing the optimization problem to a single MaxSAT instance, making use of the power of state-of-the-art MaxSAT solvers.

Figure 1 gives an overview of our maximum realizability procedure and the automata constructions it involves. As in the bounded synthesis approach, we construct a universal co-Büchi automaton $\mathcal{A}$ for the hard specification φ. For each soft specification $\Box\varphi_i$ we construct a pair of automata corresponding to the relaxations of $\Box\varphi_i$, as shown in Fig. 1. The relaxation $\Box\Diamond\varphi_i$ is treated as in bounded synthesis. For $\Box\varphi_i$ and $\Diamond\Box\varphi_i$ we construct a single universal Büchi automaton and define a corresponding annotation function as described next.

4.2 Automata and Annotations for Soft Safety Specifications

We present here the reduction to MaxSAT for the case when each soft specification is of the form $\Box\psi$ where ψ is a syntactically safe LTL formula. In this case, we construct a single automaton for both $\Box\psi$ and its relaxation $\Diamond\Box\psi$, and encode the existence of a single annotation function in the MaxSAT problem. The size of this automaton is at most exponential in the length of $\Box\psi$.

In the general case, we can treat $\Box\psi$ and $\Diamond\Box\psi$ separately, in the same way that we treat the relaxation $\Box\Diamond\psi$ of $\Box\psi$ in the presented encoding. That would require in total three instead of two annotation functions per soft specification.

We now describe the construction of a universal Büchi automaton $\mathcal{B}_{\Box\psi}$ for the safety specification $\Box\psi$ and show how we can modify it to obtain an automaton $Relax_{\Diamond\Box}(\Box\psi)$ that incorporates the relaxation of $\Box\psi$ to $\Diamond\Box\psi$.

We first construct a universal Büchi automaton $\mathcal{B}_{\Box\psi} = (Q_{\Box\psi}, q_0^{\Box\psi}, \delta_{\Box\psi}, F_{\Box\psi})$ for $\Box\psi$ such that $\mathcal{L}(\mathcal{B}_{\Box\psi}) = \{\mathcal{T} \mid \mathcal{T} \models \Box\psi\}$ and $\mathcal{B}_{\Box\psi}$ has a unique non-accepting sink state. That is, there exists a unique state $\mathsf{rej}_\psi \in Q_{\Box\psi}$ such that $F_{\Box\psi} = Q_{\Box\psi} \setminus \{\mathsf{rej}_\psi\}$, and $\{q \in Q_{\Box\psi} \mid (\mathsf{rej}_\psi, \sigma, q) \in \delta_{\Box\psi}\} = \{\mathsf{rej}_\psi\}$ for all $\sigma \in \Sigma$.

From $\mathcal{B}_{\Box\psi}$, we obtain a universal Büchi automaton $Relax_{\Diamond\Box}(\Box\psi)$ constructed by redirecting all the transitions leading to rej_ψ to the initial state $q_0^{\Box\psi}$. Formally, $Relax_{\Diamond\Box}(\Box\psi) = (Q, q_0, \delta, F)$, where $Q = Q_{\Box\psi} \setminus \{\mathsf{rej}_\psi\}$, $q_0 = q_0^{\Box\psi}$, $F = F_{\Box\psi}$ and $\delta = \left(\delta_{\Box\psi} \setminus \{(q, \sigma, q') \in \delta_{\Box\psi} \mid q' = \mathsf{rej}_\psi\}\right) \cup \{(q, \sigma, q_0) \mid (q, \sigma, \mathsf{rej}_\psi) \in \delta_{\Box\psi}\}$.

Let $Rej(Relax_{\Diamond\Box}(\Box\psi)) = \{(q, \sigma, q_0) \in \delta \mid (q, \sigma, \mathsf{rej}_\psi) \in \delta_\psi\}$ be the set of transitions in $Relax_{\Diamond\Box}(\Box\psi)$ that correspond to transitions in $\mathcal{B}_{\Box\psi}$ leading to rej_ψ.

The automaton $Relax_{\Diamond\Box}(\Box\psi)$ has the property that its run graph on a transition system $\mathcal{T}$ does not contain a reachable edge corresponding to a transition in $Rej(Relax_{\Diamond\Box}(\Box\psi))$ iff $\mathcal{T}$ is accepted by the automaton $\mathcal{B}_{\Box\psi}$, (i.e., $\mathcal{T} \models \Box\psi$). Otherwise, if the run graph of $Relax_{\Diamond\Box}(\Box\psi)$ on $\mathcal{T}$ contains a reachable edge that belongs to $Rej(Relax_{\Diamond\Box}(\Box\psi))$, then $\mathcal{T} \not\models \Box\psi$. However, if each infinite path in the run graph contains only a finite number of occurrences of such edges, then $\mathcal{T} \models \Diamond\Box\psi$. Based on these observations, we define an annotation function that annotates each node in the run graph with an upper bound on the number of edges in $Rej(Relax_{\Diamond\Box}(\Box\psi))$ visited on any path reaching the node.

A function $\pi : S \times Q \to \mathbb{N} \cup \{\bot\}$ is a $\Diamond\Box$-*valid* annotation for a transition system $\mathcal{T} = (S, s_0, \tau)$ and the automaton $Relax_{\Diamond\Box}(\Box\psi) = (Q, q_0, \delta, F)$ if

(1) $\pi(s_0, q_0) \neq \bot$, i.e., the pair of initial states is labelled with a number, and
(2) if $\pi(s, q) \neq \bot$, then for every edge $((s, q), \sigma, (s', q'))$ in the run graph of $Relax_{\Diamond\Box}(\Box\psi)$ on $\mathcal{T}$ we have that $\pi(s', q') \neq \bot$, and
  • if $(q, \sigma, q') \in Rej(Relax_{\Diamond\Box}(\Box\psi))$, then $\pi(s', q') > \pi(s, q)$, and
  • if $(q, \sigma, q') \notin Rej(Relax_{\Diamond\Box}(\Box\psi))$, then $\pi(s', q') \geq \pi(s, q)$.

This guarantees that $\mathcal{T} \models \Diamond\Box\psi$ iff there exists a $\Diamond\Box$-valid $|\mathcal{T}|$-bounded annotation π for $\mathcal{T}$ and $Relax_{\Diamond\Box}(\Box\psi)$. Moreover, if π is $|\mathcal{T}|$-bounded and $\pi(s_0, q_0) = |\mathcal{T}|$, then $\mathcal{T} \models \Box\psi$, as this means that no edge in $Rej(Relax_{\Diamond\Box}(\Box\psi))$ is reached.

4.3 MaxSAT Encoding of Bounded Maximum Realizability

Let $\mathcal{A} = (Q, q_0, \delta, F)$ be a universal co-Büchi automaton for the LTL formula φ.

For each formula $\Box\varphi_j$, $j \in \{1, \ldots, n\}$, we consider two universal automata: the universal Büchi automaton $\mathcal{B}_j = Relax_{\Diamond\Box}(\Box\varphi_j) = (Q_j, q_0^j, \delta_j, F_j)$, constructed as described in Sect. 4.2, and a universal co-Büchi automaton $\mathcal{A}_j = (\widehat{Q}_j, \widehat{q}_0^j, \widehat{\delta}_j, \widehat{F}_j)$ for the formula $\Box\Diamond\varphi_j$. Given a bound b on the size of the sought transition system, we encode the bounded maximum realizability problem as a MaxSAT problem with the following sets of variables and constraints.

Variables: The MaxSAT formulation includes the variables from the SAT formulation of the bounded synthesis problem, which represent the sought transition system $\mathcal{T}$ and the sought valid annotation of the run graph of $\mathcal{A}$ on $\mathcal{T}$. Additionally, it includes variables for representing the annotations π_j and λ_j for $\mathcal{B}_j$ and $\mathcal{A}_j$ respectively, similarly to λ in the SAT encoding. More precisely, the annotations for π_j and λ_j are represented respectively by variables $\pi_{s,q}^{\mathbb{B},j}$ and $\pi_{s,q}^{\mathbb{N},j}$ where $s \in S$ and $q \in Q_j$, and variables $\lambda_{s,q}^{\mathbb{B},j}$ and $\lambda_{s,q}^{\mathbb{N},j}$ where $s \in S$ and $q \in \widehat{Q}_j$.

The set of constraints includes C_τ and C_λ from the SAT formulation as hard constraints, as well as the following constraints for the new annotations.

Hard constraints for valid annotations: For each $j = 1, \ldots, n$, let

$$C_\pi^j \overset{\text{def}}{=} \bigwedge_{q,q' \in Q_j} \bigwedge_{s,s' \in S} \bigwedge_{\sigma_I \in 2^{\mathcal{I}}} \left((\pi_{s,q}^{\mathbb{B},j} \wedge \delta_{s,q,\sigma_I,q'}^j \wedge \tau_{s,\sigma_I,s'}) \to \mathsf{succ}_\pi^j(s, q, s', q', \sigma_I) \right),$$

$$C_\lambda^j \overset{\text{def}}{=} \bigwedge_{q,q' \in \widehat{Q}_j} \bigwedge_{s,s' \in S} \bigwedge_{\sigma_I \in 2^{\mathcal{I}}} \left((\lambda_{s,q}^{\mathbb{B},j} \wedge \widehat{\delta}_{s,q,\sigma_I,q'}^j \wedge \tau_{s,\sigma_I,s'}) \to \mathsf{succ}_\lambda^j(s, q, s', q', \sigma_I) \right),$$

where $\mathsf{succ}_\pi^j(s,q,s',q',\sigma_I) \overset{\text{def}}{=} \pi_{s',q'}^{\mathrm{B},j} \wedge \big(\mathsf{rej}^j(s,q,q',\sigma_I) \to \pi_{s',q'}^{\mathrm{N},j} > \pi_{s,q}^{\mathrm{N},j}\big) \wedge$
$$\big(\neg\mathsf{rej}^j(s,q,q',\sigma_I) \to \pi_{s',q'}^{\mathrm{N},j} \geq \pi_{s,q}^{\mathrm{N},j}\big),$$

and $\mathsf{rej}^j(s,q,q',\sigma_I)$ is a formula over o_{s,σ_I} obtained from $Rej(\mathcal{B}_j)$. The formula $\mathsf{succ}_\lambda^j(s,\widehat{q},s',\widehat{q}',\sigma_I)$ is analogous to $\mathsf{succ}_\lambda(s,q,s',q',\sigma_I)$ defined in Sect. 3.1.

Soft constraints for valid annotations: Let $b \in \mathbb{N}_{>0}$ be the bound on the size of the transition system. For each $j = 1,\ldots,n$ we define

$$\begin{aligned}
Soft_\square^j &\overset{\text{def}}{=} \pi_{s_0,q_0}^{\mathrm{B},j} \wedge (\pi_{s_0,q_0}^{\mathrm{N},j} = b) && \text{with weight } 1,\\
Soft_{\lozenge\square}^j &\overset{\text{def}}{=} \pi_{s_0,q_0}^{\mathrm{B},j} && \text{with weight } n, \text{ and}\\
Soft_{\square\lozenge}^j &\overset{\text{def}}{=} \pi_{s_0,q_0}^{\mathrm{B},j} \vee \lambda_{s_0,\widehat{q}_0}^{\mathrm{B},j} && \text{with weight } n^2.
\end{aligned}$$

The definition of the soft constraints guarantees that $\mathcal{T} \models \square\varphi_j$ if and only if there exist corresponding annotations that satisfy all three of the soft constraints for $\square\varphi_j$. Similarly, if $\mathcal{T} \models \lozenge\square\varphi_j$, then $Soft_{\lozenge\square}^j$ and $Soft_{\square\lozenge}^j$ can be satisfied.

The definition of the weights of the soft clauses reflects the ordering of transition systems with respect to their satisfaction of $\square\varphi_1 \wedge \ldots \wedge \square\varphi_n$. This guarantees that a transition system extracted from an optimal satisfying assignment for the MaxSAT problem is optimal with respect to the value of $\square\varphi_1 \wedge \ldots \wedge \square\varphi_n$, as stated in the following theorem that establishes the correctness of the encoding.

Theorem 2. *Let $\mathcal{A}$ be a given co-Büchi automaton for φ, and for each $j \in \{1,\ldots,n\}$, let $\mathcal{B}_j = Relax_{\lozenge\square}(\square\varphi_j)$ be the universal automaton for $\square\varphi_j$ constructed as in Sect. 4.2, and let $\mathcal{A}_j$ be a universal co-Büchi automaton for $\square\lozenge\varphi_j$. The constraint system for bound $b \in \mathbb{N}_{>0}$ is satisfiable if and only if there exists an implementation $\mathcal{T}$ with $|\mathcal{T}| \leq b$ such that $\mathcal{T} \models \varphi$. Furthermore, from the optimal satisfying assignment to the variables $\tau_{s,\sigma_I,s'}$ and o_{s,σ_I}, one can extract a transition system $\mathcal{T}^*$ such that for every transition system $\mathcal{T}$ with $|\mathcal{T}| \leq b$ and $\mathcal{T} \models \varphi$ it holds that $val(\mathcal{T}^*,\square\varphi_1 \wedge \ldots \wedge \square\varphi_n) \geq val(\mathcal{T},\square\varphi_1 \wedge \ldots \wedge \square\varphi_n)$.*

Figure 2 shows a transition system extracted from an optimal satisfying assignment for Example 2 with bound 3 on the implementation size. The transitions depicted in the figure are defined by the values of the variables $\tau_{s,\sigma_I,s'}$. The outputs of the implementation (omitted from the figure) are defined by the values of o_{s,σ_I}. The output in state s_1 when $r1$ is true is $table1 \wedge \neg table2$, and the output in s_2 when $r2$ is true is $\neg table1 \wedge table2$. For all other combinations of state and input the output is $\neg table1 \wedge \neg table2$.

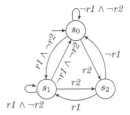

Fig. 2. An optimal implementation for Example 2

5   Experimental Evaluation

We implemented the proposed approach to maximum realizability[1] in Python 2.7. For the LTL to automata translation we use Spot [8] version 2.2.4. MaxSAT

---

[1] The code is available at https://github.com/MahsaGhasemi/max-realizability.

instances are solved by Open-WBO [16] version 2.0. We evaluated our method on instances of two examples. Each experiment was run on machine with a 2.3 GHz Intel Xeon E5-2686 v4 processor and 16 GiB of memory. While the processor is quad-core, only a single core was used. We set a time-out of 1 h.

Robotic Navigation. We applied our method to the strategy synthesis for a robotic museum guide. The robot has to give a tour of the exhibitions in a specific order, which constitutes the hard specification. Preferably, it also avoids certain locations, such as the staff's office, the library, or the passage when it is occupied. These preferences are encoded in the soft specifications. There is one input variable designating the occupancy of the passage, and eight output variables defining the position of the robot. The formal specifications are given in [7].

Table 1 summarizes the results. With implementation bound of 8, the hard specification is realizable, achieving partial satisfaction of soft specifications. This strategy always selects the passage to transition from Exhibition 1 to Exhibition 2 and hence, always avoids the library. It also temporarily violates the requirement of not entering the staff's office, to acquire access to Exhibition 2. Strategies with higher values exists, but they require larger implementation size. However, for implementation bound 10 the solver reaches a time-out.

Table 1. Results of applying the method to the robotic navigation example, with different bounds on implementation size $|T|$. We report the number of variables and clauses in the encoding, the satisfiability of hard constraints, the value (and bound) of the MaxSAT objective function, the running times of Spot and Open-WBO, and the time of the solver plus the time for generating the encoding.

$|T|$	Encoding		Solution		Time (s)		
	# vars	# clauses	Sat.	$\Sigma weights$	Spot	Open-WBO	enc.+solve
2	4051	25366	UNSAT	0 (39)	0.93	0.011	0.12
4	19965	125224	UNSAT	0 (39)	0.93	0.079	0.57
6	45897	289798	UNSAT	0 (39)	0.93	1.75	2.9
8	95617	596430	SAT	31 (39)	0.93	956	959
10	152949	954532	SAT	$-$(39)	0.93	Time-out	Time-out

Power Distribution Network. We consider the problem of dynamic reconfiguration of power distribution networks. A power network consists of a set P of power supplies (generators) and a set L of loads (consumers). The network is a bipartite graph with edges between supplies and loads, where each supply is connected to multiple loads and each load is connected to multiple supplies. Each power supply has an associated capacity, which determines how many loads it can power at a given time. It is possible that not all loads can be powered all the time. Some loads are critical and must be powered continuously, while others are not and should be powered when possible. Some loads can be initializing, meaning they must be powered only initially for several steps. Power supplies can become faulty during operation, which necessitates dynamic network reconfiguration.

We apply our method to the problem of synthesizing a relay-switching strategy from LTL specifications. The input propositions $\mathcal{I}$ determine which, if any, of the supplies are faulty at each step. We are given an upper bound on the number of supplies that can be simultaneously faulty. The set $\mathcal{O}$ of output propositions contains one proposition $s_{l \to p}$ for each load $l \in L$ and each supply $p \in P$ that are connected. The meaning of $s_{l \to p}$ is that l is powered by p.

The hard specification asserts that the critical loads must always be powered, the initializing loads should be powered initially, a load is powered by at most one supply, the capacity of supplies is not exceeded, and when a supply is faulty it is not in use. The soft specifications state that non-critical loads are always powered, and that a powered load should remain powered unless its supply fails.

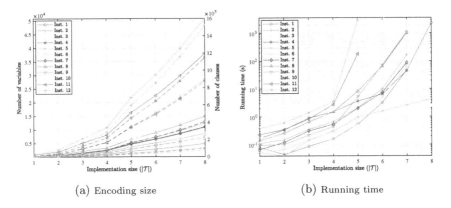

(a) Encoding size   (b) Running time

Fig. 3. Results of applying the method to the instances in Table 2, with different bounds on implementation size $|\mathcal{T}|$. (a) shows the size of the MaxSAT encoding as the number of variables (solid lines) and the number of clauses (dashed lines). (b) shows the running time of the MaxSAT solver plus the time for the encoding.

The specifications are given in [7]. Table 2 describes the instances to which we applied our synthesis method. Power supplies have the same capacity E^+ (number of loads they can power) and at most one can be faulty. We consider three categories of instances, depending on the network connectivity (full or sparse), and whether we restrict frequent switching of supplies. In Fig. 3, we show the results for the instances defined in Table 2 (detailed results in [7]). In the first set of instances, the specifications have large number of variables (due to full connectivity), and the bottleneck is the translation to automata. In the third set of instances, the limiting factor is the number of soft specifications, leading to large weights and number of variables in the MaxSAT formulation.

Table 2. Power distribution network instances. An instance is determined by the number supplies $|P|$, the number of loads $|L|$, the capacity of supplies E^+, the number of critical, non-critical and initializing loads. We also show the number of input $|\mathcal{I}|$ and output $|\mathcal{O}|$ propositions and the number of soft specifications.

Instance #	Network			Load characterization			Specifications		
	$|P|$	$|L|$	E^+	Crit.	Non-crit.	Init.	$|\mathcal{I}|$	$|\mathcal{O}|$	# soft spec.
Fully connected, switching allowed									
1	3	3	1	1	2	0	2	9	2
2	3	6	2	2	4	0	2	18	4
3	3	3	1	0	2	1	2	9	2
4	3	6	2	1	4	1	2	18	4
Sparse, switching allowed									
5	4	2	1	1	1	0	3	4	1
6	4	4	1	1	3	0	3	8	3
7	4	6	1	1	5	0	3	12	5
8	4	8	1	1	7	0	3	16	7
Sparse, switching restricted									
9	4	2	1	1	1	0	3	4	5
10	4	4	1	1	3	0	3	8	11
11	4	6	1	1	5	0	3	12	17
12	4	8	1	1	7	0	3	16	23

We observe that the number of soft specifications is an important factor affecting the scalability of the proposed method. Instance 12, on which the MaxSAT solver reaches time-out for implementation size bound 6, contains 23 soft specifications.

References

1. Almagor, S., Boker, U., Kupferman, O.: Formally reasoning about quality. J. ACM **63**(3), 24:1–24:56 (2016)
2. Alur, R., Kanade, A., Weiss, G.: Ranking automata and games for prioritized requirements. In: Gupta, A., Malik, S. (eds.) CAV 2008. LNCS, vol. 5123, pp. 240–253. Springer, Heidelberg (2008). https://doi.org/10.1007/978-3-540-70545-1_23
3. Baier, C., Katoen, J.-P.: Principles of model checking (2008)
4. Bloem, R., Chatterjee, K., Henzinger, T.A., Jobstmann, B.: Better quality in synthesis through quantitative objectives. In: Bouajjani, A., Maler, O. (eds.) CAV 2009. LNCS, vol. 5643, pp. 140–156. Springer, Heidelberg (2009). https://doi.org/10.1007/978-3-642-02658-4_14
5. Cimatti, A., Roveri, M., Schuppan, V., Tchaltsev, A.: Diagnostic information for realizability. In: Logozzo, F., Peled, D.A., Zuck, L.D. (eds.) VMCAI 2008. LNCS, vol. 4905, pp. 52–67. Springer, Heidelberg (2008). https://doi.org/10.1007/978-3-540-78163-9_9
6. Cimatti, A., Roveri, M., Schuppan, V., Tonetta, S.: Boolean abstraction for temporal logic satisfiability. In: Damm, W., Hermanns, H. (eds.) CAV 2007. LNCS, vol. 4590, pp. 532–546. Springer, Heidelberg (2007). https://doi.org/10.1007/978-3-540-73368-3_53
7. Dimitrova, R., Ghasemi, M., Topcu, U.: Maximum realizability for linear temporal logic specifications. CoRR, abs/1804.00415 (2018)
8. Duret-Lutz, A., Lewkowicz, A., Fauchille, A., Michaud, T., Renault, E., Xu, L.: Spot 2.0 - a framework for LTL and ω-automata manipulation. In: Proceedings of ATVA 2016. LNCS, vol. 9938 (2016)
9. Ehlers, R., Raman, V.: Low-effort specification debugging and analysis. In: Proceedings of SYNT 2014.EPTCS, vol. 157, pp. 117–133 (2014)
10. Finkbeiner, B., Schewe, S.: Bounded synthesis. STTT **15**(5—6), 519–539 (2013)
11. Juma, F., Hsu, E.I., McIlraith, S.A.: Preference-based planning via MaxSAT. In: Kosseim, L., Inkpen, D. (eds.) AI 2012. LNCS (LNAI), vol. 7310, pp. 109–120. Springer, Heidelberg (2012). https://doi.org/10.1007/978-3-642-30353-1_10
12. Kim, K., Fainekos, G.E., Sankaranarayanan, S.: On the minimal revision problem of specification automata. Int. J. Robot. Res. **34**(12), 1515–1535 (2015)
13. Kupferman, O., Vardi, M.Y.: Safraless decision procedures. In: Proceedings of FOCS 2005, pp. 531–542 (2005)
14. Lahijanian, M., Almagor, S., Fried, D., Kavraki, L.E., Vardi, M.Y.: This time the robot settles for a cost: a quantitative approach to temporal logic planning with partial satisfaction. In: Proceedings of AAAI 2015 (2015)
15. Lahijanian, M., Kwiatkowska, M.Z.: Specification revision for markov decision processes with optimal trade-off. In: Proceedings of CDC 2016, pp. 7411–7418 (2016)
16. Martins, R., Manquinho, V., Lynce, I.: Open-WBO: a modular MaxSAT solver. In: Sinz, C., Egly, U. (eds.) SAT 2014. LNCS, vol. 8561, pp. 438–445. Springer, Cham (2014). https://doi.org/10.1007/978-3-319-09284-3_33
17. Schewe, S., Finkbeiner, B.: Bounded synthesis. In: Namjoshi, K.S., Yoneda, T., Higashino, T., Okamura, Y. (eds.) ATVA 2007. LNCS, vol. 4762, pp. 474–488. Springer, Heidelberg (2007). https://doi.org/10.1007/978-3-540-75596-8_33

18. Tabuada, P., Neider, D.: Robust linear temporal logic. In: Proceedings of CSL 2016. LIPIcs, , vol. 62, pp. 10:1–10:21 (2016)
19. Tomita, T., Ueno, A., Shimakawa, M., Hagihara, S., Yonezaki, N.: Safraless LTL synthesis considering maximal realizability. Acta Inform. **54**(7), 655–692 (2017)
20. Tumova, J., Hall, G.C., Karaman, S., Frazzoli, E., Rus, D.: Least-violating control strategy synthesis with safety rules. In: Proceedings of HSCC 2013 (2013)

Ranking and Repulsing Supermartingales for Reachability in Probabilistic Programs

Toru Takisaka[1](✉), Yuichiro Oyabu[1,2], Natsuki Urabe[3], and Ichiro Hasuo[1,2]

[1] National Institute of Informatics, Tokyo, Japan
`takisaka@nii.ac.jp`
[2] The Graduate University for Advanced Studies (SOKENDAI), Hayama, Japan
[3] University of Tokyo, Tokyo, Japan

Abstract. Computing reachability probabilities is a fundamental problem in the analysis of probabilistic programs. This paper aims at a comprehensive and comparative account of various *martingale-based methods* for over- and underapproximating reachability probabilities. Based on the existing works that stretch across different communities (formal verification, control theory, etc.), we offer a unifying account. In particular, we emphasize the role of order-theoretic fixed points—a classic topic in computer science—in the analysis of probabilistic programs. This leads us to two new martingale-based techniques, too. We also make an experimental comparison using our implementation of template-based synthesis algorithms for those martingales.

1 Introduction

Computing *reachability probabilities* is a fundamental problem in the analysis of probabilistic systems. It is known that probabilistic model checking problems can be solved via reachability probabilities [4], much like nondeterministic model checking problems are reduced to emptiness and hence to reachability [29]. While the computation of reachability probabilities for finite-state systems is effectively solved by linear programming, the problem becomes much more challenging for *probabilistic programs*—a paradigm that attracts growing attention as a programming language foundation for machine learning [16]—because their transition graphs are infinite in general.

```
1   x := 2; y := 2; t := 0;
2   while t <= 100 do
3       t := t + 1;
4       z := Unif (−2,1);
5       if * then
6           x := x + z
7       else
8           y := y + z
9       fi
```

Fig. 1. An example of probabilistic programs. The line 4 means that the value of z is randomly sampled from the interval $[-2, 1]$.

Reachability probabilities of probabilistic programs with while loops are clearly not computable, because the problem encompasses termination of (nonprobabilistic) while programs. Therefore the existing research efforts have focused on sound *approximation methods* for reachability probabilities. An approach that is widely used in the literature is to use *ranking supermartingales*—a probabilistic analogue of *ranking functions*—as a witness for the qualitative

S. K. Lahiri and C. Wang (Eds.): ATVA 2018, LNCS 11138, pp. 476–493, 2018.
https://doi.org/10.1007/978-3-030-01090-4_28

Table 1. Martingale-based techniques for approximation of reachability probabilities. MC stands for Markov chains, and PP stands for probabilistic programs

		Certificate for	From
Ranking (super- and sub-) martingale for *under*-approximation	Additive supermartingale (ARnkSupM, Sect. 5)	$\mathbb{E}(\text{steps to } C) \leq ?$	[7, 22]
	γ-Scaled submartingale (γ-SclSubM, Sect. 6)	$\mathbb{P}(\text{reach } C) \geq ?$	This paper for PP, following categorical observations in [28] for MC
Repulsing supermartingale for *over*-approximation	ε-Decreasing supermartingale (ε-RepSupM, Sect. 3)	$\mathbb{P}(\text{reach } C) \leq ?$ $\mathbb{P}(\text{reach } C) <^? 1$	[12], derived from Azuma's martingale concentration inequality
	Nonnegative supermartingale (NNRepSupM, Sect. 4)	$\mathbb{P}(\text{reach } C) \leq ?$	This paper, derived from the Knaster–Tarski theorem ([23, 26], without nondeterminism, derived from Markov's concentration inequality)

question of almost-sure reachability. Ranking supermartingales are amenable to template-based synthesis [7,8,10], making them appealing from the automatic analysis point of view. Recently, methods for quantitatively underapproximating reachability probabilities are also proposed in [12,28].

The dual question of *overapproximating* reachability probabilities, which can then be used to qualitatively *refute* almost-sure reachability, is also considered. In the control theory, supermartingales are used as a probabilistic counterpart of *barrier certificates* [23,26]. A similar idea is recently used for the purpose of synthesizing *stochastic* invariants for probabilistic programs [12]. Here an over-approximation of reachability probability serves as quantitative verification for safety: it gives an upper bound for the probability that the system or the program reaches a bad state.

Table 1 lists four supermartingale-based techniques for over- and underapproximating reachability probabilities. The table is not meant to be exhaustive— still, it shows that multiple methods have been introduced and studied, in different communities (formal verification, control theory, etc.) and with different mathematical backgrounds (ranking functions, martingale concentration inequalities, etc.).

The current work aims at a comprehensive and comparative account of those martingale-based techniques in Table 1. Central to our account is the role of *order-theoretic fixed points*, a classic topic in theoretical computer science. More specifically, we characterize our objectives—namely reachability probability and expected reaching time—as suitable least fixed points. It turns out that a large part of the theory of martingale-based methods can be developed based on this order-theoretic characterization, without using mathematical gadgets unique to probabilistic settings such as martingale concentration inequalities. Our contributions are summarized as follows.

- A comprehensive and comparative account of different martingale-based techniques for approximating reachability probabilities. We identify their key mathematical principles to be order-theoretic fixed points and martingale concentration inequalities, and we emphasize the role of the former.
- We introduce two martingale-based techniques that seem to be new, namely γ-SclSubM and NNRepSupM in Table 1. Their purely probabilistic versions have been in the literature: γ-SclSubM is from a category-theoretic account in [28], and NNRepSupM is from control theory [26]. We extend them to probabilistic programs that additionally have nondeterminism. Moreover, completeness of ARnkSupM for probabilistic programs with real-valued variables seems to be new.
- We formalize those techniques, taking probabilistic programs (with nondeterminism) as the target of analyses. We investigate soundness and completeness of the techniques in Table 1. While the order-theoretic fixed-point foundation gives us clear theoretical guidance, additional nondeterminism requires us to carefully establish measure-theoretic arguments.
- We implemented template-based automated synthesis algorithms for γ-SclSubM, ε-RepSupM and NNRepSupM, following [7,10]. Our experimental results suggest the advantage of γ-SclSubM in quantitative reasoning, and the comparative advantage of NNRepSupM over ε-RepSupM in the quality of bounds.

The paper is organized as follows. Preliminaries are in Sect. 2, where we introduce our system models (pCFGs) for operational semantics of probabilistic programs, and review the theory of order-theoretic fixed points (the Knaster–Tarski and Cousot–Cousot theorems). In Sects. 3–6 we discuss the four techniques in Table 1, offering a unifying account based on order-theoretic fixed points, and providing some new techniques and results. In Sect. 7 we give implementations and experiment results of template-based synthesis. After discussion of related work in Sect. 8, we conclude in Sect. 9. Omitted proofs and details are in [27].

2   Preliminaries

We first fix some notations. We write $\mathbb{N}$ and $\mathbb{R}$ for the set of all natural numbers (i.e. nonnegative integers) and reals, respectively. We use subscripts to denote subsets of $\mathbb{N}$ and $\mathbb{R}$; for example, $\mathbb{R}_{\geq 0}$ denotes the set of all nonnegative reals. We write X^*, X^+, X^ω for the sets of all finite, nonempty finite, and infinite sequences of elements of X, respectively.

We use the Borel measurable structure $\mathcal{B}(\mathbb{R})$ of the set $\mathbb{R}$ of real numbers. This induces the measurable structures of all the other sets used in this paper: $\mathbb{R}^k$ where $k \in \mathbb{N}$, $X \times \mathbb{R}^k$ where X is finite, and so on. The induced measurable structures are defined in a standard manner: for example, $X \times \mathbb{R}^k$ where X is finite, it is given by $\mathcal{B}(X \times \mathbb{R}^k) = (\mathcal{B}(\mathbb{R}^k))^X$. The set of probability distributions on $(X, \mathcal{B}(X))$ is denoted by $\mathcal{D}(X)$. The Dirac measure on $x \in X$ is denoted by δ_x. The *support* $\mathrm{supp}(d)$ of $d \in \mathcal{D}(X)$ is defined by $\mathrm{supp}(d) = \{x \in X \mid \text{for any } A \in \mathcal{B}(X), x \in A \text{ implies } d(A) > 0\}$. The set of all Borel measurable function from X to Y is denoted by $\mathcal{B}(X, Y)$. The functions $\mathbf{0}$ and $\mathbf{1}$ are the real-valued constant function of which coefficient is 0 and 1, respectively.

2.1 Probabilistic Control Flow Graphs (pCFGs)

We take the notion of pCFG from [2] and use it as our model of probabilistic systems. pCFGs can be thought of as a subclass of Markov decision processes (MDPs), but tailored for operational semantics of probabilistic programs (Sect. 2.2).

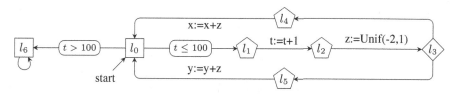

Fig. 2. The pCFG that models the probabilistic program in Fig. 1. Rectangles, diamonds, and pentagons represent deterministic, nondeterministic and assignment locations, respectively. The variables are initially set $x := 2$, $y := 2$ and $t := 0$.

Definition 2.1. (pCFG, [2]) A *probabilistic control flow graph (pCFG)* is a tuple $\Gamma = (L, V, l_{\mathrm{init}}, \boldsymbol{x}_{\mathrm{init}}, \mapsto, \mathrm{Up}, \mathrm{Pr}, G)$ consisting of the following components.

- A finite set L of *locations*, equipped with a partition $L = L_N + L_P + L_D + L_A$ into *nondeterministic*, *probabilistic*, *deterministic* and *assignment* locations.
- A finite set $V = \{x_1, \ldots, x_{|V|}\}$ of *program variables*.
- An *initial location* $l_{\mathrm{init}} \in L$, and an *initial valuation vector* $\boldsymbol{x}_{\mathrm{init}} \in \mathbb{R}^V$.
- A *transition relation* $\mapsto \subseteq L \times L$ which is total (each location has a successor). For $l \in L \setminus L_A$, we write $\mathrm{succ}(l)$ to denote the set of all successors of l, i.e. $\mathrm{succ}(l) = \{l' \in L \mid l \mapsto l'\}$. We require that each assignment location $l \in L_A$ has a unique successor; in this case, $\mathrm{succ}(l)$ denotes this unique location.
- An *update function* $\mathrm{Up} : L_A \to V \times \mathcal{U}$, where $\mathcal{U} = \mathcal{B}(\mathbb{R}^V, \mathbb{R}) \cup \mathcal{D}(\mathbb{R}) \cup \mathcal{B}(\mathbb{R})$. Here, three components of $\mathcal{U}$ represent deterministic, probabilistic and nondeterministic assignment, respectively.
- A family $\mathrm{Pr} = (\mathrm{Pr}_l \in \mathcal{D}(\mathrm{succ}(l)))_{l \in L_P}$ of probability distributions.

480   T. Takisaka et al.

- A *guard function* $G : L_D \times L \to \mathcal{B}(\mathbb{R}^V)$ such that, for each $l \in L_D$, the following hold: (collective exhaustion) $\bigcup_{l \mapsto l'} G(l, l') = \mathbb{R}^V$; and (mutual exclusion) $l \mapsto l'$, $l \mapsto l''$ and $l' \neq l''$ imply $G(l, l') \cap G(l, l'') = \emptyset$. We write $x \models G(l, l')$ if $x \in G(l, l')$.

A *configuration* of a pCFG Γ is a pair $(l, x) \in L \times \mathbb{R}^V$ of a location and a vector. A *successor* (l', x') of a configuration (l, x) is a one such that $l \mapsto l'$ and

- if $l \in L_N \cup L_P$ then $x' = x$;
- if $l \in L_D$ then $x' = x$ and $x \models G(l, l')$; and
- if $l \in L_A$ and $\mathrm{Up}(l) = (x_j, u)$, then $x' = x(x_j \leftarrow a)$. Here $x(x_j \leftarrow a)$ denotes an update of the vector (the x_j-component of x is replaced by a), and (i) $a = u(x)$ if $u \in \mathcal{B}(L \times \mathbb{R}^V, \mathbb{R})$, (ii) $a \in \mathrm{supp}(u)$ if $u \in \mathcal{D}(\mathbb{R})$, and (iii) $a \in u$ if $u \in \mathcal{B}(\mathbb{R})$.

A *finite path* of Γ is a finite sequence $c_0, c_1, \ldots, c_k$ of configurations where c_i is a successor of c_{i-1} for each i. Similarly, A *run* of Γ is an infinite sequence $c_0, c_1, \ldots$ of configurations such that each c_i is a successor of c_{i-1}.

Schedulers resolve nondeterminism. Given a history $c_0 \ldots c_i$ of configurations, it gives a distribution of the successor's location or valuation vector. We assume that a scheduler is *universally measurable*, which is standard in control theory (see e.g. [5]).

If a pCFG Γ and a scheduler σ for Γ are given, then the behavior of Γ is determined for each initial configuration c_0; we represent it by the map $\mu_-^\sigma : (L \times \mathbb{R}^V)^+ \to \mathcal{D}(L \times \mathbb{R}^V)$. For each nonempty sequence $c_0 \ldots c_i$ the distribution $\mu_{c_0 \ldots c_i}^\sigma$ is, intuitively, the distribution of the next configuration given a current history $c_0 \ldots c_i$ of configurations under the scheduler σ. For the set Sch_Γ of all schedulers for Γ we define the following.

Definition 2.2 (reachability probabilities $\mathbb{P}_{C,\sigma}^{\mathrm{reach}}, \overline{\mathbb{P}}_C^{\mathrm{reach}}, \underline{\mathbb{P}}_C^{\mathrm{reach}}$). Let Γ be a pCFG. The *reachability probability* $\mathbb{P}_{C,\sigma}^{\mathrm{reach}}(c)$ from a configuration $c_0 \in L \times \mathbb{R}^V$ to a region $C \in \mathcal{B}(L \times \mathbb{R}^V)$ under a scheduler $\sigma \in \mathrm{Sch}_\Gamma$ is defined by

$$\mathbb{P}_{C,\sigma}^{\mathrm{reach}}(c_0) = \sum_{i \geq 1} \int_{L \times \mathbb{R}^V \setminus C} \mu_{c_0}^\sigma(dc_1) \ldots \int_{L \times \mathbb{R}^V \setminus C} \mu_{c_0 \ldots c_{i-2}}^\sigma(dc_{i-1}) \int_C 1 \mu_{c_0 \ldots c_{i-1}}^\sigma(dc_i)$$

for the case of $c_0 \notin C$, and $\mathbb{P}_{C,\sigma}^{\mathrm{reach}}(c_0) = 1$ otherwise. The *upper reachability probability* $\overline{\mathbb{P}}_C^{\mathrm{reach}}(c)$ from c to C is defined by $\overline{\mathbb{P}}_C^{\mathrm{reach}}(c) = \sup_{\sigma \in \mathrm{Sch}_\Gamma} \mathbb{P}_{C,\sigma}^{\mathrm{reach}}(c)$; the *lower reachability probability* $\underline{\mathbb{P}}_C^{\mathrm{reach}}(c)$ is defined by $\underline{\mathbb{P}}_C^{\mathrm{reach}}(c) = \inf_{\sigma \in \mathrm{Sch}_\Gamma} \mathbb{P}_{C,\sigma}^{\mathrm{reach}}(c)$.

Definition 2.3 (reaching times $\mathbb{E}_{C,\sigma}^{\mathrm{steps}}, \overline{\mathbb{E}}_C^{\mathrm{steps}}, \underline{\mathbb{E}}_C^{\mathrm{steps}}$). Let Γ be a pCFG. The *expected reaching time* of Γ from a configuration $c_0 \in L \times \mathbb{R}^V$ to $C \in \mathcal{B}(L \times \mathbb{R}^V)$ under a scheduler $\sigma \in \mathrm{Sch}_\Gamma$ is defined by

$$\mathbb{E}_{C,\sigma}^{\mathrm{steps}}(c_0) = \sum_{i \geq 1} i \cdot \int_{L \times \mathbb{R}^V \setminus C} \mu_{c_0}^\sigma(dc_1) \ldots \int_{L \times \mathbb{R}^V \setminus C} \mu_{c_0 \ldots c_{i-2}}^\sigma(dc_{i-1}) \int_C 1 \mu_{c_0 \ldots c_{i-1}}^\sigma(dc_i)$$

for the case of $\mathbb{P}_{C,\sigma}^{\text{reach}}(c_0) = 1$, and $\mathbb{E}_{C,\sigma}^{\text{steps}}(c_0) = \infty$ otherwise. The *upper expected reaching time* $\overline{\mathbb{E}}_C^{\text{steps}}(c)$ of Γ from c to C is $\overline{\mathbb{E}}_C^{\text{steps}}(c) = \sup_{\sigma \in \text{Sch}_\Gamma} \mathbb{E}_{C,\sigma}^{\text{steps}}(c)$, and the *lower expected reaching time* is $\underline{\mathbb{E}}_C^{\text{steps}}(c) = \inf_{\sigma \in \text{Sch}_\Gamma} \mathbb{E}_{C,\sigma}^{\text{steps}}(c)$.

2.2   Probabilistic Programs: APP and PPP

The goal of this paper is the reachability analysis of imperative programs with probabilistic and nondeterministic branching. We consider two languages taken from [10,12], called *affine probabilistic programs* (APP) and *polynomial probabilistic programs* (PPP). The two languages differ only in the arithmetic expressions allowed in the assignment commands and Boolean expressions. For example, the assignment command $x := xy + x + 1$ is allowed in PPP but not in APP; $x := 3x + 2y - 1$ is allowed in both since its right-hand side is an affine expression.

Both APP and PPP have the standard control structure in imperative languages—such as if-branches and while-loops. APP and PPP additionally have nondeterministic and probabilistic if-branches (if $\star$ then ... and if **prob**(p) then ..., respectively, where $p \in [0,1]$). They also have nondeterministic and probabilistic assignment commands: $x := \mathbf{ndet}\ A$ where a value is chosen from a set $A \subseteq \mathbb{R}$; and $x := d$ where a value is sampled from a probability distribution d over $\mathbb{R}$.

The definition of the semantical model pCFG (Sect. 2.1) mirrors the structure of these languages. The translation from APP/PPP to pCFGs is straightforward and omitted.

2.3   Order-Theoretic Foundation of Fixed Points

Order-theoretic fixed points are central to computer science, for recursive computation, inductive/coinductive datatypes and reasoning and specification of reactive behaviors, etc. In general, a fixed-point equation can have multiple solutions; often we are interested in extremal solutions: least fixed points (lfp's, for liveness, induction, etc.) and greatest ones (gfp's, for safety, coinduction, etc.). The following fundamental results (in a simple setting of complete lattices) give two different characterizations of lfp's and gfp's.

Theorem 2.4. *Let $(L, \sqsubseteq)$ be a complete lattice, and $f \colon L \to L$ be a monotone function. Then f has the least fixed point μf and the greatest νf. Moreover,*

1. *(Knaster–Tarski) The lfp is the least pre-fixed point: $\mu f = \min\{l \in L \mid f(l) \sqsubseteq l\}$. Similarly, the gfp is the greatest post-fixed point: $\nu f = \max\{l \in L \mid l \sqsubseteq f(l)\}$.*
2. *(Cousot–Cousot [13]) The (potentially transfinite) ascending chain $\bot \sqsubseteq f(\bot) \sqsubseteq f^2(\bot) \sqsubseteq \cdots$ stabilizes to μf. Here $f^\alpha(\bot)$ is defined by obvious induction: $f^{\alpha+1}(\bot) = f(f^\alpha(\bot))$ for a successor ordinal; and $f^\alpha(\bot) = \bigsqcup_{\beta < \alpha} f^\beta(\bot)$ for a limit ordinal.*
   Similarly, the descending chain $\top \sqsupseteq f(\top) \sqsupseteq \cdots$ stabilizes to νf. □

From these characterizations we can derive the following reasoning principles.

Corollary 2.5. – **(lfp-KT)** $f(l) \sqsubseteq l$ implies $\mu f \sqsubseteq l$.
 – **(gfp-KT)** $l \sqsubseteq f(l)$ implies $l \sqsubseteq \nu f$.
 – **(lfp-CC)** For each ordinal α, $f^\alpha(\bot) \sqsubseteq \mu f$.
 – **(gfp-CC)** For each ordinal α, $\nu f \sqsubseteq f^\alpha(\top)$.   □

The arguments so far are symmetric for lfp's and gfp's. However, if one turns to the common proof methods for lfp specifications (termination, reachability, liveness) and those for gfp specifications (safety), a strong contrast emerges. Here is an example.

Lemma 2.6. Let $(S, \mapsto \subseteq S \times S)$ be a Kripke frame, $s_0 \in S$ and $C \subseteq S$.

 – **(Invariant for safety)** Let $I \subseteq S$ be an invariant, that is, $I \subseteq \Box I$. Here $\Box I$ is defined by $\Box I = \{s \in S \mid s \mapsto s' \text{ implies } s' \in I\}$. Assume also that $I \cap C = \emptyset$. Then $s_0 \in I$ implies that there is no path from s_0 to C.
 – **(Ranking function for liveness)** Let $\eta \colon S \to \mathbb{N} \cup \{\infty\}$ be a ranking function for C. That is, 1) for each $s \in S \setminus C$, there is a successor s' such that $\eta(s) \geq \eta(s') + 1$; and 2) for each $s \in S$, $\eta(s) = 0$ implies $s \in C$. Then, $\eta(s_0) \neq \infty$ implies that there is a path from s_0 to C.   □

The difference between the two methods is accounted for by the fact that, in Corollary 2.5, two items give *under*-approximations while the other two give

	Knaster–Tarski	Cousot–Cousot
lfp	overapprox.	underapprox.
gfp	underapprox.	overapprox.

over-approximations. It is clear that the invariant method in Lemma 2.6 comes from (gfp-KT) of Corollary 2.5. Its dual, (lfp-KT), gives only an overapproximation l—it can be used for refutation but not for verification. Similarly, ranking functions come from (lfp-CC)—the role of well-foundedness of the value domain $\mathbb{N}$ mirrors the structure of ordinals. Its dual (gfp-CC) only gives an overapproximation of νf. The situation is summarized in the above table.

The above foundations underpin our technical developments: this is because reachability probabilities and reaching times are characterized as least fixed points. We note that our semantical domains L in later sections need not be complete lattices. In those cases we exploit the ω- and ω^{op}-cpo structures, the corresponding continuity of f, and the *Kleene theorem*. The last is understood as a variation of the Cousot–Cousot theorem.

2.4   Invariants and the Nexttime Operations

In Sects. 3–6 the following definitions will be used.

Definition 2.7 ((pure) invariant for pCFG). Let Γ be a pCFG. A measurable set $I \in \mathcal{B}(L \times \mathbb{R}^V)$ is called a *(pure) invariant* for Γ if $(l_{\mathrm{init}}, \boldsymbol{x}_{\mathrm{init}}) \in I$, and for each $(l, \boldsymbol{x}) \in I$, if $(l', \boldsymbol{x}')$ is a successor of $(l, \boldsymbol{x})$ then $(l', \boldsymbol{x}') \in I$.

Definition 2.8 (the "nexttime" operation $\overline{\mathbb{X}}, \underline{\mathbb{X}}$). Let Γ be a pCFG, I be a pure invariant and $\mathbb{K} \in \mathcal{B}(\mathbb{R})$. For a measurable $\eta : I \to \mathbb{K}$ we define the function $\overline{\mathbb{X}}\eta$ of the same type as η as follows, provided the right-hand side of each equation is well-defined.

- For $l \in L_N$, $(\overline{\mathbb{X}}\eta)(l, \boldsymbol{x}) = \max_{l \mapsto l'} \eta(l', \boldsymbol{x})$.
- For $l \in L_P$, $(\overline{\mathbb{X}}\eta)(l, \boldsymbol{x}) = \sum_{l \mapsto l'} \mathrm{Pr}_l(l')\eta(l', \boldsymbol{x})$.
- For $l \in L_D$, $(\overline{\mathbb{X}}\eta)(l, \boldsymbol{x}) = \eta(l', \boldsymbol{x})$ where l' is the unique location s.t. $\boldsymbol{x} \models G(l, l')$.
- For $l \in L_A$, let $\mathrm{Up}(l) = (x_j, u)$.
  - $(\overline{\mathbb{X}}\eta)(l, \boldsymbol{x}) = \eta(\mathrm{succ}(l), u(\boldsymbol{x}))$ if u is a measurable function.
  - $(\overline{\mathbb{X}}\eta)(l, \boldsymbol{x}) = \int_{x \in \mathrm{supp}(u)} \eta(\mathrm{succ}(l), \boldsymbol{x}(x_j \leftarrow x))\mathrm{d}u$ if u is a distribution.
  - $(\overline{\mathbb{X}}\eta)(l, \boldsymbol{x}) = \sup_{x \in u} \eta(\mathrm{succ}(l), \boldsymbol{x}(x_j \leftarrow x))$ if u is a measurable set.

The function $\underline{\mathbb{X}}\eta : I \to \mathbb{K}$ is defined as above, but replacing max with min in the first line and sup with inf in the last.

Proposition 2.9. *We define a pointwise partial order $\sqsubseteq$ on $\mathcal{B}(I, \mathbb{K})$, i.e. $f \sqsubseteq g$ if and only if $f(c) \leq g(c)$ holds for every $c \in I$. Let $\mathbb{K}$ be a proper closed convex subset of $\mathbb{R} \cup \{\pm\infty\}$. Then $\overline{\mathbb{X}}\eta$ and $\underline{\mathbb{X}}\eta$ are well-defined for every $\eta \in \mathcal{B}(I, \mathbb{K})$, and the following hold.*

1. *The operators $\overline{\mathbb{X}}$ and $\underline{\mathbb{X}}$ are monotone endofunctions over $\mathcal{B}(I, \mathbb{K})$. In particular, $\overline{\mathbb{X}}\eta$ and $\underline{\mathbb{X}}\eta$ are Borel measurable for any $\eta \in \mathcal{B}(I, \mathbb{K})$.*
2. *$\overline{\mathbb{X}}$ is ω-continuous, and $\underline{\mathbb{X}}$ is ω^{op}-continuous.* $\square$

3 ε-Decreasing Repulsing Supermartingales (ε-RepSupM)

In Sects. 3–6 we will discuss the four martingale-based techniques in Table 1. Here we briefly review the notion of ε-decreasing repulsing supermartingale (ε-RepSupM) from [12]. It is, to the best of our knowledge, the only existing martingale-based notion for overapproximating reachability probabilities.

Definition 3.1 (ε-RepSupM [12]). Let Γ be a pCFG, I be a pure invariant, and $C \subseteq I$ be a Borel set. An ε-*repulsing supermartingale* (ε-*RepSupM*) for C supported by I is a measurable function $\eta: I \to \mathbb{R}$ such that i) $\eta(c) \geq (\overline{\mathbb{X}}\eta)(c) + \varepsilon$ for each $c \in I \setminus C$, and ii) $\eta(c) \geq 0$ for each $c \in C$.

Theorem 3.2 (soundness, [12]). *Suppose there exists an ε-RepSupM for C supported by I such that $\eta(l_{\mathrm{init}}, \boldsymbol{x}_{\mathrm{init}}) < 0$. Further assume that η has κ-bounded differences for some $\kappa > 0$, i.e. for each $c \in I$ and its successor c' it holds $|\eta(c) - \eta(c')| \leq \kappa$. Let $\gamma = e^{-\frac{\varepsilon^2}{2(\kappa+\varepsilon)^2}}$ and $\alpha = e^{\frac{\varepsilon \cdot \eta(l_{\mathrm{init}}, \boldsymbol{x}_{\mathrm{init}})}{(\kappa+\varepsilon)^2}}$.*

1. *We have the following inequality:*

$$\overline{\mathbb{P}}_C^{\mathrm{reach}}(l_{\mathrm{init}}, \boldsymbol{x}_{\mathrm{init}}) \leq \alpha \cdot \frac{\gamma^{\lceil |\eta(l_{\mathrm{init}}, \boldsymbol{x}_{\mathrm{init}})|/\kappa \rceil}}{1 - \gamma}. \tag{1}$$

2. *If the right-hand side of (1) is greater than 1, still* $\overline{\mathbb{P}}_C^{\text{reach}}(l_{\text{init}}, x_{\text{init}}) < 1$
   holds. □

We note that for any $\eta \in \mathcal{B}(I, \mathbb{R})$ that has κ-bounded differences, the function $\overline{\mathbb{X}}\eta$ is well-defined. The bound in (1) is derived from *Azuma's concentration inequality*, a well-known martingale concentration lemma that exploits κ-bounded differences. ε-RepSupM is not complete: there exist a pCFG Γ and a set C of configurations such that $\overline{\mathbb{P}}_C^{\text{reach}} < 1$ but no ε-RepSupM can prove it. See Fig. 3 below.

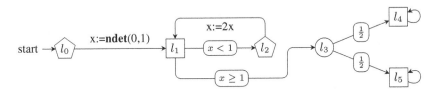

Fig. 3. An example of incompleteness of ε-RepSupM. Probabilistic locations are depicted by circles. This pCFG satisfies $\overline{\mathbb{P}}_{\{l_5\}\times\mathbb{R}}^{\text{reach}}(l_0, 0) = \frac{1}{2}$ but no ε-RepSupM can refute its a.s. reachability. Indeed, any ε-RepSupM η for $\{l_5\} \times \mathbb{R}$ must satisfy $\lim_{x\to+0} \eta(l_1, x) = \infty$ due to the ε-decreasing condition, but such an η cannot have κ-bounded differences at $(l_0, 0)$.

4 Nonnegative Repulsing Supermartingales (NNRepSupM)

We move on to another notion for overapproximating reachability probabilities, *nonnegative repulsing supermartingale* (NNRepSupM). We believe this is new. Compared to the notion of ε-RepSupM, NNRepSupM has the following features.

– NNRepSupM is derived from the theory of order-theoretic fixed points (Sect. 2.3), unlike ε-RepSupM that relies on Azuma's martingale concentration lemma.
– Consequently, we can show soundness and completeness of NNRepSupM rather easily, while ε-RepSupM is sound but not complete.
– We experimentally observe that NNRepSupM often gives better bounds (Sect. 7).

The definition of NNRepSupM resembles *probabilistic barrier certificates* used in control theory [23,26]. Our technical contributions are the following: i) we develop the theory of NNRepSupM in the presence of nondeterminism, while the settings in [23,26] are purely probabilistic; and ii) we characterize NNRepSupM in the general terms of order-theoretic fixed points (Sect. 2.3), unlike the previous theory in [23, 26] that relies on Markov's martingale concentration lemma.[1] The latter unveils the mathematical similarity between NNRepSupM and ARnkSupM (Sect. 5).

The notion comes with upper and lower variants. They are used to overapproximate $\overline{\mathbb{P}}_C^{\mathrm{reach}}$ and $\underline{\mathbb{P}}_C^{\mathrm{reach}}$, respectively (Definition 2.2). In this section we use $\mathbb{K} = [0, \infty]$.

Definition 4.1 (NNRepSupM for pCFG). Let Γ be a pCFG, I be a pure invariant, and $C \subseteq I$ be a Borel set. An *upper nonnegative repulsing supermartingale (U-NNRepSupM)* over Γ for C supported by I is a function $\eta \in \mathcal{B}(I, [0, \infty])$ s.t.

$$(i)\, \eta(c) \geq 1 \text{ for each } c \in C, \text{ and} \qquad (ii)\, \eta(c) \geq \overline{\mathbb{X}}\eta(c) \text{ for each } c \in I \setminus C.$$

The function η is a *lower nonnegative repulsing supermartingale (L-NNRepSupM)* if it satisfies the above conditions, but with $\overline{\mathbb{X}}$ replaced with $\underline{\mathbb{X}}$.

We shall prove soundness and completeness of NNRepSupM, based on the foundations in Sect. 2.3. The following characterization is fundamental.

Proposition 4.2. *In the setting of Definition 4.1, we define endofunctions $\overline{\Phi}_C$ and $\underline{\Phi}_C$ over $\mathcal{B}(I, [0, \infty])$ as follows:*

$$\overline{\Phi}_C(\eta)(x) = \begin{cases} 1 & (x \in C) \\ (\overline{\mathbb{X}}\eta)(x) & (x \notin C), \end{cases} \qquad \underline{\Phi}_C(\eta)(x) = \begin{cases} 1 & (x \in C) \\ (\underline{\mathbb{X}}\eta)(x) & (x \notin C). \end{cases}$$

Then the upper reachability probability $\overline{\mathbb{P}}_C^{\mathrm{reach}} : L \times \mathbb{R}^V \to [0, \infty]^2$ is the least fixed point (lfp) of $\overline{\Phi}_C$. Similarly, $\underline{\mathbb{P}}_C^{\mathrm{reach}}$ is the lfp of $\underline{\Phi}_C$.

Proof. (Sketch) We first need to show that $\overline{\mathbb{P}}_C^{\mathrm{reach}}$ and $\underline{\mathbb{P}}_C^{\mathrm{reach}}$ are Borel measurable. This is not very easy, as they are defined via supremum or infimum over uncountably many schedulers. We use the technique of *ε-optimal scheduler* known from control theory [5].

Checking that $\overline{\mathbb{P}}_C^{\mathrm{reach}}$ and $\underline{\mathbb{P}}_C^{\mathrm{reach}}$ are fixed points is not hard, though laborious. We use ε-optimal schedulers again for interchange between sup./inf. and integration.

Finally, the proofs for minimality differ for $\overline{\mathbb{P}}_C^{\mathrm{reach}}$ and $\underline{\mathbb{P}}_C^{\mathrm{reach}}$. For $\overline{\mathbb{P}}_C^{\mathrm{reach}}$, we first observe that $\overline{\Phi}_C$ is ω-continuous (immediate from Proposition 2.9). Therefore by the Kleene theorem, the lfp of $\overline{\Phi}_C$ is given by $\overline{\Phi}_C^{\omega}(\bot)$ (i.e. the chain in Theorem 2.4 stabilizes after ω steps). We can check the coincidence between $\overline{\Phi}_C^{\omega}(\bot)$ and $\overline{\mathbb{P}}_C^{\mathrm{reach}}$ by direct calculation.

---

[1] We note that the theory of NNRepSupM can also be developed using Markov's lemma.

[2] Precisely it is the restriction of $\overline{\mathbb{P}}_C^{\mathrm{reach}}$ to I; in what follows we do this identification for $\overline{\mathbb{P}}_C^{\mathrm{reach}}$, $\underline{\mathbb{P}}_C^{\mathrm{reach}}$, $\overline{\mathbb{E}}_C^{\mathrm{steps}}$, and $\underline{\mathbb{E}}_C^{\mathrm{steps}}$.

For $\mathbb{P}_C^{\mathrm{reach}}$, let η be a fixed point of Φ_C. Then for each $\varepsilon > 0$, we can construct a scheduler σ such that $\mathbb{P}_{C,\sigma}^{\mathrm{reach}}(c) \sqsubseteq \eta(c) + \varepsilon$ for each c (at the n-th step, σ chooses a $\varepsilon/2^n$-optimal successor). Since $\underline{\mathbb{P}}_C^{\mathrm{reach}} = \inf_\sigma \mathbb{P}_{C,\sigma}^{\mathrm{reach}}$, this proves $\underline{\mathbb{P}}_C^{\mathrm{reach}} \sqsubseteq \eta$. □

It is easy to see that a U-NNRepSupM η is nothing but a pre-fixed point of $\overline{\Phi_C}$ (i.e. $\overline{\Phi_C}(\eta) \sqsubseteq \eta$), and that an L-NNRepSupM η is a pre-fixed point of $\underline{\Phi_C}$. Therefore, soundness and completeness of NNRepSupM follow essentially from Corollary 2.5.

Corollary 4.3. *1. (Soundness) If η is a U-NNRepSupM for C supported by I, then for each $c \in I \setminus C$ we have $\overline{\mathbb{P}}_C^{\mathrm{reach}}(c) \leq \eta(c)$.*
Similarly, if η is an L-NNRepSupM for C supported by I, then for each $c \in I \setminus C$ we have $\underline{\mathbb{P}}_C^{\mathrm{reach}}(c) \leq \eta(c)$. This means, concretely, that for each $\varepsilon > 0$ there is a scheduler $\sigma \in \mathrm{Sch}_\Gamma$ such that, for any $c \in I \setminus C$, we have $\mathbb{P}_{C,\sigma}^{\mathrm{reach}}(c) \leq \eta(c) + \varepsilon$.
2. (Completeness) There exists a U-NNRepSupM η that gives the optimal bound for $\overline{\mathbb{P}}_C^{\mathrm{reach}}$. The same for L-NNRepSupM. □

5   Additive Ranking Supermartingales (ARnkSupM)

We move on to the notion of additive ranking supermartingale (ARnkSupM) in Table 1. It is the best-known martingale-based notion for analysis of probabilistic programs and is used for overapproximating the expected reaching time. That its value is finite implies almost-sure reachability, too. We review its theory; the reason is to demonstrate that the same order-theoretic structure (see Sect. 2.3) underlies ARnkSupM and NNRepSupM in the previous section. The completeness result ((2) of Corollary 5.3) for pCFGs with real-valued variables seems new, too; See Sect. 8 for a detailed comparison to existing works. Proofs are done in a much similar manner to the ones in Sect. 4. In this section we use $\mathbb{K} = [0, \infty]$.

We note that completeness of U-ARnkSupM we state below is the one for *strong* almost-sure reachability [3]. U-ARnkSupM is incomplete for *positive* almost-sure reachability [14], that is, it cannot witness the condition $\forall \sigma. \mathbb{E}_{C,\sigma}^{\mathrm{steps}}(c) < \infty$ in general.

Definition 5.1 (ARnkSupM for pCFG, [7]). Let Γ be a pCFG, $I \in \mathcal{B}(L \times \mathbb{R}^V)$ be a pure invariant, and $C \subseteq I$ be a Borel set. An *upper additive ranking supermartingale (U-ARnkSupM)* over Γ for C supported by I is a function $\eta \in \mathcal{B}(I, [0, \infty])$ that satisfies $\eta(c) \geq 1 + \overline{\mathbb{X}}\eta(c)$ for each $c \in I \setminus C$.
The function η is a *lower additive ranking supermartingale (L-ARnkSupM)* if it satisfies the above conditions, but with $\overline{\mathbb{X}}$ replaced with $\underline{\mathbb{X}}$.

Proposition 5.2. *In the setting of Definition 5.1, we define endofunctions $\overline{\Psi_C}$ and $\underline{\Psi_C}$ over $\mathcal{B}(I, [0, \infty])$ as follows:*

$$\overline{\Psi_C}(\eta)(x) = \begin{cases} 0 & (x \in C) \\ 1 + (\overline{\mathbb{X}}\eta)(x) & (x \notin C), \end{cases} \qquad \underline{\Psi_C}(\eta)(x) = \begin{cases} 0 & (x \in C) \\ 1 + (\underline{\mathbb{X}}\eta)(x) & (x \notin C). \end{cases}$$

Then the upper expected reaching time $\overline{\mathbb{E}}_C^{\text{steps}} : L \times \mathbb{R}^V \to [0, \infty]$ *is the lfp of* $\overline{\Psi_C}$. *Similarly,* $\underline{\mathbb{E}}_C^{\text{steps}}$ *is the lfp of* $\underline{\Psi_C}$. $\square$

Corollary 5.3. *1. (Soundness, e.g. [2]) If η is a U-ARnkSupM for C supported by I, then for each $c \in I \setminus C$ we have $\overline{\mathbb{E}}_C^{\text{steps}}(c) \leq \eta(c)$. In particular, for each $c \in I \setminus C$ that satisfies $\eta(c) < \infty$ we have $\mathbb{P}_C^{\text{reach}}(c) = 1$.*
Similarly, if η is an L-ARnkSupM for C supported by I, then for each $c \in I \setminus C$ we have $\underline{\mathbb{E}}_C^{\text{steps}}(c) \leq \eta(c)$. This means, concretely, that for each $\varepsilon > 0$ there is a scheduler $\sigma \in \text{Sch}_\Gamma$ such that, for any $c \in I \setminus C$, we have $\mathbb{E}_{C,\sigma}^{\text{steps}}(c) \leq \eta(c) + \varepsilon$.

In particular, for each $c \in I \setminus C$ that satisfies $\eta(c) < \infty$ we have $\overline{\mathbb{P}}_C^{\text{reach}}(c) = 1$.
2. (Completeness) There exists a U-ARnkSupM η that gives the optimal bound for $\overline{\mathbb{E}}_C^{\text{steps}}$. The same holds for L-ARnkSupM. $\square$

6 γ-Scaled Submartingales (γ-SclSubM)

Here we present the theory of γ-*scaled submartingales* (γ-SclSubM). It is for underapproximating reachability (Table 1). Compared to the well-known method of ARnkSupM, the greatest advantage is in *quantitative* reasoning: the value of a γ-SclSubM is guaranteed to be below the reachability probability (which can be less than 1), while ARnkSupM is useful only if almost reachability holds. In this section we use $\mathbb{K} = [0, 1]$.

The notion of γ-SclSubM is first introduced in [28], as an instance of a categorical abstraction of ranking functions. The current paper's contribution lies in the following: (i) the theoretical developments about γ-SclSubM in concrete (non-categorical) terms; (ii) introduction of nondeterminism (the setting of [28] is purely probabilistic); and (iii) template-based synthesis of γ-SclSubM.

Definition 6.1 (γ-SclSubM for pCFG, [28]). *Let $\gamma \in (0, 1)$ be given. An upper γ-Scaled Submartingale (U-γ-SclSubM) over Γ for C supported by I is a function $\eta \in \mathcal{B}(I, [-\infty, 1])$ that satisfies $\eta(c) \leq \gamma \cdot \overline{\mathbb{X}}\eta(c)$ for each $I \setminus C$. A lower γ-Scaled Submartingale (L-γ-SclSubM) over Γ for C supported by I is a function $\eta \in \mathcal{B}(I, [-\infty, 1])$ that satisfies $\eta(c) \leq \gamma \cdot \underline{\mathbb{X}}\eta(c)$ for each $I \setminus C$.*

The derivation of γ-SclSubM, from a categorical account in [28], can be described in the following concrete terms. A γ-SclSubM is a post-fixed point of certain functions (namely $\gamma \cdot \overline{\Phi_C}$ and $\gamma \cdot \underline{\Phi_C}$ below). According to (gfp-KT) in Corollary 2.5, γ-SclSubM underapproximates a *greatest* fixed point—but reachability is a *least* fixed point. The trick here is as follows: (1) thanks to the scaling by $\gamma \in (0, 1)$, the gfp and lfp of $\gamma \cdot \overline{\Phi_C}$ coincide; and (2) the lfp (hence the gfp) of $\gamma \cdot \overline{\Phi_C}$ is easily seen to be below the lfp of $\overline{\Phi_C}$, that is, the reachability probability that we are after. The overall argument signifies the role of the Knaster–Tarski theorem.

Proposition 6.2. *Let $\overline{\Phi_C}$ and $\underline{\Phi_C}$ be as defined in Proposition 4.2. Define endofunctions $\gamma \cdot \overline{\Phi_C}$ and $\gamma \cdot \underline{\Phi_C}$ over $\mathcal{B}(I, [0, 1])$ as follows: $(\gamma \cdot \overline{\Phi_C})(\eta)(x) =$*

$$\begin{cases} 1 & (x \in C) \\ \gamma \cdot (\overline{\mathbb{X}}\eta)(x) & (x \notin C), \end{cases} \text{ and } (\gamma \cdot \underline{\Phi_C})(\eta)(x) = \begin{cases} 1 & (x \in C) \\ \gamma \cdot (\underline{\mathbb{X}}\eta)(x) & (x \notin C). \end{cases} \text{ Then we}$$

have i) $\mu(\gamma \cdot \overline{\Phi_C}) \sqsubseteq \mu\overline{\Phi_C}$ and $\mu(\gamma \cdot \underline{\Phi_C}) \sqsubseteq \mu\underline{\Phi_C}$, and ii) $\nu(\gamma \cdot \overline{\Phi_C}) = \mu(\gamma \cdot \overline{\Phi_C})$ and $\nu(\gamma \cdot \underline{\Phi_C}) = \mu(\gamma \cdot \underline{\Phi_C})$. □

Corollary 6.3 (soundness). *If η is a U-γ-SclSubM for C supported by I, then for each $c \in I \setminus C$ we have $\overline{\mathbb{P}}_C^{\mathrm{reach}}(c) \geq \eta(c)$. This means, concretely, that for each $\varepsilon > 0$ there is a scheduler $\sigma \in \mathrm{Sch}_\Gamma$ such that, for any $c \in I \setminus C$, we have $\mathbb{P}_{C,\sigma}^{\mathrm{reach}}(c) \geq \eta(c) - \varepsilon$.*

Similarly, if η is an L-γ-SclSubM for C supported by I, then for each $c \in I \setminus C$ we have $\underline{\mathbb{P}}_C^{\mathrm{reach}}(c) \geq \eta(c)$.

Proof. Just notice that if η is an upper- or lower-γ-SclSubM, then so is $\max\{\mathbf{0}, \eta\}$. The rest is as described in the paragraph before Proposition 6.2. □

7 Implementation and Experiments

We implemented template-based automated synthesis algorithms for NNRep-SupM (Sect. 4) and γ-SclSubM (Sect. 6), and present some experimental results. We implemented the following programs:

I. synthesis of a U-NNRepSupM for an APP based on a linear template.
II. synthesis of a U-NNRepSupM for a PPP based on a polynomial template.
III. synthesis of an L-γ-SclSubM for an APP based on a linear template.

Each algorithm first translates given an APP or a PPP to a pCFG Γ and a terminal configuration C, and then solves an optimization problem of finding a U-NNRepSupM (L-γ-SclSubM) over Γ for C that gives a small (large) value as possible at the initial configuration. Reduction of optimization problems to LP or SDP ones are done in standard ways in the literature; we use *Farkas' lemma* (see e.g. [7,12]) for the case of APPs, and *Schmüdgen's Positivstellensatz* (see e.g. [8,10]) for PPPs.

We have augmented the syntax of APPs and PPPs (Sect. 2.2) so that we can specify an invariant I and a terminal configuration C. The program does not synthesize an invariant nor prove the correctness of the given invariant, and therefore the user has to provide a correct invariant by hand or by using some algorithm, e.g. [20].

All the programs are implemented in OCaml. We have used glpk (v4.63) [15] and SDPT3 [24] for the LP and SDP solvers respectively. For the implementation of Prog. II, we have also made use of a MATLAB toolbox SOSTOOLS (v3.03) [25].

We tested our implementations for several APPs and PPPs. We have used different benchmark sets for Prog. I–II and Prog. III because what is overapproximated by Prog. I–II ($\overline{\mathbb{P}}_C^{\mathrm{reach}}$) and what is underapproximated by Prog. III ($\underline{\mathbb{P}}_C^{\mathrm{reach}}$)

are different. The benchmarks implement the following probabilistic processes that are used as benchmarks in the literature. More details and codes are given in [27].

(a). **(Adversarial random walk)** A variation of a random walk, whose analysis is more challenging because of additional adversarial nondeterministic choices [11]. We have considered three variants: (a-1) 1D, (a-2) 2D and (a-3) a variant of 2D. (a-1) is a random walk over $\mathbb{R}$ modeling a *discrete queuing system*, and is parametrized by $p_1, p_2 \in [0, 1]$ that determines the distribution of the number of packets that arrive in each round. (a-2) and (a-3) are random walks over $\mathbb{R}^2$ parametrized by $M_1, M_2 \in \mathbb{R}$. They determine the distribution of movement distances in each round. We added a queue size limit for (a-1) and a time limit for (a-2) and (a-3). If the queue size exceeds 10 in (a-1) or 100 rounds were consumed in (a-2) or (a-3), the program stops, and it is not counted as termination.

(b). **(Room temperature control)** A model of an air conditioning system for adjacent two rooms [1,8]. It is parametrized by real numbers c and p: the former determines the power of the air conditioner, and the latter determines the size of perturbation. We have also added a time limit of 100 as in (a) above.

We have coded (a)–(b) as an APP. Experiments for Prog. I and III were carried out on a MacBook Pro laptop with a Core i5 processor (2.6 GHz, 2 cores) and 16 GiB RAM. That for Prog. II was carried out on an Amazon EC2 c4.large instance (May 2018, 2 vCPUs and 3.75 GiB RAM) running Ubuntu 16.04.4 LTS (64 bit). The results are in Tables 2–3. For each program, the first column ("time (s)") shows the total execution time, and the second column ("bound") shows the calculated probability bound.

(Applicability of NNRepSupM) Table 2 shows the results for Prog. I–II; the goal of these experiments is to certify the applicability of NNRepSupM to programs with nondeterminism (a-1). We have tested them for (a-1) with two combinations of parameters. Prog. I–II found a nontrivial bound for the reachability probability when $(p_1, p_2) = (0.2, 0.4)$ while it failed to find such a bound when $(p_1, p_2) = (0.8, 0.1)$. Intuitively, the random walk is more "unfavorable" in the former case in the sense that the opposite direction from a terminal configuration is chosen in higher probabilities. As expected, a polynomial NNRepSupM gives tighter bound than a linear one, but it took much longer. The bound was not improved by increasing the degree of the polynomial template.

(Applicability of γ-SclSubM) Table 3 shows the results for Prog. III; here we wish to certify applicability of our new method γ-SclSubM. For each variant of (a), we have tested Prog. III for two combinations of parameters. In each variant, Prog. III gives a nontrivial probability bound for one combination and a trivial bound for the other combination. In fact, all the cases where nontrivial bounds were "favorable" random walks where the direction to a terminal configuration tends to be chosen. In contrast, the cases where no nontrivial bound was found were "unfavorable" random walks. Note that this is the converse of the results

Table 2. Bounds by U-NNRepSupM

	param.	Prog. I (linear)		Prog. II (deg.-2 poly.)		Prog. II (deg.-3 poly.)	
		time (s)	bound	time (s)	bound	time (s)	bound
(a-1)	$p_1 = 0.2$ $p_2 = 0.4$	0.021	≤ 0.825	530.298	≤ 0.6552	572.393	≤ 0.6555
	$p_1 = 0.8$ $p_2 = 0.1$	0.024	≤ 1	526.519	≤ 1.0	561.327	≤ 1.0

Table 3. Bounds by L-γ-SclSubM with $\gamma = 0.999$

	param.	Prog. III (linear)	
		time (s)	bound
(a-1)	$p_1 = 0.2$ $p_2 = 0.4$	0.026	≥ 0
	$p_1 = 0.8$ $p_2 = 0.1$	0.022	≥ 0.751
(a-2)	$M_1 = -1$ $M_2 = 2$	0.033	≥ 0
	$M_1 = -2$ $M_2 = 1$	0.033	≥ 0.767
(a-3)	$M_1 = -1$ $M_2 = 2$	0.028	≥ 0
	$M_1 = -2$ $M_2 = 1$	0.040	≥ 0.801
(b)	$c = 0.1$ $p = 0.5$	0.056	≥ 0
	$c = 0.1$ $p = 0.1$	0.054	≥ 0.148

Table 4. Probabilistic bounds given by U-NNRepSupM and ε-RepSupM

	true reachability probability	U-NNRepSupM	1-RepSupM
(c-1)	$\frac{(0.4/0.6)^5 - (0.4/0.6)^{10}}{1-(0.4/0.6)^{10}} \approx 0.116$	0.505	< 1
(c-2)	0.5	0.5	—
(c-3)	$\int_0^1 \left(\frac{0.25}{0.75}\right)^{\lceil \log_2(1/x) \rceil} dx \approx 0.2$	0.5	—
(c-4)	$\left(\frac{0.25}{0.75}\right)^1 \approx 0.333$	—	< 1

for Prog. I–III. Prog. III also succeeded in giving a nontrivial bound for (b). However, if we increase the parameter c (i.e. if we strengthened the power of air conditioners), it failed to give a nontrivial bound.

(Comparison between NNRepSupM and ε-RepSupM) Both of NNRepSupM and ε-RepSupM (Sect. 3) overapproximate $\overline{\mathbb{P}}_C^{\mathrm{reach}}$. To compare them, we have also tested them for the following four simple pCFGs: (c-1) a bounded random walk over $[0, 10]$; (c-2) a simple system with an infinite branching where x is assigned a value taken from a geometric distribution; (c-3) a random walk over $[0, 1]$ that exhibits geometric behaviors; and (c-4) an unbounded random walk. See [27] for the concrete definitions of the pCFGs.

The results are shown in Table 4. The second column shows the true reachability probability obtained by hand calculation. The third and fourth columns show the probability bounds calculated by a linear NNRepSupM and a linear 1-RepSupM respectively.

For (c-1), both a linear NNRepSupM and a linear 1-RepSupM were found. However, while the NNRepSupM gave a non-trivial bound for the reachability probability, the probability bound calculated from the 1-RepSupM as in (1) was greater than 1 and hence trivial (cf. Theorem 3.2). Recall from Theorem 3.2.3.2 that the 1-RepSupM can still refute almost-sure reachability. For (c-2) and (c-3), whose almost-sure reachability cannot be refuted by 1-RepSupMs, our algorithm found NNRepSupMs that give non-trivial probability bounds. In contrast, for (c-4), no NNRepSupM gave non-trivial probability bound while a 1-RepSupM that refutes almost-sure reachability was found.

8   Related Work

The notion of ranking supermartingale is first proposed by [7] aiming at extending applicability of *quantitative invariants* [21,22] to probabilistic programs with real-valued variables, but nondeterminism is not considered. Soundness of the method under demonic nondeterminism is studied in [2,10,14]; among them, *lexicographic ranking supermartingales* [2] can be seen as an extension of our U-ARnkSupM. Soundness under finite demonic/angelic nondeterminism is shown in [11].

Completeness of U-ARnkSupM for strong almost-sure termination [3] has previously been shown, but only in discrete settings [3,9]. The closest result to ours is [9], where they study pCFGs with demonic nondeterminism but restrict to integer-valued variables. Our proof that also works for real-valued variables utilizes ε-optimal schedulers from control theory [5].

Several under- and overapproximation methods for *expected runtimes* of probabilistic programs, which is defined inductively on its structure rather than on its semantics, is studied in [19]. *Upper invariants of* while-*loops* among them is a U-ARnkSupM-like notion in their setting. In [19] soundness and completeness of the upper invariant technique are derived from order-theoretic considerations. They handle probabilistic programs with demonic nondeterminism, but only discrete updates are allowed.

Probabilistic barrier certificates are studied in control theory [23,26] as a tool for overapproximating reachability. While it resembles our NNRepSupMs, their setting is purely probabilistic; we extend applicability of the technique to systems with nondeterminism.

ε-RepSupM [12] is also a technique for overapproximating reachability, which is studied for the purpose of synthesizing *stochastic invariants*. It is combined with ranking supermartingales to verify the *persistence* property of programs, too [8,12]. While there are certain similarities between ε-RepSupMs and NNRepSupMs, they are technically different because ε-RepSupMs exploit the κ-*bounded differences condition*, which is not assumed in our case. Their method is sound for refuting almost-sure reachability but does not provide nontrivial probability bound in general, and is not complete (see Fig. 3).

9 Conclusions and Future Work

We gave a comprehensive and comparative account of martingale-based techniques for approximating reachability probabilities. We demonstrated that several different approximation techniques–NNRepSupM, ARnkSupM, and γ-SclSubM– had a common structure of order-theoretic fixed points in their theory, while they originally arose from different communities. The key observation was that the reachability probability and the expected reaching time were the least fixed points of certain monotone endofunctions; soundness and completeness of the first two techniques are derived as its corollaries, and it is the basis for the proof of soundness of γ-SclSubM. We also implemented the techniques above and conducted experiments, of which results suggest the advantage of γ-SclSubM in quantitative reasoning, and the comparative advantage of NNRepSupM over ε-RepSupM in the quality of bounds.

In this paper we have focused on over- and underapproximating (i.e. refuting and verifying) reachability probabilities. For future work, we wish to study more complicated specifications such as recurrence ($\mathbf{GF}\varphi$) and persistence ($\mathbf{FG}\varphi$), too. Some martingale-based techniques have already been used (see e.g. [8]); we will investigate the use of *lattice-theoretic progress measures*, introduced in [17] as a generalization of progress measures for parity games [18], in the probabilistic settings.

Acknowledgment. We thank Shin-ya Katsumata, Takamasa Okudono and the anonymous referees for useful comments. The authors are supported by JST ERATO HASUO Metamathematics for Systems Design Project (No. JPMJER1603), the JSPS-INRIA Bilateral Joint Research Project "CRECOGI," and JSPS KAKENHI Grant Numbers 15KT0012 & 15K11984. Natsuki Urabe is supported by JSPS KAKENHI Grant Number 16J08157.

References

1. Abate, A., Katoen, J., Lygeros, J., Prandini, M.: Approximate model checking of stochastic hybrid systems. Eur. J. Control **16**(6), 624–641 (2010)
2. Agrawal, S., Chatterjee, K., Novotný, P.: Lexicographic ranking supermartingales: an efficient approach to termination of probabilistic programs. PACMPL 2(POPL), 34:1–34:32 (2018)
3. Avanzini, M., Dal Lago, U., Yamada, A.: On Probabilistic Term Rewriting. In: Gallagher, J.P., Sulzmann, M. (eds.) FLOPS 2018. LNCS, vol. 10818, pp. 132–148. Springer, Cham (2018). https://doi.org/10.1007/978-3-319-90686-7_9
4. Baier, C., Katoen, J.P.: Principles of model checking. MIT Press (2008)
5. Bertsekas, D.P., Shreve, S.E.: Stochastic Optimal Control: The Discrete-Time Case. Athena Scientific (2007)
6. Bodík, R., Majumdar, R. (eds.): Proceedings of POPL 2016. ACM (2016)
7. Chakarov, A., Sankaranarayanan, S.: Probabilistic Program Analysis with Martingales. In: Sharygina, N., Veith, H. (eds.) CAV 2013. LNCS, vol. 8044, pp. 511–526. Springer, Heidelberg (2013). https://doi.org/10.1007/978-3-642-39799-8_34
8. Chakarov, A., Voronin, Y.-L., Sankaranarayanan, S.: Deductive Proofs of Almost Sure Persistence and Recurrence Properties. In: Chechik, M., Raskin, J.-F. (eds.) TACAS 2016. LNCS, vol. 9636, pp. 260–279. Springer, Heidelberg (2016). https://doi.org/10.1007/978-3-662-49674-9_15
9. Chatterjee, K., Fu, H.: Termination of nondeterministic recursive probabilistic programs. CoRR abs/1701.02944 (2017). arXiv:1701.02944
10. Chatterjee, K., Fu, H., Goharshady, A.K.: Termination Analysis of Probabilistic Programs Through Positivstellensatz?s. In: Chaudhuri, S., Farzan, A. (eds.) CAV 2016. LNCS, vol. 9779, pp. 3–22. Springer, Cham (2016). https://doi.org/10.1007/978-3-319-41528-4_1
11. Chatterjee, K., Fu, H., Novotný, P., Hasheminezhad, R.: Algorithmic analysis of qualitative and quantitative termination problems for affine probabilistic programs. In: Bodík and Majumdar [6], pp. 327–342
12. Chatterjee, K., Novotný, P., Zikelic, D.: Stochastic invariants for probabilistic termination. In: Castagna, G., Gordon, A.D. (eds.) Proceedings of POPL 2017. pp. 145–160. ACM (2017)
13. Cousot, R., Cousot, P.: Constructive versions of Tarski's fixed point theorems. Pacific Journal of Mathematics **82**(1), 43–57 (1979)

14. Fioriti, L.M.F., Hermanns, H.: Probabilistic termination: Soundness, completeness, and compositionality. In: Rajamani, S.K., Walker, D. (eds.) Proceedings of the 42nd Annual ACM SIGPLAN-SIGACT Symposium on Principles of Programming Languages, POPL 2015, Mumbai, India, January 15–17, 2015. pp. 489–501. ACM (2015). https://doi.org/10.1145/2676726.2677001

15. The GNU linear programming kit, http://www.gnu.org/software/glpk

16. Gordon, A.D., Henzinger, T.A., Nori, A.V., Rajamani, S.K.: Probabilistic programming. In: Herbsleb, J.D., Dwyer, M.B. (eds.) Proceedings of the on Future of Software Engineering, FOSE 2014. pp. 167–181. ACM (2014)

17. Hasuo, I., Shimizu, S., Cîrstea, C.: Lattice-theoretic progress measures and coalgebraic model checking. In: Bodík and Majumdar [6], pp. 718–732

18. Jurdziński, M.: Small Progress Measures for Solving Parity Games. In: Reichel, H., Tison, S. (eds.) STACS 2000. LNCS, vol. 1770, pp. 290–301. Springer, Heidelberg (2000). https://doi.org/10.1007/3-540-46541-3_24

19. Kaminski, B.L., Katoen, J., Matheja, C., Olmedo, F.: Weakest precondition reasoning for expected run-times of probabilistic programs. In: Thiemann, P. (ed.) Programming Languages and Systems - 25th European Symposium on Programming, ESOP 2016, Held as Part of the European Joint Conferences on Theory and Practice of Software, ETAPS 2016, Eindhoven, The Netherlands, April 2–8, 2016, Proceedings. Lecture Notes in Computer Science, vol. 9632, pp. 364–389. Springer (2016)

20. Katoen, J.-P., McIver, A.K., Meinicke, L.A., Morgan, C.C.: Linear-Invariant Generation for Probabilistic Programs: In: Cousot, R., Martel, M. (eds.) SAS 2010. LNCS, vol. 6337, pp. 390–406. Springer, Heidelberg (2010). https://doi.org/10.1007/978-3-642-15769-1_24

21. McIver, A., Morgan, C.: Abstraction, Refinement And Proof For Probabilistic Systems (Monographs in Computer Science). Springer Verlag (2004)

22. McIver, A., Morgan, C.: Developing and Reasoning About Probabilistic Programs in pGCL. In: Cavalcanti, A., Sampaio, A., Woodcock, J. (eds.) PSSE 2004. LNCS, vol. 3167, pp. 123–155. Springer, Heidelberg (2006). https://doi.org/10.1007/11889229_4

23. Prajna, S., Jadbabaie, A., Pappas, G.J.: Stochastic safety verification using barrier certificates. In: 2004 43rd IEEE Conference on Decision and Control. IEEE, Piscataway. pp. 929–934 (2004)

24. SDPT3, http://www.math.nus.edu.sg/~mattohkc/sdpt3.html

25. SOSTOOLS, http://sysos.eng.ox.ac.uk/sostools/

26. Steinhardt, J., Tedrake, R.: Finite-time regional verification of stochastic non-linear systems. I. J. Robotics Res. **31**(7), 901–923 (2012)

27. Takisaka, T., Oyabu, Y., Urabe, N., Hasuo, I.: Ranking and repulsing supermartingales for approximating reachability. CoRR abs/1805.10749 (2018), arXiv:1805.10749

28. Urabe, N., Hara, M., Hasuo, I.: Categorical liveness checking by corecursive algebras. In: Proc. of LICS 2017. pp. 1–12. IEEE Computer Society (2017)

29. Vardi, M.Y.: An automata-theoretic approach to linear temporal logic. In: Moller, F., Birtwistle, G. (eds.) Logics for Concurrency. LNCS, vol. 1043, pp. 238–266. Springer, Heidelberg (1996). https://doi.org/10.1007/3-540-60915-6_6

Bounded Synthesis of Register Transducers

Ayrat Khalimov[1(✉)], Benedikt Maderbacher[2], and Roderick Bloem[2]

[1] The Hebrew University, Jerusalem, Israel
ayrat.khalimov@gmail.com
[2] Graz University of Technology, Graz, Austria

Abstract. Reactive synthesis aims at automatic construction of systems from their behavioural specifications. The research mostly focuses on synthesis of systems dealing with Boolean signals. But real-life systems are often described using bit-vectors, integers, etc. Bit-blasting would make such systems unreadable, hit synthesis scalability, and is not possible for infinite data-domains. One step closer to real-life systems are register transducers [10]: they can store data-input into registers and later output the content of a register, but they do not directly depend on the data-input, only on its comparison with the registers. Previously [5] it was proven that synthesis of register transducers from register automata is undecidable, but there the authors considered transducers equipped with the unbounded queue of registers. First, we prove the problem becomes decidable if bound the number of registers in transducers, by reducing the problem to standard synthesis of Boolean systems. Second, we show how to use quantified temporal logic, instead of automata, for specifications.

1 Introduction

Reactive synthesis [2] frees hardware and software developers from tedious and error-prune coding work. Instead, the developer specifies the desired behaviour of a system, and a synthesizer produces the actual code. The research in reactive synthesis is mostly focused on synthesis of transducers dealing with *Boolean* inputs and outputs. However, most programs and hardware designs use not only Booleans, but also bit-vectors, integers, reals. Bit-blasting into Booleans makes synthesized programs unreadable and hinders the synthesis scalability.

One step closer to real-life systems are register transducers [10]. Such transducers are equipped with registers; they can read the data-input from an infinite domain; they can store the data-input into a register and later output it; they do not depend on the exact data-input value, but on its comparison with the registers. Thus, a transition of a register transducer can say "in state q: if the data-input not equals to register #1, then output the value of register #1, store the data-input into register #2, and go into state q'". Examples of a register transducer and automaton are in Figs. 2 and 1.

In [5], the authors introduced the problem of synthesis of register transducers. But their transducers are equipped with an *unbounded queue* of registers: they

© Springer Nature Switzerland AG 2018
S. K. Lahiri and C. Wang (Eds.): ATVA 2018, LNCS 11138, pp. 494–510, 2018.
https://doi.org/10.1007/978-3-030-01090-4_29

can push the data-input into the queue, and later compare the data-input with the values in the queue. For specifications, the authors use register automata with a fixed number of registers (thus, no queue). The authors show that the synthesis problem is undecidable; the proof relies on unboundedness of the queue.

We prove the problem becomes decidable if bound the number of registers in transducers. Namely, we reduce synthesis of k-register transducers wrt. register automata to synthesis of Boolean transducers wrt. Boolean automata, i.e., to standard synthesis. The reduction relies on two ideas.

The first (folklore) idea is: instead of tracking the exact register values and data-inputs, track only the *equivalences* between register values and the data-input. The second idea is: instead of checking automaton non-emptiness, we check automaton non-emptiness *modulo words of k-register transducers*.

In the second part, we suggest a temporal logic that "works well" with our approach. Among several logics suitable to the context of infinite data [3,4,9,14], we have chosen IPTL [14] (called VLTL in [9]), because of its naturalness. Using this logic, we can state properties like $\forall \ell \in \mathcal{D} : \mathsf{G}(i = \ell \rightarrow \mathsf{F}(o = \ell))$: "every data-value appearing on the input eventually appears on the output". We show how to convert a formula in this logic into a register automaton (in incomplete way; there can be no complete way) that can be used by our synthesis approach.

2 Definitions

Fix a *data-domain* $\mathcal{D}$ throughout the paper, which is an infinite set of elements (*data-values*). Calligraphic writing like i, o, ℓ, $\imath$ denotes data-variables or objects closely related to them. Sets of such objects are also written in calligraphic, like $\mathcal{D}$, $\mathcal{R}$, $\mathcal{P}$, etc. Define $\mathbb{N} = \{1, 2, ...\}$, $\mathbb{N}_0 = \{0, 1, 2, ...\}$, $[k] = \{1, ..., k\}$ for $k \in \mathbb{N}$; $\mathbb{B} = \{true, false\}$, and we often use the subscripted variants, $\mathbb{B}_i = \mathbb{B}_o = \mathbb{B}$, to clarify when $\mathbb{B}$ is related to object i or o. For an automaton A, let $L(A)$ denote the set of its accepting words.

2.1 Register Automata

A register automaton works on words from $(2^P \times \mathcal{D}^{\mathcal{P}})^\omega$, where P is a set of Boolean signals and $\mathcal{P}$ is a set of data-signals. To simplify the presentation, we assume there are only two data-signals ($\mathcal{P} = \{i, o\}$), which makes the words to be from $(2^P \times \mathcal{D}^2)^\omega$. When reading a word, a register automaton can store the value of data-signal i into its registers. Later it can compare the content of its registers with the current value of i. Register automata do not depend on actual data-values—only on the comparison with the register values. Below is a formal definition.

A *(universal co-Büchi/non-deterministic Büchi) word automaton with k registers* is a tuple $A = \langle P, \mathcal{P}, \mathcal{R}, \ell_0, Q, q_0, \delta, F \rangle$, where

- P is a set of *Boolean signals*;
- $\mathcal{P} = \{i, o\}$ is a set of *data-signals*;

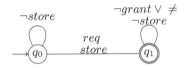

Fig. 1. A universal co-Büchi 1-register automaton: $P = \{req, grant\}$, $\mathcal{R} = \{z\}$, $F = \{q_1\}$. The labels $\neg store$ and $store$ have a special meaning: $store$ means that the automaton stores the value of data-input i into register z; $\neg store$ means it does not. The expression $o \neq z$ means that the component $\mathbb{B}_o$ of the transition is $false$. For guards and Boolean signals, the labeling is symbolic. Formally, the set of transitions is $\{(q_0, p, b_i, b_o, false, q_0) : (b_i, b_o) \in \mathbb{B}^2, p \in 2^P\} \cup \{(q_0, p, b_i, b_o, true, q_1) : (b_i, b_o) \in \mathbb{B}^2, req \in p \in 2^P\} \cup \{(q_1, p, b_i, b_o, false, q_1) : (b_i, b_o) \in \mathbb{B}^2, p \in 2^P, grant \notin p \vee b_o = false\}$.

- $\mathcal{R} = \{z_1, ..., z_k\}$ is a set of *registers*;
- $d_0 \in \mathcal{D}$ is an *initial data-value* for every register;
- Q is the set of *states* and $q_0 \in Q$ is an *initial state*;
- $F \subseteq Q$ is a set of *accepting states*;
- $\delta : Q \times 2^P \times \mathbb{B}_i^k \times \mathbb{B}_o^k \to 2^{\mathbb{B}^k \times Q}$ is a *transition function*. Intuitively, in a state, an automaton reads a finite letter from 2^P (which describes all Boolean signals whose current value is true) and a data-letter from D^2 (a data-value for i and a data-value for o). Then the automaton compares the data-letter with the content of the registers. Depending on this comparison (component $\mathbb{B}_i^k \times \mathbb{B}_o^k$, called *guard*), the automaton transits into several (for universal automaton) or one of (for non-deterministic automaton) successor states, and for each successor state, stores the value of data-signal i into one, several, or none of the registers (defined by component $\mathbb{B}^k$, called *assignment* or *store*).

An example of a register automaton is in Fig. 1.

A *configuration* is a tuple $(q, \bar{d}) \in Q \times \mathcal{D}^k$, and (q_0, d_0^k) is *initial*. A *path* is an infinite sequence $(q_0, \bar{d}_0) \xrightarrow{(l_0, i_0, o_0, \bar{a}_0)} (q_1, \bar{d}_1) \xrightarrow{(l_1, i_1, o_1, \bar{a}_1)} ...$ such that for every $j \in \mathbb{N}_0$:

- $q_j \in Q$, $\bar{d}_j \in \mathcal{D}^k$, $l_j \in 2^P$, $i_j \in \mathcal{D}$, $o_j \in \mathcal{D}$, and $\bar{a}_j \in \mathbb{B}^k$;
- $(q_{j+1}, \bar{a}_j) \in \delta(q_j, l_j, i_j = \bar{d}_j[1], ..., i_j = \bar{d}_j[k], o_j = \bar{d}_j[1], ..., o_j = \bar{d}_j[k])$;
- $\bar{d}_0 = d_0^k$; and
- for every $n \in [k]$: $\bar{d}_{j+1}[n] = \begin{cases} i_j & \text{if } \bar{a}_j[n] = true, \\ \bar{d}_j[n] & otherwise. \end{cases}$

Let $\Sigma = 2^P \times \mathcal{D}^2$. A *word* is a sequence from Σ^ω. A word is *accepted* by a universal co-Büchi automaton iff every path —whose projection into Σ equals to the word— does not visit a state from F infinitely often; otherwise the word is *rejected*. A word is *accepted* by a non-deterministic Büchi automaton iff there is a path —whose projection into Σ equals to the word— that visits a state from F infinitely often; otherwise the word is *rejected*. For example, the universal co-Büchi 1-register automaton in Fig. 1 accepts the word $(\{req\}, 5_i, *_o)(\{req, grant\}, 6_i, 5_o)(\{grant\}, *_i, 6_o)(\emptyset, *_i, *_o)^\omega$, where $\mathcal{D} = \mathbb{N}_0$, we

write subscripts i and o for clarity, and $*$ is anything from $\mathcal{D}$ (not necessary the same). The automaton describes the words where every req is followed by $grant$ with the data-value of o being equal to the data-value of i
at the moment of the request. Such words can be described by a formula
$\forall d \in \mathcal{D} : \mathsf{G}\big(req \wedge i = d \to \mathsf{XF}(grant \wedge o = d)\big)$, but we postpone the discussion of logic until Sect. 4.

2.2   Register Transducers

Register transducers is an extension of standard transducers (Mealy machines) to
an infinite domain. A register transducer can store the input data-value into its
registers. It can only output the data-value that is currently stored in one of its
registers. Similarly to register automata, the transitions of register transducers
depend on the comparison of the data-input with the registers, but not on the
actual data-values. Let us define register transducers formally.

A *k-register transducer* is a tuple $T = \langle I, O, \mathcal{I}, \mathcal{O}, \mathcal{R}, d_0, S, s_0, \tau \rangle$ where:

- I and O are sets of Boolean signals, called *Boolean inputs* and *outputs*;
- $\mathcal{I}$ and $\mathcal{O}$ are sets of data-signals, called *data-inputs* and *data-outputs*; we
  assume that $\mathcal{I} = \{i\}$ and $\mathcal{O} = \{o\}$.
- S is a (finite or infinite) set of *states* and $s_0 \in S$ is *initial*;
- $\mathcal{R} = \{t_1, ..., t_k\}$ is a set of *registers*;
- $d_0 \in \mathcal{D}$ is an *initial data-value* for every register;
- $\tau : S \times 2^I \times \mathbb{B}_i^k \to (2^O \times [k] \times \mathbb{B}^k \times S)$ is a *transition function*. Intuitively, from
  a state the transducer reads the values of the Boolean inputs (component 2^I)
  and compares the content of the registers with the data-value of i (component
  $\mathbb{B}_i^k$, called *guard*). Depending on that information, the transducer transits into
  a unique successor state (component S), stores the data-value of i into one,
  several, or none of the registers (component $\mathbb{B}^k$, called *assignment* or *store*),
  outputs a value for each Boolean output (component 2^O), and outputs a
  data-value stored in one of the registers (component $[k]$).

Figure 2 shows an example of a register transducer.

A *configuration* is a tuple $(s, \bar{d}) \in Q \times \mathcal{D}^k$; (s_0, d_0^k) is called *initial*. A *path* is
a sequence $(s_0, \bar{d}_0) \xrightarrow{(i_0, o_0, i_0, o_0, \bar{a}_0)} (s_1, \bar{d}_1) \xrightarrow{(i_1, o_1, i_1, o_1, \bar{a}_1)} ...$ where for every $j \in \mathbb{N}_0$:

- $s_j \in S$, $\bar{d}_j \in \mathcal{D}^k$, $i_j \in 2^I$, $o_j \in 2^O$, $i_j \in \mathcal{D}$, $o_j \in \mathcal{D}$, $\bar{a}_j \in \mathbb{B}^k$;
- let $(out, out, store, succ) = \tau(s_j, i_j, i_j = \bar{d}_j[1], ..., i_j = \bar{d}_j[k])$. Then:
- $s_{j+1} = succ$;
- $\bar{a}_j = store$;
- $o_j = \bar{d}_j[out]$;
- $o_j = out$;
- $\bar{d}_0 = d_0^k$; and

- for every $n \in [k]$: $\bar{d}_{j+1}[n] = \begin{cases} i_j & \text{if } \bar{a}_j[n] = true, \\ \bar{d}_j[n] & \text{otherwise.} \end{cases}$

Fig. 2. A 1-register transducer: $I = \{req\}, O = \{grant\}, \mathcal{R} = \{z\}$. The meaning of *store* and $\neg store$ is as in the previous figure. The labeling wrt. guards and Boolean signals is symbolic. The transducer always outputs the value of its only register (not shown). Formally, the set of transitions is $\{(s_0, \emptyset, b_i, \emptyset, 1, false, s_0) : b_i \in \mathbb{B}\} \cup \{(s_0, \{req\}, b_i, \emptyset, 1, true, s_1) : b_i \in \mathbb{B}\} \cup \{(s_1, \{req\}, b_i, \{grant\}, 1, true, s_1) : b_i \in \mathbb{B}\} \cup \{(s_1, \emptyset, b_i, \{grant\}, 1, false, s_0) : b_i \in \mathbb{B}\}$.

Notice that a value of the data-output refers to the current register values, not the updated ones. I.e., outputting a data-value happens before storing.

For example, a path of the register transducer in Fig. 2 can start with $(s_0, 0) \xrightarrow{(\{req\}, \emptyset, 5_i, 0_o, true)} (s_1, 5) \xrightarrow{(\{req\}, \{grant\}, 6_i, 5_o, true)} (s_1, 6) \xrightarrow{(\emptyset, \{grant\}, 4_i, 6_o, false)} (s_0, 6)$, where we assumed that $\mathcal{D} = \mathbb{N}_0$, $d_0 = 0$, and the subscripts i and o are for clarity.

A *word* is a projection of a transducer path into $2^{I \cup O} \times \mathcal{D}^2$. A register transducer *satisfies* a register automaton A, written $T \models A$, iff all transducer words are accepted by the automaton. For example, the register transducer from Fig. 2 satisfies the automaton from Fig. 1.

2.3   Synthesis Problem

Model checking and cutoffs The *model-checking problem* is:

- Given: a register transducer T, a universal co-Büchi register automaton A.
- Return: "yes" if $T \models A$, otherwise "no".

The model-checking problem is decidable, which follows from the following. Kaminski and Francez [10, Prop.4] proved the following *cutoff result* (adapted to our notions): if a data-word over an infinite domain $\mathcal{D}$ is accepted by a non-deterministic Büchi k-register automaton, then there is an accepting data-word over a finite domain $\mathcal{D}_{k+1}$ of size $k+1$. (Actually, their result is for words of finite length, but can be extended to infinite words.) Further, if we look at a given universal co-Büchi k_A-register automaton A as being non-deterministic Büchi $\tilde{A}$, then $L(\tilde{A}) = \overline{L(A)}$, i.e., it describes the error words. To do model checking, as usual, (1) build the product of the $\tilde{A}$ and a given k_T-register transducer T, then (2) check its emptiness and return "the transducer is correct" iff the product is empty. The product is easy to build, this is an easy extension of the standard product construction, we note only that it is a non-deterministic Büchi $(k_A + k_T)$-register automaton. Finally, to check emptiness of the product we can use the cutoff result, namely, restrict the data-domain to have $(k_A + k_T + 1)$ data-values. This reduces product emptiness to standard emptiness of register-less automata.

The case of deterministic Rabin register automata and transducers with more than single data-input and data-output was studied in [12], but the proof idea is similar.

In this paper we focus on the synthesis problem defined below.

Synthesis. The *bounded synthesis problem* is:

- Given: a register-transducer interface (the number of registers k_T, Boolean and data-inputs, Boolean and data-outputs), a universal co-Büchi register automaton A.
- Return: a k_T-register transducer T of a given interface such that $T \models A$, otherwise "unrealizable".

If the number of registers k_T is not given (thus we ask to find any such k_T which makes the problem realizable, or return "unrealizable" if no such k_T exists), then we get the (finite but unbounded) *synthesis problem*.

A related synthesis problem (let us call it "infinite synthesis problem") was studied in [5], but for a slightly different model of register transducers. There, the transducers operate an unbounded queue of registers (thus, it may use an infinite number of registers). They prove the infinite synthesis problem is undecidable and suggest an incomplete synthesis approach.

In the next sections, we show that the bounded synthesis problem is decidable, and suggest an approach that reduces it to the synthesis problem of register-less transducers wrt. register-less automata. The (unbounded) synthesis problem is left open.

But before proceeding to our solution, let us remark why the cutoff result does not immediately give a complete synthesis procedure.

Remark 1 (Cutoffs and synthesis). The cutoff result makes the data-domain finite, so let the values of the registers be part of the transducer states. Then a transducer has to satisfy the three conditions below, where condition (3) explains why the cutoff does not work with this naive approach.

(1) "The register values are updated according to transducer store actions."
    Introduce new Boolean outputs describing the current values of the transducer registers, and new Boolean outputs describing the store action. Then it is easy to encode the above requirement using a register-less automaton.
(2) "The value of the data-output always equals the value of one of the registers."
    With the Boolean outputs introduced in item (1), this can be easily encoded using a register-less automaton.
(3) "The transitions depend on the guard, but not on the value of data-input."
    When considered alone, this requirement can be implemented using the partial-information synthesis approach [11], where we search for a transducer that can access the guard, but not the actual value of data-input. But the partial-information synthesis approach does not allow for having partial information for transitions (needed to implement item (3)), yet full information for outputs (needed to implement items (1) and (2)).

Nevertheless, with the cutoff it is easy to get an *incomplete* synthesis approach with SMT-based bounded synthesis [6] that allows you to fine-tune transition and output functions dependencies.

3   Solving the Bounded Synthesis Problem

Recall that given a non-deterministic Büchi register automaton A, we search for a k_T-register transducer T such that $T \models \neg A$ (equiv., $T \models \tilde{A}$ where $\tilde{A}$ is dual to A and thus it is universal co-Büchi). Our approach is 5 points long.
   (**1**) We start by defining a Boolean associate $A_\mathbb{B}$ of a non-deterministic Büchi register automaton A, which is a standard register-less non-deterministic Büchi automaton derived from the description of A. Of course, we cannot directly use the Boolean associate $A_\mathbb{B}$ to answer questions about A, because $A_\mathbb{B}$ lacks the semantics of A. We also define a Boolean associate $T_\mathbb{B}$ for every register transducer T. In the end, we will synthesize $T_\mathbb{B}$ that satisfies a certain register-less automaton. For examples of such associates, look at the automaton and transducer on Figs. 1 and 2 as being standard, register-less. (**2**) We introduce a verifier automaton V, which tracks the equivalences between the registers $\mathcal{R}^A$ of A: two registers fall into the same equivalence class iff they hold the same data-value. The automaton $A_\mathbb{B}@V$ is $A_\mathbb{B}$ enhanced with this equivalence-class information. It has enough information to answer the questions like non-emptiness A and model checking wrt. A. This is because every Boolean path of $A_\mathbb{B}@V$ corresponds to some data-path in A, and vice versa (which was not the case for $A_\mathbb{B}$ and A). But $A_\mathbb{B}@V$, or rather the dual universal automaton $\overline{A_\mathbb{B}@V}$, is not suited for synthesis —we cannot synthesize from $\overline{A_\mathbb{B}@V}$— roughly because the transducer should not control the store actions of the underlying A, while the automaton $\overline{A_\mathbb{B}@V}$ gives a transducer such a control. (**3**) We add k_T fresh registers $\mathcal{R}^T$ to A that will be controlled by a transducer. To this end, we define the automaton $A \otimes T^{all}$. Additionally, the automaton T^{all} filters out data-words that do not belong to any of the transducers (e.g., data-words that have a value for o that was not seen before on i). (**4**) We enhance the Boolean associate $(A \otimes T^{all})_\mathbb{B}$ of $A \otimes T^{all}$ with information about equivalences between the registers $\mathcal{R}^T$ *and* $\mathcal{R}^A$; the resulting automaton is called $(A \otimes T^{all})_\mathbb{B}@W$. (**5**) Finally, we hide the information that should not be visible to a transducer, namely information related to the automaton registers $\mathcal{R}^A$. The resulting automaton is called $H = hide_A((A \otimes T^{all})_\mathbb{B}@W)$ and it is such that $\exists T : T \models \tilde{A}$ iff $\exists T_\mathbb{B} : T_\mathbb{B} \models \tilde{H}$, where $\tilde{H}$ is dual to H.

3.1   Boolean Associates of Register Automata and Transducers

The transition functions of k-register automata do not contain any infinite objects—data-values appear only in the semantics. Let us define Boolean associates of register automata and transducers.
   Given a k-register automaton $A = \langle P, \mathcal{P}, \mathcal{R}, \mathcal{d}_0, Q, q_0, \delta, F \rangle$, let *Boolean automaton* $A_\mathbb{B} = \langle P_\mathbb{B}, Q, q_0, \delta_\mathbb{B}, F \rangle$ be a standard register-less automaton where:

- let $G_i = \{g_{i\tau_1}, ..., g_{i\tau_k}\}$, $G_o = \{g_{o\tau_1}, ..., g_{o\tau_k}\}$, $Asgn = \{a_{\tau_1}, ..., a_{\tau_k}\}$. Then:
- $P_\mathbb{B} = P \cup G_i \cup G_o \cup Asgn$,
- $\delta_\mathbb{B} : Q \times 2^{P_\mathbb{B}} \to 2^Q$ contains $(q, l \cup g_i \cup g_o \cup a, q') \in \delta_\mathbb{B}$ iff $(q, l, \bar{b}_i, \bar{b}_o, \bar{a}, q') \in \delta$, where $l \in 2^P$, $g_i \in 2^{G_i}$, $g_o \in 2^{G_o}$, $a \in 2^{Asgn}$, $\bar{b}_i = (g_{i\tau_1} \in g_i, ..., g_{i\tau_k} \in g_i) \in \mathbb{B}^k$, $\bar{b}_o = (g_{o\tau_1} \in g_o, ..., g_{o\tau_k} \in g_o) \in \mathbb{B}^k$, $\bar{a} = (a_{\tau_1} \in a, ..., a_{\tau_k} \in a) \in \mathbb{B}^k$. Informally, we take the assignment component (on the right side) of δ and move it to the left side of $\delta_\mathbb{B}$, and introduce new Boolean signals to describe the Boolean components.

For convenience, we say that a letter $g_i \in 2^{G_i}$ encodes the guard $(g_{i\tau_1} \in g_i, ..., g_{i\tau_k} \in g_i) \in \mathbb{B}^k$, and vice versa; similarly for a letter from 2^{G_o} and 2^{Asgn}.

A *Boolean path* is an infinite sequence $q_0 \xrightarrow{l_0 \cup g_{i0} \cup g_{o0} \cup a_0} q_1 \xrightarrow{l_1 \cup g_{i1} \cup g_{o1} \cup a_1} ...$ from $(Q \times 2^{P_\mathbb{B}})^\omega$ that satisfies $\delta_\mathbb{B}$. When necessary to distinguish paths of register automata (which are in $(Q \times \mathcal{D}^k \times 2^P \times \mathcal{D}^2)^\omega$) from Boolean paths, we call the former *data-paths*. A data-path $(q_0, \bar{d}_0) \xrightarrow{(l_0, i_0, o_0, \bar{a}_0)} (q_1, \bar{d}_1) \xrightarrow{(l_1, i_1, o_1, \bar{a}_1)} ...$ *corresponds* to a Boolean path $q_0 \xrightarrow{l_0 \cup g_{i0} \cup g_{o0} \cup a_0} q_1 \xrightarrow{l_1 \cup g_{i1} \cup g_{o1} \cup a_1} ...$ where g_{ij} encodes the guard $(i_j = \bar{d}_j[1], ..., i_j = \bar{d}_j[k])$, g_{oj} encodes the guard $(o_j = \bar{d}_j[1], ..., o_j = \bar{d}_j[k])$, and $a_j \in 2^{Asgn}$ encodes $\bar{a}_j \in \mathbb{B}^k$, for $j \in \mathbb{N}_0$. From the definition of paths of register automata on page 3, it follows that for every path of a register automaton, there exists a path in the associated Boolean automaton to which the data-path corresponds. Consider the reverse direction, where we say that a Boolean path *corresponds* to a data-path iff the data-path corresponds to it. The reverse direction does not necessarily hold: there is a register automaton A (e.g., with 2 registers) where some Boolean paths of $A_\mathbb{B}$ do not have a corresponding data-path in A. This is because the letters of a Boolean path can describe contradictory guards. For example, let a transition in a Boolean path have $\bar{a} = (true, true)$, meaning that in a data-path the value of data-input is stored into the registers τ_1 and τ_2. Hence, in the next transition of the data-path, $i = \tau_1 \Leftrightarrow i = \tau_2$ must hold, but the Boolean path may have $g_i = \{g_{i\tau_2}\}$ (describing the guard $i \neq \tau_1 \wedge i = \tau_2$). Thus, we got the following.

Observation 1.

- *For every register automaton A, every data-path in A has exactly one corresponding Boolean path in $A_\mathbb{B}$.*
- *There exists a register automaton A where some Boolean paths of $A_\mathbb{B}$ do not correspond to any data-path of A.*

A *Boolean word* is a projection of a Boolean path into $2^{P_\mathbb{B}}$; note that it contains information about assignment actions.

Similarly we define Boolean transducers. Given a k-register transducer $T = \langle I, O, \mathcal{G}, \mathcal{O}, \mathcal{R}, \mathcal{d}_0, S, s_0, \tau \rangle$, a *Boolean transducer* $T_\mathbb{B} = \langle I_\mathbb{B}, O_\mathbb{B}, S, s_0, \tau_\mathbb{B} \rangle$ is a standard register-less transducer where: $I_\mathbb{B} = I \cup G_i$, $G_i = \{g_{i\tau_1}, ..., g_{i\tau_k}\}$, $O_\mathbb{B} = O \cup Asgn \cup O_k$, $Asgn = \{a_{\tau_1}, ..., a_{\tau_k}\}$, and O_k has enough Boolean signals to encode the numbers $[k]$. The transition function $\tau_\mathbb{B} : S \times 2^{I_\mathbb{B}} \to S \times 2^{O_\mathbb{B}}$ contains $(s, l \cup g_i, o \cup o_k \cup a, s')$ iff $(s, l, \bar{b}_i, o, \tilde{o}_k, \bar{a}, s') \in \tau$ where $s, s' \in S$, $l \in 2^I$, $a \in 2^{Asgn}$

encodes $\bar{a} \in \mathbb{B}^k$, $g_i \in 2^{G_i}$ encodes $\bar{b}_i \in \mathbb{B}^k$, and $o_k \in 2^{O_k}$ encodes $\tilde{o}_k \in [k]$. A *Boolean path* is an infinite sequence $s_0 \xrightarrow{l_0 \cup g_{i0}, o_0 \cup o_{k0} \cup a_0} s_1 \xrightarrow{l_1 \cup g_{i1}, o_1 \cup o_{k1} \cup a_1} \ldots$ from $(S \times 2^{I_{\mathbb{B}}} \times 2^{O_{\mathbb{B}}})^{\omega}$ that satisfies $\tau_{\mathbb{B}}$.

Because every register transducer can be viewed as a register automaton, a similar observation holds for the register transducers.

3.2   Verifier to Remove Inconsistent Guards (V_k and $A_{\mathbb{B}}@V_k$)

We introduce the automaton called verifier that filters out the Boolean paths of $A_{\mathbb{B}}$ that do not correspond to any data-paths.

$\mathbf{V_k}$. Given $k \in \mathbb{N}$, the *verifier* is a deterministic looping register-less automaton $V_k = \langle P_V, \Pi, \pi_0, \delta_V \rangle$ where

- Π is the set of all possible partitions of $\{\imath_1, ..., \imath_k\}$; the initial state $\pi_0 = \{\{\imath_1, ..., \imath_k\}\}$ contains the only partition. Later, we will a partition-state to track if the registers have the same value.
- $P_V = G_i \cup G_o \cup Asgn$ where $G_i = \{g_{i\imath_1}, ..., g_{i\imath_k}\}$, $G_o = \{g_{o\imath_1}, ..., g_{o\imath_k}\}$, $Asgn = \{a_{\imath_1}, ..., a_{\imath_k}\}$.
- $\delta_V : \Pi \times 2^{P_V} \to \Pi$ contains $\pi \xrightarrow{g_i \cup g_o \cup a} \pi'$ where:
  - the guard-letter $g_i \cup g_o$ respects the current partition:
    * for every $\imath_m = \imath_n$ of π (i.e., belonging to the same partition):
      $g_{i\imath_m} \in g_i \Leftrightarrow g_{i\imath_n} \in g_i$ and $g_{o\imath_m} \in g_o \Leftrightarrow g_{o\imath_n} \in g_o$;
    * for every $\imath_m \neq \imath_n$ of π (i.e., belonging to different partitions):
      $g_{i\imath_m} \in g_i \Rightarrow g_{i\imath_n} \notin g_i$ and $g_{o\imath_m} \in g_o \Rightarrow g_{o\imath_n} \notin g_o$;
  - the successor partition respects the assignment-letter a, formalized as follows. For every m, n in $[k]$, let e_{mn} denote that π contains $\imath_m = \imath_n$, and e'_{mn} is for π'. The value e'_{mn} is uniquely defined:

$$e'_{mn} = (a_{\imath_m} \wedge a_{\imath_n}) \vee (\neg a_{\imath_m} \wedge a_{\imath_n} \wedge g_{i\imath_m}) \vee (a_{\imath_m} \wedge \neg a_{\imath_n} \wedge g_{i\imath_n}) \vee (\neg a_{\imath_m} \wedge \neg a_{\imath_n} \wedge e_{mn}).$$

  This definition, together with the previous item, ensures that all e'_{mn} together form a partition (e.g., it is impossible to get $e'_{1,2} \wedge e'_{2,3} \wedge \neg e'_{1,3}$).
- The acceptance condition (not shown in the tuple) defines every path (infinite by definition) to be accepting; hence, every word that has a path in the automaton is accepted.

An example of a verifier is in Fig. 3.

$\mathbf{A_{\mathbb{B}}@V_k}$. Given a verifier $V_k = \langle P^V, Q^V, q_0^V, \delta^V \rangle$ and a register-less non-deterministic Büchi automaton $A_{\mathbb{B}} = \langle P^A, Q^A, q_0^A, \delta^A, F^A \rangle$, let $A_{\mathbb{B}}@V$ denote the non-deterministic Büchi automaton $\langle P, Q, q_0, \delta, F \rangle$ where:

- $P = P^V \cup P^A$;
- $Q = Q^V \times Q^A$, $q_0 = (q_0^V, q_0^A)$;
- $\delta : Q \times 2^P \to 2^Q$ has $((q_V, q_A), p, (q'_V, q'_A))$ iff $(q_V, p \cap 2^{P^V}, q'_V) \in \delta^V$ and $(q_A, p \cap 2^{P^A}, q'_A) \in \delta^A$; and
- $F = Q^V \times F^A$.

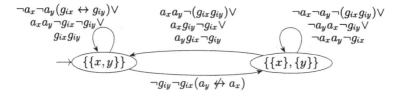

Fig. 3. A verifier automaton (a register-less looping automaton) for 2-register automata with $\mathcal{R} = \{x, y\}$. The edges have symbolic labels. Later, the left state $\{\{x, y\}\}$ will be used to denote that the registers x and y store the same value, while the right state $\{\{x\}, \{y\}\}$ will denote that they store different values. The automaton has similar restrictions for o (not shown).

Hence, $L(A_{\mathbb{B}}@V_k) = L(V_k) \cap L(A_{\mathbb{B}})$. Since $P^A = P' \cup G_i \cup G_o \cup Asgn$ (where P' are the Boolean signals of the register automaton A) and $P^V = G_i \cup G_o \cup Asgn$, the automaton $A_{\mathbb{B}}@V_k$ works on words from $(P' \cup G_i \cup G_o \cup Asgn)^\omega$. The words of $A_{\mathbb{B}}@V_k$ that do not fall out of V_k are called *consistent*, otherwise *inconsistent*.

Observation 2. *For every non-deterministic Büchi k-register automaton A:*

- *Every data-path of A has exactly one corresponding Boolean path in $A_{\mathbb{B}}@V_k$.*
- *Every Boolean path of $A_{\mathbb{B}}@V_k$ has either one or infinitely many corresponding data-paths in A.*

Corollary 1. *For every non-deterministic Büchi k-register automaton A:*
   $A_{\mathbb{B}}@V_k$ has an accepted Boolean word $\Leftrightarrow$ A has an accepted data-word.

This result, namely, decidability of non-emptiness non-deterministic Büchi register automata, was earlier established in [10, Thm.1] using cutoffs (we discussed cutoffs on page 5). Our verifier uses a similar insight, but allows us to easily extend it to the context of synthesis.

3.3   Focusing on Transducer Data-Words (T^{all} and $A \otimes T^{all}$)

For the next step to become clear, we need to look ahead at Theorem 1. There, we will be interested in data-words that belong to some register transducer, rather than general data-words. Recall that the data-words of register transducers require the signal o to have the value that appeared before in the signal i. The automaton T^{all} introduced below ensures this.

$\mathbf{T}^{all}$. Given $k_T \in \mathbb{N}$, T^{all} is a non-deterministic looping k_T-register automaton $\langle P, \mathcal{P}, \mathcal{R}, \mathcal{A}_0, Q, q_0, \delta, F \rangle$ with $P = I \cup O$, $\mathcal{P} = \{i, o\}$, $Q = F = \{q_0\}$. The transition function $\{q_0\} \times 2^P \times \mathbb{B}_i^{k_T} \times \mathbb{B}_o^{k_T} \rightarrow \{q_0\} \times 2^{\mathbb{B}^{k_T}}$, for every $\bar{g}_i \in \mathbb{B}_i^{k_T}$ and $\bar{g}_o \in \{\bar{g} \in \mathbb{B}^{k_T} \| \exists j. \bar{g}[j] = true\}$, contains $(q_0, \bar{a})$ for every $\bar{a} \in \mathbb{B}^{k_T}$. I.e., it ensures that the value of data-output o comes from a register and it does not restrict the assignment action.

Observation 3. *Fix $k_T \in \mathbb{N}$. $\forall w \in (2^{I \cup O} \times \mathcal{D}^2)^\omega$: $w \models T^{all} \Leftrightarrow \exists T: w \models T$, where T is a k_T-register transducer (possibly with $|S| = \infty$).*

In the observation, T might need infinitely many states, because an accepting path of T^{all} on w might exhibit "irregular" storing behaviour, which cannot be expressed by a finite-state transducer (recall transducers are deterministic). This is a minor technical detail though.

A ⊗ T^{all}. The product $A \otimes T^{all}$ of a non-deterministic Büchi k_A-register automaton $A = \langle P, \mathscr{P}, \mathscr{R}^A, d_0, Q^A, q_0^A, \delta^A, F^A \rangle$ and $T^{all} = \langle P, \mathscr{P}, \mathscr{R}^T, d_0, Q^T, q_0^T, \delta^T, F^T \rangle$ with k_T registers is a non-deterministic Büchi $(k_A + k_T)$-register automaton $\langle P, \mathscr{P}, \mathscr{R}, d_0, Q, q_0, \delta, F \rangle$ where $Q = Q^A \times Q^T$, $q_0 = (q_0^A, q_0^T)$, $F = F^A \times F^T$, $\mathscr{R} = \mathscr{R}^A \,\dot\cup\, \mathscr{R}^T$, and the transition function $\delta : Q \times 2^P \times \mathbb{B}_i^{k_A + k_T} \times \mathbb{B}_o^{k_A + k_T} \to 2^{Q \times \mathbb{B}^{k_A + k_T}}$ respects both the transitions functions, δ^A and δ^T.

Observation 4. *$A \otimes T^{all}$ has an accepting word $\Leftrightarrow$ A has an accepting word that belongs to some k_T-register transducer (possibly with $|S| = \infty$).*

3.4   Synthesis-tailored Verifier ($AT_{\mathbb{B}}@W$)

For brevity, let AT denote $A \otimes T^{all}$, and let $AT_{\mathbb{B}}$ be its Boolean associate.

The automaton $AT_{\mathbb{B}}@W$ introduced in this section closely resembles $AT_{\mathbb{B}}@V_k$ and $A_{\mathbb{B}}@V_k$, but it is better suited for synthesis.

Recall from Sect. 3.1 that every $T_{\mathbb{B}}$ generates words from $(2^{I \cup G_i^T} \times 2^{O \cup Asgn^T \cup O_{k_T}})^\omega$, where $Asgn^T = \{a_{\imath_1^T}, ..., a_{\imath_{k_T}^T}\}$, $G_i^T = \{g_{i\imath_1^T}, ..., g_{i\imath_{k_T}^T}\}$, and O_{k_T} has enough Boolean signals to encode the numbers $[k_T]$. In synthesis, we want our target specification automaton to have the same alphabet. The automaton $AT_{\mathbb{B}}@V_k$ uses o-guards instead of O_k signals, hence we introduce the automaton $AT_{\mathbb{B}}@W$ (we do not introduce W separately).

Suppose we have $AT_{\mathbb{B}}@V_k = \langle P, Q, q_0, \delta, F \rangle$ with $P = I \cup O \cup G_i^T \cup G_o^T \cup G_o^A \cup Asgn^T \cup Asgn^A$ and $\delta : Q \times 2^P \to 2^Q$. The automaton $AT_{\mathbb{B}}@W = \langle P', Q, q_0, \delta', F \rangle$ has the same states, but $P' = (P \setminus G_o^T) \cup O_k$ and the transition function δ' is derived from δ as follows. For every $(\pi, q) \xrightarrow{(i, o, g_i, g_o, a)} (\pi', q')$ of δ (where π and π' are partitions of $\mathscr{R}^A \cup \mathscr{R}^T$, q and q' are states of $AT_{\mathbb{B}}$, $i \in 2^I$ and $o \in 2^O$, $g_i \in 2^{G_i}$ and $g_o \in 2^{G_o}$, $a \in 2^{Asgn}$):

- let $J = \{j_1, ..., j_l\} \subset \mathbb{N}$ be such that g_o contains $o = \imath_j^T$ for every $j \in J$;
- for every $j \in J$, add to δ' the transition $(\pi, q) \xrightarrow{(i, o, g_i, \tilde{j}, a)} (\pi', q')$, where $\tilde{j} \in 2^{O_{k_T}}$ encodes the number j.
- Note that if J is empty (g_o requires that $\bigwedge_{t \in [k_T]} o \neq \imath_t^T$), then we do not add transitions to δ', because no transducer can produce such a value for o.

Observation 5. *$AT_{\mathbb{B}}@W$ has an accepting Boolean word $\Leftrightarrow$ A has an accepting data-word that belongs to some k_T-register transducer (possibly with $|S| = \infty$).*

3.5   Synthesis Using Automaton $hide_A(AT_\mathbb{B}@W)$

We cannot use $AT_\mathbb{B}@W$ for synthesis, because it uses Boolean signals that are not visible to transducers (underlined): $I \cup O \times G_i^A \cup G_i^T \cup G_o^A \cup O_{k_T} \cup \underline{Asgn^A} \cup Asgn^T$. Let us show that the simple hiding operation resolves the issue.

Given $AT_\mathbb{B}@W = \langle P, Q, q_0, \delta, F \rangle$ with $P = I \cup O \cup G_i^A \cup G_i^T \cup G_o^A \cup O_{k_T} \cup Asgn^A \cup Asgn^T$, the automaton $hide_A(AT_\mathbb{B}@W)$ is a non-deterministic Büchi automaton $\langle P', Q, q_0, \delta', F \rangle$ with $P' = I \cup O \cup G_i^T \cup O_{k_T} \cup Asgn^T$, and the transition function $\delta' : Q \times 2^I \times 2^O \times 2^{G_i^T} \times 2^{O_{k_T}} \times 2^{Asgn^T} \to 2^Q$ is such that in every transition $q \xrightarrow{(i, o, g_i^T, j, a^T)} Q'$ the destination set $Q' \subseteq Q$ contains all successor states of every transition of $AT_\mathbb{B}@W$ starting in q and having the same common labels:

$$Q' = \bigcup_{g_i^A \in 2^{G_i^A}, g_o^A \in 2^{G_o^A}, a^A \in 2^{Asgn^A}} \delta(q, i, o, g_i^A, g_i^T, g_o^A, j, a^T, a^A).$$

Observation 6. *For every non-deterministic Büchi register automaton A and $k_T \in \mathbb{N}$:*

- *Every path of $AT_\mathbb{B}@W$ corresponds to exactly one path of $hide_A(AT_\mathbb{B}@W)$.*
- *Every path of $hide_A(AT_\mathbb{B}@W)$ corresponds to at least one path of $AT_\mathbb{B}@W$.*

Observations 5 and 6 result in the following.

Lemma 1. *For every register transducer T and non-deterministic Büchi register automaton A:* $(\exists w \in L(T) : w \models A) \Leftrightarrow (\exists w_\mathbb{B} \in L(T_\mathbb{B}) : w_\mathbb{B} \models hide_A(AT_\mathbb{B}@W))$.

Theorem 1. *For every universal co-Büchi register automaton $\tilde{A}$ and $k_T \in \mathbb{N}$:*

$$(\exists T : T \models \tilde{A}) \Leftrightarrow (\exists T_\mathbb{B} : T_\mathbb{B} \models \neg hide_A(AT_\mathbb{B}@W)),$$

where T is a k_T-register transducer, A is dual to $\tilde{A}$ (thus it is non-deterministic Büchi), and $\neg hide_A(AT_\mathbb{B}@W)$ is an automaton expressing the complemented language of $hide_A(AT_\mathbb{B}@W)$ (e.g., it can be the dual universal co-Büchi automaton).

The right side of the theorem (the standard Boolean synthesis problem) holds iff it holds for finite-state transducers (e.g., see [13]). Hence we get:

Corollary 2. *A given instance of the bounded synthesis problem is realizable $\Leftrightarrow$ it is realizable by a finite-state ($|S| < \infty$) register transducer.*

Finally, Fig. 4 depicts the relation between the languages of utilized automata. It illustrates that the approach makes use of determinizable superset of AT (see point 4 in the figure). (In the resulting automaton $hide_A(AT_\mathbb{B}@W)$, when we treat it as a register automaton, the store actions are controlled by transducers *and* are deterministic, i.e., we can associate with each store action a Boolean letter controlled by a transducer.)

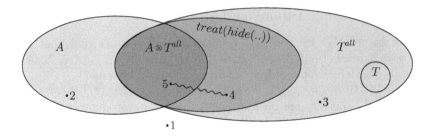

Fig. 4. Inclusion between languages. The language of $treat(hide(..))$ denotes the language of $hide_A(AT_\mathbb{B}@W)$ treated as a register automaton. The existence of points 1, 2, 3, and 5 is trivial. Figure 5 justifies the existence of point 4. The snake line indicates "if a transducer T has point 4, then it also has point 5"(follows from Lemma 1 and observations). If $T \models \neg A$ for some k_T-register transducer, then its language is located as shown by T.

Fig. 5. The automata to show the existence of point 4 in Fig.4. On the left is a non-deterministic Büchi 1-register automaton A: it accepts the words where the signal i is never equal to d_0 (and no restrictions on the values of o). On the right is $hide_A(AT_\mathbb{B}@W)$ where $k_T = 1$: if treated as a register automaton, it accepts the words whose first value of i is not d_0 (plus some restrictions on o). Hence, $L(treat(hide_A(AT_\mathbb{B}@W))) \not\subseteq L(A \otimes T^{all})$. The labels related to o are omitted.

4   Using Temporal Logic in our Synthesis Approach

We proceed to the topic of synthesis of register transducers from a temporal logic. Section 4.1 defines the first-order linear temporal logic with equality, $\text{LTL}(\text{EQ})^1$ and its variants $\exists\text{LTL}(\text{EQ})$ and $\forall\text{LTL}(\text{EQ})$, known as IPTL in [14] and VLTL in [9]. Then Sect. 4.2 defines register-guessing automata that can express $\exists\text{LTL}(\text{EQ})$ formulas.

The sound and complete conversion of $\exists\text{LTL}(\text{EQ})$ into register-guessing automata is described in Sect. 4.3. Then Sect. 4.4 describes a sound but incomplete conversion of register-guessing automata into register automata, which implies the sound but incomplete conversion of $\exists\text{LTL}(\text{EQ})$ into register automata. The latter automata are consumed by our synthesizer.

Unless explicitly stated, all automata are non-deterministic Büchi.

---

[1] The name LTL(EQ) is inspired by the names of logics in SMT-LIB [1].

4.1 LTL(EQ) (Also known as IPTL [14] and VLTL [9])

Let $\mathcal{X}$ be a set of data-variables and P be a set of Boolean propositions. An *LTL(EQ) (prenex-quantified) formula* Φ is of the form (for every $k \in \mathbb{N}$):

$$\Phi = \forall x_1...x_k.cond.\varphi | \exists x_1...x_k.cond.\varphi$$
$$cond = true | x \neq x | cond \wedge cond$$
$$\varphi = true | p | i = x | o = x | \neg\varphi | \varphi \wedge \varphi | \varphi \cup \varphi | X\varphi$$

where $x_1, ..., x_k, x \in \mathcal{X}$, $p \in P$, i and o are two data-propositions, and all the data-variables appearing in φ are quantified. As usual, define $G\varphi$ to be $\neg F\varphi$, $F\varphi = true \cup \varphi$, $\varphi_1 \vee \varphi_2$ is $\neg(\neg\varphi_1 \wedge \neg\varphi_2)$, $\varphi_1 \rightarrow \varphi_2$ is $\neg\varphi_1 \vee \varphi_2$, and *false* is $\neg true$.

Given $w = w_1 w_2... \in (2^P \times \mathcal{D}^{\{i,o\}})^\omega$, define the satisfaction $w \models \Phi$:

- $w \models \forall x_1...x_k.cond.\varphi$ iff for all $\mathit{d}_1, ..., \mathit{d}_k \in \mathcal{D}$ either $cond[x_1 \leftarrow \mathit{d}_1, ..., x_k \leftarrow \mathit{d}_k]$ does not hold or $w \models \varphi[x_1 \leftarrow \mathit{d}_1, ..., x_k \leftarrow \mathit{d}_k]$;
- $w \models \exists x_1...x_k.cond.\varphi$ iff there exists $\mathit{d}_1, ..., \mathit{d}_k \in \mathcal{D}$ such that $cond[x_1 \leftarrow \mathit{d}_1, ..., x_k \leftarrow \mathit{d}_k]$ holds and $w \models \varphi[x_1 \leftarrow \mathit{d}_1, ..., x_k \leftarrow \mathit{d}_k]$;
- let ϕ have the same grammar as φ except that instead of data-variables it has data-values; then
- $w \models true$;
- $w \not\models \phi$ iff $\neg(w \models \phi)$;
- $w \models \neg\phi$ iff $\neg(w \models \phi)$;
- $w \models p$ iff $p \in w_1$;
- $w \models \phi_1 \wedge \phi_2$ iff $w \models \phi_1$ and $w \models \phi_2$;
- for every $\mathit{d} \in \mathcal{D}$, $w \models i = \mathit{d}$ iff in w_1 the data-proposition i has the value d; similarly for o;
- for $i \in \mathbb{N}$, let $w_{[i:]}$ denote w's suffix $w_i w_{i+1}...$; then
- $w \models X\phi$ iff $w_{[2:]} \models \phi$; and
- $w \models \phi_1 \cup \phi_2$ iff $\exists i \in \mathbb{N} : \big((w_{[i:]} \models \phi_2) \wedge (\forall j < i : w_{[j:]} \models \phi_1)\big)$.

Let $\exists LTL(EQ)$ denote LTL(EQ) where formulas have existential quantifiers only, and use $\forall LTL(EQ)$ for universally quantified LTL(EQ) formulas.

4.2 Register Automata with Guessing but Without Storing

In this section we define a variation of register automata that have a non-deterministically chosen initial register values that cannot be rewritten afterwards. Such automata are a restricted version of variable automata [8].

A *k-register-guessing automaton* is a tuple $A = \langle P, \mathcal{P}, \mathcal{R}, Q, q_0, \delta, F, E \rangle$ (notice: no initial register value d_0 and a new element E) with transition function δ of the form $Q \times 2^P \times \mathbb{B}_i^k \times \mathbb{B}_o^k \rightarrow 2^Q$ (notice: no assignment component on the right), where $E \subseteq \mathcal{R} \times \mathcal{R}$ is an *inequality set*[2], while all other components are like for register automata. A path is defined similarly to a path of a register automaton, except that

---

[2] We can get away without using E (by encoding it into δ), but it proved to be convenient in Sect. 4.4.

- an initial configuration $(q_0, \bar{d}_0) \in \{q_0\} \times \mathcal{D}^k$ of the path is arbitrary provided that $\bar{d}_0$ satisfies the inequality set: $\forall (z_i, z_j) \in E : \bar{d}_0[i] \neq \bar{d}_0[j]$; and
- the automaton never stores to the registers.

An accepting word is defined as for register automata.

4.3   Converting ∃LTL(EQ) into Register-Guessing Automata

This section describes the sound and complete conversion of ∃LTL(EQ) formulas into register-guessing automata. The fact that a conversion is possible was noted in [7, Sec.4], however they did not describe the conversion itself.

Consider an ∃LTL(EQ) formula $\Phi = \exists x_1 ... x_k.cond.\varphi(i, o, x_1, ..., x_k)$. We will use the notions of $w_{\mathbb{B}}$ and $\varphi_{\mathbb{B}}$ defined below.

$(w_{\mathbb{B}})$ Given a word $w \in (2^P \times \mathcal{D}^2)^\omega$ and $x_1, ..., x_k \in \mathcal{D}$, let $w_{\mathbb{B}} \in (2^P \times \mathbb{B}_i^k \times \mathbb{B}_o^k)^\omega$ be the word derived from w by replacing every value of i and o in w by the vectors of values, $(i = x_1, ..., i = x_k)$ and $(o = x_1, ..., o = x_k)$.

$(\varphi_{\mathbb{B}})$ In $\varphi(i, o, x_1, ..., x_k)$, replace every expression $i = x_i$ with g_{ix_i} and every expression $o = x_i$ with g_{ox_i}. This introduces $2k$ new Boolean propositions, let $P_{\mathbb{B}} = P \cup \{g_{ix_1}, ..., g_{ix_k}\} \cup \{g_{ox_1}, ..., g_{ox_k}\}$. Let $\varphi_{\mathbb{B}}(g_{ix_1}, ..., g_{ix_k}, g_{ox_1}, ..., g_{ox_k})$ be the resulting LTL formula over Boolean propositions $P_{\mathbb{B}}$.

To convert a formula $\exists x_1 ... x_k.cond.\varphi$ into a k-register-guessing automaton A do the following (**conversion-1**).

- Convert $\varphi_{\mathbb{B}}$ into an NBW automaton $A_{\mathbb{B}} = \langle P_{\mathbb{B}}, Q, q_0, \delta_{\mathbb{B}}, F \rangle$ using standard approaches. Thus, for every $w_{\mathbb{B}} \in 2^{P_{\mathbb{B}}}$: $w_{\mathbb{B}} \models A_{\mathbb{B}}$ iff $w_{\mathbb{B}} \models \varphi_{\mathbb{B}}$.
- Treat $A_{\mathbb{B}}$ as a k-register-guessing automaton $A = \langle P, \mathcal{P}, \mathcal{R}, Q, q_0, \delta, F, E \rangle$, where E is derived from $cond$.

Observation 7. *For every $w \in (2^P \times \mathcal{D}^2)^\omega$: $w \models A \Leftrightarrow w \models \exists x_1 ... x_k.cond.\varphi$.*

4.4   Converting ∃LTL(EQ) into Register Automata

In this section, we describe a sound but incomplete conversion of register-guessing automata into standard register automata. Together with conversion-1 from the previous section, this gives the conversion of ∃LTL(EQ) formulas into register automata. Note that no complete conversion of ∃LTL(EQ) formulas into register automata exists: for example, the formula $\exists x.G(i \neq x)$ has no equivalent register automaton, although there is an equivalent register-guessing automaton.

In automata, we will use the definition of δ that is symbolic instead of explicit, hence the transition functions of k-register-guessing automata and of k-register automata are of the form $Q \times 2^P \times G \rightarrow 2^Q$ and $Q \times 2^P \times G \rightarrow 2^{Q \times \mathbb{B}^k}$, (previously we had $\mathbb{B}_i^k \times \mathbb{B}_o^k$ instead of G), where $g \in G$ has the form $g = true \| g \| i \sim z \| o \sim z$ where $\sim$ denotes $=$ or $\neq$, and $z \in \mathcal{R}$. Using the symbolic definition rather than the explicit one is crucial in making our conversion more applicable

Given a k-register-guessing automaton $A = \langle P, \mathcal{P}, \mathcal{R}, Q, q_0, \delta, F, E \rangle$, construct the k-register automaton $A' = \langle P, \mathcal{P}, \mathcal{R}, \bar{d}_0, Q', q_0', \delta', F' \rangle$ (**conversion-2**):

- $Q' = Q \times \mathbb{B}^k$. The Boolean component encodes, for every $z_i \in \mathcal{R}$, whether the register z_i is assigned a value or not (ignoring the initial values). The initial state $q_0' = (q_0, \textit{false}, ..., \textit{false})$. We call a register z_i with $b_i = \textit{false}$ uninitialized.
- $F' = \{(q, b_1, ..., b_k) \in Q' \| q \in F\}$.
- For every state $(q, b_1, ..., b_k) \in Q'$ and A-transition $q \xrightarrow{(l,g)} q'$ ($l \in 2^P$, $g \in G$):
  - If $g = \textit{true}$, then add to δ' the transition $(q, b_1, ..., b_k) \xrightarrow{(l,g,\textit{false}^k)} (q', b_1, ..., b_k)$.
  - Otherwise, do the following.
    * Abort point: if there exists $i \in [k]$ such that $b_i = \textit{false}$ and g contains $i \neq z_i$ or $o \sim z_i$, then abort. Because the register z_i is uninitalized ($b_i = \textit{false}$), we cannot know the valuation of $i \neq z_i$ or $o \neq z_i$. In contrast, if the guard g contains $i = z_i$, we can assume that it holds and store i into z_i (we cannot do this for $o = z_i$, because the automata do not allow for storing o).
    * Add to δ' the transition $(q, b_1, ..., b_k) \xrightarrow{(l,g',a)} (q', b_1', ..., b_k')$ where for every $i \in [k]$:
      · $b_i' = \textit{true}$ iff $b_i = \textit{true}$ or g contains $i = z_i$.
      · The action a stores i into z_i iff g contains $i = z_i$ and $b_i = \textit{false}$.
      · The guard g' contains $i \sim z_i$ iff g contains $i \sim z_i$ and $b_i = \textit{true}$; similarly for $o \sim z_i$.
    * Finally, we account for the inequality set E and update g' as follows. For every $(z_i, z_j) \in E$: if $b_i = \textit{true}$ and the action a contains $z_j = i$, then add to g' the expression $i \neq r_i$.
      (Here we assume that the A-transition is not contradictory, namely, it is not the case that $\exists (z_i, z_j) \in E : b_i = \textit{false} \wedge b_j = \textit{false} \wedge (i = z_i) \in g \wedge (i = z_j) \in g$. Such transitions cannot be executed in A and can be removed beforehand.)
- Note that the automaton A' never compares i nor o with a register that was uninitialized. Therefore, the component d_0 of A' can be anything from $\mathcal{D}$.

The automaton A' has $|Q'| = |Q| \cdot 2^k$, but the number of reachable states is $|Q| \cdot k$.

Observation 8. *If conversion-2 succeeds, then $L(A) = L(A')$.*

Theorem 2. *Given an $\exists LTL(EQ)$ $\Phi = \exists x_1, ..., x_k.cond.\varphi$. If conversion-1 and conversion-2 succeed, then $L(\Phi) = L(A')$.*

References

1. Barrett, C., Fontaine, P., Tinelli, C.: The Satisfiability Modulo Theories Library (SMT-LIB) (2016). www.SMT-LIB.org
2. Church, A.: Logic, arithmetic, and automata. In: International Congress of Mathematicians (Stockholm, 1962), pp. 23–35. Institute Mittag-Leffler, Djursholm (1963)
3. Demri, S., D'Souza, D., Gascon, R.: Temporal logics of repeating values. J. Log. Comput. **22**(5), 1059–1096 (2012). https://doi.org/10.1093/logcom/exr013

4. Demri, S., Lazić, R.: LTL with the freeze quantifier and register automata. ACM Trans. Comput. Log. **10**(3), 16:1–16:30 (2009). https://doi.org/10.1145/1507244.1507246
5. Ehlers, R., Seshia, S.A., Kress-Gazit, H.: Synthesis with identifiers. In: McMillan, K.L., Rival, X. (eds.) VMCAI 2014. LNCS, vol. 8318, pp. 415–433. Springer, Heidelberg (2014). https://doi.org/10.1007/978-3-642-54013-4_23
6. Finkbeiner, B., Schewe, S.: Bounded synthesis. STTT **15**(5–6), 519–539 (2013)
7. Frenkel, H., Grumberg, O., Sheinvald, S.: An automata-theoretic approach to modeling systems and specifications over infinite data. In: Barrett, C., Davies, M., Kahsai, T. (eds.) NFM 2017. LNCS, vol. 10227, pp. 1–18. Springer, Cham (2017). https://doi.org/10.1007/978-3-319-57288-8_1
8. Grumberg, O., Kupferman, O., Sheinvald, S.: Variable automata over infinite alphabets. In: Dediu, A.-H., Fernau, H., Martín-Vide, C. (eds.) LATA 2010. LNCS, vol. 6031, pp. 561–572. Springer, Heidelberg (2010). https://doi.org/10.1007/978-3-642-13089-2_47
9. Grumberg, O., Kupferman, O., Sheinvald, S.: Model checking systems and specifications with parameterized atomic propositions. In: Chakraborty, S., Mukund, M. (eds.) ATVA 2012. LNCS, pp. 122–136. Springer, Heidelberg (2012). https://doi.org/10.1007/978-3-642-33386-6_11
10. Kaminski, M., Francez, N.: Finite-memory automata. Theor. Comput. Sci. **134**(2), 329–363 (1994). http://www.sciencedirect.com/science/article/pii/0304397594902429
11. Kupferman, O., Vardi, M.: Synthesis with incomplete informatio. In: 2nd International Conference on Temporal Logic, pp. 91–106. Manchester (1997)
12. Lazić, R., Nowak, D.: A unifying approach to data-independence. In: Palamidessi, C. (ed.) CONCUR 2000. LNCS, vol. 1877, pp. 581–596. Springer, Heidelberg (2000). https://doi.org/10.1007/3-540-44618-4_41
13. Pnueli, A., Rosner, R.: On the synthesis of a reactive module. In: Conference Record of the Sixteenth Annual ACM Symposium on Principles of Programming Languages, pp. 179–190. ACM Press, Austin, Texas, USA, January 11–13 (1989). https://doi.org/10.1145/75277.75293
14. Wolper, P.: Expressing interesting properties of programs in propositional temporal logic. In: Proceedings of the 13th POPL, pp. 184–193. ACM, New York, NY, USA (1986). https://doi.org/10.1145/512644.512661

Tool Papers

EthIR: A Framework for High-Level Analysis of Ethereum Bytecode

Elvira Albert[1], Pablo Gordillo[1(✉)], Benjamin Livshits[2], Albert Rubio[3],
and Ilya Sergey[4]

[1] Universidad Complutense de Madrid, Madrid, Spain
pabgordi@ucm.es
[2] Imperial College London, London, UK
[3] Universitat Politècnica de Catalunya, Barcelona, Spain
[4] University College London, London, UK

Abstract. Analyzing Ethereum bytecode, rather than the source code from which it was generated, is a necessity when: (1) the source code is not available (e.g., the blockchain only stores the bytecode), (2) the information to be gathered in the analysis is only visible at the level of bytecode (e.g., gas consumption is specified at the level of EVM instructions), (3) the analysis results may be affected by optimizations performed by the compiler (thus the analysis should be done ideally *after* compilation). This paper presents EthIR, a framework for analyzing Ethereum bytecode, which relies on (an extension of) Oyente, a tool that generates CFGs; EthIR produces from the CFGs, a *rule-based representation* (RBR) of the bytecode that enables the application of (existing) high-level analyses to infer properties of EVM code.

1 Introduction

Means of creating distributed consensus have given rise to a family of distributed protocols for building a replicated transaction log (a *blockchain*). These technological advances enabled the creation of decentralised cryptocurrencies, such as Bitcoin [9]. Ethereum [12], one of Bitcoin's most prominent successors, adds Turing-complete stateful computation associated with funds-exchanging transactions—so-called *smart contracts*—to replicated distributed storage.

Smart contracts are small programs stored in a blockchain that can be invoked by transactions initiated by parties involved in the protocol, executing some business logic as automatic and trustworthy mediators. Typical applications of smart contracts involve implementations of multi-party accounting, voting and arbitration mechanisms, auctions, as well as puzzle-solving games

This work was funded partially by the Spanish MECD Salvador de Madariaga Mobility Grants PRX17/00297 and PRX17/00303, the Spanish MINECO projects TIN2015-69175-C4-2-R and TIN2015-69175-C4-3-R, the CM project S2013/ICE-3006 and by the UCM CT27/16-CT28/16 grant. Sergey's research was supported by a generous gift from Google.

S. K. Lahiri and C. Wang (Eds.): ATVA 2018, LNCS 11138, pp. 513–520, 2018.
https://doi.org/10.1007/978-3-030-01090-4_30

with reward distribution. To preserve the global consistency of the blockchain, every transaction involving an interaction with a smart contract is replicated across the system. In Ethereum, replicated execution is implemented by means of a uniform execution back-end—Ethereum Virtual Machine (EVM) [12]—a stack-based operational formalism, enriched with a number of primitives, allowing contracts to call each other, refer to the global blockchain state, initiate sub-transactions, and even create new contract instances dynamically. That is, EVM provides a convenient *compilation target* for multiple high-level programming languages for implementing Ethereum-based smart contracts. In contrast with prior low-level languages for smart contract scripting, EVM features mutable persistent state that can be modified, during a contract's lifetime, by parties interacting with it. Finally, in order to tackle the issue of possible denial-of-service attacks, EVM comes with a notion of *gas*—a cost semantics of virtual machine instructions.

All these features make EVM a very powerful execution formalism, simultaneously making it quite difficult to formally analyse its bytecode for possible inefficiencies and vulnerabilities—a challenge exacerbated by the mission-critical nature of smart contracts, which, after having been deployed, cannot be amended or taken off the blockchain.

Contributions In this work, we take a step further towards *sound* and *automated* reasoning about high-level properties of Ethereum smart contracts.

- We do so by providing ETHIR, an open-source tool for precise decompilation of EVM bytecode into a high-level representation in a rule-based form; ETHIR is available via GitHub: https://github.com/costa-group/ethIR.
- Our representation reconstructs high-level control and data-flow for EVM bytecode from the low-level encoding provided in the CFGs generated by OYENTE. It enables application of state-of-the-art analysis tools developed for high-level languages to infer properties of bytecode.
- We showcase this application by conducting an automated resource analysis of existing contracts from the blockchain inferring their loop bounds.

2   From EVM to a Rule-based Representation

The purpose of decompilation –as for other bytecode languages (see, *e.g.*, the Soot analysis and optimization framework[11])– is to make explicit in a higher-level representation the *control flow* of the program (by means of rules which indicate the continuation of the execution) and the *data flow* (by means of explicit variables, which represent the data stored in the stack, in contract fields, in local variables, and in the blockchain), so that an analysis or transformation tool can have this control flow information directly available.

2.1   Extension of Oyente to Generate the CFG

Given some EVM code, the OYENTE tool generates a set of blocks that store the information needed to represent the CFG of such EVM code. However, when the jump address of a block is not unique (depends on the flow of the program), the blocks generated by OYENTE sometimes only store the last value of the jump address. We have modified the structure of OYENTE blocks in order to include all possible jump addresses, so that the whole CFG is reconstructed. As an example, Fig. 1 shows the Solidity source code for a fragment of a contract (left), and the CFG generated from it (right). Observe that in the CFGs generated by our extension of OYENTE, the instructions SSTORE or SLOAD are annotated with an identifier of the contract field they operate on (for instance, a SSTORE operation that stores a value on the contract field 0 is replaced by SSTORE 0). Similarly, the EVM instructions MSTORE and MLOAD instructions are annotated with the memory address they operate on (such addresses will be transformed into variables in the RBR whenever possible). These annotations cannot be generated when the memory address is not statically known, though, (for instance, when we have an array access inside a loop with a variable index). In such cases, we annotate the corresponding instructions with "?".

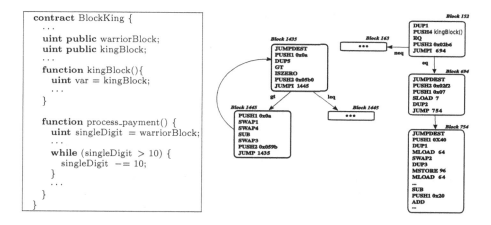

Fig. 1. Solidity code (left), and EVM code for `process_payment` within CFG (right).

Finally, when we have Solidity code available, we are able to retrieve the name of the functions invoked from the hash codes (see e.g. Block 152 in which we have annotated in the second bytecode kingBlock, the name of the function to be invoked). This allows us to statically know the continuation block.

2.2   From the CFG to Guarded Rules

The translation from EVM into our *rule-based representation* is done by applying the translation in Definition 1 to each block in a CFG. The identifiers given to the rules -*block_x* or *jump_x*- use x, the PC of the first bytecode in the block being translated. We distinguish among three cases: (1) if the last bytecode in the block is an unconditional jump (JUMP), we generate a single rule, with an invocation to the continuation block, (2) if it is a conditional jump (JUMPI) we produce two additional *guarded* rules which represent the continuation when the condition holds, and when it does not, (3) otherwise, we continue the execution in block $x+s$ (where s is the size of the EVM bytecodes in the block being translated). As regards the variables, we distinguish the following types:

1. *Stack variables*: a key ingredient of the translation is that the stack is flattened into variables, *i.e.*, the part of the stack that the block is using is represented, when it is translated into a rule, by the explicit variables $s_0, s_1, \ldots$, where s_1 is above s_0, and so on. The initial stack variables are obtained as parameters $s_0, s_1, \ldots, s_n$ and denoted as $\bar{s}_n$.
2. *Local variables*: the content of the local memory in numeric addresses appearing in the code, which are accessed through MSTORE and MLOAD with the given address, are modelled with variables $l_0, l_1, \ldots, l_r$, denoted as $\bar{l}_r$, and are passed as parameters. For the translation, we assume we are given a map `lmap` which associates a different local variable to every numeric address memory used in the code. When the address is not numeric, we represent it using a fresh variable local to the rule to indicate that we do not have information on this memory location.
3. *Contract fields*: we model fields with variables $g_0, \ldots, g_k$, denoted as $\bar{g}_k$, which are passed as parameters. Since these fields are accessed using SSTORE and SLOAD using the number of the field, we associate g_i to the ith field. As for the local memory, if the number of the field is not numeric because it is unknown (annotated as "?"), we use a fresh local variable to represent it.
4. *Blockchain data*: we model this data with variables $\overline{bc}$, which are either indexed with $md_0, \ldots, md_q$ when they represent the message data, or with corresponding names, if they are precise information of the call, like the gas, which is accessed with the opcode GAS, or about the blockchain, like the current block number, which is accessed with the opcode NUMBER. All this data is accessed through dedicated opcodes, which may consume some offsets of the stack and normally place the result on top of the stack (although some of them, like CALLDATACOPY, can store information in the local memory).

The translation uses an auxiliary function τ to translate each bytecode into corresponding high-level instructions (and updates the size of the stack m) and τ_G to translate the guard of a conditional jump. The grammar of the resulting RBR language into which the EVM is translated is given in Fig. 2. We optionally can keep in the RBR the original bytecode instructions from which the higher-level ones are obtained by simply wrapping them within a nop functor (*e.g.*, nop(DUPN)). This is relevant for a gas analyzer to assign the precise gas consumption to the higher-level instruction in which the bytecode was transformed.

Definition 1. *Given a block B with instructions $b_1, \ldots, b_i$ in a CFG starting at PC x, and local variables map* `lmap`, *the generated rules are:*

if $b_i \equiv$ *JUMP* p
$block\_x(\bar{s}_n, \bar{g}_k, \bar{l}_r, \bar{bc}_q) \Rightarrow \tau(b_1, \ldots, b_{i-1}), call(block\_p(\bar{s}_{m-1}, \bar{g}_k, \bar{l}_r, \bar{bc}_q))$
if $b_i \equiv$ *JUMPI* p
$block\_x(\bar{s}_n, \bar{g}_k, \bar{l}_r, \bar{bc}_q) \Rightarrow \tau(b_1, \ldots, b_{c-1}), call(jump\_x(\bar{s}_m, \bar{g}_k, \bar{l}_r, \bar{bc}_q))$
$jump\_x(\bar{s}_n, \bar{g}_k, \bar{l}_r, \bar{bc}_q) \Rightarrow \tau_G(b_c, \ldots, b_{i-2})\|call(block\_p(\bar{s}_m, \bar{g}_k, \bar{l}_r, \bar{bc}_q))$
$jump\_x(\bar{s}_n, \bar{g}_k, \bar{l}_r, \bar{bc}_q) \Rightarrow \neg\tau_G(b_c, \ldots, b_{i-2})\|call(block\_(x+s)(\bar{s}_m, \bar{g}_k, \bar{l}_r, \bar{bc}_q))$
if $b_i \not\equiv$ *JUMP and* $b_i \not\equiv$ *JUMPI*
$block\_x(\bar{s}_n, \bar{g}_k, \bar{l}_r, \bar{bc}_q) \Rightarrow \tau(b_1, \ldots, b_i), call(block\_(x+i)(\bar{s}_m, \bar{g}_k, \bar{l}_r, \bar{bc}_q))$

where functions τ and τ_G for some representative bytecodes are:

$\tau(JUMPDEST)$	$= \{\}; \; m := m$	
$\tau(PUSHN \; v)$	$= \{s_{m+1} = v\}; \; m := m+1$	
$\tau(DUPN)$	$= \{s_{m+1} = s_{m+1-N}\}; \; m := m+1$	
$\tau(SWAPN)$	$= \{s_{m+1} = s_m, s_m = s_{m-N}, s_{m-N} = s_{m+1}\}; \; m := m$	
$\tau(ADD\|SUB\|MUL\|DIV)$	$= \{s_{m-1} = s_m + \|-\|*\|/s_{m-1}\}; \; m := m-1$	
$\tau(SLOAD\|MLOAD \; v)$	$= \{s_m = g_v\|l_{lmap(v)}\}; \; m := m$	*if v is numeric*
	$= \{gl\|ll = s_m, s_m = \mathsf{fresh}()\}; \; m := m$	*otherwise*
$\tau(SSTORE\|MSTORE \; v)$	$= \{g_v\|l_{lmap(v)} = s_{m-1}\}; \; m := m-2$	*if v is numeric*
	$= \{gs_1\|ls_1 = s_{m-1}, gs_2\|ls_2 = s_m\}; \; m := m-2$	*otherwise*
$\ldots$		
$\tau_G(GT,ISZERO)\|\tau_G(GT)$	$= leq(s_m, s_{m-1})\|gt(s_m, s_{m-1}); \; m := m-2$	
$\tau_G(EQ,ISZERO)\|\tau_G(EQ)$	$= neq(s_m, s_{m-1})\|eq(s_m, s_{m-1}); \; m := m-2$	
$\ldots$		

RBR	$\rightarrow (B \mid J) \; RBR \mid \epsilon$
B	$\rightarrow block\_id \; (\bar{i}_n, \bar{g}_k, \bar{l}_r, \bar{bc}) \Rightarrow Instr \;\; (Call \mid \epsilon)$
J	$\rightarrow jump\_id \; (\bar{i}_n, \bar{g}_k, \bar{l}_r, \bar{bc}) \Rightarrow InstrJ$
$Instr$	$\rightarrow S \; Instr \mid \epsilon$
S	$\rightarrow s = Exp$
Exp	$\rightarrow num \mid x \mid x+y \mid x-y \mid x*y \mid x/y \mid x\%y \mid x^y$
	$\mid and(x,y) \mid or(x,y) \mid xor(x,y) \mid not(x)$
$Call$	$\rightarrow call(block\_id(\bar{i}_n, \bar{g}_k, \bar{l}_r, \bar{bc})) \mid call(jump\_id(\bar{i}_n, \bar{g}_k, \bar{l}_r, \bar{bc}))$
$InstrJ$	$\rightarrow Guard \; "\|" \; call(block\_id(\bar{i}_n, \bar{g}_k, \bar{l}_r, \bar{bc}))$
$Guard$	$\rightarrow eq(x,y) \mid neq(x,y) \mid lt(x,y) \mid leq(x,y) \mid gt(x,y) \mid geq(x,y)$

Fig. 2. Grammar of the RBR into which the EVM is translated

– c is the index of the instruction, where the guard of the conditional jump starts. Note that the condition ends at the index $i - 2$ and there is always a PUSH at $i - 1$. Since the pushed address (that we already have in p) and the result of the condition are consumed by the JUMPI, we do not store them in stack variables.

- m represents the size of the stack for the block. Initially we have $m := n$.
- variables gs_1, gs_2 and gl, and ls_1, ls_2 and ll, are local to each rule and are used to represent the use of SLOAD and SSTORE, and MLOAD and MSTORE, when the given address is not a concrete number. For SLOAD and MLOAD we also use fresh(), to denote a generator of fresh variables to safely represent the unknown value of the loaded address.

Example 1. As an example, an excerpt of the RBR obtained by translating the three blocks on the right-hand side of Fig. 1 is as follows (selected instructions keep using nop annotations the bytecode from which they have been obtained):

$block152(s_0, \overline{g_{11}}, \overline{l_8}, \overline{bc}) \Rightarrow$	$block694(s_0, \overline{g_{11}}, \overline{l_8}, \overline{bc}) \Rightarrow$	$s_5 = s_4$
$s_1 = s_0$ nop(DUP1)	$s_1 = 754$ nop(PUSH2)	$s_4 = s_2$
$s_2 = 6584849474$ nop(PUSH4)	$s_2 = 7$ nop(PUSH1)	$s_2 = s_5$ nop(SWAP2)
$call(jump152(\overline{s_2}, \overline{g_{11}}, \overline{l_8}, \overline{bc})$	$s_2 = g_7$ nop(SLOAD)	$s_5 = s_2$ nop(DUP3)
	$s_3 = s_1$ nop(DUP2)	$l_1 = s_4$ nop(MSTORE)
nop(EQ) nop(PUSH2) nop(JUMPI)	$call(block754(\overline{s_2}, \overline{g_{11}}, \overline{l_8}, \overline{bc})$	$s_3 = l_0$ nop(MLOAD)
$jump152(\overline{s_2}, \overline{g_{11}}, \overline{l_8}, \overline{bc}) \Rightarrow$		...
$eq(s_2, s_1)$	nop(JUMP)	$s_3 = s_4 - s_3$ nop(SUB)
$call(block694(s_0, \overline{g_{11}}, \overline{l_8}, \overline{bc})$	$block754(\overline{s_2}, \overline{g_{11}}, \overline{l_8}, \overline{bc}) \Rightarrow$	$s_4 = 32$ nop(PUSH1)
$jump152(\overline{s_2}, \overline{g_{11}}, \overline{l_8}, \overline{bc}) \Rightarrow$	$s_3 = 64$ nop(PUSH1)	$s_3 = s_4 + s_3$ nop(ADD)
$neq(s_2, s_1)$	$s_4 = s_3$ nop(DUP1)	...
$call(block163(s_0, \overline{g_{11}}, \overline{l_8}, \overline{bc})$	$s_4 = l_0$ nop(MLOAD)	

3   Case Study: Bounding Loops in EVM using SACO

To illustrate the applicability of our framework, we have analyzed quantitative properties of EVM code by translating it into our intermediate representation and analyzing it with the high-level static analyzer SACO [3]. SACO is able to infer, among other properties, *upper bounds* on the number of iterations of loops. Note that this is the first crucial step to infer the gas consumption of smart contracts, a property of much interest [4]. The internal representation of SACO (described in [2]) matches the grammar in Fig. 2 after minor syntactic translations (that we have solved implementing a simple translator that is available in github, named saco.py). As SACO does not have bit-operations (namely and, or, xor, and not), our translator replaces such operations by fresh variables so that the analyzer forgets the information on bit variables. After this, for our running example, we prove termination of the 6 loops that it contains and produce a linear bound for those loops. We have included in our github other smart contracts together with the loop bounds inferred by SACO for them. Other high-level analyzers that work on intermediate forms like Integer transition systems or Horn clauses (*e.g.*, APROVE, T2, VERYMAX, COFLOCO) could be easily adapted as well to work on our RBR translated programs.

4   Related Approaches and Tools

In the past two years, several approaches tackled the challenge of fully formal reasoning about Ethereum contracts implemented directly in EVM bytecode by modeling its rigorous semantics in state-of-the-art proof assistants [5,6]. While those mechanisations enabled formal machine-assisted proofs of various safety and security properties of EVM contracts [5], none of them provided means for fully *automated* sound analysis of EVM bytecode.

Concurrently, several other approaches for ensuring correctness and security of Ethereum contracts took a more aggressive approach, implementing automated toolchains for detecting bugs by symbolically executing EVM bytecode [8,10]. However, low-level EVM representation poses difficulties in applying those tools immediately for analysis of more high-level properties. For instance, representation of EVM in OYENTE, a popular tool for analysis of Ethereum smart contracts [1] is too low-level to implement analyses of high-level properties, *e.g.*, loop complexity or commutativity conditions. ZEUS, a tool for analysing Ethereum smart contracts via symbolic execution *wrt.* client-provided *policies*, operates directly on SOLIDITY sources [7]. Soundness of ZEUS as an analysis approach, thus, depends on the semantics of SOLIDITY, which is not formally defined.

References

1. Oyente: An Analysis Tool for Smart Contracts (2018). https://github.com/melonproject/oyente
2. Albert, E., et al.: Object-sensitive cost analysis for concurrent objects. STVR **25**(3), 218–271 (2015)
3. Albert, E., et al.: SACO: static analyzer for concurrent objects. In: Ábrahám, E., Havelund, K. (eds.) TACAS 2014. LNCS, vol. 8413, pp. 562–567. Springer, Heidelberg (2014). https://doi.org/10.1007/978-3-642-54862-8_46
4. Chow, J.: Ethereum, Gas, Fuel & Fees, 2016. Published online on June 23, 2016. https://media.consensys.net/ethereum-gas-fuel-and-fees-3333e17fe1dc
5. Grishchenko, I., Maffei, M., Schneidewind, C.: A semantic framework for the security analysis of ethereum smart contracts. In: Bauer, L., Küsters, R. (eds.) POST 2018. LNCS, vol. 10804, pp. 243–269. Springer, Cham (2018). https://doi.org/10.1007/978-3-319-89722-6_10
6. Hirai, Y.: Defining the ethereum virtual machine for interactive theorem provers. In: Brenner, M., Rohloff, K., Bonneau, J., Miller, A., Ryan, P.Y.A., Teague, V., Bracciali, A., Sala, M., Pintore, F., Jakobsson, M. (eds.) FC 2017. LNCS, vol. 10323, pp. 520–535. Springer, Cham (2017). https://doi.org/10.1007/978-3-319-70278-0_33
7. Kalra, S., Goel, S., Dhawan, M., Sharma, S.: Zeus: Analyzing safety of smart contracts. In: NDSS (2018, to appear)
8. Luu, L., Chu, D., Olickel, H., Saxena, P., Hobor, A.: Making smart contracts smarter. In: CCS, pp. 254–269. ACM (2016)
9. Nakamoto, S.: Bitcoin: a peer-to-peer electronic cash system (2008)
10. Nikolic, I., Kolluri, A., Sergey, I., Saxena, P., Hobor, A.: Finding the Greedy, Prodigal, and Suicidal Contracts at Scale. CoRR, abs/ arXiv:1802.06038 (2018)

11. Vallée-Rai, R., Co, P., Gagnon, E., Hendren, L.J., Lam, P., Sundaresan, V.: Soot
    - a java bytecode optimization framework. In: CASCON (1999)
12. Wood, G.: Ethereum: a secure decentralised generalised transaction ledger (2014)

MGHyper: Checking Satisfiability of HyperLTL Formulas Beyond the ∃*∀* Fragment

Bernd Finkbeiner, Christopher Hahn, and Tobias Hans[(⊠)]

Reactive Systems Group, Saarland University, Saarbrücken, Germany
{finkbeiner,hahn,hans}@react.uni-saarland.de

Abstract. Hyperproperties are properties that refer to multiple computation traces. This includes many information-flow security policies, such as observational determinism, (generalized) noninterference, and noninference, and other system properties like symmetry or Hamming distances between in error-resistant codes. We introduce MGHYPER, a tool for automatic satisfiability checking and model generation for hyperproperties expressed in HyperLTL. Unlike previous satisfiability checkers, MGHYPER is not limited to the decidable ∃*∀* fragment of HyperLTL, but provides a semi-decision procedure for the full logic. An important application of MGHYPER is to automatically check equivalences between different hyperproperties (and different formalizations of the same hyperproperty) and to build counterexamples that disprove a certain claimed implication. We describe the semi-decisionprocedure implemented in MGHYPER and report on experimental results obtained both with typical hyperproperties from the literature and with randomly generated HyperLTL formulas.

1 Introduction

HyperLTL [3] extends linear-time temporal logic (LTL) [20] with explicit quantification over traces. This makes it possible to express hyperproperties [4] like noninterference [13] or symmetry [11], which refer to multiple traces at the same time. Such properties are not expressible in LTL, or even in the branching-time temporal logics CTL [2] and CTL* [6]. For example, *noninference* [18] is a variant of noninterference stating that, for all system traces, the low-observable behavior must not change when all high inputs are replaced by a dummy input. The following HyperLTL formula expresses this policy: $\forall \pi. \exists \pi'. (\mathsf{G}\lambda_{\pi'}) \wedge \pi =_{L,out} \pi'$.

HyperLTL is supported by model checking [11] and runtime monitoring tools [9,10]. There is also a decision procedure, EAHyper [8], which checks the

---

This work was partially supported by the German Research Foundation (DFG) in the Collaborative Research Center 1223 and by the European Research Council (ERC) Grant OSARES (No. 683300).

© Springer Nature Switzerland AG 2018
S. K. Lahiri and C. Wang (Eds.): ATVA 2018, LNCS 11138, pp. 521–527, 2018.
https://doi.org/10.1007/978-3-030-01090-4_31

satisfiability of a given formula from the $\exists^*\forall^*$ fragment of HyperLTL. EAHyper is based on a reduction from HyperLTL satisfiability to LTL satisfiability [7]. A major application of EAHyper is to check equivalences between alternation-free HyperLTL formulas, i.e., formulas that either contain only universal quantifiers or only existential quantifiers. Such equivalences can be expressed in the $\exists^*\forall^*$ fragment. It is impossible, however, to handle formulas that contain a $\forall\exists$ quantifier alternation, as, for example, in noninference. This is unfortunate, because such a quantifier alternation is often needed, in particular to account for nondeterminism. A popular example is *generalized noninterference* [14]: $\forall\pi.\forall\pi'.\exists\pi''.\ \pi =_{H,in} \pi'' \wedge \pi' =_{L,out} \pi''$. The formula expresses that for every possible high-security input (seen on some trace π) and every possible low-security observations (seen on some trace π') there exists a nondeterministic execution π'' where the high-security input and the low-security observations happen together. Hence, the observer cannot conclude, after making the low-security observations, that any specific high-security input actually occurred. Other properties that need a $\forall\exists$ quantifier alternation include restrictiveness [15], separability [17], and forward correctability [19]. For formulas outside the $\exists^*\forall^*$ fragment, it is no longer possible to reduce the HyperLTL satisfiability problem to the LTL satisfiability problem: the HyperLTL satisfiability problem is, in fact, undecidable [7]. In this paper, we present the first semi-decisionprocedure for full HyperLTL. Our approach is based on a reduction to quantified boolean formulas (QBF) [12] and has been implemented in the MGHYPER tool. MGHYPER can be used to analyze and develop hyperproperties and, especially, generate models that disprove equivalences or implications between different hyperproperties or different formalizations of the same hyperproperty. For example, comparing noninference to generalized noninterference, MGHYPER instantly demonstrates that the two properties are *not* equivalent.

2   A Semi-decision Procedure for HyperLTL-SAT

A *hyperproperty* is a *set of sets of traces*. Hyperproperties can be expressed in HyperLTL, which generalizes LTL with explicit trace quantification:

$$\psi ::= \exists\pi.\ \psi \mid \forall\pi.\ \psi \mid \varphi$$
$$\varphi ::= a_\pi \mid \neg\varphi \mid \varphi \vee \varphi \mid X\varphi \mid \varphi\,U\,\varphi \mid true$$

where Q is an existential or universal quantifier, $a \in AP$ is an atomic proposition and $\pi \in \mathcal{V}$ is a trace variable of an infinitely supply $\mathcal{V}$. Logical connectives and the temporal operators F, G, W and R are defined as in LTL. The semantics of HyperLTL is defined as follows.

$$\Pi \models_T \exists \pi.\psi \quad \text{iff} \quad \text{there exists } t \in T \; : \; \Pi[\pi \mapsto t] \models_T \psi$$
$$\Pi \models_T \forall \pi.\psi \quad \text{iff} \quad \text{for all } t \in T \; : \; \Pi[\pi \mapsto t] \models_T \psi$$
$$\Pi \models_T a_\pi \quad \text{iff} \quad a \in \Pi(\pi)[0]$$
$$\Pi \models_T \neg \psi \quad \text{iff} \quad \Pi \not\models_T \psi$$
$$\Pi \models_T \psi_1 \vee \psi_2 \quad \text{iff} \quad \Pi \models_T \psi_1 \text{ or } \Pi \models_T \psi_2$$
$$\Pi \models_T X\psi \quad \text{iff} \quad \Pi[1,\infty] \models_T \psi$$
$$\Pi \models_T \psi_1 \, U \, \psi_2 \quad \text{iff} \quad \text{there exists } i \geq 0 : \Pi[i,\infty] \models_T \psi_2$$
$$\text{and for all } 0 \leq j < i \text{ we have } \Pi[j,\infty] \models_T \psi_1,$$

where $\Pi : \mathcal{V} \mapsto TR$ is the trace assignment function, which maps trace variables to traces, denoted by $\Pi[\pi \mapsto t]$. The suffixes of all traces π starting at step i is denoted by $\Pi[i,\infty]$. *HyperLTL-SAT* is the problem to decide, if a non-empty trace set T exists, such that $\{\} \models_T \psi$.

MGHYPER takes an *arbitrary* HyperLTL formula of the following form as input: $Q_0\pi_0 \ldots Q_n\pi_n.\varphi$, where $Q_i \in \{\exists, \forall\}$ and $\pi_0 \ldots \pi_n$ are vectors over $\mathcal{V}$. MGHYPER evaluates to "sat" if and only if the formula is satisfiable. Basically, MGHYPER checks whether or not there exists a trace set of size m that satisfies the HyperLTL formula under consideration. The procedure starts with trace sets of size 1, and increment m until a witness is found, leading to the following theorem.

Theorem 1. *HyperLTL-SAT is RE-complete.*

Proof. We prove membership by constructing a QBF formula φ_{QBF}^m, which is satisfiable if the given HyperLTL formula φ is satisfiable by a trace set of size m. The basic idea of the encoding of a HyperLTL formula to a QBF formula is threefold: (1) we construct a quantifier prefix that resembles the quantifier structure in the given HyperLTL formula, (2) we construct a premise that links trace variables to actual traces, and (3) we unroll the LTL suffix into a SAT-encoding. The third step follows the unrolling presented in [1] and will, due to space reasons, not be discussed. We refer to the maximum trace-unrolling bound as k (not to confuse with m), which is exponential in the size of the LTL suffix. *(1) Prefix.* Let S be a set and k a natural number, we define $Traces_S^k$ as $\{a_s^i \mid 0 \leq i < k, \forall s \in S, \forall a \in AP\}$, which we use as the trace representation inside the QBF encoding. Let $\varphi := Q_0\pi_0 \ldots Q_n\pi_n.\psi$ be a HyperLTL formula. The quantifier prefix of the resulting QBF introduces existential quantifiers, representing the trace set T of size m (the witness for satisfiability). The trace variables are quantified according to their quantifier in the HyperLTL formula:

$$Prefix(\varphi) = \exists \, Traces_T^k.Q_0 \, Traces_{\pi_0}^k.Q_1 \, Traces_{\pi_1}^k. \ldots .Q_n \, Traces_{\pi_n}^k.$$

(2) Linking. We construct a premise to link trace variables to the trace witnesses in $Traces_T^k$. For every quantifier Q_i a subpremise P_{Q_i} is constructed first, which represents the mapping of all trace variables in π_i. Mapping each trace variable to traces reassembles the trace assignment function from the HyperLTL semantics

and is encoded by ensuring that the boolean variables with the same atomic proposition in the same step share the same truth value.

$$P_{Q_i} := \left[\bigwedge_{\pi \in \pi_i} \bigvee_{t_i \in T} \left[\bigwedge_{\substack{(a_{t_i}^j, a_\pi^j) \in \\ Traces_{t_i}^k \times Traces_\pi^k}} a_{t_i}^j \leftrightarrow a_\pi^j \right] \right] \tag{1}$$

The linking mechanism is a combination of the subpremises. The boolean connective between the different supremises depends on the corresponding quantifier:

$$Linking(\varphi) := P_{Q_0}^k \circ_{Q_0} P_{Q_1}^k \circ_{Q_1} \ldots P_{Q_{n-1}}^k \circ_{Q_{n-1}} P_{Q_n}^k \circ_{Q_n}, \tag{2}$$

where $\circ_{Q_i}$ equals $\rightarrow$, if $Q_i = \forall$, and $\circ_{Q_i}$ equals $\wedge$ if $Q_i = \exists$. Together with (3) *the unrolling* of the LTL suffix [1], the constructed φ_{QBF}^m a QBF formula is satisfiable if the HyperLTL formula φ is satisfiable. Hardness follows from a reduction from Post's Correspondence Problem [7]. □

Example 1. Consider the HyperLTL formula $\varphi := \forall \pi_0 \exists \pi_1 \exists \pi_2.(a_{\pi_0} \wedge (a_{\pi_1} \rightarrow \neg b_{\pi_1} \wedge a_{\pi_2} \rightarrow b_{\pi_2}))$. Note that, for the sake of simplicity, the example LTL formula does not contain temporal operators. In the first iteration, MGHYPER tries to guess a trace set T of size 1 and will not find a satisfying assignment for the constructed QBF formula. In the second iteration, though, MGHYPER constructs the following QBF formula, with $T_2 = \{\{a_{t_0}^0, b_{t_0}^0\}, \{a_{t_1}^0, b_{t_1}^0\}\}$.

$$\exists Traces_{T_2}^0 \forall Traces_{\pi_0}^0 \exists Traces_{\pi_1}^0 \exists Traces_{\pi_2}^0 . \left[\vee \begin{pmatrix} (a_{\pi_0}^0 \leftrightarrow a_{t_0}^0 \wedge b_{\pi_0}^0 \leftrightarrow b_{t_0}^0) \\ (a_{\pi_0}^0 \leftrightarrow a_{t_1}^0 \wedge b_{\pi_0}^0 \leftrightarrow b_{t_1}^0) \end{pmatrix} \right]$$

$$\rightarrow \left(\left[\wedge \begin{pmatrix} \vee \begin{bmatrix} a_{\pi_1}^0 \leftrightarrow a_{t_0}^0 \wedge b_{\pi_1}^0 \leftrightarrow b_{t_0}^0 \\ a_{\pi_1}^0 \leftrightarrow a_{t_1}^0 \wedge b_{\pi_1}^0 \leftrightarrow b_{t_1}^0 \end{bmatrix} \\ \vee \begin{bmatrix} a_{\pi_2}^0 \leftrightarrow a_{t_0}^0 \wedge b_{\pi_2}^0 \leftrightarrow b_{t_0}^0 \\ a_{\pi_2}^0 \leftrightarrow a_{t_1}^0 \wedge b_{\pi_2}^0 \leftrightarrow b_{t_1}^0 \end{bmatrix} \end{pmatrix} \right] \wedge (a_{\pi_0}^0 \wedge (a_{\pi_1}^0 \rightarrow \neg b_{\pi_1}^0 \wedge a_{\pi_2}^0 \rightarrow b_{\pi_2}^0)) \right)$$

This QBF formula is satisfied by the assignment $\mathcal{A} = \{a_{t_0}^0, b_{t_0}^0, a_{t_1}^0, \neg b_{t_1}^0\}$ for the existentially quantified variables, which represent the traces (of length one in this example). There are four possible assignment for the universally quantified boolean variables. For $\{a_{\pi_0}^0, b_{\pi_0}^0\}$ or $\{a_{\pi_0}^0, \neg b_{\pi_0}^0\}$ we can map the existentially quantified traces variables $\pi_1 \mapsto t_1$ and $\pi_2 \mapsto t_0$, which add $\{a_{\pi_1}^0, \neg b_{\pi_1}^0, a_{\pi_2}^0, b_{\pi_2}^0\}$ to $\mathcal{A}$, such that $\mathcal{A}$ satisfies the formula. In the other two cases, $\{\neg a_{\pi_0}^0, \neg b_{\pi_0}^0\}$ or $\{\neg a_{\pi_0}^0, b_{\pi_0}^0\}$, we cannot map to $\neg a_{\pi_0}^0$, which leads to a false evaluation of $P_{Q_0}^0$ and therefore to a true evaluation of the formula. From $\mathcal{A}$ we can now follow that $\{\{a, b\}^\omega, \{a\}^\omega\}$ is a model that satisfies φ.

3   Experimental Results

MGHYPER is implemented in Ocaml and supports UNIX-based operation systems. We tested our tool against different benchmarks on a virtual machine running an Ubuntu (64-Bit) 14.04LTS installation on an Intel Core i7-4710MQ with 2,50GH on 4 kernels and 8GB RAM.

Counter Examples for Implication of Security Polices. A main application of MGHYPER is to check if two arbitrary HyperLTL formulas do not imply each other: we check if the negation of the implication is satisfiable. The first benchmark checks the implication of *General Noninterference* [4] ((GNI):$\forall \pi_1.\forall \pi_2.\exists \pi_3 G(I_{\pi_1}^{high} = I_{\pi_3}^{high}) \wedge G(O_{\pi_2}^{low} = O_{\pi_3}^{low}))$, *Noninterference* ((NI): $\forall \pi_1. \exists \pi_2. (G\lambda_{\pi_2}) \wedge G(O_{\pi_1} = O_{\pi_2}))$ and several formalizations of *Observational Determinism* [16,21,22]: (OD): $\forall \pi_1.\forall \pi_2.(I_{\pi_1}^{low} = I_{\pi_2}^{low}) \rightarrow G(O_{\pi_1}^{low} = O_{\pi_2}^{low})$, (GOD): $\forall \pi_1.\forall \pi_2.G(I_{\pi_1}^{low} = I_{\pi_2}^{low}) \rightarrow G(O_{\pi_1}^{low} = O_{\pi_2}^{low})$, and (WOD):$\forall \pi_1.\forall \pi_2.(I_{\pi_1}^{low} = I_{\pi_2}^{low}) W (O_{\pi_1}^{low} \neq O_{\pi_2}^{low})$. MGHYPER shows that none of the formalizations of observational determinism does imply general non-interference or noninference. Furthermore, it shows that generalized non-interference does not imply noninference. Every check was done in under 0.05 s.

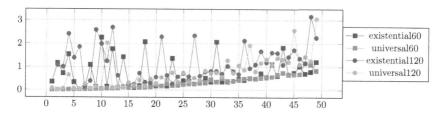

Fig. 1. Runtime for random HyperLTL formulas of size 60 and 120. A formula consists of up to 50 trace variables starting universally or existentially quantified.

Table 1. Random $\exists^n \forall^m$ formulas: instances solved (sol) in 120 s and average time (avgt) in s for 100 random formulas of size 60 with 15 atomic propositions.

avgt	sol	avgt	sol	avgt	sol	avgt	sol	avgt	sol	avgt	sol	avgt	sol	avgt	sol	avgt	sol	avgt	sol
$\exists^1\forall^1$		$\exists^1\forall^2$		$\exists^1\forall^3$		$\exists^1\forall^4$		$\exists^1\forall^5$		$\exists^1\forall^6$		$\exists^1\forall^7$		$\exists^1\forall^8$		$\exists^1\forall^9$		$\exists^1\forall^{10}$	
0.472	96	0.599	95	1.371	96	1.537	96	1.322	96	1.587	96	0.529	92	2.823	96	3.166	94	2.303	97
$\exists^2\forall^1$		$\exists^2\forall^2$		$\exists^2\forall^3$		$\exists^2\forall^4$		$\exists^2\forall^5$		$\exists^2\forall^6$		$\exists^2\forall^7$		$\exists^2\forall^8$		$\exists^2\forall^9$		$\exists^2\forall^{10}$	
6.772	80	2.743	85	2.698	93	6.319	94	4.233	97	4.107	92	3.162	87	2.906	94	4.847	92	2.131	96
$\exists^3\forall^1$		$\exists^3\forall^2$		$\exists^3\forall^3$		$\exists^3\forall^4$		$\exists^3\forall^5$		$\exists^3\forall^6$		$\exists^3\forall^7$		$\exists^3\forall^8$		$\exists^3\forall^9$		$\exists^3\forall^{10}$	
5.533	79	9.921	81	5.836	82	4.851	88	7.589	82	3.852	82	9.975	82	5.222	79	6.328	77	5.044	83
$\exists^4\forall^1$		$\exists^4\forall^2$		$\exists^4\forall^3$		$\exists^4\forall^4$		$\exists^4\forall^5$		$\exists^4\forall^6$		$\exists^4\forall^7$		$\exists^4\forall^8$		$\exists^4\forall^9$		$\exists^4\forall^{10}$	
10.316	75	8.669	80	5.631	83	3.722	83	5.843	73	5.62	81	10.074	79	6.955	76	8.037	85	5.938	79
$\exists^5\forall^1$		$\exists^5\forall^2$		$\exists^5\forall^3$		$\exists^5\forall^4$		$\exists^5\forall^5$		$\exists^5\forall^6$		$\exists^5\forall^7$		$\exists^5\forall^8$		$\exists^5\forall^9$		$\exists^5\forall^{10}$	
5.431	71	5.009	80	2.812	69	8.514	81	4.501	76	6.255	83	1.574	76	3.616	76	5.85	79	7.486	80
$\exists^6\forall^1$		$\exists^6\forall^2$		$\exists^6\forall^3$		$\exists^6\forall^4$		$\exists^6\forall^5$		$\exists^6\forall^6$		$\exists^6\forall^7$		$\exists^6\forall^8$		$\exists^6\forall^9$		$\exists^6\forall^{10}$	
3.53	78	4.378	74	3.503	71	3.057	76	4.354	71	4.513	81	3.492	79	4.836	79	6.289	80	6.0	74
$\exists^7\forall^1$		$\exists^7\forall^2$		$\exists^7\forall^3$		$\exists^7\forall^4$		$\exists^7\forall^5$		$\exists^7\forall^6$		$\exists^7\forall^7$		$\exists^7\forall^8$		$\exists^7\forall^9$		$\exists^7\forall^{10}$	
4.33	74	3.173	70	1.789	72	7.187	69	4.99	78	5.584	74	4.783	77	7.558	75	7.744	74	6.043	78
$\exists^8\forall^1$		$\exists^8\forall^2$		$\exists^8\forall^3$		$\exists^8\forall^4$		$\exists^8\forall^5$		$\exists^8\forall^6$		$\exists^8\forall^7$		$\exists^8\forall^8$		$\exists^8\forall^9$		$\exists^8\forall^{10}$	
5.681	81	4.617	79	6.803	74	5.563	75	6.219	80	5.999	74	3.013	73	2.041	72	6.146	75	3.997	75
$\exists^9\forall^1$		$\exists^9\forall^2$		$\exists^9\forall^3$		$\exists^9\forall^4$		$\exists^9\forall^5$		$\exists^9\forall^6$		$\exists^9\forall^7$		$\exists^9\forall^8$		$\exists^9\forall^9$		$\exists^9\forall^{10}$	
3.509	77	2.514	72	5.659	68	1.345	78	4.379	72	3.914	73	3.422	71	1.784	66	6.903	72	5.142	77
$\exists^{10}\forall^1$		$\exists^{10}\forall^2$		$\exists^{10}\forall^3$		$\exists^{10}\forall^4$		$\exists^{10}\forall^5$		$\exists^{10}\forall^6$		$\exists^{10}\forall^7$		$\exists^{10}\forall^8$		$\exists^{10}\forall^9$		$\exists^{10}\forall^{10}$	
3.986	81	4.553	70	5.777	70	4.791	75	8.284	75	1.534	72	4.338	71	4.18	76	5.512	65	4.529	75

Random Formulas. We tested MGHYPER against different benchmarks of random formulas. *Quantifier Alternation:* We created HyperLTL formulas with up to 49 quantifier alternations and 15 atomic proposition using randltl [5]. For each number of alternations we tested 100 formulas of size 60 and 120, where 50 start with $\exists$ and 50 with $\forall$. The size is the size argument provided for randltl [5]. The runtimes are shown in Fig. 1. *Quantifier Ordering:* $\exists^n\forall^m$ *Formulas:* For the sake of comparing MGHYPER with EAHyper, we tested MGHYPER on the largest decidable fragment of HyperLTL, which is the $\exists^*\forall^*$-fragment. We scaled in the number of existential and universal quantifiers, showing that MGHYPER is able to solve formulas with up to 10 existential and 10 universal quantifier. In comparison, EAHyper, implementing the first decision procedure for HyperLTL-SAT, already runs out of memory after 5 existential and 5 universal quantifiers.

4   Conclusion

We have presented MGHYPER, the first semi-decisionprocedure for checking the satisfiability of HyperLTL formulas beyond the decidable $\exists^*\forall^*$ fragment. An application of MGHYPER is the analysis and development of hyperproperties and, especially, the generation of models that disprove equivalences or implications between different hyperproperties. In comparison to the existing decision procedure EAHyper, MGHyper not only handles the much larger class of hyperproperties, it also outperforms, as our experiments show, EAHyper within the $\exists^*\forall^*$ fragment.

References

1. Biere, A., Cimatti, A., Clarke, E.M., Strichman, O., Zhu, Y.: Bounded model checking. Adv. Comput. (2003)
2. Clarke, E.M., Emerson, E.A.: Design and synthesis of synchronization skeletons using branching-time temporal logic. In: Logics of Programs, Workshop (1981)
3. Clarkson, M.R., Finkbeiner, B., Koleini, M., Micinski, K.K., Rabe, M.N., Sánchez, C.: Temporal logics for hyperproperties. POST (2014)
4. Clarkson, M.R., Schneider, F.B.: Hyperproperties. J. Comp. Sec. (2010)
5. Duret-Lutz, A.: Manipulating LTL formulas using spot 1.0. In: ATVA (2013)
6. Emerson, E.A., Halpern, J.Y.: "sometimes" and "not never" revisited: on branching versus linear time temporal logic. J. ACM (1986)
7. Finkbeiner, B., Hahn, C.: Deciding hyperproperties. In: CONCUR (2016)
8. Finkbeiner, B., Hahn, C., Stenger, M.: Eahyper: satisfiability, implication, and equivalence checking of hyperproperties. In: CAV (2017)
9. Finkbeiner, B., Hahn, C., Stenger, M., Tentrup, L.: Monitoring hyperproperties. In: RV (2017)
10. Finkbeiner, B., Hahn, C., Stenger, M., Tentrup, L.: Rvhyper : a runtime verification tool for temporal hyperproperties. In: TACAS (2018)
11. Finkbeiner, B., Rabe, M.N., Sánchez, C.: Algorithms for model checking hyperltl and hyperctl^*. In: CAV (2015)
12. Garey, M.R., Johnson, D.S.: Computers and Intractability: A Guide to the Theory of NP-Completeness. W. H Freeman, New York (1979)

13. Goguen, J.A., Meseguer, J.: Security policies and security models. In: S&P (1982)
14. McCullough, D.: Noninterference and the composability of security properties. In: S&P (1988)
15. McCullough, D.: A hookup theorem for multilevel security. IEEE Trans. Softw. Eng. (1990)
16. McLean, J.: Proving noninterference and functional correctness using traces. J. Comput. Secur. **1**(1), 37–58 (1992)
17. McLean, J.: A general theory of composition for trace sets closed under selective interleaving functions. In: S&P (1994)
18. McLean, J.: A general theory of composition for a class of "possibilistic" properties. IEEE Trans. Softw. Eng. (1996)
19. Millen, J.K.: Unwinding forward correctability. J. Comput. Secur. (1995)
20. Pnueli, A.: The temporal logic of programs. In: Foundations of Computer Science (1977)
21. Roscoe, A.W.: CSP and determinism in security modelling. In: S&P (1995)
22. Zdancewic, S., Myers, A.C.: Observational determinism for concurrent program security. In: CSFW-2016 (2016)

Verifying Rust Programs with SMACK

Marek Baranowski[✉], Shaobo He, and Zvonimir Rakamarić

School of Computing, University of Utah, Salt Lake City, USA
{baranows,shaobo,zvonimir}@cs.utah.edu

Abstract. Rust is an emerging systems programming language with guaranteed memory safety and modern language features that has been extensively adopted to build safety-critical software. However, there is currently a lack of automated software verifiers for Rust. In this work, we present our experience extending the SMACK verifier to enable its usage on Rust programs. We evaluate SMACK on a set of Rust programs to demonstrate a wide spectrum of language features it supports.

1 Introduction

Rust [12] is a new programming language that aims to enable safe systems programming by means of an elaborate type system, while providing advanced language features such as traits, smart pointers, and closures. It avoids memory safety issues prevalent in programs written in other low-level programming languages such as C/C++ without adding performance overhead often imposed by runtime systems or garbage collectors. Because of these merits, Rust has received a lot of attention from both academia and industry, and it has already been used to implement industrial-strength safety-critical applications, such as web browsers, cloud storage, and embedded software.

Although memory safety is enforced through type checking of Rust programs at compile time, functional correctness (e.g., no violations of user-specified assertions) is not guaranteed. Automated software verifiers based on satisfiability modulo theories (SMT) solvers [3] are a popular choice for assuring the absence of assertion violations. However, building a verifier, or extending an existing one, for a new language is often tedious and time-consuming (e.g., implement a frontend, understand and encode the language semantics). This was done in Rust2Viper [6], which translates Rust programs from the high-level intermediate representation (syntactically similar to Rust) into an intermediate verification language in order to check program correctness. CRUST [14] transforms Rust into C to verify memory safety of unsafe Rust code. As both tools use custom translators, changes to Rust necessitate these to be updated, which is a large undertaking; neither tool appears to be maintained. To the best of our knowledge, currently there are no readily available SMT-based verifiers for Rust.

Supported in part by the National Science Foundation (NSF) award CNS 1527526.

S. K. Lahiri and C. Wang (Eds.): ATVA 2018, LNCS 11138, pp. 528–535, 2018.
https://doi.org/10.1007/978-3-030-01090-4_32

In this paper, we describe how we enable the verification of Rust programs in the SMACK verifier [11,13]. An advantage of SMACK is that it is mostly input-language agnostic as it works by verifying a simple intermediate representation, specifically LLVM IR [10]. Since the official Rust compiler, rustc, can produce LLVM IR code corresponding to Rust programs, a large frontend development effort was not needed as a rich set of LLVM IR features is already supported by SMACK. Rust is an advanced, low-level programming language that controls heap sharing and aliasing using an elaborate type system. Hence, Rust's compiler emits LLVM IR code patterns that are often significantly different from code generated by the Clang compiler, which is the primary target for SMACK. In particular, it emits aliasing patterns that SMACK could not handle well. Nevertheless, we managed to extend SMACK to support the verification of a modern programming language such as Rust at a relatively small cost, and our evaluation shows that it can already handle a variety of key language features.

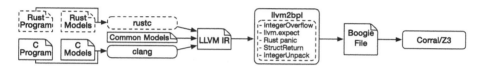

Fig. 1. Toolflow of SMACK.

2 SMACK Software Verification Toolchain

SMACK [11,13] is a software verification toolchain that translates LLVM IR code into Boogie intermediate verification language [2], which is in turn verified using back-end Boogie verifiers such as Corral [9]. Before our Rust effort, SMACK had been predominantly used to verify LLVM IR programs produced by the Clang C compiler. Figure 1 shows the toolflow of SMACK, which works as follows:

1. The SMACK top-level script automates the entire toolflow. It determines which compiler to invoke and flags to use for program compilation. In the case of C programs, it invokes Clang to generate LLVM IR code, while including SMACK's C language models. The models specify the semantics of common C library functions such as malloc, free, and string operations.
2. The common models file is then linked with the generated LLVM IR file to provide basic verification capabilities. This includes modeling dynamic memory, and support for assertions, assumptions, and nondeterministic values.
3. The core LLVM2BPL component takes an LLVM IR file as input, and produces Boogie code that captures the semantics of LLVM IR instructions; it outputs a Boogie file for verification.
4. Finally, the Corral back-end verifier is invoked on the generated Boogie file, and it uses Z3 [5] as its SMT solver. (Note that SMACK supports other back-end verifiers, which we omitted here.)

In this work, we use Corral in its bounded verification mode, meaning that it unrolls loops and recursion up to a certain user-provided bound.

3   Rust-Driven Extensions to SMACK

Figure 2 gives a Rust program illustrating the language features that our SMACK extensions leverage or support. Rust's foreign function interface (FFI) allows zero-cost interaction with C code, verification of which had already been extensively supported by SMACK. As a result, we are able to reuse SMACK's C models as well as perform cross-language verification of Rust programs containing calls to external C functions (line 13). For example, we implemented macros `assume` (line 9) and `assert` (line 14) to expand into calls to SMACK's built-in C functions.Line 8 invokes the `nondet` function that introduces nondeterministic unconstrained values. Note that we implemented these so that programs can be easily compiled into executables even with SMACK annotations present — in that case `nondet` is replaced with value 5 in the example.

Instead of being undefined or triggering wrap-around behaviors as in C, integer overflows in Rust are checked and can lead to *program panic*. For example, while not visible at the source level, the signed integer addition operation at line 5 may optionally be checked for integer overflows via the Rust compiler emitting LLVM arithmetic with overflow intrinsics; we had to extend SMACK to support such intrinsics. Finally, unlike C, standard libraries and modern language constructs such as the `Vec` library (line 10) and iterators (line 4) are abundant in Rust code. Modeling these libraries and language constructs is challenging yet essential to build a practical Rust verifier; SMACK's modeling mechanism allowed us to implement models for common Rust libraries. We describe some of these extensions in more detail next.

3.1   Supporting Rust-Generated LLVM IR Constructs

The LLVM IR code that rustc emits contains several key constructs that are not used in IR code produced by Clang. Hence, we had to extend SMACK to add support for such constructs.

Types. The Rust compiler generates load/store instructions of the LLVM `i1` data type, which is almost never emitted by Clang. We added support for such instructions by zero-extending their operands to `i8` when a store operation occurs, and casting them back when they are loaded.

Instructions operating on LLVM structure types occur frequently in rustc-generated IR code, while Clang-generated IR almost always uses only primitive types. For example, it is a common practice for Rust programmers to use the `Option` type as the return type of functions. It is generic over type `T` and represented in LLVM IR as structure type `{T,i1}`, where setting `i1` is used to indicate a valid return value. Moreover, load/store instructions over structures are frequently generated by rustc, but not by Clang. Hence, SMACK did not have elaborate support for such instructions.

```
1  #[macro_use] mod smack; use smack::*;        1  typedef unsigned long ul;
2  extern{fn fib_c(n:u64)->u64;}                2  ul fib_c(ul x) {
3  fn fib(x: usize, cache:&mut Vec<u64>) {      3    ul a = 0, b = 1;
4    for i in 2..x+1 as usize                   4    for (ul i=0; i<x-1; i++) {
5      { cache[i]=cache[i-1]+cache[i-2]; }      5      ul tmp = a;
6  }                                            6      a = b;
7  fn main() {                                  7      b = a + tmp;
8    let n=5u64.nondet();                       8    }
9    assume!(n > 2);                            9    return b;
10   let mut cache=vec![0; n+1];               10  }
11   cache[0]=0;  cache[1]=1;
12   fib(n, &mut cache);
13   let c_result=unsafe{fib_c(n)};
14   assert!(cache[n]==c_result);
15 }
```

Fig. 2. Rust program that checks the equivalence between the Rust (`fib`) and C (`fib_c`) implementations of the Fibonacci function.

We support such instructions by modeling LLVM structure types using uninterpreted functions that constrain each field. For example, value $\{v,1\}$ of type $\{T,i1\}$ is represented using an integer s with constraint $f(s,\emptyset) ==$ $v \&\& f(s,1) == 1$, where f is an uninterpreted function with the second argument being the index of a structure field. Such encoding allows us to model two basic LLVM structure instructions **extractvalue** and **insertvalue** that read and write structure fields, respectively. Loads and stores of structures into memory are recursively translated into a sequence of instructions that generate load/store for each field of primitive type, in conjunction with the two aforementioned instructions. This extension enables SMACK to handle structure constructs without us having to introduce extensive modifications to its underlying memory model.

Integer Packing. The Rust compiler frequently packs smaller structures into 8-byte integers. For example, rustc optimizes loading of a structure of type $\{i32,i32\}$ into loading of i64. This requires less scalable bit-precise reasoning to be selected in SMACK to avoid false bugs [7]. Hence, we added an analysis pass to SMACK that detects load/store instructions with pointer operands of integer element type that refer to structures. We translate such instructions to load/store directly from/into structure fields (following the encoding described earlier), thereby essentially avoiding packing. This approach helps to scale the verification of Rust programs by avoiding the need for bit-precise reasoning.

Intrinsics. We added support for two types of LLVM intrinsics heavily used by rustc: `llvm.expect` and arithmetic with overflow. The Rust compiler emits the LLVM intrinsic `llvm.expect` as an optimization hint. We modified SMACK to transform a call to this intrinsic into essentially a no-op. As future work, we will explore leveraging such hints to speed up verification.

```
1   $a2  := $zext.i8.i16($a);
2   $b2  := $zext.i8.i16($b);
3   $x2  := $add.i16($a2, $b2);
4   $x   := $trunc.i16.i8($x2);
5   $flag := $ugt.i16($x2, 255);
6   assert !$flag;
```

Fig. 3. Translation of an unsigned 8-bit checked-addition intrinsic, where $a and $b are the operands and $x is the sum.

The Rust compiler typically emits instructions for checking all integer operations for overflow through the use of LLVM arithmetic with overflow intrinsics, such as `llvm.uadd.with.overflow.i32`. The intrinsics indicate the sign and bitwidth in which to perform the given operation. We extended SMACK with an integer overflow checking pass that replaces the intrinsics with instruction sequences implementing the corresponding overflow checking. Figure 3 shows an example translation. Lines 1 and 2 extend the precision of the arguments to double the original bitwidth, thereby avoiding potential overflow. Line 3 computes the result of the addition, while line 4 converts the result back to the original bitwidth. Line 5 determines whether the operation overflowed, while line 6 checks it. Note that the translation shown in Fig. 3 is not optimal for dynamic checking since we optimized it for SMT-based verification with SMACK. Furthermore, while the conversion of the intrinsic is always performed, checking is made optional following the convention that it is disabled in the release mode.

3.2 Modeling Rust Libraries

Standard Rust libraries define most of the language's containers as generic over the contained type, and generate the corresponding code for the container when the program is compiled. However, the generated code is heavily optimized for performance, and contains constructs and functions that are difficult for SMACK to analyze, such as custom allocators. Hence, we leveraged SMACK's existing modeling capabilities to write models for popular Rust data structures, such as vector (`Vec`). Vector is a dynamically-sized array used in many Rust programs as well as for implementing other data structures such as stacks and queues. Currently, our vector model supports dynamic resizing, push, pop, get and mutable get, and indexing among other features. The model resides in a separate file, which SMACK automatically links as a Rust module.

4 Experiments

4.1 Microbenchmarks

We developed a benchmark suite containing various Rust language features to test the SMACK extensions we developed.[1] Table 1 summarizes our benchmark suite. Every category includes both correct and buggy benchmark versions. Some notable included features are:

---

[1] For our tool and benchmarks see https://github.com/smackers/smack.

Table 1. Summary of the benchmark suite we developed.

Benchmark category	#Files	LOC	Features demonstrated
Functions	8	153	Function calls, closures, recursion
Generics	6	55	Generic functions, structures, traits
IFC	4	214	Information flow control example
Loops	4	35	Range-based for loops
OPS	12	171	Basic operations, overflows
Structures	4	76	Creation, passing, returning of structures
Vector	6	88	Dynamic memory management
Memory-safety	4	58	Memory safety verification
Cross-language	4	48	Combining Rust and C

- The functions category tests recursion and passing closures as arguments.
- The generics category implements a generic trait for two generic structures. A statically dispatched function is then invoked on the structures.
- The vector category tests dynamic resizing and indexing of the Rust vector.
- The cross-language category contains Rust programs that invoke C functions, including the Fig. 2 benchmark.

Table 2. Summary of the real-world programs we verified using SMACK. Column **Time** shows the runtime of applying SMACK to verify a property.

Program	Checked property	LOC	Time
uptime	General assertion	81	2 s
expr	Signed integer overflow	137	5 min
factor	Unsigned integer overflow	100	50 s
	Functional correctness		17min

- In the memory safety category, we verify the absence of buffer overflows and memory leaks arising from C-allocated arrays in unsafe Rust programs.
- The ifc category contains the *information flow control* (IFC) example from related work [1]. IFC models an access control method where access authority can only be increased. Using nondeterministic access levels, we verify that the IFC Rust implementation only allows access to the appropriate authority.

Currently, SMACK verifies most benchmarks in under 20 minutes. The only exception is the full-blown IFC benchmark version that takes several hours to complete. The development of the benchmark suite helped us to identify key language features that SMACK struggled with, and hence it guided our efforts.

4.2   Real-World Programs

To better judge the quality of our implementation, we tested SMACK on three real-world programs, *uptime*, *expr*, and *factor*, from the *uutils* project [4]. The project is a popular repository on GitHub (starred more than 4000 times) containing Rust reimplementations of the GNU core utilities. Table 2 shows the properties we verified for each program, their size, and the runtime of SMACK. We slightly modify all the programs to simplify the verification processes. Most notably, we replace the return values of external library calls with nondeterministic values, and we ignore string literals by redefining macros that accept string arguments, such as `println!`, to empty expressions.

In the *uptime* utility, which prints the uptime of a machine, we verify that the reported uptime is 0 only when the system calls related to reporting the uptime also return 0. SMACK generates an error trace through the Rust program where an uptime of 0 is erroneously reported when certain resources are unavailable; GNU's version of *uptime* reports an error in this scenario. We reported this problem to the developers, who issued a fix.[2] The *expr* utility evaluates a string argument as an arithmetic expression. We check this program for signed integer overflows using SMACK. Our input to *expr* is the addition of two nondeterministic 64-bit integers, and SMACK discovers input values that trigger signed integer overflow. GNU's version of *expr* either reports an error, or uses unlimited precision, rather than reporting an overflowed result. We again reported the outcome to the developers, who issued a fix.[3] In the *factor* utility, we focused on verifying individual functions in its numeric library, namely `sm_mul` and `big_mul`. Both of these functions take 3 arguments a, b, and m, and compute $(a \cdot b)\%m$. We verify several properties related to integer overflows, and that `sm_mul` indeed performs the specified computation. Note that we reduced the integer bit-width to 8 bits to speed up verification.

5   Limitations and Future Work

While the described extensions we made to SMACK enable its usage on many Rust programs, some work remains. Rust programs extensively rely on Rust's standard libraries. While we implemented models for the most common ones, such as `Vec`, we plan to model a more substantial subset in the future. An additional feature we plan to add is checking of unsafe pointers to ensure they obey the semantics of the Rust's borrow system. In particular, we want to check pointers from external functions. The Rustbelt [8] project gives the conditions for which pointers generated from unsafe Rust code can be verified to be safely used. Since Rust enables legacy code to be used within a project, this feature will enable developers to verify their wrappers adhere to Rust's aliasing semantics. Finally, concurrent programming is an important feature of Rust, and we plan to support it in SMACK in the near future.

---

[2] https://github.com/uutils/coreutils/issues/1195.
[3] https://github.com/uutils/coreutils/issues/1194.

References

1. Balasubramanian, A., Baranowski, M.S., Burtsev, A., Panda, A., Rakamarić, Z., Ryzhyk, L., et al.: System programming in rust: beyond safety. In: HotOS (2017)
2. Barnett, M., Chang, B.-Y.E., DeLine, R., Jacobs, B., Leino, K.R.M.: Boogie: a modular reusable verifier for object-oriented programs. In: FMCO (2005)
3. Barrett, C., Stump, A., Tinelli, C.: The SMT-LIB standard: Version 2.0. In: SMT (2010)
4. Cross-platform Rust rewrite of the GNU coreutils. https://github.com/uutils/coreutils
5. de Moura, L.M., Bjørner, N.: Z3: an efficient SMT solver. In: TACAS (2008)
6. Hahn, F.: Rust2Viper: building a static verifier for rust. Master's thesis, ETH (2016)
7. He, S., Rakamarić, Z.: Counterexample-guided bit-precision selection. In: APLAS (2017)
8. Jung, R., Jourdan, J.-H., Krebbers, R., Dreyer, D.: RustBelt: securing the foundations of the Rust programming language. In: POPL (2017)
9. Lal, A., Qadeer, S., Lahiri, S.K.: A solver for reachability modulo theories. In: CAV (2012)
10. Lattner, C., Adve, V.: LLVM: a compilation framework for lifelong program analysis & transformation. In: CGO (2004)
11. Rakamarić, Z., Emmi, M.: SMACK: decoupling source language details from verifier implementations. In: CAV (2014)
12. The Rust programming language. https://www.rust-lang.org
13. SMACK software verifier and verification toolchain. http://smackers.github.io
14. Toman, J., Pernsteiner, S., Torlak, E.: CRUST: a bounded verifier for rust. In: ASE (2015)

$\mathcal{S}$BIP 2.0: Statistical Model Checking Stochastic Real-Time Systems

Braham Lotfi Mediouni[1(✉)], Ayoub Nouri[1], Marius Bozga[1],
Mahieddine Dellabani[1], Axel Legay[2], and Saddek Bensalem[1]

[1] Univ. Grenoble Alpes, CNRS, Grenoble INP*, VERIMAG,
38000 Grenoble, France
braham-lotfi.mediouni@univ-grenoble-alpes.fr
[2] INRIA, Rennes, France

Abstract. This paper presents a major new release of $\mathcal{S}$BIP, an extensible statistical model checker for Metric (MTL) and Linear-time Temporal Logic (LTL) properties on respectively Generalized Semi-Markov Processes (GSMP), Continuous-Time (CTMC) and Discrete-Time Markov Chain (DTMC) models. The newly added support for MTL, GSMPs, CTMCs and rare events allows to capture both real-time and stochastic aspects, allowing faithful specification, modeling and analysis of real-life systems. $\mathcal{S}$BIP is redesigned as an IDE providing project management, model edition, compilation, simulation, and statistical analysis.

1 Introduction

Statistical Model Checking (SMC) is a powerful alternative to classical numerical probabilistic model-checking that generally fail to handle large state-space systems. SMC was successfully applied in the assessment of different real-life systems in various application domains. Classical model checkers [4,8] now include SMC as part of their analysis engines and have been recently joined by a variety of specialized ones [1,6,9,12]. All these tools mainly differ in their modeling and properties specification formalisms. UPPAAL-SMC [4] considers *Networks of Priced Timed Automata*, which are high-level representations of D/CTMCs for system modeling, and weighted MTL for properties specification. PRISM [8] treats in addition *Markov Decision Processes* and *Probabilistic Timed Automata* for modeling, and *Probabilistic Computation Tree*, *Continuous Stochastic Logic* (CSL), and LTL for specification. Plasma Lab [6] is a modular statistical model checker that allows to use external simulators and checkers. Its default configuration supports DTMCs specified in a PRISM dialect and bounded LTL. Ymer [12] is one of the rare tools to implement SMC (Hypothesis testing) for GSMPs

---

The research leading to these results has received funding from the EU's H2020 programme under grant agreements no. 700665 (CITADEL), 7300080 (ESROCOS).
* Institute of Engineering Univ. Grenoble Alpes.

S. K. Lahiri and C. Wang (Eds.): ATVA 2018, LNCS 11138, pp. 536–542, 2018.
https://doi.org/10.1007/978-3-030-01090-4_33

and CSL, however it is no more maintained. Finally, COSMOS [1] relies on *Generalized Stochastic Petri Nets* as input models and *Hybrid Automata Stochastic Logic*, a more expressive formalism, for properties specifications.

In this paper, we present the newest release of $\mathcal{S}$BIP, a statistical model checker that enriches the existing BIP tool-set [2] with statistical analyses. BIP provides a general framework to support design activities ranging from specification and validation to implementation and deployment in a rigorous way. To implement this vision, a rich tool-set was built for modeling, languages embedding, functional validation, models transformation and distributed code generation.

In its previous version [9], $\mathcal{S}$BIP was limited to the analysis of DTMCs with respect to bounded LTL properties. In this release, it was redesigned and extended to support **GSMPs, CTMCs, MTL, parametric exploration of LTL and MTL properties and analysis of rare events**. The tool has also benefited from a major revision of its workflows and GUI. It now provides an Integrated Development Environment (IDE) where one can edit, compile, simulate models, and perform analyses. Additionally, $\mathcal{S}$BIP is now organized around well-structured projects that enclose models, properties and traces. It also includes support for graphical visualization of analysis results.

2 $\mathcal{S}$BIP Design and Functionalities

$\mathcal{S}$BIP is fully developed in Java and runs on GNU/Linux. It is freely available at http://www-verimag.imag.fr/Statistical-Model-Checking.html. The tool is distributed with a large set of case studies and a detailed documentation (e.g., user manual, installation details, video tutorials). For the sake of simplicity, we also provide a virtual machine with a pre-installed version of the tool.

This new release was designed in a modular fashion to allow more flexibility and extensibility. As depicted in Fig. 1, $\mathcal{S}$BIP consists of three generic functional modules: *Stochastic Simulation Engine*, *Monitoring*, and Statistical Analyses that currently include *Hypothesis Testing (HT)*, *Probability Estimation (PE)*, *Parametric Exploration (PX)* and *Importance Splitting (IP)* for rare events analysis. All these modules are fully independent and interact through well-defined Java interfaces. The latter also define a clean and easy way to extend the tool with further modules (simulators, monitors and analyzers). In practice, statistical analysis algorithms trigger the stochastic simulation engine to produce a new execution trace which is monitored against an input property to produce a local verdict. Depending on the used analysis method, several iterations are generally required, to produce the final verdict. The proposed design allows to perform different analyses in separate workflows, namely simple simulation, standard SMC analyses, parametric SMC exploration and analysis of rare events. These workflows rely on common features such as models and properties edition, compilation and generated traces inspection.

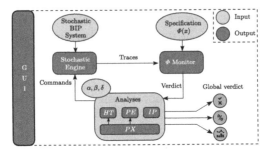

Fig. 1. SBIP architecture

Stochastic Simulation Engine. Currently, SBIP allows to use two different stochastic simulators, namely, for classical stochastic BIP [9] that enables to model discrete-time systems (DTMCs) and for the newly implemented Stochastic Real-Time BIP [10] for continuous-time systems with arbitrary distributions (GSMPs and CTMCs)[1]. The former produces untimed traces needed to verify bounded LTL properties (and to guarantee backward compatibility), whereas the latter generates timed traces necessary to verify MTL properties. We implemented simulators to produce traces in different modes, i.e., symbol-wise, piece-wise and trace-wise. We use the first mode for online monitoring and to be able to interrupt simulations as soon as a verdict is obtained. The second is primordial for rare events analysis and allows to generate traces as a concatenation of trace-fragments. Finally, we use the third mode for offline monitoring.

Monitor. The new release of the tool implements monitoring capabilities for MTL and bounded LTL formulas. Our monitoring algorithms are inspired from the rewrite-based procedures introduced in [3,11]. Given a formula and a trace, the monitor alternates rewriting and simplification phases. Rewriting consumes a symbol of the trace and partially evaluates the formula by unfolding temporal operators and evaluating atomic propositions to their truth value. Simplification applies Boolean reduction rules to the formula in order to conclude or to simplify it. The implemented MTL/LTL grammars and monitors allow for expressing properties with nested operators and having parameters, i.e., variables used to represent a range of properties in a compact way.

Statistical Analyses. In addition to classical SMC algorithms, i.e., HT [12] and PE [5], we propose in this release two additional analyses (exploitable via independent workflows) for the exploration of properties parameters, *Parametric Exploration (PX)*, and for rare events analysis, *Importance Splitting (IP)* [7]. To recall, HT allows to answer qualitative queries, i.e., given a stochastic system S and a property ϕ, it enables to assess whether the probability for S to satisfy

---

[1] SRT-BIP sources are available at https://gricad-gitlab.univ-grenoble-alpes.fr/verimag/bip/compiler/tree/stochastic-real-time

ϕ is greater or equal to a given threshold θ. *PE* addresses quantitative queries, that is to compute a probability estimate p for S to satisfy ϕ.

Parametric Exploration (PX) is an automated way to perform statistical model checking on a family of properties, in a batch mode. A family of properties is specified in a compact way as a parametric property $\phi(x)$, where x is an integer parameter ranging over a finite instantiation domain Π. Similarly to PRISM, our implemented algorithm returns a set of SMC verdicts corresponding to the verification of the parametric property instances $\phi(v_x)$ with respect to $v_x \in \Pi$. This can be very useful when exploring unknown system parameters such as, buffers sizes guaranteeing no overflow, or the amount of consumed energy. It automates the exploration for large parameters domains as opposed to tedious and time consuming manual procedures. This exploration differs from UPPAAL-SMC parametric SMC which explores the parameters of the input model.

Importance Splitting (IP) overcomes the problem of estimating the probability $P(S \models \phi)$ of a system S to satisfy a property ϕ representing a rare event. This is done by considering a set of intermediate levels l_i that corresponds to less rare properties ϕ_i, s.t., $\phi_n \Rightarrow \phi_{n-1} \Rightarrow \ldots \Rightarrow \phi_1$, where $\phi_n = \phi$. $P(S \models \phi)$ is therefore computed as the product of the conditional probabilities to reach l_i from l_{i-1}, i.e., $\Pi_{i=1}^{n} P(S \models \phi_i \mid S \models \phi_{i-1})$. In our implementation, the intermediate levels l_i and associated ϕ_i are defined via a score function given as input. To evaluate a system trace with respect to ϕ, we implemented a procedure that tells the level reached by the trace, i.e., the intermediate property it satisfies. Our algorithm is similar to the analysis procedure proposed in Plasma Lab. It iterates over levels, and for each one, it simulates m trace prefixes among which m_s reach the next level and m_f do not. The conditional probability to reach the next level is thus estimated as the ratio m_s/m. In the next iteration, the simulation of successful prefixes is resumed, while the rest (m_f) are replaced by successful ones sampled uniformly. We note that *IP* is currently limited to the analysis of DTMCs.

3   Case Studies

In this section, we briefly present experiments performed using SBIP [2]. Different case studies covering various application domains were considered to validate the new release of the tool. We implemented models for communication protocols, namely Firewire, Bluetooth, and the Precision Time Protocol (PTP), for a vehicle gear controller, a Pacemaker and a mutual exclusion scenario. All the experiments were performed on a Dell Latitude 5480 with an i7-7820HQ processor and 32 GB of RAM, running Ubuntu 16.04.

On these models, we tackled different types of requirements. For the Firewire case study, we focused on analyzing its leader election protocol in different topologies (2, 3 and 5 nodes) with respect to convergence time, by considering the impact of contention ($\phi_{1,2,3}$) and regarding the impact of a node position on its probability to become the leader (ϕ_4). In this study, except ϕ_3 performed

---

[2] See details in http://www-verimag.imag.fr/TR/TR-2018-5.pdf

using PE, the other properties were performed using PX. We also built a para-metric model of the Bluetooth device discovery mechanism with one sender and one receiver that can be either in an active (v1) or a sniff mode (v2). For this model, we were interested in studying the energy consumption of the receiver in both modes (ϕ_6) in addition to the convergence time (ϕ_5). The PTP protocol was subject to the analysis of the maximal drift between the master and the slave clocks (ϕ_7).

For the gearbox system, we investigated the minimum and maximum time required to complete a gear change (ϕ_8). We also verified requirements regarding the time relationships between atrial and ventricular events in the pacemaker model ($\phi_{9,10}$). Analyses of the Bluetooth, PTP and the gearbox models were performed using PX, while we used PE for the Pacemaker. We also considered a model of three concurrent processes arbitrarily requesting access to a shared resource. In this case study, the goal was to estimate the probability that each process is able to access the resource 10 times within 30 system steps (rare property ϕ_{11}). Using our IP implementation, we obtained 2.35×10^{-7} in less than 13 s, while it was not possible to observe the rare event using PE upon 3 min of execution.

Table 1. Summary of performance

Case study	Model	ϕ	Analysis	#smc loops	avg smc time
Firewire(2)	CTMC	ϕ_1	PX	11	1 m 21 s
		ϕ_2	PX	9	1 m 59 s
		ϕ_3	PE	–	2 m 28 s
		ϕ_4	PX	2	3 m 27 s
Firewire(3)	CTMC	ϕ_1	PX	17	1 m 53 s
		ϕ_2	PX	11	3 m 34 s
		ϕ_3	PE	–	3 m 38 s
		ϕ_4	PX	3	4 m 43 s
Firewire(5)	CTMC	ϕ_1	PX	18	3 m 54 s
		ϕ_2	PX	17	12 m 36 s
		ϕ_3	PE	–	7 m 23 s
		ϕ_4	PX	5	10 m 16 s
Bluetooth v1	CTMC	ϕ_5	PX	9	2 m 27 s
		ϕ_6	PX	16	3 m 11 s
Bluetooth v2	CTMC	ϕ_5	PX	11	3 m 0 s
		ϕ_6	PX	14	13 m 05 s
PTP	GSMP	ϕ_7	PX	15	8 m 42 s
Gear Control	CTMC	ϕ_8	PX	11	54 s
Pacemaker	CTMC	ϕ_9	PE	–	1 h 28 m
		ϕ_{10}	PE	–	1h 30m
Mutual Exclusion	DTMC	ϕ_{11}	IP	–	13 s
			PE	–	3 m 37 s

In addition to these experiments summarized in Table 1, we report in the last two columns some performance measures of the tool, namely, the number of SMC loops performed for parametric exploration, and the average SMC time for a single loop. We observed that depending on the model size and the property complexity, the time varies from some seconds to a dozen of minutes, except for the pacemaker model where it took more than an hour. In this particular case, PE required 4883 long execution traces, representing approximately 8 min of real system execution.

4   Discussion

Most SMC tools [1,4,6,8,12] use dedicated abstract models as input for verifi-cation. In contrast, $\mathcal{S}$BIP uses BIP, a full-fledged expressive component-based framework developed to support system design from specification to analysis and implementation. It allows for incrementally building complex systems from elementary components and offers real-time capabilities, in addition to high-level coordination and synchronization primitives e.g. multi-party interactions and priorities. Furthermore, it enables including external C++ code, e.g. for modeling complex data structures and integrating legacy code.

We briefly discuss $\mathcal{S}$BIP capabilities with respect to major SMC tools. Regarding the analyses, $\mathcal{S}$BIP implements the HT and PE algorithms similarly to Uppaal-smc [4], Prism [8] and Plasma Lab [6]. Besides, only Prism offers a parametric functionality similar to PX. Furthermore, to the best of our knowledge only Plasma Lab and COSMOS [1] support rare events analysis. The former is the only one implementing IP as in our tool, while the latter rather relies on importance sampling. Our underlying modeling formalism allows for expressing arbitrary probability distributions over time. It offers built-in standard distributions, e.g. Normal, and a simple mechanism for specifying custom distributions. In contrast, Prism is restricted to uniform and exponential distributions, whereas in Uppaal-smc one need to define such distributions manually by using a subset of the C language. The expressiveness of BIP together with the reliance on concrete executions result in lower runtime performance compared to Uppaal-smc and Prism. Comparatively, the authors of Plasma Lab chose to focus on modularity at the expense of performance. In the future, we plan to optimize our simulation engine to improve the overall performance.

References

1. Ballarini, P., Barbot, B., Duflot, M., Haddad, S., Pekergin, N.: Hasl: a new approach for performance evaluation and model checking from concepts to experimentation. Perform. Eval. **90**, 53–77 (2015)
2. Basu, A., et al.: Rigorous component-based system design using the BIP framework. IEEE Softw. **28**(3), 41–48 (2011)
3. Bulychev, P.E., David, A., Larsen, K.G., Legay, A., Li, G., Poulsen, D.B.: Rewrite-based statistical model checking of WMTL. RV, **7687**, 260–275 (2012)
4. David, A., Larsen, K.G., Legay, A., Mikučionis, M., Poulsen, D.B.: Uppaal SMC tutorial. STTT **17**(4), 397–415 (2015)
5. Hérault, T., Lassaigne, R., Magniette, F., Peyronnet, S.: Approximate probabilistic model checking. In: Steffen, B., Levi, G. (eds.) VMCAI 2004. LNCS, vol. 2937, pp. 73–84. Springer, Heidelberg (2004). https://doi.org/10.1007/978-3-540-24622-0_8
6. Jegourel, C., Legay, A., Sedwards, S.: A platform for high performance statistical model checking – PLASMA. In: Flanagan, C., König, B. (eds.) TACAS 2012. LNCS, vol. 7214, pp. 498–503. Springer, Heidelberg (2012). https://doi.org/10.1007/978-3-642-28756-5_37
7. Jegourel, C., Legay, A., Sedwards, S.: Importance splitting for statistical model checking rare properties. In: Sharygina, N., Veith, H. (eds.) CAV 2013. LNCS, vol. 8044, pp. 576–591. Springer, Heidelberg (2013). https://doi.org/10.1007/978-3-642-39799-8_38
8. Kwiatkowska, M., Norman, G., Parker, D.: PRISM 4.0: verification of probabilistic real-time systems. In: Gopalakrishnan, G., Qadeer, S. (eds.) CAV 2011. LNCS, vol. 6806, pp. 585–591. Springer, Heidelberg (2011). https://doi.org/10.1007/978-3-642-22110-1_47

9. Nouri, A., Bensalem, S., Bozga, M., Delahaye, B., Jegourel, C., Legay, A.: Statistical model checking QoS properties of systems with SBIP. In: STTT 2015, vol. 17, pp. 171–185
10. Nouri, A., Mediouni, B.L., Bozga, M., Combaz, J., Legay, A., Bensalem, S.: Performance evaluation of stochastic real-time systems with the SBIP framework. Technical Report TR-2017-6, Verimag Research Report (2017)
11. Roşu, G., Havelund, K.: Rewriting-based techniques for runtime verification. Autom. Softw. Eng. **12**(2), 151–197 (2005)
12. Younes, H.L.S.: Verification and Planning for Stochastic Processes with Asynchronous Events. Ph.D. thesis, Carnegie Mellon (2005)

Owl: A Library for ω-Words, Automata, and LTL

Jan Křetínský[(✉)] [ID], Tobias Meggendorfer[ID], and Salomon Sickert[ID]

Technical University of Munich, Munich, Germany
{jan.kretinsky,tobias.meggendorfer,sickert}@in.tum.de

Abstract. We present the library `Owl` (**O**mega-**W**ords, automata, and **L**TL) for ω-automata and linear temporal logic. It forms a backbone of several translations from LTL to automata and related tools by different authors. We describe the functionality of the library and the recent experience, which has already shown the library is apt for easy prototyping of new tools in this area.

1 An Owl is Born: Introduction

ω-automata are finite automata over infinite words. As opposed to finite automata over finite words, there is not a single acceptance condition, but a wide variety of possibilities, each being more appropriate for certain applications. To give a few examples, non-deterministic Büchi automata are the most used kind, useful in many contexts, including the modelling and analysis of reactive systems, where both the system and the property of interest, say in linear temporal logic (LTL) [33], are transformed into these automata. In contrast, the classical approach for synthesis of reactive systems [34] prefers deterministic parity automata. Further, while the textbook approach to probabilistic LTL model checking suggests to translate LTL formulas to deterministic Rabin automata [4], recent approaches show that deterministic generalized Rabin automata or limit-deterministic automata are more preferable [6,37,38]. Consequently, a zoo of automata arises, both due to theoretical limitations of certain kinds as well as practical efficiency. While the theoretical complexity of the transformations between the automata and of translations from LTL to automata is long settled, the research on practically more efficient approaches is flourishing, both for non-deterministic [3,7–9,15–17,39] and more recently deterministic [2,11–14,19,20,23,37] automata. Notably, while these constructions are based on diverse ideas, their implementation requires almost the same infrastructure.

Tools in this area have very different purposes, ranging from tools for one specific task, e.g. translating LTL into a particular type of automaton, e.g. [3,16,20–22],

---

This research was supported in part by the Czech Science Foundation grant No. P202/12/G061 and the the German Research Foundation (DFG) projects "Statistical Unbounded Verification" (383882557) and "Verified Model Checkers" (317422601).

S. K. Lahiri and C. Wang (Eds.): ATVA 2018, LNCS 11138, pp. 543–550, 2018.
https://doi.org/10.1007/978-3-030-01090-4_34

to educational GUI tools demonstrating the constructions, e.g. JFLAP [35], to tools implementing a comprehensive collection of algorithms from literature, e.g. GOAL [41] and Spot [9]. We contribute to this spectrum the library Owl, which enables easy and fast development of transformation/translation tools, yet yielding efficient implementations.

Owl is a full-fledged library for manipulating ω-automata and LTL. One of the main characteristics is that it links the functionality for automata and logic in a very tight and explicit way, providing additional support for "semantic" translations of LTL to automata. These are translations where states are described using structures over logical formulas, as we know it from the classical, e.g. the tableaux-based, tradition. This tradition was disrupted for deterministic automata due to Safra's construction [36], where the meaning of a state (the language it recognizes) cannot be easily described in terms of the meaning of the corresponding formulas. The "semantic" tradition has been restored recently in the works on deterministic automata cited above and Owl provides specialised operations (see below) on LTL that are the building blocks for obtaining such a translation.

Apart from this characteristics, our library has several other user-friendly traits and distinguishing features. For instance, it is built according to the on-the-fly philosophy, it is written in Java (with no memory management issues left for the user, being more accessible to students), extensive CLI support for quick and easy prototyping, and a testing framework checking correctness of translations written with the library.

In this tool paper, we briefly describe the functionality of the library and then provide a series of actual use cases (not only by the authors), demonstrating the usability and particular advantages of this library.

2   The Anatomy of the Owl: Functionality

Owl (**O**mega-**W**ords, automata, and **L**TL) arose from the needs when implementing Rabinizer 3.1 [13,22] and ltl2ldba [37]. When developing such translations a lot of infrastructure is necessary, e.g., LTL parsing and representation, while the actual construction is only a small fraction of the written code. Thus, we implemented commonly needed functionality in a reusable Java library for LTL and ω-automata and extended it with numerous features to provide a flexible infrastructure for rapid and seamless development of algorithms in these domains.

2.1   Data Structures and Algorithms

The majority of data structures and algorithms concerns LTL and automata.

LTL. The library provides an LTL parser, a simplifier with state-of-the-art rewrite rules, classification into syntactic fragments and transformation into normal forms. Additionally, a parser for the synthesis specification format TLSF [18] is available and includes a conversion to LTL.

Further, the LTL support comes with efficient rewriting according to the LTL expansion laws, e.g. [4]. This enables the decomposition of temporal formulas into directly checkable assertions on the current position and on the immediate temporal successor, e.g. $a\mathbf{U}b \equiv b \vee (a \wedge \mathbf{X}(a\mathbf{U}b))$. As such, they are a core component of both classic, e.g. tableaux-based, as well as recent semantic translations.

Automata. The library provides support for deterministic and nondeterministic ω-automata with both classic acceptance conditions, e.g., Büchi, coBüchi, Rabin and parity, as well as, e.g., like generalized Rabin [28] or Emerson-Lei acceptance [10]. Internally, acceptance is represented as transition-based acceptance and a conversion to and from state-based acceptance for interfacing with external tools is present.

Automata can either be stored and modified explicitly, meaning the whole state-space and transitions are kept in memory, or defined implicitly by specifying initial states and a method for successor computation. The latter approach has two main advantages: First, new constructions can be implemented with little effort, transferring the definition of the successor relation into code. For example, see [24] for a ca. 60 lines Java implementation of Safra's determinization procedure. Second, automata can be conveniently traversed on the fly without storing the transition system, allowing operations on huge or potentially even infinite transition structures.

For automata, classic algorithms such as decomposition into strongly connected components (SCC) and lasso-based emptiness checks are included. Furthermore, constructions such as union, intersection and degeneralization are present. In addition, modifications of the transition structure and the acceptance conditions are supported, e.g., removal of non-accepting or unreachable parts of the state space, completing the transition relation, and simplifications of the acceptance condition. Acceptance sets are stored as edge labels for efficient rewriting, supporting arbitrarily sized acceptances, compared to, e.g., Spot [9], which at the time of writing supports only an at compile-time determined bounded number of sets.

2.2   Interfacing

There are two ways to interact with Owl: On the one hand, there is a command-line interface with text-based formats, e.g., (Spot-compatible) LTL, TLSF [18], and the Hanoi ω-automaton format (HOA) [1]. This approach is completely agnostic of the implementation, but always requires a complete construction, which is prohibitively expensive for huge outputs where only a small fraction might be needed. On the other hand, there is a Java and a (specialized) C++ API offered by Owl, which allows fine-grained access and exposes the on-the-fly nature to external code.

Command-line Interface. Major functionality of the library is available via a pipe-style CLI, which makes it easy to specify the sequence of procedures (input parsing, translations, conversions, statistics and serialization) to be performed. For example, `owl ltl --- simplify-ltl ---`

ltl2dpa --- hoa reads LTL formulas from stdin line-by-line, simplifies them using the default simplifier, translates them to DPAs and
writes them to stdout in the HOA format. This can be extended
to advanced pipelines, e.g., owl -I "in.ltl" --- ltl --- ltl2dgra ---
aut-stat "DGRA:%s" --- dgra2dra --- aut-stat "DRA:%s" --- null.

This pipeline reads LTL formulas from the file in.ltl, translates them to
DGRAs and DRAs, while outputting the respective sizes of the automata, and
finally discards the actual output, saving the time needed for serialization.

Moreover, we support several sources and sinks for data. While one can simply process data from files and the command line, we also added a server mode
to reduce the JVM start-up cost, where I/O is bound to a socket. Further details
on the CLI together with an in-depth example can be found on [24].

Java and C++ API. Java and Java-like (e.g., Scala) applications can import
Owl and have fine-grained control. For C++ tools, there exists a specialized
interface to access core functionality of the library. Among other things, this
enables C++ code to iteratively explore automata state by state instead of
forcing a complete construction. This iterative exploration is a core component
of the state-of-the-art synthesis tool Strix [31] and is crucial for its performance.

2.3 Development Infrastructure and Scalable Architecture

Testing. Small changes to a translation can easily introduce bugs. Thus a test
suite is included, which provides several input sets and cross-checks each translation, developed with Owl, on hundreds of formulas [25] using ltlcross [9]. Apart
from detecting bugs, the test suite offers further conveniences, e.g., it automatically generates an image of an erroneous automaton together with an erroneous
run. Moreover, various statistics of the generated automata are displayed, usable
for performance testing. Lastly, integration of a newly developed translation can
be achieved by a few lines of JSON, see [24] for an example.

BDDs. Both the LTL part and the automata part of the library use binary decision diagrams (BDD) for some aspects of their functionality, e.g., for a compact
representation edge sets and (propositional) equivalence checks of formulas. We
implemented our own pure Java BDD library JBDD [30], to (i) achieve portability,
not requiring users to compile, e.g., CUDD, and (ii) provide an efficient and tuned
implementation for all used BDD operations, e.g. substitution of variables, called
compose. Particularly, compose is fundamental for a symbolic implementation
of the semantic constructions and greatly improves their runtime compared to
the explicit variants.

3 The Owl in the Wild: Use Cases

Owl has been successfully used for several published tools and student projects,
demonstrating versatility and usability even for less experienced users. To name a
few, the following published tools (in alphabetical order) using Owl are available:

Delag [32] translates LTL into deterministic Emerson-Lei automata.Reusing other translations based on **Owl**, see **Rabinizer** [26], it adds specialized constructions for fragments of LTL, exploiting a succinct encoding coupled to the Emerson-Lei acceptance condition. The current distribution of **Owl** includes the latest version of it.

MoChiBa [38] is an extension of **PRISM** [29] and uses limit-deterministic automata for quantitative model checking of Markov decision processes [37]. Due to a tight integration with **Owl**, additional information on the automata can be accessed, optimizing the construction.

Rabinizer [26] is a collection of tools translating LTL to various types of deterministic automata. It uses a fully BDD-based successor computation of **Owl**, improving performance over the previous versions. The current distribution of **Owl** includes the latest version of **Rabinizer** (4.0).

Strix [31] synthesises controllers (either Mealy machines or AIGER circuits) from LTL specifications via parity games. Constructing the underlying automata and solving the parity games take an incremental approach and make use of the on-the-fly implementations.

The list of student projects includes[1]

- a re-implementation of **Seminator** [5],
- a specialized translation of the $(\mathbf{F}, \mathbf{G}, \mathbf{X})$-fragment of LTL to deterministic parity automata, and
- reactive synthesis exploiting the **Owl**-supported semantic labelling of the automata produced by **Rabinizer** through learning approaches.

Furthermore, rLTL (robust LTL) [40] can be easily transformed into LTL using **Owl**[2]. Finally, to illustrate the ease with which new translations can be written, we implemented the notoriously complicated and hard-to-implement [27] Safra's determinization procedure [36], which can be found on [24]. A detailed analysis of the lines of code needed to implement the mentioned translations and the percentage of library that is used can be found on [24].

4   This is Not the End: Conclusion

We have presented the library **Owl**, which provides infrastructure for easy development of efficient prototypes in the area of LTL and automata. It has already demonstrated its re-usability in several projects, also without the presence of the library authors. For instance, our experience with Master students has demonstrated that a tool for a complex translation, such as [5], can be easily implemented using roughly 400 lines of code, achieving performance comparable to the original dedicated tool. One simply defines the mathematical type of the state space, the initial state, the successor function with the acceptance marking, whereas the rest is taken care of by the library. The library can be found at https://owl.model.in.tum.de, including code, documentation, references and an online demo. We greatly appreciate comments and suggestions.

---

[1] Authored by Florian Barta, Matthias Franze, and Sebastian Fiss, respectively.
[2] Originally implemented by Daniel Neider.

References

1. Babiak, T., et al.: The Hanoi Omega-automata format. In: Kroening, D., Păsăreanu, C.S. (eds.) CAV 2015. LNCS, vol. 9206, pp. 479–486. Springer, Cham (2015). https://doi.org/10.1007/978-3-319-21690-4_31
2. Babiak, T., Blahoudek, F., Křetínský, M., Strejček, J.: Effective translation of LTL to deterministic Rabin automata: beyond the (F,G)-fragment. In: Van Hung, D., Ogawa, M. (eds.) ATVA 2013. LNCS, vol. 8172, pp. 24–39. Springer, Cham (2013). https://doi.org/10.1007/978-3-319-02444-8_4
3. Babiak, T., Křetínský, M., Řehák, V., Strejček, J.: LTL to Büchi automata translation: fast and more deterministic. In: Flanagan, C., König, B. (eds.) TACAS 2012. LNCS, vol. 7214, pp. 95–109. Springer, Heidelberg (2012). https://doi.org/10.1007/978-3-642-28756-5_8
4. Baier, C., Katoen, J.: Principles of Model Checking. MIT Press, Cambridge (2008)
5. Blahoudek, F., Duret-Lutz, A., Klokočka, M., Křetínský, M., Strejček, J.: Seminator: a tool for semi-determinization of omega-automata. In: LPAR (2017)
6. Chatterjee, K., Gaiser, A., Křetínský, J.: Automata with generalized rabin pairs for probabilistic model checking and LTL synthesis. In: Sharygina, N., Veith, H. (eds.) CAV 2013. LNCS, vol. 8044, pp. 559–575. Springer, Heidelberg (2013). https://doi.org/10.1007/978-3-642-39799-8_37
7. Couvreur, J.-M.: On-the-fly verification of linear temporal logic. In: Wing, J.M., Woodcock, J., Davies, J. (eds.) FM 1999. LNCS, vol. 1708, pp. 253–271. Springer, Heidelberg (1999). https://doi.org/10.1007/3-540-48119-2_16
8. Daniele, M., Giunchiglia, F., Vardi, M.Y.: Improved automata generation for linear temporal logic. In: Halbwachs, N., Peled, D. (eds.) CAV 1999. LNCS, vol. 1633, pp. 249–260. Springer, Heidelberg (1999). https://doi.org/10.1007/3-540-48683-6_23
9. Duret-Lutz, A., Lewkowicz, A., Fauchille, A., Michaud, T., Renault, É., Xu, L.: Spot 2.0 — a framework for LTL and ω-automata manipulation. In: Artho, C., Legay, A., Peled, D. (eds.) ATVA 2016. LNCS, vol. 9938, pp. 122–129. Springer, Cham (2016). https://doi.org/10.1007/978-3-319-46520-3_8
10. Emerson, E.A., Lei, C.: Modalities for model checking: branching time strikes back. In: POPL (1985)
11. Esparza, J., Křetínský, J.: From LTL to deterministic automata: a safraless compositional approach. In: Biere, A., Bloem, R. (eds.) CAV 2014. LNCS, vol. 8559, pp. 192–208. Springer, Cham (2014). https://doi.org/10.1007/978-3-319-08867-9_13
12. Esparza, J., Křetínský, J., Raskin, J.-F., Sickert, S.: From LTL and limit-deterministic Büchi automata to deterministic parity automata. In: Legay, A., Margaria, T. (eds.) TACAS 2017. LNCS, vol. 10205, pp. 426–442. Springer, Heidelberg (2017). https://doi.org/10.1007/978-3-662-54577-5_25
13. Esparza, J., Křetínský, J., Sickert, S.: From LTL to deterministic automata - a safraless compositional approach. Form. Methods Syst. Des. (2016)
14. Esparza, J., Křetínský, J., Sickert, S.: One theorem to rule them all: a unified translation of LTL into ω-automata. In: LICS (2018)
15. Etessami, K., Holzmann, G.J.: Optimizing Büchi automata. In: Palamidessi, C. (ed.) CONCUR 2000. LNCS, vol. 1877, pp. 153–168. Springer, Heidelberg (2000). https://doi.org/10.1007/3-540-44618-4_13
16. Gastin, P., Oddoux, D.: Fast LTL to Büchi automata translation. In: CAV (2001). Tool accessible at http://www.lsv.ens-cachan.fr/~gastin/ltl2ba/
17. Giannakopoulou, D., Lerda, F.: From states to transitions: improving translation of LTL formulae to Büchi automata. In: Peled, D.A., Vardi, M.Y. (eds.) FORTE

2002. LNCS, vol. 2529, pp. 308–326. Springer, Heidelberg (2002). https://doi.org/10.1007/3-540-36135-9_20

18. Jacobs, S., Klein, F., Schirmer, S.: A high-level LTL synthesis format: TLSF v1.1. In: Fifth Workshop on Synthesis (SYNT@CAV) (2016)

19. Kini, D., Viswanathan, M.: Limit deterministic and probabilistic automata for LTL \ GU. In: Baier, C., Tinelli, C. (eds.) TACAS 2015. LNCS, vol. 9035, pp. 628–642. Springer, Heidelberg (2015). https://doi.org/10.1007/978-3-662-46681-0_57

20. Kini, D., Viswanathan, M.: Optimal translation of LTL to limit deterministic automata. In: Legay, A., Margaria, T. (eds.) TACAS 2017. LNCS, vol. 10206, pp. 113–129. Springer, Heidelberg (2017). https://doi.org/10.1007/978-3-662-54580-5_7

21. Klein, J.: ltl2dstar - LTL to deterministic Streett and Rabin automata. http://www.ltl2dstar.de/

22. Komárková, Z., Křetínský, J.: Rabinizer 3: safraless translation of LTL to small deterministic automata. In: Cassez, F., Raskin, J.-F. (eds.) ATVA 2014. LNCS, vol. 8837, pp. 235–241. Springer, Cham (2014). https://doi.org/10.1007/978-3-319-11936-6_17

23. Křetínský, J., Esparza, J.: Deterministic automata for the (F,G)-fragment of LTL. In: Madhusudan, P., Seshia, S.A. (eds.) CAV 2012. LNCS, vol. 7358, pp. 7–22. Springer, Heidelberg (2012). https://doi.org/10.1007/978-3-642-31424-7_7

24. Křetínský, J., Meggendorfer, T., Sickert, S.: Owl: a library for ω-words, automata, and LTL. https://owl.model.in.tum.de. Accessed July 2018

25. Křetínský, J., Meggendorfer, T., Sickert, S.: LTL store: repository of LTL formulae from literature and case studies. CoRR, abs/1807.03296 (2018)

26. Křetínský, J., Meggendorfer, T., Sickert, S., Ziegler, C.: Rabinizer 4: from LTL to your favourite deterministic automaton. In: Chockler, H., Weissenbacher, G. (eds.) CAV 2018. LNCS, vol. 10981, pp. 567–577. Springer, Cham (2018). https://doi.org/10.1007/978-3-319-96145-3_30

27. Kupferman, O.: Recent challenges and ideas in temporal synthesis. In: Bieliková, M., Friedrich, G., Gottlob, G., Katzenbeisser, S., Turán, G. (eds.) SOFSEM 2012. LNCS, vol. 7147, pp. 88–98. Springer, Heidelberg (2012). https://doi.org/10.1007/978-3-642-27660-6_8

28. Křetínský, J., Esparza, J.: Deterministic automata for the (F,G)-fragment of LTL. In: Madhusudan, P., Seshia, S.A. (eds.) CAV 2012. LNCS, vol. 7358, pp. 7–22. Springer, Heidelberg (2012). https://doi.org/10.1007/978-3-642-31424-7_7

29. Kwiatkowska, M., Norman, G., Parker, D.: PRISM 4.0: verification of probabilistic real-time systems. In: Gopalakrishnan, G., Qadeer, S. (eds.) CAV 2011. LNCS, vol. 6806, pp. 585–591. Springer, Heidelberg (2011). https://doi.org/10.1007/978-3-642-22110-1_47

30. Meggendorfer, T.: JBDD: a java BDD library. https://github.com/incaseoftrouble/jbdd. Accessed July 2018

31. Meyer, P.J., Sickert, S., Luttenberger, M.: Strix: explicit reactive synthesis strikes back!. In: Chockler, H., Weissenbacher, G. (eds.) CAV 2018. LNCS, vol. 10981, pp. 578–586. Springer, Cham (2018). https://doi.org/10.1007/978-3-319-96145-3_31

32. Müller, D., Sickert, S.: LTL to deterministic Emerson-Lei automata. In: Gandalf (2017)

33. Pnueli, A.: The temporal logic of programs. In: FOCS (1977)

34. Pnueli, A., Rosner, R.: On the synthesis of a reactive module. In: POPL (1989)

35. Rodger, S.H., Qin, H., Su, J.: Changes to JFLAP to increase its use in courses. In: SIGCSE (2011)

36. Safra, S.: On the complexity of omega-automata. In: FOCS (1988)

37. Sickert, S., Esparza, J., Jaax, S., Křetínský, J.: Limit-deterministic Büchi automata for linear temporal logic. In: Chaudhuri, S., Farzan, A. (eds.) CAV 2016. LNCS, vol. 9780, pp. 312–332. Springer, Cham (2016). https://doi.org/10.1007/978-3-319-41540-6_17

38. Sickert, S., Křetínský, J.: MoChiBA: probabilistic LTL model checking using limit-deterministic Büchi automata. In: Artho, C., Legay, A., Peled, D. (eds.) ATVA 2016. LNCS, vol. 9938, pp. 130–137. Springer, Cham (2016). https://doi.org/10.1007/978-3-319-46520-3_9

39. Somenzi, F., Bloem, R.: Efficient Büchi automata from LTL formulae. In: Emerson, E.A., Sistla, A.P. (eds.) CAV 2000. LNCS, vol. 1855, pp. 248–263. Springer, Heidelberg (2000). https://doi.org/10.1007/10722167_21

40. Donzé, A., Maler, O.: Robust satisfaction of temporal logic over real-valued signals. In: Chatterjee, K., Henzinger, T.A. (eds.) FORMATS 2010. LNCS, vol. 6246, pp. 92–106. Springer, Heidelberg (2010). https://doi.org/10.1007/978-3-642-15297-9_9

41. Tsai, M.-H., Tsay, Y.-K., Hwang, Y.-S.: GOAL for games, omega-automata, and logics. In: Sharygina, N., Veith, H. (eds.) CAV 2013. LNCS, vol. 8044, pp. 883–889. Springer, Heidelberg (2013). https://doi.org/10.1007/978-3-642-39799-8_62

EVE: A Tool for Temporal Equilibrium Analysis

Julian Gutierrez, Muhammad Najib$^{(\boxtimes)}$, Giuseppe Perelli, and Michael Wooldridge

Department of Computer Science, University of Oxford, Oxford, UK
{julian.gutierrez,mnajib,giuseppe.perelli,michael.wooldridge}@cs.ox.ac.uk

Abstract. We present EVE (Equilibrium Verification Environment), a formal verification tool for the automated analysis of temporal equilibrium properties of concurrent and multi-agent systems. In EVE, systems are modelled using the Simple Reactive Module Language (SRML) as a collection of independent system components (players/agents in a game) and players' goals are expressed using Linear Temporal Logic (LTL) formulae. EVE can be used to automatically check the existence of pure strategy Nash equilibria in such concurrent and multi-agent systems and to verify which temporal logic properties are satisfied in the equilibria.

1 Introduction

We are interested in the verification of concurrent and multi-agent systems in which system components are modelled as open systems using a game-theoretic approach. In this approach, multi-agent/concurrent systems correspond to multi-player games, agents/processes to (rational) players, computation runs to plays of the game, and individual component behaviours to player strategies. Since the classical notion of correctness is not appropriate in this multi-agent setting [21], one needs different concepts to analyse such systems, and game theory provides a natural set of mathematical tools and solution concepts for that [16]. Among the proposed solution concepts, Nash equilibrium (NE) [17] is considered as the most important in non-cooperative and multi-player settings. In our framework, NE is characterised [1] as follows: given a game G, with $N = \{1, \ldots, n\}$ the set of players and $\vec{a}$ a strategy profile, $\vec{a}$ is a NE if for every player $i \in N$ that does not get her LTL goal formula satisfied in the play resulting from $\vec{a}$, she cannot get her goal satisfied by unilaterally changing her strategy.

In this paper, we present EVE (Equilibrium Verification Environment), which can be used to solve three key decision problems in rational synthesis and verification [9,21]: NON-EMPTINESS, E-NASH, and A-NASH. These problems ask, respectively, whether a multi-player game has at least one NE, whether an LTL [18] formula holds on *some* NE, and whether an LTL formula holds on *all*

---

[1] We refer to [9,21] for the formal characterisation of NE.

© Springer Nature Switzerland AG 2018
S. K. Lahiri and C. Wang (Eds.): ATVA 2018, LNCS 11138, pp. 551–557, 2018.
https://doi.org/10.1007/978-3-030-01090-4_35

NE. EVE uses a technique based on parity games to check for the existence of NE in a concurrent and multi-player game, and a model of strategies that is *memoryful* and *bisimulation invariant*. The latter property is a (desirable) key feature of our modelling framework since bisimilarity is a fundamental equivalence in concurrency which allows one to perform modular and compositional reasoning for the semantic analysis of several concurrent, reactive, and distributed systems.

There are only a few of existing tools that can be used to reason about NE in multi-player games; PRALINE [2] and MCMAS [20] are the most comparable to EVE, and yet both are different from EVE in critical ways. PRALINE does not support LTL goals and uses a model of strategies that is sensitive to bisimilar transformations, meaning that in PRALINE two games on bisimilar systems may have different sets of NE; cf., [7]. On the other hand, MCMAS can check the existence of NE in memoryless strategies only and, like PRALINE, uses a model of strategies that does not allow for bisimulation-invariant transformations, which are made, *e.g.*, when using symbolic methods via OBDDs or some model-minimisation techniques. Another tool is UPPAAL [15], which has been used to study NE in wireless networks [3]. Unlike EVE, UPPAAL works in a quantitative setting, uses Statistical Model Checking, and computes approximate NE.

2   Tool Description

Modelling Language. Each system component (agent/player) in EVE is represented as a SRML *module*, which consists of an *interface* that defines the name of the module and lists a non-empty set of Boolean variables controlled by the module, and a set of *guarded commands*, which define the choices available to the module at each state. There are two kinds of guarded commands: **init**, used for initialising the variables, and **update**, used for updating variables subsequently; we refer to [13] for further details on the semantics of SRML. In addition, we associate each module with a goal, which is specified as an LTL formula.

Implementation and Usage. EVE was developed in Python and is available online from https://github.com/eve-mas/eve-parity. EVE takes as input a concurrent and multi-agent system described in SRML, with player goals and a property ϕ to be checked specified in LTL. For NON-EMPTINESS, EVE returns "YES" (along with a set of winning players W) if the set of NE in the system is not empty, and returns "NO" otherwise. For E-NASH (A-NASH), EVE returns "YES" if ϕ holds on *some* (*all*) NE of the system, and "NO" otherwise. EVE also returns a witness for each "YES" instance as a synthesised strategy profile.

3   Case Studies

We now present two examples from the literature of distributed systems to show the practical usage of EVE. Among other things, these two examples differ in the way they are modelled as a concurrent game. While the first one is played in an arena implicitly given by the specification of the players in the game (as done in [9]), the second one is played on a graph, *e.g.*, as done in [1] with the use of concurrent game structures. Both of these modelling approaches can be used within our tool. We also use these two examples to evaluate EVE's performance in practice (and compare it against MCMAS and PRALINE) in Sect. 4.

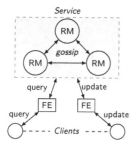

Fig. 1. Gossip framework structure.

```
module RM1 controls s1
init
:: true ~> s1':=true;
update
:: s1 ~> s1':=false;
:: s1 ~> s1':=true;
:: !s1 and (!s2 or ... or !sn)
   ~> s1':=true;
goal
:: G F (!s1);
```

Fig. 2. SRML code modelling RM$_1$.

Gossip Protocol. *Gossip protocols* mimic the way social networks disseminate information and have been used to solve problems in many large-scale distributed systems, such as *peer-to-peer* and *cloud* computing systems. Ladin *et al.* [14] developed a framework to provide high availability services based on the gossip approach first introduced in [4,22]. The main feature of this framework is the use of *replica managers* (RMs) which exchange "gossip" messages periodically to keep the data updated. The architecture of such an approach is shown in Fig. 1.

We model each RM as follows: (1) When in *servicing mode*, an RM can choose either to keep in servicing mode or to switch to gossiping mode; (2) If it is in gossiping mode and there is at least another RM also in gossiping mode[2], since the information during gossip exchange is of (small) bounded size, it goes back to servicing mode in the subsequent step. The goal of each RM is to be able to gossip infinitely often. As shown in Fig. 2, the module RM1 controls a variable: s1. Its value being true signifies that RM1 is in servicing mode; otherwise in gossiping mode. Behaviour (1) is reflected in the first and second update commands, while behaviour (2) is reflected in the third update command. The goal of RM1 is specified with the LTL formula **GF** ¬ s1, which expresses that RM1's goal is to gossip infinitely often: "always" (**G**) "eventually" (**F**) gossip (¬s1).

Observe that with all RMs rationally pursuing their goals, they will adopt any strategy which induces a run where each RM can gossip (with at least one other RM) infinitely often. This kind of game-like modelling gives rise to a powerful characteristic: on *all* runs sustained by a NE, the distributed system is guaranteed to have two crucial *non-starvation/liveness* properties; RMs can gossip infinitely often and clients are served infinitely often. These properties are verified in the experiments; E-NASH: no NE sustains "all RMs forever gossiping"; and with A-NASH: in all NE at least one RM is in servicing mode infinitely often.

---

[2] The core of the protocol involves (at least) pairwise interactions periodically.

Replica Control Protocol. Consensus is a fundamental issue in distributed computing and multi-agent systems. Gifford [6] used a quorum-based voting protocol to ensure data consistency in an information system by not allowing more than one processes in the system to read or write the same data item concurrently. To do this, each copy of a replicated data item is assigned a vote.

We can model a (modified version of) Gifford's protocol as a game as follows. The set of players $N = \{1, \ldots, n\}$ in the game is arranged in a request queue represented by a sequence of states $q_1, \ldots, q_n$, where q_i means that player i is requesting to read/write the data item. At state q_i, other players in $N \setminus \{i\}$ can then vote whether to allow player i to read/write. If the majority of players in N vote "yes", then the transition goes to q_0, i.e., player i is allowed to read/write, and otherwise it goes to q_{i+1}[3]. The voting process then restarts from q_1. The protocol's structure is shown in Fig. 3. Notice that at the last state, q_n, there is only one outgoing

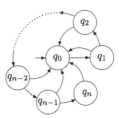

Fig. 3. Gifford's protocol modelled as a game.

arrow to q_0. The goal of each player i is to visit q_0 right after q_i infinitely often, so that the desired behaviour of the system is sustained on all NE of the system: a data item is not accessed by two processes concurrently and the data is updated in *every* round. The associated properties are verified in the experiments in Sect. 4. With E-NASH: there is no Nash equilibrium in which the data is never updated; with A-NASH: on all NE, each player is allowed to request to read/write infinitely often. This example uses a (deterministic) module, called "Environment", modelling the underlying concurrent game structure, shown in Fig. 3, where the game is played.

4   Experimental Evaluation and Conclusions

Experiments. In order to evaluate the practical preformance of our tool and approach against MCMAS[4] and PRALINE, we present results on the temporal equilibrium analysis for the examples in Sect. 3. We ran the tools on the two examples with different numbers of players ("P"), states ("S"), and edges ("E"). The experiments were obtained on a PC with Intel i5-4690S CPU 3.20 GHz machine with 8 GB of RAM running Linux kernel version 4.12.14-300.fc26.x86_64. We report the running time[5] for solving NON-EMPTINESS ("ν"), E-NASH ("ϵ"), and A-NASH ("α"). For the last two problems, since there is no direct support in PRALINE and MCMAS, we used the reduction of E/A-NASH

---

[3] We assume arithmetic modulo $(|N| + 1)$ in this example.

[4] The tool to automatically convert EVE's input (SRML code) into MCMAS's input (ISPL code) is available online from https://github.com/eve-mas/sevia.

[5] To carry out a fairer comparison (since PRALINE accepts Büchi objectives), we added to PRALINE's running time, the time needed to convert LTL games into its input. Translating parity games to PRALINE's input is possible in our particular examples since in those cases we can map the colours/priorities directly into Büchi condition.

to NON-EMPTINESS presented in [5]. Time-out ("TO") was fixed to be 7200 seconds (2 hours).

From the experiments we observe that, in general, EVE has the best performance, followed by PRALINE and MCMAS. Although PRALINE performed better than MCMAS, both struggled (timed-out) with inputs with more than 100 edges, while EVE could handle up to about 6000 edges (for NON-EMPTINESS) (Tables 1 and 2).

Table 1. Gossip Protocol experiment results.

P	S	E	EVE			PRALINE			MCMAS		
			ν (s)	ϵ (s)	α (s)	ν (s)	ϵ (s)	α (s)	ν (s)	ϵ (s)	α (s)
2	4	9	0.02	0.24	0.08	0.02	1.71	1.73	**0.01**	**0.01**	**0.01**
3	8	27	0.09	0.43	0.26	0.33	26.74	27.85	**0.02**	**0.06**	**0.06**
4	16	81	**0.42**	**3.51**	**1.41**	0.76	547.97	548.82	760.65	3257.56	3272.57
5	32	243	**2.30**	**35.80**	**25.77**	10.06	TO	TO	TO	TO	TO
6	64	729	**16.63**	**633.68**	**336.42**	255.02	TO	TO	TO	TO	TO
7	128	2187	**203.05**	TO	TO	5156.48	TO	TO	TO	TO	TO
8	256	6561	**4697.49**	TO	TO	TO	TO	TO	TO	TO	TO

Table 2. Replica control experiment results.

P	S	E	EVE			PRALINE			MCMAS		
			ν (s)	ϵ (s)	α (s)	ν (s)	ϵ (s)	α (s)	ν (s)	ϵ (s)	α (s)
2	3	8	0.04	0.11	0.10	0.05	0.64	0.74	**0.01**	**0.01**	**0.02**
3	4	20	0.11	1.53	0.22	0.12	4.96	5.46	**0.02**	**0.06**	**0.11**
4	5	48	**0.34**	**1.73**	**0.68**	0.56	65.50	67.45	1.99	4.15	11.28
5	6	112	**1.43**	**2.66**	**2.91**	6.86	1546.90	1554.80	1728.73	6590.53	TO
6	7	256	**5.87**	**13.69**	**16.03**	94.39	TO	TO	TO	TO	TO
7	8	576	**32.84**	**76.50**	**102.12**	2159.88	TO	TO	TO	TO	TO
8	9	1280	**166.60**	**485.99**	**746.55**	TO	TO	TO	TO	TO	TO

Conclusion. We have presented EVE, a tool to analyse temporal equilibrium properties in concurrent games modelling multi-agent systems. Although there are other tools to compute pure NE (*e.g.*, PRALINE and MCMAS), they work in different settings. Moreover, while EVE uses a *richer* (bisimulation-invariant) model of strategies, it still performed better than the other two tools. In addition, this model of strategies is amenable to the use of powerful techniques for symbolic reasoning and model minimisation. Another important feature is that, in addition to NON-EMPTINESS, EVE has direct support for other problems in the rational verification framework [8,9,21], namely E-NASH and A-NASH. These two problems can be considered as counterparts to model checking in game-theoretic settings, making them very relevant in the analysis of multi-agent systems. We foresee many avenues for further work: games with imperfect information [12], quantitative payoffs [11], or branching-time goals [10,19].

Acknowledgments. The authors acknowledge with gratitude the financial support of the ERC Advanced Investigator Grant 291528 ("RACE") at Oxford. Muhammad Najib is supported by the Indonesian Endowment Fund for Education (LPDP).

References

1. Alur, R., Henzinger, T.A., Kupferman, O.: Alternating-time temporal logic. J. ACM **49**(5), 672–713 (2002)
2. Brenguier, R.: Praline: a tool for computing nash equilibria in concurrent games. In: Sharygina, N., Veith, H. (eds.) CAV 2013. LNCS, vol. 8044, pp. 890–895. Springer, Heidelberg (2013). https://doi.org/10.1007/978-3-642-39799-8_63
3. Bulychev, P.E., David, A., Larsen, K.G., Legay, A., Mikucionis, M.: Computing nash equilibrium in wireless ad hoc networks: A simulation-based approach. In: Proceedings Second International Workshop on Interactions, Games and Protocols, IWIGP 2012, Tallinn, Estonia, 25th March 2012, pp. 1–14 (2012)
4. Fischer, M.J., Michael, A.: Sacrificing serializability to attain high availability of data in an unreliable network. In: PODS, pp. 70–75. ACM, New York (1982)
5. Gao, T., Gutierrez, J., Wooldridge, M.: Iterated boolean games for rational verification. In: AAMAS, pp. 705–713. ACM, Sao Paulo, Brazil (2017)
6. Gifford, D.K.: Weighted voting for replicated data. In: Proceedings of the Seventh ACM Symposium on Operating Systems Principles SOSP '79, pp. 150–162. ACM, New York (1979)
7. Gutierrez, J., Harrenstein, P., Perelli, G., Wooldridge, M.: Nash equilibrium and bisimulation invariance. In: CONCUR. LIPIcs, vol. 85, pp. 17:1–17:16. Schloss Dagstuhl, Berlin, Germany (2017)
8. Gutierrez, J., Harrenstein, P., Wooldridge, M.: Iterated boolean games. Inf. Comput. **242**, 53–79 (2015)
9. Gutierrez, J., Harrenstein, P., Wooldridge, M.: From model checking to equilibrium checking: reactive modules for rational verification. Artif. Intell. **248**, 123–157 (2017)
10. Gutierrez, J., Harrenstein, P., Wooldridge, M.: Reasoning about equilibria in game-like concurrent systems. Ann. Pure Appl. Log. **168**(2), 373–403 (2017)
11. Gutierrez, J., Murano, A., Perelli, G., Rubin, S., Wooldridge, M.: Nash equilibria in concurrent games with lexicographic preferences. In: Sierra, C. (ed.) Proceedings of the Twenty-Sixth International Joint Conference on Artificial Intelligence, IJCAI 2017, Melbourne, Australia, August 19–25, 2017, pp. 1067–1073 (2017) (ijcai.org)
12. Gutierrez, J., Perelli, G., Wooldridge, M.: Imperfect information in reactive modules games. Inf. Comput. **261**, 650–675 (2018)
13. van der Hoek, W., Lomuscio, A., Wooldridge, M.: On the complexity of practical ATL model checking. In: Proceedings of the Fifth International Joint Conference on Autonomous Agents and Multiagent Systems AAMAS '06, pp. 201–208. ACM, New York, NY, USA (2006)
14. Ladin, R., Liskov, B., Shrira, L., Ghemawat, S.: Providing high availability using lazy replication. ACM Trans. Comput. Syst. **10**(4), 360–391 (1992)
15. Larsen, K.G., Pettersson, P., Yi, W.: Uppaal in a nutshell (1997)

16. Nisan, N.: Introduction to mechanism design (for computer scientists). In: Nisan, N., Roughgarden, T., Tardos, E., Vazirani, V.V. (eds.) Algorithmic Game Theory, pp. 209–242. Cambridge University Press, Cambridge (2007)

17. Osborne, M.J., Rubinstein, A.: A Course in Game Theory. MIT Press, Cambridge (1994)

18. Pnueli, A.: The temporal logic of programs. In: FOCS, pp. 46–57. IEEE, Rhode Island, USA (1977)

19. Toumi, A., Gutierrez, J., Wooldridge, M.: A tool for the automated verification of nash equilibria in concurrent games. In: Leucker, M., Rueda, C., Valencia, F.D. (eds.) ICTAC 2015. LNCS, vol. 9399, pp. 583–594. Springer, Cham (2015). https://doi.org/10.1007/978-3-319-25150-9_34

20. Čermák, P., Lomuscio, A., Mogavero, F., Murano, A.: MCMAS-SLK: a model checker for the verification of strategy logic specifications. In: Biere, A., Bloem, R. (eds.) CAV 2014. LNCS, vol. 8559, pp. 525–532. Springer, Cham (2014). https://doi.org/10.1007/978-3-319-08867-9_34

21. Wooldridge, M., Gutierrez, J., Harrenstein, P., Marchioni, E., Perelli, G., Toumi, A.: Rational verification: From model checking to equilibrium checking. In: Proceedings of the Thirtieth AAAI Conference on Artificial Intelligence, February 12–17, 2016, Phoenix, Arizona, USA, pp. 4184–4191 (2016)

22. Wuu, G.T., Bernstein, A.J.: Efficient solutions to the replicated log and dictionary problems. In: Proceedings of the Third Annual ACM Symposium on Principles of Distributed Computing PODC '84, pp. 233–242. ACM, New York, USA (1984)

Author Index

Printed in the United States
By Bookmasters